SERVICES MARKETING

INTEGRATING CUSTOMER FOCUS ACROSS THE FIRM

Alan Wilson,
Valarie A. Zeithaml,
Mary Jo Bitner
and Dwayne D. Gremler

**FOURTH
EDITION**

SERVICES MARKETING

INTEGRATING CUSTOMER FOCUS ACROSS THE FIRM

FOURTH EDITION

Services Marketing, Fourth Edition
Alan Wilson, Valarie A. Zeithaml, Mary Jo Bitner and Dwayne D. Gremler"
ISBN-13 9781526847805
ISBN-10 1526847809

Published by McGraw Hill
338 Euston Road
London
NW1 3BH
Telephone: +44 (0) 203 429 3400

Website: www.mheducation.co.uk

British Library Cataloguing in Publication Data
A catalogue record for this book is available from the British Library
Library of Congress Cataloguing in Publication Data
The Library of Congress data for this book has been applied for from the Library of Congress

Portfolio Manager: Rosie Churchill
Content Developer: Rebekah Taylor
Content Product Manager: Ali Davis
Marketing Manager: Vee Suchak

Text Design by Kamae Design, Oxford
Cover Design by Adam Renvoize

ISBN-13 9781526847805
ISBN-10 1526847809

Brief Table of Contents

About the authors   xi
Preface   xii
Acknowledgements   xv
Guided tour   xvi
Technology to enhance learning and teaching: Connect   xviii

PART 1: Foundations for services marketing   1

1   Introduction to services   2
2   Conceptual framework of the book: the gaps model of service quality   25

PART 2: Focus on the customer   39

3   Consumer behaviour in services   40
4   Customer expectations of service   61
5   Customer perceptions of service   81

PART 3: Understanding customer requirements   103

6   Listening to customers   104
7   Building customer relationships   129

PART 4: Aligning service design and standards   156

8   Service innovation and design   157
9   Customer-defined service standards   183
10 The physical and virtual servicescape   203

PART 5: Delivering and performing service   226

11 Employees' roles in service delivery   227
12 Customers' roles in service delivery   252
13 Delivering service through electronic channels and intermediaries   274
14 Managing demand and capacity   293
15 Service recovery   318

PART 6: Managing service promises   345

16 Managing external and internal communications   346
17 Pricing of services   369

PART 7: Service and the bottom line   **386**

18   The financial impact of service quality   387

Case section   **404**

Endnotes   473

Index   492

Detailed Table of Contents

About the authors   xi
Preface   xii
Acknowledgements   xv
Guided tour   xvi
Technology to enhance learning and teaching: Connect   xviii

PART 1: Foundations for services marketing   1

Chapter 1: Introduction to services   2

What are services?   3
Service contexts   6
Service dominant logic   9
Technology and evolution of services   11
Why services marketing?   14
Characteristics of services impacting on marketing activities   15
Services marketing mix   19
Staying focused on the customer   22

Chapter 2: Conceptual framework of the book: the gaps model of service quality   25

The customer gap   27
The provider gaps   28
Putting it all together: closing the gaps   34

PART 2: Focus on the customer   39

Chapter 3: Consumer behaviour in services   40

Search, experience and credence properties   42
Consumer choice of service   43
Consumer experience during service delivery   48
Post-experience evaluation   52
Understanding differences among consumers   54

Chapter 4: Customer expectations of service   61

Importance of customer expectations   63
Meaning and types of service expectations   63
Factors that influence customer expectations of service   68
Issues involving the management of customer service expectations   74

Chapter 5: Customer perceptions of service   81

Customer perceptions   82
Customer satisfaction   84

Ensuring high customer satisfaction   88
Service quality   89
Service encounters: the building blocks for customer
perceptions   94
The evidence of service   99

PART 3: Understanding customer requirements   103

Chapter 6: Listening to customers   104

Customer databases and big data analytics   106
Monitoring user-generated content and netnography   108
Using marketing research to understand customer expectations   109
Elements in an effective services marketing research programme   110
Analysing and interpreting marketing research findings   121
Using marketing research information   123
Ethics in marketing research   123
Upward communication through employees   124

Chapter 7: Building customer relationships   129

Relationship marketing   131
Relationship value of customers   137
Customer profitability segments   140
Relationship development strategies   143
Relationship challenges   149

PART 4: Aligning service design and standards   156

Chapter 8: Service innovation and design   157

Challenges of service innovation policy   158
New service development processes   160
Types of new services   161
Service innovation through the Internet of Things   163
Stages in service innovation and development   164
Service blueprinting   170
High-performance service innovations   179

Chapter 9: Customer-defined service standards   183

Factors necessary for appropriate service standards   185
Types of customer-defined service standards   189
Development of customer-defined service standards   191

Chapter 10: The physical and virtual servicescape   203

Physical and virtual evidence   205
Typology of servicescapes   208
Strategic roles of the servicescape   210
Framework for understanding servicescape effects on
behaviour   212
Guidelines for physical evidence strategy   220

PART 5: Delivering and performing service 226

Chapter 11: Employees' roles in service delivery 227

Service culture 229
The critical importance of service employees 231
Boundary-spanning roles 234
Strategies for delivering service quality through people 239
Customer-oriented service delivery 248

Chapter 12: Customers' roles in service delivery 252

The importance of customers in service co-creation and delivery 254
Customers' roles 257
Self-service technologies – the ultimate in customer participation 262
Strategies for enhancing customer participation 265

Chapter 13: Delivering service through electronic channels and intermediaries 274

Multi-channel versus omni-channel delivery 275
Delivering service through electronic channels 276
Delivering service through mobile channels 280
Other forms of service distribution 281
Direct or company-owned channels 282
Franchising 283
Agents and brokers 285
Common issues involving intermediaries 288
Strategies for effective service delivery through intermediaries 289

Chapter 14: Managing demand and capacity 293

The underlying issue: lack of inventory capability 295
Capacity constraints 296
Demand patterns 299
Strategies for matching capacity and demand 300
Revenue management 306
Queuing strategies: when demand and capacity cannot be matched 310

Chapter 15: Service recovery 318

The impact of service failure and recovery 320
How customers respond to service failures 323
Customers' recovery expectations 326
Cultural differences in customers' recovery expectations 329
Switching versus loyalty following service recovery 330
Service recovery strategies 331
Service guarantees 338

PART 6: Managing service promises 345

Chapter 16: Managing external and internal communications 346

The need for coordination in online and offline marketing communication channels 348
Key service communication challenges 350
Five categories of strategy to overcome communication challenges 353

Chapter 17: Pricing of services   369

    Three key ways that service prices are different for consumers   371
    Approaches to pricing services   375
    Dynamic pricing   379
    Adapting the price   380

PART 7: Service and the bottom line   386

Chapter 18: The financial impact of service quality   387

    Service and profitability: the direct relationship   389
    Offensive marketing effects of service: attracting more and
    better customers   391
    Defensive marketing effects of service: customer retention   392
    The key drivers of service quality, customer retention and profits   394
    Customer equity and return on marketing   394
    Company performance measurement: the balanced performance
    scorecard   397

Case Section   404

1   CitizenM: redesigning consumers' hotel experiences   405
2   Amazon: delivering service through electronic channels
    and intermediaries   413
3   The John Lewis and Partners customer experience   422
4   McDonald's: designing services processes and innovations   430
5   Music festivals and the price of live performances   438
6   Marriott International: opportunity window
    for customer experience   448
7   Turkish Airlines: enhancing the customer experience   456
8   Starbucks: key elements of the 'Starbucks experience'   465

Endnotes   473
Index   492

About the Authors

Alan Wilson is Professor of Marketing and was previous Head of the Marketing Department within the University of Strathclyde Business School. Before joining the university, he was a senior consultant and executive trainer within the services division of a London-based marketing consultancy practice and prior to that an Associate Director of a leading London-based marketing research agency. He specializes in the marketing of services and has a PhD in the subject. He is a Fellow of both the Chartered Institute of Marketing and the Market Research Society. His book, *Marketing Research: Delivering Customer Insight*, is in its fourth edition and he has published in a wide range of marketing and service management journals, for which he has won a number of awards and prizes. Professor Wilson has delivered high-level executive training to a wide range of service organizations in the banking, hospitality, professional service and business-to-business service sectors and has been invited to deliver lectures and seminars on both services marketing and marketing research in a variety of countries throughout the world.

Valarie Zeithaml is an award-winning teacher and researcher, and an internationally recognized pioneer of services marketing. Dr. Zeithaml has researched customer expectations in more than 50 industries. She has consulted with service and product companies, including IBM, Kaiser Permanente, GE, John Hancock Financial Services, Aetna, AT&T, Metropolitan Life Insurance, Bank of America, Chase Manhattan Bank, Allstate, and Procter and Gamble. For her work that is influencing the future direction of marketing, she was named a Thomson Reuters Highly Cited Researcher in the report on "The World's Most Influential Scientific Minds." The American Marketing Association (AMA) named her a Marketing Legend in 2016. She was selected for its inaugural cohort of AMA Fellows for her significant contributions to the research, theory and practice of marketing and service to the AMA in 2015. Amongst other accolades, in 2008 the AMA awarded her with the Paul D. Converse Award, which is granted every four years to individuals who have made outstanding and enduring contributions to marketing through journal articles, books or a body of work.

Mary Jo Bitner serves as Academic Director for the Center for Services Leadership at Arizona State University. Dr. Bitner was a founding faculty member of the Center for Services Leadership created for the study of services marketing and management. Dr. Bitner has published more than 50 articles and has received a number of awards for her research in leading journals, including the Journal of Marketing, Journal of the Academy of Marketing Science, Journal of Business Research, Journal of Retailing, International Journal of Service Industry Management, and Academy of Management Executive. She has consulted with and presented seminars and workshops for numerous businesses.

Dwayne D Gremler, Bowling Green State University, received his MBA and PhD degrees from Arizona State University. He is a passionate advocate for the research and instruction of services marketing issues. He has served as Chair of the American Marketing Association's Services Marketing Special Interest Group and has helped organize services marketing conferences in Australia, The Netherlands, France, and the United States. He has been the recipient of several research awards and while a professor at the University of Idaho, Dr. Gremler received the First Interstate Bank Student Excellence in Award for teaching, an award determined by students in the College of Business and Economics.

Preface

This fourth European edition of this highly successful *Services Marketing* text is for students and business people who recognize the vital role that services play in the economy and our lives. European economies are now dominated by services, and virtually all companies view service as critical to retaining their customers today and in the future. Even manufacturing companies that, in the past, have depended on physical products for their livelihood now recognize that service provides one of their few sustainable competitive advantages.

The new edition takes the theories, concepts and frameworks that exist in the original American version of the text and applies them to the European and International context. Examples, cases and readings are used to provide a true International flavour to the material. The material in this fourth edition has also been updated and restructured to reflect the latest services marketing thinking.

The foundation of the text is the recognition that services present special challenges that must be identified and addressed. Issues commonly encountered in service organizations – the inability to inventory, the difficulty in synchronizing demand and supply, and challenges in controlling the performance quality of human interactions – need to be articulated and tackled by managers. This text aims to help students and managers understand and address these special challenges of services marketing.

The development of strong customer relationships through quality service (and services) is at the heart of the book's content. The topics covered are equally applicable to organizations whose core product is service (such as banks, transportation companies, hotels, hospitals, educational institutions, professional services, telecommunication) and to organizations that depend on service excellence for competitive advantage (high-technology manufacturers, automotive and industrial products, and so on).

The book's content focuses on the knowledge needed to implement service strategies for competitive advantage across industries. Included are frameworks for customer-focused management, and strategies for increasing customer satisfaction and retention through service. In addition to standard marketing topics (such as pricing), this text introduces students to topics that include: management and measurement of service quality; service recovery; the linking of customer measurement to performance measurement; service blueprinting; customer co-creation and co-production; and cross-functional treatment of issues through integration of marketing with disciplines such as operations and human resources. Each of these topics represents pivotal content for tomorrow's businesses as they structure around process rather than task, engage in digital marketing, mass customize their offerings, deliver services using mobile and digital platforms as well as through the Internet of Things, and attempt to build strong relationships with their customers.

As the writing of the book was largely completed before the Covid 19 pandemic, it is worth noting the impact of the pandemic on many service industries. In particular, the delivery of services remotely through online channels has become increasingly important and the role of logistic services in maintaining home deliveries has grown significantly. Hospitality, retail and travel organisations have had to rethink their operations to safeguard staff and customers whilst still delivering and marketing a valued customer experience. Finally, the importance of the dedicated support provided by health workers worldwide clearly demonstrates the vital role that certain services continue to play in all our lives.

Distinguishing Content Features

The distinguishing features of the text, some of which are new to this fourth edition, include the following:
- **Cross-functional treatment** of issues through integration of marketing with other disciplines such as operations and human resources management.
- Introducing the conceptual framework of the of the book based on the **gaps model**.

- Greater emphasis on the topic of **service quality** than existing marketing and service marketing texts.
- Increased focus on **customer expectations and perceptions** and what they imply for marketers.
- Increased **technology, social media and digital coverage** throughout the text.
- A chapter on **service recovery** that includes a conceptual framework for understanding the topic.
- A chapter on **listening to customers through research, big data, netnography and monitoring user-generated content**.
- A chapter on **customer-defined service standards**.
- A chapter on **consumer-based pricing**.
- A chapter on **integrated services marketing communications**.
- Increased focus on **customer relationships, brand communities and relationship marketing strategies**.
- An entire chapter that recognizes **human resource challenges, human resource strategies and the role of robots and chatbots** for delivering customer-focused services.
- Coverage of **new service development processes, radical innovation, crowd sourcing ideas** and a detailed and complete introduction to **service blueprinting** – a tool for describing, designing and positioning services.
- Coverage of the customer's role in service delivery, self-service technologies and strategies for **co-production**.
- A chapter on the role of **physical evidence,** including the '**physical and virtual servicescapes**'.
- A chapter on the **financial impact** of service quality.

    To support these topics, there are:

- **European and International cases and opening examples** at the start of each chapter, which provide a real-life context for the chapter content.
- **'Service Spotlights'** in each chapter providing short **examples** to illustrate services marketing in action.
- **Discussion questions** and **exercises** appropriate to the **European context** in each chapter.
- **Up-to-date Suggestions for further reading** in each chapter.
- Short revision lists of **Key concepts** provided at the end of each chapter.

    The framework of the book continues to be managerially focused, with every chapter presenting company examples and strategies for addressing key issues. There are integrating frameworks in most chapters. For example, there are frameworks for understanding service recovery strategies, service pricing, integrated marketing communications, customer relationships, customer roles and internal marketing.

Unique Structure

The text features a structure completely different from the standard 4Ps (marketing mix) structure of introductory marketing texts. It starts by introducing the reader to the key foundations for service marketing by introducing services and services marketing (Chapter 1). The remainder of the text is organized around the gaps model of service quality, which is described fully in (Chapter 2). The focus is then on understanding the customer, in terms of behaviour (Chapter 2), expectations (Chapter 3) and perceptions (Chapter 4). Beginning with Chapter 6, the text is organized into parts around the provider gaps in the gaps model. For example, Chapters 6 and 7 deal with understanding customer requirements; Chapters 8, 9 and 10 with aligning service design and standards; Chapters 11 through to 15 address delivering and performing services; and Chapters 16 and 17 managing service promises. Chapter 18 then focuses on the total picture of service and the bottom line.

What Courses and Which Students Should Use this Text?

Students need to have completed at least a basic marketing course as a prerequisite to using this text. The primary target audience for the text is services marketing classes at the undergraduate, postgraduate (both master's and doctoral courses), and executive education levels. Other target audiences are (1) service management classes at both the undergraduate and postgraduate levels and (2) postgraduate-level marketing management classes in which a lecturer wishes to provide a more comprehensive teaching of services than is possible with a standard marketing management text. A subset of chapters would also provide a more concise text for use in a specialized mini-semester course. A further reduced set of chapters may be used to supplement undergraduate and graduate basic marketing courses to enhance the treatment of services.

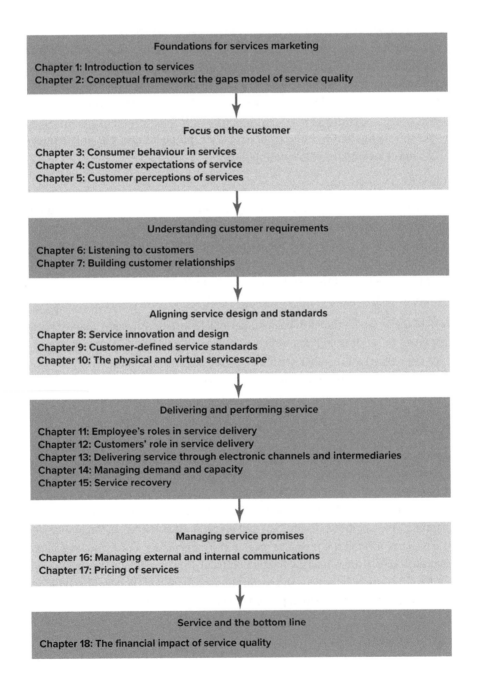

Acknowledgements

I would like to acknowledge the suggestions for improvements made by the reviewers of the book. Their feedback on the book and on the stages of the draft manuscript has helped me to improve the fourth edition for academics' teaching and for their students' learning. My thanks go to the following reviewers for their comments at various stages in the text's development:

Adele Berndt, Jönköping International Business School
Jill Brown, University of Portsmouth
Joyce Byrne-Walsh, Institute of Technology Tallaght
Klaes Eringa, NHL Stenden University of Applied Sciences
David Ermen, University of Applied Sciences of the Grisons
Annouk Lievens, University of Antwerp

I would also like to thank the following case contributors and those who contributed to the Connect resources:

Kate Daunt, Cardiff University
Klaes Eringa, NHL Stenden University of Applied Sciences
Orla Higgins, National University of Ireland Galway
David Kooijker, Stenden University
Annouk Lievens, University of Antwerp
Sarah Montano, University of Birmingham
Christopher Pich, Nottingham Trent University
Sheilagh Resnick, Nottingham Trent University
Mariusz Soltanifar, Hanze University of Applied Sciences Groningen
Fiona Whelan-Ryan, Waterford Institute of Technology

I would further like to acknowledge the professional efforts of the McGraw Hill staff. My sincere thanks to Rosie Churchill, Ali Davis, Nina O'Reilly and Rebekah Taylor.

Finally I would like to thank my wife and family, Sandra, Duncan and Kirsty for their continued love and support.

Guided Tour

Learning Objectives

This chapter's objectives are to:

1 Explain what services are and identify important trends in services.
2 Explain the need for special services marketing concepts and practices and why the need has developed and is accelerating.
3 Introduce the concept of service dominant logic.
4 Explore the profound impact of technology on service.
5 Outline the basic differences between goods and services and the resulting challenges and opportunities for service businesses.
6 Introduce the expanded marketing mix for services and the philosophy of customer focus, as powerful frameworks and themes that are fundamental to the rest of the text.
7 Introduce the servuction system model and the concept of the services triangle.

Learning Objectives

Each chapter opens with a set of learning objectives, summarizing what knowledge, skills or understanding readers should acquire from each chapter.

Opening Example
Airbnb – Understanding Peer-to-Peer Room Rental

Airbnb is part of the broader 'sharing economy', a socio-economic system facilitated by the internet that allows individuals to rent out anything, from spare seats in their cars, to rooms in their homes, tools from their shed or clothes from their wardrobe. The sharing economy is an alternative to the constant accumulation and ownership of things. Since its beginnings, Airbnb has provided peer-to-peer room rental service beds for more than 11 million guests in 192 different countries.

Airbnb was started in 2008 by cash-strapped flat-mates Brian Chesky, Nathan Blecharczyk and Joe Gebbia, who had space to share and hosted three

Source: ©Koay Shi Chian/Shutterstock

Opening Examples

Each chapter opens with an example of service marketing in action or a services marketing issue that helps you to understand how the theory explored in the chapter is relevant to real practice. Examples include Airbnb, Skyscanner, Starbucks, and KLM.

★ SERVICE SPOTLIGHT

Ford, along with other car manufacturers, has added value to their cars by adding the service provided by their Ford's Sync Emergency Assistance technology. This technology can potentially reduce the time taken to respond to accidents by assisting vehicle occupants to place a direct emergency call with location details in the correct local language. It helps notify the emergency services in that vital 'golden hour' after a serious crash when rapid medical attention can be the difference between life and death.

The vehicle's SYNC system initiates an emergency call through the occupant's Bluetooth-connected mobile phone following the deployment of an airbag. The system plays an introductory message and then relays the accident location co-ordinates using the on-board GPS unit, map and mobile network information. Emergency Assist saves crucial seconds by placing a call directly to emergency service operators rather than first routing through a third-party call centre. The value is co-created through a network of the car manufacturer, the driver switching on the Bluetooth function, the mobile phone manufacturer and the emergency services.

Source: www.euroncap.com/rewards/ford_sync_emergency_assistance.aspx.

Service Spotlights

Each chapter is interspersed with numerous short service spotlights that tie theory to practice and show how companies bring services to their customers. Examples come from a variety of customer and business-to-business servers, and include Amex, Ford Hilton and Disneyland Paris.

Summary

This chapter has set the stage for further learning about services marketing by presenting information on changes in the world economy and business practice that have driven the focus on service: the fact that services dominate the modern economies of the world; the focus on service as a competitive business imperative; specific needs of the deregulated and professional service industries; the role of new service concepts growing from technological advances; and the realization that the characteristics of services result in unique challenges and opportunities. The chapter presented a broad definition of services as activities, processes and performances, and it drew distinctions among pure services, value-added services, service experiences and customer service. It also introduced the concept of service dominant logic.

Building on this fundamental understanding of the service economy, the chapter went on to present the key characteristics of services that underlie the need for distinct strategies and concepts for managing service businesses. These basic characteristics are that services are intangible, heterogeneous, produced and consumed simultaneously, and perishable. Because of these characteristics, service managers face a number

Chapter Summary

This briefly reviews and reinforces the main topics covered in each chapter to ensure that you have developed a solid understanding of the key topics. Use it in conjunction with the learning objectives as a quick reference.

Key Concepts

Heterogeneity	16	Self-service technologies	12
Inseparability	17	Service dominant logic	9
Intangibility	6	Services marketing mix	19
People	19	Services marketing triangle	18
Perishability	17	Servuction system	21

Key Concepts

An ideal tool for revision or to check definitions as you read, key concepts are highlighted in bold, with page number references at the end of each chapter so they can be found easily.

Further Reading

Akaka, M.A. and Vargo, S. L. (2015). Extending the context of service: From encounters *Journal of Services Marketing*, 29(6/7), 453–462.
Anderson, L., Ostrom, A., Corus, C., Fisk, R., Gallan, A., Giraldo, M., Mende, M., Mulder S., Rosenbaum, M., Shirahada, K. and Williams, J. (2013). Transformative service resea for the future. *Journal of Business Research*, 66, 1203–1210.
Grönroos, C. (2011). Value co-creation in service logic: A critical analysis. *Marketing Theory*,
Grönroos, C. and Gummerus, J. (2014). The service revolution and its marketing implic logic vs service-dominant logic. *Managing Service Quality*, 24(3), 206–29.
IfM and IBM (2008). *Succeeding through Service Innovation: A Service Perspective* Research, Business and Government. Cambridge, United Kingdom: University of Caml for Manufacturing.
Lovelock, C. and Gummesson, E. (2004). Whither services marketing? In search of a new fresh perspectives. *Journal of Service Research*, 7(1), 20–41.

Further Reading

Each chapter ends with a list of suggested reading, listing international research in services marketing.

Discussion Questions

1 What distinguishes service offerings from customer service? Provide specific examples.

2 How is technology changing the nature of customer service and service offerings?

3 What are the basic characteristics of services v. goods? What are the implications of these char for Accenture or for easyJet?

4 One of the underlying frameworks for the text is the services marketing mix. Discuss why e three new mix elements (process, people and physical evidence) is included. How might eac communicate with or help to satisfy an organization's customers?

5 Think of a service job you have had or currently have. How effective, in your opinion, was or i nization in managing the elements of the services marketing mix?

6 Think of a service and examine how technology is used or could be used to improve its deliver

Discussion Questions and Exercises

Discussion questions encourage you to review and apply the knowledge you have developed from each chapter. Exercises require a little more time and thought, and can be used as group assignments or exam practice.

CASE 2 **AMAZON: DELIVERING SERVICE THROUGH ELECTRONIC CHANNELS AND INTERMEDIARIES**

This case was written by Dr Fiona Whelan-Ryan, WIT School of Business, Waterford Institute of Technology, Ireland.

Source: ©rvlsoft/Shutterstock

arrangement enhances customer experience in gaining access to a wider choice of products from a range of suppliers with the convenience of purchasing them through a single check-out process (Chaffey, 2018). Today, Amazon offers more than 390 million products sold by other companies (Duhigg, 2019). Amazon warehouses, referred to as fulfilment centres, employ a workforce of the more than 250,000 full-time associates to support this global network. Amazon Fulfilment comprises employees, technol-

Case Studies

The book includes a case study section designed to test how well you can apply the main ideas presented throughout the book to real company examples. The cases integrate a number of service ideas into a fuller example that needs deeper analysis and understanding. Each case study has its own set of questions. Cases include: Amazon, McDonald's, Music Festivals, and Turkish Airlines.

Transform learning with Connect®

Boost grades, stimulate engagement and deliver an amazing course

McGraw Hill connect®

Connect® is an online platform that integrates the science of learning with award-winning adaptive technology, to offer students and teachers a more effective teaching and learning experience.

> " Connect increases my students' knowledge and has made my teaching more effective.
>
> University of Birmingham Business School, UK "

The Three Pillars of Connect®

Flexible and high quality content tailored to your course

Use a combination of your content with McGraw Hill and OER resources to customise your course with the support of our dedicated academic and implementation consultants.

Detailed reporting and analytics

Monitor progress and improve efficiency with detailed Connect® reports. Students and teachers can use real-time performance measurement tools to monitor learning and focus on the gaps that require more attention.

Ease of set-up and continuous support

McGraw Hill offers comprehensive service, support and training - face-to-face, online or over the phone, throughout every phase of working with us to ensure easy set-up and access to the platform.

Bring theory to life **within Connect®**

Students can **test and apply their knowledge** with our engaging excercises and activities within Connect®

Discover the features on offer for your discipline on the next page!

Connect® for Marketing

We have a wide selection of activities on hand to help students gain valuable practice during their course. By applying what they have learned to real world scenarios, these exercises help test their knowledge and skills in preparation for the real world of marketing.

Application-Based Activities (ABAs)

The Application-Based Activities provide students with valuable practice, using problem solving skills to apply their knowledge to realistic scenarios. Students progress from understanding basic concepts to using their knowledge to analyse complex scenarios and solve problems. The following activities are available for your courses:

- Planning and the Marketing Mix
- Buyer Behaviour
- Integrated Marketing Communication
- Pricing Strategies & Their Impact on Sales Results
- Retail Strategy

Each activity has been created to align with higher order thinking skills, from Bloom's Taxonomy to ensure students are developing from simple memorisation, to concept application. They are also categorised by difficulty to cater to each student's abilities.

Question Bank

Build your own question banks relating to end-of-chapter material and featuring video case content to both test student knowledge and ability, and ensure engagement with existing real world cases.

Smarter studying with

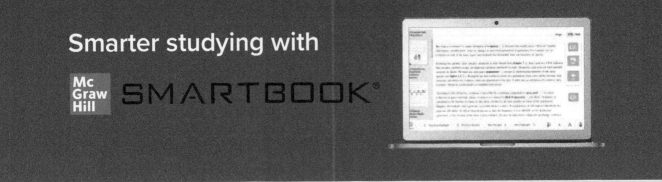

Mc Graw Hill SMARTBOOK®

The **Smartbook 2.0**® tool integrated within Connect® maximises learning by helping students study more efficiently, highlighting the most important points in the chapter, asking verification questions and indicating additional resources.

More Personalised

Smartbook 2.0® constantly adapts to students' needs, creating a personalised learning experience.

More Productive

Smartbook 2.0® creates an extremely productive learning experience, focusing students' attention on the concepts they need to learn.

More Prepared

Smartbook 2.0® helps students prepare for lessons, allowing you to use class time more dynamically.

> I liked the idea of continuous assessment online as it helped me to keep track of student performance while it freed up my time spent marking and meant I could focus on my research.
>
> **Alejandra Ramos, Trinity College Dublin, Ireland**

The ReadAnywhere App

To help you study anywhere, anytime! Gain mobile freedom to access your eBook anywhere, even offline, on your smartphone or tablet.

You can:
- Read offline and data-free by downloading the entire text or only the chapters you need.
- Never lose an assignment, a note, or your place. ReadAnywhere includes the same functionality as the eBook offered in Connect® with auto-sync across both platforms.
- Start studying anytime, anywhere.

Available on:

Create & Custom Publishing

It's easy to create your perfect
customised reader

At McGraw Hill it's easy to create a bespoke reading
resource for our students right from the comfort of your desk.

Using our tool Create you can browse and select material from our extensive library of texts and collections
and if desired, you can even include your own materials, which can be organised in the order in which you'd
like your students to work from them.

Available in both print and eBook format, you can offer your students a learning solution that works
best for them, in addition you can add digital materials to go alongside your reader too.

What are the benefits of having a custom reader?

- You have one **tailor-made** learning resource
- **McGraw Hill are here to support you** throughout your custom journey
- Students get **value for money**; they only need to purchase & read the required course material
- **Convenient** and students can easily find resources **all in one place**
- Students are **more prepared** for class

How do I Get Started?

1 **Find** and **Select** your content in **Create**

2 **Arrange** and **Integrate** your own content

3 **Personalise** your design and **Choose** the format

Learn more
https://www.mheducation.co.uk/higher-education/services/creating-custom-publishing

Contact the Team
marketing.emea@mheducation.com

OPEN UNIVERSITY PRESS
McGraw-Hill

Improve your Study, Research & Writing Skills

Clear and accessible guides on improving your reading, writing and researching skills. From undergraduate level to career researcher, we have a book to help you with your study and academic progression.

Our Study Skills books are packed with practical advice and tips that are easy to put into practice and will really improve the way you study.

- Develop your study skills
- Learn how to undertake a research project
- Enhance your academic writing and avoid plagiarism
- Learn effective ways to prep for exams
- Improve time management
- Increase your grades
- Get the job you want!

Discount Code: STUDY20

Special Offer!

As a valued customer, buy online and receive **20% off** any of our Study Skills books by entering the above promo code.

DOING YOUR RESEARCH PROJECT
A Guide for First-time Researchers

Over 300,000 copies sold across editions

JUDITH BELL AND STEPHEN WATERS

Open UP Study Skills

The Complete Guide to Referencing and Avoiding Plagiarism

3rd edition

Colin Neville

Open UP Study Skills

Succeeding with your University Essay
A Step-By-Step Handbook

John Biggam

Open UP Study Skills

The Good Research Guide
For small-scale social research projects

6th edition

Martyn Denscombe

Learn more
https://www.mheducation.co.uk/open-university-press/study-skills

Contact the Team
marketing.emea@mheducation.com

Part 1
Foundations for Services Marketing

Chapter 1   Introduction to Services

Chapter 2   Conceptual Framework of the Book: The Gaps Model
of Service Quality

This first part of the text provides you with the foundations needed to begin your study of services marketing. The first chapter identifies up-to-date trends, issues, and opportunities in services as a backdrop for the strategies addressed in the remaining chapters. The second chapter introduces the gaps model of service quality, the framework that provides the structure for the rest of the text. The remaining parts of the book will include information and strategies to address the specific gaps identified by this model, giving you the tools and knowledge to become a services marketing leader.

Chapter 1

Introduction to Services

Chapter Outline

What are Services?	3
Service Contexts	6
Service Dominant Logic	9
Technology and Evolution of Services	11
Why Services Marketing?	14
Characteristics of Services Impacting on Marketing Activities	15
Services Marketing Mix	19
Staying Focused on the Customer	22
Summary	22
Key Concepts	23
Exercises	23
Discussion Questions	23
Further Reading	24

Learning Objectives

This chapter's objectives are to:

1 Explain what services are and identify important trends in services.
2 Explain the need for special services marketing concepts and practices and why the need has developed and is accelerating.
3 Introduce the concept of service dominant logic.
4 Explore the profound impact of technology on service.
5 Outline the basic differences between goods and services and the resulting challenges and opportunities for service businesses.
6 Introduce the expanded marketing mix for services and the philosophy of customer focus, as powerful frameworks and themes that are fundamental to the rest of the text.
7 Introduce the servuction system model and the concept of the services triangle.

Opening Example
Europe's Service Industries

The service sector is a critical component of Europe's economy. It directly contributes to GDP and job creation and indirectly supports growth in other businesses by providing: financial services such as banking, investment, accountancy and insurance; infrastructure services such as energy, telecommunications, sanitation and transportation; education services for a well-trained work-force; legal services to regulate and maintain order; retail services to sell and distribute products; health, tourism and leisure services for a healthy and motivated work-force.

Source: ©Shutterstock/canadastock

In 2018 there were 29 European companies within the world's top 100 organizations. Of these, 11 of the companies were directly involved in the provision of services such as banking/financial services (HSBC Holdings, BNP Paribas, Banco Santander, ING Group, Intesa Sanpaolo and Lloyds Banking Group), insurance (Allianz, AXA Group and Prudential), energy and utilities (ENEL), and telecommunication services (Deutsche Telekom).

These organizations operate in the sectors that are traditionally associated with, and classified as, services. However, almost all of the other European companies that appear in the top 100 rely on service and services to sell their products. For example, Siemens offers consultancy services to develop and sell their product solutions to their customers. Volkswagen and BMW provide after-sales service, warranties, breakdown cover and financial packages as part of their offering and rely on the service provided by their dealers to attract custom. Shell and the other large oil companies in the top 100 aim to improve their corporate customers' business performance by providing leading-edge energy consulting supported by innovative technology.

Services are therefore critical to today's economy and although the organizations in the top 100 organizations only represent the tip of the iceberg of the European service sector, they clearly demonstrate Europe's position as a key global player in the provision of services and highlight the need to study and understand services marketing.

Source: Data extracted from www.forbes.com.[1]

What are Services?

This week, you have probably experienced a multitude of services, which may have included:

- Transport services (using buses, trains and taxis to bring you to university or your place of work)
- Hospitality services (buying coffee from Starbucks or going to a nightclub)
- Medical services (making a visit to the doctor or dentist)
- Communication services (using your mobile phone or receiving emails)
- Entertainment services (watching movies on Netflix or attending a concert)
- Leisure services (working out at the gym or planning a holiday)

Tangibility Spectrum

The broad definition of services implies that intangibility is a key determinant of whether an offering is a service. Although this is true, it is also true that very few products are purely intangible or totally tangible. Instead, services tend to be *more intangible* than manufactured products, and manufactured products tend to be *more tangible* than services. For example, the fast-food industry, while classified as a service, also has many tangible components such as the food, the packaging, and so on. Cars, while classified within the manufacturing sector, also supply many intangibles, such as transportation and navigation services. The tangibility spectrum shown in Figure 1.2 captures this idea. Throughout this text, when we refer to services we will be assuming the broad definition of services and acknowledging that there are very few 'pure services' or 'pure goods'. However, the issues and approaches we discuss are directed more toward those offerings that lie on the right-hand side, the intangible side, of the spectrum.

Figure 1.2   Tangibility spectrum

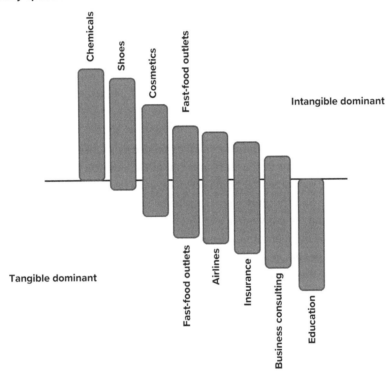

Source: Adapted from G. Lynn Shostack, 'Breaking free from product marketing', *Journal of Marketing* 41 (April 1977), pp. 73–80.

Service Contexts

However broadly or narrowly we define a service, it is important at this point to draw distinctions between *service organizations, services as products, services as experiences, customer service* and *transformative service.* Sometimes when people think of service, they think only of customer service, but service can be divided into five distinct contexts. The tools and strategies you will learn in this text can be applied to any of these contexts.

1   *Service organizations* include those industries typically classified within the service sector whose core product is a service. All of the following organizations can be considered pure service companies: Accor (hotels such as Novotel and Ibis), Lufthansa (transportation) and HSBC (banking). The total services sector comprises a wide range of service organizations, as suggested by Figure 1.2. Organizations in these sectors provide or sell services as their core offering.

There is a growing market for services and increasing dominance of services in economies worldwide, and not just in Europe. The tremendous growth and economic contributions of the service sector have drawn increasing attention to the issues and challenges of service sector industries worldwide.

Specific demand for services marketing concepts has come from the deregulated industries and professional services as both these groups have gone through rapid changes in the ways they do business. In recent decades many very large service industries, including airlines, banking, telecommunications and energy supply, have been deregulated by European governments. As a result, marketing decisions that used to be tightly controlled by the government are now partially, and in some cases totally, within the control of individual firms.[5]

For example, until the late 1990s all UK electricity supply pricing was determined and monitored by the government. A householder could only buy electricity from the one designated local supplier. Since that time electricity companies have been free to set their own pricing structures and bundle the purchase of electricity with the supply of other utilities, such as gas and telephony. Similar changes have happened across other countries in Europe, such as Sweden, Finland, Germany, Spain, Netherlands, Austria and Denmark. Needless to say, deregulation initially creates turmoil in the electricity generation and supply industry, accelerating the need for more sophisticated, customer-based and competition-sensitive marketing.

★ SERVICE SPOTLIGHT

One company to take advantage of deregulation in energy markets is EDF Energy. It is now one of the UK's largest energy companies providing generation, trading, transmission, distribution, supply and other energy services. It is a wholly owned subsidiary of the EDF Group, headquartered in France, and as one of Europe's largest energy groups, it generates around one-fifth of the UK's electricity and employs around 13,000 people. It supplies electricity and gas to around 6 million residential and business customers, making it the biggest supplier of electricity by volume. Elsewhere in Europe it has over 37 million customers, with over 28 million of these in France. It has over 152,000 employees worldwide and offers services in 19 countries (13 of these in Europe).

Source: www.edfenergy.com.

Providers of professional services (such as dentists, lawyers, accountants, engineers and architects) have also demanded new concepts and approaches for their businesses as these industries have become increasingly competitive and as professional standards have been modified to allow advertising. Whereas traditionally the professions avoided even using the word *marketing*, they are now seeking better ways to understand and segment their customers, to ensure the delivery of quality services, and to strengthen their position amid a growing number of competitors.

2 *Services as products* represent a wide range of intangible product offerings that customers value and pay for in the marketplace. Service products are sold by service companies and by non-service companies, such as manufacturers and technology companies. For example, IBM and Hewlett-Packard offer information technology consulting services to the marketplace, competing with firms such as Accenture and Capita, which are traditional pure services firms. Other industry examples include retailers, like Carrefour, that sell services such as insurance and travel services.

Early in the development of the field of services marketing and management, most of the impetus came from service industries such as banking, transportation and retailing. As these traditional service industries evolve and become more competitive, the need for effective services management and marketing strategies continues. Now, manufacturing and technology industries, such as cars, computers and software, are also recognizing the need to provide quality service and revenue-producing services in order to compete worldwide.

From Ericsson and Apple to Hewlett-Packard and Siemens, companies are recognizing the opportunity to grow and profit through services.[6] Why? Because the quick pace of developing technologies and increasing competition make it difficult to gain strategic competitive advantage through physical products alone. Moreover, customers are more demanding. Not only do they expect excellent, high-quality goods and technology, they also expect high levels of customer service and total service solutions along with them.

⭐ SERVICE SPOTLIGHT

Siemens design and manufacture products and systems ranging from traffic lights, gas turbines and turbine spares to the superconducting magnets used in medical scanners and the drives that are behind many of Europe's manufacturing plants. In the UK, more than half of Siemens's turnover comes from the provision of services. For example, the industry solutions division is the systems and solutions integrator for processing plant business. It provides services ranging from planning and construction to operation and maintenance over a plant's entire life-cycle. The division aims to use its process know-how for increasing the productivity and competitiveness of enterprises in various industries.

Other divisions of Siemens generate around 40 per cent of the UK's wind energy; they install, maintain and read meters in nearly 9 million homes and businesses; maintain a fleet of electric trains; and repair and maintain traffic lights in towns and cities. This service portfolio is aimed at supporting technology (including non-Siemens technology) to provide solutions for customers.

Source: **www.siemens.com.**

As manufacturers such as Siemens and IT companies such as IBM move to become services organizations, the need for special concepts and approaches for managing and marketing services is becoming increasingly apparent.[7]

3 *Services as experiences* The term 'Experience Economy' was first described in an article published in 1999 by Pine and Gilmore.[8] The article argued that service companies would evolve from simply providing a service to creating memorable events for their customers, with the memory of the experience becoming the product. Rather than the service company charging for the activities it performs, it would be charging for the feelings that customers derive from engaging in the service. Many organizations in the hospitality (boutique hotels) and entertainment sectors (Disneyland Paris) have focused on experiences for many years. However, we are now seeing other services including retailers (Nike Stores) and airlines (Virgin Atlantic) doing likewise.

4 *Customer service* is also a critical aspect of what we mean by 'service'. Customer service is the service provided in support of a company's core products. Companies typically do not charge for customer service. Customer service can occur on-site (as when a retail employee helps a customer find a desired item or answers a question), or it can occur over the telephone or via the Internet (e.g. Dell computer provides real-time chat sessions to help customers diagnose hardware problems). Many companies operate customer service call centres or helplines, often staffed around the clock. Quality customer service is essential to building customer relationships. It should not, however, be confused with the services provided for sale by the company.

5 *Transformative service* is about developing and delivering services that create positive changes and improvements in the well-being of individuals, communities and ecosystems. In addition to customer satisfaction and loyalty, services can impact on well-being outcomes, such as access, decreasing disparity, and health.[9] Well-designed services can bring happiness to individuals and communities reducing aspects of tension, fear and stress. For example, a city authority may improve the life of its inhabitants by developing public transport systems, better policing, hosting festivals and providing innovative

social care initiatives. Transformative service is also about the well-being of the environment, providing services that create positive changes for people today but also protect the planet in a way that ensures the well-being of people in the future. This may encompass areas such as managing the sustainable delivery and consumption of energy, water waste management and transportation service offerings.

Service Dominant Logic

Service dominant logic is another way to look at what service means. In an article in the *Journal of Marketing*, Steve Vargo and Bob Lusch argue for a new dominant logic for marketing that suggests that all products and physical goods are valued for the services they provide.[10] Drawing on the work of respected economists, marketers and philosophers, the two authors suggest that the value derived from physical goods is really the service provided by the good, not the good itself. For example, they suggest that a pharmaceutical product provides medical services, a razor provides shaving services, and computers provide information and data manipulation services. Although this view is somewhat abstract, it suggests an even broader, more inclusive, view of the meaning of service. Their argument is that companies provide service solutions for customers and should therefore offer the best combinations of service and products to create that solution. The over-arching concept is that it is the knowledge and competencies of the providers and the customers that represent the essential source of value creation rather than the products on their own. In the traditional view of goods, a product is delivered to a customer who uses and consumes it. The thinking behind service dominant logic is that value is not something that is simply created and delivered to the customer; the value is co-created in a process that requires the active participation of the producer, its customers and possibly other stakeholders (of the producer and the customer).

Value is created not at the time of the exchange between the producer and the customer but when the customer integrates, applies and uses the resources of a particular producer. A car has limited value unless it can provide a way of getting people to work; or it can provide a way of communicating a person's self-image; or it provides a sense of freedom for some. This is termed 'value in use' and is supported by warranties, advertising, branding and finance schemes as well as the physical product itself. It is also co-created by the customer, as the customer is expected to perform in certain ways in order to ensure their optimum achievement of the 'value in use'. It will depend on their driving skills, their knowledge of cars, roads and destinations as well as the manner in which they display the car (how clean they keep it, the accessories they use and the manner in which they drive). The value also varies contextually in relation to time and place dimensions. This 'value-in-context'[11] concept takes account of external influences and other stakeholders covering government-imposed laws and restrictions; traffic congestion, fuel prices; ecological and social pressures relating to emissions or fast driving and fuel consumption. Producers and customers may work together to influence these external forces in order to co-create better value for each other. This may mean that in the future, car manufacturers do not simply develop and sell electric cars but also work with customers and other stakeholders to provide solutions that allow householders to generate sufficient power for the cars, as well as charging points in city centres, or better road layouts in addition to education programmes on energy conservation.

To fully understand service dominant logic, it is also important to consider the role of interaction in creating value. This was highlighted by Christian Grönroos[12] but also stems from the traditional view of services (see Figure 1.5 and the servuction system later in the chapter) that a service involves interaction between a service provider and a customer.

A company is producing an offering of potential value to the customer through product development, design, manufacture and delivery. This may happen with or without direct interaction with the customer. The customers, in turn, are responsible for the value-creating processes, where value is created or emerges as value in use. Where customers interact through being engaged with the company in product design or with the company's personnel in delivery, installation or customer service activities, co-production of the resources can occur and/or co-creation of value in use is made possible (see Figure 1.3). If there are no direct interactions, customers are engaged in independent value creation with products or resources obtained from the independent activities undertaken by the company aimed at facilitating the customer's future value creation. The value generation process can therefore be seen as comprising three spheres: a *provider sphere* that is closed to customers, where the service provider compiles resources to be offered to customers to enable their value creation; *a joint sphere* where the service provider and customers interact directly to co-create value; and *a customer sphere*, where the customers independently create value without the direct involvement of the service provider.[13]

Figure 1.3   A value-in-use creation model

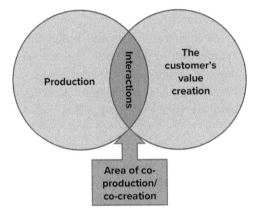

In many markets, the Internet and other technologies have enabled the complexity and dynamism of these interactions and inter-relationships to evolve further, with websites, online forums, review sites, real-time data, mobile applications and location-based services, all adding to the value created for the customer and the producer. Therefore service dominant logic moves thinking away from the fallacy that products are different from services because they only create value in a linear and sequential set of stages: creation, exchange and consumption. Instead it puts forward a much more complex and dynamic system of stakeholders, communications and technology that creates value and the context in which it is obtained.[14] This is evident in the following service spotlight.

SERVICE SPOTLIGHT

Ford, along with other car manufacturers, has added value to their cars by adding the service provided by their Ford's Sync Emergency Assistance technology. This technology can potentially reduce the time taken to respond to accidents by assisting vehicle occupants to place a direct emergency call with location details in the correct local language. It helps notify the emergency services in that vital 'golden hour' after a serious crash when rapid medical attention can be the difference between life and death.

The vehicle's SYNC system initiates an emergency call through the occupant's Bluetooth-connected mobile phone following the deployment of an airbag. The system plays an introductory message and then relays the accident location co-ordinates using the on-board GPS unit, map and mobile network information. Emergency Assist saves crucial seconds by placing a call directly to emergency service operators rather than first routing through a third-party call centre. The value is co-created through a network of the car manufacturer, the driver switching on the Bluetooth function, the mobile phone manufacturer and the emergency services.

Source: **www.euroncap.com/rewards/ford_sync_emergency_assistance.aspx.**

Technology and Evolution of Services

The preceding sections examined the roots of services marketing and the reasons why the field exists. Today, technology is currently shaping the field and profoundly influencing the practice of services marketing. In this section we explore trends in service technology (positive *and* negative) to set the stage for topics that will be discussed throughout this text.

Innovative Service Offerings

Looking to the recent past, it is apparent how technology has been the basic force behind service innovations that are now taken for granted. Video streaming services, interactive voice response systems, mobile phone apps, location-based services, self service checkouts and other common services only became possible because of new technologies. Just think how dramatically different your world would be without these basic technology services.

The Internet has also resulted in a host of new services. Internet-based companies like Amazon, Facebook and eBay offer services previously unheard of. And companies established in the pre-digital era are also finding that the Internet provides a way to offer new services as well.[15] For example, the *Financial Times* offers an interactive edition that allows customers to organize the newspaper's content to suit their individual preferences and needs.

Developments in integrated computing and artificial intelligence have led to the emergence of Internet of Things (IoT) technologies. As a result, many new technology services are on the horizon. For example, the 'connected car' allows people to access all kinds of existing and new services while on the road. Already many cars are equipped with satellite navigation systems that direct drivers to specific locations. The most advanced in-car systems can provide recommendations for shopping by informing drivers when they are in close proximity to their preferred retailer. On a long journey, the systems can provide weather forecasts and warnings, and when it is time to stop for the night, the car's system can book a room at a nearby hotel, recommend a restaurant and make dinner reservations. The computing capabilities of the mobile phone are also making it possible for whole suites of service applications, including airline check-in, theatre booking or the provision of tourist information to be available in a person's pocket. Voice assistants like Google Home or Amazon's Alexa can provide answers to your questions without you needing to pick up your phone or turn on your computer. They can adjust your heating, lighting and music whilst ordering a pizza from the local takeaway and, as they gather more data from you, they quickly learn your likes as well as dislikes, tailoring services to your preferences.

Other technological advances are making it possible for medical professionals to monitor patients' conditions remotely and even to provide medical diagnoses, treatment, and surgery guidance via technology interfaces. Similarly, a company such as Rolls-Royce can now remotely monitor and adjust jet engines on commercial aeroplanes, as well as providing sophisticated information and data about each engine to the airlines remotely through the Internet.

New Ways to Deliver Service

In addition to providing opportunities for new service offerings, technology is providing vehicles for delivering existing services in more accessible, convenient, productive ways. Technology facilitates basic customer service functions (bill-paying, questions, bank account records, tracking orders), transactions (both retail and business to business) and learning or information seeking. Companies have moved from face-to-face service to telephone-based service to widespread use of interactive voice response systems to Internet-based customer service and now to mobile services. Interestingly, many companies are coming full circle and now offer human contact as the ultimate form of customer service!

Technology also facilitates transactions by offering a direct vehicle for making purchases. Technology giant Dell offers virtually all its customer service and ordering functions to its business customers via technology. Over 90 per cent of its transactions with customers are completed online. On the consumer side, online shopping and transactions have already revolutionized the music, travel and book businesses.

Finally, technology, specifically the Internet, provides an easy way for customers to learn and research. Access to information has never been easier. For example, health-related websites are now among the most frequently accessed sites on the Internet with current estimates indicating that there are now over 100,000 sites offering health-related information.[16] There can be dangers with this, as the public is often unsure as to which sites are providing accurate information and which are providing spurious cures for serious health conditions.

★ SERVICE SPOTLIGHT

As there are so many online sites and mobile applications addressing health and medicines, the National Health Service (NHS) in the UK has set up an online site to help people easily find safe and trusted mobile apps. The NHS Choices Health Apps Library (www.nhs.uk/apps-library) provides access to a range of applications aimed at assisting patients manage their health and medical conditions through mobile phones and tablet computers. The apps range from those addressing certain conditions, treatments and body parts, to those supporting healthy living and providing health information. All the apps in the Health Apps Library are reviewed to ensure that they are clinically safe.

Source: **www.nhs.uk/apps-library.**

Enabling Both Customers and Employees

Technology enables both customers and employees to be more effective in getting and providing service.[17] Through **self-service technologies**, customers can serve themselves more effectively. Via online or mobile phone banking, customers can access their accounts, check balances, apply for loans, shift money between accounts and take care of just about any banking need they might have – all without the assistance of the bank's employees. These online and mobile banking services are just one example of the types of self-service technologies that are proliferating across industries.

For employees, technology can provide tremendous support in making them more effective and efficient in delivering service. Customer relationship management and sales support software are broad categories of technology that can aid front-line employees in providing better service. By having immediate access to information about their product and service offerings, as well as about particular customers, employees are better able to serve them. This type of information allows employees to customize services to fit the customer's needs. They can also be much more efficient and timely than in the old days when most customer and product information was in paper files or in the heads of sales and customer service representatives.

Smart cities are also on the rise, and IoT developers are devising ways to use the IoT to monitor city conditions such as traffic, air quality, electric/water usage, and environmental factors. Doing so can assist city planners as well as residents to conserve resources and come up with solutions to current issues. Such solutions may include the sequencing of traffic lights, more efficient routing of public transport and alerting the public to specific situations as they occur.

Extending The Global Reach of Services

Technology infusion results in the potential for reaching out to customers around the globe in ways not possible before. The Internet itself knows no boundaries, and therefore information, customer service and transactions can move across countries and across continents, reaching any customer who has access to the Web. Internet technology, in combination with mobile communications and renewable energy services, can also act as *transformative service* tools supporting human well-being and making a valuable contribution to some of the poorest and least developed areas of the world.

⭐ SERVICE SPOTLIGHT

easyJet offers an online flight tracker service for all of its flights in Europe. It is possible to track any of its flights in real time on a map, allowing friends, relatives or business partners picking up passengers from an airport to check the most up-to-date status of a flight using a tablet or smartphone. This enhances the service for the customer and increases consumer confidence in the easyJet brand and the quality of its operations.

Technology also allows employees of international companies to stay in touch easily – to share information, to ask questions, or to serve on virtual teams together. All this technology facilitates the global reach as well as the effectiveness of service businesses.

The Internet *is* a Service

An interesting way to look at the influence of technology is to realize that the Internet is just 'one big service'. All businesses and organizations that operate on the Internet are essentially providing a service – whether they are giving information, performing basic customer service functions or facilitating transactions. Thus, all the tools, concepts and strategies you learn in studying services marketing and management have direct application in an Internet or e-business world. Although technology and the Internet are profoundly changing how people do business and what offerings are possible, it is clear that customers still want basic service. They want what they have always wanted: dependable outcomes, easy access, responsive systems, flexibility, apologies and compensation when things go wrong. But now they expect these same outcomes from technology-based businesses and from e-commerce solutions.[18] With hindsight it is obvious that many dot-com start-ups suffered and even failed because of lack of basic customer knowledge and failure of implementation, logistics, and service follow-up.[19]

The Paradoxes and Dark Side of Technology and Service

Although there is clearly great potential for technology to support and enhance services, there are potential negative outcomes as well. Customer concerns about privacy and confidentiality raise major issues for firms as they seek to learn about and interact directly with customers through the Internet. These types of concerns are what have stymied and precluded many efforts to advance technology applications in the healthcare industry, for example. Nor are all customers equally interested in using technology as a means of interacting with companies. Research exploring 'customer technology readiness' suggests that some customers are simply not interested in, or ready to use, technology.[20] Employees can also be reluctant to accept and integrate technology into their work lives – especially when they perceive, rightly or wrongly, that the technology will become a substitute for human labour and perhaps eliminate their jobs.

With technology infusion comes a loss of human contact, which many people believe is detrimental purely from the perspective of human relationships and quality of life. Parents may lament that their children spend hours in front of screens, interacting with games, seeking information and relating to their friends only through instant messaging without any face-to-face human contact. And workers in organizations become more and more reliant on communicating through technology – even communicating via email with the person in the next office!

Finally, the payback in technology investments is often uncertain. It may take a long time for an investment to result in productivity or customer satisfaction gains. Airlines, such as British Airways and KLM, originally had to use ticket discounting to get passengers to migrate to Internet booking services.

Why Services Marketing?

Why is it important to learn about services marketing, service quality and service management? What are the differences in services versus product marketing that have led to the demand for books and courses on services? Many forces have led to the growth of services marketing, and many industries, companies and individuals have defined the scope of the concepts, frameworks and strategies that define the field. The field of services marketing and management has evolved as a result of these combined forces.

Services Marketing is Different

Over time, business people have realized that marketing and managing services presents issues and challenges not faced in the marketing of products. As service businesses began to turn to marketing and decided to employ marketing people, they naturally recruited from the best marketers in the world – Procter & Gamble, General Foods and Unilever. People who moved from marketing in packaged goods industries to marketing in airlines, banking and other service industries found that their skills and experiences were not directly transferable. They faced issues and dilemmas in marketing services that their experiences in packaged goods and manufacturing had not prepared them for. These people realized the need for new concepts and approaches for marketing and managing service businesses.

Service marketers responded to these forces and began to work across disciplines and with academics and business practitioners from around the world to develop and document marketing practices for services. As the field evolved, it expanded to address the concerns and needs of *any* business in which service is an integral part of the offering. Frameworks, concepts and strategies have been developed to address the fact that 'services marketing is different'. As the field continues to evolve in the twenty-first century, new trends will shape it and accelerate the need for services marketing concepts and tools.

In the final decades of the twentieth century, many firms jumped on the service bandwagon, investing in service initiatives and promoting service quality as ways to differentiate themselves and create competitive advantage. Many of these investments were based on faith and intuition by managers who believed in serving customers well and who believed in their hearts that quality service made good business sense. Indeed, a dedication to quality service has been the foundation for success for many firms, across industries. In his book *Discovering the Soul of Service*, Leonard Berry describes in detail 14 such companies.[21] The companies featured in his book had been in business for an average of 31 years in 1999 when the book was written. These companies had been profitable in all but five of their combined 407 years of existence. Dr Berry discovered through his research that these successful businesses share devotion to nine common service themes. Among these are values-driven leadership, commitment to investment in employee success, and trust-based relationships with customers and other partners at the foundation of the organization.

Since the mid-1990s, firms have demanded hard evidence of the bottom-line effectiveness of service strategies, and researchers are building a convincing case that service strategies, implemented appropriately, can be very profitable. Work sponsored by the Marketing Science Institute suggests that corporate strategies focused on customer satisfaction, revenue generation, and service quality may actually be more profitable than strategies focused on cost-cutting or strategies that attempt to do both simultaneously.[22] Research from the Harvard Business School builds a case for the 'service–profit chain', linking internal service and employee satisfaction to customer value and ultimately to profits.[23] Also, considerable research shows linkages from customer satisfaction (often driven by service outcomes) to profits.[24]

An important key to these successes is that the right strategies are chosen and that these strategies are implemented appropriately and well. Much of what you learn from this text will guide you in making such correct choices and in providing superior implementation. Throughout the text we will point out the profit implications and trade-offs to be made with service strategies.

Characteristics of Services Impacting on Marketing Activities

There is general agreement that the distinctive characteristics discussed in this section result in challenges (as well as advantages) for managers of services.[25] It is also important to realize that each of these characteristics could be arranged on a continuum similar to the tangibility spectrum shown in Figure 1.2. That is, services tend to be more heterogeneous, more intangible and more difficult to evaluate than goods, but the differences between goods and services are not black and white by any means.[26]

Table 1.1 summarizes the traditional view of the differences between goods and services and the implications of these characteristics. Many of the strategies, tools and frameworks in this text were developed to address these characteristics. It has been suggested that these distinctive characteristics should not be viewed as unique to services but that they are also relevant to goods, as all products are simply tools or objects used to provide a service to the customer and that 'economic exchange is fundamentally about service provision'.[27] This is complicated by the fact there is a growing diversity of activities within the service sector, many of which involve a combination of goods and services within the offering.

Table 1.1   Goods versus services

Goods	Services	Resulting Implications
Tangible	Intangible	Services cannot be inventoried
		Services cannot be easily patented
		Services cannot be readily displayed or communicated
		Pricing is difficult
Standardized	Heterogeneous	Service delivery and customer satisfaction depend on employee and customer actions
		Service quality depends on many uncontrollable factors
		There is no sure knowledge that the service delivered matches what was planned and promoted
Production separate from consumption	Inseparability – simultaneous production and consumption	Customers participate in and affect the transaction
		Customers affect each other
		Employees affect the service outcome
		Decentralization may be essential
		Mass production is difficult
Non-perishable	Perishable	It is difficult to synchronize supply and demand with services
		Services cannot be returned or resold

Source: A. Parasuraman, V.A. Zeithaml and L.L. Berry, 'A conceptual model of service quality and its implications for future research', *Journal of Marketing* 49 (Fall 1985), pp. 41–50.

However, the continuing importance of understanding these differences can be explained as follows:[28]

1   The identification of these characteristics provided the impetus and legitimacy necessary to launch the new field of services marketing and the related academic research.
2   The characteristics identified enabled service researchers to recognize that achieving quality in manufacturing requires a different approach to that required for a service quality improvement.
3   Each of the characteristics taken separately or in combination continues to inform research and management in specific service industries, categories and situations.

Intangibility

The most basic distinguishing characteristic of services is intangibility. Because services are performances or actions rather than objects, they cannot be seen, felt, tasted or touched in the same manner as tangible goods. For example, healthcare services are actions (such as surgery, diagnosis, examination and treatment) performed by providers and directed towards patients and their families. These services cannot actually be seen or touched by the patient, although the patient may be able to see and touch certain tangible components of the service (such as the equipment or hospital room). In fact, many services such as healthcare are difficult for the consumer to grasp even mentally. Even after a diagnosis or surgery has been completed, the patient may not fully comprehend the service performed, although tangible evidence of the service (e.g. incision, bandaging, pain) may be quite apparent.

Resulting Marketing Implications

Intangibility presents several marketing challenges. Services cannot be patented easily, and new service concepts can therefore easily be copied by competitors. Services cannot be readily displayed or easily communicated to customers, so quality may be difficult for consumers to assess. Decisions about what to include in advertising and other promotional materials are challenging, as is pricing. The actual costs of a 'unit of service' are hard to determine, and the price–quality relationship is complex.

Heterogeneity

Because services are performances, frequently produced by humans, no two services will be precisely alike. The employees delivering the service frequently *are* the service in the customer's eyes, and people may differ in their performance from day to day or even hour to hour. Heterogeneity also results because no two customers are precisely alike: each will have unique demands or experience the service in a unique way. Thus, the heterogeneity connected with services is largely the result of human interaction (between and among employees and customers) and all of the vagaries that accompany it. For example, a tax accountant may provide a different service experience to two different customers on the same day, depending on their individual needs and personalities and on whether the accountant is interviewing them when he or she is fresh in the morning or tired at the end of a long day of meetings.

Resulting Marketing Implications

Because services are heterogeneous across time, organizations and people, ensuring consistent service quality is challenging. Quality actually depends on many factors that cannot be fully controlled by the service supplier, such as the ability of the consumer to articulate his or her needs, the ability and willingness of personnel to satisfy those needs, the presence (or absence) of other customers and the level of demand for the service. Because of these complicating factors, the service manager cannot always know for sure that the service is being delivered in a manner consistent with what was originally planned and promoted. This can be a particular challenge for service brands such as hotels and restaurants that attempt to deliver a consistent brand offering throughout the world in each of their locations. If customers receive inconsistent service that doesn't match the brand promise, this may impact on their future brand choice. Sometimes services may be provided by a third party (for example, baggage handling agents and check-in agents for an airline), further increasing the potential heterogeneity of the offering. Some of the variation can be reduced by replacing human inputs by automation (automated teller machines and self-service check-in facilities) or through the adoption of rigorous quality control improvement procedures.

Inseparability

Whereas most goods are produced first, then sold and consumed, most services are sold first and then produced and consumed simultaneously. For example, a car can be manufactured in Japan, shipped to Paris, sold four months later and consumed over a period of years. By contrast, restaurant services cannot be provided until they have been sold, and the dining experience is essentially produced and consumed at the same time. Frequently this situation also means that the customer is present while the service is being produced, and thus views and may even take part in the production process. Inseparability also means that customers will frequently interact with each other during the service production process and thus may affect each other's experiences. For example, strangers seated next to each other in an aeroplane may well affect the nature of the service experience for each other. That passengers understand this fact is clearly apparent in the way business travellers will often go to great lengths to be sure they are not seated next to families with small children. Another outcome of simultaneous production and consumption is that service producers find themselves playing a role as part of the product itself and as an essential ingredient in the service experience for the consumer.

Resulting Marketing Implications

Because services are often produced and consumed at the same time, mass production is difficult. The quality of service and customer satisfaction will be highly dependent on what happens in 'real time', including actions of employees and the interactions between employees and customers. Clearly the real-time nature of services also results in advantages in terms of opportunities to customize offerings for individual consumers. Simultaneous production and consumption also means that it is not usually possible to gain significant economies of scale through centralization. Often, operations need to be relatively decentralized so that the service can be delivered directly to the consumer in a convenient location, although the growth of technology-delivered services is changing this requirement for many services. Also, because of simultaneous production and consumption, the customer is involved in, and observes, the production process and thus may affect (positively or negatively) the outcome of the service transaction. However, advances in the Internet and telecommunications have made it possible in some information-based sectors to separate customers in both time and space from production.

Perishability

Perishability refers to the fact that services cannot be saved, stored, resold or returned. A seat on a flight or in a restaurant, an hour of a lawyer's time or telephone line capacity not used cannot be reclaimed and used or resold at a later time. Perishability is in contrast to goods (with the exception of fresh food products) that can be stored in inventory or resold another day, or even returned if the consumer is unhappy. Would it not be nice if a bad haircut could be returned or resold to another consumer? Perishability makes this action an unlikely possibility for most services, although it should be noted that there are services, such as education and entertainment, where performances can be captured and replayed or rebroadcast time and time again.

Resulting Marketing Implications

A primary issue that marketers face in relation to service perishability is the inability to hold stock. Demand forecasting and creative planning for capacity utilization are therefore important and challenging decision areas. For example, there is tremendous demand for resort accommodation in the French Alps for skiing in February, but much less demand in July. Yet hotel and chalet owners have the same number of rooms to sell all year round. The fact that services cannot typically be returned or resold also implies a need for strong recovery strategies when things do go wrong. For example, although a bad haircut cannot be returned, the hairdresser can and should have strategies for recovering the customer's goodwill if and when such a problem occurs.

Challenges and Questions for Service Marketers

Because of the basic characteristics of services, marketers of services face some very real and quite distinctive challenges. Answers to questions such as those listed here still elude managers of services:

- *How can service quality be defined and improved* when the product is intangible and non-standardized?
- *How can new services be designed and tested effectively* when the service is essentially an intangible process?

- *How can the firm be certain it is communicating a consistent and relevant image* when so many elements of the marketing mix communicate to customers and some of these elements are the service providers themselves?
- *How does the firm accommodate fluctuating demand* when capacity is fixed and the service itself is perishable?
- *How can the firm best motivate and select service employees* who, because the service is delivered in real time, become a critical part of the product itself?
- *How should prices be set when* it is difficult to determine actual costs of production and price may be inextricably intertwined with perceptions of quality?
- *How should the firm be organized so that good strategic and tactical decisions are made* when a decision in any of the functional areas of marketing, operations and human resources may have significant impact on the other two areas?
- *How can the balance between standardization and personalization be determined* to maximize both the efficiency of the organization and the satisfaction of its customers?
- *How can the organization protect new service concepts from competitors* when service processes cannot be readily patented?
- *How does the firm communicate quality and value to consumers* when the offering is intangible and cannot be readily tried or displayed?
- *How can the organization ensure the delivery of consistent quality service* when both the organization's employees and the customers themselves can affect the service outcome?

The Services Triangle

To answer some of these questions, it is important to understand that services marketing is about promises – promises made and promises kept to customers. A strategic framework known as the *services marketing triangle* (illustrated in Figure 1.4) shows the three interlinked groups that work together to develop, promote and deliver these service promises. These key players are labelled on the points of the triangle: the *company* (or strategic business unit (SBU) or department or 'management'), the *customers* and the *employees/technology*. This last group can be the firm's employees and subcontractors that deliver the company's services or it can be the technology such as automated teller machines that supply the service. Between these three points on the triangle, three types of marketing must be successfully carried out for a service to succeed: external marketing, interactive marketing, and internal marketing.

Figure 1.4   The services marketing triangle

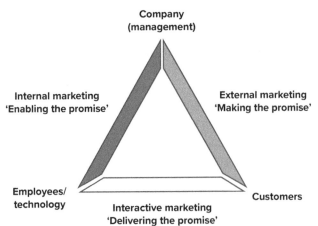

Source: Adapted from M.J. Bitner, 'Building service relationships: it's all about promises', *Journal of the Academy of Marketing Science* 23, no. 4 (1995), pp. 246–51; C. Grönroos, *Service Management and Marketing* (Lexington, MA: Lexington Books, 1990); and P. Kotler, *Marketing Management: Analysis, Planning, Implementation, and Control*, 8th edn (Englewood Cliffs, NJ: Prentice Hall, 1994), p. 470.

On the right-hand side of the triangle are the *external marketing* efforts that the firm engages in to set up its customers' expectations and promise them what is to be delivered. Anything or anyone that communicates to the customer before service delivery can be viewed as part of this external marketing function. But external marketing is just the beginning for services marketers: promises made must be kept. On the bottom of the triangle is what has been termed *interactive marketing* or *real-time marketing*. Here is where promises are kept or broken by the firm's employees, technology, subcontractors or agents. If promises are not kept, customers become dissatisfied and eventually leave. The left-hand side of the triangle suggests the critical role played by *internal marketing*. Management engages in these activities to aid the providers in their ability to deliver on the service promise: recruiting, training, motivating, rewarding, and providing equipment and technology. Unless service employees are able and willing to deliver on the promises made, the firm will not be successful, and the services triangle will collapse.

All three sides of the triangle are essential to complete the whole, and the sides of the triangle should be aligned – that is, what is promised through external marketing should be the same as what is delivered; and the enabling activities inside the organization should be aligned with what is expected of service providers and employees.

Services Marketing Mix

One of the most basic concepts in marketing is the marketing mix, defined as the elements an organization controls that can be used to satisfy or communicate with customers. The traditional marketing mix is composed of the four Ps: *product, price, place* (distribution) and *promotion*.[29] These elements appear as core decision variables in any marketing text or marketing plan. The notion of a mix implies that all the variables are interrelated and depend on each other to some extent. Further, the marketing mix philosophy implies an optimal mix of the four factors for a given market segment at a given point in time.

Key strategy decision areas for each of the four Ps are captured in the four columns in Table 1.2. Careful management of product, place, promotion and price will clearly be essential to the successful marketing of services. However, the strategies for the four Ps require some modifications when applied to services. For example, traditionally promotion is thought of as involving decisions related to sales, advertising, sales promotions and publicity. In services these factors are also important, but because services are produced and consumed simultaneously, service delivery people (such as checkout operators, ticket collectors, nurses and telephone personnel) are involved in real-time promotion of the service even if their jobs are typically defined in terms of the operational function they perform.

Because services are usually produced and consumed simultaneously, customers are often present in the firm's factory, interact directly with the firm's personnel and are actually part of the service production process. Also, because services are intangible, customers will often be looking for any tangible cue to help them understand the nature of the service experience. For example, in the hotel industry the design and decor of the hotel as well as the appearance and attitudes of its employees will influence customer perceptions and experiences.

Acknowledgement of the importance of these additional variables has led services marketers to adopt the concept of an expanded marketing mix for services. In addition to the traditional four Ps, the services marketing mix includes people, physical evidence and process.[30]

> *People* All human actors who play a part in service delivery and thus influence the buyer's perceptions: namely, the firm's personnel, the customer, and other customers in the service environment.

All the human actors participating in the delivery of a service provide cues to the customer regarding the nature of the service itself. How these people are dressed, their personal appearance, and their attitudes and behaviours all influence the customer's perceptions of the service. The service provider or contact person

Table 1.2 Expanded marketing mix for services

Product	Place	Promotion	Price
Physical good features	Channel type	Promotion blend	Flexibility
Quality level	Exposure	Salespeople	Price level
Accessories	Intermediaries	Selection	Terms
Packaging	Outlet locations	Training	Differentiation
Warranties	Transportation	Incentives	Discounts
Product lines	Storage	Advertising	Allowances
Branding	Managing channels	Media types	
		Types of ads	
		Sales promotion	
		Publicity	
		Digital media	

People	Physical Evidence	Process	
Employees	Facility design	Flow of activities	
Recruiting	Equipment	Standardized	
Training	Signage	Customized	
Motivation	Employee dress	Number of steps	
Rewards	Other tangibles	Simple	
Teamwork	Reports	Complex	
Customers	Business cards	Customer involvement	
Education	Statements		
Training	Guarantees		
	Web page design		

can be very important. In fact, for some services, such as consulting, counselling, teaching and other professional relationship-based services, the provider *is* the service. In other cases the contact person may play what appears to be a relatively small part in service delivery – for instance, a telephone installer, an airline baggage handler or an equipment delivery dispatcher. Yet research suggests that even these providers may be the focal point of service encounters that can prove critical for the organization.

In many service situations, customers themselves can also influence service delivery, thus affecting service quality and their own satisfaction. For example, a client of a consulting company can influence the quality of service received by providing needed and timely information and by implementing recommendations provided by the consultant. Similarly, healthcare patients greatly affect the quality of service they receive when they either comply or do not comply with health regimes prescribed by the provider.

Customers not only influence their own service outcomes, but they can influence other customers as well. In a theatre, at a football match or in a classroom, customers can influence the quality of service received by others – either enhancing or detracting from other customers' experiences.

Physical evidence The environment in which the service is delivered and where the firm and customer interact, and any tangible components that facilitate performance or communication of the service.

The physical evidence of service includes all the tangible representations of the service such as brochures, letterhead, business cards, report formats, signage and equipment. In some cases it includes the physical facility where the service is offered – the 'servicescape' – for example, the retail bank branch facility. In other cases, such as telecommunication services, the physical facility may be irrelevant. In this case other tangibles, such as billing statements and appearance of the telephone engineer's van, may be important indicators of quality. Especially when consumers have little on which to judge the actual quality of service, they will rely on these cues, just as they rely on the cues provided by the people and the service process. Physical evidence cues provide excellent opportunities for the firm to send consistent and strong messages regarding the organization's purpose, the intended market segments and the nature of the service.

Process *The actual procedures, mechanisms, and flow of activities by which the service is delivered – the service delivery and operating systems.*

The actual delivery steps that the customer experiences, or the operational flow of the service, also give customers evidence on which to judge the service. Some services are very complex, requiring the customer to follow a complicated and extensive series of actions to complete the process. Highly bureaucratized services frequently follow this pattern, and the logic of the steps involved often escapes the customer. Another distinguishing characteristic of the process that can provide evidence to the customer is whether the service follows a production line/standardized approach or whether the process is an empowered/customized one. None of these characteristics of the service is inherently better or worse than another. Rather, the point is that these process characteristics are another form of evidence used by the consumer to judge service. For example, two successful airline companies, easyJet and Singapore Airlines, follow extremely different process models. easyJet is a no-frills (no food, no assigned seats), low-priced airline that offers frequent, relatively short flights within Europe. All the evidence it provides is consistent with its vision and market position. Singapore Airlines, on the other hand, focuses on the business traveller and is concerned with meeting individual traveller needs. Thus, its process is highly customized to the individual, and employees are empowered to provide non-standard service when needed. Both airlines have been very successful.

The three new marketing mix elements (people, physical evidence, and process) are included in the marketing mix as separate elements because they are within the control of the firm *and* because any or all of them may influence the customer's initial decision to purchase a service as well as the customer's level of satisfaction and repurchase decisions. Their impact is evident in the servuction system model (Figure 1.5), developed by two French academics.[31] This model breaks the service delivery process that a customer receives into two parts: that which is visible to the customer and that which is not. The invisible part is the process element from the extended marketing mix consisting of systems, backroom procedures

Figure 1.5   The servuction system model[32]

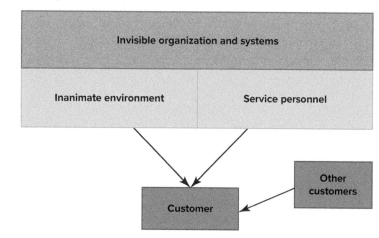

and the technology or equipment needed to produce the service. In a restaurant this would involve the ordering of ingredients, the cooking facilities and the procedures involved in preparing the food.

The visible part is broken into the inanimate environment (physical evidence) and the service providers or the individuals (people) who interact with the customer during the service experience. The inanimate environment consists of the physical design elements that the customer comes into contact with. This could include aspects such as the lighting, place settings, colour schemes, staff uniforms and the final bill. The model also suggests that customers interact with each other. Their behaviour and characteristics impact on each other's experience. Therefore the benefits derived by a customer come from the interaction with the physical environment and the people (service providers and other customers). Each of those elements is supported and influenced by the process, much of which may be invisible to the customer.

These new marketing mix elements as well as the traditional elements are explored in depth in future chapters.

Staying Focused on the Customer

A critical theme running throughout this text is *customer focus*. In fact, the subtitle of the book is 'Integrating customer focus across the firm'. From the firm's point of view, all strategies are developed with an eye on the customer, and all implementations are carried out with an understanding of their impact on the customer. From a practical perspective, decisions regarding new services and communication plans will integrate the customer's point of view; operations and human resource decisions will be considered in terms of their impact on customers. All the tools, strategies and frameworks included in this text have customers at their foundation. The services marketing mix just described is clearly an important tool that addresses the uniqueness of services, keeping the customer at the centre.

In this text we also view customers as assets to be valued, developed and retained. The strategies and tools we offer thus focus on customer relationship-building and loyalty as opposed to a more transactional focus in which customers are viewed as one-time revenue producers. This text looks at customer relationship management not as a software program but as an entire architecture or business philosophy. Every chapter in the text can be considered a component needed to build a complete customer relationship management approach.

Summary

This chapter has set the stage for further learning about services marketing by presenting information on changes in the world economy and business practice that have driven the focus on service: the fact that services dominate the modern economies of the world; the focus on service as a competitive business imperative; specific needs of the deregulated and professional service industries; the role of new service concepts growing from technological advances; and the realization that the characteristics of services result in unique challenges and opportunities. The chapter presented a broad definition of services as activities, processes and performances, and it drew distinctions among pure services, value-added services, service experiences and customer service. It also introduced the concept of service dominant logic.

Building on this fundamental understanding of the service economy, the chapter went on to present the key characteristics of services that underlie the need for distinct strategies and concepts for managing service businesses. These basic characteristics are that services are intangible, heterogeneous, produced and consumed simultaneously, and perishable. Because of these characteristics, service managers face a number of challenges in marketing, including the complex problem of how to deliver quality services consistently.

The chapter described two themes that provide the foundation for future chapters: the expanded marketing mix for services; and customer focus as a unifying theme. It also introduced the concept of the services triangle and the servuction system. The remainder of the text focused on exploring the unique opportunities and challenges faced by organizations that sell and deliver services, and on developing solutions that will help you become an effective services champion and manager.

Key Concepts

Heterogeneity	16	Self-service technologies	12
Inseparability	17	Service dominant logic	9
Intangibility	6	Services marketing mix	19
People	19	Services marketing triangle	18
Perishability	17	Servuction system	21
Physical evidence	20	Tangibility spectrum	6
Process	21		

Exercises

1   Roughly calculate your budget for an average month. What percentage of your budget goes for services versus goods? Do the services you purchase have value? In what sense? If you had to cut back on your expenses, what would you cut out?

2   Visit two local retail service providers that you believe are positioned very differently (such as IKEA and a local family-owned furniture store, or Burger King and a fine-dining restaurant). From your own observations, compare their strategies on the elements of the services marketing mix.

3   Try a service you have never tried before on the Internet. Analyse the benefits of this service. Was enough information provided to make it easy to use? How would you compare this service to other methods of obtaining the same benefits?

4   Select a service and use the servuction system model to highlight the key components and interactions impacting on the customer during service delivery.

Discussion Questions

1   What distinguishes service offerings from customer service? Provide specific examples.

2   How is technology changing the nature of customer service and service offerings?

3   What are the basic characteristics of services v. goods? What are the implications of these characteristics for Accenture or for easyJet?

4   One of the underlying frameworks for the text is the services marketing mix. Discuss why each of the three new mix elements (process, people and physical evidence) is included. How might each of these communicate with or help to satisfy an organization's customers?

5   Think of a service job you have had or currently have. How effective, in your opinion, was or is the organization in managing the elements of the services marketing mix?

6   Think of a service and examine how technology is used or could be used to improve its delivery.

7 How can quality service be used in a manufacturing context for competitive advantage? Think of your answer in the context of cars or computers or some other manufactured product that you have actually purchased.

8 Discuss the concept that the value a customer derives from a physical good such as a vacuum cleaner is really the cleaning service provided by the good, not the good itself.

Further Reading

Akaka, M.A. and Vargo, S. L. (2015). Extending the context of service: From encounters to ecosystems *Journal of Services Marketing*, *29*(6/7), 453–462.

Anderson, L., Ostrom, A., Corus, C., Fisk, R., Gallan, A., Giraldo, M., Mende, M., Mulder, M., Rayburn, S., Rosenbaum, M., Shirahada, K. and Williams, J. (2013). Transformative service research: An agenda for the future. *Journal of Business Research*, 66, 1203–1210.

Grönroos, C. (2011). Value co-creation in service logic: A critical analysis. *Marketing Theory*, 11(3), 279–301.

Grönroos, C. and Gummerus, J. (2014). The service revolution and its marketing implications: Service logic vs service-dominant logic. *Managing Service Quality*, 24(3), 206–29.

IfM and IBM (2008). *Succeeding through Service Innovation: A Service Perspective for Education, Research, Business and Government*. Cambridge, United Kingdom: University of Cambridge Institute for Manufacturing.

Lovelock, C. and Gummesson, E. (2004). Whither services marketing? In search of a new paradigm and fresh perspectives. *Journal of Service Research*, 7(1), 20–41.

Lusch, R. and Vargo, S. (2006). Service dominant logic: Reactions, reflections, and refinements. *Marketing Theory*, 6 (3), 281–88.

Vargo, S.L. and Lusch, R.F. (2004). The four service marketing myths: Remnants of a goods-based, manufacturing model. *Journal of Service Research*, 6(4), 324–35.

Vargo, S.L. and Lusch, R.F. (2008). Service-dominant logic: Continuing the evolution. *Journal of the Academy of Marketing Science*, 36(1), 1–10.

Chapter 2

Conceptual Framework of the Book: The Gaps Model of Service Quality

Chapter Outline

The Customer Gap   27
The Provider Gaps   28
Putting it All Together: Closing the Gaps   34
Summary   35
Example   35
Key Concepts   38
Exercises   38
Discussion Questions   38
Further Reading   38

Learning Objectives

This chapter's objectives are to:

1 Introduce a framework, called the gaps model of service quality, which is used to organize the remainder of this textbook.
2 Demonstrate that the gaps model is a useful framework for understanding service quality in an organization.
3 Demonstrate that the most critical service quality gap to close is the customer gap, the difference between customer expectations and perceptions.
4 Show that four gaps that occur in companies, which we call 'provider gaps', are responsible for the customer gap.
5 Identify the factors responsible for each of the four provider gaps.

Opening Example

Ritz-Carlton Hotels – Providing Excellent Service

How does a hotel chain provide excellent service, identify customer expectations and meet them? Ritz-Carlton, owned by Marriott International, is a hotel brand that exemplifies the use of the strategies needed to provide consistent, accurate and high quality service.

Understanding customer expectations is a key focus of Ritz-Carlton. The company uses a research agency to contact a sample of individual guests around the world by phone to gain feedback on their experiences with the hotels. This is in addition to the customer satisfaction questionnaire that is sent by

Source: ©Image Source

email to every guest following their stay. Furthermore, personalization is achieved through a customer relationship system called Mystique which holds data about guests' preferences based on their previous stays at the hotel chain. This system enables all staff to demonstrate an understanding of a guest and their likely needs.

Customer-defined standards are critical for ensuring that high quality service is maintained. Training is extremely important at Ritz-Carlton, each employee is required to complete 250 hours of training every year. This is a mix of classroom training, online training and one-to-one coaching with all new employees requiring to be certified in the operational standards of their positions. The focus is on creating a consistent standard of service at all the company's hotel properties throughout the world.

Service performance is where Ritz-Carlton excels. Two of Ritz-Carlton's service values state, 'I am empowered to create unique, memorable and personal experiences for our guests,' and 'I own and immediately resolve guest problems.' All hotel employees, no matter what position they hold, can spend up to $2000 to resolve any situation involving a guest, without seeking approval from a manager. As such, they have the potential to create excellent service experiences and this is reinforced by each employee being dedicated to the organization's three steps of service:

1 Provide a warm and sincere greeting.
2 Use the guest's name as well as anticipating and fulfilling each guest's needs.
3 Provide a fond farewell (give a warm good-bye and use the guest's name).

To ensure that Ritz-Carlton's customer service is maintained at a consistently high level, department managers gather staff members together on a daily basis to share customer feedback and discuss the actions and events planned for that day.

Managing service promises is handled by clear communication to all customers and employees. Each member of staff carries a small, multi-folded Credo Card the size of a business card. This sets out the service promises for the brand. These are:

1 The Ritz-Carlton is a place where the genuine care and comfort of our guests is our highest mission.
2 We pledge to provide the finest personal service and facilities for our guests who will always enjoy a warm, relaxed, yet refined ambience.
3 The Ritz-Carlton experience enlivens the senses, instils well-being, and fulfils even the unexpressed wishes and needs of our guests.

These are also published on the organization's website alongside the other values and philosophy of Ritz-Carlton. Having clarity about these promises and values sets the tone for the organization's culture. No guest should have to guess what Ritz-Carlton is trying to deliver. And significant effort is made to ensure each guest receives excellent service.

Source: Adapted from multiple sources including www.ritzcarlton.com

Effective services marketing similar to that provided by Ritz-Carlton is a complex undertaking that involves many different strategies, skills and tasks. Executives of service organizations have long been confused about how to approach this complicated topic in an organized manner. This textbook is designed around one approach: viewing services in a structured, integrated way called the *gaps model of service quality*.[1] This model positions the key concepts, strategies and decisions in services marketing and is used to give the rest of this book its structure, with one Part section devoted to each of the gaps described in this chapter.

The Customer Gap

The customer gap (sometimes known as Gap 5) is the difference between customer expectations and perceptions (see Figure 2.1). Customer expectations are standards or reference points that customers bring to the service experience, whereas customer perceptions are subjective assessments of actual service experiences. Customer expectations often consist of what a customer believes should or will happen. For example, when you visit an expensive restaurant, you expect a high level of service, one that is considerably superior to the level you would expect in a fast-food restaurant. Closing the gap between what customers expect and what they perceive is critical to delivering quality service; it forms the basis for the gaps model.

Figure 2.1   The customer gap

In a perfect world, expectations and perceptions would be identical: customers would perceive that they have received what they thought they would and should. In practice these concepts are often, even usually, separated by some distance. Broadly, it is the goal of services marketing to bridge this distance, and we devote the remainder of this textbook to describing strategies and practices designed to close this customer gap.

The Provider Gaps

To close the all-important customer gap (*Gap 5*), the gaps model suggests that four other gaps – the *provider gaps* – also need to be closed. These gaps occur within the organization providing the service (hence the term provider gaps) and include:

- *Gap 1:* Not knowing what customers expect
- *Gap 2:* Not selecting the right service quality designs and standards
- *Gap 3:* Not delivering to service designs and standards
- *Gap 4:* Not matching performance to promises.

The rest of this chapter describes the full gaps model. Alternative views of the gaps model can be found in the Further Reading section at the end of this chapter.

Provider Gap 1: Not Knowing What Customers Expect

Provider gap 1 is the difference between customer expectations of service and a company's understanding of those expectations. A primary cause of why many firms fail to meet customers' expectations is that they lack accurate understanding of exactly what those expectations are. Many reasons exist for managers not being aware of what customers expect: they may not interact directly with customers, they may be unwilling to ask about expectations or they may be unprepared to address them. When people with the authority and responsibility for setting priorities do not fully understand customers' service expectations, they may trigger a chain of bad decisions and suboptimal resource allocations which result in perceptions of poor service quality. In this text, we broaden the responsibility for the provider gap 1 from managers alone to any employee in the organization with the authority to change or influence service policies and procedures. In today's changing organizations, the authority to make adjustments in service delivery is often delegated to empowered teams and front-line people. This is particularly true of business-to-business situations, where account teams make their own decisions about how to address their clients' unique expectations.

Figure 2.2 shows the key factors responsible for provider gap 1. An inadequate marketing research orientation is one of the critical factors. When management or empowered employees do not acquire accurate information about customers' expectations, provider gap 1 is large. Formal and informal methods to capture information about customer expectations must be developed through marketing research. Techniques involving a variety of traditional research approaches – among them customer interviews, survey research, complaint systems and customer panels – must be used to stay close to the customer. More innovative techniques, such as structured brainstorming and service quality gap analysis, are often needed.

Another key factor that is related to provider gap 1 is lack of upward communication. Front-line employees often know a great deal about customers; if management is not in contact with front-line employees and does not understand what they know, the gap widens.

Also related to provider gap 1 is a lack of company strategies to retain customers and strengthen relationships with them, an approach called *relationship marketing*. When organizations have strong relationships with existing customers, provider gap 1 is less likely to occur. Relationship marketing is distinct from *transactional marketing*, the term used to describe the more conventional emphasis on acquiring new customers rather than on retaining them. Relationship marketing has always been a practice with large clients of business-to-business firms (such as IBM or Siemens), but firms that sell to end customers often view such situations as sales or transactions rather than as ongoing relationships. When companies focus too much on attracting new customers, they may fail to understand the changing needs and expectations of their current customers. Technology affords companies the ability to acquire and integrate vast quantities of data on customers that can be used to build relationships. Frequent-flyer travel programmes conducted by airlines, car rental companies and hotel chains are among the most familiar programmes of this type.

Figure 2.2   Key factors leading to provider gap 1

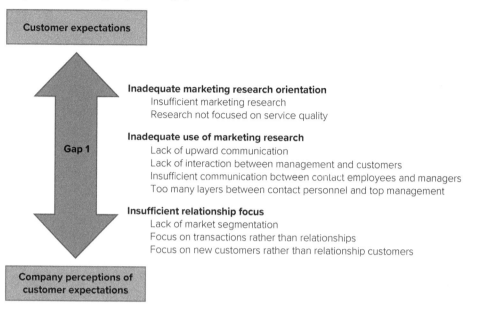

To address the factors in provider gap 1, this text covers topics that include how to understand customers through multiple research strategies (Chapter 6), and how to build strong relationships and understand customer needs over time (Chapter 7). Through these strategies, provider gap 1 can be minimised.

Provider Gap 2: Not Selecting the Right Service Quality Designs and Standards

Accurate perceptions of customers' expectations are necessary, but not sufficient, for delivering superior quality service. Another prerequisite is the presence of service designs and performance standards that reflect those accurate perceptions. A recurring theme in service companies is the difficulty experienced in translating customer expectations into service quality specifications that employees can understand and execute. These problems are reflected in provider gap 2, the difference between company understanding of customer expectations and development of customer-driven service designs and standards. Customer-driven standards differ from the conventional performance standards that companies establish for service in that they are based on pivotal customer requirements that are visible to, and measured by, customers. They are operations standards set to correspond to customer expectations and priorities, rather than responses to company concerns such as productivity or efficiency.

Figure 2.3 illustrates a variety of reasons why provider gap 2 exists in service organizations. Those people responsible for setting standards, typically management, sometimes believe that customer expectations are unreasonable or unrealistic. They may also believe that the degree of variability inherent in service defies standardization and that setting standards, therefore, will not achieve the desired goal. Although these assumptions are valid in some situations, they often are mere rationalizations of management's reluctance to tackle head-on the difficult challenges of creating service standards to deliver excellent service.

Because services are intangible, they are difficult to describe and communicate. This difficulty becomes especially evident when new services are being developed. It is critical that all people involved (managers, front-line employees and behind-the-scenes support staff) work with the same concepts of the new service, based on customer needs and expectations. For a service that already exists, any attempt to improve it will also suffer unless everyone has the same vision of the service and associated issues. One of the most important ways to avoid provider gap 2 is clearly to design services without oversimplification, incompleteness, subjectivity and bias. To do so, tools are needed to ensure that new and existing services are developed and

Figure 2.3   Key factors leading to provider gap 2

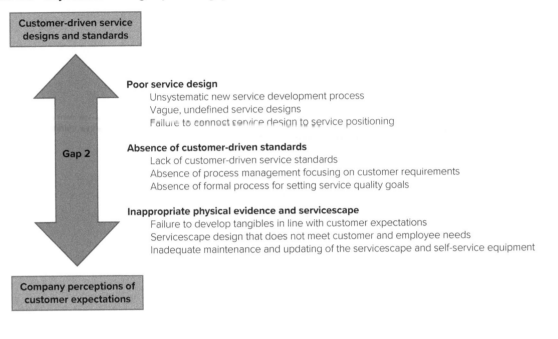

improved in as careful a manner as possible. Chapter 8 describes the tools that are most effective in service development and design, including service blueprinting, a unique tool for services.

The quality of service delivered by customer-contact personnel is critically influenced by the standards against which they are evaluated and compensated. Standards signal to contact personnel what the management priorities are and which types of performance really count. When service standards are absent, or when the standards in place do not reflect customers' expectations, the customers' perception of service quality is likely to suffer. When standards do reflect what customers expect, the quality of service they receive is likely to be enhanced. Chapter 9 develops further the topic of customer-defined service standards and shows that, if they are developed appropriately, they can have a powerful positive impact on closing both provider gap 2 and the customer gap.

In Chapter 10 we explore the importance of physical evidence, the variety of roles it plays, and strategies for effectively designing physical evidence and the servicescape to meet customer expectations. By *physical evidence*, we mean everything from business cards to reports, signage, Internet presence, self-service equipment, and other facilities used to deliver the service. The *servicescape*, the physical setting where the service is delivered, is a particular focus of Chapter 10. Think of a restaurant, a hotel, a theme park, a health club, a hospital or a university. In these industries, the servicescape – the physical facility – is critical in terms of communicating information about the service and making the entire experience pleasurable. In these cases, the servicescape plays a variety of roles, from serving as a visual metaphor for what the company stands for, to actually facilitating the activities of both consumers and employees through technology such as self-service equipment.

⭐ **SERVICE SPOTLIGHT**

Standards may be set by external bodies, for example, Ofgem is the UK Office of Gas and Electricity Markets. It is a government department and an independent National Regulatory Authority which has the principal objective of protecting the interests of existing and future electricity and gas consumers. It sets a number of 'Quality of Service Guaranteed Standards' which are service levels that should be met by each gas and electricity provider. If any supplier fails to meet the level of service required, then customers may be entitled to a payment. The amount paid to customers depends on many factors, such as the cause of an interruption to supply and the amount of time the supply was interrupted. Payments under the guaranteed standards recognise the inconvenience caused to customers. *Source: www.ofgem.gov.uk*

Provider Gap 3: Not Delivering to Service Designs and Standards

Once service designs and standards are put in place, it would seem that the firm is well on its way to delivering high-quality services. This assumption is true, but is still not enough to deliver excellent service. The firm must have systems, processes and people in place to ensure that service delivery actually matches (or exceeds) the designs and standards in place.

Provider gap 3 is the discrepancy between development of customer-driven service standards and actual service performance by company employees. Even when guidelines exist for performing services well and treating customers correctly, high-quality service performance is not a certainty. Standards must be backed by appropriate resources (people, systems and technology) and must be enforced in order to be effective – that is, employees must be measured and compensated on the basis of performance along those standards. Thus, even when standards accurately reflect customers' expectations, if the company fails to provide support for those standards – if it does not facilitate, encourage and require their achievement – standards are of little use. When the level of service delivery falls short of the standards, it falls short of what customers expect as well. Narrowing gap 3 – by ensuring that all the resources needed to achieve the standards are in place – reduces the customer gap.

Research has identified many of the critical inhibitors to closing gap 3 (see Figure 2.4). These factors include employees who do not clearly understand the roles they are to play in the company, employees who experience conflict between customers and company management, poor employee selection, inadequate technology, inappropriate compensation and recognition, and lack of empowerment and teamwork. These factors all relate to the company's human resource function and involve internal practices, such as recruitment, training, feedback, job design and building motivation, as well as organizational structure. In order to deliver better service performance, these issues must be addressed across functions, such as involving both marketing and human resources. In addition, technology advances have allowed customer-contact employees to become more efficient and effective in serving customers. For example, today's technology allows customer service agents in call centres to have several online 'chats' with many customers simultaneously. Such capability allows employees to resolve problems much faster, increasing employee efficiency and generally creating a more satisfying customer experience. Self-service technologies, for example in retail stores or at airport check-in desks, can also be used to overcome any inconsistencies in services traditionally provided by employees.

Another important variable in provider gap 3 is the customer. Even if contact employees and intermediaries are 100 per cent consistent in their service delivery, the uncontrollable customer variables can have a positive or negative impact on service delivery. If customers do not perform their roles appropriately – if, for example, they fail to provide all the information necessary to the provider or neglect to read and follow instructions – service quality is jeopardized. Customers can also negatively influence the quality of service received by others if they are disruptive or take more than their share of a service provider's time. Understanding customer roles and how customers themselves can influence service delivery and outcomes is critical.

A third difficulty associated with provider gap 3 involves the challenge in delivering service through such intermediaries as retailers, franchisees, agents and brokers. Because quality in service occurs in the human interaction between customers and service providers, control over the service encounter by the company is crucial, yet rarely is it fully possible. Most service (and many manufacturing) companies face an

Figure 2.4 Key factors leading to provider gap 3

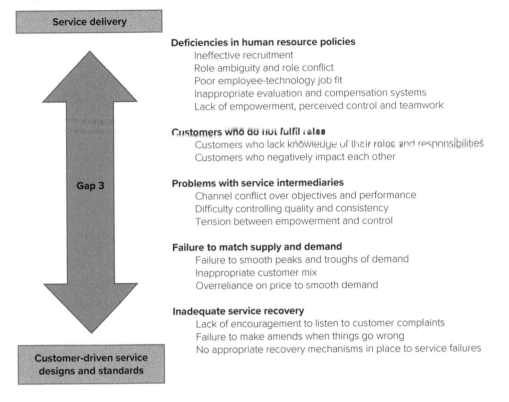

Deficiencies in human resource policies
Ineffective recruitment
Role ambiguity and role conflict
Poor employee-technology job fit
Inappropriate evaluation and compensation systems
Lack of empowerment, perceived control and teamwork

Customers who do not fulfil roles
Customers who lack knowledge of their roles and responsibilities
Customers who negatively impact each other

Problems with service intermediaries
Channel conflict over objectives and performance
Difficulty controlling quality and consistency
Tension between empowerment and control

Failure to match supply and demand
Failure to smooth peaks and troughs of demand
Inappropriate customer mix
Overreliance on price to smooth demand

Inadequate service recovery
Lack of encouragement to listen to customer complaints
Failure to make amends when things go wrong
No appropriate recovery mechanisms in place to service failures

even more formidable task: attaining service excellence and consistency in the presence of intermediaries who represent them and interact with their customers yet are not under their direct control. Franchisers of services depend on their franchisees to execute service delivery as they have specified it. And it is in the execution by the franchisee that the customer evaluates the service quality of the company. With franchises and other types of intermediaries, someone other than the producer is responsible for the fulfilment of quality service. For this reason, a firm must develop ways to either control or motivate these intermediaries to meet company standards.

Another issue in provider gap 3 is the need in service firms to synchronize demand and capacity. Because services are perishable and cannot be inventoried, service companies frequently face situations of over-demand or under-demand. Lacking inventories to handle over-demand, companies lose sales when capacity is inadequate to handle customer needs. On the other hand, capacity is frequently underutilized in slow periods. Most companies rely on operations strategies such as cross-training or varying the size of the employee pool to synchronize supply and demand. Marketing strategies for managing demand – such as price changes, advertising, promotion and alternative service offerings – can supplement approaches for managing supply.

The final key factor associated with provider gap 3 is lack of service recovery. Even the best companies, with the best of intentions and clear understanding of their customers' expectations, sometimes fail. It is critical for an organization to understand the importance of service recovery – why people complain, what they expect when they complain, and how to develop effective service recovery strategies for dealing with inevitable service failures. Such strategies might involve a well-defined complaint-handling procedure and an emphasis on empowering employees to react on the spot, in real time, to fix the failure; at other times it involves a service guarantee or ways to compensate the customer for the unfulfilled promise.

We discuss strategies to deal with the roles of employees in Chapter 11, customers in Chapter 12, intermediaries in Chapter 13, demand and capacity in Chapter 14 and service recovery in Chapter 15.

Provider Gap 4: Not Matching Performance to Promises

Provider gap 4 illustrates the difference between service delivery and the service provider's external communications. Promises made by a service company through its sales force, media advertising and other communications may potentially raise customer expectations, the standards against which customers assess service quality. The discrepancy between actual and promised service therefore has an adverse effect on the customer gap. Broken promises can occur for many reasons: over-promising in advertising or personal selling, inadequate coordination between operations and marketing, or differences in policies and procedures across service outlets. Figure 2.5 shows the key factors that lead to provider gap 4.

Figure 2.5   Key factors leading to provider gap 4

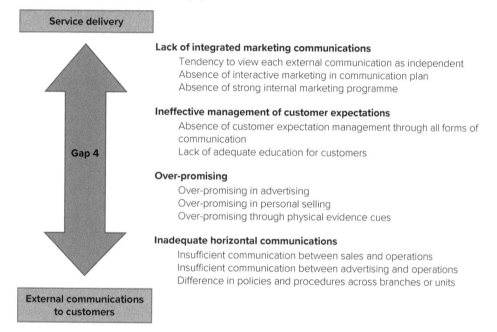

In addition to unduly elevating expectations through exaggerated claims, there are other, less obvious ways in which external communications influence customers' service quality assessments. Service companies frequently fail to capitalize on opportunities to educate customers to use services appropriately. They also neglect to manage customer expectations of what will be delivered in service transactions and relationships.

The growth in online brand communities and review sites can significantly influence customer expectations. As such, service companies need to monitor these sites to ensure that the information delivered through these channels is accurate and in order to rectify any service failings that are highlighted. Any responses that a company makes to a negative review need to demonstrate a genuine concern about the issue rather than discounting the issue as being wrong or unimportant.

One of the major difficulties associated with provider gap 4 is that communications to consumers involve issues that cross organizational boundaries. Because service advertising promises what people do, and because what *people* do cannot be controlled like machines that produce physical goods can be controlled, this type of communication involves functions other than the marketing department. This type of marketing is what we call *interactive marketing* – the marketing between contact people and customers – and it must be coordinated with the conventional types of *external marketing* used in product and service firms. When employees who promote the service do not fully understand the reality of service delivery, they are likely to make exaggerated promises or fail to communicate to customers aspects of the service which are intended to serve them well. The result is poor service quality perceptions. Effectively coordinating actual service delivery with external communications, therefore, narrows provider gap 4 and favourably affects the customer gap as well.

Another issue linked with provider gap 4 is pricing of services. In packaged goods (and even in durable goods), customers possess enough price knowledge before purchase to be able to judge whether a price is fair or in line with competition. With services, customers often have no internal reference points for prices before purchase and consumption. Pricing strategies such as discounting, 'everyday prices' and couponing, obviously need to be different in service cases in which the customer has no initial sensitivity to prices. Techniques for developing prices for services are more complicated than those for pricing tangible goods.

In summary, external communications – whether from marketing communications or pricing – can create a larger customer gap by raising expectations about service delivery.

In addition to improving service delivery, companies must also manage all communications to customers so that inflated promises do not lead to higher expectations. Chapter 16 discusses integrated services marketing communications, and Chapter 17 covers pricing to accomplish these objectives.

Putting it all Together: Closing the Gaps

The full conceptual model shown in Figure 2.6 conveys a clear message to managers wishing to improve their quality of service: the key to closing the customer gap (gap 5) is to close provider gaps 1 to 4 and keep them closed. To the extent that one or more of provider gaps 1 to 4 exist, customers perceive service quality shortfalls. The gaps model of service quality serves as a framework for service organizations attempting to improve quality service and services marketing.

Figure 2.6   Gaps model of service quality

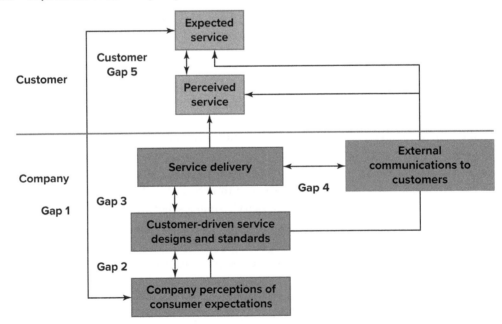

Example   35

Summary

This chapter presented the integrated gaps model of service quality (shown in Figure 2.6), a framework for understanding and improving service delivery. The remainder of the text is organized around this model of service quality, and focuses on the four provider gaps involved in delivering and marketing a service:

- *Provider gap 1:* Not knowing what customers expect
- *Provider gap 2:* Not selecting the right service quality designs and standards
- *Provider gap 3:* Not delivering to service designs and standards
- *Provider gap 4:* Not matching performance to promises

The gaps model positions the key concepts, strategies and decisions in services marketing in a manner that begins with the customer and builds the organization's tasks around what is needed to close the gap between customer expectations and perceptions. The final chapter in this book, Chapter 18, discusses the financial implications of service quality, reviewing the research and company data that indicate linkages between service quality and financial performance.

Example

Using the Gaps Model to Assess an Organization's Service Strategy

The gaps model featured in this chapter is a useful way to audit the service performance and capabilities of an organization. It is the framework that many companies use as an assessment or service audit tool because it is comprehensive and it offers a way for companies to examine all the factors that influence service quality. To use it as an audit tool, a company documents what it knows about each gap and the factors that affect the size of the gap. Although you will learn much more about each of these gaps throughout this book, we provide a basic gaps audit below. In Exercise 1 at the end of the chapter, we propose that you use this audit with a company of your own choosing to determine its service quality gaps.

Service Quality Gaps Model Audit

For each of the following factors in the gaps, indicate the effectiveness of the organization. Use a 1 to 10 scale where 1 is 'poor' and 10 is 'excellent'.

Table 2.1   Customer gap audit form

Customer Gap 1	Maximum Score	Organization Score 1 = poor 10 = excellent	Organization Score/ Maximum Score
1 How well does the company understand customer expectations of service quality?	10		
2 How well does the company understand customer perceptions of service?	10		
Total score for customer gap 1	**20**		
Provider Gap 1	**Maximum Score**	**Organization Score 1 = poor 10 = excellent**	**Organization Score/ Maximum Score**
Market research orientation: Is the amount and type of market research adequate to understand customer expectations of service?	10		

(Continued)

Provider Gap 1 (continued)	Maximum Score	Organization Score 1 = poor 10 = excellent	Organization Score/ Maximum Score
Market research orientation: Does the company use this information in decisions about service provision?	10		
Upward communication: Do managers and customers interact enough for management to know what customers expect?	10		
Upward communication: Do contact people tell management what customers expect?	10		
Relationship focus: To what extent does the company understand the expectations of different customer segments?	10		
Relationship focus: To what extent does the company focus on relationships with customers rather than transactions?	10		
Total score for Provider gap 1	60		
Provider Gap 2	Maximum Score	Organization Score 1 = poor 10 = excellent	Organization Score/ Maximum Score
Systematic service design: How effective is the company's service development process?	10		
Systematic service design: How well are new services defined for customers and employees?	10		
Presence of customer-defined standards: How effective are the company's service standards?	10		
Presence of customer-defined standards: Are they defined to correspond to customer expectations?	10		
Presence of customer-defined standards: How effective is the process for setting and tracking service quality goals?	10		
Appropriate physical evidence and servicescape: How appropriate, attractive and effective are the company's physical facilities, equipment and other tangibles?	10		
Total score for Provider gap 2	60		
Provider Gap 3	Maximum Score	Organization Score 1 = poor 10 = excellent	Organization Score/ Maximum Score
Effective human resource policies: How effectively does the company recruit, hire, train, compensate and empower employees?	10		
Effective human resource policies: Is service quality delivery consistent across employees, teams, units and branches?	10		
Effective role fulfilment by customers: Do customers understand their roles and responsibilities?	10		

(Continued)

Example 37

Provider Gap 3 (continued)	Maximum Score	Organization Score 1 = poor 10 = excellent	Organization Score/ Maximum Score
Effective role fulfilment by customers: Does the company manage customers to fulfil their roles, especially customers that are incompatible?	10		
Effective alignment with service intermediaries: How well are service intermediaries aligned with the company?	10		
Effective alignment with service intermediaries: Is there conflict over objectives and performance, costs and rewards?	10		
Effective alignment with service intermediaries: Is service quality delivery consistent across the outlets?	10		
Alignment of supply and demand: How well is the company able to match supply with demand fluctuations?	10		
Service recovery: How effective are the service recovery efforts of the organization?	10		
Service recovery: How well does the organization plan for service failures?	10		
Total score for Provider gap 3	**100**		
Provider Gap 4	Maximum Score	Organization Score 1 = poor 10 = excellent	Organization Score/ Maximum Score
Integrated marketing communications: How well do all company communications – including the interactions between company employees and customers – express the same message and level of service quality?	10		
Effective management of customer expectations: How well does the company communicate to customers about what will be provided to them?	10		
Accurate promising in advertising and personal selling: Does the company avoid overpromising and overselling?	10		
Adequate horizontal communications: How well do different parts of the organization communicate with each other so that service quality equals what is promised?	10		
Total score for Provider gap 4	**40**		

The score for each gap should be compared to the maximum score possible. Are particular gaps weaker than others? Which areas in each gap need attention? As you go through the rest of the book, we will provide more detail about how to improve the factors in each of the gaps.

Key Concepts

Customer gap	27	Provider gaps	28
Gaps model	27		

Exercises

1   Choose an organization to interview, and use the integrated gaps model of service quality as a framework. Ask the manager whether the organization suffers from any of the factors listed in the figures in this chapter. Which factor in each of Figures 2.2 through to 2.5 does the manager consider the most troublesome?

2   What does the company do to try to address the problems?

3   Use the Internet to access the website of Ritz-Carlton, IKEA, KLM or any other well-known service organization. Which provider gaps has the company closed? How can you tell?

4   Interview a non-profit or public sector organization in your area (it could be some part of your university or college). Find out if the integrated gaps model of service quality framework makes sense in the context of that organization.

Discussion Questions

1   Think about a service you receive. Is there a gap between your expectations and your perceptions of that service? What do you expect to receive that you do not?

2   Think about a service that you receive regularly. How would you change it and the way it is provided to make it better for the customer?

3   If you were the manager of a service organization and wanted to apply the gaps model to improve service, which gap would you start with? Why? In what order would you proceed to close the gaps?

4   Can provider gap 4 be closed prior to closing any of the other three provider gaps? How?

5   Which of the four provider gaps do you believe is hardest to close? Why?

Further Reading

Bitner, M.J., Zeithaml, V.A. and Gremler, D.D. (2010). Technology's impact on the gaps model of service quality, in Maglio, P.P., Kieliszewski, C.A. and Spoher, J.C. (eds). *Handbook of Service Science*, New York: Springer.

Blut, M., Chowdhry, N., Mittal, V. and Brock, C. (2015). E-service quality: A meta-analytic review. *Journal of Retailing*, 91(4), 679–700.

Ladhari, R. (2009). A review of twenty years of SERVQUAL research. *International Journal of Quality and Service Sciences*, 1(2), 172–98.

Mauri, A.G., Minazzi, R., and Muccio, S. (2013). A review of literature on the gaps model on service quality: a 3-decades period: 1985–2013. *International Business Research*, 6(12), 134–44.

Part 2
Focus on the Customer

Chapter 3   Consumer Behaviour in Services

Chapter 4   Customer Expectations of Service

Chapter 5   Customer Perceptions of Service

The Customer Gap

Knowing what customers want and how they assess what they receive is the foundation for designing effective services. The customer gap from the gaps model of service quality corresponds to two concepts - customer expectations and customer perceptions, both of which are critical to successful services marketing.

Part 2 focuses on the customer, their behaviour and the nature of their expectations and perceptions. Chapter 3 focuses on how consumers choose and evaluate services. Chapter 4 looks at the types and sources of customer expectations from a service. Chapter 5 considers the factors that influence customer perceptions of service and the relationships among customer satisfaction, service quality and individual service encounters.

Expected Service

Customer Gap

Perceived Service

Chapter 3

Consumer Behaviour in Services

Chapter Outline

Search, Experience and Credence Properties	42
Consumer Choice of Service	43
Consumer Experience During Service Delivery	48
Post-Experience Evaluation	52
Understanding Differences Among Consumers	54
Summary	58
Key Concepts	58
Exercises	59
Discussion Questions	59
Further Reading	60

Learning Objectives

The chapter's objectives are to:

1 Enhance understanding of how consumers choose and evaluate services, through focusing on factors that are particularly relevant for services.
2 Describe how consumers judge goods versus services in terms of search, experience and credence criteria.
3 Develop the elements of consumer behaviour that a services marketer must understand: choice behaviour, consumer experiences and post-experience evaluation.
4 Examine attitudes towards the use of self-service technologies.
5 Explore how differences among consumers (cultural differences, group decision-making) affect consumer behaviour and influence services marketing strategies.

Opening Example
The Travelling Millennials and their Buying Behaviour

TripAdvisor, the world's largest travel website, regularly undertakes research to gain insight into the attitudes and behaviours of consumers in the travel industry. The research is based upon an annual online survey, the TripBarometer, which in 2017 had 23,198 respondents from 33 countries.

One research theme explored between 2015 and 2017 has highlighted some of the unique characteristics of the millennial traveller. This generation of travellers born between the early 1980s and early 2000s is two to three times more likely than older travellers to leave booking their trips until less than

Source: ©Twinsterphoto/Shutterstock

two weeks before departure. They are often less fixed on a specific destination when they start planning a trip and regularly browse TripAdvisor with no particular destination in mind. Recommendations from friends and social media are particularly important to this age group. They are also likely to change their selected destination if they can find a cheaper flight to an alternative destination.

Compared to earlier generations, millennials are 39 per cent more likely to go on city breaks in comparison to other age groups. The most common reasons for choosing city breaks is that these millennials are seeking excitement and fun rather than relaxation. Tourist attractions and activities are a huge draw for them, and steadily become less influential for older travellers. Online reviews are an important factor for this group when choosing where to travel and if they do book in advance, they are more likely to book through a travel review site than through the property's own website.

Sources: www.tripadvisor.com/tripadvisorinsights; 2015, 2016 and 2017.

The primary objectives of services producers and marketers are identical to those of all marketers: to develop and provide offerings that satisfy consumer needs and expectations, thereby ensuring their own economic survival. To achieve these objectives, service providers need to understand how consumers choose, experience and evaluate their service offerings. However, most of what is known about consumer evaluation processes pertains specifically to goods. The assumption appears to be that services, if not identical to goods, are at least similar enough in the consumer's mind that they are chosen, experienced and evaluated in the same manner.

This chapter challenges that assumption and shows that services' characteristics result in some differences in consumer evaluation processes compared with those used in assessing goods. Recognizing these differences and thoroughly understanding consumer evaluation processes are critical for the customer focus on which effective services marketing is based. Because the premise of this text is that the customer is at the heart of effective services marketing, we begin with the customer and maintain this focus throughout the text.

Consumers have a more difficult time evaluating and choosing among services than they have choosing between goods. In part this is because services are intangible and non-standardized, but also because consumption is so closely intertwined with production. These characteristics lead to differences in consumer evaluation processes for goods and services in all stages of the buying and consumption process.

Search, Experience and Credence Properties

One framework for isolating differences in evaluation processes between goods and services is a classi-fication of properties of offerings proposed by economists.[1] Economists first distinguished between two categories of properties of consumer products: search qualities, attributes that a consumer can deter-mine before purchasing a product; and experience qualities, attributes that can be discerned only after purchase or during consumption. Search qualities include colour, style, price, fit, feel, hardness and smell; experience qualities include taste and wearability. Products such as cars, clothing, furniture, and jewellery are high in search qualities because their attributes can be almost completely determined and evaluated before purchase. Products such as holidays and restaurant meals are high in experience qualities, because their attributes cannot be fully known or assessed until they have been purchased and are being consumed. A third category, credence qualities, includes characteristics that the consumer may find impossible to evaluate even after purchase and consumption.[2] Examples of offerings high in credence qualities are insur-ance and brake replacement on cars. Few consumers possess sufficient knowledge of risk or the mechanical skills required to evaluate whether these services are necessary or are performed properly, even after they have been prescribed and produced by the seller.

Figure 3.1 arrays products high in search, experience or credence qualities along a continuum of evalu-ation ranging from easy to evaluate to difficult to evaluate. Products high in search qualities are the easiest to evaluate (left-hand end of the continuum). Products high in experience qualities are more difficult to eval-uate, because they must be purchased and consumed before assessment is possible (centre of continuum). Products high in credence qualities are the most difficult to evaluate, because the consumer may be unaware of or may lack sufficient knowledge to appraise whether the offerings satisfy given wants or needs even after consumption (right-hand end of the continuum). The major premise of this chapter is that most goods fall to the left of the continuum, whereas most services fall to the right because of the distinguishing charac-teristics described in Chapter 1. These characteristics make services more difficult to evaluate than goods, particularly in advance of purchase. Difficulty in evaluation, in turn, forces consumers to rely on different cues and processes when assessing services.

Figure 3.1   Continuum of evaluation for different types of products

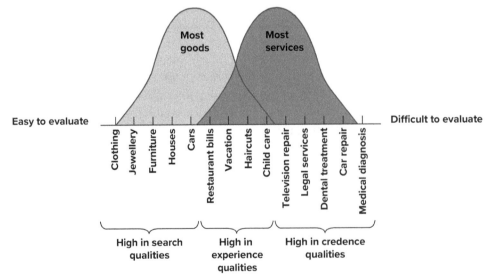

The following sections of this chapter build from these basic differences to explore the stages of con-sumer decision-making and evaluation for services. This discussion is organized around three broad stages of consumer behaviour, as shown in Figure 3.2: a) **consumer choice of service** involving: need recognition, information search, evaluation of alternatives and purchase; b) **consumer experience of the service during its delivery**, and c) **post-experience evaluation of the service**. Within each of these stages, you will see similarities and differences between goods and services.

Figure 3.2   Stages in consumer decision-making and evaluation of services

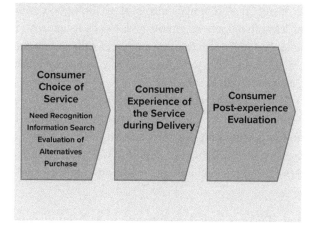

Consumer Choice of Service

The first important area of consumer behaviour that marketers are concerned with is how customers choose and make decisions and the steps that lead to the purchase of a particular service. This process is similar to that used for goods in some ways and different in others. Customers follow a logical sequence, including need recognition, information search, evaluation of alternatives, and purchase. The following sections discuss this sequence, particularly focusing on the ways in which services decision-making is different from goods decision-making.

Need Recognition

The process of buying a service begins with the recognition that a need or want exists. Although there are many different ways to characterize needs, the most widely known is Maslow's hierarchy, which specifies five need categories arranged in a sequence from basic lower-level needs to higher-level needs. Services can fill all these needs, and they become increasingly important for higher-level social, ego and self-actualization needs.

1 *Physiological needs* are *biological needs such as food, water and sleep*. The recognition of these basic needs is fairly straightforward. Recall the last time you were on holiday, perhaps sightseeing in a new place. At some point around lunchtime you recognized that you were thirsty and hungry and needed to stop and have lunch. Restaurants, coffee shops, bistros and other service establishments that provided food and water were more likely to become noticeable at this point.

2 *Safety and security needs* include *shelter, protection and security*. When visiting cities, people will seek accommodation in safe areas. They will travel with airlines that have good safety records. They seek bank accounts that provide security for their money as well as insurance products to protect them from future negative events. They seek reliable suppliers of electricity, gas and telecommunications. Organizations will promote reassurance, trust and professionalism to address these needs. For example, Vodafone emphasize coverage, reliability and business continuity.

3 *Social needs* are for *affection, friendship and acceptance*. Social needs are critical to all cultures but are particularly important in Asia. In countries like Japan and China, consumers place a great deal of

value on social and belonging needs. They spend more time with their families and work colleagues than do those in Europe and therefore consume more services that can be shared. The Japanese spend more annually per capita in restaurants, than people from any other country. Consumers in all cultures use many types of services to address social needs, including health and dance clubs, dating services and packaged holidays (like Club Med) in which socializing is encouraged.

4 *Ego needs* are for *prestige, success, accomplishment and self-esteem.* Food, safety and belonging are not enough for many consumers. Individuals also seek to look good to others and to feel good about themselves because of what they have accomplished. Needs to improve oneself and achieve success are responsible for the growth of education, training and other services that increase the skills and prestige of consumers. Personal services such as spa services, plastic surgery, teeth-whitening and gym membership also satisfy these needs.

5 *Self-actualization* involves *self-fulfilment and enriching experiences.* Consumers desire to live up to their full potential and enjoy themselves. Some consumers purchase experiences such as skydiving, jungle safaris and bungee-jumping for the pure thrill of the experience, a need quite different from the others in Maslow's hierarchy. Other people self-actualize through classes in oil painting or poetry-writing, thereby expressing feelings and meanings that are unrelated to the basic needs of day-to-day living.

The hierarchical nature of Maslow's need categorization has been disputed, and evidence exists that people with unfilled basic needs can be motivated to self-actualize. We are not concerned with the hierarchy of needs in this section; we use it only as a way to discuss different drivers that lead customers to the next stages of consumer behaviour in services.

Information Search

Once they recognize a need, consumers obtain information about goods and services that might satisfy this need. Seeking information may be an extensive, formalized process if the service or good is important to the consumer or it represents a major investment (for example, an Australian holiday package or a professional landscape service). In other cases, the information search may be quick and relatively automatic (for example, a restaurant for a quick lunch or a service station for fuel). Consumers use both customer opinion sources (such as friends or online customer review sites) and promotional sources (such as advertising and corporate websites) to gain information about goods and services. Seeking information is a way of reducing risk, helping consumers feel more confident about their choices.

Customer Opinion, Social Media and Online Review Sites

When purchasing goods, consumers make use of both customer opinion and promotional sources because both effectively convey information about search qualities. When purchasing services, on the other hand, consumers seek and rely to a greater extent on online review sites and talking to friends and family directly or through social media. There are a number of reasons for this.

First, promotional sources can convey information about search qualities but can communicate far less about experience qualities. Checking online customer review sites or asking friends directly or through social media can provide consumers with information about the experience qualities of a service. Review sites such as TripAdvisor are used extensively by consumers when they are choosing hotels, restaurants and visitor attractions. This type of site allows users to post 'content' online in a number of formats from text reviews to images and pictures. Based on this content, other consumers are likely to avoid a service provider with too many negative comments and choose a provider with positive comments. When Jeff Bezos, the founder and CEO of Amazon, was asked why he allowed negative reviews about products on his site, as this may impact on sales, he stated: 'We don't make money when we sell things. We make money when we help customers make purchase decisions.' As such, customers are more likely to find a helpful site with reviews and detailed information more appealing than a site that may simply push the manufacturer's view of a product.

A second reason for greater use of customer opinion sources of information for services is that many types of promotional sources of information are not as readily available for services. Many service providers are local, independent merchants with neither the experience nor the funds to advertise. If you want to choose a hairdresser in your local area, you are more likely to ask friends and work colleagues directly or through social media rather than relying on local advertisements or web-pages. Furthermore, cooperative advertising (advertising funded jointly by the retailer and the manufacturer) is used infrequently with services because most local providers are both producer and retailer of the service. And, because professional associations representing lawyers, architects, etc. banned advertising for so long, both professionals and consumers tend to resist its use even though it is now permitted.

Finally, because consumers can assess few attributes before purchase of a service, they may feel there is a greater risk in selecting a little-known alternative. Personal influence becomes pivotal as product complexity increases and when objective standards by which to evaluate a product decrease (that is, when experience qualities are high).[3] Managers in service industries clearly recognize the strong influence of word-of-mouth communication.

⭐ SERVICE SPOTLIGHT

The Crowne Plaza Hotel in London Docklands recognizes the importance of word of mouth. The Guest Services Manager responds to every comment about the hotel posted by guests on TripAdvisor. It makes no difference whether the comment is positive or negative, a reply is provided. Guests are thanked for their comment and, if there has been a specific problem, information is provided regarding how the problem will be rectified either for the dissatisfied customer or for future guests. This demonstrates that the hotel is listening to its customers and that it is concerned about providing an appropriate service level for their guests. Potential customers may look more positively on an organization that is seen to be willing to address problems and satisfy its guests.

Perceived Risk

Although some degree of perceived risk probably accompanies all purchase transactions, more risk appears to be involved in the purchase of services than in the purchase of goods because services are typically more intangible, variable and perishable. Risk can come in various forms: financial, time, performance, social or psychological, any of which may be greater for services.

The intangible nature of services and their high level of experience qualities imply that services generally must be selected on the basis of less pre-purchase information than is the case for goods. There is clear evidence that greater intangibility (whether for goods or services) increases perceptions of risk.[4] Also, because services are non-standardized, the consumer will feel some uncertainty about the outcome and consequences each time a service is purchased. In addition, services purchases may involve more perceived risk than other purchases because, with some exceptions, services are not accompanied by warranties or guarantees. Dissatisfied customers can rarely 'return' a service; they have already consumed it by the time they realize their dissatisfaction. Finally, many services are so technical or specialized (such as healthcare or legal services) that consumers possess neither the knowledge nor the experience to evaluate whether they are satisfied, even after they have consumed the service.

The increase in perceived risk in purchasing services suggests the use of strategies to reduce risk. Risk reduction can be accomplished through tactics that reduce risk directly (e.g. guarantees) or by addressing the factors that contribute to the perception of risk (e.g. making the service more tangible).[5] For example,

DHL provides tracking numbers for customers so they can follow their shipments online and know exactly where a package is. This system helps reduce the risk for consumers. Offering a free or reduced-cost trial period for a service would be another means to reduce risk. For example, gyms and health clubs often encourage a free trial day for prospective clients to reduce the sense of risk in this important decision. To the extent that it is possible, service providers should emphasize employee training and other procedures to standardize their offerings so that consumers learn to expect a given level of quality, again reducing perceived risk.

Evaluation of Service Alternatives

The evoked set of alternatives – that group of products that a consumer considers acceptable options in a given product category – has traditionally been smaller with services than with goods. One reason involved differences in retailing between goods and services. To purchase goods, consumers generally shop in retail stores that display competing products in close proximity, clearly demonstrating the possible alternatives. To purchase services, on the other hand, the consumer had to visit an establishment (such as a bank, a dry cleaner or a hair salon) that almost always offered only a single 'brand' for sale. A second reason for the smaller evoked set was that consumers were unlikely to find more than one or two businesses providing the same services in a given geographic area, whereas they may find numerous retail stores carrying the identical manufacturer's product. A third reason for a smaller evoked set was the difficulty of obtaining adequate pre-purchase information about services. The Internet is changing this as it widens the set of alternatives. This trend is most notable in areas such as insurance, airlines and hotels with comparison websites where a wide range of information on suppliers and prices can be accessed in one place.

For non-professional services, consumers' decisions often entail the choice between performing the services for themselves or hiring someone to perform them.[6] Working people may choose between cleaning their own homes or hiring housekeepers, between altering their families' clothes or taking them to a tailor, even between staying home to take care of their children or engaging a nursery to provide child care. Consumers may consider themselves as sources of supply for many services, including lawn care, tax preparation and preparing meals. Thus, the customer's evoked set frequently includes self-provision of the service. Self-service via technology is also a viable alternative for many services.

Service Purchase

Following consideration of alternatives (whether an extensive process or more automatic), consumers make the decision to purchase a particular service or to do it themselves. One of the most interesting differences between goods and services is that many goods are fully produced (at the factory) prior to being purchased by consumers. Thus, consumers, prior to making their final purchase decision, can see and frequently try the exact object that they will buy. For services, much is still unknown at the point of purchase. In many cases, the service is purchased and produced almost simultaneously – as with a restaurant meal or live entertainment. In other cases, consumers pay all or part of the purchase price up front for a service they will not fully experience until it is produced for them much later. This situation arises with services such as packaged holidays or kitchen design, or ongoing services such as health club memberships or university education. In business-to-business situations, long-term contracts for services (such as payroll, network integration or landscaping) may be signed prior to anything being produced at all.

Because of the inherent risk in the purchase decision for services, some providers offer 'free' (or 'deeply discounted') initial trials or extensive tours of their facilities (for example, prospective student and parent tours at universities) in order to reduce risk in the final purchase decision. In business-to-business situations, trust in the provider is paramount when customers sign long-term service contracts, and frequently the contracts themselves spell out in detail the service level agreements and penalties for non-performance.

⭐ **SERVICE SPOTLIGHT**

Spotify, the Swedish audio streaming platform that provides music and podcasts from record labels and media companies, offers a 30-day free trial of its premium service. This enables potential new members to try out the service before taking out a full membership. This is aimed at reducing the perceived risk to the consumer by allowing them to experience the benefits that the premium service offers over the free Spotify version.

EXAMPLE
Evaluating Self-Service

One of the major recent changes in consumer behaviour is the growing tendency for consumers to interact with technology to create services instead of interacting with a live service firm employee. Self-service technologies (SSTs) are technological interfaces that allow customers to produce services independent of direct service employee involvement. Examples that you are probably very familiar with are bank ATM machines, pay-at-the-pump terminals at service stations and automated airline check-in. All forms of services over the Internet are also self-service technologies, many of which are very innovative. In the UK, for example, users can complete their tax return online rather than use the usual paper forms. Electronic self-ordering is being developed at fast-food chains, and self-scanning at grocery stores is available in many supermarkets.

Table 3.1 shows a comprehensive set of categories and examples of self-service technologies in use today. The columns of the matrix represent the types of technologies that companies are using to interface with customers in self-service encounters, and the rows show purposes of the technologies from the customer perspective. As you can see, customers use the technologies to provide customer service (deal with questions about accounts, bill-paying and delivery-tracking), to conduct transactions (order, buy and exchange resources with companies without direct interaction), and to provide self-help (learn, receive information, train themselves and provide their own services).

Table 3.1   Categories and examples of self-service technologies

Interface Purpose	Telephone/Interactive Voice Response	Online/Internet	Interactive
Customer service	• Telephone banking • Flight information • Order status	• Package tracking • Account information	• ATMs • Hotel checkout
Transactions	• Telephone banking • Prescription refills	• Retail purchasing • Financial transactions	• Pay at the pump • Hotel checkout • Car rental
Self-help	• Information telephone lines	• Internet information search • Distance learning	• Blood pressure machines • Tourist information

Customers may have strong feelings about self-service technologies,[7] they love them when:

- ***They bail them out of difficult situations***. A single parent with a sleeping child in the car needs to get fuel and a fast meal. Using a pay-at-the-pump service station and drive-up fast-food restaurant allows the parent to accomplish these tasks without leaving the sleeping child.

- **They are better than the interpersonal alternative**. Self-service technology has the potential to save customers time, money and psychological costs. The Internet, in particular, allows customers to shop at any time and complete transactions more quickly than they could in person. Internet loans and finance also allow customers to avoid the anxiety of meeting a banker in person and feeling judged.
- **They work as they are supposed to**. When self-service technologies work as they are supposed to, customers are impressed. Many of you have had the experience of using one-click ordering at Amazon. When these transactions work smoothly, as they usually do after the proper setup, they are satisfying.

On the other hand, customers hate self-service technology when the following problems occur:

- **They fail to work**. Broken machines, failed PIN numbers, websites that are down or crash, and items not shipped as promised all frustrate consumers.
- **They are poorly designed**. Poorly designed technologies that are difficult to use or understand create hassles for customers, making them feel as though the technology is not worth using. Websites that are difficult to navigate are particularly troublesome. If customers cannot reach information they need within a few clicks (some researchers say that two clicks are all that customers will tolerate), then they shun the website.
- **The customer messes up**. Customers dislike technologies that they don't feel they can use adequately. Even though they feel partially responsible, they will avoid using them in the future. A common frustration is having various user names and passwords for different websites. When confronted with a screen requiring this information – and not recalling it accurately – many customers will give up and go elsewhere.
- **There is no service recovery**. When the process or technology fails, self-service technologies rarely provide ways to recover on the spot. For example, a vending machine may take a customer's money but fail to deliver the product requested. In these cases customers must then call or visit the company, precisely what they were trying to avoid by using the self-service technology.

It is increasingly evident that these technological innovations are a critical component of many customer–firm interactions. If these technologies are to succeed, they must become more reliable, be better than the interpersonal alternatives and have recovery systems in place when they fail.

Consumer Experience During Service Delivery

Because the choice process for services is inherently risky with many unknowns, the experience itself often dominates the evaluation process. As noted, services are high in experience and credence qualities relative to goods; thus, how consumers evaluate the actual experience of the service is critical in their evaluation process and their decision to repurchase later. In fact, noted customer experience experts have stated that 'the experience is the marketing'.[8]

Much has been written recently about customer experiences and their important role in influencing consumer behaviour. Goods and services companies alike are being urged to create 'memorable experiences for their customers'.[9]

In this section we describe elements of consumer behaviour that are relevant to understanding service experiences and how customers evaluate them. We do not limit our discussion to fun, exciting or memorable experiences only. Instead, we use the term *customer experience* to encompass service processes that span the mundane to the spectacular. Customers purchasing building maintenance and dry-cleaning services still have experiences, albeit less exciting ones than customers of entertainment or travel services. All services *are* experiences – some are long in duration and some are short; some are complex and others are simple; some are mundane, whereas others are exciting and unique. Creating and managing effective processes and experiences are always essential management tasks for service organizations. Many subsequent chapters in this book will provide you with tools and approaches for managing specific elements of the customer experience – the heart of services marketing and management.

Services as Processes

Because services are actions or performances done for and with customers, they typically involve a sequence of steps, actions and activities. Consider medical services. Some of the steps in medical care involve customers interacting with providers (e.g. patients interacting with their doctor), other steps may be carried out by the customers themselves (e.g. 'following the doctor's orders', taking medications) and other steps may involve third parties (e.g. going to a hospital for tests). The combination of these steps, and many others along the way, constitute a process, a service experience that is evaluated by the consumer. It is the combination of steps, the flow of the activities or the 'experience' that is evaluated by the customer. In many cases, the customer's experience comprises interactions with multiple, interconnected organizations, as in the case of medical services, car insurance or home buying. Diverse sets of experiences across the network of firms (e.g. a doctor's office, a pharmacy, hospital and physiotherapy clinic) will likely influence consumers' overall impressions of their experience. Whether or not the provider acknowledges it or seeks to control this experience in a particular way, it is inevitable that the customer will have an experience – good, bad or indifferent.

Service Provision as Drama

The metaphor of service as theatre is a useful framework for describing and analysing service performances. Both the theatre and service organizations aim to create and maintain a desirable impression before an audience and recognize that the way to accomplish this is by carefully managing the actors and the physical setting of their behaviour.[10] The service marketer must play many drama-related roles – including director, choreographer and writer – to be sure the performances of the actors are pleasing to the audience. The Walt Disney Company explicitly considers its service provision a 'performance', even using show business terms such as *cast member, onstage* and *show* to describe the operations at Disneyland Paris.[11]

The skill of the service *actors* in performing their routines, the way they appear and their commitment to the 'show' are all essential to service delivery. Although service actors are present in most service performances, their importance increases in three conditions. First, service actors are critical when the degree of direct personal contact is high. Consider the difference between a visit to see a lawyer in comparison to a visit to a fast-food restaurant. The second condition in which service actors' skills are critical is when the services involve repeat contact. Nurses in hospitals, favourite waiters or tennis coaches in resorts or captains on cruises are essential characters in service theatre, and their individual performances can make or break the success of the services. The third condition in which contact personnel are critical is when they have discretion in determining the nature of the service and how it is delivered. When you consider the quality of the education you are receiving in university, you are certain to focus much of your evaluation on your lecturers' delivery of classes. In education, as in other services such as medical and legal services, the professional is the key actor in the performance.[12]

Ray Fisk and Steve Grove, two experts in the area of service dramaturgy, point out that service actors' performances can be characterized as sincere or cynical.[13] A sincere performance occurs when an actor becomes one with the role that he or she is playing, whereas a cynical performance occurs when an actor views a performance only as a means to an end, such as getting paid for doing the job. When a service employee takes the time to listen and help, the performance is sincere and often noteworthy. Unfortunately, too many examples of cynical performances exist in which front-line 'actors' seem to care little about the 'audience' of customers. As Grove and Fisk point out, a single employee can ruin the service experience by ridiculing other cast members' efforts, failing to perform his or her role correctly or projecting the wrong image. To create the right impression, three characteristics are necessary: loyalty, discipline and circumspection.[14]

The physical setting of the service can be likened to the staging of a theatrical production, including scenery, props and other physical cues to create desired impressions. Among a setting's features that may influence the character of a service are the colours or brightness of the service's surroundings; the volume and pitch of sounds in the setting; the smells, movement, freshness and temperature of the air; the use of space; the style and comfort of the furnishings; and the setting's design and cleanliness.[15] As an example, the service provided by a cruise ship features its layout (cabins and entertainment/eating areas), decor and comfort (large, cushioned deckchairs), furnishings (lots of polished wood and brass) and cleanliness ('shipshape'). The setting increases in importance when the environment distinguishes the service. Consider how critical the setting is for a city-centre law firm, which must appear professional, capable, even imposing.[16] In essence, the delivery of service can be conceived as drama, where service personnel are the actors, service customers are the audience, physical evidence of the service is the setting and the process of service assembly is the performance. The drama metaphor offers a useful way to improve service performances.[17] Selection of personnel can be viewed as auditioning the actors. An actor's personal appearance, manner, facial expression, gestures, personality and demographic profile can be determined in large part in the interview or audition. Training of personnel can become rehearsing. Clearly defining the role can be seen as scripting the performance. Creation of the service environment involves setting the stage. Finally, deciding which aspects of the service should be performed in the presence of the customer (onstage) and which should be performed in the back room (backstage) helps define the performances that the customer experiences.

Service Roles and Scripts

Service roles are combinations of social cues that guide and direct behaviour in a given setting.[18] Just as there are roles in dramatic performances, there are roles in service delivery. For example, the role of a hostess in a restaurant is to acknowledge and greet customers, find out how many people are in their group, and then lead them to a table where they will eat. The success of any service performance depends in part on how well the role is performed by the service actor and how well the team of players – the 'role set' of both service employees and customers – act out their roles.[19] Service employees need to perform their roles according to the expectations of the customer; if they do not, the customer may be frustrated and disappointed. If customers are informed and educated about their roles and if they cooperate with the provider in following the script, successful service provision is likely.

One factor that influences the effectiveness of role performance is the service script – the logical sequence of events expected by the customer, involving him or her as either a participant or an observer.[20] Service scripts consist of sequences of actions associated with actors and objects that, through repeated involvement, define what the customer expects.[21] Receiving a dental check-up is a service experience for which a well-defined script exists. For a check-up, the consumer expects the following sequence: enter the reception area, greet a receptionist, sit in a waiting room, follow the dental nurse to a separate room, recline in a chair while teeth are examined by the dentist, then pay for the services. When the service conforms to this script, the customer has a feeling of confirmed expectations and satisfaction. Deviations from the service script lead to confusion and dissatisfaction. Suppose, on moving to a new town, you went to a dentist who had no receptionist and no waiting area, only a doorbell in a cubicle. Suppose, on answering the doorbell, an employee in shorts took you to a large room where all patients were in a dental chairs facing each other. These actions and objects are certainly not in the traditional service script for dentistry and might create considerable uncertainty and doubt in patients.

Some services are more scripted than others. Customers would expect very expensive, customized services such as spa breaks to be less scripted than mass-produced services such as fast food ('Have a nice day!') and airline travel.

The Compatibility of Service Customers

We have just discussed the roles of employees and customers receiving service. We now want to focus on the role of *other customers* receiving service at the same time. Consider how central the mere presence of other customers is in churches, restaurants, dances, bars, clubs and spectator sports: if no one else shows up, customers will not get to socialize with others; one of the primary expectations in these types of services. However, if customers become so dense that crowding occurs, customers may also be dissatisfied.[22] The way other customers behave with many services – such as airlines, education, clubs and social organizations – also exerts a major influence on a customer's experience.[23] In general, the presence, behaviour and similarity of other customers receiving services has a strong impact on the satisfaction and dissatisfaction of any given customer.[24]

Customers can be incompatible for many reasons – differences in beliefs, values, experiences, ability to pay, appearance, age and health, to name just a few. The service marketer must anticipate, acknowledge and deal with heterogeneous consumers who have the potential to be incompatible. The service marketer can also bring homogeneous customers together and solidify relationships between them, which increases the cost to the customer of switching service providers.[25] Customer compatibility is a factor that influences customer satisfaction, particularly in high-contact services.

Customer Co-Production

In addition to being audience members, as suggested by the drama metaphor, service users also play a customer co-production role that can have profound influence on the service experience.[26] For example, counselling, personal training or educational services have little value without the full participation of the client, who will most likely have extensive work to do between sessions. In this sense, the client co-produces the service. In business-to-business contexts such as consulting, architecture, accounting and almost any outsourced service, customers also co-produce the service.[27] It has been suggested that customers therefore need to understand their roles and be 'trained' in ways that are similar to the training of service employees, so that they will have the motivation, ability and role clarity to perform.[28]

The idea of customers as 'partners' in the co-creation of products is gaining ground across all industries, not just services.[29] Postmodern consumer behaviour experts propose an even broader interpretation of this idea. They suggest that a fundamental characteristic of the postmodern era is consumers' assertiveness as active participants in creating their world – often evidenced in their demands to adjust, change and use products in customized ways.[30]

> **★ SERVICE SPOTLIGHT**
>
> In IKEA customers co-produce the service. They identify the items they want, collect them from the warehouse, deliver them to their homes and assemble them. To enable customers to understand their role in these tasks and complete them successfully, IKEA provides a catalogue setting out the product range and instructions as to how to purchase the items. IKEA makes use of comprehensive in-store signage, including arrows on the floor, to direct customers around the store and enable them to find the items they require in the warehouse area. Instructions are also provided on how to assemble items when the customer gets them home. These elements can all be seen as a form of customer training similar to that given to service employees, so that customers will have the motivation, ability and role clarity to co-produce effectively.

Emotion and Mood

Emotion and mood are feeling states that influence people's (and therefore customers') perceptions and evaluations of their experiences. Moods are distinguished from emotions in that *moods* are transient feeling states that occur at specific times and in specific situations, whereas *emotions* are more intense, stable and pervasive.[31]

Because services are experiences, moods and emotions are critical factors that shape the perceived effectiveness of service encounters. If a service customer is in a bad mood when he or she enters a service establishment, service provision will likely be interpreted more negatively than if he or she were in a buoyant, positive mood. Similarly, if a service provider is irritable or sullen, his or her interaction with customers will likely be coloured by that mood. Furthermore, when other customers in a service establishment are cranky or frustrated, whether from problems with the service or from existing emotions unrelated to the service, their mood affects the provision of service for all customers who sense the negative mood. In sum, any service characterized by human interaction is strongly dependent on the moods and emotions of the service provider, the service customer and other customers receiving the service at the same time.

In what specific ways can mood affect the behaviour of service customers? First, positive moods can make customers more obliging and willing to participate in behaviours that help service encounters succeed.[32] Customers in a good emotional state are probably more willing to follow an exercise regimen prescribed by a personal trainer, clear their own dishes at a fast-food restaurant and overlook delays in service. Customers in a negative mood may be less likely to engage in behaviours essential to the effectiveness of the service: abstaining from chocolates when on a diet programme for a weight loss club, taking frequent aerobic classes from a health club or completing homework assigned in a class.

A second way that moods and emotions influence service customers is to bias the way they judge service encounters and providers. Mood and emotions enhance and amplify experiences, making them either more positive or more negative than they might seem in the absence of these same moods and emotions.[33] After losing a big account, a salesperson catching an airline flight will be more incensed with delays and crowding than he or she might be on a day when business went well. Conversely, the positive mood of a services customer at a dance or restaurant will heighten the experience, leading to positive evaluations of the service establishment. The direction of the bias in evaluation is consistent with the polarity (positive or negative) of the mood or emotion.

Finally, moods and emotions affect the way information about service is absorbed and retrieved in memory. As memories about a service are encoded by a consumer, the feelings associated with the encounter become an inseparable part of the memory. If travellers fall in love while on holiday in Greece, they may hold favourable assessments of the destination due more to their emotional state than to the destination itself. Conversely, if a customer first becomes aware of his or her poor level of fitness when on a guest pass in a health club, the negative feelings may be encoded and retrieved every time he or she thinks of the health club or, for that matter, any health club.

Because emotions and moods play such important roles in influencing customer experiences, 'organizations must manage the emotional component of experiences with the same rigour they bring to the management of product and service functionality'.[34] Organizations may observe customers' emotional responses and attempt to create places, processes and interactions to enhance certain emotions. Some firms believe that consumers' emotional responses may be the best predictors of their ultimate loyalty. Thus, many companies are now beginning to measure emotional responses and connections as well – going beyond traditional measures of satisfaction and behavioural loyalty.

Post-Experience Evaluation

Following the service experience, customers form an evaluation that determines to a large degree whether they will return or continue to patronize the service organization (see Figure 3.2). Historically within the field of marketing, much more attention has been paid to pre-purchase evaluations and consumer choice. Yet, post-purchase and post-experience evaluations are typically most important in predicting subsequent consumer behaviours and repurchase, particularly for services.

Post-experience evaluation is captured by companies in measures of satisfaction, service quality, loyalty and, sometimes, emotional engagement. We devote an entire chapter (Chapter 5) to exploring the specifics of customer satisfaction and service quality. Another chapter (Chapter 7) examines the topic of relationships and loyalty.

Word-of-Mouth Communication

Post-experience evaluations will significantly impact what consumers tell others about the service. Because service consumers are strongly influenced by the personal opinions of others, understanding and controlling word-of-mouth communication becomes even more important for service companies. The best way to get positive word of mouth is, of course, to create memorable and positive service experiences. When service is unsatisfactory, it is critical to have an effective service recovery strategy (see Chapter 15) to curb negative word of mouth.

Attribution of Dissatisfaction

When consumers are disappointed with purchases – because the products did not fulfil the intended needs, did not perform satisfactorily or were not worth the price – their attribution of dissatisfaction may be to a number of different sources, among them the producers, the retailers, or themselves. Because consumers participate to a greater extent in the definition and production of services, they may feel more responsible for their dissatisfaction when they purchase services than when they purchase goods. As an example, consider a consumer purchasing a haircut; receiving the cut that he or she desires depends in part on communicating clear specifications to the stylist. If disappointed, he or she may blame either the stylist (for lack of skill) or him or herself (for choosing the wrong stylist or for not communicating his or her own needs clearly).

The quality of many services depends on the information the customer brings to the service encounter: a pharmacist's accurate diagnosis requires a conscientious case history and a clear articulation of symptoms; a dry cleaner's success in removing a spot depends on the consumer's knowledge of its cause; and a tax adviser's satisfactory performance relies on the receipts saved by the consumer. Failure to obtain satisfaction with any of these services may not be blamed completely on the retailer or producer, because consumers must adequately perform their part in the production process also.

With products, on the other hand, a consumer's main form of participation is the act of purchase. The consumer may attribute failure to receive satisfaction to his or her own decision-making error, but he or she holds the producer responsible for product performance. Goods usually carry warranties or guarantees with purchase, emphasizing that the producer believes that if something goes wrong, it is not the fault of the consumer. With services, consumers attribute some of their dissatisfaction to their own inability to specify or perform their part of the service. They may also complain less frequently about services than about goods because of their belief that they themselves are partly responsible for their dissatisfaction.

Positive or Negative Biases

There is a long history of research in psychology and consumer behaviour that suggests that people remember negative events and occurrences more than positive ones and are more influenced by negative information than by positive information. Research and personal observation suggest that it is easier for consumers to remember the negative service experiences they have than to think of the many routine, or even positive, experiences.

There is also a long stream of research that says that customers will weigh negative information about a product attribute more heavily than positive information in forming their overall brand attitudes. Yet some very interesting and recent research suggests 'positivity bias' for services.[35] The research showed that consumers tend to infer positive qualities for the firm and its employees if they have a good experience with one service employee. When individual service providers are regarded positively, customers' positive perceptions of other service providers in the company are also raised. On the other hand, customers who have a negative experience with one employee are less likely to draw a negative inference about all employees or the firm. That is, customers are more likely to attribute that negative experience to the individual provider, not the entire firm. Although this study is just one piece of research, the results and implications are very intriguing.

Brand Loyalty

The degree to which consumers are committed to particular brands of goods or services depends on a number of factors: the cost of changing brands (switching cost), the availability of substitutes, social ties to the company, the perceived risk associated with the purchase, and the satisfaction obtained in the past. Because it may be more costly to change brands of services, because awareness of substitutes is limited and because higher risks may accompany services, consumers are more likely to remain customers of particular companies with services than with goods.

The difficulty of obtaining information about services means that consumers may be unaware of alternatives or substitutes for their brands, or they may be uncertain about the ability of alternatives to increase satisfaction over present brands. Monetary fees may accompany brand switching in many services: dentists sometimes demand new X-rays on the initial visit and health clubs frequently charge 'membership fees' at the outset to obtain long-term commitments from customers.

If consumers perceive greater risks with services, as is hypothesized here, they probably depend on brand names to a greater extent than when they purchase products. Brand loyalty, described as a means of economizing decision effort by substituting habit for repeated, deliberate decision, functions as a device for reducing the risks of consumer decisions.

A final reason that consumers may be more brand loyal with services is the recognition of the need for repeated patronage in order to obtain optimum satisfaction from the seller. Becoming a 'regular customer' allows the seller to gain knowledge of the customer's tastes and preferences, ensures better treatment and encourages more interest in the consumer's satisfaction. Thus a consumer may exhibit brand loyalty to cultivate a satisfying relationship with the seller.

Brand loyalty has two sides. The fact that a service provider's own customers are brand loyal is, of course, desirable. The fact that the customers of the provider's competition are difficult to capture, however, creates special challenges. The marketer may need to direct communications and strategy to the customers of competitors, emphasizing attributes and strengths that their firm possesses and the competitor lacks. Marketers can also facilitate switching from competitors' services by reducing switching costs.

Understanding Differences Among Consumers

To this point in the chapter, we have discussed consumer decision-making and evaluation processes that are applicable across a wide range of consumers and types of services. In the remaining sections, we examine two broad topics that shed light on some of the differences *among* consumers. First, we examine the role of national and ethnic cultures in shaping consumer behaviour. Then we discuss some of the unique differences in consumer decision-making for organizations and households.

Global Differences: The Role of Culture

Culture represents the common values, norms and behaviours of a particular group and is often identified with nations or ethnicity. Culture is learned, shared, multidimensional and transmitted from one generation to the next. Understanding cultural differences is important in services marketing because of its effects on the ways that customers evaluate and use services. Culture also influences how companies and their service employees interact with customers. Culture is important in international services marketing – taking services from one country and offering them in others – but it is also critical within countries. More and more, individual countries are becoming multicultural, and organizations need to understand how this factor affects evaluation, purchase and use of services even within countries.

Research provides considerable evidence that there are differences in how consumers perceive services across cultures. For example, a study showed notable differences in how fast-food and grocery consumers in eight different countries (Australia, China, Germany, India, Morocco, the Netherlands, Sweden and the United States) evaluate these services.[36] Differences in how services are evaluated across cultures can be traced to basic factors that distinguish cultures from each other. In the next sections, we highlight some of the major differences that can influence how people choose, use and evaluate services, including values and attitudes, manners and customers, material culture, and aesthetics. Language, another obvious cultural difference particularly important for services, is discussed in Chapter 16.

Values and Attitudes Differ Across Cultures.   Values and attitudes help determine what members of a culture think is right, important and/or desirable. Because behaviours, including consumer behaviours, flow from values and attitudes, services marketers who want their services adopted across cultures must understand these differences.

⭐ SERVICE SPOTLIGHT

In 2014, Starbucks withdrew from the Australian market, selling its 24 remaining local stores to 7-Eleven operator Withers Group. Starbucks as a chain was never successful in Australia, owing to the pressure of Australia's thriving independent coffee shop scene. Australians are certainly big purchasers of 'coffee to go' but the coffee shop market is mature and sophisticated. Australians did not need to be introduced to the concept of coffee as many other countries in Asia and Northern Europe did. Early Italian and Greek immigrants introduced Australia to coffee drinking and independent boutique-type coffee shops have served the office-working populations in the large cities for decades. There is a strong sense in Australia of buying local, supporting the community, having relationships with the people you buy from and supporting ethically minded businesses. The Starbucks brand did not take full account of these differences in cultural values and attitudes.

Manners and Customs.   Manners and customs represent a culture's views of appropriate ways of behaving. It is important to monitor differences in manners and customs because they can have a direct effect on the service encounter. For example in fast-food restaurants, Central and Eastern Europeans are perplexed by Western expectations that unhappy workers put on a 'happy face' when dealing with customers. As an example, McDonald's requires Polish employees to smile whenever they interact with customers. Such a requirement strikes many employees as artificial and insincere. The fast-food giant has learned to encourage managers in Poland to probe employee problems and to assign troubled workers to the kitchen rather than to the food counter.[37]

Material Culture.   Material culture consists of the tangible products of culture. What people own and how they use and display material possessions vary around the world. Cars, houses, clothes and furniture are examples of material culture.

The importance of owning your own home varies significantly from country to country, reflecting the different cultural traditions existing within each society. Table 3.2 shows the percentage of residential dwellings that are owner-occupied (with and without a mortgage) in a number of European countries. The difference between Switzerland and Romania is particularly striking. Such differences will impact on property-related services such as decorating, garden maintenance, estate agents, lawyers, architects (for extensions/home improvements) and even do-it-yourself (DIY) retailers.

Aesthetics.   Aesthetics refer to cultural ideas about beauty and good taste. These ideas are reflected in music, art, drama and dance as well as the appreciation of colour and form.

Table 3.2   Housing ownership in European countries

Country	% of Population in Owner-Occupied Housing with Mortgage	% of Population in Owner-Occupied Housing without Mortgage	% of Population in Owner-Occupied Housing
Romania	1	96	97
Lithuania	10	80	90
Croatia	6	04	90
Slovakia	12	78	90
Hungary	16	69	85
Poland	12	72	84
Bulgaria	3	80	83
Estonia	19	63	82
Norway	62	19	81
Latvia	10	71	81
Malta	22	59	81
Czech Republic	19	59	78
Spain	31	46	77
Slovenia	11	65	76
Portugal	37	38	75
Greece	14	59	73
Italy	16	56	72
Belgium	41	31	72
Finland	42	29	71
Ireland	32	37	69
Netherlands	61	8	69
Sweden	55	10	65
United Kingdom	35	30	65
France	31	33	64
Denmark	47	15	62
Austria	25	30	55
Germany	26	25	51
Switzerland	38	4	42

Source: Eurostat (2017). Distribution of population by tenure status.

Attitudes towards style in clothing, cars, restaurants, retail stores and hotels vary internationally relating to the expectations of local culture. A French café is very different from a Starbucks in terms of atmosphere. Many Scandinavian hotels such as Radisson Blu have very clean lines with utilitarian furniture supported by decor that is striking but simple. The internal design of a French car is generally more 'chic' or quirky than would be the case for a German-built car. These all reflect the aesthetic characteristics of the culture they serve. Care must therefore be taken in designing service environments to ensure that the target market is comfortable with the aesthetic qualities being presented.

Group Decision-Making

A group is defined as two or more individuals who have implicitly or explicitly defined relationships to one another such that their behaviour is interdependent.[38] When groups make decisions about services – a household purchasing a family holiday or a kitchen redesign, or an organization purchasing information technology consulting or marketing research services – many of the same issues arise as for individuals. Groups purchasing services encounter greater perceived risk, more reliance on word-of-mouth communication, greater difficulty in comparing alternatives and often a higher level of customer participation than do groups purchasing goods. For example, although many large organizations have very clear evaluation processes for buying goods, their processes and decision rules for purchasing services are often not as well defined. The intangibility and variability of business services make them more risky and often difficult to compare. Thus, organizations often rely on established partnerships, long-term relationships or referrals from others when it comes to major service purchases. Similar issues arise for households who rely heavily on personal referrals in making significant services purchases such as home repair, landscaping and annual vacations. Even smaller household decisions – where to eat dinner or the choice of a dry cleaner – may be influenced by referrals and may involve a great deal of risk, depending on the occasion. A special anniversary or birthday dinner, or where to have an heirloom such as Grandmother's 40-year-old wedding dress dry cleaned, can be decisions that carry considerable personal risk.

Despite these similarities, some differences in group decision-making should be considered for a fuller understanding of consumer behaviour in services. Among the aspects that are different for group buying are collective decision-making, mixed motives or goals, roles in the purchasing process, and group culture. We will highlight some of these differences for two major groups: households and organizations.

Households

When a family makes a service purchase decision, it has a collective style of decision-making that often differs from what any of the individuals would use if making an independent choice. When a family chooses a holiday destination, for example, its style may involve one of the following: (1) one parent makes a unilateral decision that the family will go on holiday to Disneyland Paris; (2) the family discusses possible holiday destinations at the dinner table, taking each person's ideas and suggestions into account, and selects three locations that a parent will investigate further; (3) the parents provide a budget and a list of the destinations that can be visited within that budget, then allow the children to choose among them. Once a destination has been chosen, the mix of motives or goals of the group comes into play. The mother may want to sightsee, the father to rest and the children to visit local theme parks. In this and other group purchasing decisions, the needs and goals of the various members must be balanced so that the service (in this case the holiday) delivers optimal satisfaction for as many members as possible. Group roles are also a key consideration. In a household, one individual often identifies a need and initiates the purchase, someone else may influence which service provider is selected, someone else may pay and someone else may become the ultimate user of the service. For example, the father may decide that the family needs to visit an optician for an eye test, a teenager may recommend an optician that a friend uses, the mother may pay the bills, and all the family members may go to get their eyes tested. Finally, national and ethnic culture affects household purchase and consumption behaviours. For example, ethnic groups vary, with some being very patriarchal, others egalitarian and still others autocratic.

Organizations

Organizational consumers are a special category of group consumers. These days, companies spend millions on information technology services, call centres, travel management, payroll services and outsourced services for human resource management. Making the right decision on service purchases can be absolutely critical for an organization's success. How do companies make these important decisions? How, for example, do certain companies choose to outsource their call-centre operations to a company in India?

For routine and even complex purchases, organizations often rely on a small number of buyers within the company, many of whom specialize in purchasing. These buyers are typically organized either formally or informally into **buying centres**, which include all people involved in the decision process.[39] Each of these roles may be taken by a different person, or one person may assume all roles in some cases.

- The *initiator* identifies the organization's service needs.
- The *gatekeeper* collects and controls information about the purchase.
- The *decider* determines what service to purchase.
- The *buyer* or purchasing agent physically acquires the service.
- The *user* consumes the service and may or may not have any influence over the purchase decision.

Among the characteristics that distinguish organizational from individual decision-making are economic forces such as current business climate and technology trends; organizational strategies and culture; whether purchasing is a centralized or decentralized function; and the group forces that influence purchasing decisions.[40] Organizational purchases also tend to differ by magnitude and include new task purchases (large purchases that require careful consideration of needs and evaluation of alternative), straight rebuys (simple reorders of past service purchases) and modified rebuys (a mix of new and straight rebuy features).[41]

As companies outsource more services, and particularly when these services are outsourced around the globe, purchase decisions become complex and difficult. Often companies must rely on outside consultants, such as Accenture or PriceWaterhouseCoopers, to help them with these multifaceted and financially risky decisions.

Organizational purchasers also rely on references and the experience of other organizations in making their service purchase decisions. Referrals and testimonials can be very helpful to other organizations considering similar business service purchases. In fact, many business service providers have customer stories, cases and testimonials on their websites to help reduce the risk of these complex decisions.

Summary

The intention of this chapter was to provide understanding about how consumers choose and evaluate services. Services possess high levels of experience and credence properties, which in turn make them challenging to evaluate, particularly prior to purchase. The chapter isolated and discussed three stages of consumer behaviour for services, and it looked at how experience and credence properties result in challenges and opportunities in all three stages. The three stages are consumer choice (including need recognition, information search, evaluation of alternatives and service purchase); consumer experience; and post-experience evaluation. Consumer behaviour theories, current research and insights for managers were highlighted in each of these sections.

Although the three stages are relevant for all types of consumer behaviour in services, important differences exist in behaviour across global cultures and for groups versus individuals. Global differences in consumer behaviour were presented, particularly as they relate to service consumption. The chapter ended with a discussion of the differences in group versus individual consumer decision-making related to households and organizations.

Key Concepts

Attribution of dissatisfaction	53	Culture	54
Buying centres	58	Customer co-production	51

Evaluation of alternatives	43	Search vs. experience vs. credence qualities	42
Information search	43	Self-service technologies	47
Moods and emotions	52	Service as theatre	49
Need recognition	43	Service roles	50
Perceived risk	45	Service script	50
Purchase	43	Word-of-mouth communication	53

Exercises

1   Choose a particular end-consumer services industry and one type of service provided in that industry (such as the financial services industry for mortgage loans, the legal services industry for wills or the travel industry for a holiday package). Talk to five customers who have purchased that service and determine to what extent the information in this chapter described their behaviour in terms of consumer choice, consumer experience and post-experience evaluation for that service.

2   Choose a particular business-to-business service industry and one type of service provided in that industry (such as the information services industry for computer maintenance services or the consulting industry for management consulting). Talk to five customers in that industry and determine to what extent the information in this chapter described their behaviour in terms of consumer choice, consumer experience and post-experience evaluation for that service.

3   Visit a service provider of your choice. Experience the service at first hand if possible and observe other customers for a period of time. Describe the consumer (service) experience in detail in terms of what happened throughout the process and how customers, including yourself, felt about it. How could the service experience be improved?

4   Interview three people who come from countries other than your own. Ask them about their consumer behaviour patterns with regard to a variety of services. Note the differences and similarities to your own consumer behaviour. What are some possible causes of the differences?

Discussion Questions

1   Based on the chapter, which aspects of consumer behaviour are similar and which are different for services versus goods?

2   Where does a college or university education fit on the continuum of evaluation for different types of products? Where does computer software fit? Consulting? Retailing? Fast food? What are the implications for consumer behaviour?

3   What are examples (other than those given in the chapter) of services that are high in credence properties? How do high credence properties affect consumer behaviour for these services?

4   Which services do you consider to be unsuited to the introduction of self-service technology? Why?

5   How do you reduce risk when choosing a restaurant in a city you haven't visited before?

6   Why are consumer experiences so important in the evaluation process for services?

7   Using the service drama metaphor, describe the services provided by a health club, a fine restaurant or a cruise liner.

8   What are some differences in service choice, purchase and consumption processes for organizations and households compared with individuals? What are some similarities?

Further Reading

Collier, J.E., Moore, R.S., Horky, A. and Moore, M.L. (2015). Why the little things matter: Exploring situational influences on customers' self-service technology decisions. *Journal of Business Research,* 68(3), 703–710.

Girard, T. and Dion, P. (2010). Validating the search, experience and credence product classification framework. *Journal of Business Research,* 63(9–10), 1079–87.

Hofstede, G. (2003). *Culture's Consequences: Comparing Values, Behaviours, Institutions and Organisations across Nations,* 2nd edn. London: Sage Publications.

Kim, Y. and Peterson, R.A. (2017). A meta-analysis of online trust relationships in e-commerce. *Journal of Interactive Marketing,* 38, 44–54.

Larivière, B., Bowen, D., Andreassen, T.W., Kunz, W., Sirianni, N.J., Voss, C. and De Keyser, A. (2017). 'Service Encounter 2.0': An investigation into the roles of technology, employees and customers. *Journal of Business Research,* 79, 238–246.

McKoll-Kennedy, J.R. and Fetter, R. (1999). Dimensions of consumer search behaviour in services. *Journal of Services Marketing,* 13(3), 242–63.

Pappas, N. (2016). Marketing strategies, perceived risks, and consumer trust in online buying behaviour. *Journal of Retailing and Consumer Services,* 29, 92–103.

Schmitt, B. (2011). Experience marketing: concepts, frameworks and consumer insights. *Foundations and Trends® in Marketing,* 5 (2), 55–112.

Sparks, B. and Browning V. (2011). The impact of online reviews on hotel booking intentions and perception of trust. *Tourism Management,* 32(6), 1310–1323.

Wilson, A., Murphy, H. and Cambra Fierro, J. (2012). Hospitality and travel: The nature and implications of user-generated content. *Cornell Hospitality Quarterly,* 53(3), 220–229.

Chapter 4

Customer Expectations of Service

Chapter Outline

Importance of Customer Expectations	63
Meaning and Types of Service Expectations	63
Factors that Influence Customer Expectations of Service	68
Issues Involving the Management of Customer Service Expectations	74
Summary	79
Key Concepts	79
Exercises	79
Discussion Questions	80
Further Reading	80

Learning Objectives

This chapter's objectives are to:

1 Recognize that customers hold different types of expectations for service performance.

2 Discuss the sources of customer expectations of service, including those that are controllable and uncontrollable by marketers.

3 Acknowledge that the types and sources of expectations are similar for end consumers and business customers, for pure service and product-related service, for experienced customers and inexperienced customers.

4 Understand the most important current issues surrounding the management of customer expectations.

Opening Example

KLM – Using Social Media to Meet Customer Expectations

In 2010, a volcanic eruption in south Iceland grounded thousands of flights and left millions of passengers stranded. During the eruption more than 75 per cent of European airspace was closed for a week, affecting more than 90,000 flights and 10 million passengers. While the circumstances were beyond the control of the airlines, the main expectation of the stranded passengers was that their airlines would keep them updated with information. In tense, time-sensitive circumstances, consumers were increasingly turning to social media for real-time information and advice. In the seven days when most of Europe's largest air-

Source: ©J. Helgason/Shutterstock

lines were grounded, there were more than 55,000 mentions on Twitter of #ashtag, as people tried to source information about flights, accommodation and up-to-date news of their situation. The rapidly evolving situation meant that the flight information on static websites quickly became obsolete. This led to airlines following customer demand and turning to social media – some for the first time – to update their customers. Although this was a struggle for many, the crisis did highlight KLM, which excelled at meeting customer expectations by issuing updates via social media channels. KLM not only provided users with flight status updates, but also engaged in public conversations and looked to make the answers to frequently asked questions easily available. The airline sent out regular Twitter updates filled with advice on re-booking, information about local areas and links to news stories, and dedicated time to reply to many individual customer questions, comments and concerns. KLM also created a bespoke 'Volcanic Eruption' Q&A sidebar on its Facebook page and had official representatives available to respond to questions continuously. Using their social media platforms, KLM was able not just to update a large number of customers and people affected by the ash cloud, but also to grow its number of followers on Twitter by more than 4,000 in that one week. Not only did KLM show its competence in managing a crisis, but the organized way in which it provided information and responded to questions had a very positive effect on their brand perceptions. The explosion in social media created a critical tipping point with organizations struggling to cope with the 'noise' and potential damage it can create, but for KLM, the ash cloud did it no lasting harm.

Since 2010, KLM has grown its social media usage significantly to make obtaining feedback from passengers easy. The company aims to respond to each Twitter tweet or Facebook post within one hour and resolve all issues within 24 hours. KLM receives around 60,000 questions every week on social media: 75 per cent of these are posted on Facebook, with the other 25 per cent coming predominantly via Twitter.

KLM has 150 employees fully focused on social customer care. The average response time is 23 minutes. It is a 24/7 service available in 14 languages.

Flight attendants also carry an iPad on board to field any social enquiries from passengers on their flight. The customer care team can ask the cabin crew to take the enquiries offline, solve any problems and report back. An example of such social customer care is when a customer complained about being given a cold meal on a flight. On the return flight, the cabin crew made sure this passenger was among the first to get their meal and received an apology for what happened on the outbound journey.

Source: Adapted from 'Every ash cloud has a silver lining' on MyCustomer.com by Dee Roche 3/5/2011 and www.klm.com

Importance of Customer Expectations

Customer expectations are beliefs about service delivery that serve as standards, or reference points, against which performance is judged. Because customers compare their perceptions of performance with these reference points when evaluating service quality, thorough knowledge about customer expectations is critical to services marketers. Knowing what the customer expects is the first and possibly most critical step in delivering good-quality service. Being wrong about what customers want can mean losing a customer's business when another company hits the target exactly. Being wrong can also mean expending money, time and other resources on things that do not matter to the customer. Being wrong can even mean not surviving in a fiercely competitive market.

Among the aspects of expectations that need to be explored and understood for successful services marketing are the following: what types of expectation standards do customers hold about services? What factors most influence the formation of these expectations? What role do these factors play in changing expectations? How can a service company meet or exceed customer expectations?

In this chapter we provide a framework for thinking about customer expectations.[1] The chapter is divided into three main sections: (1) the meaning and types of expected service, (2) factors that influence customer expectations of service, and (3) current issues involving customer service expectations.

Meaning and Types of Service Expectations

To say that expectations are reference points against which service delivery is compared is only a beginning. The level of expectation can vary widely depending on the reference point the customer holds. Although almost everyone has an intuitive sense of what expectations are, service marketers need a far more thorough and clear definition of expectations if they are to comprehend, measure and manage them.

Imagine that you are planning to go to a restaurant. Figure 4.1 shows a continuum along which different possible types of service expectations can be arrayed from low to high. On the left of the continuum are different types or levels of expectations, ranging from high (top) to low (bottom). At each point we give a name to the type of expectation, and illustrate what it might mean in terms of a restaurant you are considering. Note how important the expectation you hold will be to your eventual assessment of the restaurant's performance. Suppose you went into the restaurant for which you held the minimum tolerable expectation, paid very little money and were served immediately with good food. Next suppose that you went to the restaurant for which you had the highest (ideal) expectations, paid a lot of money and were served good (but not fantastic) food. Which restaurant experience would you judge to be best? The answer is likely to depend a great deal on the reference point that you brought to the experience.

Because the idea of customer expectations is so critical to evaluation of service, we start this chapter by talking about the levels of expectations.

Expected Service: Levels of Expectations

As we show in Figure 4.1, customers hold different types of expectations about service. For purposes of our discussion in the rest of this chapter, we focus on two types. The highest can be termed *desired service:* the level of service the customer hopes to receive – the 'wished for' level of performance. Desired service is a blend of what the customer believes 'can be' and 'should be'. For example, consumers who sign up for a computer dating service expect to find compatible, attractive, interesting people to date and perhaps even someone to marry. The expectation reflects the hopes and wishes of these consumers; without these hopes and wishes and the belief that they may be fulfilled, consumers would probably not purchase the dating service. In a similar way, you may use an online travel-planning and flight-booking site such as Expedia to book a short holiday to Venice at Easter. What are your expectations of the service? In all likelihood you want

Figure 4.1 Possible levels of customer expectations

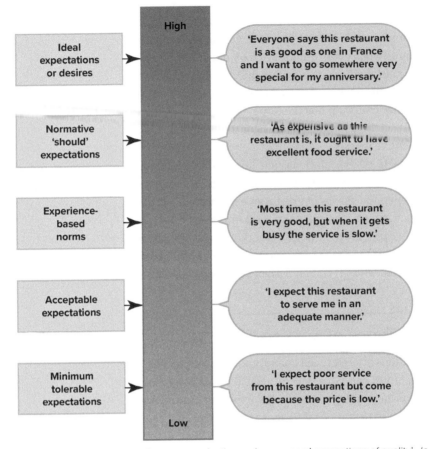

Source: Adapted from R.K. Teas, 'Expectations, performance evaluation and consumers' perceptions of quality', *Journal of Marketing* (October 1993), pp. 18–34.

Expedia to find you a flight exactly when you want to travel and a hotel close to the key sights in Piazza San Marco at a price you can afford – because that is what you hope and wish for.

However, you probably also see that demand at Easter may constrain the availability of airline seats and hotel rooms. And not all airlines or hotels you may be interested in may have a relationship with Expedia. In this situation, and in general, customers hope to achieve their service desires but recognize that this is not always possible. We call the threshold level of acceptable service *adequate service* – the level of service the customer will accept.[2] So the customer may put up with a flight at a less than ideal time and stay at a hotel further away from the key Venetian sites if he or she really wants to travel at Easter. Adequate service represents the 'minimum tolerable expectation',[3] the bottom level of performance acceptable to the customer.

Figure 4.2 shows these two expectation standards as the upper and lower boundaries for customer expectations. This figure portrays the idea that customers assess service performance on the basis of two standard boundaries: what they desire and what they deem acceptable.

Among the intriguing questions about service expectations is whether customers hold the same or different expectation levels for service firms in the same industry. For example, are desired service expectations the same for all restaurants? Or just for all fast-food restaurants? Do the levels of adequate service expectations vary across restaurants? Consider the following quotation:

> *Levels of expectation are why two organizations in the same business can offer far different levels of service and still keep customers happy. It is why McDonald's can extend excellent industrialized service with few employees per customer and why an expensive restaurant with many tuxedoed waiters may be unable to do as well from the customer's point of view.*[4]

Figure 4.2   Dual customer expectation levels

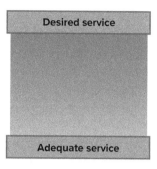

Customers typically hold similar desired expectations across categories of service, but these categories are not as broad as whole industries. Among subcategories of restaurants are expensive restaurants, ethnic restaurants, fast-food restaurants and airport restaurants. A customer's desired service expectation for fast-food restaurants is quick, convenient, tasty food in a clean setting. The desired service expectation for an expensive restaurant, on the other hand, usually involves elegant surroundings, gracious employees, candle-light and fine food. In essence, desired service expectations seem to be the same for service providers within industry categories or subcategories that are viewed as similar by customers.

The adequate service expectation level, on the other hand, may vary for different firms within a category or subcategory. Within fast-food restaurants, a customer may hold a higher expectation for McDonald's than for Burger King, having experienced consistent service at McDonald's over time and somewhat inconsistent service at Burger King. It is possible therefore that a customer can be more disappointed with service from McDonald's than from Burger King, even though the actual level of service at McDonald's may be higher than the level at Burger King.

⭐ SERVICE SPOTLIGHT

In the past, hotels built their business around employing highly attentive people. In the future, they may replace many of their staff with technology. As a regular guest, on the day of your arrival, when you get within 10 kilometres of the hotel, an alert from your phone ensures that the temperature and humidity levels of your room are automatically adjusted to your liking so they will meet your expectations when you arrive.

Upon arrival, you will be greeted by an automated luggage attendant using auto-tracking technology designed to quickly transfer your bags to your room. Upon entering the hotel lobby, you will be automatically registered without having to check in. Your room number and directions to the room will display on your smartphone. Virtual receptionists will be positioned at key locations in the hotel to help out whenever the need arises. As you approach your room, the door will automatically unlock and you will see your luggage already waiting for you. Upon entering your room, the sound system will automatically be playing music that syncs with your personality at the perfect volume. Temperature and humidity will have been programmed into the room-electrics specifically for you. Window shades will open or close depending on your position in the room, time of day, and intensity of the sunlight. Even when stepping into the shower, the controls will anticipate your desired water temperature, spray selection, and pressure.

Although this may seem far off in the future, Citizen M hotels already provide a smart tablet in each room which commands all essential room functions from lighting to room temperature and air conditioning, TV and entertainment, whilst also serving as a portal for all branded hotel services and as a regular web browsing device. Hotel chains such as Hilton have self-check-in facilities and bedrooms that are unlocked using your smartphone. In Japan, there are hotels where robots deliver room-service meals from the kitchens to guests in their rooms.

Source: Adapted from Thomas Frey, www.futuristspeaker.com.

The Zone of Tolerance

As we discussed in earlier chapters, services are heterogeneous in that performance may vary across providers, across employees from the same provider, and even with the same service employee. The extent to which customers recognize and are willing to accept this variation is called the zone of tolerance and is shown in Figure 4.3. If service drops below adequate – the minimum level considered acceptable – customers will be frustrated and their satisfaction with the company will be undermined. If service performance is higher than the zone of tolerance at the top end – where performance exceeds desired service – customers will be very pleased and probably quite surprised as well. You might consider the zone of tolerance as the range within which customers do not particularly notice service performance. When it falls outside the range (either very low or very high), the service gets the customer's attention in either a positive or negative way. As an example, consider the service at a checkout queue in a grocery shop. Most customers hold a range of acceptable times for this service encounter – probably somewhere between five and ten minutes. If service consumes that period of time, customers probably do not pay much attention to the wait. If a customer joins the queue and finds sufficient checkout staff to serve them in the first two or three minutes, they may notice the service and judge it as excellent. On the other hand, if a customer has to wait in a queue for 15 minutes, they may begin to grumble and start checking the time. The longer the wait is below the zone of tolerance, the more frustrated the customer becomes.

Figure 4.3   The zone of tolerance

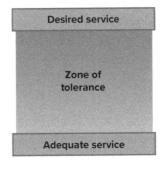

Customers' service expectations are characterized by a range of levels (like those shown in Figure 4.3), bounded by desired and adequate service, rather than a single level. This tolerance zone, representing the difference between desired service and the level of service considered adequate, can expand and contract with each customer. An airline customer's zone of tolerance will narrow when he or she is running late and is concerned about making it in time for his or her plane. A minute seems much longer, and the customer's adequate service level increases. On the other hand, a customer who arrives at the airport early may have a larger tolerance zone, making the wait in line far less noticeable than when he or she is pressed for time. This example shows that the marketer must understand not just the size and boundary levels for the zone of tolerance but also when and how the tolerance zone fluctuates with a given customer.

⭐ **SERVICE SPOTLIGHT**

The budget hotel sector has become very commoditized, with many chains competing on price combined with standard-sized rooms and a basic level of service. Premier Inn has developed the Premier Inn Hub, a compact city centre hotel concept to address the expectations of a particular segment of the market. Research undertaken by Whitbread, the parent company of Premier Inn, found that some customers were not concerned about the size of the room. Their expectations valued price, location and design over space. To meet these expectations, hub bedrooms are only 11.4 square metres with

> every centimetre optimized. The rooms have a modern design combining a desk that folds into the bed, luggage storage under the bed, an en-suite bathroom with power shower, free wi-fi and a 40-inch smart screen TV. The concept has been targeted at major UK city centres with eight in London and three in Edinburgh.
>
> *Source:* **www.premierinn.com.**

Different Customers Possess Different Zones of Tolerance

Another aspect of variability in the range of reasonable services is that different customers possess different tolerance zones. Some customers have narrow zones of tolerance, requiring a tighter range of service from providers, whereas other customers allow a greater range of service. For example, very busy customers are likely always to be pressed for time, desire short wait times in general and hold a constrained range for the length of acceptable wait times. When it comes to meeting plumbers or repair personnel at their home for problems with leaking pipes or domestic appliances, customers who work outside the home have a more restricted window of acceptable time duration for that appointment than do customers who work in their homes or who do not work at all.

The zone of tolerance of an individual customer increases or decreases depending on a number of factors, including company-controlled factors such as price. When prices increase, customers tend to be less tolerant of poor service. In this case, the zone of tolerance decreases because the adequate service level shifts upward. Later in this chapter we will describe many different factors, some company-controlled and others customer-controlled, that lead to the narrowing or widening of the tolerance zone.

Zones of Tolerance Vary for Service Dimensions

Customers' tolerance zones also vary for different service attributes or dimensions. The more important the factor, the narrower the zone of tolerance is likely to be. In general, customers are likely to be less tolerant about unreliable service (broken promises or service errors) than about other types of service deficiency, which means that they have higher expectations for this factor. In addition to higher expectations for the most important service dimensions and attributes, customers are likely to be less willing to relax these expectations than those for less important factors, making the zone of tolerance for the most important service dimension smaller and the desired and adequate service levels higher.[5] Figure 4.4 portrays the likely difference in tolerance zones for the most important and the least important factors showing that customers have higher expectations of reliability than tangibles. They are also less tolerant about unreliable service than they are about deficiencies in the tangibles.[6] This could mean that in the example of a railway journey, a passenger will be less tolerant of a train running late than of a train being dirty.

The fluctuation in the individual customer's zone of tolerance is more a function of changes in the adequate service level, which moves readily up and down because of situational circumstances, than in the desired service level, which tends to move upward incrementally because of accumulated experiences. Desired service is relatively idiosyncratic and stable compared with adequate service, which moves up and down and in response to competition and other factors. Fluctuation in the zone of tolerance can be likened to an accordion's movement, but with most of the movement coming from one side (the adequate service level) rather than the other (the desired service level).

In summary, we can express the boundaries of customer expectations of service with two different levels of expectations: desired service and adequate service. The desired service level is less subject to change than the adequate service level. A zone of tolerance separates these two levels. This zone of tolerance varies across customers and expands or contracts with the same customer.

Figure 4.4   Zones of tolerance for different service dimensions

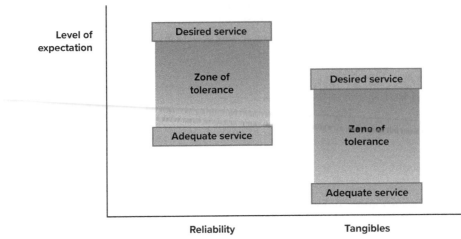

Source: Adapted from L.L. Berry, A. Parasuraman and V.A. Zeithaml, 'Ten lessons for improving service quality', Marketing Science Institute, Report No. 93–104 (May 1993).

Factors that Influence Customer Expectations of Service

Because expectations play such a critical role in customer evaluation of services, marketers need and want to understand the factors that shape them. Marketers would also like to have control over these factors as well, but many of the forces that influence customer expectations are uncontrollable. In this section, we try to separate the many influences on customer expectations.

Sources of Desired Service Expectations

As shown in Figure 4.5, the two largest influences on desired service level are personal needs and philosophies about service. **Personal needs**, those states or conditions essential to the physical or psychological well-being of the customer, are pivotal factors that shape what customers desire in service. Personal needs can fall into many categories, including physical, social, psychological and functional. A cinema-goer who regularly goes to see films straight from work, and is therefore thirsty and hungry, hopes and desires that the food and drink counters at the cinema will have short queues and attentive staff, whereas a cinema-goer who regularly has dinner elsewhere has a low or zero level of desired service from the food and drink counters. A customer with high social and dependency needs may have relatively high expectations for a hotel's ancillary services, hoping, for example, that the hotel has a bar with live music and dancing.

Some customers are more demanding than others, having greater sensitivity to, and higher expectations of, service. **Lasting service intensifiers** are individual, stable factors that lead the customer to a heightened

Figure 4.5   Factors that influence desired service

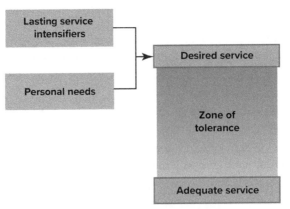

sensitivity to service. One of the most important of these factors can be called *derived service expectations*, which occur when customer expectations are driven by another person or group of people. For example, a niece from a big family who is planning a ninetieth birthday party for a favourite aunt is representing the entire family in selecting a restaurant for a successful celebration. Her needs are driven in part by the derived expectations from the other family members. A parent choosing a holiday for the family, a spouse selecting a home-cleaning service, an employee choosing an office for the firm – all these customers' individual expectations are intensified because they represent and must answer to other parties who will receive the service. In the context of business-to-business service, customer expectations are driven by the expectations of their own customers. The head of an information technology department in an insurance company, who is the business customer of a large computer company, has expectations based on those of the insurance customers he or she serves: when the computer equipment is down, his or her customers complain. The need to keep the system up and running is not just his or her own expectation but is derived from the pressure of customers.

Business-to-business customers may also derive their expectations from their managers and supervisors. Employees of a marketing research department may speed up project cycles (increase their expectations for speed of delivery) when pressured by their management to deliver the study results. Corporate buyers may increase demands for faster delivery at lower costs when company management is emphasizing cost reduction in the company.

Another lasting service intensifier is *personal service philosophy* – the customer's underlying generic attitude about the meaning of service and the proper conduct of service providers. If you have ever been employed as a member of waiting staff in a restaurant, you are likely to have standards for restaurant service that were shaped by your training and experience in that role. You might, for example, believe that waiters should not keep customers waiting longer than 15 minutes to take their orders. Knowing the way a kitchen operates, you may be less tolerant of lukewarm food or errors in the order than customers who have not held the role of waiter or waitress. In general, customers who are themselves in service businesses or have worked for them in the past seem to have especially strong service philosophies.

To the extent that customers have personal philosophies about service provision, their expectations of service providers will be intensified. Personal service philosophies and derived service expectations elevate the level of desired service.

Sources of Adequate Service Expectations

A different set of determinants affects adequate service, the level of service the customer finds acceptable. In general, these influences are short term and tend to fluctuate more than the factors that influence desired service. In this section we explain the five factors shown in Figure 4.6 that influence adequate service: (1) temporary service intensifiers, (2) perceived service alternatives, (3) customer self-perceived service role, (4) situational factors, and (5) predicted service.

The first set of elements, *temporary service intensifiers*, consists of short-term, individual factors that make a customer more aware of the need for service. Personal emergency situations in which service is urgently needed (such as an accident and the need for car insurance or a breakdown in office equipment during a busy period) raise the level of adequate service expectation, particularly the level of responsiveness required and considered acceptable. A mail-order company that depends on freephone numbers for receiving all customer orders will tend to be more demanding of the telephone service during peak periods of the week, month and year. Any system breakdown or lack of clarity on the lines will be tolerated less during these intense periods than at other times.

Problems with the initial service can also lead to heightened expectations. Performing a service right the first time is very important because customers value service reliability above all other dimensions. If the service fails in the recovery phase, putting it right the second time (that is, being reliable in service recovery) is even more critical than it was the first time. Car repair service provides a case in point. If a problem with your car's brakes sends you to a car repairer, you expect the company to fix the brakes. But if you experience further problems with the brakes after the repair (a not uncommon situation with car repairs), your

Figure 4.6 Factors that influence adequate service

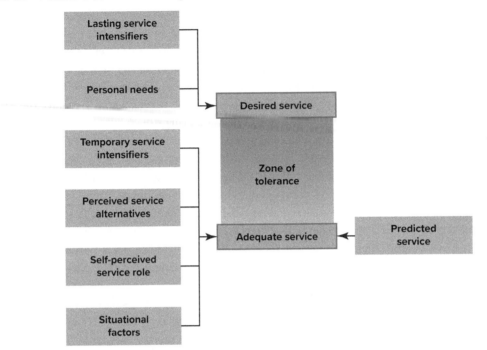

adequate service level will increase. In these and other situations where temporary service intensifiers are present, the level of adequate service will increase and the zone of tolerance will narrow.

Perceived service alternatives are other providers from whom the customer can obtain service. If customers have multiple service providers to choose from, or if they can provide the service for themselves (such as lawn care or personal grooming), their levels of adequate service are higher than those of customers who believe it is not possible to get better service elsewhere. An airline customer who lives in a provincial town with a small airport, for example, has a reduced set of options in airline travel. This customer will be more tolerant of the service performance of the carriers in the town because few alternatives exist. He or she will accept the scheduling and lower levels of service more readily than will the customer in a big city who has a multitude of flights and airlines to choose from. The customer's perception that service alternatives exist raises the level of adequate service and narrows the zone of tolerance.

It is important that service marketers fully understand the complete set of options that customers view as perceived alternatives. In the provincial town, small airport example just discussed, the set of alternatives from the customer's point of view is likely to include more than just other airlines: taxi service to a nearby large city, rail service or driving. In general, service marketers must discover the alternatives that the customer views as comparable rather than those in the company's competitive set.

A third factor affecting the level of adequate service is the *customer's self-perceived service role*. We define this as customer perceptions of the degree to which customers exert an influence on the level of service they receive. In other words, customers' expectations are partly shaped by how well they believe they are performing their own roles in service delivery.[7] One role of the customer is to specify the level of service expected. A customer who is very explicit with a waiter about how rare he or she wants his or her steak cooked in a restaurant will probably be more dissatisfied if the meat comes to the table overcooked than a customer who does not articulate the degree of cooking expected. The customer's active participation in the service also affects this factor. A customer who does not get his or her car serviced regularly is likely to be more lenient on the car manufacturer when he or she experiences problems than one who conscientiously follows the manufacturer's service schedule.

A final way the customer defines his or her role is in assuming the responsibility for complaining when service is poor. A dissatisfied customer who complains will be less tolerant than one who does not voice his or her concerns. A car insurance customer acknowledged responsibility in service provision this way: 'You can't blame it all on the insurance broker. You need to be responsible too and let the broker know what exactly you want.'

Customers' zones of tolerance seem to expand when they sense they are not fulfilling their roles. When, on the other hand, customers believe they are doing their part in delivery, their expectations of adequate service are heightened and the zone of tolerance contracts. The comment of a car repair customer illustrates this: 'Service staff don't listen when you tell them what is wrong. I now prepare a written list of problems in advance, take it to the car dealership, and tell them to fix these.' This customer will expect more than one who did not prepare so well.

Levels of adequate service are also influenced by *situational factors*, defined as service performance conditions that customers view as beyond the control of the service provider. For example, where personal emergencies such as serious car accidents would be likely to intensify customer service expectations of insurance companies (because they are temporary service intensifiers), catastrophes that affect a large number of people at one time (floods or storms) may lower service expectations because customers recognize that insurers are inundated with demands for their services. Customers who recognize that situational factors are not the fault of the service company may accept lower levels of adequate service, given the context. In general, situational factors temporarily lower the level of adequate service, widening the zone of tolerance.

The final factor that influences adequate service is *predicted service*, the level of service that customers believe they are likely to get (Figure 4.7). This type of service expectation can be viewed as predictions made by customers about what is likely to happen during an impending transaction or exchange. Predicted service performance implies some objective calculation of the probability of performance or estimate of anticipated service performance level. If customers predict good service, their levels of adequate service are likely to be higher than if they predict poor service. For example, travellers may expect poorer service from some of the no-frills airlines, such as Ryanair or easyJet, in comparison to some of the full-cost airlines, such as British Airways, KLM or Air France. This prediction will mean that higher standards for adequate service will exist in the full-cost airlines. On the other hand, customers of mobile phone companies may know that the companies' call centre operations will provide poor service around Christmas time when many people are setting up the mobiles that they have received as gifts. In this case, levels of adequate service decrease and zones of tolerance widen.

Figure 4.7   Factors that influence desired and predicted service

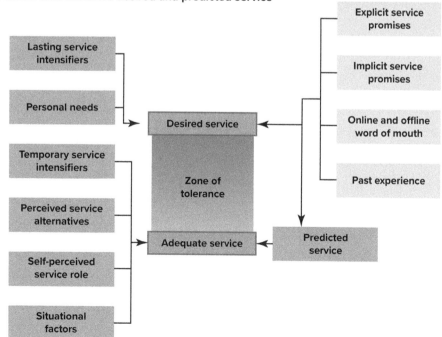

Predicted service is typically an estimate or calculation of the service that a customer will receive in an individual transaction rather than in the overall relationship with a service provider. Whereas desired and adequate service expectations are global assessments, comprising many individual service transactions, predicted service is almost always an estimate of what will happen in the next service encounter or transaction that the customer experiences. For this reason, predicted service is viewed in this model as an influencer of adequate service.

Because predictions are about individual service encounters, they are likely to be more concrete and specific than the types of expectation levels customers hold for adequate service or desired service. For example, your predicted service expectations about the length of time you will spend in the waiting room the next time you visit your doctor are most likely to be expressed in terms of the number of minutes or hours you have spent in the waiting room on your last visit.

Service Encounter Expectations Versus Overall Service Expectations

In Chapter 5 we discuss the difference between overall service quality and service encounter quality, viewing the service encounter as a discrete event occurring over a definable period of time (such as a particular hotel stay or a particular check-in experience at the hotel). Customers hold expectations of the quality of each service encounter, just as they hold expectations about the overall service quality of a firm. When the expectations are about individual service encounters, they are likely to be more specific and concrete (such as the number of minutes one must wait for a receptionist) than the expectations about overall service quality (like speedy service).

Sources of Both Desired and Predicted Service Expectations

When consumers are interested in purchasing services, they are likely to seek or take in information from several different sources. For example, they may call a store, ask a friend or track prices online to find the needed service at the lowest price. They may also receive service information by watching television or hearing an unsolicited comment from a colleague about a service that was performed well. In addition to these active and passive types of external search for information, consumers may conduct an internal search by reviewing the information held in their memory about the service. This section discusses one internal and three external factors that influence both desired service and predicted service expectations: (1) **explicit service promises**, (2) **implicit service promises**, (3) **online and offline word-of-mouth communications** and (4) **past experience**.

Explicit service promises are personal and non-personal statements about the service made by the organization to customers. The statements are personal when they are communicated by salespeople or service or repair personnel; they are non-personal when they come from advertising, brochures and other written publications. Explicit service promises are one of the few influences on expectations that are completely in the control of the service provider.

Promising exactly what will ultimately be delivered would seem a logical and appropriate way to manage customer expectations and ensure that reality fits the promises. However, companies and the personnel who represent them often deliberately over-promise to obtain business or inadvertently over-promise by stating their best estimates about delivery of a service in the future. In addition to over-promising, company representatives simply do not always know the appropriate promises to make because services are often customized and therefore not easily defined and repeated; the representative may not know when or in what final form the service will be delivered.

All types of explicit service promises have a direct effect on desired service expectation. If the sales visit portrays a banking service that is available 24 hours a day, the customer's desires for that service (as well as the service of competitors) will be shaped by this promise.

Explicit service promises influence the levels of both desired service and predicted service. They shape what customers desire in general as well as what they predict will happen in the next service encounter from a particular service provider or in a certain service encounter.

> ### ⭐ SERVICE SPOTLIGHT
>
> The 15-Minute Satisfaction Guarantee offered by Ibis hotels is an example of explicit service promise. This guarantee is a contractual agreement between Ibis and every hotel guest. Ibis invites every guest to immediately report any issue that may arise. If the hotel is responsible and the issue takes more than 15 minutes to resolve, the affected service will be free of charge.
>
> *Source:* **www.ibis.com.**

Implicit service promises are service-related cues other than explicit promises that lead to inferences about what the service should and will be like. These quality cues are dominated by price and the tangibles associated with the service. In general, the higher the price and the more impressive the tangibles, the more a customer will expect from the service. Consider a customer who shops for insurance, finding two firms charging radically different prices. He or she may infer that the firm with the higher price should and will provide higher-quality service and better coverage. Similarly, a customer who stays at a five-star hotel is likely to desire and predict a higher standard of service than from a hotel with less impressive facilities.

The importance of online and offline word-of-mouth communication in shaping expectations of service is well documented.[8] These personal and sometimes non-personal statements made by parties other than the organization convey to customers what the service will be like and influence both predicted and desired service. Word-of-mouth communication carries particular weight as an information source, because it is perceived as unbiased. Word of mouth tends to be very important in services that are difficult to evaluate before purchase and before direct experience of them. Online reviews, such as those on TripAdvisor, friends and family, and individuals on social media platforms as well as industry experts are all word-of-mouth sources that can affect the levels of desired and predicted service. Positive comments on social media or posted on a review site about a restaurant may result in customers having overinflated expectations of the service offering they will receive. This could ultimately lead to disappointment when they visit the restaurant. However, if the comments are neutral or negative, the same restaurant experience may result in the customers being reasonably satisfied, as they would not have high expectations for the service.

Past experience, the customer's previous exposure to service that is relevant to the focal service is another force in shaping predictions and desires. The service relevant for prediction can be previous exposure to the focal firm's service. For example, you probably compare each stay in a particular hotel with all previous stays in that hotel. But past experience with the focal hotel is likely to be a very limited view of your past experience. You may also compare each stay with your experiences in other hotels and hotel chains. Customers also compare across industries: hospital patients, for example, compare hospital stays against the standard of hotel visits. In a general sense, past experience may incorporate previous experience with the focal brand, typical performance of a favourite brand, experience with the brand last purchased or the top-selling brand, and the average performance a customer believes represents a group of similar brands.[9]

The Management of Customer Expectations

How might a manager of a service organization use the information we have developed in this chapter to create, improve, or market services? First, managers need to know the pertinent expectation sources and their relative importance for a customer population, a customer segment and, perhaps, even a particular customer. They need to know, for instance, the relative weight of word of mouth, explicit service promises and implicit service promises in shaping desired service and predicted service. Some of these sources are more stable and permanent in their influence (such as lasting service intensifiers and personal needs) than the others, which fluctuate considerably over time (like perceived service alternatives and situational factors).

The different sources vary in terms of their credibility as well as their potential to be influenced by the marketer. Table 4.1 shows the breakdown of various factors and how services marketers can influence them. Chapter 16 details these and other strategies that services marketers can use to match delivery to promises and thereby manage expectations.

Table 4.1   How services marketers can influence factors

Factor	Possible Influence Strategies
Explicit service promises	Make realistic and accurate promises that reflect the service actually delivered rather than an idealized version of the service.
	Ask contact people for feedback on the accuracy of promises made in advertising and personal selling.
	Avoid engaging in price or advertising wars with competitors because they take the focus off customers and escalate promises beyond the level at which they can be met.
	Formalize service promises through a service guarantee that focuses company employees on the promise and that provides feedback on the number of times promises are not fulfilled.
Implicit service promises	Ensure that service tangibles accurately reflect the type and level of service provided. Ensure that price premiums can be justified by higher levels of performance by the company on important customer attributes.
Lasting service intensifiers	Use market research to determine sources of derived service expectations and their requirements. Focus advertising and marketing strategy on ways the service allows the focal customer to satisfy the requirements of the influencing customer.
	Use market research to profile personal service philosophies of customers and use this information in designing and delivering services.
Personal needs	Educate customers on ways the service addresses their needs.
Temporary service intensifiers	Increase service delivery during peak periods or in emergencies.
Perceived service alternatives	Be fully aware of competitive offerings and, where possible and appropriate, match them.
Self-perceived service role	Educate customers to understand their roles and perform them better.
Word-of-mouth communications	Simulate word of mouth in advertising by using testimonials and opinion leaders. Identify influencers and opinion leaders for the service and concentrate marketing efforts on them.
	Use incentives with existing customers to encourage them to say positive things about the service.
Past experience	Use marketing research to profile customers' previous experience with similar services.
Situational factors	Use service guarantees to assure customers about service recovery regardless of the situational factors that occur.
Predicted service	Tell customers when service provision is higher than what can normally be expected so that predictions of future service encounters will not be inflated.

Issues Involving the Management of Customer Service Expectations

The following issues represent current topics of particular interest to service marketers about customer expectations. In this section we discuss five of the most frequently asked questions about customer expectations:

1   What does a service marketer do if customer expectations are 'unrealistic'?
2   Should a company try to delight the customer?

3 How does a company exceed customer service expectations?

4 Do customer service expectations continually escalate?

5 How does a service company stay ahead of competition in meeting customer expectations?

What does a Services Marketer do if Customer Expectations are 'Unrealistic'?

One inhibitor to learning about customer expectations is management's and employees' fear of asking. This apprehension often stems from the belief that customer expectations will be extravagant and unrealistic and that, by asking about them, a company will set itself up for even loftier expectation levels (that is, 'unrealistic' levels). Compelling evidence, shown in Table 4.2, suggests that customers' main expectations of

Table 4.2 Service customers want the basics

Type of Service	Type of Customer	Principal Expectations
Car repair	Consumers	Be competent. ('Fix it right the first time.') Explain things. ('Explain why I need the suggested repairs – provide an itemized list.') Be respectful. ('Don't treat me like I am stupid.')
Car insurance	Consumers	Keep me informed. ('I shouldn't have to learn about insurance law changes from the newspaper.') Be on my side. ('I don't want them to treat me like a criminal just because I have a claim.') Play fair. ('Don't drop me when something goes wrong.') Protect me from catastrophe. ('Make sure my family is provided for in the event of a major accident.') Provide prompt service. ('I want fast settlement of claims.')
Hotel	Consumers	Provide a clean room. ('Don't have a deep-pile carpet that can't be completely cleaned ... you can literally see germs down there.') Provide a secure room. ('Good bolts and peephole on door.') Treat me like a guest. ('It is almost like they're looking you over to decide whether they're going to let you have a room.') Keep your promise. ('They said the room would be ready, but it wasn't at the promised time.')
Property and accident insurance	Business customers	Fulfil obligations. ('Pay up.') Learn my business and work with me. ('I expect them to know me and my company.') Protect me from catastrophe. ('They should cover my risk exposure so there is no single big loss.') Provide prompt service. ('Fast claim service.')
Equipment repair	Business customers	Share my sense of urgency. ('Speed of response. One time I had to buy a second piece of equipment because of the huge downtime with the first piece.') Be competent. ('Sometimes they are quoting stuff from their instruction manuals to their own people and they don't even know what it means.') Be prepared. ('Have all the parts ready.')
Vehicle rental/leasing	Business customers	Keep the equipment running. ('Need to have equipment working all of the time – that is the key.') Be flexible. ('The leasing company should have the flexibility to rent us equipment when we need it.') Provide full service. ('Get rid of all the paperwork and headaches.')

Source: Adapted from 'Understanding customer expectations of service' by A. Parasuraman, L.L. Berry and V.A. Zeithaml, *MIT Sloan Management Review* (Spring 1991), pp. 33–46, Copyright © 1991 by Massachusetts Institute of Technology. All rights reserved.

service are quite simple and basic: 'Simply put, customers expect service companies to do what they are supposed to do. They expect fundamentals, not fanciness; performance, not empty promises.'[10] Customers want service to be delivered as promised. They want planes to take off on time, hotel rooms to be clean, food to be hot and service providers to show up when scheduled. Unfortunately, many service customers are disappointed and let down by companies' inability to meet these basic service expectations.

Asking customers about their expectations does not so much raise the levels of the expectations themselves but rather heightens the belief that the company will do something with the information that surfaces. Arguably the worst thing a company can do is show a strong interest in understanding what customers expect and then never act on the information. At a minimum, a company should acknowledge to customers that it has received and heard their input and that it will expend effort trying to address their issues. The company may not be able to – and indeed does not always have to – deliver to expressed expectations. An alternative and appropriate response would be to let customers know the reasons that desired service is not being provided at the present time and describe the efforts planned to address them. Another approach could be a campaign to educate customers about ways to use and improve the service they currently receive.

Giving customers progress updates as service is improved to address their needs and desires is sensible, because it allows the company to get credit for incremental efforts to improve service.

Some observers recommend deliberately under-promising the service to increase the likelihood of meeting or **exceeding customer expectations**.[11] While under-promising makes service expectations more realistic, thereby narrowing the gap between expectations and perceptions, it may also reduce the competitive appeal of the offer. Some research has indicated that under-promising may also have the inadvertent effect of lowering customer *perceptions* of service, particularly in situations in which customers have little experience with a service.[12] In these situations customer expectations may be self-fulfilling; that is, if the customer goes into the service experience expecting good service, he or she will focus on the aspects of service provision that are positive, but if he or she expects low service, then that customer may focus on the negative. Thus a salesperson who sells to a customer with a realistic promise may lose the sale to another who inflates the offering. In Chapter 16 we describe various techniques for controlling a firm's promises, but for now consider two options.

First, if the salesperson knows that no competitor can meet an inflated sales promise in an industry, he or she could point that fact out to the customer, thereby refuting the promise made by competitive salespeople.

The second option is for the provider to follow a sale with a 'reality check' about service delivery. Imagine buying a new house from a builder. In order to make the sale, typical sales promises are made about the quality of the home, some less than accurate. Before you are given the keys to the new house, the builder accompanies you on a final check of everything. At the front door the builder points out that each new home has between 3,000 and 5,000 individual elements and that, in his experience, the typical new home has 100 to 150 defects. Armed with this reality check, you would perceive a total of 30–40 defects found in your house as being good. Consider your response in the absence of that reality check.

Should a Company try to Delight the Customer?

Some management consultants urge service companies to 'delight' customers to gain a competitive edge. The *delight* that they refer to is a profoundly positive emotional state that results from having one's expectations exceeded to a surprising degree.[13] One author describes the type of service that results in delight as 'positively outrageous service' – that which is unexpected, random, extraordinary and disproportionately positive.[14]

A way that managers can conceive of delight is to consider product and service features in terms of concentric rings.[15] The innermost bull's-eye refers to attributes that are central to the basic function of the product or service, called *musts*. Their provision is not particularly noticeable, but their absence would be. Around the musts is a ring called *satisfiers*: features that have the potential to further satisfaction beyond the basic function of the product. At the next and final outer level are *delights,* or product features that are unexpected and surprisingly enjoyable. These features are things that consumers would not expect to find and they are therefore highly surprised and sometimes excited when they receive them. For example, a student may consider the musts to consist of lecturers, rooms, class outlines and lectures/seminars. Satisfiers might include lecturers who are entertaining or friendly, interesting lectures and good audiovisual aids. A delight might include a free textbook for students signing up for the course.

Delighting customers may seem like a good idea, but this level of service provision comes with extra effort and cost to the firm. Therefore, the benefits of providing delight must be weighed. Among the considerations are the staying power and competitive implications of delight.

Staying power involves the question of how long a company can expect an experience of delight to maintain the consumer's attention. If it is fleeting and the customer forgets it immediately, it may not be worth the cost. Alternatively, if the customer remembers the delight and adjusts his or her level of expectation upward accordingly, it will cost the company more just to satisfy, effectively raising the bar for the future. Recent research indicates that delighting customers does in fact raise expectations and makes it more difficult for a company to satisfy customers in the future.[16]

The competitive implication of delight relates to its impact on expectations of other firms in the same industry. If a competitor in the same industry is unable to copy the delight strategy, it will be disadvantaged by the consumer's increased expectations. If students were offered that free textbook in one of their classes, they might then expect to receive one in each of their classes. Those classes not offering the free textbook might not have high enrolment levels compared with the delighting class. If a competitor can easily copy the delight strategy, however, neither firm benefits (although the consumer does!), and all firms may be hurt because their costs increase and profits erode. The implication is that if companies choose to delight, they should do so in areas that cannot be copied by other firms.

How does a Company Exceed Customer Service Expectations?

Many companies today talk about exceeding customer expectations – delighting and surprising them by giving more than they expect. This philosophy raises the question: should a service provider try simply to meet customer expectations or to exceed them?

First, it is essential to recognize that exceeding customer expectations of the basics is virtually impossible. Honouring promises – having the reserved room available, meeting deadlines, showing up for meetings, delivering the core service – is what the company is supposed to do. Companies are *supposed* to be accurate and dependable and provide the service they promised to provide.[17] As you examine the examples of basic expectations of customers in Table 4.2, ask yourself if a provider doing any of these things would delight you. The conclusion you should reach is that it is very difficult to surprise or delight customers consistently by delivering reliable service.

How, then, does a company delight its customers and exceed their expectations? In virtually any service, developing a customer relationship is one approach for exceeding service expectations. Ritz-Carlton Hotels provide highly personalized attention to their customers. In each hotel within the chain, a special database called guest recognition is used to remember over 800,000 guests and generate information for all relevant staff. It stores: likes/dislikes; previous difficulties; family interests; personal interests; preferred credit card; recency/frequency of stays; lifetime usage/amount of purchase. In this way staff are able to understand what is 'new or different' about an individual customer.[18]

Another way to exceed expectations is to deliberately under-promise the service to increase the likelihood of exceeding customer expectations. The strategy is to under-promise and over-deliver. If every service promise is less than what will eventually happen, customers can be delighted frequently. Although this reasoning sounds logical, a firm should weigh two potential problems before using this strategy.

Firstly, customers with whom a company interacts regularly are likely to notice the under-promising and adjust their expectations accordingly, negating the desired benefit of delight. Customers will recognize the pattern of under-promising when time after time a firm promises one delivery time (we cannot get that to you before 5 p.m. tomorrow) yet constantly exceeds it (by delivering at noon).

⭐ **SERVICE SPOTLIGHT**

Many airlines have adopted under-performing strategies with regard to flight duration. easyJet produces a timetable that suggests that flights will be longer than they actually are, allowing them to give the impression that their timekeeping is good as most flights will arrive early or on time. However, with experience, regular customers may come to expect an early arrival and be disappointed when this does not happen.

Secondly, under-promising in a sales situation potentially reduces the competitive appeal of an offering and must be tempered by what the competition is offering. When competitive pressures are high, presenting a cohesive and honest portrayal of the service both explicitly (through advertising and personal selling) and implicitly (such as through the appearance of service facilities and the price of the service) may be wiser. Controlling the firm's promises, making them consistent with the deliverable service, may be a better approach.

A final way to exceed expectations without raising them in the future is to position unusual service as unique rather than standard: emphasizing that because of special circumstances or a special situation, the service will deviate from the norm. For example, a restaurant may offer customers a free dessert by claiming that the chef is trying out some new recipes/creations.

Do Customer Service Expectations Continually Escalate?

As we illustrated at the beginning of this chapter, customer service expectations are dynamic. In the credit card industry, as in many competitive service industries, battling companies seek to outdo each other and thereby raise their level of service above that of competing companies. Service expectations – in this case adequate service expectations – rise in step with service delivery or promises. In a highly competitive and rapidly changing industry, expectations can thus rise quickly. For this reason, companies need continually to monitor adequate service expectations – the more turbulent the industry, the more frequent the monitoring that is needed.

Desired service expectations, on the other hand, are far more stable. Because they are driven by more enduring factors, such as personal needs and lasting service intensifiers, they tend to be high to begin with and remain high.

How does a Service Company Stay Ahead of Competition in Meeting Customer Expectations?

All else being equal, a company's goal is to meet customer expectations better than its competitors can. Given the fact that adequate service expectations change rapidly in a turbulent environment, how can a company ensure that it stays ahead of competition?

The adequate service level reflects the minimum performance level expected by customers after they consider a variety of personal and external factors (Figure 4.6), including the availability of service options from other providers. Companies whose service performance falls short of this level are clearly at a competitive disadvantage, with the disadvantage escalating as the gap widens. These companies' customers may well be 'reluctant' customers, ready to take their business elsewhere the moment they perceive an alternative.

If they are to use service quality for competitive advantage, companies must perform above the adequate service level. This level, however, may signal only a temporary advantage. Customers' adequate service levels, which are less stable than desired service levels, will rise rapidly when competitors promise and deliver a higher level of service. If a company's level of service is barely above the adequate service level to begin with, a competitor can quickly erode that advantage. Companies currently performing in the region of competitive advantage must stay alert to the need for service increases to meet or beat competition.

To develop a true customer franchise with customer loyalty, companies must not only consistently exceed the adequate service level but also reach the desired service level. Exceptional service can intensify customers' loyalty to a point at which they are impervious to competitive options.

Summary

Using a conceptual framework of the nature and determinants of customer expectations of service, we showed in this chapter that customers hold different types of service expectations: (1) desired service, which reflects what customers want; (2) adequate service, or what customers are willing to accept; and (3) predicted service, or what customers believe they are likely to get. These different levels of service are reflected within the customer's zone of tolerance which establishes the variability in the service delivery that the customer is willing to accept.

Customer expectations and tolerance levels are influenced by a variety of factors. The types and sources of these are the same for end consumers and business customers, for pure service and product-related service, and for experienced customers and inexperienced customers.

Key Concepts

Customer expectations	63	Perceived service alternatives	69, 70
Customer self-perceived service role	69, 70	Personal needs	68
Exceeding customer expectations	76	Predicted service	69, 71
Explicit and implicit service promises	72, 73	Self-perceived service role	69
Lasting service intensifiers	68	Situational factors	69, 71
Online and offline word-of-mouth		Temporary service intensifiers	69
communications	72, 73	Zone of tolerance	66
Past experience	72, 73		

Exercises

1 Keep a service journal for a day and document your use of services. Record your predicted service before every service encounter. Then, following the encounter, note whether your expectations were met or exceeded. How does your journal log relate to your desire to do business with that service firm again?

2 List five incidents in which a service company has exceeded your expectations. How did you react to the service? Did these incidents change the way you viewed subsequent interactions with the companies? In what way?

3 Map out your expectations for a course delivered by a University or College. Consider whether these expectations are being met.

4 Compare your expectations for a service with friends and with people from different ages and backgrounds. How do they differ?

Discussion Questions

1 What is the difference between desired service and adequate service? Why would a services marketer need to understand both types of service expectations?

2 Consider a recent service purchase that you have made. Which of the factors influencing expectations were the most important in your decision? Why?

3 Why are desired service expectations more stable than adequate service expectations?

4 How do the technology changes such as the Internet and social media influence customer expectations?

5 Describe several instances in which a service company's explicit service promises were inflated and led you to be disappointed with the service outcome.

6 Do you believe that any of your service expectations are unrealistic? Which ones? Should a service marketer try to address unrealistic customer expectations?

7 Intuitively, it would seem that managers would want their customers to have wide tolerance zones for service. But if customers do have these wide zones of tolerance for service, is it more difficult for firms with superior service to earn customer loyalty? Would superior service firms be better off attempting to narrow customers' tolerance zones to reduce the competitive appeal of mediocre providers?

8 Should service marketers delight their customers?

Further Reading

Bebko, C.P. (2000). Service intangibility and its impact on customer expectations of service quality. *Journal of Services Marketing*, 14(1), 9–26.

Habel, J., Alavi, S., Schmitz, C., Schneider, J.V. and Wieseke, J. (2016). When do customers get what they expect? Understanding the ambivalent effects of customers' service expectations on satisfaction. *Journal of Service Research*, 19(4), 361–379.

Licata, J.W., Chakraborty, G. and Krishnan, B.C. (2008). The consumer's expectation formation process over time. *Journal of Services Marketing*, 22(3), 176–87.

Nath, P., Devlin, J. and Reid, V. (2018). The effects of online reviews on service expectations: Do cultural value orientations matter? *Journal of Business Research*, 90, 123–133.

Schneider, B. and Bowen, D.E. (2010). *Winning the Service Game*. Springer US.

Sparks, B.A. and Browning, V. (2011). The impact of online reviews on hotel booking intentions and perception of trust. *Tourism Management*, 32(6), 1310–23.

Wilson, A., Murphy, H. and Fierro, J.C. (2012). Hospitality and travel: The nature and implications of user-generated content. *Cornell Hospitality Quarterly*, 53(3), 220–28.

Yap, K.B. and Sweeney, J.C. (2007). Zone of tolerance moderates the service quality-outcome relationship. *Journal of Services Marketing*, 21(2), 137–48.

Chapter 5

Customer Perceptions of Service

Chapter Outline

Customer Perceptions   82
Customer Satisfaction   84
Ensuring High Customer Satisfaction   88
Service Quality   89
Service Encounters: The Building Blocks for Customer Perceptions   94
The Evidence of Service   99
Summary   100
Key Concepts   100
Exercises   101
Discussion Questions   101
Further Reading   102

Learning Objectives

This chapter's objectives are to:

1 Provide a solid basis for understanding what influences customer perceptions of service and the relationships among customer satisfaction, service quality and individual service encounters.
2 Demonstrate the importance of customer satisfaction – what it is, the factors that influence it and the significant outcomes resulting from it.
3 Develop critical knowledge of service quality and its five key dimensions: reliability, responsiveness, empathy, assurance and tangibles.
4 Show that service encounters or the 'moments of truth' are the essential building blocks from which customers form their perceptions.

Opening Example
Changing Perceptions – Virgin Money

Virgin Money is attempting to change customers' perceptions of the service delivered by bank branches through the opening of five Virgin Money Lounges in major cities. These lounges do have areas where customers can do their online banking or receive service relating to their Virgin Money products, but they are about more than money and banking. They are designed to be places where customers can relax and local communities come together. They provide free hot and cold drinks, fruit and snacks as well as free Wi-Fi and access to free iPads. Television is available all day as well as newspapers and

Source: ©Chris Ratcliffe via Bloomberg/Getty Images

a selection of magazines. Children are welcomed; there is a dedicated children's area in every Lounge, complete with toys, books and games consoles. There are also customer toilets and baby changing facilities. The Glasgow lounge even has a fish tank, a dance floor and a cinema room.

Customers can come in to relax with friends or family-members, use the lounge facility to brush up on a few points before a meeting, or simply unwind with a newspaper. The lounges are furnished with a mix of sofas and writing desks.

Often social and entertainment events are put on in the evenings for customers. In addition, local communities are able to benefit from the proximity of a Lounge by booking it for free to hold a community event or meeting. In 2019, the lounges were used for after-hours community events like exhibitions, talks and book signings.

Brian Brodie, Virgin Money's sales and marketing director said: 'We know our customers expect something different and this is a real key manifestation of that.'

Source: Cameron, G. (2014). Virgin Money unveils latest bank lounge. [online] HeraldScotland.com. Available at: https:// www.heraldscotland.com/business_hq/13171165.virgin-money-unveils-latest-bank-lounge/ [Accessed 22 Oct. 2019].

Customer Perceptions

How customers perceive services, how they assess whether they have experienced quality service, and whether they are satisfied with their overall experience are the subjects of this chapter. Companies today recognize that they can compete more effectively by distinguishing themselves with respect to service quality and improved customer satisfaction.

Satisfaction Versus Service Quality

Practitioners and writers in the popular press tend to use the terms *satisfaction* and *quality* interchangeably, but researchers have attempted to be more precise about the meanings and measurement of the two concepts, resulting in considerable debate.[1] Consensus is that the two concepts are fundamentally different in terms of their underlying causes and outcomes.[2] Although they have certain things in common, satisfaction is generally viewed as a broader concept, whereas service quality focuses specifically on dimensions of service. Based on this view, *perceived service quality* is a component of customer satisfaction. Figure 5.1 graphically illustrates the relationships between the two concepts.

Figure 5.1   The quality–satisfaction link

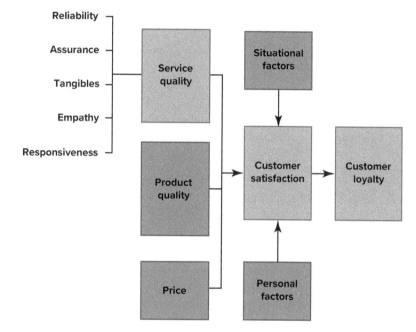

Service quality is a focused evaluation that reflects the customer's perception of reliability, assurance, tangibles, empathy, responsiveness (the acronym, RATER is a good way to remember these).[3] Satisfaction, on the other hand, is more inclusive: it is influenced by perceptions of service quality, product quality and price as well as situational factors and personal factors. For example, the *service quality* of a health club is judged on attributes such as whether equipment is available and in working order when needed, how responsive the staff are to customer needs, how skilled the trainers are and whether the facility is well maintained. *Customer satisfaction* with the health club is a broader concept that will certainly be influenced by perceptions of service quality but will also include perceptions of product quality (such as quality of products sold in the bar/restaurant), price of membership,[4] personal factors (such as the consumer's emotional state), and even uncontrollable situational factors (such as weather conditions and experiences driving to and from the health club).[5]

Transaction Versus Cumulative Perceptions

In considering perceptions, it is also important to recognize that customers will have perceptions of single, transaction-specific encounters as well as overall perceptions of a company based on all their experiences.[6] For example, a bank customer will have a perception of how he or she was treated in a particular encounter with a bank employee at a branch and will form a perception based on elements of the service experienced during that specific transaction. That perception is at a very micro, transaction-specific level. The same bank customer will also have overall perceptions of the bank based on his or her encounters over a period of time. These experiences might include multiple in-person encounters at the bank branch, online banking experiences and experiences using the bank's ATMs across many different cities. At an even more general level, the customer may have perceptions of banking services or the whole banking industry as a result of all his or her experiences with banks and everything he or she knows about banking.

Research suggests that it is important to understand all these types of perceptions for different reasons and that they reveal complementary rather than competing points of view.[7] Understanding perceptions at the transaction-specific level is critical for diagnosing service issues and making immediate changes. These isolated encounters are also the building blocks for overall, cumulative experience evaluations, as you will learn later in this chapter. On the other hand, cumulative experience evaluations are likely to be better predictors of overall loyalty to a company. That is, customer loyalty most often results from the customer's assessment of all his or her experiences, not just from one single encounter.

Customer Satisfaction

'Everyone knows what satisfaction is, until asked to give a definition. Then, it seems, nobody knows.'[8] This quote from Richard L. Oliver, respected expert and long-time writer and researcher on the topic of customer satisfaction, expresses the challenge of defining this most basic of customer concepts.

What is Customer Satisfaction?

Building from previous definitions, Oliver offers his own formal definition (p. 13): 'Satisfaction is the consumer's fulfillment response. It is a judgment that a product or service feature, or the product or service itself, provides a pleasurable level of consumption-related fulfillment.' In less technical terms, we interpret this definition to mean that *satisfaction* is the customer's evaluation of a product or service in terms of whether that product or service has met the customer's needs and expectations. Failure to meet needs and expectations is assumed to result in *dissatisfaction* with the product or service.

In addition to a sense of *fulfilment* in the knowledge that one's needs have been met, satisfaction can also be related to other types of feelings, depending on the particular context or type of service.[9] For example, satisfaction can be viewed as *contentment* – more of a passive response that consumers may associate with services they do not think a lot about or services that they receive routinely over time. Satisfaction may also be associated with feelings of *pleasure* for services that make the consumer feel good or are associated with a sense of happiness. For those services that really surprise the consumer in a positive way, satisfaction may mean *delight*. In some situations, where the removal of a negative leads to satisfaction, the consumer may associate a sense of *relief* with satisfaction. Finally, satisfaction may be associated with feelings of *ambivalence* when there is a mix of positive and negative experiences associated with the product or service.

Although consumer satisfaction tends to be measured at a particular point in time as if it were static, satisfaction is a dynamic, moving target that may evolve over time, influenced by a variety of factors.[10] Particularly when product usage or the service experience takes place over time, satisfaction may be highly variable depending on which point in the usage or experience cycle one is focusing on. Similarly, in the case of very new services or a service not previously experienced, customer expectations may be barely forming at the point of initial purchase; these expectations will solidify as the process unfolds and the consumer begins to form his or her perceptions. Through the service cycle the consumer may have a variety of different experiences – some good, some not good – and each will ultimately impact satisfaction.

What Determines Customer Satisfaction?

As shown in Figure 5.1, customer satisfaction is influenced by specific product or service features, perceptions of product and service quality, and price. In addition, personal factors, such as the customer's mood or emotional state, and situational factors, such as the opinions of family members, will also influence satisfaction.

Product and Service Features

Customer satisfaction with a product or service is influenced significantly by the customer's evaluation of product or service features.[11] For a service such as a resort hotel, important features might include the pool area, access to golf facilities, restaurants, room comfort and privacy, helpfulness and courtesy of staff, room price, and so on. In conducting satisfaction studies, most firms will determine through some means (often focus groups) what the important features and attributes are for their service and then measure perceptions of those features as well as overall service satisfaction. Research has shown that customers of services will make trade-offs among different service features (for example, price level versus quality versus friendliness of personnel versus level of customization), depending on the type of service being evaluated and the criticality of the service.[12]

Consumer Emotions

Customers' emotions can also affect their perceptions of satisfaction with products and services.[13] These emotions can be stable, pre-existing emotions – for example, mood state or life satisfaction. Think of times when you are at a very happy stage in your life (such as when you are on holiday), and your good, happy mood and positive frame of mind influence how you feel about the services you experience. Alternatively, when you are in a bad mood, your negative feelings may carry over into how you respond to services, causing you to overreact or respond negatively to any little problem.

Specific emotions may also be induced by the consumption experience itself, influencing a consumer's satisfaction with the service. Research done in a white-water rafting context showed that the guides had a strong effect on their customers' emotional responses to the trip and that those feelings (both positive and negative) were linked to overall trip satisfaction.[14] Positive emotions, such as happiness, pleasure, elation and a sense of warm-heartedness, enhanced customers' satisfaction with the rafting trip. In turn, negative emotions, such as sadness, sorrow, regret and anger, led to diminished customer satisfaction. Overall, in the rafting context, positive emotions had a stronger effect than negative ones. In online services, the usability of a website or mobile app may also impact on the emotions of the user, producing feelings of pleasure or frustration which result in satisfaction or dissatisfaction.

⭐ SERVICE SPOTLIGHT

Similar effects of emotions on satisfaction were found in a Portuguese study that looked at consumers' satisfaction with fitness centres.[15] In that study, negative emotions, including fear, nervousness and feelings of abandonment had a strong effect on customers' dissatisfaction ratings. On the other hand, positive emotions such as enthusiasm, excitement and delight had a significant positive effect for enhancing the level of overall satisfaction.

Attributions for Service Success or Failure

Attributions – the perceived causes of events – influence perceptions of satisfaction as well.[16] When they have been surprised by an outcome (the service is either much better or much worse than expected), consumers tend to look for the reasons, and their assessments of the reasons can influence their satisfaction. For example, if a customer of a weight-loss organization fails to lose weight as hoped for, the person will probably search for the causes – was it something they did, was the diet plan ineffective or did circumstances simply not allow them to follow the diet regime? – before determining their level of satisfaction or dissatisfaction with the weight-loss company.[17] For many services, customers take at least partial responsibility for how things turn out. This is often the case in online services where customers may blame their own technical abilities for failing to get a service to work correctly.

Even when customers do not take responsibility for the outcome, customer satisfaction may be influenced by other kinds of attributions. For example, research done in a travel agency context found that customers were less dissatisfied with a pricing error made by the agent if they felt that the reason was outside the agent's control or if they felt that it was a rare mistake, unlikely to occur again.[18]

Perceptions of Equity and Fairness

Customer satisfaction is also influenced by perceptions of equity and fairness.[19] Customers ask themselves: have I been treated fairly compared with other customers? Did other customers get better treatment, better prices, or better quality service? Did I pay a fair price for the service? Was I treated well in exchange for what I paid and the effort I expended? Notions of fairness are central to customers' perceptions of satisfaction with products and services, particularly in service recovery situations. As you will learn in Chapter 15, satisfaction with a service provider following a service failure is largely determined by perceptions of fair treatment.

Other Consumers, Family Members and Co-Workers

In addition to product and service features and one's own individual feelings and beliefs, consumer satisfaction is often influenced by other people.[20] For example, satisfaction with a family holiday is a dynamic phenomenon, influenced by the reactions and expressions of individual family members over the duration of the holiday. Later, what family members express in terms of satisfaction or dissatisfaction with the holiday will be influenced by stories that are retold among the family and selective memories of the events. Similarly, the satisfaction of people on a white-water rafting adventure is certainly influenced by individual perceptions, but it is also influenced greatly by the experiences, behaviour and views of the other rafters. In a business setting, satisfaction with a new service or technology – for example, a new customer relationship management software service – will be influenced not only by individuals' personal experiences with the software itself, but also by what others say about it in the company, how others use it and feel about it, and how widely it is adopted in the organization.

National Customer Satisfaction Indices

Because of the importance of customer satisfaction to firms and overall quality of life, many countries have a national index that measures and tracks customer satisfaction at a macro level.[21] Many public policymakers believe that these measures could and should be used as tools for evaluating the health of the nation's economy, along with traditional measures of productivity and price. National customer satisfaction indices aim to measure the *quality* of economic output, whereas more traditional economic indicators tend to focus only on *quantity*. The first such index was the Swedish Customer Satisfaction Barometer introduced in 1989.[22] Throughout the 1990s similar indices were introduced in Germany (Deutsche Kundenbarometer, or DK, in 1992), the United States (American Customer Satisfaction Index, ACSI, in 1994), Norway (Norsk Kundebarometer, in 1996) and Switzerland (Swiss Index of Customer Satisfaction, SWICS, in 1998).[23] These indices measure customer satisfaction over a wide range of different industries and organizations, including public sector organizations. They are intended to be complementary to productivity measures, with productivity reflecting the quantity of output and customer satisfaction measuring the customers' view of quality of output. In the UK, the UKCSI has been published twice a year since 2008 by the Institute of Customer Service. It is based on 46,500 responses from an online panel which is geographically and demographically representative of the UK population. Customers are asked to rate their experiences of dealing with an organization on over 30 customer experience metrics using a scale of 1 to 10. The customer satisfaction index score for an organization is based on an average of all its customers' responses and is expressed as a score out of 100. The sector score is the mean average of all responses for that sector. The research regularly demonstrates that organizations which have consistently higher levels of customer satisfaction than their sector average have tended to achieve stronger revenue growth, profit and employee productivity. The research also shows that females tend to report higher levels of satisfaction than males, with younger customers on average being the least satisfied and older customers being the most satisfied with organizations.

There are very many different ways to measure customer satisfaction, loyalty and quality, and all are not equally useful. Some are too complex, others are too simple, and yet others measure the wrong things.

Some are better for predicting outcomes such as growth and performance, while other types of satisfaction and quality measures are needed for diagnosing underlying problems and making improvements.

One measurement approach, 'Net Promoter', was developed by loyalty expert Frederick Reichheld.[24] This was based on business case studies conducted by his firm. Net Promoter has gained tremendous popularity across industries in a very short time. The research promotes *one* customer loyalty question as the best for most industries in terms of predicting repeat customer purchases, growth, or referrals. The question is: 'How likely is it that you would recommend [company X] to a friend or colleague?'

Customers respond using a standard scale that ranges from 0 (not at all likely) to 10 (extremely likely). Based on their responses, each customer is classified into one of three groups:

Promoters (those giving scores of 9 or 10) are the customers who are loyal and enthusiastic about the organization, will continue buying and referring others and are exceptionally enthusiastic fans.

Passives (those giving scores of 7 or 8) are generally satisfied customers, but lack the enthusiasm of Promoters. They may be vulnerable to competitive offerings and not immune to trying other suppliers.

Detractors (those giving scores of 6 or less) are less happy with the service provider and may communicate negative word of mouth.

Once customers have been classified, an index score is calculated by subtracting the percentage of Detractors from the percentage of Promoters. As shown in Figure 5.2, the score is generally displayed as a whole number by dropping the per cent sign for the final number and scores range from anywhere between −100 (all Detractors) to +100 (all Promoters).

Figure 5.2   The Net Promoter Score

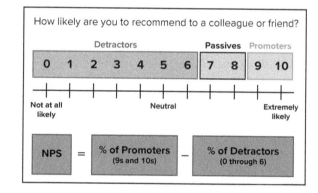

Many firms now use Reichheld's Net Promoter metric (the proportional difference between a firm's promoters and detractors, based on the single question '*How likely are you to recommend …*') to predict growth and loyalty. While the measure enjoys tremendous popularity, there is continuing controversy about its superiority as a predictor. Academic researcher Timothy Keiningham and colleagues have concluded that it is no better at predicting growth than other measures such as a Customer Satisfaction Index.[25] However, it can be used over time to track a firm's service delivery performance (if the score is going up or going down).

Although tools such as Net Promoter or customer satisfaction indices help firms to determine where they stand with their customers and to monitor trends, these global measures do not provide the detail that companies need to diagnose underlying causes or to make improvements. Additional, deeper, and more detailed assessment (as discussed in this chapter and Chapter 6) can help firms evaluate potential issues and what improvements may be needed.

Improving service and satisfaction most often involves a series of strategic and tactical actions related to employees, service operations and customers. A successful corporate-wide customer satisfaction, loyalty, or service strategy will involve all the functional areas that can influence it.

Temkin Group (part of the experience management and software company, Qualtrics), produces Net Promoter Industry Benchmarks for airlines, car dealerships, insurance, banks, computers, fast food, hotels, car rental, retailers, streaming media, supermarkets, internet service providers, utilities and mobile networks. Its benchmark results for 2017 suggest the brands with the highest scores in the UK are Nationwide Building Society, John Lewis, Aldi, Home Bargains, Nando's, IKEA, M&S Food, Spotify and Waitrose. The results are based on detailed responses from more than 10,000 UK consumers who had purchased products or services from each company within the previous 12 months.

Source: **www.temkingroup.com.**

Ensuring High Customer Satisfaction

A qualitative study[26] undertaken by *Marketing Magazine* looking at consumers' satisfaction with brands identified the following critical requirements in customer comments:

1 **Be Customer Centric** – *'Fit service around me – knowing what I said, and calling me back when I have got the time. That would show me I'm really valued, rather than just offering me a discount.'*

   Brands need to look at each situation from a customer's point of view and work from the assumption that their customers are reasonable people. Consumers are demanding that brands fit around their hectic schedules, and availability and 24/7 access are becoming more important.

2 **Have Superior Staff** – *'Brand X is just let down by dreadful unknowledgeable weekend staff – they have no idea what they're talking about.'*

   Spending millions on a TV campaign when staff don't know the basics about the product or service doesn't cut it with consumers. Communication skills on the ground are essential: BMW and Virgin Atlantic are great examples of this – sexy, aspirational brands – the personalities of which permeate their staff.

3 **Delight the Customer** – *'When my flowers from Brand X arrived at my wife's doorstep wilted, I phoned the company and they sent me £50 in vouchers. It was really good of them.'*

   A maxim that brands often overlook: over-delivering, whether through excellent customer service or exceeding post-purchase expectations.

4 **Keep your Promises** – *'I was on hold with my insurance company and then an automated message tells me it will call me back in 10 minutes – and you know what, they actually did.'*

   Well-articulated promises that set clear expectations are the key to customer satisfaction.

5 **Sort out Service Recovery** – *'Everyone understands that things go wrong … The art is how you put it right. Having a manager on hand so that you can speak to someone who actually knows what they are talking about really does help.'*

   Inevitably, services or products sometimes fail. Dealing with this promptly and effectively is paramount to maintaining a brand's reputation.

6 **Build a Relationship** – *'With Brand X, you can never trace who you've spoken to and which country they're in. There's no relationship at all, it's confusing.'*

   Being put on hold for a lengthy period only to discover that the person you finally get through to knows nothing about your problem and wants to put you through to another department is the bugbear of many a consumer. The 'one-stop-shop' concept – where the left hand of a company knows what the right is doing – is essential.

Service Quality

We now turn to service quality, a critical element of customer perceptions. In the case of pure services (e.g. healthcare, financial services, education), service quality will be the dominant element in customers' evaluations. In cases in which customer service or services are offered in combination with a physical product (e.g. IT services, car repairs), service quality may also be very critical in determining customer satisfaction. Figure 5.1 highlighted these relationships. We will focus here on the left-hand side of Figure 5.1, examining the underlying factors that influence perceptions of service quality. First we discuss *what* customers evaluate; then we look specifically at the five dimensions of service that customers rely on in forming their judgements.

Outcome, Interaction and Physical Environment Quality

What is it that consumers evaluate when judging service quality? Grönroos's 1984 Nordic model of the service experience categorized the dimensions into those relating to technical quality and those relating to functional quality.[27] For example, in the case of a lawsuit, a client will judge the quality of the technical outcome, or how the court case was resolved, and the quality of the interaction. Interaction quality would include such factors as the lawyer's timeliness in returning telephone calls, his or her empathy for the client, and his or her courtesy and listening skills. Similarly, a restaurant customer will judge the service on his or her perceptions of the meal (technical outcome quality), how the meal was served and how the employees interacted with him or her (interaction quality). Rust and Oliver[28] developed these two dimensions further into a three-component model consisting of service product, service delivery and service environment. The service product relates to the service offering and outcome, service delivery relates to the process of consuming the service and the service environment relates to the internal culture and external physical environment associated with the supplier.

This depiction of service quality as outcome quality, interaction quality and physical environment quality is most recently captured by Michael Brady and Joseph Cronin in their empirical research published in the *Journal of Marketing*.[29] Other researchers have defined similar aspects of service in their examinations of service quality.[30]

Service Quality Dimensions

Research suggests that customers do not perceive quality in a unidimensional way but rather judge quality based on multiple factors relevant to the context. The dimensions of service quality have been identified through the pioneering research of Parsu Parasuraman, Valarie Zeithaml and Leonard Berry. Their research identified five specific dimensions of service quality that apply across a variety of service contexts.[31] The five dimensions defined here are shown in Figure 5.1 as drivers of service quality. These five dimensions appear again in Chapter 6, along with the scale developed to measure them, SERVQUAL.

- *R*   **Reliability:** ability to perform the promised service dependably and accurately
- *A*   **Assurance:** employees' knowledge and courtesy and their ability to inspire trust and confidence
- *T*   **Tangibles:** appearance of physical facilities, equipment, personnel and written materials
- *E*   **Empathy:** caring, individualized attention given to customers
- *R*   **Responsiveness:** willingness to help customers and provide prompt service

These dimensions represent how consumers organize information about service quality in their minds. On the basis of exploratory and quantitative research, these five dimensions were found relevant for banking, insurance, appliance repair and maintenance, securities brokerage, long-distance telephone service, car repairs and others. The dimensions are also applicable to retail and business services, and logic suggests they would be relevant for internal services as well. At times customers will use all the dimensions to determine service quality perceptions, at other times not. For example, for an ATM, empathy is not likely to be a relevant dimension, while in a telephone encounter to schedule a repair, tangibles will not be relevant. Research suggests that cultural differences may also affect the relative importance placed on the five dimensions in different countries. In the following pages we expand on each of the dimensions and provide illustrations of how customers judge them.

Reliability: Delivering on Promises

Of the five dimensions, reliability has been consistently shown to be the most important determinant of perceptions of service quality.[32] Reliability is defined as the ability to perform the promised service dependably and accurately. In its broadest sense, reliability means that the company delivers on its promises – about delivery, service provision, problem resolution and pricing. Customers want to do business with companies that keep their promises, particularly when it comes to service outcomes and core service attributes.

⭐ **SERVICE SPOTLIGHT**

One company that communicates effectively and delivers on the reliability dimension is Whistl, the express parcel service. The reliability message of Whistl is evident in its aim: 'To satisfy customers every time' – this reflects the company's service positioning. But even when firms do not choose to position themselves explicitly on reliability, as Whistl has, this dimension is extremely important to consumers.

All firms need to be aware of customer expectations of reliability. Firms that do not provide the core service that customers think they are buying, fail them in the most direct way.

Assurance: Inspiring Trust and Confidence

Assurance is defined as employees' knowledge and courtesy and the ability of the firm and its employees to inspire trust and confidence. This dimension is likely to be particularly important for services that customers perceive as high risk or for services whose outcomes customers do not feel they can evaluate properly – for example, banking, insurance, medical and legal services.

Trust and confidence may be embodied in the person who links the customer to the company, such as insurance agents, lawyers or advisers. In such service contexts the company seeks to build trust and loyalty between key contact people and individual customers. The 'personal banker' concept captures this idea: customers are assigned to a banker who will get to know them individually and who will coordinate all their banking services.

In certain situations, trust and confidence are embodied in the organization itself. Financial services companies such as AXA Insurance ('Be Life Confident') and ING Direct ('It's Your Money We're Saving') illustrate efforts to create trusting relationships between customers and the company as a whole.

Tangibles: Representing the Service Physically and Virtually

Tangibles are defined as the appearance of physical facilities, equipment, personnel, websites, mobile phone apps and communication materials. Tangibles provide physical and virtual representations or images of the service that customers, particularly new customers, will use to evaluate quality. Service industries that emphasize physical tangibles in their strategies include hospitality services in which the customer visits the establishment to receive the service, such as restaurants and hotels, retail stores and entertainment companies. However, there is growing importance of the virtual tangibles through online services and apps in travel, banking and even government services.

Although tangibles are often used by service companies to enhance their image, provide continuity and signal quality to customers, most companies combine tangibles with another dimension to create a service quality strategy for the firm.

Emirates Airline promotes its quality by emphasizing world-class service from its staff and by advertising the fact that it flies one of the youngest fleets of aircraft in the world. It highlights that Emirates employees work hard to anticipate a customer's every need and supports this with a range of high-quality tangibles. These include the ICE inflight entertainment system, flat bed seating, the latest cabin design, interesting menus, luxurious lounges and a user-friendly online booking site. This combination is also evident in their promotional messaging: 'Making your Emirates experience world class in every class'.

In contrast, firms that do not pay attention to the tangibles dimension of the service strategy can confuse and even negate an otherwise good strategy.

Empathy: Treating Customers as Individuals

Empathy is defined as the caring, individualized attention that the firm provides its customers. The essence of empathy is conveying, through personalized or customized service, that customers are unique and special and that their needs are understood. Customers want to feel that they are understood by, and important to, the firms that provide them with a service. Personnel at small service firms often know customers by name and build relationships that reflect their personal knowledge of customer requirements and preferences. When such a small firm competes with larger firms, the ability to be empathetic may give it a clear advantage.

In business-to-business services, customers want supplier firms to understand their industries and issues. Many small computer consulting firms successfully compete with large vendors by positioning themselves as specialists in particular industries. Even though larger firms have superior resources, the small firms are perceived as more knowledgeable about customers' issues and needs and are able to offer more customized services.

Responsiveness: Being Willing to Help

Responsiveness is the willingness to help customers and to provide prompt service. This dimension emphasizes attentiveness and promptness in dealing with customer requests, questions, complaints and problems. Responsiveness is communicated to customers by the length of time they have to wait for assistance, answers to questions or attention to problems. Responsiveness also captures the notion of flexibility and ability to customize the service to customer needs.

To excel on the dimension of responsiveness, a company must view the process of service delivery and the handling of requests from the customer's point of view rather than from the company's point of view. Standards for speed and promptness that reflect the company's view of internal process requirements may be very different from the customer's requirements for speed and promptness. To truly distinguish themselves on responsiveness, companies need well-staffed customer service departments as well as responsive front-line people in all contact positions. Responsiveness perceptions diminish when customers wait to get through to a company by telephone, are put on hold, are put through to a complex voice mail system, or have trouble accessing the firm's website.

Table 5.1 provides examples of how customers judge each of the five dimensions of service quality across a variety of service contexts.

E-Service Quality

The growth of e-tailing and e-services has led many companies to wonder how consumers evaluate service quality on the Web and whether the criteria are different from those used to judge the quality of non-Internet services.[33] Some commercial groups, such as the online comparison sites Bizrate and Kelkoo, capture customer perceptions of specific sites. A more systematic study, sponsored by the Marketing Science Institute, has been conducted to understand how consumers judge e-service quality (e-SQ).[34] In that study, e-SQ is defined as the extent to which a website facilitates efficient and effective shopping, purchasing and delivery. Through exploratory focus groups and two phases of empirical data collection and analysis, this research

Table 5.1   Examples of how customers judge the five dimensions of service quality

	Reliability	Assurance	Tangibles	Empathy	Responsiveness
Car repair (consumer)	Problem fixed the first time and ready when promised	Knowledgeable mechanics	Repair facility; waiting area; uniforms; equipment	Acknowledges customer by name; remembers previous problems and preferences	Accessible; no waiting; responds to requests
Airline (consumer)	Flights to promised destinations depart and arrive on schedule	Trusted name; good safety record; competent employees	Aircraft; ticketing counters; baggage area; website; mobile apps; uniforms	Understands special individual needs; anticipates customer needs	Prompt and speedy system for ticketing, in-flight baggage handling
Dental care (consumer)	Appointments are kept on schedule; diagnoses prove accurate	Knowledge; skills; credentials; reputation	Waiting room; examination room; equipment; written materials	Acknowledges patient as a person; remembers previous problems; listens well; has patience	Accessible; no waiting; willingness to listen
Architecture (business)	Delivers plans when promised and within budget	Credentials; reputation; name in the community; knowledge and skills	Office area; reports; plans themselves; billing statements; website; dress of employees	Understands client's industry; acknowledges and adapts to specific client needs; gets to know the client	Returns telephone calls; adapts to changes
Information processing (internal)	Provides needed information when requested	Knowledgeable staff; well trained; credentials	Internal reports; office area; intranet provision; dress of employees	Knows internal customers as individuals; understands individual and departmental needs	Prompt response to requests; not 'bureaucratic'; deals with problems promptly
Internet brokerage (consumer and business)	Provides correct information and executes customer requests accurately	Credible information sources on the site; brand recognition; credentials apparent on site	Appearance of the website and collateral	Responds with human interaction as needed	Quick website with easy access and no down time

identified seven dimensions that are critical for core service evaluation (four dimensions) and service recovery evaluation (three dimensions).

The four core dimensions that customers use to judge websites at which they experience no questions or problems are:

1 *Efficiency:* the ability of customers to access the website, find their desired product and information associated with it, and check out with minimal effort.
2 *Fulfilment:* the accuracy of service promises, having products in stock, and delivering the products in the promised time. In other words, customers receive what they thought they ordered based on the description on the website, receive it when expected and are billed the correct amount.
3 *Reliability:* the technical functioning of the site, particularly the extent to which it is available and functioning properly.
4 *Privacy:* the assurance that shopping behaviour data are not shared and that credit information is secure.

Table 5.2   Service encounter themes

THEME 1: RECOVERY	
Satisfactory	**Unsatisfactory**
They lost my room reservation but the manager gave me the top suite for the same price.	We had made advance online reservations at the hotel. When we arrived we found we had no room – no explanation, no apologies and no assistance in finding another hotel.
Even though I did not make any complaint about the hour-and-a-half wait, the waitress kept apologizing and said the bill was on the house.	One of my suitcases was damaged and looked like it had been dropped from 30,000 feet. When I tried to make a claim for the damage, the employee insinuated that I was lying and trying to cheat them.

THEME 2: ADAPTABILITY	
Satisfactory	**Unsatisfactory**
I did not have an appointment to see a doctor; however, the practice nurse spoke to the doctor's receptionist and worked me into the schedule. I received treatment after a 10-minute wait. I was very satisfied with the special treatment I received, the short wait and the quality of the service.	My young son, flying alone, was to be assisted by the flight attendant from start to finish. She left him alone in the airport with no one to escort him to his connecting flight.
It was snowing outside – my car had broken down. I checked 10 hotels and there were no rooms. Finally, one understood my situation and offered to rent me a bed and set it up in a small banquet room.	Despite our repeated requests, the hotel staff would not deal with the noisy people partying in the corridor at 3 a.m.

THEME 3: SPONTANEITY	
Satisfactory	**Unsatisfactory**
Our children always travel with their teddy bears. When we got back to our room at the hotel we saw that the cleaning person had arranged the bears very comfortably in a chair. The bears were holding hands.	The lady at the front desk acted as if we were bothering her. She was watching television and paying more attention to the television than to the hotel guests.
The medical staff took extra time to explain exactly what I would be aware of and promised to take special care in making sure I did not wake up during the surgical operation.	I needed a few more minutes to choose from the menu. The waitress said, 'If you would read the menu and put down your mobile phone, you would know what you want to order'.

THEME 4: COPING	
Satisfactory	**Unsatisfactory**
A person who became intoxicated on a flight started speaking loudly, annoying the other passengers. The flight attendant asked the passenger if he would be driving when the plane landed and offered him coffee. He accepted the coffee and became quieter and friendlier.	An intoxicated man began pinching the female flight attendants. One attendant told him to stop, but he continued and then hit another passenger. The co-pilot was called and asked the man to sit down and leave the others alone, but the passenger refused. The co-pilot then placed the man's hands in restraints.

Recovery – Employee Response to Service Delivery System Failures

The first theme includes all incidents in which there has been a failure of the service delivery system and an employee is required to respond in some way to consumer complaints and disappointments. The failure may be, for example, a hotel room that is not available, a flight that is delayed six hours, an incorrect item sent from a mail-order company or a critical error on an internal document. The content or form of the employee's response is what causes the customer to remember the event either favourably or unfavourably.

Adaptability – Employee Response to Customer Needs and Requests

A second theme underlying satisfaction/dissatisfaction in service encounters is how adaptable the service delivery system is when the customer has special needs or requests that place demands on the process. In these cases, customers judge service encounter quality in terms of the flexibility of the employees and the system. Incidents categorized within this theme all contain an implicit or explicit request for customization of the service to meet a need. Much of what customers see as special needs or requests may actually be rather routine from the employee's point of view; what is important is that the customer perceives that something special is being done for him or her based on his or her own individual needs. External customers and internal customers alike are pleased when the service provider makes an effort to accommodate and adjust the system to meet their requirements. On the flip side, they are angered and frustrated by an unwillingness to try to accommodate and by promises that are never followed through. Contact employees also see their abilities to adapt the system as being a prominent source of customer satisfaction, and often they are equally frustrated by constraints that keep them from being flexible.

Spontaneity – Unprompted and Unsolicited Employee Actions

Even when there is no system failure and no special request or need, customers can still remember service encounters as being very satisfying or very dissatisfying. Employee spontaneity in delivering memorably good or poor service is the third theme. Satisfying incidents in this group represent very pleasant surprises for the customer (special attention, being treated like royalty, receiving something nice but not requested), whereas dissatisfying incidents in this group represent negative and unacceptable employee behaviours (rudeness, stealing, discrimination, ignoring the customer).

Coping – Employee Response to Problem Customers

The incidents categorized in this group came to light when employees were asked to describe service encounter incidents in which customers were either very satisfied or dissatisfied. In addition to describing incidents of the types outlined under the first three themes, employees described many incidents in which customers were the cause of their own dissatisfaction. Such customers were basically uncooperative – that is, unwilling to cooperate with the service provider, other customers, industry regulations and/or laws. In these cases, nothing the employee could do would result in the customer feeling pleased about the encounter. The term *coping* is used to describe these incidents because coping is the behaviour generally required of employees to handle problem customer encounters. Rarely are such encounters satisfying from the customer's point of view.[43] Also of interest is that customers themselves did not relate any 'problem customer' incidents. That is, customers either do not see, or choose not to remember or retell, stories of the times when they themselves were unreasonable to the point of causing their own unsatisfactory service encounter.

Table 5.3 summarizes the specific employee behaviours that cause satisfaction and dissatisfaction in service encounters according to the four themes just presented: recovery, adaptability, spontaneity and coping. The left-hand side of the table suggests what employees do that result in positive encounters, whereas the right-hand side summarizes negative behaviours within each theme.

Table 5.3   General service behaviours based on service encounter themes – dos and don'ts

Theme	Do	Don't
Recovery	Acknowledge problem	Ignore customer
	Explain causes	Blame customer
	Apologize	Leave customer to fend for himself or herself
	Compensate/upgrade	Downgrade
	Lay out options	Act as if nothing is wrong
	Take responsibility	Blame the problem on someone else
Adaptability	Recognize the seriousness of the need	Ignore
	Acknowledge	Promise, but fail to follow through
	Anticipate	Show unwillingness to try
	Attempt to accommodate	Embarrass the customer
	Adjust the system	Laugh at the customer
	Explain rules/policies	Avoid responsibility
	Take responsibility	Blame the problem on someone else
Spontaneity	Take time	Exhibit impatience
	Be attentive	Ignore
	Anticipate needs	Yell/laugh/swear
	Listen	Steal from customers
	Provide information	Discriminate
	Show empathy	
Coping	Listen	Take customer's dissatisfaction personally
	Try to accommodate	Let customer's dissatisfaction affect others
	Explain	
	Let go of the customer	

The Evidence of Service

Because services are intangible, customers are searching for evidence of service in every interaction they have with an organization.[44] Figure 5.4 depicts the three major categories of evidence as experienced by the customer: people, process and physical evidence. Together, these categories represent the service and provide the evidence that makes the offering tangible. The new mix elements essentially *are* the evidence of service in each moment of truth.

All these evidence elements, or a subset of them, are present in every service encounter a customer has with a service firm and are critically important in managing service encounter quality and creating customer satisfaction. For example, when a dental patient has an appointment with a local dentist, the first encounter is frequently with a receptionist in a waiting area. The quality of that encounter will be judged by how the appointment registration *process* works (Is there a queue? How long is the wait? Is the registration system computerized and accurate?), the actions and attitude of the *people* (Is the receptionist courteous, helpful, knowledgeable? Does he or she treat the patient as an individual? Does he or she handle enquiries fairly and

Figure 5.4   The evidence of service (from the customer's point of view)

- Flow of activities
- Steps in process
- Personalization versus standardization
- Level of automation

- Tangible communication
- Servicescape
- Guarantees
- Technology
- Website

Process

Physical evidence

People

- Contact employees
- The customer's role
- Other customers

Source: Adapted from 'Managing the evidence of service' by M.J. Bitner from *The Service Quality Handbook*, eds E.E. Scheuing and W.F. Christopher.

efficiently?) and the *physical evidence* of the service (Is the waiting area clean and comfortable? Is the signage clear?). The three types of evidence may be differentially important depending on the type of service encounter (remote, telephone, face-to-face). All three types will operate in face-to-face service encounters like the one just described.

Summary

This chapter described customer perceptions of service by first introducing you to two critical concepts: customer satisfaction and service quality. These critical customer perceptions were defined and discussed in terms of the factors that influence each of them. You learned that customer satisfaction is a broad perception influenced by features and attributes of the product as well as by customers' emotional responses, their attributions and their perceptions of fairness. Service quality, the customer's perception of the service component of a product, is also a critical determinant of customer satisfaction. Sometimes, as in the case of a pure service, service quality may be the *most* critical determinant of satisfaction. You learned that perceptions of service quality are based on five dimensions: reliability, assurance, tangibles, empathy and responsiveness.

Another major purpose of this chapter was to introduce the idea of service encounters, or 'moments of truth', as the building blocks for both satisfaction and quality. You learned that every service encounter (whether remote, over the telephone or in person) is an opportunity to build perceptions of quality and satisfaction. The underlying themes of pleasure and displeasure in service encounters were also described. The importance of managing the evidence of service in each and every encounter was discussed.

Key Concepts

Assurance	90	Empathy	91
Critical incident technique (CIT)	96	Equity and fairness	86
E-service quality	91	Moment of truth	94

National customer satisfaction indices	86	Satisfaction	82
Net Promoter Score	87	Service encounter	94
Nordic model of service quality	89	Service encounter cascade	94
Reliability	90	Service quality	83
Remote encounters	95	Service recovery	96
Responsiveness	91	Tangibles	90

Exercises

1   Keep a journal of your service encounters with at least five different organizations during the week. For each journal entry, ask yourself the following questions: what circumstances led up to this encounter? What did the employee say or do? How did you evaluate this encounter? What exactly made you evaluate the encounter that way? What should the organization have done differently (if anything)? Categorize your encounters according to the four themes of service encounter satisfaction/dissatisfaction (recovery, adaptability, spontaneity, coping).

2   Interview someone with a non-European cultural background about service quality. Inquire whether the five dimensions of quality are relevant in his or her home culture and which are seen as most important in determining quality of banking services (or some other type of service).

3   Think of an important service experience you have had in the past several weeks. Analyse the encounter according to the evidence of service provided (see Figure 5.4). Which of the three evidence components was (or were) most important for you in evaluating the experience, and why?

4   Interview an employee of a local service business. Ask this person to discuss each of the five dimensions of quality as it relates to his or her company. Which dimensions are most important? Are any dimensions *not* relevant in this context? Which dimensions does the company do best? Why? Which dimensions could benefit from improvement? Why?

5   Interview a manager, owner or director of a business. Discuss with this person the strategies he or she uses to ensure customer satisfaction. Does service quality enter into these strategies, and if so, how? Find out how this person's organization measures customer satisfaction and/or service quality.

6   Visit the Amazon website and a traditional bookshop. How would you compare the two experiences? Compare and contrast the factors that most influenced your satisfaction and perceptions of service quality in the two different situations. When would you choose to use one versus the other?

Discussion Questions

1   What is customer satisfaction, and why is it so important? Discuss how customer satisfaction can be influenced by each of the following: product attributes and features, customer emotions, attributions for success or failure, perceptions of fairness, and family members or other customers.

2   Discuss the differences between perceptions of service quality and customer satisfaction.

3   List and define the five dimensions of service quality. Describe the services provided by a firm you do business with (your bank, your dentist, your favourite restaurant) on each of the dimensions. In your mind, has this organization distinguished itself from its competitors on any particular service quality dimension?

4   Describe a remote encounter, a telephone encounter and a face-to-face encounter that you have had recently. In each case, how did you evaluate the encounter, and what were the most important factors determining your satisfaction/dissatisfaction?

5   Describe an 'encounter cascade' for a commercial flight. In your opinion, what are the most important encounters in this cascade for determining your overall impression of the quality of the airline?

6   Assume that you are a manager of a health club. Discuss general strategies you might use to maximize customers' positive perceptions of your club. How would you know if you were successful?

7   Consider a service and explain how satisfaction with this service could be influenced by the reactions and opinions of other people.

8   Examine the website of a service organization. What aspects of the site do you find satisfying and what aspects do you find dissatisfying? How do these satisfiers and dissatisfiers compare with the service quality dimensions introduced in this chapter?

Further Reading

Blut, M., Chowdhry, N., Mittal, V. and Brock, C. (2015). E-service quality: A meta-analytic review. *Journal of Retailing*, 91(4), 679–700.

Carlson, J. and O'Cass, A. (2010). Exploring the relationships between e-service quality, satisfaction, attitudes and behaviours in content-driven e-service websites. *Journal of Services Marketing*, 24(2), 112–27.

Keiningham, T.L., Cooil, B., Aksoy, L., Andreassen, T.W. and Weiner, J. (2007). The value of different customer satisfaction and loyalty metrics in predicting customer retention, recommendation and share-of-wallet. *Managing Service Quality*, 17(4), 361–84.

Morgan, N.A. and Rego, L.L. (2006). The value of different customer satisfaction and loyalty metrics in predicting business performance. *Marketing Science*, 25(5), 426–39.

Morgeson, F.V., Mithas, S., Keiningham, T.L. and Aksoy, L. (2011). An investigation of the cross-national determinants of customer satisfaction. *Journal of the Academy of Marketing Science*, 39(2), 198–215.

Reichheld, F.F. (2003). The one number you need to grow. *Harvard Business Review*, 81(12), 46–55.

Part 3
Understanding Customer Requirements

Chapter 6	Listening to Customers
Chapter 7	Building Customer Relationships

The Listening Gap

Not knowing what customers expect is one of the root causes of not delivering to customer expectations. Provider gap 1 is the difference between customer expectations of service and company understanding of those expectations. Note that in its graphic representation we created a link between the customer and the company, showing customer expectations above the line that dissects the model and provider perceptions of customer expectations below that line. This alignment signifies that what customers expect is not always the same as what companies believe they expect.

Part 2 describes two ways to close provider gap 1. In Chapter 6 we detail ways that companies listen to customers through research. Both formal and informal methods of customer research are described, including surveys, critical incident studies and complaint solicitation. Upward communication from front-line employees to managers, another key factor in listening to customers, is also discussed.

Chapter 7 covers company strategies to retain customers and strengthen relationships with them, an approach called relationship marketing. Relationship marketing is distinct from transactional marketing, the more conventional approach that tends to focus on acquiring new customers rather than retaining them. When organizations have strong relationships with existing customers, opportunities for in-depth listening increase over time and provider gap 1 is less likely to occur. A variety of strategies, including the creation of switching barriers and the development of relationship bonds, are suggested as a means of relationship development and, ultimately, the cultivation of customer loyalty.

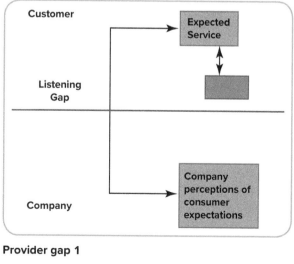

Provider gap 1

Chapter 6

Listening to Customers

Chapter Outline

Customer Databases and Big Data Analytics	106
Monitoring User-Generated Content and Netnography	108
Using Marketing Research to Understand Customer Expectations	109
Elements in an Effective Services Marketing Research Programme	110
Analysing and Interpreting Marketing Research Findings	121
Using Marketing Research Information	123
Ethics in Marketing Research	123
Upward Communication through Employees	124
Summary and Key Concepts	126
Exercises	127
Discussion Questions	128
Further Reading	128

Learning Objectives

This chapter's objectives are to:

1 Understand the role of customer databases and big data.
2 Present the types of, and guidelines for, marketing research in services.
3 Show how marketing research information can and should be used for services.
4 Describe the strategies by which companies can facilitate interaction and communication between management and customers.
5 Present ways that companies can and do facilitate upward communication of customer information from contact people to management.

solutions (sometimes known as listening platforms) developed by providers such as Cision (www.uk.cision .com/uk) and Radian6 (www.radian6.com) which simply identify all information appearing about a brand or company. These tools often provide sophisticated dashboards with easy-to-use reporting features.

Cleaning and relevance checking is needed with user-generated content, as the automated systems struggle with inaccurate spelling, grammar and punctuation. They may also fail to understand the context in which things are being said. However, improved artificial intelligence (AI) systems are getting better at interpreting textual data including the context and sentiment behind the data. These systems use natural language processing which includes techniques ranging from statistical and machine learning methods to rules-based and algorithmic approaches. These approaches break down language into shorter, elemental pieces, aiming to understand relationships between the pieces and explore how the pieces work together to create meaning. It is also important to understand the mood or subjective opinions being expressed and these techniques are used for sentiment analysis. When a hotel chain opens a new hotel they can use these systems to monitor customers' opinions towards any features of the hotel design, staffing and operations.

In addition to these hands-off-type monitoring approaches, service organizations may also use their own social networking or websites to create a community that will attract user-generated content.

For example, My Starbucks Idea (ideas.starbucks.com/) is a site run by Starbucks to generate ideas, opinions and feedback from customers. British Airways post new initiatives and advertisements on their Facebook site to get customer reactions to them.

Netnography, sometimes known as *online ethnography*, is the ethnographic study of online communities. It generally involves a researcher participating fully as a member of the community. Communities which are relevant to the service organization (e.g. world travel), and where there are high levels of interaction and comments, are likely to provide the richest sources of information. Customers may speak more freely within their online community than when they are taking part in traditional marketing, as they perhaps feel they are not under as much scrutiny. Balanced against this, however, is the concern that these customers may not be accurately posting their views but may instead be posting comments that enhance their own reputation or reinforce the online persona that they are trying to create. This may lead to new ideas for the design of new services or service components. Data are collected by copying discussions from the forum, or by the researcher taking notes on observations of interactions. There are ethical issues that stem from this type of research, however, particularly around the issue of a researcher taking an active part in the discussions/ conversations of a community without the participants being aware of the researcher's identity. In such situations, best practice suggests that the researcher should disclose fully his or her presence, job function, and research intentions to online community members during any research assignment.[2]

Using Marketing Research to Understand Customer Expectations

Although behavioural information may be available from customer databases and user generated content, finding out through marketing research what customers expect is essential to providing service quality. Marketing research is the key vehicle for understanding customer expectations and perceptions of services. In services, as with any offering, a firm that does no marketing research at all is unlikely to understand its customers. Similarly, a firm that does marketing research, but not on the topic of customer expectations, may fail to uncover what is needed to stay in tune with changing customer requirements. Marketing research must focus on service issues such as what features are most important to customers, what levels of these features customers expect, and what customers think the company can and should do when problems occur in service delivery. Even when a service firm is small and has limited resources to conduct research, avenues are open to explore what customers expect.

In this section we discuss the elements of services marketing research programmes that help companies identify customer expectations and perceptions. In the sections that follow, we will discuss ways in which the tactics of general marketing research may need to be adjusted to maximize its effectiveness in services.

Research Objectives for Services

The first step in designing services marketing research is without doubt the most critical: defining the problem and research objectives. This is where the services marketer poses the questions to be answered or problems to be solved with research. Does the company want to know what customer requirements are, how customers view the service provided by the company, how they will respond to a new service introduction or what they will want from the company five years from now? Each of these research questions requires a different research strategy. Thus, it is essential to devote time and resources to define the problem thoroughly and accurately. In spite of the importance of this first stage, many marketing research studies are initiated without adequate attention to objectives.

Research objectives translate into action questions. While many different questions are likely to enter into a marketing research programme, the following are the most common research objectives in services:

- to discover customer requirements or expectations for service
- to develop customer-defined standards for service delivery (see Chapter 9)
- to monitor and track service performance
- to assess overall company performance compared with that of competitors
- to assess gaps between customer expectations and perceptions
- to identify dissatisfied customers, so that service recovery can be attempted
- to gauge the effectiveness of changes in service delivery
- to appraise the service performance of individuals and teams for evaluation, recognition and rewards
- to determine customer expectations for a new service
- to monitor changing customer expectations in an industry
- to forecast future expectations of customers.

These research objectives are similar in many ways to the research conducted for physical products: both aim to assess customer requirements, dissatisfaction and demand. Services research, however, incorporates additional elements that require specific attention.

Services research must continually monitor and track service performance, because performance is subject to human variability and heterogeneity. Conducting performance research at a single point in time, as might be done for a physical product such as a car, would be insufficient in services. A major focus of services research involves capturing human performance – at the level of individual employee, team, branch, organization as a whole and competition. Another focus of services research involves documenting the process by which service is performed. Even when service employees are performing well, a service provider must continue to track performance because the potential for variation in service delivery always exists.

Table 6.1 lists a number of potential services research objectives. Once objectives such as these have been identified, they will point the way to decisions about the most appropriate type of research, methods of data collection, and ways to use the information. The research approaches in this table are described in later sections of this chapter.

Elements in an Effective Services Marketing Research Programme

A good services marketing research programme includes multiple types of information sources and research studies. The composite of information and types of research will differ by company because the range of uses for service quality research – from employee performance assessment to advertising campaign development to strategic planning – requires a rich, multifaceted flow of information. If an organization were to engage

Table 6.1   Research approaches and primary objectives

Research Approaches	Primary Objectives
Complaint solicitation	To identify/attend to dissatisfied customers
	To identify common service failure points
Critical incident studies	To identify 'best practices' at transaction level
	To identify customer requirements as input for quantitative studies
	To identify common service failure points
	To identify systemic strengths and weaknesses in customer-contact services
Researching customer needs	To identify customer requirements as input for quantitative research
Customer satisfaction surveys and SERVQUAL surveys	To monitor and track service performance
	To assess overall company performance compared with that of competition
	To determine links between satisfaction and behavioural intentions
	To assess gaps between customer expectations and perceptions
Database marketing research	To identify the individual requirements of customers using information technology and database information
Exit surveys	To obtain immediate feedback on performance of service transactions
	To measure effectiveness of changes in service delivery
	To assess service performance of individuals and teams
	To use as input for process improvements
	To identify common service failure points
Service expectation meetings and reviews	To create dialogue with important customers
	To identify what individual large customers expect and then to ensure that it is delivered
	To close the loop with important customers
Market-oriented ethnography	To research customers in natural settings
	To study customers while they are in a service encounter
Mystery shopping	To measure individual employee performance for evaluation, recognition and rewards
	To identify systemic strengths and weaknesses in customer-contact services
Customer panels	To monitor changes in customer expectations over time
	To provide a forum for customers to suggest and evaluate new service ideas
Lost customer follow-up	To identify reasons for customer defection
	To assess gaps between customer expectations and perceptions
Future expectations research	To forecast future expectations of customers
	To develop and test new service ideas

in virtually all types of service research, the portfolio would look like Table 6.1, but few organizations do all types of research. The particular portfolio for any organization will match organization resources and address the key areas needed to understand the customers of the business. So that it will be easier for you to identify the appropriate type of research for different research objectives, we list the objectives in column 2 of Table 6.1. In the following sections we describe each major type of research and show the way each type addresses the criteria associated with it.

⭐ SERVICE SPOTLIGHT

easyJet gauges customer purchasing behaviour and motivation by using their online customer community of around 3,000 people located across various countries that represent both leisure and business segments. Each week, these community members are sent an email asking for their input into a couple of research topics related to the airline's future activities. Participants are incentivized with a monthly prize draw and the information provides guidance for both strategic and tactical decision making. A customer satisfaction programme is also run in tandem with this activity. Every month, interviews are conducted with between 35,000 and 40,000 customers from across Europe, all contacted the day after travel. They are invited by email to take part in an online survey with a view to gaining insight into their experience across different stages of their trip: from booking, to departure, flight, arrival and return journey. Information from the survey is reported back regularly via online dashboards and easyJet operational managers at each airport use the data to understand how they are performing and how they compare to other similar airport operations. It may also identify service delivery problems that need to be addressed on a route or at an airport.

Complaint Solicitation

Many of you must have complained to employees of service organizations, only to find that nothing happens with your complaint. No one rushes to solve it and the next time you experience the service, the same problem is present. How frustrating! Good service organizations take complaints seriously. Not only do they listen to complaints – they also seek complaints as communications about what can be done to improve their service and the performance of their service employees.

To be effective, complaint solicitation requires rigorous recording of numbers and types of complaints through many channels, and then working to eliminate the most frequent problems. Complaint channels include employees at the front line, intermediary organizations like retailers who deliver service, managers, and third parties such as consumer pressure groups who field complaints. Companies must both solve individual customer problems and seek overall patterns to eliminate failure points. More sophisticated forms of complaint resolution define 'complaint' broadly to include all comments – both negative and positive – as well as questions from customers. Firms should build depositories for this information and report results frequently, perhaps weekly or monthly.

Firms that use complaints as research collect and document them, then use the information to identify dissatisfied customers, correct individual problems where possible and identify common service failure points. Although this research is used for both goods and services, it has a critical real-time purpose in services – to improve failure points and to boost or correct the performance of contact personnel. Research on complaints is one of the easiest types of research for firms to conduct, leading many companies to depend solely on complaints to stay in touch with customers. Unfortunately, there is convincing research evidence that customer complaints alone are a woefully inadequate source of information: only a small percentage of customers with problems actually complain to the company. The rest will stay dissatisfied, telling other people about their dissatisfaction.

Critical Incident Studies

In Chapter 5 we discussed the critical incident technique (CIT), a qualitative interview procedure in which customers are asked to provide verbatim stories about satisfying and dissatisfying service encounters they have experienced. According to a summary of the use of the technique in services, CIT has been reported in hotels, restaurants, airlines, amusement parks, car repair, retailing, banking, cable television, public transportation and education.[3] The studies have explored a wide range of service topics: consumer evaluation of services, service failure and recovery, employees, customer participation in service delivery, and service experience.

The critical incident technique has many benefits. First, data are collected from the respondent's perspective and are usually vivid because they are expressed in consumers' own words and reflect the way they think. Second, the method provides concrete information about the way the company and its employees behave and react, thereby making the research easy to translate into action. Third, like most qualitative methods, the research is particularly useful when the topic or service is new and very little other information exists. Finally, the method is well suited for assessing perceptions of customers from different cultures because it allows respondents to share their perceptions rather than answer researcher-defined questions.[4]

SERVICE SPOTLIGHT

Asda, the major UK grocery chain which is part of the Walmart group, tracks customer satisfaction via a customer-perception tracker survey with 40,000 shoppers a month. In addition, the company undertakes targeted projects on specific customer types such as mothers. The Mums Immersion project had the objective of developing a better understanding of what life looks like to a mother. The project involved senior managers immersing themselves in the day-to-day life of mothers with group discussions, a mobile app where mothers could record the pain and pleasures of their daily lives in real time and online discussion forums. Insights were delivered in the form of events and a report to all senior managers in the company. This research has led to improvements in store design, product offerings and service standards.

Researching Customer Needs

Researching customer needs involves identifying the benefits and attributes that customers expect in a service. This type of research is very basic and essential because it determines the type of questions that will be asked in surveys and, ultimately, the improvements that will be attempted by the firm. Because these studies are so foundational, qualitative techniques are often appropriate to begin them. Quantitative techniques may follow, using the qualitative research as a pre-test stage of survey development. Unfortunately, many companies do superficial research, often developing surveys on the basis of intuition or company direction rather than through customer probing.

SERVICE SPOTLIGHT

Telefónica O_2 used research to create a loyalty programme for its mobile phone customers. The development of the Priority loyalty programme began by talking to customers to understand what really mattered to them. This insight informed the structure and content of the programme and continues to do so with ongoing research, social media tracking and behavioural analysis. In order to target and influence customers positively, both qualitative and quantitative research into customer preferences and behaviour were used to identify their favourite brands, moments when they needed a boost (e.g. Monday mornings) and celebratory rewards.

The research helped reveal the moments in the customers' relationship with O2 when their attitude shifted, evidenced in a dip in the net promoter score (NPS) and when the risk of churn increased. It also helped to create customer segmentation based on value. This understanding led to the creation of a tiered reward structure in which each type of reward performs a special function, including to encourage everyday engagement, acquire or reactivate a lapsed user, reward customers based on spend and increase overall satisfaction.

Source: **https://priority.o2.co.uk/.**

Another approach to researching customer needs that has been effective in services industries is to examine existing research about customer requirements in similar service industries. The five dimensions of quality service are generalizable across industries, and sometimes the way these dimensions are manifest is also remarkably similar. Customers of travel agencies and customers of banks, for example, expect many of the same features when using these two services. Besides expert advice, customers at travel agents expect short queues, brochures, informative websites and a friendly empathetic service – the same features that are desired by bank customers. In these and other industries that share common customer expectations, managers may find it helpful to seek knowledge from existing research in a related service industry.

Relationship and SERVQUAL Surveys

One category of surveys could appropriately be named *relationship surveys* because they pose questions about all elements in the customer's relationship with the company (including service, product and price). This comprehensive approach can help a company diagnose its relationship strengths and weaknesses. These surveys typically monitor and track service performance annually with an initial survey providing a baseline. Relationship surveys are also effective in comparing company performance with that of competitors, often focusing on the best competitor's performance as a benchmark. When used for this purpose, the sponsor of the survey is not identified and questions are asked about both the anonymous company and one or more of its competitors.

A sound measure of service quality is necessary for identifying which aspects of service need performance improvement, assessing how much improvement is needed on each aspect, and evaluating the impact of improvement efforts. Unlike goods quality, which can be measured objectively by such indicators as durability and number of defects, service quality is abstract and is best captured by surveys that measure customer evaluations of service. One of the first measures to be developed specifically to measure service quality was the SERVQUAL survey.

The original SERVQUAL scale published in 1988 involved a survey containing 21 service attributes, grouped into the five service quality dimensions (discussed in Chapter 5) of reliability, responsiveness, assurance, empathy and tangibles. Although many different formats of the SERVQUAL scale are now in use, Table 6.2 sets out the basic 21 perception items used in a typical survey. Each item is rated on a 1 (strongly disagree) to 7 (strongly agree) scale.

The survey sometimes asks customers to provide two different ratings on each attribute – one reflecting the level of service they would expect from excellent companies in a sector and the other reflecting their perception of the service delivered by a specific company within that sector. The difference between the expectation and perception ratings constitutes a quantified measure of service quality.

Table 6.2   Perception statements in a typical SERVQUAL survey

Reliability Dimension

When *Company X* promises to do something by a certain time, it does so.
Company X performs the service right first time.
Company X provides its services at the time it promises to do so.
Company X insists on error-free records.

Responsiveness Dimension

Company X keeps customers informed about when services will be performed.
Employees in *Company X* give you prompt service.
Employees in *Company X* are always willing to help you.
Employees in *Company X* are never too busy to respond to your request.

Assurance Dimension

The behaviour of employees in *Company X* instils confidence in you.
You feel safe in your transactions with *Company X*.
Employees in *Company X* are consistently courteous with you.
Employees in *Company X* have the knowledge to answer your questions.

Empathy Dimension

Company X gives you individual attention.
Company X has employees who give you personal attention.
Company X has your best interest at heart.
Employees of *Company X* understand your specific needs.
Company X has operating hours that are convenient to all customers.

Tangibles Dimension

Company X has modern-looking equipment.
Company X's physical facilities are visually appealing.
Company X's employees appear neat.
Materials associated with the service (such as leaflets or statements) are visually appealing at *Company X*.

Source: A. Parasuraman, V.A. Zeithaml, and L.L. Berry, 'SERVQUAL: A multiple-item scale for measuring consumer perceptions of service quality'. *Journal of Retailing*, 64 (Spring 1988), 12–40.

Data gathered through a SERVQUAL survey can be used for a variety of purposes:

- to determine the average gap score (between customers' perceptions and expectations) for each service attribute
- to assess a company's service quality along each of the five SERVQUAL dimensions
- to track customers' expectations and perceptions (on individual service attributes and/or on the SERVQUAL dimensions) over time
- to compare a company's SERVQUAL scores against those of competitors
- to identify and examine customer segments that differ significantly in their assessments of a company's service performance
- to assess internal service quality (that is, the quality of service rendered by one department or division to others within the same company).

The SERVQUAL instrument spawned many studies focusing on service quality assessment and is used in many service industries. Despite the fact that SERVQUAL has been productively used in multiple contexts, cultures and countries for measuring service quality, the SERVQUAL instrument has been the centre of criticism from a range of academic researchers. The main criticisms identified by Buttle[5] relate to the instrument's dimensions and shortcomings associated with the **disconfirmation paradigm**.

There are concerns that the attributes used in the original SERVQUAL instrument are not appropriate for all service offerings and need to be contextualized to reflect different service activities. Therefore, as with any method, care must be taken to ensure that the dimensions that are being measured are appropriate to the situation in which it is to be used. The attributes of the original SERVQUAL instrument do provide a valuable starting point for the development of an appropriate tool; however, it may be necessary to add or delete some of them depending on the context.

Disconfirmation Paradigm

Grönroos[6] suggested three problems when measuring comparisons between expectations and experiences over a number of attributes:

1 If expectations are measured after the service experience has taken place, which frequently happens for practical reasons, then what is measured is not really expectation but something which has been influenced by the service experience.

2 It may not make sense to measure expectations prior to the service experience, because the expectations that exist before a service is delivered may not be the same as the factors that a person uses when evaluating their experiences. For example, a customer in a restaurant may place no importance on the background music playing before the meal, but the quality or volume of the music heard during the meal may alter a customer's view of the factors to consider in evaluating the quality of the dining experience.

3 A customer's view of their experience in a service encounter is influenced by their prior expectations. Consequently, if expectations are measured and then experiences are measured, then the measures are not independent of each other and the expectations are actually being measured twice.

These issues do not necessarily invalidate the measurement of service quality. However, it has led to researchers looking for alternative ways of measuring service quality. One of the better known alternatives is the **SERVPERF** instrument, developed by Cronin and Taylor,[7] which measures experiences only and does not ask respondents about their expectations. Experiences are measured over a range of attributes that the researcher has developed to describe the service as conclusively as possible. The resultant instrument may be easier to administer and the data may be easier to analyse. However, SERVPERF has not reached the same level of popularity as exists for SERVQUAL.

Exit Surveys or Post-Transaction Surveys

Whereas the purpose of SERVQUAL surveys is usually to gauge the overall relationship with the customer, the purpose of transaction surveys is to capture information about one or all of the key service encounters with the customer. In this method, customers are asked a short list of questions immediately after a particular transaction (hence the name *exit surveys*) about their satisfaction with the transaction and contact personnel with whom they interacted. Because the surveys are administered continuously to a broad spectrum of customers, they are more effective than complaint solicitation (where the information comes only from dissatisfied customers).

Sport and Leisure Management,[8] which provides leisure management services for the public sector in the UK, needed to refresh its collection of post-transaction customer feedback surveys in order to improve its decision-making. Rather than use paper-based systems, it has installed user-friendly computer terminals in the foyer of leisure centres. These collect customer attitudes about the service experience from users before they leave the premises.

In other companies, transaction surveys are administered by telephone several days after a transaction, such as installation of durable goods or claims adjustment in insurance. Because they are timed to occur close to service transactions, these surveys are useful in identifying sources of dissatisfaction and satisfaction. For example, Kwik Fit, which sells car exhausts and tyres, often calls or emails customers a day after a car has been serviced to ensure that customers are satisfied with the work. A strong benefit of this type of research is that it often appears to customers that the company is following up to ensure that they are satisfied; consequently, the contact does double duty as a market research tool and as customer service.

This type of research is simple and provides management with continuous information about interactions with customers. Further, the research allows management to associate service quality performance with individual contact personnel so that high performance can be rewarded and low performance corrected. It also serves as an incentive for employees to provide better service, because they understand how and when they are being evaluated. One type of post-transaction survey that is becoming more familiar is on websites following online purchases. When a consumer makes a purchase, a message automatically pops up on the site and invites consumers to fill out a survey. Consumers who agree are asked questions about ease of ordering, product selection, website navigation and customer support.

Service Expectation Meetings and Reviews

In business-to-business situations, when large accounts are involved, a highly effective form of customer research involves eliciting the expectations of the client at a specified time of the year and then following up later (usually after a year) to determine whether the expectations were fulfilled. Even when the company produces a physical product, the meetings deal almost completely with the service expected and provided by an account or sales team assigned to the client. Unlike other forms of research we have discussed, these meetings are not conducted by objective and unbiased researchers but are instead initiated and facilitated by senior members of the account team so that they can listen carefully to the client's expectations. You may be surprised to find that such interaction does not come naturally to sales teams who are used to talking *to* clients rather than listening carefully to their needs. Consequently, teams have to be carefully trained to not defend or explain but rather to comprehend. One company found that the only way it could teach its salespeople not to talk on these interviews was to take a marketing researcher along to gently kick the salesperson under the table whenever he or she strayed from the format!

The format, when appropriate, consists of: (1) asking clients what they expect in terms of eight to ten basic requirements determined from focus group research, (2) enquiring what particular aspects of these requirements the account team performed well in the past and what aspects need improvement, and (3) requesting that the client rank the relative importance of the requirements. After getting the input, senior account members go back to their teams and plan their goals for the year around client requirements. The next step is verifying with the client that the account plan will satisfy requirements or, when it will not, managing expectations to let the client know what cannot be accomplished. After executing the plan for the year, the senior account personnel then return to the client, determine whether the plan has been successfully executed and expectations met, then establish a new set of expectations for the coming year.

Process Checkpoint Evaluations

With professional services such as consulting, construction and architecture, services are provided over a long period, and there are no obvious ways or times to collect customer information. Waiting until the entire project is complete – which could be years – is undesirable because myriad unresolvable problems could have occurred by then. But discrete service encounters to calibrate customer perceptions are also not usually available. In these situations the smart service provider defines a process for delivering the services and then structures the feedback around the process, checking in at frequent points to ensure that the client's expectations are being met. For example, a management consulting firm might establish the following process for delivering its services to clients: (1) collect information, (2) diagnose problems, (3) recommend alternative solutions, (4) select alternatives, and (5) implement solutions. Next, it could agree with the client up front that it will communicate at major process checkpoints – after diagnosing the problem, before selecting the alternative, and so on – to make certain that the job is progressing as planned.

Market-Oriented Ethnography

Structured questionnaires make key assumptions about what people are conscious of or can recall about their behaviour and what they are willing to explain to researchers about their opinions. Even focus group interviews depend on norms of participation, or what people are willing to say in front of others and to researchers. To understand fully how customers assess and use services, it may be necessary and effective to use other approaches, such as market-oriented ethnography. This set of approaches allows researchers to observe consumption behaviour in natural settings. The goal is to enter the consumer's world as much as possible – observing how and when a service is used in an actual home environment or consumption environment, such as watching consumers eat in restaurants or attend concerts. Among the techniques used are observation, interviews, documents and examination of material possessions such as artefacts. Observation involves entering the experience as a participant observer and watching what occurs rather than asking questions about it. Such approaches provide valuable insights, especially about lifestyles and usage patterns.[9]

★ SERVICE SPOTLIGHT

Given that one of Volvo's central claims is 'designed around you', the car manufacturer is keen to identify the features and services that customers want from their cars and their car dealers. An ethnographic approach is used where teams of researchers and engineers visit customers, look at their lives, talk about what's important to them, their relationship with their car, visit them in their home, and drive around with them. In addition, to supplement quantitative data from surveys, Volvo carries out early-buyer research, where people who have purchased a vehicle are visited in their homes, with their cars, and asked extensively about their experience of buying the car, their first drive, their impressions after two or three months of owning it, and so on. This results in identifying features and service support that people either aren't using, or don't understand how to use properly.

Mystery Shopping

In this form of research, which is unique to services, companies employ outside research organizations to send people into service establishments and experience the service as if they were customers. These 'mystery shoppers' are trained in the criteria important to customers of the establishment. They deliver objective assessments about service performance by completing questionnaires about service standards. Questionnaires contain items that represent important quality or service issues to customers.

In Europe mystery shopping is used quite extensively by organizations in financial services, retailing, motor dealerships, hotels and catering, passenger transportation, public utilities and, even, government departments. Unlike customer satisfaction surveys, the mystery shopping approach is being used to measure the process rather than the outcomes of a service encounter. The emphasis is on the service experience as it unfolds, looking at which activities and procedures do or do not happen rather than gathering opinions about the service experience. Mystery shopping studies are used for three main purposes:

- to act as a diagnostic tool, identifying failings and weak points in an organization's service delivery
- to encourage, develop and motivate service personnel by linking with appraisal, training and reward mechanisms
- to assess the competitiveness of an organization's service provision by benchmarking it against the offerings of others in an industry.

Mystery shopping aims to collect facts rather than perceptions. These facts can relate to basic enquiries, purchases and transactions covering questions such as:

- How many rings did it take before the telephone was answered?
- How long was the queue?
- What form of greeting was used?

They can also relate to more complex encounters, such as in the purchase of a mortgage where the procedures adopted in a two-hour fact-finding meeting can be assessed in terms of service quality and financial compliance.

All the areas on which mystery shoppers need to report are highly structured to minimize the impact of the shoppers' own preferences in terms of areas such as service or cleanliness. Shoppers are often shown videos or photographs of service environments or encounters to illustrate the appropriate rating for a specific type of encounter. Shoppers also receive a detailed briefing on the scenario that they are to enact, focusing on their personal characteristics, the questions they should ask and the behaviours they should adopt. They are then tested on these elements to ensure that the service encounter is realistic and to reduce the risk that service personnel might detect their true purpose as mystery shoppers.

Mystery shopping keeps workers alert because they know they may be evaluated at any time. They know they are being judged on the company's service standards and therefore carry out the standards more consistently than if they were not going to be judged. Mystery shopping can be a very effective way of reinforcing service standards.

★ SERVICE SPOTLIGHT

Transport for London, which operates the underground public transport network in and around London, uses mystery shopping for monitoring and measuring the level and consistency of the Underground's tangible and intangible service performance.

Mystery shoppers travel around the network and follow strictly specified routes, assessing trains and stations on measures such as: cleanliness and environment; lighting; maps and information; comfort factors; staff; ticket purchase; safety; and customer mobility and access. The shoppers' routes are organized in such a way that, in each quarter, a number of visits are made to each platform of the 270 London Underground stations. Each shopper is supplied with a questionnaire which includes descriptions of the rating scale to be used for each service measure, together with a short statement explaining what the measure covers. The survey is designed to allow shoppers enough time to complete the train measures between station visits.

When shoppers arrive at the nominated station, they move from the platform, along a route way, through the booking hall and then exit the building. The shoppers then retrace their steps to a designated platform and move on to the next station in the assignment, carrying out a train assessment en route. All of the areas where responses are required are highly structured to minimize the impact of the shoppers' own individual preferences in terms of areas such as service or cleanliness. Shoppers are often shown videos or photographs of service environments or encounters to illustrate the appropriate rating for each type of encounter. London Underground use the mystery shopping scores for setting targets for staff and contractors as well as for developing appropriate action plans to improve performance.[10]

Customer Panels

Customer **panels** are ongoing groups of customers assembled to provide attitudes and perceptions about a service over time. They offer companies regular and timely customer information – virtually a pulse on the market. Firms can use customer panels to represent large segments of end-customers.

Customer panels are used in the entertainment industry to screen movies before they are released to the public. After a rough cut of a film has been created, the movie is viewed by a panel of consumers that matches the demographic target. In the most basic of these panels, consumers participate in post-screening interviews or focus groups in which they report on their responses to the movie. They may be asked questions as general as their reactions to the ending of the movie and as specific as whether they understood different aspects of the plot line. On the basis of these panels' results, movies are revised and edited to ensure that they are communicating the desired message and that they will succeed in the marketplace. In extreme situations, entire movie endings have been changed to be more consistent with customer attitudes. In some of the most sophisticated consumer panel research on movies (also used for television shows and commercials), consumers have digital devices in their seats through which they indicate their responses as they watch films. This instantaneous response allows the producers, directors and editors to make changes at the appropriate places in the film to ensure that the story line, characters and scenery are 'tracking'.

Lost Customer Research

This type of research involves deliberately seeking out customers who have dropped the company's service to inquire about their reasons for leaving. Some lost customer research is similar to exit interviews with employees in that it asks open-ended, in-depth questions to expose the reasons for defection and the particular events that led to dissatisfaction. It is also possible to use more standard surveys on lost customers. For example, many utility companies (e.g. Eon), mobile phone operators (e.g. Vodafone) and bank customers (e.g. BNP Paribas) contact former customers, asking them about service performance during different stages of the customer–vendor relationship. The surveys also seek specific reasons for customers' defections and ask customers to describe the problems that triggered the move.

One benefit of this type of research is that it identifies failure points and common problems in the service, and can help establish an early-warning system for future defectors. Another benefit is that the research can be used to calculate the cost of lost customers.

Future Expectations Research

Customer expectations are dynamic and can change very rapidly in markets that are highly competitive and volatile. As competition increases, as tastes change and as consumers become more knowledgeable, companies must continue to update their information and strategies. One such 'industry' is interactive video, representing the merger of computer, telecommunications and cable television. The technologies available in this industry are revolutionary. In dynamic market situations, companies want to understand not just current customer expectations but also future expectations – the service features desired in the future. Future expectations research is new and consists of different types. First, *features research* involves environmental scanning and querying of customers about desirable features of possible services. *Lead user research* brings in customers who are opinion leaders/innovators and asks them what requirements are not being met by existing products or services.

The question of customer involvement in expectation studies is often debated. Designers and developers claim that consumers do not know what they might want, especially in industries or services that are new and rapidly changing. Consumers and marketing researchers, on the other hand, counter that services developed independent of customer input are likely to be targeted at needs that do not exist. To study this question, researchers assessed the contributions made by users compared with professional developers for end-user telecom services. Three groups were studied: users alone, developers alone and users with a design expert present to provide information on feasibility. Findings showed that users created more original but less producible ideas. However, inviting users to test and explore possibilities once a prototype has been created can produce positive results.[11]

Analysing and Interpreting Marketing Research Findings

One of the biggest challenges facing a marketing researcher is converting a complex set of data to a form that can be read and understood quickly by executives, managers and other employees who will make decisions from the research. Many of the people who use marketing research findings have not been trained in statistics and have neither the time nor the expertise to analyse computer printouts and other technical research information. The goal in this stage of the marketing research process is to communicate information clearly to the right people in a timely fashion. Among considerations are the following: who gets this information? Why do they need it? How will they use it? When users feel confident that they understand the data, they are far more likely to apply it appropriately. When managers do not understand how to interpret the data, or when they lack confidence in the research, the investment of time, skill and effort will be lost.

Depicting marketing research findings graphically is a powerful way to communicate research information. Here is a sample of graphic representations of the types of marketing research data we have discussed throughout this chapter.

Tracking of Performance, Gap Scores and Competition

A simple way of tracking performance is shown in Figure 6.1. Both expectations and perceptions are plotted, and the gap between them shows the service quality shortfall. Although any attribute or dimension of service can be tracked in this way, Figure 6.1 shows the scores for service reliability. Competitor service performance is another measurement of service quality that is tracked frequently. It allows managers to have a better grasp of service improvement priorities for their firm by comparing the firm's service strengths and weaknesses against those of key competitors.[12]

Zones of Tolerance Charts

When companies collect data on the dual expectation levels described in Chapter 4 – desired service and adequate service – and performance data, they can convey the information concisely on zones of tolerance charts. Figure 6.2 plots customer service quality perceptions relative to customers' zones of tolerance. Perceptions

Figure 6.1   Tracking of customer expectations and perceptions of service reliability

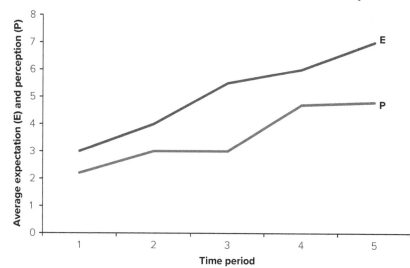

Source: Data from E. Sivadas, 'Europeans have a different take on CS [Customer Satisfaction] programs', *Marketing News*, 26 October 1998, p. 39.

of company performance are indicated by the circles, and the zones of tolerance boxes are bounded at the top by the desired service score and at the bottom by the adequate service score. When the perception scores are within the boxes or above, the company is delivering service that is above customers' minimum level of expectations. When the perception scores are below the boxes, the company's service performance is lower than the minimum level, and customers are dissatisfied with the company's service.[13]

Figure 6.2   Service quality perceptions relative to zones of tolerance by dimensions

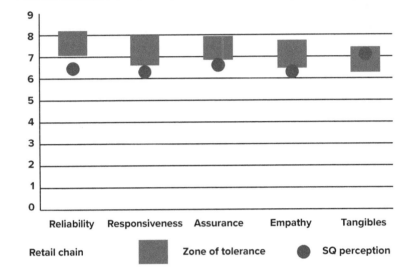

Importance/Performance Matrices

One of the most useful forms of analysis in marketing research is the importance/performance matrix. This chart combines information about customer perceptions and importance ratings. An example is shown in Figure 6.3. Attribute importance is represented on the vertical axis from high (top) to low (bottom). Performance is shown on the horizontal axis from low (left) to high (right). There are many variations of these matrices: some companies define the horizontal axis as the gap between expectations and perceptions, or as performance relative to competition. The shading on the chart indicates the area of highest leverage for service quality improvements – where importance is high and performance is low. In this quadrant are the attributes that most need to be improved. In the adjacent upper quadrant are attributes to be maintained, those that a company performs well and that are very important to customers. The lower two quadrants contain attributes that are less important, some of which are performed well and others poorly. Neither of these quadrants merit as much attention in terms of service improvements as the upper quadrants because customers are not as concerned about the attributes that are plotted in them as they are the attributes in the upper quadrants.

Figure 6.3   Importance/performance matrix

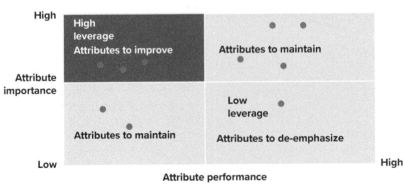

⭐ **SERVICE SPOTLIGHT**

The InterContinental Hotels Group (IHG), responsible for leading brands such as Holiday Inn, InterContinental and Crowne Plaza, is keen to identify customer needs for all of its branded offerings. There is a vast amount of data collected through market research, reservation data and sources such as TripAdvisor and social media channels. Up to date business-critical information is vital because the company operates in a hugely competitive sector. It is also important to make all this material available to decision makers across the group. IHG has therefore invested in KnowledgeNet, which is a machine-learning, knowledge-management platform used by 3,700 people across IHG with dashboards for everyone from the group CEO to local sales teams. This helps managers in setting priorities and better understanding customer attitudes and decision making across the hospitality sector.

Using Marketing Research Information

Conducting research about customer expectations is only the first part of understanding the customer, even if the research is appropriately designed, executed and presented. A service firm must also use the research findings in a meaningful way – to drive change or improvement in the way service is delivered. The misuse (or even non-use) of research data can lead to a large gap in understanding customer expectations. When managers are too busy dealing with the day-to-day challenges of the business to read research reports, companies fail to use the resources available to them. And when customers participate in marketing research studies but never see changes in the way the company does business, they feel frustrated and annoyed with the company. Understanding how to make the best use of research – to apply what has been learned to the business – is a key way to close the gap between customer expectations and management perceptions of customer expectations. Managers must learn to turn research information and insights into action, to recognize that the purpose of research is to drive improvement and customer satisfaction.

The research plan should specify the mechanism by which customer data will be used. The research should be actionable, timely, specific and credible. It can also have a mechanism that allows a company to respond immediately to dissatisfied customers.

Ethics in Marketing Research

Ethics in the undertaking of research is particularly important in marketing research, as the industry is dependent upon:[14]

- *Goodwill:* the goodwill of the individual respondents is their willingness to volunteer information on their awareness, attitudes and behaviours. Any practice that erodes that goodwill makes future marketing research studies more difficult to undertake.
- *Trust:* marketing decision makers trust researchers to provide accurate information that has been collected in a professional manner. Researchers also trust decision makers to divulge all information that may have an impact on the completion of a marketing research study.
- *Professionalism:* if respondents are to answer questionnaires in a serious and thoughtful manner, they have to feel that the research is going to be used in a professional manner.
- *Confidentiality:* respondents are more willing to express their views and opinions if they know that the information is going to be used in a confidential manner (in other words, taking part in marketing research will not result in the respondent becoming subject to follow-up sales calls).

The behaviour of marketing researchers is therefore controlled by the data protection laws enforced by the government of the country in which the research is being carried out and also by the relevant self-regulatory codes of conduct drawn up by the professional bodies, such as ESOMAR and the Market Research Society, that represent the marketing research industry. In Europe, the European Union (EU) has launched an updated legal framework for data protection entitled the General Data Protection Regulation (GDPR), which has applied since May 2018 with the aim of protecting all EU citizens from privacy and data breaches.

Upward Communication through Employees

In some service firms, especially small and localized firms, owners or managers may be in constant contact with customers, thereby gaining first-hand knowledge of customer expectations and perceptions. However, in large service organizations managers do not always get the opportunity to experience at first-hand what their customers want.

The larger a company is, the more difficult it will be for managers to interact directly with the customer, and the less first-hand information they will have about customer expectations. Even when they read and digest research reports, managers can lose touch with the reality of the customer if they never get the opportunity to experience the actual service. A theoretical view of how things are supposed to work cannot provide the richness of the service encounter. To truly understand customer needs, management benefits from hands-on knowledge of what really happens in stores, on customer service telephone lines, in service queues and in face-to-face service encounters.

Objectives for Upward Communication

Table 6.3 shows the major research objectives for improving upward communication in an organization. These objectives include gaining first-hand knowledge about customers, improving internal service quality, gaining first-hand knowledge of employees and obtaining ideas for service improvement. These objectives

Table 6.3   Elements in an effective programme of upward communication

Type of Interaction or Research	Research Objective	Qualitative/ Quantitative	Cost of Information		
			Money	Time	Frequency
Executive visits to customers	To gain first-hand knowledge about customers	Qualitative	Moderate	Moderate	Continuous
Executive listenings	To gain first-hand knowledge about customers	Qualitative	Low	Low	Continuous
Research on intermediate customers	To gain in-depth information on end customers	Quantitative	Moderate	Moderate	Annual
Employee internal satisfaction surveys	To improve internal service quality	Quantitative	Moderate	Moderate	Annual
Employee visits or listenings	To gain first-hand knowledge about employees	Qualitative	Moderate	Moderate	Continuous
Employee suggestions	To obtain ideas for service improvements	Qualitative	Low	Low	Continuous

can be met by two types of interactive activities in the organization: one designed to improve the type and effectiveness of communications from customers to management, and the other designed to improve communications between employees and management.

Research for Upward Communication

Executive Visits to Customers

This approach is frequently used in business-to-business services marketing. In some visits, executives of the company make sales or service calls with customer contact personnel (salespeople). In other situations, executives of the selling company arrange meetings with executives at a similar level in client companies.

Executive or Management Listening to Customers

Direct interaction with customers adds clarity and depth to managers' understanding of customer expectations and needs. Many companies require executives to perform entry-level jobs on a regular basis to promote understanding of their customers. A growing number of service companies, including Disney, Amazon and Sysco require that managers spend time in call centres, interacting with customers and experiencing service delivery. A formal programme for encouraging informal interaction is often the best way to ensure that the contact takes place.

⭐ **SERVICE SPOTLIGHT**

Asda, the major UK grocery chain which is part of the Walmart Group, runs a customer listening programme in which managers from head office and from individual stores accompany shoppers around their stores.

'It is tremendously powerful in getting your managers to think about the customer,' says Asda's head of market research. 'What better way to see the customer's perspective than to accompany them on a shopping trip?' The information collected helps in the redesign of store layouts, signage, shelving displays, lighting, shelf restocking policies and customer service practices.[15]

Given the growth in online communities and blogs where consumers post comments about products, services and organizations, it is important for an organization to monitor such communication. This will give another insight into how customers perceive an organization's offering. Travel sites, in particular, have consumer-generated reviews on hotels, airlines and visitor attractions which may influence the purchasing decisions of other customers. Self-publishing tools and enhanced/user-friendly communication technologies have made consumer-generated content increasingly popular. It is important that managers are aware of the content of such communications. Some organizations may establish their own blogging site, where they treat contributors as VIPs with exclusive previews and consultation on areas such as new products and plans and opportunities to air their views. Software providers such as Microsoft have been doing this for some time but now companies such as BT, Accenture, Tui, Benetton and, even, local and national governments are establishing communication channels of this type.

Research on Intermediate Customers

Intermediate customers (such as contact employees, dealers, distributors, agents and brokers) are people the company serves and who, in turn, serve the end-customer. Researching the needs and expectations of these customers *in serving the end-customer* can be a useful and efficient way to both improve service to, and obtain information about, end-users. The interaction with intermediate customers provides opportunities for understanding end-customers' expectations and problems. It can also help the company learn about the service expectations of intermediate customers and how to satisfy those, a process critical in their providing quality service to end-customers.

Research on Internal Customers

Employees who perform services are themselves customers of internal services on which they depend heavily to do their jobs well. There is a strong and direct link between the quality of internal service that employees receive and the quality of service they provide to their own customers. For this reason it is important to conduct employee research that focuses on the service that internal customers give and receive. In many companies this focus requires adapting existing employee opinion research to focus on service satisfaction. Employee research complements customer research when service quality is the issue being investigated. Customer research provides insight into what is occurring, whereas employee research provides insight into why. The two types of research play unique and equally important roles in improving service quality. Companies that focus service quality research exclusively on external customers are missing a rich and vital source of information.[16]

Executive or Management Listening Approaches to Employees

Employees who actually perform the service have the best possible vantage point for observing the service and identifying impediments to its quality. Customer contact personnel are in regular touch with customers and thereby come to understand a great deal about customer expectations and perceptions.[17] If the information they know can be passed on to top management, senior managers' understanding of the customer may improve. In fact, it could be said that in many companies, top management's understanding of the customer depends largely on the extent and types of communication received from customer contact personnel and from non-company contact personnel (such as independent insurance agents and retailers) who represent the company and its services. When these channels of communication are closed, management may not get feedback about problems encountered in service delivery and about how customer expectations are changing.

Upward communication provides information to upper-level managers about activities and levels of performance throughout the organization. Specific types of communication that may be relevant are formal (such as reports of problems and exceptions in service delivery) and informal (like discussions between contact personnel and upper-level managers). Managers who stay close to their contact people benefit not only by keeping their employees happy, but also by learning more about their customers.[18] These companies encourage, appreciate and reward upward communication from contact people. Through this important channel, management learns about customer expectations from employees in regular contact with customers and can thereby reduce the size of gap 1.

Employee Suggestions

Most companies have some form of employee suggestion programme, whereby contact personnel can communicate to management their ideas for improving work. Suggestion systems have come a long way from the traditional suggestion box. Effective suggestion systems are those in which employees are empowered to see their suggestions through and are active participants in continuous improvement for their jobs, where supervisors can respond quickly to ideas and implement proposals immediately, and where coaching is provided in ways to handle suggestions.[19] In today's companies, suggestions from employees are facilitated by self-directed work teams that encourage employees to identify problems and then work to develop solutions to those problems.

Summary

This chapter discussed the role of marketing research in understanding customer perceptions and expectations. It defined key forms of services research, including critical incidents studies, mystery shopping, service expectation meetings and reviews, process checkpoint evaluations and database research. Important topics in researching services – including developing research objectives and presenting data – were also described. Finally, upward communication, the ways in which management obtains and uses information from customers and customer contact personnel, was discussed. These topics combine to close gap 1 between customer expectations and company understanding of customer expectations, the first of four provider gaps in the gaps model of service quality.

Key Concepts

Big data	107	Netnography	109
Complaint solicitation	112	Panels	119
Critical incident technique	113	Post-transaction survey	117
Data analytics	108	Research objectives	110
Data mining	108	Research programme	109
Disconfirmation paradigm	116	SERVPERF	116
Ethnography	118	SERVQUAL	114
Lost customer research	120	Upward communication	124
Marketing research	106	User-generated content monitoring	108
Mystery shopping	118	Zones of tolerance charts	121

Exercises

1 Choose a local services organization to interview about its marketing research. Find out what the firm's objectives are and the types of marketing research it currently uses. Using the information in this chapter, think about the effectiveness of its marketing research. What are its strengths and weaknesses?

2 Choose one of the services you consume. If you were in charge of creating a survey for that service, what questions would you include? Give several examples. What type of survey (relationship versus transaction based) would be most appropriate for this service? What recommendations would you give to management of the company about making such a survey actionable?

3 If you were the marketing director of your college or university, what types of research (see Table 6.1) would be essential for understanding both external and internal customers? If you could choose only three types of research, which ones would you select? Why?

4 Using the SERVQUAL scale presented in this chapter (see Table 6.2), create a questionnaire for a service firm that you use. Give the questionnaire to ten people, and describe what you learn.

5 To get an idea of the power of the critical incidents technique, try it yourself with reference to restaurant service. Think of a time when, as a customer, you had a particularly satisfying interaction with a restaurant. Follow the instructions below (they are identical to the instructions in an actual study) and observe the insights you obtain about your requirements in restaurant service:

a When did the incident happen?

b What specific circumstances led up to this situation?

c Exactly what did the employee (or firm) say or do?

d What resulted that made you feel the interaction was satisfying?

e What could or should have been done differently?

Discussion Questions

1   Give five reasons why research objectives must be established before marketing research is conducted.

2   Why are both qualitative and quantitative research methods needed in a services marketing research programme?

3   Why does the frequency of research differ across the research methods shown in Table 6.1?

4   Compare and contrast the types of research that help a company identify common failure points. Which of the types do you think produces better information? Why?

5   Why would a company undertake a mystery shopping study when it could simply ask customers if they are satisfied?

6   What reasons can you give for companies' lack of use of research information? How might you motivate managers to use the information to a greater extent? How might you motivate front-line workers to use the information?

7   Given a specific marketing research budget, what would be your recommendations for the percentage to be spent on customer research versus upward communication? How would you justify it?

8   What kinds of information could be gleaned from research on intermediate customers? What would intermediate customers know that service providers might not?

9   For what types of products and services would monitoring user-generated content be preferable to traditional research?

10 What challenges exist when measuring comparisons between expectations and experiences?

Further Reading

Buttle, F. (1996). SERVQUAL: review, critique, research agenda. *European Journal of Marketing,* 30(1), 8–32.

Chintagunta, P., Hanssens, D.M. and Hauser, J.R. (2016). Marketing and data science: Together the future is ours. *GfK Marketing Intelligence Review,* 8(2), 18–23.

Costello, L., McDermott, M.L. and Wallace, R. (2017). Netnography: Range of practices, misperceptions, and missed opportunities. *International Journal of Qualitative Methods,* 16(1), 1–12.

Cronin, J. and Taylor, S.A. (1994). SERVPERF versus SERVQUAL: Reconciling performance-based and perceptions-minus-expectations measurement of service quality. *Journal of Marketing,* 58(1), 125–31.

Douglas, J. (2015). Mystery shoppers: An evaluation of their use in monitoring performance. *The TQM Journal,* 27(6), 705–715.

Erevelles, S., Fukawa, N. and Swayne, L. (2016). Big Data consumer analytics and the transformation of marketing. *Journal of Business Research,* 69(2), 897–904.

Kozinets, R.V. (2015). *Netnography: Redefined.* London: Sage.

Ladhari, R. (2010). Developing E-service quality scales: a literature review. *Journal of Retailing and Consumer Services,* 17(6), 464–77.

Parasuraman, A., Berry, L.L. and Zeithanl, V.A. (1991). Refinement and reassessment of the SERVQUAL scale. *Journal of Retailing,* 67(4), 420–50.

Poynter, R. (2014). *The Handbook of Online and Social Media Research: Tools and Techniques for Market Researchers.* London: Wiley.

Wilson, A. (2011). *Marketing Research: Delivering Customer Insight.* London: Red Global Press.

Wilson, A.M. (2001). Mystery shopping: Using deception to measure service performance. *Psychology & Marketing,* 18(7), 721–734.

Chapter 7

Building Customer Relationships

Chapter Outline

Relationship Marketing	131
Relationship Value of Customers	137
Customer Profitability Segments	140
Relationship Development Strategies	143
Relationship Challenges	149
Summary and Key Concepts	153
Exercises	153
Discussion Questions	154
Further Reading	154

Learning Objectives

This chapter's objectives are to:

1. Explain relationship marketing, its goals, and the benefits of long-term relationships for firms and customers.
2. Explain why and how to estimate customer relationship value.
3. Introduce the concept of customer profitability segments as a strategy for focusing relationship marketing efforts.
4. Present relationship development strategies – including quality core service, switching barriers and relationship bonds.
5. Identify challenges in relationship development, including the somewhat controversial idea that 'the customer is not always right'.

Opening Example
The Starbucks App

Starbucks attempts to build digital relationships with its customers through the Starbucks app and the Starbucks Rewards programme. The app aims to provides a user friendly mobile experience.

Using the geo-location feature, a user can see where the closest Starbucks location is, the menu at each location, and even place an order that can be ready upon the customer's arrival. The app also allows for personalization, maintaining details of the customer's favourite order and suggesting what food items might pair well with that order. Also, the app provides Starbucks Rewards programme members

Source: ©JARIRIYAWAT/Shutterstock

with a free beverage on their birthday and 'challenges' that can earn them rewards points toward free food and drinks.

The rewards programme gives a number of benefits for app users. In addition to earning points for purchases, rewards members can receive free in-store refills, special member offers/events, and the ability to pay by phone and order ahead.

Starbucks' mobile app makes online ordering and paying easy, with dedicated stations for mobile order-ahead customers, distinct from existing in-store registers, and giving baristas new tablets.

The mobile ordering system acts as a digital marketing tool, allowing customers to see new items ahead of time. In-store payments are also encouraged through the app, which utilizes a Starbucks gift card to process the payments with the mobile app or Apple watch being scanned at the till to process the payment.

Starbucks has also integrated its app with Spotify, the online music streaming service. The Starbucks app allows users to identify songs being played in stores, then download and save those they like to a playlist on Spotify's app.

Loyalty programmes can be very valuable in building a customer base, but once launched they can be very difficult to change or withdraw. For Starbucks, providing all of these benefits resulted in increased loyalty; however, there was a major outcry from programme members when they made changes to the reward scheme. In early 2019, Starbucks rolled out its new rewards programme, changing the number of points customers had to earn to receive free food and beverages. Some customers were concerned about losing stars, others were worried about stars being devalued. A large outpouring of negative comments appeared on Twitter and Facebook. The new format did not necessarily change the scale of the rewards but most of the complaints came from customer confusion with the new system. With any loyalty programme, tweaking the rewards and benefits can be a challenging task.

Source: Information from www.starbucks.com and www.businessinsider.com/starbucks-rewards-program-changes-explained-2019-4?r=US&IR=T.

Starbucks provides a strong example of a company that has focused on keeping its customers and building long-term relationships with them. Unlike Starbucks, however, many companies do not have an accurate understanding of their customers because they fail to focus on customer relationships. They tend to fixate on acquiring new customers rather than viewing existing customers as assets that they need to nurture and retain. By concentrating on customer acquisition, firms can easily fall into the traps of short-term promotions, price discounts or catchy advertisements that bring customers in but are not enough to bring them back. By adopting a relationship philosophy, on the other hand, companies develop in-depth understanding of their customers and are better able to meet their changing needs and expectations.

Marketing strategies for understanding customers over time and building long-term relationships are the subjects of this chapter.

Relationship Marketing

Over the past few decades firms have shifted from a transaction focus to a relationship focus in their marketing efforts. Customers have become partners and co-creators as firms have attempted to maintain relationships through the provision of higher quality service and long-term customer benefits.

Relationship marketing essentially represents a paradigm shift within marketing – away from an acquisitions/transaction focus toward a retention/relationship focus. Relationship marketing (or relationship management) is a philosophy of doing business, a strategic orientation, that focuses on *keeping and improving* relationships with current customers rather than on acquiring new customers. This philosophy assumes that many consumers and business customers prefer to have an ongoing relationship with one organization than to switch continually among providers in their search for value. Building on this assumption, and the fact that it is usually much cheaper to keep a current customer than to attract a new one, successful marketers work on effective strategies for retaining customers. Our opening example showed how Starbucks has built its business around a relationship philosophy.

It has been suggested that firms frequently focus on attracting customers (the 'first act') but then pay little attention to what they should do to keep them (the 'second act').[1] Ideas expressed in an interview with James L. Schorr, then executive vice president of marketing at Holiday Inns, illustrate this point.[2] Schorr stated that he was famous at Holiday Inns for what is called the 'bucket theory of marketing'. By this he meant that marketing can be thought of as a big bucket: it is what the sales, advertising and promotion programmes do that pours business into the top of the bucket. As long as these programmes are effective, the bucket stays full. However, 'There's only one problem,' he said, 'there's a hole in the bucket.' When the business is running well and the hotel is delivering on its promises, the hole is small and few customers are leaving. When the operation is weak and customers are not satisfied with what they get, however, they start falling out through the holes in the bucket faster than they can be replaced by new customers.

The bucket theory (see Figure 7.1) illustrates why a relationship approach that focuses on plugging the holes in the bucket makes so much sense. Historically, marketers have been more concerned with acquisition of customers, so a shift to a relationship approach often represents changes in mindset, organizational culture and employee reward systems. For example, the sales incentive systems in many organizations are set up to reward bringing in new customers. Often, there are fewer (or no) rewards for retaining current accounts. Thus, even when people see the logic of customer retention, the existing organizational systems may not support its implementation.

Figure 7.1 **There is a hole in the bucket: why relationship development makes sense**

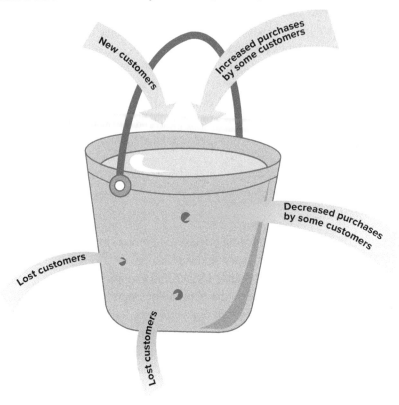

The Evolution of Customer Relationships

Firms' relationships with their customers, like other social relationships, tend to evolve over time. Scholars have suggested that marketing exchange relationships between providers and customers often have the potential to evolve from strangers to acquaintances to friends to partners.[3]

Customers as Strangers

Strangers are those customers who are not aware of, or those who have not yet had any transactions (interactions) with, a firm. At the industry level, strangers may be thought of as customers who have not yet entered the market; at the firm level, they may include customers of competitors. Clearly the firm has no relationship with them at this point. Consequently, the firm's primary goal with these strangers (potential customers) is to initiate communication with them in order to *attract* and *acquire* their business. Thus, the primary marketing efforts directed towards such customers deal with familiarizing them with the firm's offerings and, subsequently, encouraging them to give the firm a try.

Customers as Acquaintances

Once customer awareness and trial are achieved, familiarity is established and the customer and the firm become acquaintances, creating the basis for an exchange relationship. A primary goal for the firm at this stage of the relationship is *satisfying* the customer. In the acquaintance stage, firms are generally concerned about providing a value proposition to customers that is comparable with that of competitors. For a customer, an acquaintanceship is effective as long as the customer is relatively satisfied and what is being received in the exchange is perceived as fair value. With repeat interactions, the customer becomes more familiar with the firm's product offerings. These encounters can help reduce uncertainty about the benefits expected in the exchange and, therefore, increase the attractiveness of the company relative to the competition.

Repeat interactions improve the firm's knowledge of the customer, helping to facilitate marketing, sales and service efforts. Thus, an acquaintance relationship facilitates transactions primarily through the reduction of the customer's perceived risk and the provider's costs.

In acquaintance relationships, firms generally focus on providing value comparable to the competition, often through the repetitive provision of standardized offerings. As a result, the potential to develop a sustainable competitive advantage through relationship activities is limited. However, firms that already have acquaintance relationships with their customers can create value for them by learning from all their transactions. For example, Amazon has created value for its acquaintances through a highly developed order-processing system. By processing and organizing historical transaction data from a customer and comparing it with data from other customers demonstrating similar purchase behaviours, the system is able to identify additional products of potential interest to the acquaintance customer and to generate cross-selling opportunities.

Customers as Friends

As a customer continues to make purchases from a firm and to receive value in the exchange relationship, the firm begins to acquire specific knowledge of that customer's needs, allowing it to create an offering that directly addresses the customer's situation. The provision of a unique offering (a differential value) transforms the exchange relationship from acquaintance to friendship. This transition requires the development of trust, particularly in service exchange relationships.[4] As discussed in Chapter 3, customers may not be able to assess a service outcome prior to purchase and consumption, and in the case of services high in credence qualities, customers may not be able to discern service performance even after experiencing it. Therefore, customers must trust the provider to deliver what is promised. As customers become friends, they not only become familiar with the company but they also come to trust that it provides superior value.

A primary goal for firms at the friendship stage of the relationship is customer *retention*. Given their likelihood of past satisfying experiences and repeated purchases, these customers ('friends') are more likely to appreciate the firm's product offerings and are, perhaps, more open to other related services. A firm's potential to develop sustainable competitive advantage through friends should be higher than for acquaintances, because the offering is more unique (and more difficult for competition to imitate) and the customer comes to trust that uniqueness.[5]

Customers as Partners

As a customer continues to interact with a firm, the level of trust often deepens and the customer may receive more customized product offerings and interactions. The trust developed in the friendship stage is a necessary but not sufficient condition for a customer–firm partnership to develop.[6] That is, the creation of trust leads to (ideally) the creation of commitment – and that is the condition necessary for customers to extend the time perspective of a relationship.[7] The deepening of trust and the establishment of commitment reduce the customer's need to solve problems in the traditional sense of 'finding a better alternative'. Thus, in order to move the relationship into a partner relationship, a firm must use customer knowledge and information systems to deliver highly personalized and customized offerings.

The key to success in the partnership stage is the firm's ability to organize and use information about individual customers more effectively than competitors. Customers benefit from, and therefore desire to commit to, relationships with firms whose knowledge of their needs translates into the delivery of highly personalized and customized offerings.[8] Over time, the customer–firm relationship may evolve through continuous adaptation and commitment, and the parties may become increasingly interdependent. At this point the relationship has advanced from having the purpose of merely meeting the customer's needs to a situation in which both parties sense a deep appreciation of each other. However, in order to continue to receive such benefits, customers generally must be willing to pay a price premium or to commit themselves to the firm for an extended period of time.

> ⭐ **SERVICE SPOTLIGHT**
>
> The American Express Centurion Card is an example of an exclusive and expensive partnership, Nicknamed the 'Black Card' because of its distinctive colour, obtained from the anodized titanium used to make it, The Amex Centurion is unlike most credit cards, for which anyone can apply. To get a Centurion card, you must be invited. Centurion cardholders earn Membership Rewards points, and enjoy exclusive benefits, including concierge-style perks like guaranteed tables at three-star restaurants, priority bookings at luxury hotels, invitations to private cultural events, personal shoppers at major retailers, access to private jets and the unique status of having a metal card.
>
> The concierge service is able to arrange just about any service or perk for Amex Centurion cardholders. The Amex Centurion, available for personal or business accounts, is a charge card with no interest rate, no pre-set spending limit, and no foreign transaction fees. It requires a one-time initiation fee of around 4,000 euros and a 2,000 euro annual fee. In order to maintain Centurion membership, a cardholder is expected to make and pay off around 200,000 euros-worth of purchases a year.

At the partnership stage, the firm is concerned with *enhancing* the relationship. Customers are more likely to stay in the relationship if they feel that the company understands their changing needs and is willing to invest in the relationship by constantly improving and evolving its product and service mix. By enhancing these relationships, the firm expects that customers will be less likely to be lured away by competitors and more likely to buy additional products and services from the company over time. These loyal customers not only provide a solid base for the organization, they may represent growth potential. For example, a bank current account customer becomes a better customer when he or she sets up a savings account, takes out a loan and/or uses the financial advisory services of the bank; likewise, a corporate account becomes a better customer when it chooses to do 75 per cent of its business with a particular supplier rather than splitting the business equally among three suppliers. In recent years, in fact, many companies have aspired to be the 'exclusive supplier' of a particular product or service for their customers. Over time these enhanced relationships can increase market share and profits for the organization.

However, it is important to note that not all customers may be interested in forming relationships with their suppliers or service providers. Depending on the product or service, the level of interest from some customers may vary from a situation where some only want to transact the business, and others want the service provider to have ongoing knowledge of their changing requirements. Grönroos divided customer expectations into three types:[9]

1 *Transactional expectations* – where the customer is looking for solutions to their needs at an acceptable price, and they do not appreciate contacts from the supplier or service provider in between purchases.
2 *Active relational expectations* – where the customer is looking for opportunities to interact with the supplier or service provider in order to get additional value. A lack of contact leaves them disappointed because the value inherent in the relationship is missing.
3 *Passive relational expectations* – where customers are looking for the knowledge that they could contact the service provider if they wanted to. In this sense, they are also seeking contact, but they seldom respond to invitations to interact.

It is important for a service provider to be aware of the relationship expectations of their customers if the most appropriate relationship management strategy is to be adopted.

The Goal of Relationship Marketing

The discussion of the evolution of customer relationships demonstrates how a firm's relationship with its customers might be enhanced as customers move further along this relationship continuum. As the relationship value of a customer increases, the provider is more likely to pursue a closer relationship. Thus, the primary goal of relationship marketing is *to build and maintain a base of committed customers who are profitable for the organization.* From a customer's problem-solving perspective, the formation of satisfaction, trust and commitment corresponds to the customer's willingness to engage in an exchange relationship as an acquaintance, friend and partner, respectively. From a firm's resource-allocation perspective, the delivery of differential, and perhaps customized, value corresponds to the extent of its ability and/or desire to create an acquaintance, friend or partner relationship with the customer. As customers make the transition from satisfaction-based acquaintanceships to trust-based friendships to commitment-based partnerships, increases are required in both the value received and the level of cooperation.

Benefits for Customers and Firms

Both parties in the customer–firm relationship can benefit from customer retention. That is, it is not only in the best interest of the organization to build and maintain a loyal customer base, but customers themselves also benefit from long-term associations.

Benefits for Customers

Assuming they have a choice, customers will remain loyal to a firm when they receive greater value relative to what they expect from competing firms. *Value* represents a trade-off for the consumer between the 'give' and the 'get' components. Consumers are more likely to stay in a relationship when the gets (quality, satisfaction, specific benefits) exceed the gives (monetary and non-monetary costs). When firms can consistently deliver value from the customer's point of view, clearly the customer benefits and has an incentive to stay in the relationship.

Beyond the specific inherent benefits of receiving service value, customers also benefit in other ways from long-term associations with firms. Sometimes these relationship benefits keep customers loyal to a firm more than the attributes of the core service. Research has uncovered specific types of relational benefits that customers experience in long-term service relationships, including confidence benefits, social benefits and special treatment benefits.[10]

Confidence Benefits

Confidence benefits comprise feelings of trust or confidence in the provider, along with a sense of reduced anxiety and comfort in knowing what to expect. Across all the services studied in the research just cited, confidence benefits were the most important to customers.

Human nature is such that most consumers would prefer not to change service providers, particularly when they are considerably invested in the relationship. The costs of switching are frequently high in terms of the monetary costs of transferring business and the associated psychological and time-related costs. Most consumers (whether individuals or businesses) face many competing demands on their time and money, and are continually searching for ways to balance and simplify decision-making to improve the quality of their lives. When they can maintain a relationship with a service provider, it frees up time for other concerns and priorities.

Social Benefits

Over time, customers develop a sense of familiarity and, even, a social relationship with their service providers. These ties make it less likely that they will switch, even if they learn about a competitor that might have better quality or a lower price. This customer's description of her hair stylist illustrates the concept of social benefits: 'I like him . . . He's really funny and always has lots of good jokes. He's kind of like a friend now . . . It's more fun to deal with somebody that you're used to. You enjoy doing business with them.'

In some long-term customer–firm relationships, a service provider may actually become part of the consumer's social support system.[11] Hairdressers, as in the example just cited, often serve as personal confidants.

Less common examples include proprietors of local retail stores who become central figures in local communities; the health club or restaurant manager who knows his or her customers personally; the pharmacist who knows an entire family and its special needs; or the tour guide who befriends passengers on a long coach tour.[12]

These types of personal relationships can develop for business-to-business customers as well as for end consumers of services. The social support benefits resulting from these relationships are important to the consumer's quality of life (personal and/or work life) above and beyond the technical benefits of the service provided. Many times the close personal and professional relationships that develop between service providers and clients are the basis for the customer's loyalty. The flip side of this customer benefit is the risk to the firm of losing customers when a valued employee leaves and takes customers with him or her.[13]

Special Treatment Benefits

Special treatment includes getting the benefit of the doubt, being given a special deal or price, or getting preferential treatment, as exemplified by the following quote from the research:[14]

> *You should get the benefit of the doubt in many situations. For example, I always pay my VISA bill on time, before a service charge is assessed. One time my payment didn't quite arrive on time. When I called them, by looking at my past history, they realized that I always make an early payment. Therefore, they waived the service charge.*

Interestingly, the research showed that special treatment benefits, while important, were deemed less important than the other types of benefits received in service relationships. Although special treatment benefits can clearly be critical for customer loyalty in some industries (think of frequent-flyer benefits in the airline industry), they seem to be less important to customers overall.

Benefits for Firms

The benefits to organizations of maintaining and developing a loyal customer base are numerous. In addition to the economic benefits that a firm receives from cultivating close relationships with its customers, a variety of customer behaviour benefits and human resource management benefits are also often received.

Economic Benefits

One of the most commonly cited economic benefits of customer retention is increased purchases over time. As customers get to know a firm, and are satisfied with the quality of its services relative to that of its competitors, they tend to give more of their business to the firm.

Another economic benefit is lower costs. Some estimates suggest that repeat purchases by established customers require as much as 90 per cent less marketing expenditure.[15] Many start-up costs are associated with attracting new customers, including advertising and other promotion costs, the operating costs of setting up new accounts and time costs of getting to know the customers. Sometimes these initial costs can outweigh the revenue expected from the new customers in the short term, so it is to the firm's advantage to cultivate long-term relationships. Even ongoing relationship maintenance costs are likely to drop over time. For example, early in a relationship a customer is likely to have questions and encounter problems as he or she learns to use the service; an experienced customer will likely have fewer problems and questions, and the firm will incur fewer costs in serving the latter. In Chapter 18 we provide more specifics on the financial impact of customer retention.

Customer Behaviour Benefits

The contribution that loyal customers make to a service business can go well beyond their direct financial impact on the firm.[16] The first, and maybe the most easily recognized, customer behaviour benefit that a firm receives from long-term customers is the free advertising provided through word-of-mouth communication.

When a complex product is difficult to evaluate and – as is the case with many services – when risk is involved in the decision to buy it, consumers often look to others for advice on which providers to consider. Satisfied, loyal customers are likely to provide strong word-of-mouth endorsements. Such endorsements may also take the form of online reviews or blogs. This form of communication can be more effective than any paid advertising that the firm might use, and it has the added benefit of reducing the costs of attracting new customers. Indeed, loyal customers often talk a great deal about a company and may be responsible for generating much new business over the years.

In addition to word-of-mouth communication, a second consumer behaviour benefit is one that is sometimes labelled customer voluntary performance.[17] In a restaurant, such behaviour might include customers clearing their own tables, reporting messy washrooms to an employee or picking up litter in the car park. Such behaviours support the firm's ability to deliver quality services. Although customer voluntary performance could be engaged in by anyone, those customers who have a long-term relationship with the firm are perhaps more likely to do so because they may want to see the provider do well. Third, for some services loyal customers may provide social benefits to other customers in the form of friendships or encouragement. At a health club, for example, a new member is likely to think more highly of the club when fellow members provide encouragement and guidance during fitness sessions and classes. Finally, loyal customers may serve as mentors and, because of their experience with the provider, help other customers understand the explicitly or implicitly stated rules of conduct.[18]

Human Resource Management Benefits

Loyal customers may also provide a firm with human resource management benefits. First, loyal customers may, because of their experience with and knowledge of the provider, be able to contribute to the co-production of the service by assisting in service delivery; often the more experienced customers can make the service employees' job easier. For example, a regular patient of a medical clinic is likely to know how the system works; she would know to bring her medication with her on a visit, and to schedule an annual mammogram without waiting for her doctor to prompt her. A second benefit relates to one of the benefits for customers that we have already discussed. We noted that loyal customers receive social benefits as a result of being in a relationship with a firm; employees who regularly interact with the same customers may also receive similar social benefits.[19] A third benefit of customer retention is employee retention. It is easier for a firm to retain employees when it has a stable base of satisfied customers. People like to work for companies whose customers are happy and loyal. Their jobs are more satisfying, and they are able to spend more of their time fostering relationships than scrambling for new customers. In turn, customers are more satisfied and become even better customers – a positive upward spiral. When employees stay with the firm longer, service quality improves and costs of turnover are reduced, adding further to profits.

Relationship Value of Customers

Relationship value of a customer is a concept or calculation that looks at customers from the point of view of their lifetime revenue and/or profitability contributions to a company. This type of calculation is obviously needed when companies start thinking of building long-term relationships with their customers. Just what is the potential financial value of those long-term relationships? And what are the financial implications of *losing* a customer? Here we will first summarize the factors that influence a customer's relationship value, and then show some ways it can be estimated. In Chapter 18 we provide more detail on lifetime value financial calculations.

Factors that Influence Relationship Value

The lifetime or relationship value of a customer is influenced by the length of an average 'lifetime', the average revenues generated per relevant time period over that lifetime, sales of additional products and services over time, referrals generated by the customer over time, and costs associated with serving the customer. *Lifetime value* sometimes refers to lifetime revenue stream only, but when costs are considered, lifetime value truly means 'lifetime profitability'.

Estimating Customer Lifetime Value

If companies knew how much it really costs to lose a customer, they would be able accurately to evaluate investments designed to retain customers. One way of documenting the value of loyal customers is to estimate the increased value or profits that accrue for each additional customer who remains loyal to the company rather than defecting to the competition. Past research has found that when the retention or loyalty rate rises by 5 percentage points the total firm profits can increase from 35 per cent to 95 per cent.[20]

With sophisticated accounting systems to document actual costs and revenue streams over time, a firm can be quite precise in documenting the value and costs of retaining customers. These systems attempt to estimate the value of *all* the benefits and costs associated with a loyal customer, not just the long-term revenue stream. The value of word-of-mouth advertising, employee retention and declining account maintenance costs can also enter into the calculation.[21]

Table 7.1 sets out an example of customer lifetime value calculation. The example assumes that the initial cost of acquiring the customer in terms of sales effort and set-up costs is 200 euros and this is incurred in Year 0 before any revenue is generated. The retention rate is assumed to be 75 per cent each year, so the number of customers that were acquired in year 1 reduces by 25 per cent each year. The discount rate of 10 per cent adjusts any revenue, costs and profit to the present-day value (taking account of inflation). So revenue and costs increase by 10 per cent each year and the relative value of the profit from a year 0 viewpoint reduces by 10 per cent each year. The running total on the bottom of the table shows the cumulative customer lifetime value over time. Based on five years of revenue and costs, the end customer lifetime value calculation works out to be 349 euros after five years. If the retention rate were increased by 5 per cent to 80 per cent each year, the end customer lifetime value would rise to 413 euros after five years. In other words, this example shows that a 5 per cent increase in retention can lead to an 18 per cent increase in profits over five years. This multiplier effect is part of the reason that many companies are focusing a large part of their activities on customer retention.

Table 7.1   Example customer lifetime value calculation

	Year 0	Year 1	Year 2	Year 3	Year 4	Year 5
Initial acquisition cost per customer	200					
Average customer revenue (of customers who are retained)		400	440	480	520	560
Average customer cost		200	220	240	260	280
Average profit contribution		200	220	240	260	280
% of customers retained each year at a 75% retention rate		100%	75%	56%	42%	32%
Average profit contribution of retained customers only		**200**	**165**	**134**	**109**	**87**
Discount rate applied each year at 10% discount rate	1.00	1.10	1.21	1.33	1.46	1.61
Discounted average profit contribution per retained customer		190	136	101	75	47
Running total of average profit contribution	**−200**	**−10**	**126**	**227**	**302**	**349**

Linking Customer Relationship Value to Firm Value

The emphasis on estimating the relationship value of customers has increased substantially in the past decade. Part of this emphasis has resulted from an increased appreciation of the economic benefits that companies accrue with the retention of loyal customers. Interestingly, previous research suggests that customer retention has a large impact on company value and that relationship value calculations can also provide a useful proxy for assessing the value of a firm.[22] That is, a company's market value can be roughly determined by carefully calculating customer lifetime value. The approach is straightforward: estimate the relationship value of a customer, forecast the future growth of the number of customers and use these figures to determine the value of a company's current and future base. To the extent that the customer base forms a large part of a company's overall value, such a calculation can provide an estimate of a company's value – a particularly useful figure for young, high-growth companies for which traditional financial methods (e.g. discounted cash flow) do not work well.

Relationship Value from the Service Dominant Logic Perspective

In goods dominated logic, value is intrinsic to goods; it is created by the organization and distributed to those who consume it. In service dominant logic, the organization cannot create value on its own but can only offer value propositions through the use of its resources and then collaboratively create value with the customer. In commercial services, the organization provides inputs for the customer's value-creating activities and the customer does the same for the organization. The customer provides a supply of money but may also:

- help in promoting the service brand
- offer new ideas and feedback for the service
- or contribute to the atmosphere for other customers (e.g. in a nightclub or football stadium).

The value created may develop over time: the restaurant meal may spark interest in a new cuisine, leading to the customer attending cooking classes and making menu suggestions when they next visit the restaurant, and finally resulting in their tweeting favourably about the restaurant. This co-creational nature of value is relational in the sense that the extended activities of both parties (as well as those of other parties: the cooking school) interactively and interdependently combine, over time, to create value.[23] It is through these joint, collaborative and reciprocal roles in value co-creation that service dominant logic conceptualizes relationships. Organizations may be seeking to obtain the direct goal of repeat or long-term business from a customer, but there may be value from other types of relationship that do not result in repeat business. The service dominant logic concept of relationship is of the importance of a service oriented and customer oriented view that results in a much broader value creation perspective.

This broader view not only reflects the type of value obtained but also the range of actors involved in the co-creation of value. Customers and organizations operate in markets that are often complex with networks of suppliers, intermediaries, advisers, friends and families. If a restaurant patron only visits a restaurant once, they may influence other restaurant patrons sitting at adjoining tables and their experience may be communicated to friends or reported on review sites. The value created for the customer on that single visit is impacted upon by the supplier of the meal ingredients to the restaurant, the staff recruitment agency, the interior designer, the credit card processing company and many others. Therefore relationships are not limited to a dyad between the restaurant and the customer but are instead nested within dynamic networks of relationships which achieve mutual benefit for all parties through service provision. As such, the relationship with the one-time customer or occasional purchaser is often as important as the relationships with long-term providers and long-term customers.

Customer Profitability Segments

Companies may want to treat all customers with excellent service, but they generally find that customers differ in their relationship value and that it may be neither practical nor profitable to meet (and certainly not to exceed) *all* customers' expectations.[24]

Traditional segmentation approaches using demographics or lifestyles are showing their limitations as individual behaviour becomes more hybridized, as in the case of an individual being ready to spend large amounts on certain services whilst at the same time being very frugal on other services. An example of this would be spending thousands of euros in a destination at a luxury hotel or spa but flying easyJet to travel to the destination and eating Subway sandwiches at the hotel. For the marketer, it may be that they are addressing one consumer, but two segments, exhibiting opposite characteristics. The individual may be price-conscious and frugal in the morning but indulgent and free-spending in the afternoon. Understanding and tracking behaviour becomes very important, as is the need to look after loyal and valuable customers.

> **⭐ SERVICE SPOTLIGHT**
>
> Virgin Airlines' Flying Club rewards customers according to their value to the airline. It inducts members at the Red tier, then moves them up through Silver and Gold. Red tier members earn frequent flyer miles and get discounts on rental cars and hotels. Silver tier members earn 30 per cent more points on flights, expedited check-in, and anytime seat choice. Gold tier members get 60 per cent more points on flights, priority boarding, and access to exclusive clubhouses where they can grab a drink or get a massage before their flight. It is important to offer a benefit scheme; Red tier benefits aim to hook the customer into coming back. Once they do, they realize that making it to the next tier, 'silver' or 'gold' isn't unattainable, and they may keep flying with Virgin.

As the Starbucks example at the start of this chapter illustrates, companies do try to identify segments – or, more appropriately, tiers of customers – that differ in current and/or future profitability to a firm. This approach goes beyond usage or volume segmentation because it tracks costs and revenues for segments of customers, thereby capturing their financial worth to companies. The hotel guest who eats and drinks on the premises is more valuable than the guest who rents a room but goes outside the hotel to eat and drink. After identifying profitability bands, the firm offers services and service levels in line with the identified segments. Building a high-loyalty customer base of the right customers increases profits.

Profitability Tiers – The Customer Pyramid

Virtually all firms are aware at some level that their customers differ in profitability, and in particular, that a minority of their customers account for the highest proportion of sales or profit. This finding has often been called the '80/20 rule' – 20 per cent of customers produce 80 per cent of sales or profit.

In this version of tiering, 20 per cent of the customers constitute the top tier, those who can be identified as the most profitable in the company. The rest are indistinguishable from each other but differ from the top tier in profitability. Most companies realize that there are differences among customers within this tier but do not possess the data or capabilities to analyse the distinctions. The 80/20 two-tier scheme assumes that consumers within the two tiers are similar, just as conventional market segmentation schemes typically assume that consumers within segments are similar.

However, it is likely that more than two tiers exist, and provided a company has sufficient data to segment customer tiers more precisely, they can be analysed. Different systems and labels can be helpful. One useful four-tier system, shown in Figure 7.2, includes the following:

Figure 7.2   The customer pyramid

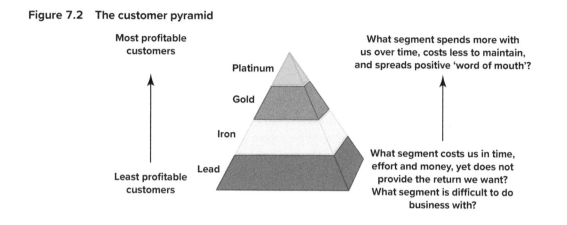

1 The *platinum tier* describes the company's most profitable customers, typically those who are heavy users of the product, are not overly price sensitive, are willing to invest in and try new offerings, and are committed customers of the firm.

2 The *gold tier* differs from the platinum tier in that profitability levels are not as high, perhaps because the customers want price discounts that limit margins or they are not as loyal. They may be heavy users who minimize risk by working with multiple vendors rather than just the focal company.

3 The *iron tier* contains essential customers who provide the volume needed to utilize the firm's capacity, but their spending levels, loyalty and profitability are not substantial enough for special treatment.

4 The *lead tier* consists of customers who are costing the company money. They demand more attention than they are due given their spending and profitability, and are sometimes problem customers – complaining about the firm to others and tying up the firm's resources.

Note that this classification is superficially reminiscent of, but very different from, traditional usage segmentation performed by airlines such as Virgin. Two differences are obvious. First, in the customer pyramid profitability rather than usage defines all levels. Second, the lower levels actually articulate classes of customers who require a different sort of attention. The firm must work either to change the customers' behaviour – to make them more profitable through increases in revenue – or to change the firm's cost structure to make them more profitable through decreases in costs.

Once a system has been established for categorizing customers, the multiple levels can be identified, motivated, served and expected to deliver differential levels of profit. Companies improve their opportunities for profit when they increase shares of purchases by customers who either have the greatest need for the services or show the greatest loyalty to a single provider. By strengthening relationships with the loyal customers, increasing sales with existing customers and increasing the profitability on each sale opportunity, companies increase the potential of each customer.

The Customer's View of Profitability Tiers

Whereas profitability tiers make sense from the company's point of view, customers are not always understanding, nor do they appreciate being categorized into a less desirable segment.[25] For example, at some companies the top clients have their own individual account representative whom they can contact personally. The next tier of clients may be handled by representatives who each have 100 clients. Meanwhile, most clients are served by a call centre, an automated voice response system or referral to a website. Customers are aware of this unequal treatment, and many resist and resent it. It makes perfect sense from a business perspective, but customers are often disappointed in the level of service they receive and give firms poor marks for quality as a result.

Therefore, it is increasingly important that firms communicate with customers so they understand what level of service they can expect and what they would need to do or pay to receive faster or more personalized service. The most significant issues result when customers do not understand this and believe they have been singled out for poor service, or feel that the system is unfair. Although many customers refuse to pay for quality service, they react negatively if they believe it has been taken away from them unfairly.

The ability to segment customers narrowly, based on profitability implications, also raises questions of privacy for customers. In order to know who is profitable and who is not, companies must collect large amounts of individualized behavioural and personal data on consumers. Many consumers today resent what they perceive as an intrusion into their lives in this way, especially when it results in differential treatment that they perceive is unfair.

Making Business Decisions Using Profitability Tiers

Prudent business managers are well aware that past customer purchasing behaviour, although useful in making predictions, can be misleading.[26] What a customer spends today, or has spent in the past, may not necessarily reflect what he or she will do (or be worth) in the future. Banks serving students know this well – a typical student generally has minimal financial services needs (i.e. a current account) and tends not to have a high level of deposits. However, within a few years that student may embark on a professional career, start a family and/or purchase a house, and thus require several financial services and become a potentially very profitable customer. Generally, a firm would like to keep its consistent big spenders and lose the erratic small spenders. But all too often a firm also has two other groups they must consider: erratic big spenders and consistent small spenders. So, in some situations where consistent cash flow is a concern, it may be helpful to a firm to have a portfolio of customers that includes steady customers, even if they have a history of being less profitable. Some service providers have actually been quite successful in targeting customers who were previously considered to be unworthy of another firm's marketing efforts.[27] Firms, therefore, need to be cautious in blindly applying customer value calculations without thinking carefully about the implications.

★ SERVICE SPOTLIGHT

Triodos Bank was founded in the Netherlands in 1980 and has branches in the Netherlands, Belgium, Spain, the United Kingdom and Germany. Its mission is to make money for positive social, environmental and cultural change, and in particular:

- to help create a society that promotes people's quality of life and that has human dignity at its core
- to enable individuals, institutions and businesses to use money more consciously in ways that benefit people and the environment, and promote sustainable development
- to offer customers sustainable financial products and high-quality service.

It targets individuals and organizations that are poorly served by traditional banks. For example, it provides tailored services to charities, social enterprise and values-based businesses providing vital support for disadvantaged people. Although charities may not provide the profitable returns that other banks seek, Triodos attracts charity clients by promoting the following message: 'We care about your aims as a charity. We believe banking can be a catalyst for making greater social and environmental impact by putting money to work for good. That's why we're interested in how your organisation is working for positive change, and we want to help you change the world for the better.'

Source: https://www.triodos.com/about-us; https://www.triodos.co.uk/charity.

Relationship Development Strategies

To this point in the chapter we have focused on the rationale for relationship marketing, the benefits (to both firms and customers) of the development of strong exchange relationships, and an understanding of the relationship value of a customer. In this section we examine a variety of factors that influence the development of strong customer relationships, including the customer's overall evaluation of a firm's offering, bonds created with customers by the firm, and barriers that the customer faces in leaving a relationship. These factors, illustrated in Figure 7.3, provide the rationale for specific strategies that firms often use to keep their current customers.

Figure 7.3   Relationship development model

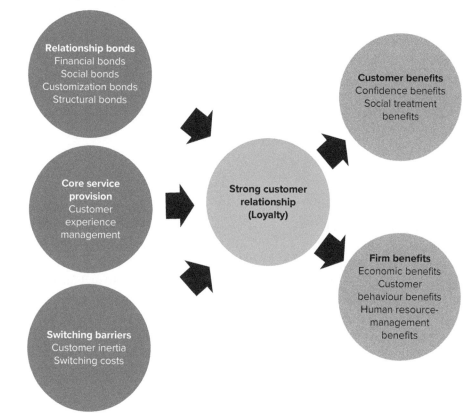

Source: Created using information from D.D. Gremler and S.W. Brown, 'Service loyalty: antecedents, components, and outcomes', in *1998 AMA Winter Educators' Conference: Marketing Theory and Applications,* vol. 9, D. Grewal and C. Pechmann, eds. Chicago, IL: American Marketing Association, pp. 165–6.

Core Service Provision

Customer Experience Management

Clearly, a firm needs to begin the relationship development process by providing a good core service delivery that, at a minimum, meets customer expectations; it does no good to design relationship strategies for inferior services. Managing the customer experience during the service encounter, including the interactions with the organization, its facilities and interactions with the service firm's representatives and other customers, is therefore critically important. A company needs to know what is important to customers at each stage of the process and at each 'touchpoint' they experience.[28] This involves identifying the key criteria and putting in place measurement tools to assess whether these criteria are being delivered. There is a need to look at the organization from the viewpoint of the customer, and not at the customer from the viewpoint of the organization. To be effective, customer experience management needs to involve the whole organization and not be seen as the responsibility of a customer service department. It is only effective when it is seen as a priority of senior management and when an organization's work processes, systems and structure change to best serve the customer. In seeking consistency of service across all touchpoints, it is necessary to understand the journey that the customer goes through when doing business with the organization and determine where things go very well and where goodwill is destroyed. Developing this understanding makes it possible to create a better customer journey and, as a result, an improved customer experience. Implementing customer experience management is an ongoing and continuous process of listening to customers with the voice of the customer being captured at every opportunity through surveys, focus groups and user panels. This insight is then used to continually enhance the delivery of the service in every 'touchpoint'. Retention strategies will have little long-term success unless the firm has a solid base of service quality and customer experience management on which to build. The firm does not necessarily have to be the very best among its competitors or be world-class in terms of quality and customer satisfaction. It must be competitive, however, and frequently better than that. All the retention strategies that we describe in this section are built on the assumption of competitive quality and value being offered. The following example of Boots provides convincing support for the argument that excellence in the core service or product offered is essential to a successful relationship approach. Boots has benefited tremendously from its loyal customer base; it offers excellent quality and uses relationship strategies to enhance its success.

★ SERVICE SPOTLIGHT

Boots the Chemists is one of the best-known and trusted brands in the UK. At the heart of the company's loyalty strategy is its Advantage Card, launched in 1997. By 2019, the number of active Boots Advantage Card members totalled 14.4 million, reflecting the programme's well-established position as one of the largest and most valued loyalty schemes in the UK. The Advantage Card uses Smart chip technology enabling customers to be able to spend their points in any store and for Boots to identify the customer when they use their card at the point of purchase. Members collect four points for every £1 spent in store or online. However, building customer relationships is not solely dependent on loyalty cards. Boots emphasizes that it is also about customer service. Each week Boots continues to analyse more than 20,000 customer responses to in-store questionnaires to better understand customers' evolving needs. Boots attributes its success to its passionate focus on customer service and care, with the customer relationship being very much at the heart of its business strategy.

Source: **www.boots.com.**

Switching Barriers

When considering a switch in service providers, a customer may face a number of barriers that make it difficult to leave one service provider and begin a relationship with another. Literature suggests that switching barriers influence consumers' decisions to exit from relationships with firms and, therefore, facilitate customer retention.[29]

Customer Inertia

One reason that customers commit to developing relationships with firms is that a certain amount of effort may be required to change firms. Sometimes consumers simplistically state that 'it's just not worth it' to switch providers. Inertia may even explain why some dissatisfied customers stay with a provider. In discussing why people remain in relationships (in general) that they no longer find satisfying, scholars suggest that people may stay because breaking the relationship would require them to restructure their life – to develop new habits of living, to refashion old friendships and to find new ones.[30] In other words, people do not like to change their behaviour.

To retain customers, firms might consider increasing the perceived effort required on the part of the customer to switch service providers. If a customer believes that a great deal of effort is needed to change companies, he or she is more likely to stay put. For example, car repair facilities might keep a complete and detailed maintenance history of a customer's vehicle. These records remove from the customer the burden of having to remember all the services performed on the vehicle and would force the customer to expend considerable effort in providing a complete maintenance history if the vehicle is taken to a new mechanic. Conversely, if a firm is looking to attract a competitor's customers, it might automate the process for switching providers as much as possible in order to reduce the effort required to switch. Utility companies supplying electricity and gas generally make switching providers as simple as saying 'yes' on the Internet or to a company representative – thereby removing any action required of the customer.

Switching Costs

In many instances, customers develop loyalty to an organization in part because of costs involved in changing to and purchasing from a different firm. These monetary and non-monetary costs, both real and perceived, are termed *switching costs*. Switching costs include investments of time, money or effort – such as set-up costs, search costs, learning costs and contractual costs – that make it challenging for the customer to move to another provider.[31] To illustrate: a patient may *incur set-up costs* such as paying for new X-rays when switching dentists or paying for a property survey when changing mortgage/housing loan provider. Because services often have characteristics that make them difficult to evaluate – including intangibility, non-standardization, inseparability of production and consumption, as well as high experience and credence qualities – high *search costs* may be required to obtain suitable information about alternative services. *Learning costs* are those costs associated with learning the idiosyncrasies of how to use a product or service; in many situations a customer who wishes to switch firms may need to accumulate new user skills or customer know-how. *Contractual costs* arise when the customer is required to pay a penalty to switch providers (e.g. penalty charges for customer-initiated switching of mortgage companies or mobile phone services), making it financially difficult, if not impossible, for the customer to initiate an early termination of the relationship.

In order to retain customers, firms might consider increasing their switching costs to make it difficult for customers to exit the relationship (or at least create the perception of difficulty). Indeed, many firms explicitly specify such costs in the contracts that they require their customers to sign (e.g. mobile phone services, health clubs). In order to attract new customers, a service provider might consider implementing strategies designed to *lower* the switching costs of customers not currently using the provider. To reduce the set-up costs involved when switching, providers could complete the paperwork required from the customer. Banks, for example, could offer to do all the paperwork to set up a current account, including direct debits and standing orders.

Relationship Bonds

Switching barriers tend to serve as constraints that keep customers in relationships with firms because they 'have to'.[32] However, firms can engage in activities that encourage customers to remain in the relationship bond because they 'want to'. Leonard Berry and A. Parasuraman have developed a framework for understanding the types of retention strategies that focus on developing bonds with customers.[33] The framework suggests that relationship marketing can occur at different levels and that each successive level of strategy results in ties that bind the customer a little closer to the firm. At each successive level, the potential for sustained competitive advantage is also increased. Building on the levels of the retention strategy idea, Figure 7.4 illustrates four types of retention strategies, which are discussed in the following sections. Recall, however, that the most successful retention strategies will be built on foundations of core service excellence.

Figure 7.4   Levels of relationship strategies

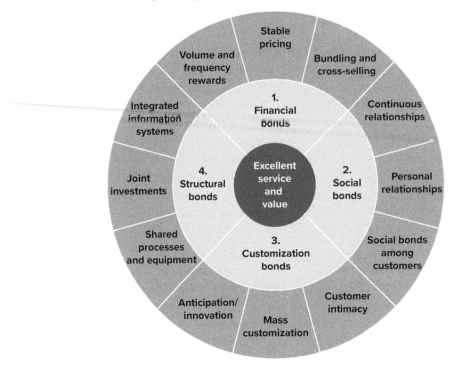

Level 1 – Financial Bonds

At level 1 the customer is tied to the firm primarily through financial incentives – lower prices for greater volume purchases or lower prices for customers who have been with the firm a long time. Examples of level 1 relationship marketing are not hard to find. Think about the airline industry and related travel service industries like hotels and car rental companies. Frequent-flyer programmes provide financial incentives and rewards for travellers who bring more of their business to a particular airline. Hotels and car rental companies do the same. Mobile phone companies have engaged in a similar battle, trying to provide volume discounts and other price incentives to retain market share and build a loyal customer base. One reason these financial incentive programmes proliferate is that they are not difficult to initiate and frequently result in at least short-term profit gains. Unfortunately, financial incentives do not generally provide long-term advantages to a firm because, unless combined with another relationship approach, they do not differentiate the firm from its competitors in the long run. Many travellers belong to several frequent-flyer programmes and do not hesitate to trade off among them. Although price and other financial incentives are important to customers, they are generally not difficult for competitors to imitate because the primary customized element of the marketing mix is price.

Other types of retention strategies that depend primarily on financial rewards are focused on bundling and cross-selling of services. Frequent-flyer programmes again provide a common example. Many airlines link their reward programmes with hotel chains, car rental and, in some cases, credit card usage. By linking airline mileage points earned to usage of other firms' services, customers can enjoy even greater financial benefits in exchange for their loyalty.

In other cases, firms aim to retain their customers by simply offering their most loyal customers the assurance of stable prices, or at least lower price increases than those paid by new customers. In this way firms reward their loyal customers by sharing with them some of the cost savings and increased revenue that the firm receives through serving them over time.

Although widely and increasingly used as retention tactics, loyalty programmes based on financial rewards merit caution.[34] These programmes are often easily imitated. Thus, any increased usage or loyalty from customers may be short-lived. Second, these strategies are not likely to be successful unless they are structured so that they truly lead to repeat or increased usage rather than serving as a means to attract new customers and potentially causing endless switching among competitors.

⭐ SERVICE SPOTLIGHT

Mastercard decided that it needed to deepen the brand's relationship with customers and position itself as more than just a payment-card company. It therefore developed a Priceless Cities programme available exclusively to Mastercard cardholders providing discounted access to 'unforgettable experiences' in major cities throughout the world. The experiences are categorized into: entertainment; arts and culture; sports; culinary; travel and sport. Discounts can only be obtained if payment is made using Mastercard. The overall aim is to build loyalty to the Mastercard brand.

Level 2 – Social Bonds

Level 2 strategies bind customers to the firm through more than financial incentives. Although price is still assumed to be important, level 2 retention marketers build long-term relationships through social and interpersonal as well as financial bonds. Customers are viewed as 'clients', not nameless faces, and become individuals whose needs and wants the firm seeks to understand.

Social, interpersonal bonds are common among professional service providers (lawyers, accountants, architects) and their clients as well as among personal care providers (hairdressers, counsellors, healthcare providers) and their clients. A dentist who takes a few minutes to review his or her patient's file before an appointment jogs his or her memory on personal facts about the patient (occupation, family details, interests, dental health history). By bringing these personal details into the conversation, the dentist reveals a genuine interest in the patient as an individual and builds social bonds. Interpersonal bonds are also common in business-to-business relationships in which customers develop relationships with salespeople and/or relationship managers working with their firms.

Sometimes relationships are formed with the organization because of the social bonds that develop *among customers* rather than between customers and the provider of the service. Such bonds are often formed in health clubs, country clubs, educational settings and other service environments where customers interact with each other. Over time the social relationships they have with other customers are important factors that prevent them from switching to another organization. One company that has built a significant strategy around customer-to-customer bonds is Harley Davidson, with its local Harley Owners Groups (HOGs). Throughout Europe (in Belgium, Germany, Spain, France, Italy, Luxembourg, Netherlands, Austria, Switzerland and the UK) HOGs are involved in local rallies, tours and parties as well as in national HOG events organized by the company. Through the HOGs, Harley customers come to know each other and develop a sense of community around their common interest – motorcycle riding.

These communities can also exist virtually as online brand communities hosted by the organization acting as an important tool for building social bonds and engaging with customers and potential customers. In addition, such communities can be seen as a source of customer data as customers interact with their views on the organization and the strengths and weaknesses of the service it offers. Online communities have been found to strengthen the relationship with the brand, enhance brand commitment, and online community members have been found to build stronger associations with the brand than non-participating consumers.[35] Leading organizations such as Apple, Red Bull, Starbucks, Go Pro, Ing Direct and SAP, all have their own online communities.

Managing an online brand community can be a difficult task as members need to feel the freedom to express their opinions to other community members. However, there is the potential for online brand communities to become a magnet for negative brand comments and discussion. As the community is closely linked with the organization in the minds of its members, everything that takes place within the community becomes associated with the brand. As a result, anti-brand comments or inappropriate responses from the organization can result in a reduction in brand loyalty. Managing and responding to comments on the community site requires the allocation of sufficient resources and the development of appropriate expertise.

Social bonds alone may not tie the customer permanently to the firm, but they are much more difficult for competitors to imitate than are price incentives. In the absence of strong reasons to shift to another provider, interpersonal bonds can encourage customers to stay in a relationship.[36] In combination with financial incentives, social bonding strategies may be very effective.

⭐ SERVICE SPOTLIGHT

Social bonds can also be created through social media by setting up a Facebook page and getting customers to visit the site and interact with it. For example, Vapiano, the German-owned Italian food chain, has more than 500,000 Facebook followers. It also has Instagram and Twitter feeds. There is interaction on these site relating to menu items, competitions, individual stores and special offers. However, interaction only occurs if staff are dedicated to updating the site and posting interesting material.

Level 3 – Customization Bonds

Level 3 strategies involve more than social ties and financial incentives, although there are common elements of level 1 and 2 strategies encompassed within a customization strategy. A customization approach suggests that customer loyalty can be encouraged through intimate knowledge of individual customers and through the development of one-to-one solutions that fit the individual customer's needs. For example, regular returning guests at exclusive hotels, such as Claridges in London, will find that their room is set up in a similar manner to that which they had on their previous visit with regard to the positioning of the furniture, the specific pillows/bedding used and the guests' preferences for flowers, drinks etc. They do this by keeping a detailed record of guest preferences and by taking photographs of the room when the guest departs. Customization in this form can result in significant effort for the service provider; in less exclusive services, mass customization approaches are adopted.

Mass customization has been defined as 'the use of flexible processes and organizational structures to produce varied and often individually customized products and services at the price of standardized, mass-produced alternatives'.[37] Mass customization does not mean providing customers with endless solutions or choices that only make them work harder for what they want; rather, it means providing them through little effort on their part with tailored services to fit their individual needs. To illustrate mass customization bonds, consider organizations such as Amazon, Netflix and Spotify that make recommendations to customers based on their previous choices and purchases. These aim to enable customers to quickly find offerings that they may like and reduce the time and effort involved in searching for them. The effort needed by the service provider to provide such customization is relatively limited, but it can be very effective in building loyalty.

⭐ SERVICE SPOTLIGHT

Royal Caribbean Cruises enables customers to customize their ocean cruise by combining dining packages, beverage packages, internet packages, photography options, on-board activities and on-shore excursions in their cruise planner. This is often done long before the cruise takes place and provides a level of customization that previously didn't exist when purchasing a cruise holiday only involved passengers choosing the class of cabin.

was awakened at 4.00 a.m. by drunken customers who were arguing with each other in a room above; management eventually called the police and asked them to escort the customers off the property. An Enterprise Rent-A-Car customer demanded that she not be charged for any of the two weeks that she had a car because, near the end of the rental period, she found a small stain in the back seat.[41] These customers often have the objective of gaining faster, superior or perhaps free service, but their behaviour is considered dysfunctional from the perspective of the service provider and perhaps fellow customers.

Dysfunctional customer behaviour can affect employees, other customers and the organization. Research suggests that exposure to dysfunctional customer behaviour can have psychological, emotional, behavioural and physical effects on employees.[42] For example, customer-contact employees who are exposed to rude, threatening, obstructive, aggressive or disruptive behaviour by customers often have their mood or temper negatively affected as well as their motivation and morale. Such customers are difficult to work with and often create stress for employees. The dysfunctional behaviour of some customers can also have an impact on other customers: it can spoil the service experience for other customers, and it may become contagious for other customers witnessing it, particularly if it includes vociferous or illegitimate complaining. Finally, dysfunctional customer behaviour can create both direct costs and indirect costs for the organization. Direct costs can include the expense of restoring damaged property, increased insurance premiums, property loss by theft, costs incurred in compensating customers affected by the dysfunctional behaviour of others, and the costs incurred through illegitimate claims by dysfunctional customers. Indirect costs might include increased workloads for staff required to deal with dysfunctional behaviour as well as increased costs for attracting and retaining appropriate personnel and, perhaps, for absenteeism payments.

Although often these difficult customers will be accommodated and employees can be trained to recognize and deal with them appropriately, at times the best choice may be to not maintain the relationship at all – especially at the business-to-business level, where long-term costs to the firm can be substantial.

Some Customers May Not Want Relationships

Some customers may simply not want a relationship. This may be due to them seeing relationship marketing activities as being:[43]

- *Irritating* – If customers feel they are being forced into a relationship that isn't genuine and a service company's employees are only acting as if they want to be friendly and caring, then the customer may become irritated. The waiter who is over friendly and continually checks on the customer's perceptions of the meal may become annoying particularly if the guest thinks the waiter is only seeking a bigger tip.
- *Intrusive* – Organizations that overuse their databases to communicate with the customer can be seen as being intrusive and taking advantage of the information held about the customers. Customers may feel exploited in such a one-sided relationship and may raise questions about privacy issues, etc. The mobile phone companies that continuously text their customers about offers may lead to customers moving supplier.
- *Time-consuming* – To establish a relationship with an organization by applying for a loyalty card, for example, a customer may have to expend a large amount of time and effort completing paperwork or registering personal details online. Some customers may consider this as being too much effort for the limited rewards they will get.
- *Unattractive* – Some customers will not value the benefits offered. The rewards for loyalty may seem trivial to a customer if they are difficult to redeem or if so many points or tokens need collecting before anything of any value can be claimed.

Service organizations need to take account of these points and segment their customers as to the relationships and rewards that different customers require. Understanding who wants to remain anonymous and who wants to be recognized as a loyal customer is important. Not all customers want to have a relationship with all their service providers; they may be happy to provide detailed information about their likes and dislikes to hotels and airlines, but be unwilling to do so with their bank and grocery store. Similarly, there will be differences in customer perceptions about being tied into long-term relationships and loyalty programmes. It is therefore unlikely that one relationship solution will be appropriate for all of a service organization's customers. Service organizations need to develop a sensitivity to ways of satisfying each customer in a manner that is relevant and attractive to that particular customer.

SERVICE SPOTLIGHT

It is quite common for advertising agencies to choose not to work for certain clients. Difficult clients can paralyse an advertising agency in a variety of ways. Some ask for complex campaigns to be undertaken on limited budgets. Others require so much up-front work, and the development of creative ideas during the bidding process, that the companies who aren't selected in the end essentially do much of the preliminary design work for free. Other clients are stingy; require many meetings before settling on an agency; or insist on a lot of direct, frequently disruptive, involvement in the design of campaigns or choice of media. As a result, agencies have become more wary of chasing every client brief that comes along.

Ending Business Relationships

For the effective management of service relationships, managers should not only know how to establish a relationship but also how to end one. As suggested earlier in this chapter, firms may identify some customers who are not in their targeted segment, who are not profitable in the long run, may be difficult to work with or are dysfunctional. A company may *not* want to continue in a relationship with every customer. However, gracefully exiting a relationship may not be easy. Customers may end up feeling disappointed, confused or hurt if a firm attempts to terminate the relationship.

Relationship Endings

Relationships end in different ways – depending on the type of relationship in place.[44] In some situations, a relationship is established for a certain purpose and/or time period and then dissolves when it has served its purpose or the time frame has elapsed. For example, a house-painting service may be engaged with the customer for four days while painting the house exterior, but both parties understand that the end of the relationship is predetermined – the end occurs when the house has been painted and the customer has paid for the service. Sometimes a relationship has a natural ending. Piano lessons for children, for example, often cease as the child gets older and develops interests in other musical areas (such as singing or playing the clarinet); in such situations, the need for the relationship has diminished or become obsolete. In other situations an event may occur that forces the relationship to end; a provider who relocates to the other side of town may force some customers to select a different company. Or a relationship ending may occur because the customer is not fulfilling his or her obligations. For example, a bank may choose to end the relationship with a customer who regularly has insufficient funds in their account. Whatever the reason for ending the relationship, firms should clearly communicate their reasons for wanting (or needing) to terminate it so that customers understand what is occurring and why.

Should Firms Fire their Customers?

A logical conclusion to be drawn from the discussion of the challenges firms face in customer relationships is that perhaps firms should seek to get rid of those customers who are not right for them. More and more companies are making these types of decisions based on the belief that troublesome customers are usually less profitable and less loyal, and that attempting to retain their business may be counterproductive.[45] Another reason for 'firing' a customer is the negative effect that these customers can have on employee quality of life and morale. Troublesome airline passengers who are disruptive on a flight may find that the airline refuses to carry them on any future flight.

Although it may sound like a good idea, firing customers is not that simple and needs to be done in a way that avoids negative publicity or negative word of mouth. Sometimes raising prices or charging for services that previously had been given away for free can move unprofitable customers out of the company. Helping a client find a new supplier who can better meet their needs is another way to gracefully exit a non-productive relationship. If the customer has become too demanding, the relationship may be salvaged by negotiating expectations or finding more efficient ways to serve the client. If not, both parties may find an agreeable way to end the relationship.

Summary

In this chapter we focused on the rationale for, benefits of, and strategies for developing long-term relationships with customers. It should be obvious by now that organizations that focus only on acquiring new customers may well fail to understand their current customers; thus, while a company may be bringing customers in through the front door, equal or greater numbers may be exiting. Estimates of lifetime relationship value accentuate the importance of retaining current customers.

The particular strategy that an organization uses to retain its current customers can and should be customized to fit the industry, the culture and the customer needs of the organization. However, in general, customer relationships are driven by a variety of factors that influence the development of strong customer relationships, including (1) the customer's overall evaluation of the quality of a firm's core service offering, (2) the switching barriers that the customer faces in leaving a relationship, and (3) the relationship bonds developed with that customer by the firm. By developing strong relationships with customers and by focusing on factors that influence customer relationships, the organization will accurately understand customer expectations over time and consequently will narrow service quality gap 1.

Although long-term customer relationships are critical and can be very profitable, firms should not attempt to build relationships with just any customer. In other words, 'the customer is not always right'. Indeed, in some situations it may be best for firms to discontinue relationships with some customers – for the sake of the customer, the firm, or both.

Key Concepts

Customer experience management	144	Relationship endings	152
Customer pyramid	141	Relationship marketing	131
Lifetime value	138	Retention strategies	144
Online brand communities	147	Switching barriers	144
Profitability tiers	141	Touchpoints	144
Relationship bonds	145		

Exercises

1 Interview the manager of a local service organization. Discuss the target market(s) for the service. Estimate the lifetime value of a customer in one or more of the target segments. To do this estimate, you will need to get as much information from the manager as you can. If the manager cannot answer your questions, make some assumptions.

2   In small groups in class, debate the question, 'Is the customer always right?' In other words, are there times when a customer may be the wrong customer for the organization?

3   Design a customer appreciation programme for the organization with whom you currently work. Why would you have such a programme, and to whom would it be directed?

4   Choose a specific company context (your class project company, the company you work for or a company in an industry you are familiar with). Calculate the lifetime value of a customer for this company. You will need to make assumptions to do this calculation, so state them clearly. Using ideas and concepts from this chapter, describe a relationship marketing strategy to increase the number of lifetime customers for this firm.

Discussion Questions

1   Discuss how relationship marketing or retention marketing is different from the traditional emphasis in marketing.

2   Describe how a firm's relationships with customers may evolve over time. For each level of relationship discussed in the chapter, identify a firm with which you have that level of relationship and discuss how its marketing efforts differ from other firms.

3   Think about a service organization that retains you as a loyal customer. Why are you loyal to this provider? What are the benefits to you of staying loyal and not switching to another provider? What would it take for you to switch?

4   With regard to the same service organization, what are the benefits to the organization of keeping you as a customer? Calculate your 'lifetime value' to the organization.

5   Describe the logic behind 'customer profitability segmentation' from the company's point of view. Also discuss what customers may think of the practice.

6   Describe the various switching barriers discussed in the text. What switching barriers might you face in switching banks, mobile phone service providers, or universities?

7   Describe the four levels of retention strategies, and give examples of each type. Again, think of a service organization to which you are loyal. Can you describe the reason(s) you are loyal in terms of the different levels? In other words, what ties you to the organization?

8   Have you ever worked as a front-line service employee? Can you remember having to deal with difficult or 'problem' customers? Discuss how you handled such situations. As a manager of front-line employees, how would you help your employees deal with difficult customers?

9   Which types of service organization would you want to have a relationship with and what types would you not want to have a relationship? Explain your selections.

10   How can an organization's online brand community help to build relationships? Will this only work for certain types of services?

Further Reading

Breugelmans, E., Bijmolt, T.H., Zhang, J., Basso, L.J., Dorotic, M., Kopalle, P. and Wünderlich, N.V. (2015). Advancing research on loyalty programs: A future research agenda. *Marketing Letters*, 26(2), 127–139.

Grönroos, C. (2017). Relationship marketing readiness: Theoretical background and measurement directions. *Journal of Services Marketing*, 31(3), 218–225.

Gummesson, E. (2008). *Total Relationship Marketing.* Oxford: Butterworth-Heinemann.

Johnston, R. and Kong, X. (2011). The customer experience: A road-map for improvement. *Managing Service Quality,* 21(1), 5–24.

MacGillavry, K. and Wilson, A. (2014). Delivering loyalty via customer experience management at DHL freight. *Global Business and Organizational Excellence,* 33(6), 6–20.

Stathopoulou, A. and Balabanis, G. (2016). The effects of loyalty programs on customer satisfaction, trust, and loyalty toward high-and low-end fashion retailers. *Journal of Business Research,* 69(12), 5801–5808.

Vargo, S. (2009). Toward a transcending conceptualization of relationship: A service-dominant logic perspective. *Journal of Business & Industrial Marketing,* 24(5/6), 373–79.

Wirtz, J., Den Ambtman, A., Bloemer, J., Horváth, C., Ramaseshan, B., Van De Klundert, J. and Kandampully, J. (2013). Managing brands and customer engagement in online brand communities. *Journal of Service Management,* 24(3), 223–44.

Part 4
Aligning Service Design and Standards

Chapter 8   Service Innovation and Design

Chapter 9   Customer-Defined Service Standards

Chapter 10   The Physical and Virtual Servicescape

Meeting customer expectations of service requires not only understanding what the expectations are, it also requires taking action on that knowledge. Action takes several forms: designing services based on customer requirements, setting service standards to ensure that employees perform as customers expect, and providing physical evidence that creates the appropriate cues and ambience for service. When action does not take place, there is a gap – service design and standards gap – as shown in the accompanying figure. In this section you will learn to identify the causes of gap 2 as well as effective strategies for closing this gap.

Chapter 8 describes the tools that are most effective in service development and design, especially a tool called *service blueprinting*. Chapter 9 helps you differentiate between company-defined standards and customer–provider gap 2-defined standards, and to recognize how they can be developed. Chapter 10 explores the strategic importance of physical evidence, the variety of roles it plays, and strategies for effectively designing physical evidence and the servicescape to meet customer expectations.

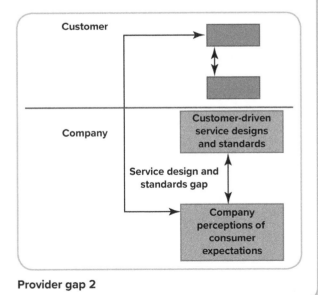

Provider gap 2

Chapter 8

Service Innovation and Design

Chapter Outline

Challenges of Service Innovation Policy	158
New Service Development Processes	160
Types of New Services	161
Service Innovation through the Internet of Things	163
Stages in Service Innovation and Development	164
Service Blueprinting	170
High-Performance Service Innovations	179
Summary and Key Concepts	180
Exercises	181
Discussion Questions	181
Further Reading	182

Learning Objectives

This chapter's objectives are to:

1 Describe the challenges inherent in service innovation and design.
2 Present the stages and unique elements of the service innovation and development process.
3 Demonstrate the value of service blueprinting and how to develop and read service blueprints.
4 Present lessons learned in choosing and implementing high-performance service innovations.

Opening Example
Crowdsourcing Innovation – Giffgaff

Giffgaff, the mobile phone network, is the third largest operator in the UK and is run by its 400,000 customers. It refers to its customers as members because they cocreate the service provided by the company. The company only runs a small call centre as most queries are answered online by its existing members. Customers now raise 5,000 posts (queries) per week, with over 90 per cent resolved by other members. On average, customer questions are frequently answered by fellow customers within 90 seconds. The community votes on the best answers so the best ones rise to the top; the members are also self-policing, and flag anything inappropriate.

Source: ©olesea vetrila/Shutterstock

The core of the company's business model is supported by its community: members assist other customers, draw new customers to the network, and devise strategies to expand the business. Members are incentivized to undertake these tasks by rewarding them with points through its Giffgaff PayBack scheme. These points can be converted into cash, credit or a donation to charity. Giffgaff has now paid out over £11 million to members for the services provided.

In terms of innovation and new service design, the members are also tasked with coming up with new ideas for the company. These ideas relate to how members want their mobile network run and what they want from Giffgaff in the future. Over 14,000 ideas from the members have been submitted and 10 per cent of these have now been implemented. Giffgaff lists the best ideas on its website.

Source: Based on information from https://www.telegraph.co.uk/finance/newsbysector/mediatechnologyandtelecoms/ telecoms/11630738/Giffgaff-the-bonkers-mobile-network-proves-that-the-crowd-can-run-your-business-for-you.html.

So what causes new products and services such as those offered by Giffgaff to fail or succeed? If you decide to start your own business, what can you do to protect yourself as much as possible from failure?

An analysis of more than 60 studies on new product and service success showed that the dominant and most reliable predictors of success for new introductions relate to ***product/service characteristics*** (product meeting customer needs, product advantage over competing products, technological sophistication); ***strategy characteristics*** (dedicated human resources to support the initiative, dedicated research and development (R&D) focused on the new product initiative); ***process characteristics*** (marketing, predevelopment, technological and launch proficiencies); and ***marketplace characteristics*** (market potential).[1]

Frequently, a good service idea fails because of development, design and specification flaws: topics that are emphasized in this chapter. As more firms across industries move into services as a growth strategy, the challenges and opportunities of developing and delivering service offerings become a reality.

Challenges of Service Innovation Policy

Because services are largely intangible and process oriented (such as a visit to the dentist, a golf lesson or a Champions League football game), they are difficult to describe and communicate. When services are delivered over a long period – a week's holiday, a six-month consulting engagement, 10 weeks on a diet club programme – their complexity increases, and they become even more difficult to define and describe. Further, because services are delivered by employees to customers, they are variable. Rarely are two services alike or experienced in the same way. These characteristics of services, which we explored in Chapter 1, are the heart of the challenge involved in designing services. Global companies and governments around the world are awakening to these challenges and the recognition that, despite the dominance of services in the world's economies, there is relatively little formal focus on service research and innovation.[2] The Organisation for Economic Co-operation and Development (OECD) produced a report in 2005 entitled 'Promoting Innovation in Services' in which they stated:

> *Boosting innovation in services is central to improving performance of the service sector . . . the sector has traditionally been seen as less innovative than manufacturing and as playing only a supportive role in the innovation system. As the importance of service innovation becomes more and more apparent, significant initiatives are beginning to emerge in countries around the world.*[3]

A 2015 study on 'Service Research Priorities in a Rapidly Changing Context'[4] identified' stimulating service innovation' as one of the top priorities. Seeking to identify priorities for both practice and research, this study was based on input from academics and business practitioners from around the world and across disciplines and functions. Interviews, surveys and roundtables were conducted with people from 37 countries. The study's findings identified priorities for research as well as knowledge gaps. The following five topics were seen as specific areas where knowledge is needed to advance service innovation in companies and countries:

- Innovating within complex service systems and value networks
- Identifying drivers of sustained service innovation
- Managing customers' and partners' collaboration throughout the service innovation process
- Innovating services through crowd-sourcing and open innovation
- Understanding the interrelationships among service- product, service- product, service-process, and business-model innovation.

Despite the importance of innovation, a benchmarking review of service innovation policies in Europe[5] reported great diversity in policies and intensity of focus on service innovation across countries. The authors of the report identified a few countries that are very advanced in service innovation policies and procedures: namely, Finland, Sweden and Ireland. They also mention Austria, Germany and Denmark as being among other countries that have maintained a policy interest in service innovation.

In addition to specific support mechanisms, many European countries are applying the concept of geographical service clusters, providing eco-systems for services innovation in a region. These clusters involve providing the correct infrastructure and conditions to attract certain types of businesses to coalesce in an area. The most common services in these clusters are in: information and communication technology; education and research; creative industries; financial services; health and well-being; tourism; transport and logistics. Service-related cluster initiatives can be found in Austria, Belgium, Bulgaria, Cyprus, Estonia, Finland, France, Iceland, Ireland, Italy, Luxembourg, Malta, the Netherlands, Norway, Portugal, Spain, Sweden, Switzerland and the UK. For example in France, the Finance Innovation Competitiveness Cluster brings together in one location major financial firms in banking, insurance and asset management, regulators, business schools, universities and academics, as well as public institutions. This cluster aims to become a 'global competitiveness cluster' meaning that it has a mission to compete on the world stage.

Describing Service Innovations

Because services cannot be touched, examined or easily tried out, people have historically resorted to words in their efforts to describe them. Yet, there are a number of risks inherent in attempting to describe services with words alone. The first is *oversimplification*. To say that 'portfolio management' means 'buying and selling stocks' is like describing the space shuttle as 'something that flies'. Some people will picture a bird, some a helicopter, and some an angel.'[6] Words are simply inadequate to describe a complex service system such as financial portfolio management. In our modern-day global economy, service systems have significantly increased in complexity, often involving networks of service firms and customers, and evolution of offerings over time. Within these complex systems, the risks of oversimplification are even more apparent.

The second risk of using words alone is *incompleteness*. In describing services, people (employees, managers, customers) tend to omit details or elements of the service with which they are not familiar. A person might do a fairly credible job of describing how a discount stockbroker service takes orders from customers. But would that person be able to describe fully how the monthly statements are created, how the interactive computer system works, and how these two elements of the service are integrated into the order-taking process?

The third risk is *subjectivity*. Any one person describing a service in words will be biased by personal experiences and degree of exposure to the service. There is a natural (and mistaken) tendency to assume that because all people have gone to a fast-food restaurant, they all understand what that service is. Persons working in different functional areas of the same service organization (a marketing person, an operations person, a finance person) are likely to describe the service very differently as well, biased by their own functional background.

A final risk of describing services using words alone is *biased interpretation*. No two people will define 'responsive', 'quick' or 'flexible' in exactly the same way. For example, a supervisor or manager may suggest to a front-line service employee that he or she should try to be more flexible or responsive in providing service to the customer. Unless the term 'flexibility' is further defined, the employee is likely to interpret the word differently from the manager.

All these risks become very apparent in the innovation and service development process, when organizations attempt to design complex services never before experienced by customers or when they attempt to change existing services. In the sections that follow, we present approaches for new service development and design to address these unique challenges.

New Service Development Processes

Research suggests that products that are designed and introduced via the steps in a structured planning framework have a greater likelihood of ultimate success than those not developed within a framework. Despite the proven value of a structured and analytic approach to innovation, often new services are introduced on the basis of managers' and employees' subjective opinions about what the services should be and whether they will succeed, rather than on objective designs incorporating data about customer perceptions, market needs and feasibility. A new service design process may be imprecise in defining the nature of the service concept because the people involved believe either that service processes cannot be defined precisely or that 'everyone knows what we mean'. None of these rationalizations for imprecision or lack of planning are justifiable, as we illustrate in this chapter's model for new service innovation and development.[7]

Because services are produced and consumed and co-created in real time, often involving interaction between employees and customers, it is also critical that innovation and the new-service development process involve both employees and customers. Employees frequently *are* the service, or at least they perform or deliver the service, and thus their involvement in choosing which new services to develop and how they should be designed and implemented can be very beneficial. Contact employees are psychologically and physically close to customers and can be very helpful in identifying customer needs for new services. Involving employees in the design and development process also increases the likelihood of new service success because employees can identify the organizational issues that need to be addressed to support the delivery of the service to customers.[8]

Because customers often actively participate in service delivery, they too should be involved in the new service development process. Beyond just providing input on their own needs, customers can help design the service concept and the delivery process, particularly in situations in which the customer personally carries out part of the service process. Examples include:

1. IKEA: Well known for involving its customers in the design of its stores to ensure that the layout will work for the shoppers and not just for the staff or the architects who design the stores.
2. Banco Santander: A significant amount of market research was undertaken by the UK arm of Banco Santander in determining the future of its retail banking branches. As a result, new designs have been developed, some of which incorporate Costa Coffee outlets.

★ SERVICE SPOTLIGHT

Marriott International uses a variety of methods to develop and test out its new hotel concepts. For the Marriott hotel brand, the company created a Marriott Beta hotel in Charlotte, USA in 2016. This was a fully functioning hotel that doubled as a 'live beta' testbed where rapid prototyping could be undertaken with real-time feedback from guests. Innovations such as keyless entry to digital experiences in the fitness studio were trialled in this way, ultimately shaping the future Marriott hotel experience.

In 2017, Marriott also developed a pop-up innovation lab to crowdsource real-time feedback on new designs for their Aloft and Element hotel brands. The lab enabled industry professionals, hotel guests, employees and the general public to explore some of the innovations planned for the hotels. All of the people who visited the lab were invited to provide feedback on what they saw, touched or tasted using a mobile phone based survey tool. The information received influenced the new Aloft and Element designs that have been rolled out worldwide.

Types of New Services

As we describe the service innovation and development process, remember that not all new services are 'new' to the same degree. New service options can run the gamut from major innovations to minor style changes:

- *Major or radical innovations* are new services for markets as yet undefined. Past examples include the first broadcast television services and the creation of eBay Internet-based auction sites. Many innovations now and in the future will evolve from information, computer and Internet-based technologies. Often these major innovations create brand-new markets.
- *Start-up businesses* consist of new services for a market that is already served by existing products that meet the same generic needs. Service examples include the creation of Amazon to provide an alternative to bookstores, online banking for financial transactions and door-to-door airport shuttle services that compete with traditional taxi and limousine services.
- *New services for the currently served market* represent attempts to offer existing customers of the organization a service not previously available from the company (although it may be available from other companies). Examples include Tesco offering insurance services, a health club offering nutrition classes and airlines offering telephone and Internet service during flights.
- *Service line extensions* represent augmentations of the existing service line, such as a restaurant adding new menu items, an airline offering new routes, a law firm offering additional legal services and a university adding new courses or degrees.
- *Service improvements* represent perhaps the most common type of service innovation. Changes in features of services that are already offered might involve faster execution of an existing service process,

extended hours of service, or augmentations such as added amenities in a hotel room (e.g. the addition of wireless Internet connections).

- *Style changes* represent the most modest service innovations, although they are often highly visible and can have significant effects on customer perceptions, emotions and attitudes. Changing the colour scheme of a restaurant, revising the logo for an organization, redesigning a website or painting aircraft a different colour all represent style changes. These innovations do not fundamentally change the service, only its appearance, similar to how packaging changes are used for consumer products.

These types of service innovations are tied to the offerings themselves, suggesting that innovation occurs when a service offering is altered or expanded in some way – either radically on one extreme or stylistically at the other extreme. It is also possible that service innovations may come about when the customer's usage or co-creation role is redefined. For example, assuming the customer plays the role of user, buyer, or payer in a service context, new services can result when the previous role is redefined.[9]

Many radical innovations effectively redefine the customer's role in these ways. For example, Netflix totally redefined customers' role for movie rentals. While customers used to visit their local video store to rent one or more movies for a predetermined period of time and pay for them on a per movie basis, Netflix allows customers to stream movies directly to their Internet-enabled devices. Thus, while movie watching in the home has not changed, the entire service process for renting, receiving, paying for and returning movies is radically different. Similar changes in the process have occurred within other sectors (see Table 8.1).

Table 8.1   Radical service innovations

Sector	Company
Transportation	Uber/Lyft
Media purchasing	iTunes
Music listening	Spotify
Hospitality	Airbnb
Food deliveries	Deliveroo
Bicycling	City Bike Schemes
Payment	PayPal

Firms in many industries are discovering the value of strategically focusing on service innovations to provide value for their customers as well as profits and growth for the firm. Using this strategic approach, services are developed to enhance relationships with customers by providing them with total packages of offerings, sometimes referred to as 'solutions'. By adding services to their traditional offerings, firms can differentiate themselves from their competitors and frequently make higher profit margins on the new services compared with traditional manufactured offerings.

SERVICE SPOTLIGHT

Philips electronics

Companies such as Philips Electronics, the European electronics giant, are faced with the realities of price competition from cheaper products produced primarily in Asia. The results for many companies are declining sales and growing losses from their products. Part of the solution for these companies is a venture into services.

For Philips this has meant branching out into healthcare by marrying its expertise in consumer marketing and the knowledge in its professional medical division with an unmet demand for personal healthcare monitoring. The Philips Lifeline service is a medical-alert system that allows elderly patients immediate connection to a call centre, where Personal Response Associates, with access to their health profiles, can help them. The immediate access is gained by pushing a button on an electronic bracelet that the patient wears.

Other services which Philips have in the works include one that allows doctors to monitor patients' vital signs from their homes via the Internet, and an intelligent pill box that can detect when a person has not taken his or her medication. A box with excess pills would automatically alert the system and an operator would call the patient to remind them.

For Philips the move was dramatic as it began to understand a whole new industry in healthcare delivery. Yet the potential rewards were great and customer demands for services and solutions are real. These rewards and demands are what compel more and more firms to pursue the strategic service path.

Source: **www.medical.philips.com.**

Service Innovation through the Internet of Things

One of the most ubiquitous and far-reaching trends in business today is the digitalization of products. This digital transformation of products is known as the 'Internet of Things' or IOT, where products include sensors that are connected to the Internet. The IOT has allowed an explosion in services based on the data that passes between interconnected products. Everything from home appliances to industrial equipment to medical equipment, clothing and communication devices, can have sensors embedded in them; and everything can communicate. Through embedded sensors, products continuously produce data which can be captured, connected and transformed into information. Ultimately the information can be transformed into innovative services, frequently based on new service models.

Here are just a few examples of the types of services that have been innovated through connected products: traffic signals that help monitor and optimize traffic flow, trucks that are equipped with sensors to monitor performance and predict failures and maintenance needs, onboard diagnostics in cars to enhance performance and safety, athletic shoes that monitor and communicate usage and appliances and home heating that can be controlled remotely. In all cases, it is not the data itself that provides a service, but the use of that data to solve a customer problem, amplify the customer's knowledge and abilities, or create new capabilities.

The IOT is affecting almost every industry, and its potential grows daily. Interconnected products may create the greatest change and opportunity impacting on service innovation over the next decade.

★ SERVICE SPOTLIGHT

Rolls-Royce

Many of the Rolls-Royce engines on commercial aeroplanes are owned by Rolls-Royce rather than the airline or the plane manufacturer. The company's TotalCare® is a flexible and comprehensive cost-per-flight-hour leasing service, designed to deliver engines with an engine maintenance programme. Engine management plans are developed that combine engine condition monitoring, customer-specific operational information and fleet-wide experience to produce tailored repair and engine overhaul schedules. The TotalCare® programme covers lease engine costs and also covers the cost of repairing or replacing parts. There is minimal interruption to flying for scheduled engine maintenance as Rolls-Royce guarantees access to spare engines. Rolls-Royce also uses computer and satellite technology to track in-flight engine performance from its information centre in Derby in the UK. The company can direct replacement parts and repair teams to the airport locations where they are needed. As Rolls-Royce takes responsibility for the performance of the aircraft engines, the airlines can concentrate more of their efforts on delivering their core services of flying and looking after passengers. TotalCare® also allows Rolls Royce to build close relationships with airlines as well as a continuous income stream and higher margins.

Source: **https://www.rolls-royce.com/products-and-services/civil-aerospace/aftermarket-services/airlines.aspx.**

Stages in Service Innovation and Development

In this section we focus on the actual steps to be followed in service innovation and development. The steps can be applied to any type of new service. Much of what is presented in this section has direct parallels in the new product development process for manufactured goods. Because of the inherent characteristics of services, however, the development process for new services requires adaptations.[10] Figure 8.1 shows the basic principles and steps in new service development. Although these steps may be similar to those for

Figure 8.1 Service innovation and development process

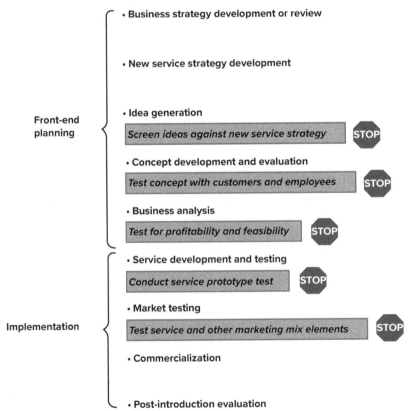

Sources: Booz-Allen & Hamilton, *New Product Management for the 1980s* (New York: Booz-Allen & Hamilton, 1982); M.J. Bowers (1985) 'An exploration into new service development: organization, process, and structure', doctoral dissertation, Texas: A&M University; A. Khurana and S.R. Rosenthal (1997) 'Integrating the fuzzy front end of new product development', *Sloan Management Review* (Winter 1997), pp. 103–20; and R.G. Cooper (2001) *Winning at New Products,* 3rd edn, Cambridge, MA: Perseus Publishing.

manufactured goods, their implementation is different for services. The challenges typically lie in defining the concept in the early stages of the development process and again at the prototype development stage. Other challenges come about in the design and implementation of the new service because it can involve coordinating human resources, technology, internal processes and facilities within already existing systems. Partly because of these challenges, service firms are generally less likely to carry out a structured development process for new innovations than are their manufacturing and consumer-goods counterparts.[11]

An underlying assumption of new product development process models is that new product ideas can be dropped at any stage of the process if they do not satisfy the criteria for success at that particular stage.[12] Figure 8.1 shows the checkpoints (represented by stop signs) that separate critical stages of the development process. The checkpoints specify requirements that a new service must meet before it can proceed to the next stage of development. Despite what Figure 8.1 suggests, however, new service or product development is rarely a completely linear process. Many companies are finding that to speed up new service innovation, some steps can be worked on simultaneously, and in some instances a step may even be skipped, particularly for simple products and services. The overlapping of steps and simultaneous development of various pieces of the new service/product development process has been referred to as 'flexible product development'. This type of flexible, speedy process is particularly important in technology and digital industries, in which products and services evolve extremely quickly. In these environments, computer technology lets companies monitor customer opinions and needs during development and change the final offering right up until it is launched. Often, the next version of the service is in planning stages at the same time that the current version is being launched.[13] Even if the stages are handled simultaneously, the important checkpoints noted in Figure 8.1 must be assessed to maximize chances of success.

The process shown in Figure 8.1 is divided into two sections: front-end planning and implementation. The front end determines what service concepts will be developed, whereas the back end executes or implements the service concept. When asked where the greatest weaknesses in product and service innovation occur, managers typically report problems with the 'fuzzy front end'.[14] The front end is called 'fuzzy' because of its relative abstractness, which is even more apparent with intangible and variable services than with manufactured products.

Front-End Planning

Business Strategy Development or Review

It is assumed that an organization will have an overall strategic orientation, vision and mission. Clearly a first step in new service development is to review that mission and vision. The new service strategy and specific new service ideas must fit within the larger strategic mission and vision of the organization.

⭐ **SERVICE SPOTLIGHT**

Alibaba sets its mission as being **'To make it easy to do business anywhere'.** This mission has led to the development of a host of new services, such as: e-commerce and retail service platforms; cloud computing and AI technology; FinTech and online payment platforms; entertainment services and internet services.

In addition to its strategic mission, the company's underlying orientation toward growth will affect how it defines its new services strategy. Becoming aware of the organization's overall strategic orientation is fundamental to plotting a direction for growth. Noted strategy researchers suggest four primary strategic orientations that are taken by companies:[15] (1) *prospectors* seek to be innovative, searching out new opportunities and taking on risks; (2) *defenders* are experts in their own areas and tend not to seek new opportunities outside their domain of expertise; (3) *analysers* maintain stability in certain areas of operation but are open to experimenting and seeking out opportunities on the margin; (4) *reactors* seldom make adjustments unless forced to do so by environmental pressures. Another noted management strategist suggests that firms can be distinguished by whether they primarily pursue a cost-leadership strategy, a differentiation strategy or a focused strategy.[16] An organization's strategic orientation will affect how it views growth through new service development.

New-Service Strategy Development

Research suggests that without a clear new product or service strategy, a well-planned portfolio of new products and services, and an organizational structure that facilitates product development via ongoing communications and cross-functional sharing of responsibilities, front-end decisions become ineffective.[17] Thus, a product portfolio strategy and a defined organizational structure for new product or service development are critical – and are the foundations – for success.

The types of new services that will be appropriate will depend on the organization's goals, vision, capabilities and growth plans. By defining a new service strategy (possibly in terms of markets, types of services, time horizon for development, profit criteria or other relevant factors), the organization will be in a better position to begin generating specific ideas. For example, it may focus its growth on new services at a particular level of the described continuum from major innovations to style changes. Or the organization may define its new service strategy even more specifically in terms of particular markets or market segments or in terms of specific profit-generation goals.

One way to begin formulating a new service strategy is to use the framework shown in Table 8.2 for identifying growth opportunities. The framework allows an organization to identify possible directions for growth and can be helpful as a catalyst for creative ideas. The framework may also later serve as an initial idea screen if, for example, the organization chooses to focus its growth efforts on one or two of the four cells in the matrix. The matrix suggests that companies can develop a growth strategy around current customers or for new customers, and can focus on current offerings or new service offerings.

Table 8.2 New service strategy matrix for identifying growth opportunities

Offerings	Markets	
	Current Customers	**New Customers**
Existing services	Share building	Market development
New services	Service development	Diversification

Sources: Adapted from H.I. Ansoff (1965) *Corporate Strategy,* New York: McGraw-Hill.

Idea Generation

The next step in the process is the generation of new ideas that can be passed through the new service strategy screen described in the preceding step. Many methods and avenues are available for services idea generation. Formal brainstorming, solicitation of ideas from employees and customers, lead user research and learning about competitors' offerings are some of the most common approaches. Some companies are even collaborating with outsiders (e.g. competitors, vendors, alliance partners) or developing licensing agreements and joint ventures in an effort to exploit all possible sources of new ideas.[18] Observing customers and how they use the firm's products and services can also generate creative ideas for new innovations. Sometimes referred to as *empathic design,* observation is particularly effective in situations in which customers may not be able to recognize or verbalize their needs.[19] In service businesses, contact personnel, who actually deliver the services and interact directly with consumers, can be particularly good sources of ideas for complementary services and ways to improve current offerings.

Social media and networks can also be a good source of new ideas. Crowdsourcing seeks out feedback and ideas from the people who know the services best: the customers. The Starbucks example at the start of this chapter is an example of crowdsourcing of ideas. Lego is another well-known brand that encourages customers to redesign its product offerings. The idea has been popularized by various authors including James Surowiecki's book, *The Wisdom of Crowds*.[20] And it has been transformed by the power and popularity of the Internet which allows major international brands to easily engage a crowd of customers. In 2013, Marriott Hotels evolved their crowdsourcing of ideas through a dedicated website by asking guests to help the hotel chain shape innovative ideas and concepts that are closer to being rolled out. The website solicited theme-travel ideas for design, culinary, wellness and technology. Guests choose their favourite improvement ideas via voting and comments on Facebook. The campaign delivered numerous new ideas, including easier access to healthier foods and pop-up shops stocked with bona fide local gifts, as well as loaning guests digital equipment to socially share their experience, and regional touches that let a hotel really reflect its location.

Other organizations have found that internal networks of employees, across functions and disciplines, can be great sources of innovative ideas; thus, organizational practices that encourage networking and make collaboration easy are also ways to encourage new ideas.[21] Whether the source of a new idea is inside or outside the organization, some established mechanism should exist for ensuring an ongoing stream of new service possibilities. This mechanism might include: a formal service innovation, service R&D department or function with responsibility for generating new ideas; suggestion boxes for employees and customers; new-service development teams that meet regularly; surveys and focus groups with customers and employees; or formal competitive analysis to identify new services.

Service Concept Development and Evaluation

Once an idea surfaces that is regarded as a good fit with both the business and the new service strategies, it is ready for initial development. In the case of a tangible product, this next step in service concept development and evaluation would mean formulating the basic product definition and then presenting consumers with descriptions and drawings to get their reactions.

The inherent characteristics of services, particularly intangibility and simultaneous production and consumption, place complex demands on this phase of the process. Drawing pictures and describing an intangible service in concrete terms is difficult. It is, therefore, important that agreement be reached at this stage on exactly what the concept is and what customer need it fills. The service concept is made up of the core benefit provided to the customer, supported by a variety of tangible and intangible elements that assist in the delivery of that benefit. The core benefit of a passenger flight is getting a customer to a particular destination, but the service concept also involves: booking and check-in procedures; the frequency of in-flight service; the design of the aeroplane; the configuration of the seating; food and drink, etc. The service concept for no-frills airlines is very different from that of the traditional carriers even though the core benefit is the same. It may be necessary to involve multiple parties in sharpening the definition of the service concept. For example, Lynn Shostack relates that the design and development of a new discount share-dealing service was initially described by the bank as a way 'to buy and sell stocks for customers at low prices'.[22] Through the initial concept development phase it became clear that not everyone in the organization had the same idea about how this description would translate into an actual service and that there was a variety of ways the concept could be developed. Only through multiple iterations of the service – and the raising of hundreds of issues, large and small – was an agreement finally reached on the discounted share-dealing concept.

After clear definition of the concept, it is important to produce a description of the service that represents its specific features and characteristics, and then to determine initial customer and employee responses to the concept. The service design document would describe the problem addressed by the service, discuss the reasons for offering the new service, itemize the service process and its benefits and provide a rationale for purchasing the service.[23] The roles of customers and employees in the delivery process would also be described. The new service concept would then be evaluated by asking employees and customers whether they understand the idea of the proposed service, whether they are favourable to the concept and whether they feel it satisfies an unmet need.

Business Analysis

Assuming that, at the concept development stage, the service idea is favourably evaluated by customers and employees, the next step is to estimate its economic feasibility and potential profit implications. Demand analysis, revenue projections, cost analyses and operational feasibility studies are assessed at this stage. Because the development of service concepts is so closely tied to the operational system of the organization, this stage will involve preliminary assumptions about the costs of staff recruitment and training, delivery system enhancements, facility changes and any other projected operations costs. The organization will pass the results of the business analysis through its profitability and feasibility screen to determine whether the new service idea meets the minimum requirements.

Implementation

Once the new service concept has passed all the front-end planning hurdles, it is ready for the implementation stages of the process.

Service Development and Testing

In the development of new tangible products, the development and testing stage involves construction of product prototypes and testing for consumer acceptance. Again, because services are intangible and simultaneously produced, consumed and frequently co-created, this step presents unique challenges. To address these challenges, this stage of service development should involve all who have a stake in the new service: customers and contact employees as well as functional representatives from marketing, operations and human resources. During this phase, the concept is refined to the point at which a detailed service blueprint representing the implementation plan for the service can be produced. The blueprint is likely to evolve over a series of iterations on the basis of input from all the involved parties.

A final step is for each area involved in rendering the service to translate the final blueprint into specific implementation plans for its part of the service delivery process. Because service development, design and delivery are so intricately intertwined, all parties involved in any aspect of the new service must work together at this stage to delineate the details of the new service. If not, seemingly minor operational details can be overlooked and cause an otherwise good new service idea to fail.

⭐ SERVICE SPOTLIGHT

In 2017, Hilton established the Hilton Innovation Gallery as an experiential showcase for cutting-edge product developments that will shape the future of hospitality. Open to invited guests including Hilton Team Members, hotel owners and technology partners, the 4,300-square-foot gallery brings together all elements of Hilton's innovation process. It is a physical space where conversations between thought leaders, design experts and hospitality professionals deliver new products and solutions for Hilton's guests. Upon entering the space, visitors will make their way through five experiences including:

1. Product Showcase: A space for visitors to interact with physical and virtual products that Hilton is exploring for use in hotels.
2. Food & Beverage Concept Studio: A show kitchen which offers an opportunity to experience and showcase the latest Food and Beverage concepts.
3. Virtual Reality Stage: A dedicated space for visitors to use virtual reality headsets to experience new Hilton concepts.

> **4.** Darkroom: A progressive model guestroom dedicated to showing cutting-edge material technologies.
>
> **5.** Innovation Theatre: A gathering space to brainstorm and collaborate around innovative ideas.
>
> *Source:* **https://newsroom.hilton.com/corporate/news/hilton-launces-incubator-to-fasttrack-guest-innovations.**

Market Testing

At the **market testing** stage of the development process, a tangible product might be test marketed in a limited number of trading areas to determine marketplace acceptance of the product as well as other marketing mix variables, such as promotion, pricing and distribution systems. Because new service offerings are often intertwined with the delivery system for existing services, it is difficult to test new services in isolation. Also, in some cases, such as a one-site retailer, it may not be possible to introduce the service to an isolated market area because the organization has only one point of delivery. There are alternative ways of testing the response to marketing mix variables, however. The new service might be offered to employees of the organization and their families for a time to assess their responses to variations in the marketing mix. Alternatively, the organization might decide to test variations in pricing and promotion in less realistic contexts by presenting customers with hypothetical mixes and getting responses on whether they would try the service under varying circumstances. This approach certainly has limitations compared with an actual market test, but it is better than not assessing market response at all.

It is also extremely important at this stage in the development process to do a pilot run of the service to be sure that the operational details are functioning smoothly. Frequently this step is overlooked, and the actual market introduction may be the first test of whether the service system functions as planned. By this point, mistakes in design are harder to correct. As one noted service expert says, 'There is simply no substitute for a proper rehearsal' when introducing a new service.[24] In the case of the discount share-dealing service described earlier, the bank ran a pilot test by offering employees a special price for one month. The offer was marketed internally, allowing the bank to observe the service process in action before it was actually introduced to the external market.

Commercialization

During the commercialization stage, the service goes live and is introduced to the marketplace. This stage has two primary objectives. The first is to build and maintain acceptance of the new service among large numbers of service delivery personnel who will be responsible day to day for service quality. This task is made easier if acceptance has been built in by involving key groups in the design and development process all along. However, it will still be a challenge to maintain enthusiasm and communicate the new service throughout the system; excellent internal marketing will help.

The second objective is to monitor all aspects of the service during introduction and through the complete service cycle. If the customer needs six months to experience the entire service, then careful monitoring must be maintained through at least six months. Every detail of the service should be assessed: telephone calls, face-to-face transactions, billing, complaints and delivery problems. Operating efficiency and costs should also be tracked.

Post-Introduction Evaluation

At this point, the information gathered during commercialization of the service can be reviewed and changes made to the delivery process, staffing or marketing mix variables on the basis of actual market response to the offering.

An example of post-introduction evaluation is when Expedia.com, the travel website, realized that despite pre-launch testing, restrictions on Expedia bargain fares were confusing to customers. A 'hot fix' team was called in to remedy the problem.[25] Within a day, the project team redesigned the presentation of information so that the fare restrictions would be clear to customers.

No service will ever stay the same. Whether deliberate or unplanned, changes will always occur. Therefore, formalizing the review process is critical to make those changes that enhance service quality from the customer's point of view.

Service Blueprinting

A stumbling block in service innovation and development is the difficulty of describing and depicting the service at the concept development, service development and market test stages. One of the keys to matching service specifications to customer expectations is the ability to describe critical service process characteristics objectively and to depict them so that employees, customers and managers alike know what the service is, can see their role in its delivery and understand all the steps and flows involved in the service process. In this section we look in depth at service blueprinting, a useful tool for designing and specifying intangible service processes.[26]

What is a Service Blueprint?

The manufacturing and construction industries have a long tradition of engineering and design. Can you imagine a house being built without detailed plans? Can you imagine a car, a computer or, even, a simple product like a child's toy or a shampoo being produced without concrete and detailed plans, written specifications and engineering drawings? Yet services commonly lack concrete specifications. A service, even a complex one, might be introduced without any formal, objective depiction of the process.

A service blueprint is a picture, or a map, that accurately portrays the service system so that the different people involved in providing it can understand and deal with it objectively, regardless of their roles or their individual points of view. Blueprints are particularly useful at the design stage of service development. A service blueprint visually displays the service by simultaneously depicting the process of service delivery, the points of customer contact, the roles of customers and employees, and the visible elements of the service (see Figure 8.2). It provides a way to break down a service into its logical components and to depict the steps or tasks in the process, the means by which the tasks are executed and the evidence of service as the customer experiences it.

Figure 8.2   Service blueprinting

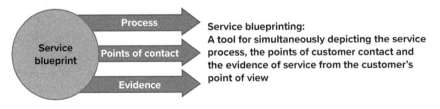

Service blueprinting:
A tool for simultaneously depicting the service process, the points of customer contact and the evidence of service from the customer's point of view

Blueprinting has its origins in a variety of fields and techniques, including logistics, industrial engineering, decision theory and computer systems analysis – all of which deal with the definition and explanation of processes.[27] Because services are 'experiences' rather than objects, blueprinting is a particularly useful tool for describing them.

Blueprint Components

The key components of service blueprints are shown in Figure 8.3.[28] They are customer actions, 'onstage' contact employee actions, 'backstage' contact employee actions, and support processes. The conventions for drawing service blueprints are not rigidly defined, and thus the particular symbols used, the number of horizontal lines in the blueprint, and the particular labels for each part of the blueprint may vary somewhat depending on what you read and the complexity of the service being described. These variations are not a problem as long as you keep in mind the purpose of the blueprint and view it as a useful tool rather than as a set of rigid rules for designing services.

Figure 8.3   Service blueprint components

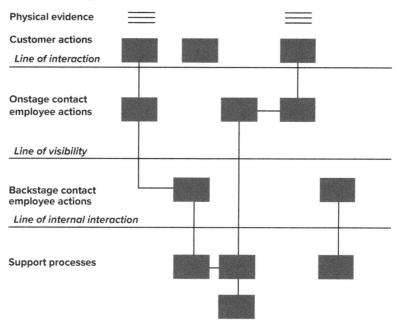

The *customer actions* area encompasses the steps, choices, activities and interactions that the customer performs in the process of purchasing, consuming and evaluating the service. The total customer experience is apparent in this area of the blueprint. In a legal services example, the customer actions might include a decision to contact a lawyer, telephone calls to the lawyer, face-to-face meetings, receipt of documents and receipt of a bill.

In parallel to the customer actions are two areas of contact employee actions. The steps and activities that the contact employee performs that are visible to the customer are the *onstage contact employee actions*. In the legal services setting, the actions of the lawyer (the contact employee) that are visible to the client are, for example, the initial interview, intermediate meetings and final delivery of legal documents. Those contact employee actions that occur behind the scenes to support the onstage activities are the *backstage contact employee actions*. In the example, anything the lawyer does behind the scenes to prepare for the meetings or to prepare the final documents will appear in this section of the blueprint, together with telephone call contacts the customer has with the lawyer or other front-line staff in the firm. All *non-visible* contact employee actions are shown in this area of the blueprint.

The *support processes* section of the blueprint covers the internal services, steps and interactions that take place to support the contact employees in delivering the service. Again, in our legal example, any

The examples in this chapter are very much simplified versions of a blueprint and any of the steps in the blueprint could be exploded into a detailed blueprint if needed for a particular purpose. For example, if the hotel learned that the 'room service' step was taking too long and causing unacceptable delays, that step could be blueprinted in much greater detail to isolate the problems.

Blueprints for Technology-Delivered Self-Service

Up to this point our discussion of service blueprints has only related to services that are delivered in person, services in which employees interact directly with customers at some point in the process. But what about technology-delivered services like self-service websites (Expedia's travel information site, Dell's customer self-service site) and interactive kiosks (ATMs, airline self-check-in machines)? Can service blueprinting be used effectively to design these types of services? Certainly it can, but the lines of demarcation change, and some blueprint labels may need to be adapted (see Figure 8.5).

As Figure 8.5 shows, if no employees are involved in the service (except when there is a problem or the service does not function as planned), the contact person areas of the blueprint are not needed. Instead, the area above the line of visibility can be used to illustrate the interface between the customer and the computer website or the physical interaction with the kiosk. This area can be relabelled onstage/visible technology. The backstage contact person actions area would be irrelevant in this case.

If the service involves a combination of human and technology interfaces, as with airline computerized check-in, the onstage area can be cut into two distinct spaces divided by an additional horizontal line. In the airline computerized check-in example, the human contact with the airline employee who takes the bags and checks identification would be shown in one area and the technology interactions with the check-in computer kiosk would be shown in the second area, both above the line of visibility.

Reading and Using Service Blueprints

A service blueprint can be read in a variety of ways, depending on the purpose. If the purpose is to understand the customer's view of the process or the customer experience, the blueprint can be read from left to right, tracking the events in the customer action area. Questions that might be asked include: how is the service initiated by the customer? What choices does the customer make? Is the customer highly involved in creating the service or are few actions required of the customer? What is the physical evidence of the service from the customer's point of view? Is the evidence consistent with the organization's strategy and positioning?

If the purpose is to understand contact employees' roles, the blueprint can also be read horizontally, but this time focusing on the activities directly above and below the line of visibility. Questions that might be asked include: how rational, efficient and effective is the process? Who interacts with customers, when and how often? Is one person responsible for the customer, or is the customer passed off from one contact employee to another?

If the purpose is to understand the integration of the various elements of the service process, or to identify where particular employees fit into the bigger picture, the blueprint can be analysed vertically. In this analysis, it becomes clear what tasks and which employees are essential in the delivery of service to the customer. The linkages from internal actions deep within the organization to front-line effects on the customer can also be seen in the blueprint. Questions that might be asked include: what actions are being performed backstage to support critical customer interaction points? What are the associated support actions? How are handoffs from one employee to another taking place?

If the purpose is service redesign, the blueprint can be looked at as a whole to assess the complexity of the process, how it might be changed, and how changes from the customer's point of view would impact the contact employee and other internal processes, and vice versa. Blueprints can also be used to assess the overall efficiency and productivity of the service system and to evaluate how potential changes will impact the system.[29] The blueprint can also be analysed to determine likely failure points or bottlenecks in

Figure 8.5   Blueprint for a bank cash machine

Physical Evidence	Appearance of cash machine	Appearance of cash machine	Appearance of cash machine	Appearance of the dispensed notes	Appearance of the receipt and quality of printing	Details provided on card or machine regarding customer service number
User actions	Approach the cash machine	Insert debit card and enter PIN	Select cash with-drawal with receipt and enter amount	Remove debit card	Remove cash	Any problems with machine or debit card, make phone call
Frontstage	Screen shows various banking options		Releases debit card	Releases cash	Prints and releases receipt	Call centre staff explain complaints process
Backstage		Computer checks ID details and either rejects or accepts transaction	Computer checks balance in customer's account and either accepts or rejects transaction	Computer updates account balance		Procedures in place to check and rectify complaints
Support Processes	Technology maintenance –ensuring full functionality		Account details kept up to date	Machine is kept topped up with cash	Machine is kept topped up with paper and printing ink	Provision of 24/7 call centre

the process. When such points are discovered, a firm can introduce measures to track failures, or that part of the blueprint can be exploded so that the firm can focus in much greater detail on that piece of the system.

Blueprinting applications in a variety of contexts have demonstrated benefits and uses including:[30]

- Providing a platform for innovation
- Recognizing roles and interdependencies among functions, people and organizations
- Facilitating both strategic and tactical innovations
- Transferring and storing innovation and service knowledge
- Designing moments of truth from the customer's point of view
- Suggesting critical points for measurement and feedback in the service process
- Clarifying competitive positioning
- Understanding the ideal customer experience.

Clearly, one of the greatest benefits of blueprinting is education.[31] When people begin to develop a blueprint, what is actually known about the service quickly becomes apparent. Sometimes the shared knowledge is minimal. Biases and prejudices are made explicit, and agreements and compromises must be reached. The process itself promotes cross-functional integration and understanding. In the attempt to visualize the entire service system, people are forced to consider the service in new and more comprehensive ways.

Building a Blueprint

Recall that many of the benefits and purposes of building a blueprint evolve from the process of doing it. Thus the final product is not necessarily the only goal. Through the process of developing the blueprint, many intermediate goals can be achieved: clarification of the concept, development of a shared service vision, recognition of complexities and intricacies of the service that are not initially apparent, and delineation of roles and responsibilities, to name a few. The development of the blueprint needs to involve a variety of functional representatives as well as information from customers. Drawing or building a blueprint is not a task that should be assigned to one person or one functional area. Figure 8.6 identifies the basic steps in building a blueprint.

Figure 8.6   Building a service blueprint

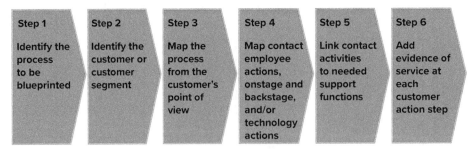

Step 1	Step 2	Step 3	Step 4	Step 5	Step 6
Identify the process to be blueprinted	Identify the customer or customer segment	Map the process from the customer's point of view	Map contact employee actions, onstage and backstage, and/or technology actions	Link contact activities to needed support functions	Add evidence of service at each customer action step

---

EXAMPLE

Frequently Asked Questions about Service Blueprinting

The following provides answers to frequently asked questions about service blueprints.

What Process Should be Blueprinted?

What process to map depends on the team or organization's objectives. If these are not clearly defined, then identifying the process can present a challenge. Questions to ask: why are we blueprinting the service? What is our objective? Where does the service process begin and end? Are we focusing on the entire service, a component of the service, or a period of time?

Can Multiple Market Segments be Included on One Blueprint?

Generally, the answer to this question is no. Assuming that market segments require different service processes or attributes, the blueprint for one segment may look very different from the blueprint for another. Only at a very high level (sometimes called a *concept blueprint*) might it be relevant to map multiple segments simultaneously.

Who Should 'Draw' the Blueprint?

A blueprint is a team effort. It should not be assigned as an individual task, certainly not in the development stages. All relevant parties should be involved or represented in the development effort. The task might include employees across multiple functions in the organization (marketing, operations, human resources, facilities design) as well as customers in some cases.

Should the Actual or Desired Service Process be Blueprinted?

If a new service is being designed, then clearly it is important to start with the desired service process. However, in cases of service improvement or service redesign, it is very important to map (at least at a conceptual level) the actual service process first. Once the group knows how the service is actually functioning, then the blueprint can be modified or used as a basis for changes and improvements.

Should Exceptions or Recovery Processes be Incorporated within the Blueprint?

It may be possible to map relatively simple, commonly occurring recovery processes onto a blueprint, assuming there are not a lot of these. However, this process can quickly become complex and cause the blueprint to be confusing or unreadable. Often a better strategy is to indicate common fail points on the blueprint and, if needed, develop sub-blueprints for the service recovery processes.

What is the Appropriate Level of Detail?

The answer to this question depends again on the objective or purpose for doing the blueprint in the first place. If it is to be used primarily to communicate the general nature of the service, then a concept blueprint with few details is best. If it is being used to focus on diagnosing and improving the service process, then more detail is needed. Because some people are more detail oriented than others, this particular question will always arise and needs to be resolved in any team blueprinting effort.

What Symbols should be Used?

At this point in time, there is not a lexicon of blueprinting symbols that is commonly used or accepted across companies. What is most important is that the symbols be defined, be kept relatively simple, and be used consistently by the team and across the organization if blueprints are being shared internally.

Should Time or Financial Costs be Included on the Blueprint?

Blueprints are very versatile. If reducing the time taken for various parts of the service process is an objective of the blueprinting effort, then time can definitely be included. The same is true for financial costs or anything else that is relevant as an objective. However, it is not advisable to put such information on the blueprint unless it is of central concern.

Step 1: Identify the Service Process to be Blueprinted

Blueprints can be developed at a variety of levels, and there needs to be agreement on the starting point. For example, in an express mail delivery blueprint, specific blueprints could be developed for two-day express mail, large accounts, Internet-facilitated services and/or high street drop-off centres. Each of these blueprints would share some features but would also include unique features. Or if the 'sort packages' and 'loading' elements of the process were found to be problem areas or bottlenecks that were slowing service to customers, a detailed blueprint of the sub-processes at work in those two steps could be developed. A firm can identify the process to be mapped once it has determined the underlying purpose for building the blueprint.

Step 2: Identify the Customer or Customer Segment Experiencing the Service

A common rationale for market segmentation is that each segment's needs are different and therefore will require variations in the service or product features. Thus, blueprints are most useful when developed for a particular customer or customer segment, assuming that the service process varies across segments. At a very abstract or conceptual level it may be possible to combine customer segments on one blueprint. However, once almost any level of detail is reached, separate blueprints should be developed to avoid confusion and maximize their usefulness.

Step 3: Map the Service Process From the Customer's Point of View

Step 3 involves charting the choices and actions that the customer performs or experiences in purchasing, consuming and evaluating the service. Identifying the service from the customer's point of view first will help avoid focusing on processes and steps that have no customer impact.

This step forces agreement on who the customer is (sometimes no small task) and may involve considerable research to determine exactly how the customer experiences the service.

Sometimes the beginning and ending of the service from the customer's point of view may not be obvious. For example, research in a haircutting context revealed that customers viewed the process as beginning with the telephone call to the salon and making the appointment, whereas the hairstylists did not typically view the making of appointments as part of the service process.[32] Similarly, in a mammogram screening service, patients viewed driving to the clinic, parking and locating the screening office as part of the service experience. If the blueprint is being developed for an existing service, it may be helpful at this point in the process to videotape or photograph the service process from the customer's point of view. Managers, and others who are not on the front line, often do not actually know what the customers are experiencing and may be quite surprised when they view the actual service experience.

Step 4: Map Contact Employee Actions, Both Onstage and Backstage, and/or Technology Actions

First the lines of interaction and visibility are drawn, and then the process from the customer-contact person's point of view is mapped, distinguishing visible or onstage activities from invisible backstage activities. For existing services this step involves questioning front-line operations employees to learn what they do and which activities are performed in full view of the customer versus which activities are carried out behind the scenes.

For technology-delivered services or those that combine technology and human delivery, the required actions of the technology interface will be mapped above the line of visibility as well. If no employees are involved in the service, the area can be relabelled 'onstage technology actions'. An additional horizontal line can separate 'onstage contact employee actions' from 'onstage technology actions' if both human and technology interactions are involved. Using the additional line will facilitate reading and interpretation of the service blueprint.

Step 5: Link Contact Activities to Needed Support Functions

The line of internal interaction can then be drawn and linkages from contact activities to internal support functions can be identified. In this process, the direct and indirect impact of internal actions on customers becomes apparent. Internal service processes take on added importance when viewed in connection with their link to the customer. Alternatively, certain steps in the process may be viewed as unnecessary if there is no clear link to the customer's experience or to an essential internal support service.

Step 6: Add Evidence of Service at Each Customer Action Step

Finally, the evidence of service can be added to the blueprint to illustrate what the customer sees and receives as tangible evidence of the service at each step in the customer experience. A photographic blueprint, including photos, slides or video of the process, can be very useful at this stage to aid in analysing the impact of tangible evidence and its consistency with the overall strategy and service positioning.

High-Performance Service Innovations

Up to this point in the chapter we have discussed approaches and tools for developing and designing new services. A dilemma in most companies is that there are too many new ideas from which to choose. New technologies, changing customer needs, deregulation, competitors' actions – all these areas result in myriad potential new offerings to consider. The question is which to pursue. How can a company decide which new offerings will likely be major successes, and which may be less successful or even fail? How can they decide which are worthy of investment and which are not?

In this section we summarize some of what has been learned about successful new services in terms of measures of success, key success drivers and the importance of integrating new services.

Choose the Right Projects

Success with new services is going to be determined by two things: choosing the right projects and doing the projects right.[33] Researchers confirm that following the new service development process discussed earlier in this chapter and illustrated in Table 8.2 will help with both these goals.[34] Service blueprinting, also presented in this chapter, will help as well, primarily with the second goal of getting the projects rights.

Another concept, *portfolio management for new products*, is very useful in helping companies choose the right projects in the first place.[35] Using this approach, companies manage their product portfolio like they manage their financial portfolio. The approach helps companies prioritize projects, choose which ones to accelerate, and determine the best balance between risk versus return, maintenance versus growth and short-term versus long-term projects. Methods for portfolio management include financial models, scoring models and checklists, mapping approaches, and behavioural approaches.[36]

Integrate New Services

Because of the nature of services – they are processes, typically delivered at least in part by people, consumed and produced simultaneously – any new service introduction will affect the existing systems and services. Unlike when a manufacturer adds a new product to its production facility, new service introductions are frequently visible to customers and may even require their participation. Explicit recognition of these potential impacts, and planning for the integration of people, processes and physical evidence, will facilitate success.[37] This recognition will help in both (1) deciding which projects to pursue – sometimes the disruptive effect on existing systems is too great to warrant the investment – and (2) knowing how to proceed with implementation – what elements of existing processes, people and physical facilities will need to be adjusted, added or changed.

Consider Multiple Measures of Success

In predicting the success of a new service, multiple performance measures may be considered.[38] First, and most commonly used, is near-term *financial performance* including revenue growth, profitability, market share and return on investment (ROI). In other cases, *relationship enhancement* may be a more appropriate measure of success. This measurement might include (1) the new service's effect on customer loyalty, (2) image enhancement and (3) the effect on the success of other products and services. Or success may be measured in terms of *market development* – the degree to which the new service opens up new markets or new customer segments. Successful projects will lead to increases in one, or perhaps more than one, of these measures.

Maintain Some Flexibility

New service success depends on market-driven, customer-focused new product processes; emphasis on planning for and executing the launch; integration of services within existing processes (including staff training); and strong marketing communications, both external and internal. Yet, firms must be cautioned about being too rigid in their service innovation approach. Steps in the development process should be allowed some flexibility, and there will no doubt be overlapping processes. Initial service development, for example, can be occurring simultaneously with additional gathering of customer information. Because services, particularly business-to-business services, are often very complex, some creativity and 'out of order' decisions will be needed. There must be some elements of improvisation, anarchy and internal competition in the development of new services. 'Consequently, the innovation and adoption of new services must be both a planned process and a happening!'[39]

Summary

Service providers must effectively match customer expectations to new service innovations and actual service process designs. However, because of the very nature of services – their intangibility and variability and co-creation elements – the design and development of service offerings are complex and challenging. Many services are only vaguely defined before their introduction to the marketplace. This chapter has outlined some of the challenges involved in innovating and designing services and some strategies for effectively overcoming the challenges.

Through adaptations of the new product development process that is commonplace in goods production and manufacturing companies, service providers can begin to not only make their offerings more explicit but also avoid failures. The new service development process presented in the chapter includes nine stages, beginning with the development of a business and new service strategy and ending with post-introduction evaluation of the new service. Between these initial and ending stages are a number of steps and checkpoints designed to maximize the likelihood of new service success. Carrying out the stages requires the inclusion of customers, contact employees, business partners and anyone else who will affect or be affected by the new service. Because successful new service introduction is often highly dependent on service employees (often they are the service), integration of employees at each stage is critical.

Service blueprinting is a particularly useful tool in the new service development process. A blueprint can make a complex and intangible service concrete through its visual depiction of all the steps, actors, processes and physical evidence of the service. The key feature of service blueprints is their focus on the customer – the customer's experience is documented first and is kept fully in view as the other features of the blueprint are developed.

The final section of the chapter summarized some of the key factors driving successful new service innovations, including the need for portfolio planning and integration of new services with existing processes and systems. The need to consider multiple measures of success was highlighted as well as the importance of maintaining flexibility in the innovation and new service development process.

Key Concepts

Business analysis	168	Market testing	169
Crowdsourcing	167	New service development	160
Idea generation	166	Service blueprint	168
Internet of Things	163	Service concept development and evaluation	167

Exercises

1 Think of a new service you would like to develop if you were an entrepreneur. How would you go about it? Describe what you would do and where you would get your information.

2 Find a new and interesting service in your local area, or a service offered on your campus. Document the service process via a service blueprint. To do this exercise, you will probably need to interview one of the service employees. After you have documented the existing service, use blueprinting concepts to redesign the service or change it in some way.

3 Choose a service you are familiar with and document the customer action steps through a photographic blueprint. What is the 'evidence of service' from your point of view as a customer?

4 Develop a service blueprint for a technology-delivered service (such as an Internet-based travel service). Compare and contrast this blueprint with one for the same service delivered via more traditional channels (such as a personal travel agent).

5 Compare two services on the Internet. Discuss the design of each in terms of whether it meets your expectations. How could the design or the service process be changed? Which one is most effective, and why?

Discussion Questions

1 Why is it challenging to design and develop services?

2 Why is service innovation so critical for firms and countries?

3 Identify where ideas for service innovation might come from.

4 What are the risks of attempting to describe services in words alone?

5 Compare and contrast the blueprints in Figures 8.4 and 8.5.

6 How might a service blueprint be used for marketing, human resource and operations decisions? Focus on the blueprint example in Figure 8.4 as a context for your answer.

7 Assume that you are a multi-product service company that wants to grow through adding new services. Describe a logical process you might use to introduce a new service to the marketplace. What steps in the process might be most difficult and why? How might you incorporate service blueprinting into the process?

8 Discuss Table 8.2 in terms of the four types of opportunities for growth represented there. Choose a company or service, and explain how it could grow by developing new services in each of the four cells.

9 What role can social media play in innovation?

Further Reading

Barrett, M., Davidson, E., Prabhu, J. and Vargo, S.L. (2015). Service innovation in the digital age: Key contributions and future directions. *MIS Quarterly*, 39(1), 135–54.

Bitner, M.J., Ostrom, A.L. and Morgan, F.N. (2008). Service blueprinting: A practical technique for service innovation. *California Management Review*, 50(3), 66–94

Den Hertog, P., van der Aa, W. and de Jong, M.W. (2010). Capabilities for managing service innovation: Towards a conceptual framework. *Journal of Service Management*, 21(4), pp. 490–514.

Poetz, M.K. and Schreier, M. (2012). The value of crowdsourcing: Can users really compete with professionals in generating new product ideas? *Journal of Product Innovation Management*, 29(2), 245–56.

Ramaswamy, V. and Gouillart, F. (2010). Building the co-creative enterprise. *Harvard Business Review*, October, 100–109.

Storey, C., Cankurtaran, P., Papastathopoulou, P. and Hultink, E.J. (2016). Success factors for service innovation: A meta-analysis. *Journal of Product Innovation Management*, 33(5), 527–48.

Witell, L., Gebauer, H., Jaakkola, E., Hammedi, W., Patricio, L. and Perks, H. (2017). A bricolage perspective on service innovation. *Journal of Business Research*, 79, 290–98.

Witell, L., Snyder, H., Gustafsson, A., Fombelle, P. and Kristensson, P. (2016). Defining service innovation: A review and synthesis. *Journal of Business Research*, 69(8), 2863–72.

Chapter Outline

Factors Necessary for Appropriate Service Standards	185
Types of Customer-Defined Service Standards	189
Development of Customer-Defined Service Standards	191
Summary and Key Concepts	201
Exercises	201
Discussion Questions	202
Further Reading	202

Learning Objectives

This chapter's objectives are to:

1 Distinguish between company-defined and customer-defined service standards.
2 Differentiate among one-time service fixes and 'hard' and 'soft' customer-defined standards.
3 Explain the critical role of the service encounter sequence in developing customer-defined standards.
4 Illustrate how to translate customer expectations into behaviours and actions that are definable, repeatable and actionable.
5 Explain the process of developing customer-defined service standards.
6 Emphasize the importance of service performance indexes in implementing strategy for service delivery.

Opening Example

DHL Freight – Understanding Service Standards from a Customer Perspective

DHL Freight is a leading provider of international road transportation solutions in Europe and beyond. The road freight market is highly fragmented, with many providers offering seemingly similar services. Unlike many consumer businesses, the level of emotional engagement between the customer and the provider is low and the relationship is often reduced to a negotiation around operational service quality (e.g., on-time delivery) and price. This results in price competition and yield erosion for the road freight provider. Customers tend to switch provider easily and do not demonstrate any loyalty behaviour. It is therefore important for DHL Freight to deliver the highest standard of service that meets the needs of customers.

Source: ©Bjoern Wylezich/ Shutterstock

In order to determine if shippers are truly driven by price alone, DHL Freight undertook a survey with 700 road freight customers in five countries (France, Germany, the Netherlands, Poland, and Sweden) and asked them to identify the most important attributes of a road freight provider as well as what they would most like their current provider to improve. The research demonstrated that shippers care about more than just operational quality; they are also concerned with the quality of the service support and the ease of doing business with the road freight provider.

DHL Freight found that there was a big difference between the operating standards used by the company to measure performance and the factors used by customers to rate the quality of the service. Like most companies, DHL Freight uses functional scorecards to measure how well their functions perform in terms of aspects such as deliveries made, invoice claims, invoice correctness and number of complaints, but the performance of DHL Freight on these measures did not correlate with customer survey results relating to satisfaction, loyalty or likelihood of recommending the road freight provider to others.

From a customer's perspective, operational quality and price were considered very important, as was expected, but they are not the only or most important aspects. The survey identified that ease of contact with the freight provider, acting quickly and having knowledgeable staff are equally important, or even more so. DHL Freight has therefore introduced standards and customer satisfaction and net promoter score measures to address these softer attributes.

Clearly the relationship between a company and its customers in road freight is more complex than is widely assumed.

Source: Adapted from K. MacGillavry and A. Wilson (2014) 'Delivering loyalty via customer experience management at DHL Freight', Global Business and Organizational Excellence, 33(6), 6–20.

As we saw in Chapters 6 and 7, understanding customer requirements is the first step in delivering high service quality. Once managers of service businesses accurately understand what customers expect, they face a second critical challenge: using this knowledge to set service quality standards and goals for the organization. Service companies often experience difficulty in setting standards to match or exceed customer expectations – partly because doing so requires that the marketing and operations departments within a company work together. In most service companies, integrating the work of the marketing function and the operations function (appropriately called *functional integration*) is not a typical approach; more frequently these two functions operate separately – setting and achieving their own internal goals – rather than pursuing a joint goal of developing the operations standards that best meet customer expectations.

Creating service standards that address customer expectations is not a common practice in service firms. Doing so often requires altering the very process by which work is accomplished, which is ingrained in tradition in most companies. Often change requires new equipment or technology. Change also necessitates aligning executives from different parts of the firm to understand collectively the comprehensive view of service quality from the customer's perspective. And, almost always, change requires a willingness to be open to different ways of structuring, calibrating and monitoring the way service is provided.

Factors Necessary for Appropriate Service Standards

The translation of customer expectations into specific service quality standards depends on the degree to which tasks and behaviours to be performed can be standardized or routinized. Some executives and managers believe that services cannot be standardized – that customization is essential for providing high-quality service. Managers also may feel that standardizing tasks is inconsistent with employee empowerment – that employees will feel controlled by the company if tasks are standardized. Further, they feel that services are too intangible to be measured. This view leads to vague and loose standard setting with little or no measurement or feedback.

In reality, many service tasks are routine (such as those needed for opening bank accounts or servicing domestic gas central heating boilers) and, for these, specific rules and standards can be fairly easily established and effectively executed. Employees may welcome knowing how to perform actions most efficiently: it frees them to use their ingenuity in the more personal and individual aspects of their jobs.

Standardization of Service Behaviours and Actions

Standardization of service can take three forms: (1) substitution of technology for personal contact and human effort, (2) improvement in work methods, and (3) combinations of these two methods.[1] Examples of technology substitution include automatic teller machines, automatic car washes and airport X-ray machines. Improvements in work methods are illustrated by restaurant salad bars and routinized tax and accounting services developed by firms such as Pizza Hut and Sage (Accounting Software).

Technology and work improvement methods facilitate the standardization of service necessary to provide consistent delivery to customers. By breaking tasks down and providing them efficiently, technology also allows the firm to calibrate service standards such as the length of time a transaction takes, the accuracy with which operations are performed and the number of problems that occur. In developing work improvements, the firm comes to understand completely the process by which the service is delivered. With this understanding, the firm more easily establishes appropriate service standards.

Standardization, whether accomplished by technology or by improvements in work processes, reduces gap 2. Standardization does not mean that service is performed in a rigid, mechanical way. Customer-defined standardization ensures that the most critical elements of a service are performed as expected by customers, not that every action in a service is executed in a uniform manner. In fact, using customer-defined standardization can allow for, and be compatible with, employee empowerment. One example of this compatibility involves the time limits many companies establish for customer service calls. If their customers' highest priorities involve feeling good about the call or resolving problems, then setting a limit for calls would be decidedly company-defined and not in customers' best interests.

SERVICE SPOTLIGHT

Some companies use customer priorities rather than company priorities to determine service standards. Zappos, the online shoe retailer has no set standard for the amount of time an employee should spend on the telephone with a customer. Instead, they have defined standards that focus on making the customer satisfied and comfortable, letting telephone representatives use their own judgement about the duration of calls. They recognize that standardization of service is not appropriate in some situations.

When is the Strategy of Customization Better than Standardization?

This chapter focuses on the benefits of customer-defined standards in the context of situations – hotels, retail stores, service outlets – in which it is important to provide the same service to all or most customers. In these situations, standards establish strong guidelines for technology and employees in order to ensure consistency and reliability. In other services, providing standardization is neither appropriate nor possible, and customization – providing unique types and levels of service to customers – is a deliberate strategy.

In most 'expert' services – such as accounting, consulting, engineering and dentistry, for example – professionals provide customized and individualized services; standardization of the tasks is perceived as being impersonal, inadequate and not in the customer's best interests. Because patient and client needs differ, these professionals offer very customized services that address individual requirements. They must adapt their offerings to the particular needs of each customer because each situation is different. Even within a given medical specialty, few patients have the same illness with precisely the same symptoms and the same medical history. Therefore, standardizing the amount of time a doctor spends with a patient is rarely possible, one of the reasons why patients usually must wait before receiving medical services even though they have advance appointments. Because professionals such as accountants and lawyers cannot usually standardize what they provide, they often charge by the hour rather than by the job, which allows them to be compensated for the customized periods of time they spend with clients. It is important to recognize, however, that even in highly customized services, some aspects of service provision can be routinized. Physiotherapists and dentists, for example, can and do standardize recurring and non-technical aspects such as checking patients in, weighing patients, taking routine measurements, billing patients and collecting payment. In delegating these routine tasks to assistants, the professional staff can spend more of their time on the expert service of diagnosis or patient care.

Another situation in which customization is the chosen strategy is in business-to-business contexts, particularly with key accounts. When accounts are large and critical to a provider, most aspects of service provision are customized. At a very basic level, this customization takes the form of service contracts such as those described for ISS (see Service Spotlight on page 187) in which the client and the provider agree on issues such as cleaning standards, speed of response, etc. At a higher level, customization involves creative problem-solving and innovative ideas (as in consulting services).

Finally, many consumer services are designed to be (or appear) very customized. These services include spa and upmarket hotel visits, exotic vacations such as safaris, and even haircuts from expensive salons. In these situations, the steps taken to ensure the successful delivery of service are often standardized behind the scenes but appear to the customer to be very individualized. Even Disney theme parks use this approach, employing hundreds of standards to ensure the delivery of 'magic' to each individual customer.

Formal Service Targets and Goals

Companies that have been successful in delivering consistently high service quality are noted for establishing formal standards to guide employees in providing service. These companies have an accurate sense of how well they are performing service that is critical to their customers – how long it takes to conduct transactions, how frequently service fails, how quickly they settle customer complaints – and strive to improve by defining goals that lead them to meet or exceed customer expectations.

One type of formal goal-setting that is relevant in service businesses involves specific targets for individual behaviours or actions. As an example, consider the behaviour 'calls the customer back quickly', an action that signals responsiveness in contact employees. If the service goal for employee behaviour is stated in such a general term as 'call the customer back quickly', the standard provides little direction for service employees. Different employees will interpret this vague objective in their own ways, leading to inconsistent service: some may call the customer back in ten minutes whereas others may wait two to four days. And the firm itself will not be able to determine when or if individual employees meet the goal because its expression is not measurable – one could justify virtually any amount of time as 'quickly'. On the other hand, if the individual employee's service goal is to call each customer back within four hours, employees have a specific, unambiguous guideline about how quickly they should execute the action (four hours). Whether the goal is met is also unequivocal: if the call occurs within four hours the company meets the goal; otherwise it does not.

Another type of formal goal setting involves the overall department or company target, most frequently expressed as a percentage, across all executions of the behaviour or action. For example, a department might set as its overall goal 'to call the customer back within four hours 97 per cent of the time' and collect data over a month's or years' time to evaluate the extent to which it meets the target.

Service firms that produce consistently excellent service – firms such as Disneyland Paris, DHL and British Airways – have very specific, quantified, measurable service goals. Disneyland calibrates employee performance on myriad behaviours and actions that contribute to guest perceptions of high service quality. Whether they are set and monitored using audits (such as timed actions) or customer perceptions (such as opinions about courtesy), service standards provide a means for formal goal setting.

⭐ SERVICE SPOTLIGHT

Integrated Service Solutions (ISS), headquartered in Copenhagen, Denmark, is one of the world's largest facility service providers, with market presence in Europe, Asia, South America and Australia. ISS employs more than 480,000 people serving 200,000 public and private-sector customers in over 50 countries. It offers services such as catering, office support, security, cleaning, property services and facility management. ISS's service offering has been developed to meet customer needs. ISS has to meet standards of service set by its customers. For example, in Singapore, where the company cleans the Raffles Link shopping area, the standards for cleanliness may be among the most challenging in the world. ISS Singapore uses the most modern and environmentally friendly cleaning equipment, chemicals and methods to serve their demanding customers in Singapore.

Source: **www.issworld.com**

Customer- not *Company*-Defined Standards

Virtually all companies possess service standards and measures that are *company defined* – they are established to reach internal company goals for productivity, efficiency, cost or technical quality. A current company-defined standard that does not meet customer expectations is the common practice of voice-activated telephone support systems that do not allow consumers to speak to humans. Because these systems save companies money (and actually provide faster service to some customers), many organizations have switched from the labour-intensive practice of having customer representatives to using these systems.

To close gap 2, standards set by companies must be based on customer requirements and expectations (identified using some of the methods outlined in Chapter 6) rather than just on internal company goals. In this chapter we make the case that company-defined standards are not typically successful in driving behaviours that close provider gap 2. Instead, a company must set *customer-defined standards:* operational standards based on pivotal customer requirements that are visible to and measured by customers. These standards are deliberately chosen to match customer expectations and to be calibrated the way the customer views and expresses them. Because these goals are essential to the provision of excellent service, the rest of this chapter focuses on customer-defined standards.

As explained in Chapter 4, knowing customer requirements, priorities and expectation levels can be both effective and efficient. Anchoring service standards on customers can save money by identifying what the customer values, thus eliminating activities and features that the customer either does not notice or will not pay for. Through precise measurement of expectations, the company often discovers that it has been over-delivering to many customer needs.

A bank might add several extra tellers and reduce the average peak waiting time in queues from seven minutes to five minutes. If customers expect, however, to wait up to eight minutes during peak time, the investment in extra tellers may not be effective. An opportunity thus exists to capture the value of this information through reduced teller costs and higher profits.[2]

Although customer-defined standards need not conflict with productivity and efficiency, they are not developed for these reasons. Rather, they are anchored in and steered by customer perceptual measures of service quality or satisfaction. The service standards that evolve from a customer perspective are likely to be different from company-defined service standards.

Virtually all organizations have lists of actions that they measure regularly, most of which fall into the category of company-defined standards. Often these standards deal with activities or actions that reflect the history of the business rather than the reality of today's competitive marketplace or the needs of current customers.

★ SERVICE SPOTLIGHT

Scottish and Southern Energy, a supplier of gas and electricity to domestic consumers, follows the Energy Supplier Guaranteed Standards set by the UK energy regulator (Ofgem). These standards are aimed at meeting customer expectations and requirements, including:

- **Keeping appointments** – Scottish and Southern Energy (SSE) issues guarantees about punctuality when it sets appointments with customers in relation to their gas or electricity supply. Customers can select either a morning or afternoon slot, Monday to Friday, and can also specify a two-hour window. If SSE cannot keep this appointment, or fails to give advance notice, customers receive £30 off their bill.
- **Electricity bill queries** – SSE promises to reply in writing within five working days with an explanation about customer billing enquiries; for example, if customers think that they are due a refund, have noticed a billing error or if they are in disagreement with SSE about changes to their mode of payment. If not, the company pays the customer £30.
- **Meter disputes** – When customers believe that their meter is faulty and SSE is unable to resolve the query over the telephone, the company sends a written explanation within five working days or offers an appointment to visit within seven working days. If the company fails to do so, it promises to send the customers a £30 payment.
- SSE also ensures that its customers are compensated quickly, and promises payment within 10 working days, or the customer receives a further £30.

Types of Customer-Defined Service Standards

The type of standards that close provider gap 2 are *customer-defined standards:* operational goals and measures based on pivotal customer requirements that are visible to and measured by customers rather than on company concerns such as productivity or efficiency. Take a typical operations standard such as inventory control. Most firms control inventory from the company's point of view.

However, supermarkets such as Tesco and Sainsbury's capture every single service measurement related to inventory control *from the customer's point of view*. The companies begin with the question, 'What does the customer see?' and answer, 'The average number of stockouts per week'. These supermarkets then design a customer-focused measurement system based on measures such as the number of empty shelves, the number of unfulfilled product requests and complaints as well as transaction-based data linked to the use of customer loyalty cards at the tills. These and other customer-defined standards allow for the translation of customer requirements into goals and guidelines for employee performance. Two major types of customer-defined service standards can be distinguished: 'hard' and 'soft'. These standards are discussed in the following two sections.

Hard Customer-Defined Standards

As we stressed in Chapter 4, customer expectations of reliability – fulfilment of service promises – are high. Studies across numerous industries have found that the most frequent customer complaints are associated with service mistakes or problems (32 per cent of all complaints) or poor product performance (30 per cent of all complaints).[3]

To address the need for reliability, companies can institute a 'do it right the first time' and an 'honour your promises' value system by establishing reliability standards. An example of a generic reliability standard that would be relevant to virtually any service company is 'right first time', which means that the service performed is done correctly the first time according to the customer's assessment. If the service involves delivery of products, 'right first time' to the customer might mean that the shipment is accurate – that it contains all that the customer ordered and nothing that the customer did not order. If the service involves installation of equipment, 'right the first time' would likely mean that the equipment was installed correctly and could be used immediately by the customer. Another example of a reliability standard is 'right on time', which means that the service is performed at the scheduled time. The company representative arrives when promised or the delivery is made at the time the customer expects it. In more complex services, such as disaster recovery or systems integration in computer service, 'right on time' would likely mean that the service was completed by the promised date.

Reliability is often the single most important concern of service customers. In online retailing, on time and accurate fulfilment of orders is one of the most important aspects of reliability. One of the best examples of hard customer-defined service standards in the Internet context is the single summary metric used by Dell technologies for fulfilment.[4] This metric is the Perfect Order Metric, which Dell developed in response to a declining Net Promoter Score. After talking to many customers, Dell learned that customers simply wanted Dell to deliver what the customer ordered when Dell said they would. Based on this feedback, the Perfect Order Metric is calculated as follows: (% of on-time deliveries) X (% of complete orders) X (% of orders delivered damage-free) X (% of orders delivered with accurate documentation). Dell tracks its performance on this reliability metric and rewards employees based on how well they do, ensuring employees are working toward goals that are most important to the customer.

Hard service standards for responsiveness are set to ensure the speed or promptness with which companies deliver products (within two working days), handle complaints (by sundown each day), answer questions (within two hours), answer the telephone and arrive for repair calls (within 30 minutes of the estimated time). Table 9.1 displays several examples of hard customer-defined standards. In addition to standard-setting that specifies levels of response, companies must have well-staffed customer service departments. Responsiveness perceptions diminish when customers wait to get through to the company by telephone, are put on hold, or are dumped into a telephone mail system.

Table 9.1   Examples of hard standards include:

Company	Customer Priorities	Customer-Defined Standards
DHL	On-time delivery	% of packages delivered late on the correct day % of packages wrong day % of missed pickups
Dell Computer	On-time delivery Computer works properly	% On-time deliveries % Complete orders % Orders delivered damage -free % Orders with accurate documentation

Soft Customer-Defined Standards

Not all customer priorities can be counted, timed or observed through audits. As Albert Einstein once said, 'Not everything that counts can be counted, and not everything that can be counted counts'. For example, 'understanding and knowing the customer' is not a customer priority that can be adequately captured by a standard that counts, times or observes employees. In contrast to hard measures, soft measures are those that must be documented using perceptual data. We call the second category of customer-defined standards soft standards and measures because they are opinion-based measures and cannot be directly observed. They must be collected by talking to customers, employees or others. Soft customer-defined service standards provide direction, guidance and feedback to employees in ways to achieve customer satisfaction and can be quantified by measuring customer perceptions and beliefs. Soft standards are especially important for person-to-person interactions such as the selling process and the delivery process for professional services. Table 9.2 displays several examples of soft customer-defined standards. Many firms have both hard and soft customer-defined standards. For example a student administration service within a university may have hard standards such as: all enquiries in person to receive attention within two minutes; acknowledge all written enquiries within two working days; and answer all telephone enquiries during working hours within thirty seconds. These hard standards may sit alongside soft standards such as staff are: committed to providing accurate information; are approachable, helpful, respectful and professional; are committed to equitable treatment for all; respect client confidentiality.

One-Time Fixes

When customer research is undertaken to find out what aspects of service need to be changed, requirements can sometimes be met using one-time fixes. One-time fixes are *technology, policy or procedure changes that, when instituted, address customer requirements.* We further define one-time fixes as those company standards that can be met by an outlet (a franchisee, for example) making a one-time change that does not involve employees and therefore does not require motivation and monitoring to ensure compliance. We include one-time fixes in our discussion of standards because organizations with multiple outlets often must clearly define these standards to ensure consistency.

Examples of successful one-time fixes include Europcar and other car rental companies' express check-in, Tesco's self-scanning tills or KLM's online check-in facility. In each of these examples, customers expressed a desire to be served in ways different from the past. All had clearly indicated their frustration at waiting in long lines. Whereas most companies in these industries decided for various reasons not to address these customer requirements, Europcar, Tesco and KLM each responded with one-time fixes that virtually

Table 9.2 Examples of soft customer-defined standards include:

Company	Customer Priorities	Customer-Defined Standards
Ritz-Carlton*	Being treated with respect	'Gold Standards' Uniforms are to be immaculate Wear proper and safe footwear Wear name tag Adhere to grooming standards Notify supervisor immediately of hazards Use proper telephone etiquette Ask the caller, 'May I place you on hold?' Do not screen calls Eliminate call transfers when possible
American Express	Resolution of problems	Resolve problem at first contact (no transfers, other calls or multiple contacts) Communicate and give adequate instructions; take all the time necessary
	Treatment	Listen Do everything possible to help Be appropriately reassuring (open and honest)
	Courtesy of representative	Put card member at ease Be patient in explaining billing process Display sincere interest in helping card member Listen attentively Address card member by name Thank card member at end of call

Source: 'The Ritz-Carlton Basics', flyer distributed by Ritz-Carlton to all employees and www.Americanexpress.com.

revolutionized the service quality delivered by their companies. One-time fixes are often accomplished by technology. Technology can simplify and improve customer service, particularly when it frees company personnel by handling routine, repetitive tasks and transactions. Customer service employees can then spend more time on the personal and possibly more essential portions of the job. Some technology, in particular computer databases that contain information on individual needs and interests of customers, allows the company to standardize the essential elements of service delivery.

One-time fixes also deal with the aspects of service relating to rules and policies, operating hours, product quality and price. An example of a one-time fix involving a policy change is that of allowing front-line employees to refund money to dissatisfied customers. An example of operating-hour changes is extending the operating hours of call centres to include Sundays.

⭐ **SERVICE SPOTLIGHT**

Many hotels are implementing one-time fixes to address consumer environmental concerns relating to sustainability. Such fixes may include: moving away from bottled water as the standard and offering conveniently located filtered water dispensers and complimentary refillable bottles; adding recycling systems for newspapers and bathroom amenity containers; implementing food waste composting programmes; and introducing linen and towel reuse programmes.

Development of Customer-Defined Service Standards

How have firms such as Ritz Carlton, KLM and DHL been able to develop commendable customer-defined service standards? Figure 9.1 shows the general process for setting customer-defined service standards.

Figure 9.1   Process for setting customer-defined standards

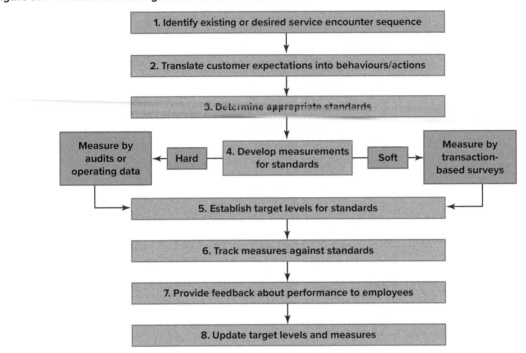

Step 1: Identify Existing or Desired Service Encounter Sequence

As stated in Chapter 4, a customer's expectations and overall service quality evaluations are the accumulation of evaluations of multiple service experiences. Service encounters are the component pieces needed to establish service standards in a company. In establishing standards we are concerned with service encounter quality, because we want to understand for each service encounter the specific requirements and priorities of the customer. When we know these priorities, we can focus on them as the aspects of service encounters for which standards should be established. Therefore, one of the first steps in establishing customer-defined standards is to delineate the service encounter sequence. Identifying the sequence can be done by listing the sequential steps and activities that the customer experiences in receiving the service. Alternatively, service blueprints (see Chapter 8) can be used to identify the sequence by noting all the customers' activities across the top of the blueprint. Vertical lines from customer activities into the lower levels of the blueprint signal the points at which service encounters take place. Standards that meet customer expectations can then be established.

Because many services have multiple encounters, companies and researchers have examined whether some encounters (for example, the first or the last) are more important than others. The Marriott Corporation identified the encounters that occur in the first ten minutes of a hotel stay as the most critical, leading the hospitality company to focus on hotel front-desk experiences (such as express check-in) when making improvements. Although service practice and management literature have emphasized strong starts, recent research indicates that strong finishes in the final event of the encounter have a greater impact on overall satisfaction. Further, the research shows that consistent performance throughout the encounter – widely believed to produce the most favourable evaluations – is not as effective as a pattern of improving performance that culminates in a strong finish.[5] An implication of this research for hotels is that managers should focus on the 'back end' of the hotel experience – checkout, parking, concierge services – to leave a strong final impression.

Step 2: Translate Customer Expectations Into Behaviours and Actions

Setting a standard in broad conceptual terms, such as 'improve skills in the company', is ineffective because the standard is difficult to interpret, measure and achieve. When a company collects data, it often captures customer requirements in very abstract terms. In general, contact or field people often find that data are not diagnostic – they are too broad and general. Research neither tells them specifically what is wrong and right in their customer relationships nor helps them understand what activities can be eliminated so that the most important actions can be accomplished. In most cases, field people need help translating the data into specific actions to deliver better customer service.

Effective service standards are defined in very specific ways that enable employees to understand what they are being asked to deliver. At best, these standards are set and measured in terms of specific responses of human behaviours and actions.

Figure 9.2 shows different levels of abstraction/concreteness for standards in a service firm, arrayed from top (most abstract) to bottom (most concrete and specific). At the very abstract level are customer requirements that are too general to be useful to employees: customers want satisfaction, value and relationships. One level under these very general requirements are abstract dimensions of service quality already discussed in this text: reliability, responsiveness, empathy, assurance and tangibles. One level further down are attributes more specific in describing requirements. If we dig still deeper beneath the attribute level, we get to specific behaviours and actions that are at the right level of specificity for setting standards.

Figure 9.2   What customers expect: getting to actionable steps

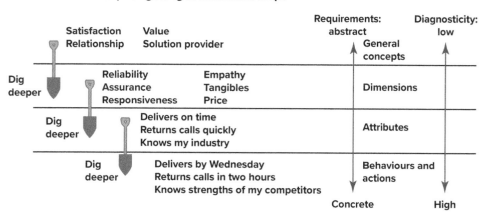

A real-world example of the difference in requirements across these levels will illustrate their practical significance. In a traditional measurement system for a major company's training division, only one aspect of the instructor was included in its class evaluation: ability of instructor. During qualitative research relating to the attributes that satisfy students, three somewhat more specific requirements were elicited: (1) instructor's style, (2) instructor's expertise and (3) instructor's management of class. Although the articulation of the three attributes was more helpful to instructors than the broad 'ability of instructor', management found that the attributes were still too broad to help instructors wanting to improve their course delivery. When the company invested in a customer-defined standards project, the resulting measurement system was far more useful in diagnosing student requirements because the research focused on *specific behaviours and actions* of instructors that met student requirements. Instead of a single broad requirement or three general attributes, the requirements of students were articulated in 14 specific behaviours and actions that related to the instructor and 11 specific behaviours and actions that related to the course content. These behaviours and actions were clearly more diagnostic for communicating what was good and bad in the courses.

An additional benefit of this approach was that feedback on behaviours and actions was less personal than feedback on traits or personal characteristics. It was also easier for employees of the company to make changes that related to behaviours rather than to personality traits.

Step 3: Determine Appropriate Standards

The next step involves deciding whether hard or soft standards should be used to capture the behaviour and action. One of the biggest mistakes companies make in this step is to choose a hard standard hastily. Companies are accustomed to operational measures and have a bias towards them. However, unless the hard standard adequately captures the expected behaviour and action, it is not customer defined. The best way to decide whether a hard standard is appropriate is first to establish a soft standard by means of follow-up satisfaction surveys and then determine over time which operational aspect most correlates to this soft measure. Figure 9.3 shows the linkage between speed of complaint handling (a hard measure) and satisfaction (a soft measure), and illustrates that satisfaction strongly depends on the number of hours it takes to resolve a complaint.

Figure 9.3   Linkage between soft and hard measures for speed of complaint handling

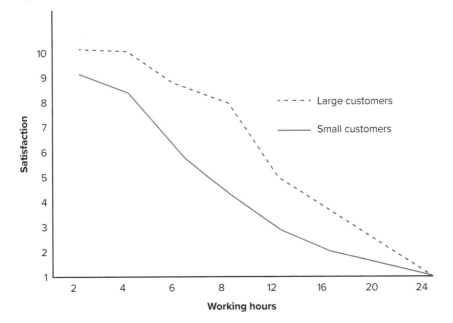

This involves prioritizing the behaviours and actions, of which there will be many, into those for which customer-defined standards will be established. The following are the most important criteria for creation of the standards.

1. *The standards are based on behaviours and actions that are very important to customers.* Customers have many requirements for the products and services that companies provide. Customer-defined standards need to focus on what is *very important* to customers. Unless very important behaviours/actions are chosen, a company could show improvement in delivering to standards with no impact on overall customer satisfaction or business goals.

2. *The standards cover performance that needs to be improved or maintained.* Customer-defined standards should be established for behaviour that needs to be improved or maintained. The company gets the highest leverage or biggest impact from focusing on behaviours and actions that need to be improved.

3. *The standards cover behaviours and actions employees can improve.* Employees perform consistently according to standards only if they understand, accept and have control over the behaviours and actions specified in the standards. Holding contact people to standards that they cannot control (such as product quality or time lag in introduction of new products) does not result in improvement. For this reason, service standards should cover controllable aspects of employees' jobs.

4. *The standards are accepted by employees.* Employees will perform to standards consistently only if they understand and accept the standards. Imposing standards on unwilling employees often leads to resistance, resentment, absenteeism, even turnover. Many companies establish standards for the amount of time it should take (rather than for the time it does take) for each service job and gradually cut back on the time to reduce labour costs. This practice inevitably leads to increasing tensions among employees. In these situations, managers, financial personnel and union representatives can work together to determine new standards for the tasks.

5. *The standards are predictive rather than reactive.* Customer-defined standards should not be established on the basis of complaints or other forms of reactive feedback. Reactive feedback deals with past concerns of customers rather than with current and future customer expectations. Rather than waiting for dissatisfied customers to complain, the company should actively seek both positive and negative perceptions of customers in advance of complaints.

6. *The standards are challenging but realistic.* A large number of studies on goal-setting show that highest performance levels are obtained when standards are challenging but realistic. If standards are not challenging, employees get little reinforcement for mastering them. On the other hand, unrealistically high standards leave an employee feeling dissatisfied with performance and frustrated by not being able to attain the goal.

Table 9.3 shows an example of the set of behaviours and actions selected by a company for its complaint-handling service encounter. Some of these are different across the two segments of customers for which standards were set (small and large customers). Three other behaviours were chosen for standards across all customers.

Table 9.3   Customer-defined standards for complaint handling by segment

Large Customers	All Complaint-Handling Personnel Trained to
Are assigned an individual to call with complaints Have a 4-hour standard for resolving problems	Paraphrase problems Ask customers what solution they prefer
Small Customers	
Can call service centre or individual Have an 8-hour standard for resolving problems	Verify that problem has been fixed

⭐ **SERVICE SPOTLIGHT**

It isn't only commercial bodies that develop service standards. Public bodies such as government departments and local government set standards for delivery. The following service standards are used by the Department of Education in Northern Ireland.

Customer service standards

The Department of Education (DE) staff will aim to:
- treat all customers with respect
- be polite

- listen
- be helpful
- ensure that people take responsibility for handling enquiries
- be clear and avoid the use of jargon
- be honest and fair in all our dealings.

Telephone

When you contact the Department of Education (DE) by telephone we will:
- respond to all telephone calls in a courteous and professional manner
- identify ourselves by name on the telephone and answer all telephone calls promptly
- endeavour to answer all telephone queries immediately; where this is not possible you will be advised as to why a delay is necessary and a reply will be made within one working day
- use a text phone relay service for those who are hearing impaired.

If you begin the conversation in Irish, Ulster Scots or another language, and the person you are speaking to is not able to respond in that language, they will offer the following options:
- to continue the call in English
- to write to us in the other language, or
- in the case of Irish or Ulster Scots, to transfer you to our voicemail where you can leave a message.

Letter or email

When you contact the Department of Education in writing – by letter or email – we will:
- acknowledge all written communication (received by postal communication or email) within two working days
- provide a written reply to an enquiry/communication within 15 working days (if DE cannot provide a definitive response within this timeframe, we will send you an interim reply explaining the reasons for this, and how the matter is to be progressed)
- when requested, and in line with departmental policies, supply information, materials and publications in alternative formats and languages, where reasonably practicable to do so.

In person

When you visit the Department of Education we will ensure that you are:
- made to feel welcome and are greeted appropriately by reception staff
- met promptly by a member of staff and
- advised of any safety or security procedures
- we will ensure that our reception area is:
  - clean and comfortable and
  - easily accessible to visitors with disabilities.

Source: **https://www.education-ni.gov.uk/customer-service-standards.**

Step 4: Develop Measurements for Standards

Once companies have determined whether hard or soft standards are appropriate and which specific standards best capture customer requirements, they must develop feedback measures that adequately capture the standards. Two types of measures are hard measurements and soft measurements.

Hard Measurements

Hard measurements for *measuring behaviours and actions* consist of counts or audits or timed actions that provide feedback about the operational performance of a service standard. What distinguishes these data from soft measurements is that they can be captured continuously and operationally without asking the customer's opinion about them.

⭐ SERVICE SPOTLIGHT

Here are some of the actual hard measurements used by Federal Express in its international operations:

- *Missing proofs of delivery:* the number of invoices that do not include proof-of-delivery paperwork
- *Overgoods:* lost and found packages that lack, or have lost, identifying labels for the sender and the addressee, and are sent to the Overgoods Department
- *Wrong day late deliveries:* number of packages delivered after the commitment date
- *Traces:* the number of 'proof of performance' requests from customers that cannot be answered through data contained in the computer system.[6]

In these and other hard measurements, the actual gauge involves a count of the number and type of actions or behaviours that are correct or incorrect. Somewhere in the operation system these actions and behaviours are tabulated, frequently through information technology. Other gauges of hard measures include service guarantee lapses (the number of times a service guarantee is invoked because the service did not meet the promise), amounts of time (as in the number of hours or days to respond to a question or complaint or of minutes spent in a queue) and frequencies associated with relevant standards (such as the number of visits made to customers).

The appropriate hard measure to deliver to customer requirements is not always intuitive or obvious, and the potential for counting or tracking an irrelevant aspect of operations is high. For this reason it is desirable to link the measure of operational performance with soft measures (relationship surveys or follow-up satisfaction surveys) to be sure that they are strongly correlated.

Soft Measurements

Two types of perceptual measurement that were described in Chapter 6 can document customers' opinions about whether performance met the standards established: satisfaction surveys and relationship surveys. Relationship and SERVQUAL surveys cover all aspects of the customer's relationship with the company, are typically expressed in attributes, and are usually completed once a year. Follow-up satisfaction surveys, possibly including a Net Promoter Score measure, are associated with specific service encounters, are short (approximately six or seven questions) and are administered as close in time to a specific service encounter as possible. Such surveys can be administered in various ways: company-initiated telephone calls following the interactions, customer-initiated calls to a freephone number or online electronic surveys. Follow-up satisfaction surveys are administered continuously, whenever a customer experiences a service encounter of the type being considered, and they provide data on a continuous basis. For requirements that are longer term, such as in a long-term business to business contract, annual relationship surveys can document customer perceptions on a periodic basis.

Employee monitoring can also be used for soft measurement. This is illustrated by the practice of supervisors listening in on employee calls. You may have experienced this practice when you called customer service numbers for many organizations and noticed that the voice prompts tell you that calls may be monitored for quality purposes. The purpose of this monitoring is to provide feedback on employee performance to the standards set by the organization to meet customer needs. One critical aspect of developing feedback mechanisms is ensuring that performance captures the process from the customer's view rather than the company's perspective. A supervisor monitoring an employee's handling of a customer service call, for example, should focus less on how quickly the employee gets the customer off the telephone and more on how adequately he or she handles the customer's request.

★ **SERVICE SPOTLIGHT**

The airlines Air France and KLM have developed seven service standards to ensure a consistent quality of customer service. These soft standards apply for all who maintain direct contact with customers. These standards also supplement harder standards that are measured by the airlines around aspects of safety, security, reliability, punctuality and sustainability. The seven soft service standards are as follows:

1. **Be willing to help customers and be attentive to their needs**
   Being willing to help means adopting an easy-to-approach attitude, encouraging customers to express their needs sooner. Being attentive means showing customers a willingness to help and listening carefully to customers to better identify their needs.
2. **Be involved and proactive**
   Being involved means taking an interest in customers, showing concern and making them feel at ease. Customers should feel their needs are being taken into account and that their expectations can be met. Being proactive means anticipating customers' requirements and taking spontaneous action to ensure that customers are comfortable.
3. **Be courteous and friendly**
   Being courteous and tactful means treating customers in a friendly, respectful and discreet manner. Being warm and friendly means having a smile and staff showing the customer that they enjoy their job.
4. **Be impeccably dressed and well mannered**
   Being impeccably dressed means looking immaculate and wearing the uniform in accordance with the uniform manual. Being well mannered means respecting the rules of etiquette.
5. **Deliver a high level of expertise**
   Delivering a high level of expertise means being knowledgeable about all aspects of one's job. Knowing where to get hold of the right information. Knowing how to use appropriate skills to provide customers with reliable top-quality service. Being able to adapt to different situations.
6. **Provide relevant information regularly**
   Providing relevant information that is useful to customers at all stages of their journey. The information provided is comprehensible and consistent, and is given at the right time and place. Ensuring that information is provided on an ongoing basis reassures customers that their needs are being attended to.
7. **Create a welcoming environment**
   Creating a clean, peaceful and inviting environment that contributes towards determining the airline's image and reflecting the company's high service standards.

Source: **www.klm.com.**

Step 5: Establish Target Levels for Standards

The next step requires that companies establish target levels for the standards. Without this step the company lacks a way to quantify whether the standards have been met. Figure 9.3 provided a good example of the approach used to set standards for timeliness in a service company. Each time a complaint was made to the company, and each time a complaint was resolved, employees logged in the times. They also asked each customer his or her satisfaction with the performance in resolving the complaint. The company was then able to plot the information from each complaint on the chart to determine how well the company was performing as well as where the company wished to be in the future. The vertical axis in Figure 9.3 shows the satisfaction levels of customers, and the horizontal axis shows the number of hours it took the company to resolve customer problems. This technique is one of several for determining the target level.

Another technique is a simple perception–action correlation study. When the service consists of repetitive processes, companies can relate levels of customer satisfaction with actual performance of a behaviour or task. Consider, for example, a study to determine the standard for customers' wait time in a queue. The information needed includes customer perceptions of their queuing up (soft perceptual measure) and the amount of time they actually stand in the queue (hard operations measure). The joint collection of these data over many transactions provides evidence of the sensitivity of customers to different wait times.

An airline conducted precisely this study by having airline staff intercept customers as they approached the check-in counter. As each customer entered the line, the attendant stamped the entry time on a ticket and handed the customer the stamped ticket. As the customer exited the queue at the end of the transaction, airline staff restamped the ticket with the exit time and asked the customer three or four questions about their perceptions of queuing up and their satisfaction with the transaction. Aggregating the individual customer data provided a graph that allowed the company to evaluate the impact on perceptions of various levels of line waits.

Step 6: Track Measures Against Standards

Successful service businesses such as Royal Bank of Scotland and London Underground (part of Transport for London) have careful and comprehensive fact-based systems about their operations.

Royal Bank of Scotland uses customer satisfaction, actual performance and operational measures as the drivers of service performance measurement. Qualitative research involving trade-off analysis was used to identify customers' perceptions of the key service attributes from a bank. These attributes were then established as service standards which were measured through an index which was constructed from scores relating to:

- Customer satisfaction questionnaire (70 per cent)
- Mystery shopping activity (20 per cent)
- An inventory of tangibles relating to physical aspects of each branch (10 per cent).

Table 9.4   The attributes that were measured by each method

Attributes	Satisfaction Questionnaire	Mystery Shopping	Inventory
Courtesy	X	X	
Telephone handling	X	X	
Queuing	X	X	
Product/service knowledge	X	X	
Problem-solving	X		
Efficiency	X		
Appearance	X	X	
Loyalty	X		
Tangibles			X

London Underground measures service quality through customer satisfaction surveys, mystery shopping activities and the monitoring of complaints. However, the quality of service is also measured through operational information relating to areas such as:

- Percentage of trains cancelled
- Percentage of ticket offices open
- Percentage of ticket machines in operation
- Average journey times
- Headway: the average time between each train arriving at a platform.

These combine with the other service quality measures to provide guidance for management priorities and investment decisions.

Step 7: Provide Feedback about Performance to Employees

Data and facts need to be analysed and distributed to support evaluation and decision-making at multiple levels within the company. The data also must be deployed quickly enough that the people who need it to make decisions about service or processes can do so. Responsibility for meeting service requirements must also be communicated throughout the organization. All parts of the organization must be measuring their services to internal customers and, ultimately, measuring how that performance relates to external customer requirements. Many organizations use dashboards that employees can access through their computers that set out performance measures in a relatively simple and straightforward manner. Data is visualized on a dashboard as tables, line charts, bar charts and gauges. Symbols can also be used in the form of traffic lights with red showing a drop in performance, amber showing no change and green showing an improvement in performance.

Step 8: Update Target Levels and Measures

The final step involves revising the target levels, measures and, even, customer requirements regularly enough to keep up with customer expectations.

Developing Service Performance Indices

One outcome from following the process for developing customer-defined standards is a service performance index. **Service performance indices** are comprehensive composites of the most critical performance standards. Development of an index begins by identifying the set of customer-defined standards that the company will use to drive behaviour. Not all service performance indices contain customer-defined standards, but the best are based on them. Most companies build these indices by: (1) understanding the most important requirements of the customer, (2) linking these requirements to tangible and measurable aspects of service provision, and (3) using the feedback from these indices to identify and improve service problems. The most progressive companies also use the feedback for reward and recognition systems within the company.

Among the issues that companies must tackle when developing service performance indices are: (1) the number of components to be contained, (2) what overall or summary measures will be included, (3) whether the index should be weighted or unweighted (to put greater emphasis on the performance of the attributes considered most important to customers), and (4) whether all parts of the business (departments, sectors or business units) will be held to the same performance measures. One of the most important goals of an index is to simply and clearly communicate business performance in operational and perceptual terms. Companies must develop the same rigour in these measurement areas that they have in financial performance.

Summary

This chapter discussed the discrepancy between company perceptions of customer expectations and the standards they set to deliver to these expectations. Among the major causes for provider gap 2 are inadequate standardization of service behaviours and actions, absence of formal processes for setting service quality goals, and lack of customer-defined standards. These problems were discussed and detailed, along with strategies to close the gap. To close the service design and standards gap, standards set by companies must be based on customer requirements and expectations rather than just on internal company goals. That is, the company-defined standards are typically not successful in driving behaviours that close provider gap 2 and a company must set customer-defined standards based on key customer requirements visible to and measured by customers.

In this chapter we described two types of service standards: hard standards, those that can be counted, timed or observed through audits; and soft standards, customer perceptions that cannot be directly observed. Customer-defined standards are at the heart of delivery of service that customers expect: they are the link between customers' expressed expectations and company actions to deliver to those expectations. Creating these service standards is not always done by service organizations. Doing so requires that companies' marketing and operations departments work together by using the marketing research as input for operations design. Unless the operations standards are defined by customer priorities, they are not likely to have an impact on customer perceptions of service.

Key Concepts

Customization v. standardization	186	One-time fixes	190
Goal-setting	187	Service performance indices	200
Hard customer-defined service standards	189	Service standards	185
Measuring behaviours and actions	197	Soft customer-defined service standards	190

Exercises

1 Select a local service firm. Visit the firm and ascertain the service measurements that the company tracks. What hard measures does it monitor? What soft measures? On the basis of what you find, develop a service performance index.

2 Choose one of the peripheral services (such as computer, library, placement) provided by your university or college. What hard standards would be useful to track to meet student expectations? What soft standards? What one-time fixes would improve service?

3 Think about a specific service that you have delivered or received. Using Figure 9.2, write in the customer requirements at each of the levels. How far down in the chart can you describe requirements? Is that far enough? What would you need to do to find out more?

4 Look at three websites from which you can order products (such as amazon.co.uk or tesco.com). What are the companies' delivery promises? What types of standards might they set for these promises? Are these customer- or company-defined standards?

Discussion Questions

1   In what types of service industries are standards most difficult to develop? Why? Recommend three standards that might be developed in one of the firms from the industries you specify. How would employees react to these standards? How could you gain buy-in for them?

2   Given the need for customer defined service standards, do firms need company-defined standards at all? Could all standards in a company be customer defined? Why or why not? What functional departments in a firm would object to having all standards customer defined?

3   What is the difference between hard and soft standards? Which do you think would be more readily accepted by employees? By management? Why?

4   Consider the university or college you currently attend. What are examples of hard standards, soft standards and one-time fixes that would address student requirements? Does the university or college currently use these standards for delivery of service to students? Why or why not? Do you think your reasons would apply to private sector companies as well? To public or non-profit companies?

5   Think about a service that you currently use, and then map out the service encounter sequence for that service. What is your most important requirement in each interaction? Document these requirements and make certain that they are expressed at the concrete level of behaviours and actions.

6   From a customer perspective, what standards would you expect the following customer service personnel to meet:
    a. a hotel receptionist?
    b. a lawyer?
    c. a hospital cleaner?

Further Reading

Boksberger, P.E. and Melsen, L. (2011). Perceived value: A critical examination of definitions, concepts and measures for the service industry. *Journal of Services Marketing*, 25(3), 229–40.

Caemmerer, B. and Wilson, A. (2010). Customer feedback mechanisms and organisational learning in service operations. *International Journal of Operations and Production Management*, 30(3), 288–311.

Chun Wang, J., Wang, Y.C. and Tai, Y.F. (2016). Systematic review of the elements and service standards of delightful service. *International Journal of Contemporary Hospitality Management*, 28(7), 1310–1337.

Kwan, S.K. and Hottum, P. (2014). Maintaining consistent customer experience in service system networks. *Service Science*, 6(2), 136–147.

Taticchi, P., Tonelli, F. and Cagnazzo, L. (2010). Performance measurement and management: A literature review and a research agenda. *Measuring Business Excellence*, 14(1), 4–18.

Wilson, A. (2000). The use of performance information in the management of service delivery. *Marketing Intelligence and Planning*, 18(3), 127–34.

Chapter 10

The Physical and Virtual Servicescape

Chapter Outline

Physical and Virtual Evidence	205
Typology of Servicescapes	208
Strategic Roles of the Servicescape	210
Framework for Understanding Servicescape Effects on Behaviour	212
Guidelines for Physical Evidence Strategy	220
Summary and Key Concepts	222
Exercises	224
Discussion Questions	224
Further Reading	225

Learning Objectives

This chapter's objectives are to:

1 Explain the profound impact of physical evidence, particularly the servicescape, on customer perceptions and experiences.
2 Illustrate differences in types of physical and virtual servicescapes, the roles played by the servicescape, and the implications for strategy.
3 Explain *why* the servicescape affects customer and employee behaviour, using a framework based in marketing, organizational behaviour and environmental psychology.
4 Present elements of an effective physical evidence strategy.

Redesigning the Costa Coffee Experience

Costa, the coffee store, now owned by Coca Cola, has over 2,300 coffee outlets in over 30 countries with plans to expand into countries such as Bulgaria, Greece, Hungary, Poland, Romania, Russia and Switzerland in 2020.

Source: ©Sorbis/Shutterstock

Costa operates in a market which is highly competitive with other coffee outlets such as Starbucks, Cafe Nero, McDonald's and many small independent coffee shops. It is therefore critical that the Costa customer experience is consistent across all outlets. However, historically within the UK, store designs and the materials used in each store varied.

In 2016, a design agency was appointed to enhance the customer experience and improve the efficiency of over 1,000 UK branches. Research was undertaken to break down the customer journey into its individual component parts and provide guidance in the creation of a more relaxed environment that was easier for the customer to navigate. The improved design also aimed to make life easier for the baristas in terms of coffee preparation, cleaning and in the general efficiency of the outlets. Following a trial in nine branches, the new design was rolled out across the UK.

The counter of a coffee shop is the main focus of attention, where the initial service encounter occurs and the customer interacts with the barista and the coffee making process. The aim was to make the crafting of the coffee more visible to the customer by reorienting the coffee machines and removing the clutter created by the promotional material on the counter. The seating environment was also improved with a brighter and more contemporary colour scheme of oranges and blues to complement the brand's red logo. In certain zones, screens were installed along with sections of opaque glass in the windows to provide some privacy to customers. Lighting levels were also enhanced and this was combined with improved seating to create a more relaxed feel for the customer. Externally, outlets were designed to be more eye catching with a reduction in promotional materials and signage.

Source: Adapted from Costa redesign to roll out to 1,000 branches, Edge, 16 Sept, https://edgegb.com/news/costa-branch-roll-out.

In this chapter we explore the importance of physical evidence for communicating service quality attributes, setting customer expectations, and creating the service experience. In Chapter 1, when we introduced the expanded marketing mix for services, we defined physical evidence as *the environment in which the service is delivered and in which the firm and the customer interact, and any tangible commodities that facilitate performance or communication of the service.* The first part of this definition encompasses the actual physical or virtual facility in which the service is performed, delivered and consumed; throughout this chapter this facility is referred to as the **servicescape**.[1]

Physical evidence is particularly important for communicating about credence services (such as hairstyling), but it is also important for services such as hotels, hospitals and theme parks that are dominated by experience attributes. Think of how effectively Disney uses the physical evidence of its service to excite its customers. The brightly coloured displays, the music, the fantastic rides and the costumed characters all reinforce the feelings of fun and excitement that Disney seeks to generate in its customers. Think also of how effective Disney is in portraying consistent physical evidence that is compatible with its goals. The physical evidence and servicescape, or the 'stage' in Disney's terms, is always stimulating to the extreme, is always clean, is always in top repair and never fails to deliver what it has promised to consumers, and more. In this chapter we present many examples of how physical evidence communicates with customers and how it can play a role in creating the service experience, in satisfying customers, and in enhancing customers' perceptions of quality.

Physical and Virtual Evidence

What is Physical and Virtual Evidence?

Customers often rely on tangible cues, or physical and virtual evidence, to evaluate the service before its purchase and to assess their satisfaction with the service during and after consumption. Effective design of physical and virtual evidence is important for closing provider gap 2.

General elements of physical evidence are shown in Table 10.1. They include all aspects of the organization's physical facility (the servicescape) as well as other forms of tangible communication. Elements of the servicescape that affect customers include both exterior attributes (such as signage, parking and the landscape) and interior attributes (such as design, layout, equipment and decor). Note that web pages and virtual servicescapes conveyed over the Internet are increasingly important forms of physical evidence that companies can use to communicate about the service experience, making services more tangible for customers both before and after purchase. For example, travellers can now preview destinations, tour natural environments and 'experience' entertainment venues online before booking their trips or even deciding where to travel. Virtual tours and 360-degree views of hotels and their rooms allow potential guests to view the facilities in and out before booking.

Table 10.1   Elements of physical evidence

Exterior Servicescape	Interior Servicescape	Virtual Servicescape	Other Tangibles
Exterior design	Interior design	Web page design	Business cards
Signage	Equipment/technology	Web-cams	Stationery
Parking	Signage	Photographs	Billing statements
Landscape	Floor layout	360 degree views	Reports
Surrounding environment	Air quality/temperature	Virtual reality	Uniforms/Employee dress
	Lighting	Augmented reality	Brochures
	Floor coverings	Online chat facilities	
	Aromas/scents		

Virtual reality (VR) can be used to immerse consumers in a 360-degree digital environment. It is most commonly experienced via a headset or head-mounted display. A person using virtual reality equipment is able to look around the artificial world and move about in it. Hotels and travel companies such as Marriott, Tui and Qantas Airways have created promotional experiences using VR. The technology gives would-be travellers a taste of their possible destinations, and hotel facilities. It could also be used to enable consumers to experience a full retail experience whilst sitting at home. VR viewers are considered to be more emotionally engaged than when the same content is viewed in 2D or in a 360-degree video on a flat screen. However, that might simply be as a result of the novelty of the experience.

Augmented reality (AR) is the integration of the physical, real-world environment, with computer-generated digital information. It is often called mediated reality, in which a view of the surrounding real world is digitally manipulated. Whilst virtual reality requires a headset, augmented reality can be viewed on a mobile phone or tablet. The popularity of Pokémon GO, in 2016, led to many organizations looking at the potential of augmented reality. McDonald's, the restaurant chain, became the game's first official partner when it launched in Japan, turning 2,900 restaurants into venues where people were guaranteed to snag a new creature. Some brands that have their own mobile apps have upgraded to offer AR functionality. IKEA has developed IKEA Place, a mobile AR application that allows people to virtually place IKEA home furnishings in their rooms before purchasing. The app experience involves the customer viewing their room through their phone and virtually placing images of IKEA products into the image.

SERVICE SPOTLIGHT

Australian airline Qantas partnered with Hamilton Island, an island off the Queensland coast, to create a virtual reality experience that gave viewers the opportunity to immerse themselves in a 360-degree experience of the island and the Great Barrier Reef. The film was shown in Qantas lounges and in the first-class cabins on some of its flights. The project used Samsung Gear headsets. The objective was to showcase the destination in a different way, bringing it to life by exploring the destination from the cockpit of a helicopter and through swimming in the reef with turtles. Qantas has now extended this to other destinations and has produced a cardboard viewer that users can use to experience the virtual reality on their mobile phone.

Source: **www.qantas.com.**

Digital and virtual/augmented reality technology clearly provides tremendous opportunities for firms to communicate about their services. Online images create expectations for customers that set standards for service delivery, and it is critical that the actual services live up to these expectations. These digital tools also need to support the positioning of the service brand and be consistent with other marketing messages.

Physical and virtual evidence examples from different service contexts are given in Table 10.2. It is apparent that some services (like hospitals, resorts and child care) rely heavily on such evidence to communicate and create customer experiences. Others (like insurance, express mail) provide limited physical evidence for customers. All the elements of evidence listed for each service communicate something about the service to consumers, facilitate performance of the service and/or add to the customer's total experience. Although we focus in this chapter primarily on the servicescape and its effects, keep in mind that what is said applies to the other forms of tangible evidence as well.

How Does Physical Evidence Affect the Customer Experience?

Physical evidence, particularly the servicescape, can have a profound effect on the customer experience. This is true whether the experience is mundane (e.g. a bus or train ride), personally meaningful (e.g. a wedding or a birthday celebration), or spectacular (e.g. a week-long travel adventure). In all cases, the physical evidence of the service will influence the flow of the experience, the meaning customers attach to it, their satisfaction and their emotional connections with the organization delivering the experience.

As marketers and corporate strategists begin to pay more attention to experiences, they have recognized the impact of physical space and tangibles in creating those experiences. Lewis Carbone, a leading consultant on experience management, has developed an entire lexicon and management process around the basic idea of 'experience engineering' through 'clue management'.[2] *Clue management* refers to the process of

Table 10.2   Examples of physical evidence from the customer's point of view

Service	Physical Evidence	
	Servicescape	**Other Tangibles**
Insurance	Website	Policy itself Billing statements Periodic updates Company brochure Letters/cards Claims forms
Hotel	Building exterior Parking Reception area Lift/corridors Bedroom Bathroom Restaurant layout Bar Leisure facilities Website 360° views Virtual reality images	Uniforms Reports/stationery Billing statements
Airline	Airline check-in area Airline gate area Aeroplane exterior Aeroplane interior (decor, seats, air quality) Self-service check-in terminals Website 360° views	Boarding cards Food Uniforms
Express mail	Drop-off service points Website	Packaging Vehicles Uniforms Computers
Sporting event	Parking Stadium exterior Ticketing area Entrance Seating Toilets Catering outlets Playing field Website 360° views	Signs Tickets Programmes Employee uniforms Streaming sites

clearly identifying and managing *all* the various clues that customers use to form their impressions and feelings about the company. Included in this set of clues are what Carbone refers to as *mechanics clues,* or the physical and tangible clues that we focus on in this chapter. Other writers and consultants who focus on managing customer experiences also zero in on the importance of tangible evidence and physical facilities in shaping those experiences.[3] Throughout this chapter there are numerous examples of how physical evidence communicates with customers and shapes their experiences.

Italian bank ChiantiBanca has opened a string of new branches that are designed to look more like traditional local eateries than financial institutions. Italian design studio DINN! and branding agency Crea International devised the Restaurant Experience Banking concept to integrate ChiantiBanca's customer services with a relaxing and familiar local environment to enhance the social and economic potential of the branches.

Traditional cash desks are nowhere to be seen; they are replaced by clusters of tables surrounded by bar stools, chairs and cushioned seating cubes. Brochures displayed on the tables are arranged to look like restaurant menus. Digital technologies include video teller machines (VTMs), which replace the standard ATMs, and a touch-screen wall displaying information and advertisements. This showcase, called 'Bacheca del Chianti', communicates the values and identity of the bank through information and graphical tools that mirror the physical design of the branch office. Informal spaces at the front of the banks function as welcome zones, complete with play areas for young children. Each branch shares a similar colour and materials palette, including timber, Corten steel and earthy shades of brown and green. The first four branches are located in Florence, Poggibonsi, Fontebecci and Monteriggioni.

Source: **www.chiantibanca.it.**

Typology of Servicescapes

In this chapter we explain the roles played by the servicescape and how it affects employees and customers, and their interactions. The chapter relies heavily on ideas and concepts from environmental psychology, a field that encompasses the study of human beings and their relationships with built (human-made), natural and social environments.[4] The physical setting may be more or less important in achieving the organization's marketing and other goals, depending on certain factors. Table 10.3 is a framework for categorizing service

Table 10.3   Typology of service organizations based on variations in form and use of the servicescape

Complexity of the Servicescape		
Servicescape Usage	**Elaborate**	**Lean**
Self-service (customer involvement and limited interaction with employees)	Golf course eBay Amazon	ATM Electric vehicle charging station Mobile banking app
Interpersonal services (customer and employee interaction and involvement)	Restaurant Hospital Airline School	Car repair Hair salon
Remote service (employee involvement with limited interaction with customers and limited customer involvement)	Mobile network provision House insurance Electricity supply	Warehousing Provision of traffic information

Source: Adapted from M.J. Bitner (1992) 'Servicescapes: The impact of physical surroundings on customers and employees', *Journal of Marketing* 56 (April), pp. 57–71.

organizations on two dimensions that capture some of the key differences that will impact the management of the servicescape. Organizations that share a cell in the matrix will face similar issues and decisions regarding their physical spaces.

Servicescape Usage

First, organizations differ in terms of *whom* the servicescape will actually affect. That is, who actually comes into the service facility and thus is potentially influenced by its design – customers, employees, or both groups? The first column of Table 10.3 suggests three types of service organizations that differ on this dimension.

At one extreme is the *self-service* environment, in which the customer performs most of the activities and few if any employees are involved. Examples of self-service environments include ATMs, cinemas, self-service entertainment, such as golf courses and theme parks, and online services. In these primarily self-service environments the organization can plan the servicescape to focus exclusively on marketing goals such as attracting the right market segment, making the facility pleasing and easy to use, and creating the desired service experience.

At the other extreme of the use dimension is the *remote service*, which has little or no customer involvement with the servicescape. Telecommunications, online services, utilities, financial consultants and mail-order services are examples of services that can be provided without the customer ever seeing the service facility. In fact, the facility may be in a different region or a different country. In remote services, the facility can be set up to keep employees motivated and to facilitate productivity, teamwork, operational efficiency or whatever organizational behaviour goal is desired without any consideration of customers because they will never need to see the servicescape.

Interpersonal services are placed between these two extremes and represent situations in which both the customer and the employee are present and active in the servicescape. Examples abound, such as hotels, restaurants, hospitals, educational settings and airlines. In these situations, the servicescape must be planned to attract, satisfy and facilitate the activities of both customers and employees simultaneously. Special attention must also be given to how the servicescape affects the nature and quality of the social interactions between and among customers and employees. A cruise ship provides a good example of a setting in which the servicescape must support customers and the employees who work there, and facilitate interactions between the two groups.

Servicescape Complexity

The horizontal dimension of Table 10.3 suggests another factor that will influence servicescape management. Some service environments are very simple, with few elements, few spaces and few pieces of equipment. Such environments are termed *lean*. Electric vehicle charging stations and ATMs would be considered lean environments because both provide service from one simple structure. For lean servicescapes, design decisions are relatively straightforward, especially in self-service or remote service situations in which there is no interaction among employees and customers.

Other servicescapes are very complicated, with many elements and many forms. They are termed *elaborate* environments. An example is a hotel with its many floors and rooms, sophisticated equipment and complex variability in functions performed within the physical facility. In such an elaborate environment, the full range of marketing and organizational objectives theoretically can be approached through careful management of the servicescape. For example, a guest's hotel room can be designed to enhance comfort and satisfaction while simultaneously facilitating low-energy usage and costs. Firms such as hotels that are positioned in the elaborate interpersonal service cell face the most complex servicescape decisions.

Strategic Roles of the Servicescape

Within the cells of the typology, the servicescape can play many strategic roles simultaneously. An examination of the variety of roles and how they interact makes clear how strategically important it is to provide appropriate physical evidence of the service. In fact, the servicescape is frequently one of the most important elements used in positioning a service organization.

Package

Similar to a tangible product's package, the servicescape and other elements of physical evidence essentially 'wrap' the service and convey to consumers an external image of what is 'inside'. Product packages are designed to portray a particular image as well as to evoke a particular sensory or emotional reaction. The physical setting of a service does the same thing through the interaction of many complex stimuli. The servicescape is the outward appearance of the organization, and thus can be critical in forming initial impressions or setting up customer expectations – it is a visual metaphor for the intangible service. This packaging role is particularly important in creating expectations for new customers and for newly established service organizations that are trying to build a particular image. The physical surroundings offer an organization the opportunity to convey an image in a way not unlike the way an individual chooses to 'dress for success'. The packaging role extends to the appearance of contact personnel through their uniforms or dress and other elements of their outward appearance.[5]

⭐ SERVICE SPOTLIGHT

Eurostar, the operators of the trains running between the UK and France, has ditched the contemporary styling of their customer areas for a retro look evocative of the 'golden age of travel'. The makeover aims to create a 'less pedestrian travel experience'.

The London Ticket Hall combines Art Nouveau and Victorian Gothic. In the Eurostar terminal at St Pancras station, furniture and fittings for both the standard and business class ticket offices have been styled to incorporate materials and shapes common in the late 19th and early 20th century. Christopher Jenner, Eurostar's creative director stated, 'A good travel brand is judged by how it responds to its clients' needs. We've designed a space which is functional, yet embodies the narrative of connection and journey within its DNA.'

A Venetian plaster wall in the business class office is interrupted with curvy panels of walnut edged in brass. The same combination of wood and metal is used for the cabinetry, and bespoke blown-glass lampshades are suspended over the ticket desk made of formed Corian edged with wood. A 30-metre-long hand-drawn illustration of the journey from London to Paris is recreated on photo-etched stainless steel to cover the main walls of the standard class office. Curved desks are formed out of Corian, edged in steel and English oak. Limestone has been used to create new flooring for both spaces, which will retain their glazed frontages.

Art Nouveau and Victorian Gothic were radical movements which shared common values. These values – fluidity, organic, enriched and symbolic – were key inspiration points in the development of Eurostar's design.[6]

Interestingly, the same care and resource expenditures given to package design in product marketing are often not provided for services, even though the service package serves a variety of important roles. There are many exceptions to this generality, however. Smart companies like H&M, KLM and Novotel spend a lot of time and money relating their servicescape design to their brand, providing their customers with strong visual metaphors and 'service packaging' that conveys the brand positioning.

Facilitator

The servicescape can also serve as a facilitator in aiding the performance of persons in the environment. How the setting is designed can enhance or inhibit the efficient flow of activities in the service setting, making it easier or harder for customers and employees to accomplish their goals. A well-designed, functional facility can make the service a pleasure to experience from the customer's point of view and a pleasure to perform from the employee's. On the other hand, poor and inefficient design may frustrate both customers and employees. For example, an international air traveller who finds him or herself in a poorly designed airport with few signs, poor ventilation and few places to sit or eat will find the experience quite dissatisfying, and employees who work there will probably be unmotivated as well.

The same international traveller will appreciate seats on the aeroplane that are conducive to work and sleep. The seating itself, part of the physical surroundings of the service, has been improved over the years better to facilitate travellers' needs to sleep. In fact, the competition for better seat design continues as a major point of contention among the international airline carriers, and the results have translated into greater customer satisfaction for business travellers.[7] In first class travel airlines are competing to have the best suites on their planes, Singapore Airlines' first class offering not only features a Poltrona Frau upholstered leather reclining swivel chair but also offers couples travelling together the option of a double bed.

Citizen M boutique hotels located in the Netherlands and the UK provide all guests with a Phillips moodpad which is described as a technological personal assistant. It wakes you up, opens the blinds, turns on the lights, controls the television and adapts the room to your chosen theme in terms of colour, digital art and music.[8] Amazon's website is designed in such a way as to enable the user to quickly find products to purchase using a very clear search facility and simple shopping cart controls to speedily process payment. All these examples emphasize the facilitator role of the servicescape.

Socializer

The design of the servicescape serves as a socializer of both employees and customers in the sense that it helps convey expected roles, behaviours and relationships. For example, a new employee in a professional services firm would come to understand his or her position in the hierarchy partly through noting the office he or she has been allocated, the quality of the office furnishings and his or her location relative to others in the organization.

The design of the facility can also suggest to customers what their role is relative to employees, what parts of the servicescape they are welcome in and which are for employees only, how they should behave while in the environment and what types of interactions are encouraged. For example, consider a Club Med holiday environment that is set up to facilitate customer–customer interactions as well as guest interactions with Club Med staff. The organization also recognizes the need for privacy, providing areas that encourage solitary activities. To illustrate further, in many Starbucks locations, the company has shifted to more of a traditional coffeehouse environment in which customers spend social time rather than just coming in for a quick cup of coffee on the run. To encourage this type of socializing, these Starbucks locations have comfortable lounge chairs and tables set up to encourage customers to interact and to stay longer.

Differentiator

The design of the physical facility can differentiate a firm from its competitors and signal the market segment that the service is intended for. Given its power as a differentiator, changes in the physical environment can be used to reposition a firm and/or to attract new market segments. In shopping malls the signage, the colours used in decor and displays, and the type of music wafting from a store signal the intended market segment.

APS Bank, a long-established bank with branches in Malta, has redesigned its branch interiors to communicate a feeling of 'Natural Solidity'. The aim being to portray the bank as dependable, transparent and a partner that can be counted on. The branch interiors, focus on simplicity, minimalism, transparency, and clean lines, that provide guidance and reassurance to existing and future customers. In the Sliema branch, one of the key features is the brand wall, with integrated plasma screens showing informative content and lifestyle imagery relevant to the branch's location. There is a 24-hour lobby offering a self-service area, which can be accessed even when the other parts of the bank are closed. The Welcome area is built to have an approachable contemporary feel similar to a lounge, with a mix of upholstered furniture and soft seating. There are also meeting pods, as well as semi-private meeting rooms with glass screens, which allows for a sense of intimacy and transparency all at the same time.

Source: **Adapted from: https://i-amonline.com/case-study/aps-maltese-branch-design/.**

The design of a physical setting can also differentiate one area of a service organization from another. For example, in the hotel industry, one large hotel may have several levels of dining possibilities, each signalled by differences in design. Price differentiation is also often partly achieved through variations in physical setting. Bigger rooms with more physical amenities cost more, just as larger seats with more leg room (generally in business class) are more expensive on an airline.

Framework for Understanding Servicescape Effects on Behaviour

Although it is useful from a strategic point of view to think about the multiple roles of the servicescape and how they interact, making actual decisions about servicescape design requires an understanding of why the effects occur and how to manage them. The next sections of this chapter present a framework or model of the environment and behaviour relationships in service settings.

The Underlying Framework – The Physical Servicescape

The framework for understanding the physical servicescape effects on behaviour follows from basic *stimulus–organism–response theory*. In the framework the multidimensional environment is the *stimulus*, consumers and employees are the *organisms* that respond to the stimuli, and behaviours directed at the environment are the *responses*. The assumptions are that dimensions of the servicescape will impact customers and employees and that they will behave in certain ways depending on their internal reactions to the servicescape.

A specific example will help illustrate the theory in action. Assume there is a fresh coffee outlet close to the lecture theatres on a university campus. This coffee outlet has large comfortable sofas, and an aroma of fresh coffee wafts from it. The design and the aroma are two elements of the servicescape that will impact customers in some way. Now assume you are a tired student, just out of class, strolling across campus. The comfortable sofas attract your attention and, simultaneously, you smell the coffee. The furniture and the delicious smell cause you to feel happy, relaxed and thirsty at the same time. You are attracted to the coffee outlet and decide to buy a coffee and cookie because you have another class to attend before lunch. The movement toward the outlet and the purchase of a coffee are behaviours directed at the servicescape. Depending on how much time you have, you may even choose to relax in a sofa and read a newspaper with your coffee, other forms of behaviour directed at the servicescape.

The framework shown in Figure 10.1 is detailed in the next sections. It represents a comprehensive stimulus–organism–response model that recognizes complex dimensions of the environment, impacts on multiple parties (customers, employees and their interactions), multiple types of internal responses (cognitive, emotional and physiological) and a variety of individual and social behaviours that can result.

Figure 10.1   A framework for understanding physical environment–user relationships in service organizations

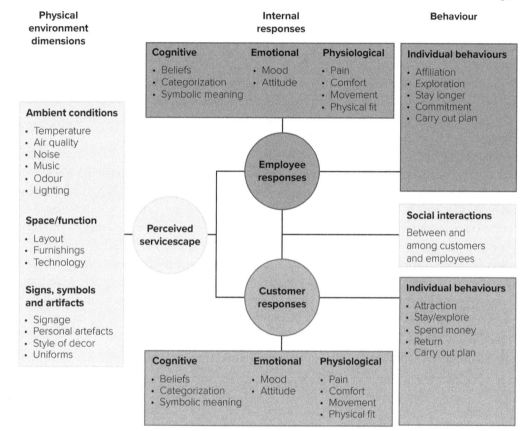

Source: Adapted from M.J. Bitner (1992) 'Servicescapes: The impact of physical surroundings on customers and employees', *Journal of Marketing* 56 (April), pp. 57–71.

Our discussion of the framework begins on the left side of the model with *physical environment dimensions*. Next we explain and develop the *internal responses* portion of the model. Finally we turn to the dimensions of the *behaviours*.

Environmental Dimensions of the Physical Servicescape

In this section we consider the complex mix of environmental features that influence responses and behaviours (the left-hand portion of Figure 10.1). Specifically, environmental dimensions of the physical surroundings can include all the objective physical factors that can be controlled by the firm to enhance (or constrain) employee and customer actions. There is an endless list of possibilities: lighting, colour, signage, textures, quality of materials, style of furnishings, layout, wall decor, temperature, and so on. In Figure 10.1, and in the discussion that follows here, the hundreds of potential elements have been categorized into three composite dimensions: ambient conditions; spatial layout and functionality; and signs, symbols and artefacts.

Although we discuss the three dimensions separately, environmental psychology explains that people respond to their environments holistically. That is, although individuals perceive discrete stimuli (for example, they can perceive noise level, colour and decor as distinct elements), it is the total configuration of stimuli that determines their reactions to a place. Hence, though the dimensions of the environment are defined independently in the following sections, it is important to recognize that they are perceived by employees and customers as a holistic pattern of interdependent stimuli. This holistic response is shown in Figure 10.1 as the 'perceived servicescape'.

SERVICE SPOTLIGHT

An example of architectural design and the servicescape has been designed by London architect Farshid Moussavi, who created the first physical retail space for Victoria Beckham's fashion label in London's West End.

The ground floor space features concrete floors and a ceiling covered with mirrored stainless steel, and is fitted with bespoke pieces of furniture. A four-metre-wide flight of polished concrete stairs located at the back leads up to a flat white wall at the rear of the top floor that is used to project images of Beckham's collections. A similar flight leads down to the basement level.

Diagonal sections of the floor and ceiling have been cut away with the intention of creating a visual connection between all three levels of the 560-square-metre space. These triangular holes accommodate the staircases, while clear glass balustrades maintain a sense of openness. Lengths of blonde-gold coloured chain are used to display clothes throughout the store. These are suspended from recessed tracks in the ceiling and can be moved to make way for installations and other displays. Further hanging space is proved by zig-zagging strips of metal in the same colour, suspended on wires.

Shelving has been designed to be 'wafer thin' and can retract into the walls. American walnut wood and bottle-green coloured glass have been used to create the fitting rooms and cash desk. The same wood is used to create bespoke modular benches that rest on the tips of triangular shaped bottoms. Stainless steel has been used to wrap display counters, with built-in glass display cases, as well as columns and the ceiling of the lower-ground floor.

Source: www.dezeen.com/2014/10/01/farshid-moussavi-victoria-beckham-36-dover-street-london-shop-interior/.

Ambient Conditions

Ambient conditions include background characteristics of the environment such as temperature, lighting, noise, music, scent and colour. All these factors can profoundly affect how people feel, think, and respond to a particular service establishment. For example, a number of studies have documented the effects of music on consumers' perceptions of products, their perceptions of how long they have waited for service, and the amount of money they spend.[9] When there is music, shoppers tend to perceive that they spend less time shopping or in queues than when there is no music. Slower music tempos at lower volumes tend to make people shop in a more leisurely style and, in some cases, they spend more. Shoppers also spend more time when the music 'fits' the product or matches their musical tastes. Other studies have similarly shown the effects of scent on consumer responses.[10] Scent in bakeries, coffee shops and cheese shops, for example, can be used to draw people in, and pleasant scents can increase lingering time. The presence of a scent can reduce perceptions of time spent and improve store evaluations. There is a distinct scent in the cabins of Singapore Airlines. They have used the same cologne since the airline was founded. The cologne, Stefan Floridian Waters, originates and is available to buy in Singapore perfumeries. It is blended into the hot towels and is infused into the entire fleet. The perfume is described as exotic and feminine. Combined with the sound, touch, sight and taste sensations of Singapore Airlines, the scent aims to make the airline stand out in the increasingly competitive airline industry. Singapore Airlines markets itself as an experience, not just a means of travel.[11]

The effects of ambient conditions are especially noticeable when they are extreme. For example, people attending a music concert in a hall which is hot and stuffy, because the air conditioning has failed, will be uncomfortable, and their discomfort will be reflected in how they feel about the concert. If the temperature and air quality were within a comfort tolerance zone, these ambient factors would probably go unnoticed. Ambient conditions also have a greater effect when the customer or employee spends considerable time in the servicescape. The impact of temperature, music, odours and colours builds over time. Another instance in which ambient conditions will be particularly influential is when they conflict with what the customer or employee expects. As a general rule, ambient conditions affect the five senses. Sometimes such dimensions may be totally imperceptible (gases, chemicals, equipment noise) yet have profound effects, particularly on employees who spend long hours in the environment.

★ SERVICE SPOTLIGHT

Abercrombie & Fitch is well known for the musky scent of its stores. This unmistakable scent is that of Abercrombie's signature cologne, Fierce. Employees regularly spray it into the air at Abercrombie stores to keep the scent fresh. Hollister Co., which is part of the same retail group, uses a different scent called SoCal and staff are required to go around spraying the cologne every 30 minutes.

Source: **www.abercrombie.co.uk**

Spatial Layout and Functionality

Because service environments generally exist to fulfil specific purposes or needs of customers, spatial layout and functionality of the physical surroundings are particularly important. *Spatial layout* refers to the ways in which machinery, equipment and furnishings are arranged, the size and shape of those items, and the spatial relationships among them. *Functionality* refers to the ability of the same items to facilitate the accomplishment of customer and employee goals. The spatial layout and functionality of the environment are particularly important for customers in self-service environments, where they must perform the service on their own and cannot rely on employees to assist them. Thus, the functionality of an ATM machine and of self-service restaurants are critical to success and customer satisfaction.

The importance of facility layout is particularly apparent in retail, hospitality and leisure settings, where research shows it can influence customer satisfaction, store performance and consumer search behaviour.[12]

Signs, Symbols and Artefacts

Many items in the physical environment serve as explicit or implicit signals that communicate about the place to its users. Signs displayed on the exterior and interior of a structure are examples of explicit communicators. They can be used as labels (name of company, name of department, and so on), for directional purposes (entrances, exits) and to communicate rules of behaviour (no smoking, children must be accompanied by an adult). Adequate signs have even been shown to reduce perceived crowding and stress.

Other environmental symbols and artefacts may communicate less directly than signs, giving implicit cues to users about the meaning of the place and norms and expectations for behaviour in the place. Quality construction materials, artwork, certificates and photographs, floor coverings, and personal objects displayed in the environment can all communicate symbolic meaning and create an overall aesthetic impression. Restaurant managers, for example, know that white tablecloths and subdued lighting symbolically convey full service and relatively high prices, whereas counter service, plastic furnishings and bright lighting symbolize the opposite. In office environments, certain cues such as desk size and placement symbolize status and may be used to reinforce professional image.[13]

Signs, symbols and artefacts are particularly important in forming first impressions and for communicating service concepts. When customers are unfamiliar with a particular service establishment, they look for environmental cues to help them categorize the place and form their expectations. A study of dentists' offices found that consumers use the environment, in particular its style of decoration and level of quality, as a clue to the competence and manner of the service provider.[14]

Internal Responses to the Servicescape

Employees and customers respond to dimensions of their physical surroundings cognitively, emotionally and physiologically, and those responses are what influence their behaviours in the environment (as shown in the middle portion of Figure 10.1). Although the internal responses are discussed independently here, they are clearly interdependent: a person's beliefs about a place, a cognitive response, may well influence the person's emotional response, and vice versa. For example, patients who come into a dentist's waiting room that is designed to calm and soothe their anxieties (emotional responses) may believe as a result that the dentist is caring and competent (cognitive responses).

Environment and Cognition

The perceived servicescape can have an effect on people's beliefs about a place and their beliefs about the people and products found in that place. In a sense the servicescape can be viewed as a form of non-verbal communication, imparting meaning through what is called 'object language'.[15] For example, particular environmental cues such as the type of office furniture and decor and the clothing worn by a lawyer may influence a potential client's beliefs about whether the lawyer is successful, expensive and trustworthy. In a consumer study, variations in descriptions of store atmospheres were found to alter beliefs about a product (perfume) sold in the store.[16] Another study showed that a travel agent's office decor affected customer attributions and beliefs about the travel agent's behaviour.[17] Travel agents whose facilities were more organized and professional were viewed more positively than were those whose facilities were disorganized and unprofessional.

In other cases, perceptions of the servicescape may simply help people distinguish a firm by influencing how it is categorized. The overall perception of the servicescape enables the consumer or employee to categorize the firm mentally. Research shows that in the restaurant industry a particular configuration of environmental cues such as hard furnishings suggests 'fast food', whereas another configuration (soft furnishings) suggests 'elegant sit-down restaurant'.[18] In such situations, environmental cues serve as a shortcut device that enables customers to categorize and distinguish among types of restaurants.

Environment and Emotion

In addition to influencing beliefs, the perceived servicescape can directly elicit emotional responses that, in turn, influence behaviours. Just being in a particular place can make a person feel happy, light-hearted and relaxed; whereas being in another place may make that person feel sad, depressed and gloomy. The colours, decor, music and other elements of the atmosphere can have an unexplainable and sometimes subconscious effect on the moods of people in the place. For some people, certain environmental stimuli (noises, smells) common in a dental office can bring on immediate feelings of fear and anxiety. In very different contexts, the marble interior and grandeur of a government building or palace may call up feelings of pride and respect; lively music and bright decor in a local night spot may cause people to feel excited and happy. In all these examples, the response from the consumer probably does not involve thinking but, rather, is just an unexplained feeling. Consumers' responses to Nike Town (on page 217) are in large part emotional.

⭐ **SERVICE SPOTLIGHT**

Nike Towns epitomize the role of servicescape design in building the brand, providing customers with a way to interact with the brand, and making Nike come alive. Nike Town represents the height of retail theatre.

So what is so special about Nike Town? What sets it apart from other retail environments? First, it is a showcase for the full range of Nike products. A common reaction of consumers is that they had no idea Nike made and carried all of the products displayed. In addition, every designed element of the services-cape encourages impulsive behaviour, inviting instant gratification. But the prices are very high – higher than prices on the same items in other stores. This is by design. Here the servicescape and the experience of Nike Town are meant to build the brand – not necessarily to sell the products, and especially not to compete with other Nike stores and dealers.

The Nike Town store in London is a concept 'town'. Buildings, each housing a specific sport, sur-round a central square, the store's focal point. In its centre sits the core – a three-storey high, 360-degree projector screen – which springs to life every 20 minutes as window blinds snap shut and customers are surrounded by Nike sports images. Nike Town is more than just a shop; each week there are special events: athletes come in for interviews, and they even organize a running club. With 70,000 square feet of shopping space Nike Town manages to fit everything in, and more besides. The store boasts the larg-est women's sports clothing and footwear area in Europe.[19]

Environmental psychologists have researched people's emotional responses to physical settings.[20] They have concluded that any environment, whether natural or engineered, will elicit emotions that can be captured by two basic dimensions: (1) pleasure/displeasure; and (2) degree of arousal (amount of stimulation or excitement). Servicescapes that are both pleasant and arousing would be termed *exciting*, whereas those that are pleasant and non-arousing, or sleepy, would be termed *relaxing*. Unpleasant servicescapes that are arousing would be called *distressing*, whereas unpleasant, sleepy servicescapes would be *gloomy*. These basic emotional responses to environments can be used to begin predicting the expected behaviours of consumers and employees who find themselves in a particular type of place. Certain organizations may try to stimulate strong emotional responses; for examples of this, look at the following hotel websites: www.kakslauttanen.fi, www.icehotel.com and www.conradmaldives.com.

Environment and Physiology

The perceived servicescape may also affect people in purely physiological ways. Noise that is too loud may cause physical discomfort, the temperature of a room may cause people to shiver or perspire, the air quality may make it difficult to breathe, and the glare of lighting may decrease ability to see and may induce physi-cal discomfort. All these physical responses may, in turn, directly influence whether people stay in and enjoy a particular environment. It is well known that the comfort of seating in a restaurant influences how long people stay. The hard seats in fast-food restaurants cause most people to leave within a predictable period of time, whereas the soft, cosy chairs of Starbucks coffee shops have the opposite effect, encouraging people to stay. Similarly, environmental design and related physiological responses affect whether employees can perform their job functions well.

A vast amount of research in engineering and design has addressed human physiological responses to ambient conditions as well as physiological responses to equipment design.[21] Such research fits under the rubric of **human factors design or ergonomics**. Human factors research systematically applies relevant information about human capabilities and limitations to the design of items and procedures that people use. For example, First Group, one of the largest bus operators in the UK, has introduced new low-floor buses to offer easier access for parents with pushchairs, wheelchairs and the elderly.

Variations in Individual Responses

In general, people respond to the environment in the ways just described – cognitively, emotionally, physiologically – and their responses influence how they behave in the environment. However, the response will not be the same for every individual, every time. Personality differences as well as temporary conditions such as moods or the purpose for being there can cause variations in how people respond to the servicescape.[22]

One personality trait that has been shown to affect how people respond to environments is *arousal-seeking*. Arousal-seekers enjoy and look for high levels of stimulation, whereas arousal-avoiders prefer lower levels of stimulation. Thus an arousal-avoider in a loud, bright disco with flashing lights might feel strong dislike for the environment, whereas an arousal-seeker would be very happy. In a related vein, it has been suggested that some people are better *screeners* of environmental stimuli than others.[23] Screeners of stimuli would be able to experience a high level of stimulation but not be affected by it. Non-screeners would be highly affected and might exhibit extreme responses even to low levels of stimulation.

The particular purpose for being in a servicescape can also affect a person's response to it. A passenger on an aeroplane for a one-hour flight will likely be less affected by the atmosphere on the plane than will the traveller who is embarking on a 14-hour long-haul flight. Similarly, a day-surgery hospital patient will likely be less sensitive and demanding of the hospital environment than would a patient who is spending two weeks in the hospital. And a person who is staying at a hotel for a business meeting will respond differently to the environment than will a couple on their honeymoon.

Temporary mood states can also cause people to respond differently to environmental stimuli. A person who is feeling frustrated and fatigued after a long day at work is likely to be affected differently by a highly arousing restaurant than the person would be after a relaxing three-day weekend.

Behaviours in the Servicescape

That human behaviour is influenced by the physical setting in which it occurs is essentially a truism. Interestingly, however, until the 1960s psychologists largely ignored the effects of physical setting in their attempts to predict and explain behaviour. Since that time a large and steadily growing body of literature within the field of environmental psychology has addressed the relationships between human beings and their built environments. Recent marketing focus on the customer experience has also drawn attention to the effects of physical spaces and design on customer behaviour.[24]

Individual Behaviours

Environmental psychologists suggest that individuals react to places with two general, and opposite, forms of behaviour: approach and avoidance. Approach behaviours include all positive behaviours that might be directed at a particular place, such as desire to stay, explore, work and affiliate.[25] Avoidance behaviours reflect the opposite – a desire not to stay, to explore, to work or to affiliate. In a study of consumers in retail environments, researchers found that approach behaviours (including shopping enjoyment, returning, attraction and friendliness towards others, spending money, time spent browsing, and exploration of the store) were influenced by perceptions of the environment.[26] At one 7-Eleven store, the owners played 'easy-listening music' to drive away the youthful market segment that was detracting from the store's image. And our coffee outlet example is reminiscent of bakeries in supermarkets that attract patrons through the power of smell.

In addition to attracting or deterring entry, the servicescape can actually influence the degree of success that consumers and employees experience in executing their plans once inside. Each individual comes to a particular service organization with a goal or purpose that may be aided or hindered by the setting.

Sports fans are aided in their enjoyment of the game by adequate and easy-access parking, clear signage directing them to their seats, efficient food service and clean washrooms. The ability of employees to do their jobs effectively is also influenced by the servicescape. Adequate space, proper equipment, and comfortable temperature and air quality all contribute to an employee's comfort and job satisfaction, causing him or her to be more productive, stay longer and affiliate positively with co-workers.

⭐ SERVICE SPOTLIGHT

The impact of the environment on behaviour is demonstrated by the actions of Tyne and Wear Metro. The passenger transport operator in Northern England had problems with youths hanging around stations, not getting up to criminal activities, but involved in low-level anti-social behaviour. Passengers complained and the company felt compelled to respond. Their solution was to play classical music at some of their stations. The young people seemed to detest the music and it became completely uncool to hang around a location where Mozart was playing. The music completely eliminated the problem.

Social Interactions

In addition to its effects on their individual behaviours, the servicescape influences the nature and quality of customer and employee interactions, most directly in interpersonal services. It has been stated that 'all social interaction is affected by the physical container in which it occurs'.[27] The 'physical container' can affect the nature of social interaction in terms of the duration of interaction and the actual progression of events. In many service situations, a firm may want to ensure a particular progression of events (a 'standard script') and limit the duration of the service. Environmental variables such as physical proximity, seating arrangements, size and flexibility can define the possibilities and limits of social episodes such as those occurring between customers and employees, or customers and other customers. The design of the servicescape can help define the social rules, conventions and expectations in force in a given setting, thus serving to define the nature of social interaction.[28] The close physical proximity of passengers on the sunbathing deck on a cruise ship will in and of itself prescribe certain patterns of behaviour. This type of holiday is not designed for a social recluse! Some researchers have implied that recurring social behaviour patterns are associated with particular physical settings and that when people encounter typical settings, their social behaviours can be predicted.[29]

Examples of how environments shape social interactions – and how these interactions in turn influence the environment – are abundant.[30] Even casual observation of the retail phenomenon 'Nike Town' (page 217) shows how this form of 'entertainment retail' shapes the behaviours of consumers but at the same time allows them to interpret and create their own realities and experiences.[31] In a mountain biking trip, the 'wilderness servicescape' profoundly influences the behaviours, interactions and total experiences of cyclist consumers and their guides. In this case the natural, and for the most part uncontrollable, environment is the setting for the service.[32]

The Underlying Framework – The Virtual Servicescape

Although the framework in Figure 10.1 was originally developed for physical servicescapes, a large part of it (excluding the employee responses) could also be seen to be relevant to virtual servicescapes such as online services and websites. A number of the environmental dimensions would be different, but the perceived servicescape would create similar customer responses and behaviours. Figure 10.2 sets out an adapted framework suitable for websites. In the web environment, ambient conditions may include music/sound effects, colour schemes and fonts. Spatial layout and functionality may include: procedures for signing in or

⭐ **SERVICE SPOTLIGHT**

In the UK, McDonald's has been redesigning its restaurants to improve on the McDonald's customer service experience. The colour scheme of the restaurants has been changed to incorporate more greens and creams to suggest a fresher and healthier service offering. There has also been a focus on providing customers with more choice as to how they order and pay through digital technology. Self-order touch screen panels have been installed to enable customers to browse the entire menu and related nutritional information. Customers can then order using these panels, pay by card and approach a designated area of the counter to pick up their order or receive table service. The new design also includes wireless charging points for customers' mobile devices and the provision of integrated tablets for web browsing or children's gaming activities.

Be Prepared to Update and Modernize the Evidence

Some aspects of the evidence, particularly the servicescape, require frequent or at least periodic updating and modernizing. Even if the vision, goals and objectives of the company do not change, time itself takes a toll on physical and virtual evidence, necessitating change and modernization. Clearly, an element of fashion is involved, and over time different colours, designs and styles may come to communicate different messages. Organizations obviously understand this concept when it comes to advertising strategy, but sometimes they overlook other elements of physical evidence.

Work Cross-Functionally

In presenting itself to the consumer, a service brand is concerned with communicating a desired image, with sending consistent and compatible messages through all forms of evidence, and with providing the type of service evidence the target customers want and can understand. Frequently, however, physical and virtual evidence decisions are made over time and by various functions within the organization. For example: decisions regarding employee uniforms may be made by the human resources area; servicescape design decisions may be made by the facilities management group; process design decisions are most frequently made by operations managers; webpages are designed by the IT department; and advertising and pricing decisions may be made by the marketing department. Thus, it is not surprising that the physical and virtual evidence of the service may at times be less than consistent. Service blueprinting and wireframing can be a valuable tool for communicating within the firm, identifying existing service evidence and providing a springboard for changing or providing new forms of evidence.

A multi-function team approach to service evidence strategy is often necessary, particularly for making decisions about the servicescape. It has been said that 'Facility planning and management . . . is a problem-solving activity that lies on the boundaries between architecture, interior space planning and product design, organizational [and consumer] behaviour, planning and environmental psychology'.[34]

Summary

In this chapter we explored the roles of physical and virtual evidence in forming customer and employee perceptions and shaping customer experiences. Because services are intangible and because they are often produced and consumed at the same time, they can be difficult to comprehend or evaluate before their purchase. The physical and virtual evidence of the service thus serves as a primary cue for setting customer expectations before purchase. These tangible cues, particularly the servicescape, also influence customers' responses as they experience the service. Because customers and employees often interact in the servicescape, the physical surroundings also influence employees and the nature of employee–customer interactions.

The chapter focused primarily on the physical and virtual servicescapes – the facilities and platforms where the service is produced, delivered and consumed. We presented a typology of servicescapes that illustrated their range of complexity and usage. By locating itself in the appropriate cell of the typology, an organization can quickly see who needs to be consulted regarding servicescape decisions, what objectives might be achieved through careful design of the facility, and how complex the decisions are likely to be. General strategic roles of the servicescape were also described. The servicescape can serve as a package (a 'visual metaphor' for the service itself), a facilitator in aiding the accomplishment of customer and employee goals, a socializer in prescribing behaviours in the environment and a differentiator to distinguish the organization from its competitors.

With this grounding in the importance of physical evidence, in particular the servicescape, we presented a general framework for understanding physical and virtual servicescape effects on employee and customer behaviours. The servicescape can affect the approach and avoidance behaviours of individual customers and employees as well as their social interactions. These behavioural responses come about because the servicel environment influences: (1) people's beliefs or cognitions about the service organization, (2) their feelings or emotions in response to the place, and (3) their actual physiological reactions while in the physical facility or on the website. The chapter also pointed out that individuals may respond differently to the servicescape depending on their personality traits, the mood they are in or the goals they are trying to accomplish.

Three categories of environmental dimensions capture the complex nature of the servicescape: ambient conditions; spatial layout and functionality; and signs, symbols and artefacts. These dimensions affect people's beliefs, emotions and physical responses, causing them to behave in certain ways while in the servicescape.

Given the importance of physical and virtual evidence and its potentially powerful influence on both customers and employees, it is important for firms to think strategically about the management of the tangible evidence of service. The impact of service evidence and design decisions needs to be researched and planned as part of the marketing strategy. The chapter concluded with specific guidelines for physical and virtual evidence strategy. If such evidence is researched, planned and implemented effectively, key problems leading to service quality shortcomings can be avoided. Through careful thinking about service evidence decisions, an organization can avoid miscommunicating to customers via incompatible or inconsistent evidence or over-promising and raising customer expectations unrealistically. Beyond its role in helping avoid these negative outcomes, an effective service evidence strategy can play a critically important role in communicating to customers and in guiding them in understanding the firm's offerings and setting up accurate expectations. During the service experience, the physical and virtual servicescape can play a major role in creating memorable outcomes and emotional connections with customers.

Key Concepts

Clue management	206	Servicescape	204
Environmental dimensions	213	Socializer	211
Environmental psychology	208	Stimulus–organism–response theory	212
Human factors design or ergonomics	217	Virtual servicescapes	205
Package v. facilitator v. differentiator	210–211	Wireframes	221

Exercises

1 Choose two very different firms (different market segments or service levels) in the same industry. Observe both establishments. Describe the service 'package' in both cases. How does the package help distinguish the two firms? Do you believe that the package sets accurate expectations for what the firm delivers? Is either firm over-promising through the manner in which its servicescape (or other types of physical or virtual evidence) communicates with customers?

2 Think of a particular service organization (it can be a class project company, the company you work for or some other organization) for which you believe physical or virtual evidence is particularly important in communicating with and satisfying customers. Prepare the text of a presentation you would give to the manager of that organization to convince him or her of the importance of physical or virtual evidence in the organization's marketing strategy.

3 Choose a service organization and collect all forms of physical and virtual evidence that the organization uses to communicate with its customers. If customers see the firm's facility, also take a photograph of the servicescape. Analyse the evidence in terms of compatibility, consistency and whether it over-promises or under-promises what the firm can deliver.

4 Visit the websites of several service providers. Does the virtual evidence of the website portray an image consistent with other forms of evidence provided by the organizations?

5 Visit a hotel review site such as tripadvisor.com and examine what proportion of reviews mention elements of the physical or virtual environment. What aspects of the environment do reviewers specifically focus on?

Discussion Questions

1 What is physical/ virtual evidence, and why have we devoted an entire chapter to it in a marketing text?

2 Describe and give an example of how servicescapes play each of the following strategic roles: package, facilitator, socializer and differentiator.

3 Imagine that you own an independent copying and printing shop. In which cell would you locate your business in the typology of servicescapes shown in Table 10.3? What are the implications for designing your physical facility?

4 How can an effective physical or virtual evidence strategy help close provider gap 2? Explain.

5 Why are both customers and employees included in the framework for understanding servicescape effects on behaviour (Figure 10.1)? What types of behaviours are influenced by the servicescape according to the framework? Think of examples.

6 Using your own experiences, give examples of times when you have been affected cognitively, emotionally and physiologically by elements of the servicescape (in any service context).

7 Why is everyone not affected in exactly the same way by the servicescape?

8 Describe the physical environment of your favourite restaurant in terms of the three categories of servicescape dimensions: ambient conditions; spatial layout and functionality; and signs, symbols and artefacts.

9 Imagine that you are serving as a consultant to a local health club. How would you advise the health club to begin the process of developing an effective physical evidence strategy?

10 How can virtual servicescapes on the Internet be used by companies? Do they have any weaknesses?

Further Reading

Dedeoglu, B.B., Bilgihan, A., Ye, B.H., Buonincontri, P. and Okumus, F. (2018). The impact of servicescape on hedonic value and behavioral intentions: The importance of previous experience. *International Journal of Hospitality Management*, 72, 10–20.

Harris, L.C. and Ezeh, C. (2008). Servicescape and loyalty intentions: An empirical investigation. *European Journal of Marketing*, 42(3/4), 390–422.

Harris, L.C. and Goode, M.M.H. (2010). Online servicescapes, trust and purchase intentions. *Journal of Services Marketing*, 24(3) 230–43.

Kaminakis, K., Karantinou, K., Koritos, C. and Gounaris, S. (2019). Hospitality servicescape effects on customer–employee interactions: A multilevel study. *Tourism Management*, 72, 130–144.

Lee, S. and Jeong, M. (2012). Effects of e-servicescape on consumers' flow experiences. *Journal of Hospitality and Tourism Technology*, 3(1), 47–59.

Leenders, M.A., Smidts, A. and El Haji, A. (2016). Ambient scent as a mood inducer in supermarkets: The role of scent intensity and time-pressure of shoppers. *Journal of Retailing and Consumer Services*, **48** (270–280).

Mari, M. and Poggesi, S. (2013). Servicescape cues and customer behavior: A systematic literature review and research agenda. *The Service Industries Journal*, 33(2), 171–99.

Rosenbaum, M.S. and Massiah, C. (2011). An expanded servicescape perspective. *Journal of Service Management*, 22(4), 471–90.

Part 5

Delivering and Performing Service

Chapter 11   Employees' Roles in Service Delivery

Chapter 12   Customers' Roles in Service Delivery

Chapter 13   Delivering Service through Electronic Channels and Intermediaries

Chapter 14   Managing Demand and Capacity

Chapter 15   Service Recovery

In the gaps model of service quality, provider gap 3 (the service performance gap) is the discrepancy between customer-driven service standards and actual service delivery (see the accompanying figure). Even when guidelines exist for performing service well and treating customers correctly, high-quality service performance is not a certainty. Part 5 deals with all the ways in which companies ensure services are performed according to customer-defined designs and standards.

In Chapter 11, we focus on the key roles that employees play in service delivery and strategies that ensure they are effective in their roles.

In Chapter 12 we discuss the variability in service performance caused by customers. If customers do not perform appropriately – if they do not follow instructions or if they disturb other customers receiving service at the same time – service quality is jeopardized.

Chapter 13 describes service delivery through electronic channels and intermediaries such as retailers, franchisees, agents and brokers. Firms must develop ways to either control or motivate these intermediaries to meet company goals and deliver consistent quality service.

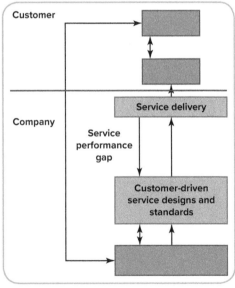

Provider gap 3

Chapter 14 emphasizes the need to synchronize demand and capacity in service organizations in order to deliver consistent, high-quality service.

Chapter 15 describes service recovery management, which involves understanding why customers complain, what they expect when they complain, and how to deal with service failures.

The underlying logic connecting employee satisfaction and loyalty to customer satisfaction and loyalty, and ultimately profits, is illustrated by the service profit chain shown in Figure 11.1.[13] In earlier chapters we focused on customer satisfaction and retention; here we focus on employee satisfaction and employee retention. The service profit chain suggests that there are critical linkages among internal service quality; employee satisfaction/productivity; the value of services provided to the customer; and, ultimately, customer satisfaction, retention and profits.

Figure 11.1   The service profit chain

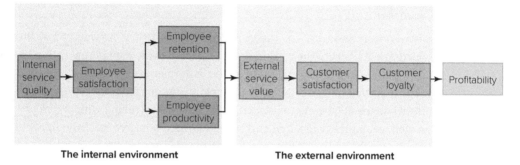

Source: Adapted from J.L. Heskett, T.O. Jones, G.W. Loveman, W.E. Sasser Jr and L.A. Schlesinger (1994), 'Putting the service–profit chain to work', *Harvard Business Review* (March–April).

Service profit chain researchers are careful to point out that the model does not suggest causality. That is, employee satisfaction does not *cause* customer satisfaction; rather the two are interrelated and feed off each other. The model does imply that companies that exhibit high levels of success on the elements of the model will be more successful and profitable than those that do not. This finding is borne out in other research, which reports that companies that manage people right will outperform by 30 to 40 per cent companies that do not.[14]

The Effect of Employee Behaviours on Service Quality Dimensions

Customers' perceptions of service quality will be impacted by the customer-oriented behaviours of employees.[15] In fact, all five dimensions of service quality (reliability, responsiveness, assurance, empathy and tangibles) can be influenced directly by service employees.

Delivering the service as promised – *reliability* – is often totally within the control of front-line employees. Even in the case of automated services (such as ATMs, automated ticketing machines or self-serve service stations), behind-the-scenes employees are critical for making sure all the systems are working properly. When services fail or errors are made, employees are essential for setting things right and using their judgement to determine the best course of action for service recovery.

Front-line employees directly influence customer perceptions of *responsiveness* through their personal willingness to help and their promptness in serving customers. Consider the range of responses you receive from different retail staff when you need help finding a particular item of clothing. One employee may ignore your presence, whereas another offers to help you search and calls other stores to locate the item. One may help you immediately and efficiently, whereas another may move slowly in accommodating even the simplest request.

The *assurance* dimension of service quality is highly dependent on employees' ability to communicate their credibility and to inspire trust and confidence. The reputation of the organization will help, but in the end, individual employees with whom the customer interacts confirm and build trust in the organization or detract from its reputation and ultimately destroy trust. For start-up or relatively unknown organizations, credibility, trust and confidence will be tied totally to employee actions.

It is difficult to imagine how an organization would deliver 'caring, individualized attention' to customers independent of its employees. *Empathy* implies that employees will pay attention, listen, adapt and be flexible in delivering what individual customers need.[16] For example, research documents that when employees are customer oriented, have good rapport with customers and exhibit perceptive and attentive listening skills, customers will evaluate the service more highly and be more likely to return.[17] Employee appearance and dress are important aspects of the *tangibles* dimension of quality, along with many other factors that are independent of service employees (the service facility, decor, brochures, signage, and so on).

★ SERVICE SPOTLIGHT

In order to demonstrate responsiveness and assurance, airlines such as British Airways, KLM, Iberia and Air France have provided Apple iPads to their cabin crews. These provide cabin crew with a library of information on the popular computer tablet. Safety manuals, customer service updates and timetables are all at the cabin crew's fingertips, allowing them to answer any questions from passengers. The device also helps staff identify where each customer is seated, who they are travelling with and their Loyalty Programme status, as well as any meal requirements. Overall, the iPads give staff the opportunity to offer a more personalized service and the ability to log incidents that happen both on the ground and in the air. These can then be synced with a main database once the devices are brought back to an airport.

Boundary-Spanning Roles

Our focus in this chapter is on front-line service employees who interact directly with customers, although much of what is described and recommended can be applied to internal service employees as well. The front-line service employees are referred to as *boundary spanners* because they operate at the organization's boundary. Boundary spanners provide a link between the external customer and environment and the internal operations of the organization. They serve a critical function in understanding, filtering and interpreting information and resources to and from the organization and its external constituencies.

Who are these boundary spanners? What types of people and positions comprise critical boundary-spanning roles? Their skills and experience cover the full spectrum of jobs and careers. In some industries, boundary spanners are well-paid, highly educated professionals – for example, doctors, lawyers, accountants, consultants, architects and teachers. In other industries, such as fast food, hotels, telecommunication and retail, the boundary spanners are often the least skilled, lowest-paid employees in the organization. They are order-takers, front-desk employees, telephone operators, store clerks, truck drivers and delivery people. In many cases, they may not even work directly for the organization, but be part of what is termed 'the *gig economy*'. In the gig economy, instead of a regular wage, workers are classed as independent contractors and only receive payment for the 'gigs' they do. This is a particularly common practice in areas such as food delivery, courier services, ride-hailing services and call handling. Proponents of the gig economy claim that people can benefit from flexible hours with control over how much time they work; for employers, the flexible nature means that they only pay for work when it is done and don't incur staff costs when market demand is low. However, the approach is controversial as it means that workers have no protection against unfair dismissal, no right to redundancy payments, and no right to receive the national minimum wage, paid holiday or sickness pay. When market demand is low, they receive no income.

No matter what the level of skill, pay or employment status, boundary-spanning positions are often high-stress jobs. In addition to mental and physical skills, these positions require extraordinary levels of *emotional labour*, frequently demand an ability to handle interpersonal and inter-organizational conflict, and call on the employee to make real-time trade-offs between quality and productivity on the job. These stresses and trade-offs can result in failure to deliver services as specified, which widens the service performance gap.

Emotional Labour

The term *emotional labour* was coined by Arlie Hochschild to refer to the labour that goes beyond the physical or mental skills needed to deliver quality service.[18] In general, boundary-spanning service employees are expected to align their displayed emotions with organizationally desired emotions via their use of emotional labour.[19] Such labour includes delivering smiles, making eye contact, showing sincere interest and engaging in friendly conversation with people who are essentially strangers and who may or may not ever be seen again. Friendliness, courtesy, empathy and responsiveness directed towards customers all require huge amounts of emotional labour from the front-line employees who shoulder this responsibility for the organization. Emotional labour draws on people's feelings (often requiring them to suppress their true feelings) to be effective in their jobs. A front-line service employee who is having a bad day, or is not feeling just right, is still expected to put on the face of the organization when dealing with customers. One of the clearest examples of emotional labour is the story (probably apocryphal) of the flight attendant who was approached by a businessman who said, 'Let's have a smile.' 'Okay,' she replied, 'I'll tell you what, first you smile and then I'll smile, okay?' He smiled. 'Good,' she said. 'Now hold that for 15 hours,' and walked away.[20]

Many of the strategies we will discuss later in this chapter can help organizations and employees deal with the realities of emotional labour on the job. For the organization, such strategies include carefully selecting people who can handle emotional stress, training them in the required skills (like listening and problem-solving) and teaching or giving them coping abilities and strategies (via job rotation, scheduled breaks, teamwork or other techniques).[21]

Strategies for Managing Emotional Labour

Customer-contact employees in service positions are often required to display (or, conversely, to hide) a variety of emotions. In many situations, such employees are increasingly being required to invest personal identity and expression into their work. The following description suggests how the experience of the service employee, even in the most routine of occupations, is markedly different from that of the traditional manufacturing worker:

> *The assembly-line worker could openly hate his job, despise his supervisor, and even dislike his coworkers, and while this might be an unpleasant state of affairs, if he [completes] his assigned tasks efficiently, his attitude [is] his own problem. For the service worker, inhabiting the job means, at the very least, pretending to like it, and, at most, actually bringing his whole self into the job, liking it, and genuinely caring about the people with whom he interacts.*[22]

Emotional labour occurs more often when the job requires frequent and long durations of voice contact or face-to-face contact with customers. Employees in these roles often need emotional management to deal with such situations. The following activities help to foster an environment that helps employees deal with the realities of emotional labour on the job:

1 Screen for emotional labour abilities
2 Teach emotional management skills and appropriate behaviours
3 Carefully fashion the physical work environment
4 Allow employees to air their views
5 Put management on the front line
6 Give employees a break
7 Pass demanding customers to managers.

Screen for Emotional Labour Abilities

Many firms look to hire employees who are well suited to meet the emotional labour requirements of the job. Retailers, such as Marks and Spencer or Asda (Wal-Mart), put prospective employees through simulated customer contact exercises to see the kind of friendliness and warmth they naturally communicate. Such practices help in identifying employees whose values, background and personalities match the job's emotional labour requirements.

Teach Emotional Management Skills and Appropriate Behaviours

Most customer-contact employees are taught that they need to be courteous to customers. However, customers have no obligation to return empathy or courtesy. In situations in which customers exercise the privilege of 'the customer is always right', employees face real challenges in suppressing their true feelings. Seldom do firms provide much training to assist employees in facing these challenges. Arlie Hochschild identifies two forms of emotional labour: *surface acting*, in which employees pretend to feel emotions that are not really present and, in doing so, deliberately and consciously create an outward appearance in order to deceive others; and *deep acting*, in which employees attempt to experience the real feelings they must express to the customer, including the active invocation of 'thoughts, images, and memories to induce the associated emotion'.[23] Hair salon stylists and airline flight attendants are often encouraged to engage in deep acting strategies, such as imagining that the client is a friend or that the passenger is a frightened little child flying for the first time. Often, in order to persuade clients to buy hair products or colour their hair, stylists have to moderate their language or behaviour; they may use deep acting to justify these behaviours to themselves. Companies may also train employees in how to avoid absorbing a customer's bad mood, perhaps by having employees spend hours role-playing to suppress their natural reaction to retaliate with their own negative emotions.

Carefully Fashion the Physical Work Environment

As we discussed in Chapter 10, the environment in which the service is delivered can have an impact on employee behaviours and emotions. Many of the better call centres working for insurance companies or banks attempt to reduce staff stress and boredom through bright airy decoration with windows that allow employees to see the weather, trees, grass, people and cars driving by.

Allow Employees to Air Their Views

Employees who must exert emotional labour often need to have an outlet to 'let off steam'. Allowing employees to air their views lets them get rid of their frustrations. If such venting is done in a group setting, it can provide emotional support and encouragement, as well as allowing employees to see that others are experiencing the same problems and that they are not alone. If part of the work day (or week) is explicitly set aside to allow employees to share their frustrations, it delivers a message to employees that the company is aware of, and acknowledges, the emotional contribution that they have made. Ritz-Carlton, Wal-Mart and other companies regularly set aside time for such venting. In addition to the cathartic benefit this experience can provide, other employees may reveal coping strategies that they have found useful.

Put Management on the Front Line

Customer-contact employees often feel that management does not truly understand or appreciate the emotional labour they must expend. Managers should regularly be required to interact with customers. The utility company, Scottish and Southern Energy, has its management team work alongside its customer service representatives in fielding customers' telephone calls. In addition to understanding what the issues are, managers are truly able to empathize with employees. Managers who do so not only have an appreciation for the emotional labour requirements of their employees, but they are also in a better position to serve as role models and mentors in using emotional management skills.

Give Employees a Break

In situations in which an employee has just handled a particularly tough customer, especially if the employee has frequent and long durations of voice or face-to-face contact with customers, a particularly helpful strategy is to allow the employee a short break to regroup. Retailers rotate employees into different positions throughout the day so that they do not spend the entire time working on checkouts. Customer contact employees can be re-energized and refreshed after spending a little time away from the situation, even if they take only a few minutes to finish paperwork or complete some other job responsibility.

Pass Demanding Customers to Managers

Some customers may be too much for an employee to handle. In such situations, to alleviate pressure on the customer-contact employee, firms may shift responsibility for the interaction to managers. Norwich Union Insurance call-centre operators are trained to pass difficult customers on to supervisors or managers.

Sources of Conflict

Front-line employees often face interpersonal and inter-organizational conflicts on the job. Many, such as waiters, bus drivers and hotel receptionists may perceive themselves performing roles that give them a status below that of the customer. This is often described as a subordinate service role.[24] They may feel that the customer has more control over their role than they do. As a result some employees may develop their own approach to get even and overcome the perceived inequality between customers and themselves. For instance, the hotel receptionist who speaks French when dealing with English guests, despite being able to speak excellent English, is shifting the balance of power to give herself greater control over the situation.

The frustration and confusion of front-line employees can, if left unattended, lead to stress, job dissatisfaction, a diminished ability to serve customers and burnout.[25] Managers need to understand the perceived roles and challenges faced by their front-line employees and in particular the conflicts that they have to deal with, including person/role conflicts, organization/client conflicts and inter-client conflicts, as discussed in the next three points.[26]

Person/Role Conflicts

In some situations, boundary spanners feel conflicts between what they are asked to do and their own personalities, orientations or values. Service workers may feel role conflict when they are required to subordinate their feelings or beliefs, as when they are asked to live by the motto 'The customer is always right – even when he [or she] is wrong'. Sometimes there is a conflict between role requirements and the self-image or self-esteem of the employee.

Person/role conflict also arises when employees are required to wear specific clothing or change some aspect of their appearance to conform to the job requirements. A young lawyer, just out of school, may feel an internal conflict with his new role when his employer requires him to cut his long hair and trade his casual clothes for a formal suit.

Organization/Client Conflict

A more common type of conflict for front-line service employees is the conflict between their two bosses: the organization and the individual customer. Service employees are typically rewarded for following certain standards, rules and procedures. Ideally these rules and standards are customer based, as described in Chapter 10. When they are not, or when a customer makes excessive demands, the employee has to choose whether to follow the rules or satisfy the demands. The conflict is greatest when the employee believes the organization is wrong in its policies and must decide whether to accommodate the client and risk losing his or her job, or to follow the policies. The employee may attempt to apply the agreed policies but, given the potential stressful situation with the customer, they can frequently side with the customer against the organization or show signs of frustration and irritation. Such conflicts are especially severe when service employees depend directly on the customer for income. For example, employees who depend on tips or commissions are likely to face greater levels of organization/client conflict because they have even greater incentives to identify with the customer.

Inter-Client Conflict

Sometimes conflict occurs for boundary spanners when incompatible expectations and requirements arise from two or more customers. This situation occurs most often when the service provider is serving customers in turn (a bank teller, a supermarket checkout operator, a doctor) or is serving many customers simultaneously (a teacher, an entertainer).

When serving customers in turn, the provider may satisfy one customer by spending additional time, customizing the service, and being very flexible in meeting the customer's needs. Meanwhile, waiting customers are becoming dissatisfied because their needs are not being met in a timely way. Beyond the timing issue, different clients may prefer different modes of service delivery. Having to serve one client who prefers personal recognition and a degree of familiarity in the presence of another client, who is business-focused and would prefer little interpersonal interaction, can also create conflict for the employee.

When serving many customers at the same time, employees often find it difficult or impossible simultaneously to serve the full range of needs of a group of heterogeneous customers. This type of conflict is readily apparent in any classroom in which the teacher must meet a multitude of expectations and different preferences for formats and style.

Quality/Productivity Trade-Offs

Front-line service workers are asked to be both effective and efficient: they are expected to deliver satisfying service to customers and at the same time to be cost-effective and productive in what they do. A dentist, for example, is expected to deliver caring, quality, individualized service to his or her patients, but at the same time to serve a certain number of patients within a specified time frame. A checkout operator in a grocery shop is expected to know his or her customers and to be polite and courteous, yet also to process the groceries accurately and move people through the line quickly. An architectural draftsperson is expected to create quality drawings, yet to produce a required quantity of drawings in a given period of time. These essential trade-offs between quality and quantity, and between maximum effectiveness and efficiency, place real-time demands and pressures on service employees.

Research suggests that these trade-offs are more difficult for service businesses than for manufacturing and packaged goods businesses, and that pursuing goals of customer satisfaction and productivity simultaneously is particularly challenging in situations in which service employees are required to customize service offerings to meet customer needs.[27]

One way to improve productivity whilst maintaining consistent quality is to replace employees with automated alternatives, such as chatbots or robots. Chatbots are computer programmes developed to automatically engage with received messages/enquiries. They can be programmed to respond the same way each time, to respond differently to messages containing certain keywords and even to use machine learning to adapt their responses to fit the situation. By automating telephone or online conversations that would otherwise require an employee to answer, organizations save time and money that can then be allocated to other efforts. They can also be used to enable customer agents to better serve the customer by automating the initial interaction and screening of an enquiry. They can speed up the response time and can also offer 24-hour support when an office is closed. For example, a cinema can use a chatbot to answer queries from customers about screening schedules and prices without involving an employee. The use of robots for service is at a very early stage but hotel chains, such as Aloft, have been experimenting with robots delivering room service to hotel rooms. Robots are also being used by hotels for cleaning and maintenance in the form of vacuum cleaners, lawn mowers and pool cleaners. It is possible to have a WiFi Enabled Robot Vacuum stored under the bed in each hotel room. After a guest checks out, the housekeeping staff can initiate a remote cleaning from anywhere using the robot vacuum's phone app via a wireless connection. While it vacuums, the staff can clean another room or clean the bathroom. This speeds up the overall cleaning process as the robot and the staff clean in tandem. And the staff don't have to waste energy vacuuming and moving the cleaner from room to room, ultimately helping them to do their job faster and more easily.

Strategies for Delivering Service Quality through People

A complex combination of strategies is needed to ensure that service employees are willing and able to deliver quality services and that they stay motivated to perform in customer-oriented, service-minded ways. These strategies for enabling service promises are often referred to as *internal marketing*, as shown in the service triangle (Figure 1.4) in Chapter 1.[28] By approaching human resource decisions and strategies with the primary goal to motivate and enable employees to deliver customer-oriented promises successfully, an organization will move towards delivering service quality through its people. The strategies presented here are organized around four basic themes. To build a customer-oriented, service-minded workforce, an organization must: (1) hire the right people, (2) develop people to deliver service quality, (3) provide the needed support systems, and (4) retain the best people. Within each of these basic strategies are a number of specific sub-strategies for accomplishing the goal, as shown in Figure 11.2.

Figure 11.2   Human resource strategies for delivering service quality through people

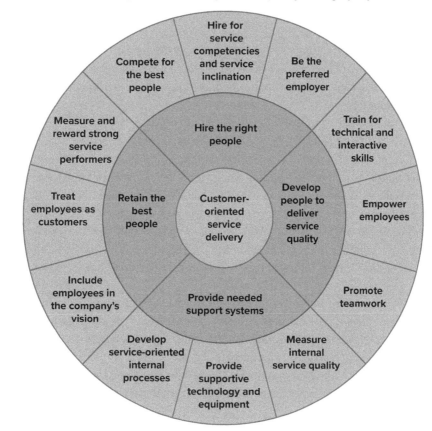

Hire the Right People

To effectively deliver service quality, considerable attention should be focused on recruiting and hiring service employees. Such attention is contrary to traditional practices in many service industries, where service personnel are the lowest on the corporate ladder and work for a minimum wage. At the other end of the spectrum, in the professional services, the most important recruiting criteria are typically technical training, certifications and expertise. However, successful service organizations generally look beyond the technical qualifications of applicants to assess their customer and service orientation as well. Figure 11.2 shows three ways to go about hiring the right people.

Compete for the Best People

To get the best people, an organization needs to identify them and compete with other organizations to hire them. L. Berry and A. Parasuraman refer to this approach as 'competing for talent market share'.[29] They suggest that firms act as marketers in their pursuit of the best employees, just as they use their marketing expertise to compete for customers. Firms that think of recruiting as a marketing activity will address issues of market (employee) segmentation, product (job) design and promotion of job availability in ways that attract potential long-term employees.

Hire for Service Competencies and Service Inclination

Once potential employees have been identified, organizations need to be conscientious in interviewing and screening them to truly select the best people from the pool of candidates. Service employees need two complementary capacities: *service competencies* and *service inclination*.[30]

Service competencies are the skills and knowledge necessary to do the job. In many cases, employees validate competencies by achieving particular degrees and certifications, such as attaining a degree and passing the relevant professional qualifications. These are required of doctors, airline pilots, university professors, teachers and many other job seekers before they are ever interviewed for service jobs in their fields. In other cases, service competencies may not be degree related but may instead relate to basic intelligence or physical requirements. A checkout assistant, for example, must possess basic mathematical skills and the potential to operate a cash till.

Given the multidimensional nature of service quality, service employees should be screened for more than their service competencies. They must also be screened for *service inclination* – their interest in doing service-related work – which is reflected in their attitudes towards service and orientation toward serving customers and others on the job. Self-selection suggests that most service jobs will draw applicants with some level of service inclination and that most employees in service organizations are inclined towards service. However, some employees clearly have a greater service inclination than others. Research has shown that service effectiveness is correlated with service-oriented personality characteristics such as helpfulness, thoughtfulness and sociability.[31] An ideal selection process for service employees assesses both service competencies and service inclination, resulting in employee hires who are high on both dimensions.[32]

In many cases a component of the selection process will include a form of work simulation that allows employees to demonstrate how they would actually perform on the job. A simulation may take the form of role-playing or a series of exercises that parallel the demands of the actual job. In addition to being a good way to assess potential employee abilities, simulations can give the potential recruit a better view of what the job is actually like. Those candidates who do not like what they experience can withdraw their application before being hired and then finding out that the job is not what they had expected.

Be the Preferred Employer

One way to attract the best people is to be known as the preferred employer in a particular industry or in a particular location. This is often called employer branding and is achieved through extensive training, career and advancement opportunities, excellent internal support, attractive incentives, and quality goods and services that employees are proud to be associated with. In other words, employer branding is how you market your company to job seekers, as well as internal employees. A positive reputation as an employer can lead to an increase in employee loyalty and the ability to attract the best talent. Organizations such as British Airways, Hilton, Ritz-Carlton, Mercedes and Accenture invest a large amount of money and effort in promoting themselves to potential applicants in order to be seen as preferred employers in their sector.

★ SERVICE SPOTLIGHT

Starbucks attempts to cultivate a strong community among its employees. It refers to current employees as partners, instilling a sense of pride in each employee. It has also set up Instagram and Twitter accounts to promote its employer brand and interact with job seekers. These social media accounts are used to share its company mission, training opportunities and personal employee stories. They also demonstrate the organization's commitment to diversity and inclusion.

Develop People to Deliver Service Quality

To grow and maintain a workforce that is customer oriented and focused on delivering quality, an organization must develop its employees to deliver service quality. That is, once it has hired the right individuals, the organization must train and work with these employees to ensure service performance.

Train for Technical and Interactive Skills

To provide quality service, employees need ongoing training in the necessary technical skills and knowledge and in process or interactive skills.[33] Examples of technical skills and knowledge are working with accounting systems in hotels, cash machine procedures in a retail store, underwriting procedures in an insurance company and any operational rules the company has for running its business. Most service organizations are quite conscious of, and relatively effective at, training employees in technical skills. These skills may be taught through formal education, as is the case at McDonald's Hamburger University. Additionally, technical skills are often taught through on-the-job training, as when education students work with experienced teachers in internship programmes or when call centre trainees listen in on the conversations of experienced employees. Companies are increasing their use of information technology to train employees in the technical skills and knowledge needed on the job.

★ SERVICE SPOTLIGHT

CitizenM, the Dutch boutique hotel chain, uses employer branding in order to be the preferred employer by emphasizing the following benefits in its human resource strategy:

- **Training programme:** Our first gift to you is a special training programme in the language and lifestyle of citizenM. We inspire, empower and coach you as a professional in:
  - citizenM hospitality
  - citizenM knowledge and know-how
  - citizenM (food) retail
  - citizenM Barista and professional cocktail shaker.
- **Personal development plan:** Our second gift to you is a personal development plan. Whether you like to learn more about hospitality, personal presentation or sushi, you can pick your flavour from our à la carte system.
- **Pays & perks:** We love to reward our ambassadors for good performance, excellent guest service and overall team success. The basic salary is set to meet market conditions and a performance-based reward. We also love to give you and your family the opportunity of a good night's sleep in one of our hotels at a very special rate.

- **Food:** We offer free delicious and healthy food and beverages.
- **Multi-tasking job:** Working for citizenM is never dull or standard. Every employee has a mobile job being responsible for a variety of tasks. But we have one thing in common: we are all ambassadors to our guests.
- **Outfit:** We want you to be mobile. So no dull, impractical uniforms but a stylish, easy and fitting citizenM outfit.
- **Community:** As a citizen you are automatically part of the citizenM community. Here you can chat with your colleagues and keep yourself up-to-date about what's new on citizenM.

Source: **www.citizenm.com**

Service employees also need training in interactive skills that allow them to provide courteous, caring, responsive and empathetic service. Successful companies invest heavily in training and make sure that the training fits their business goals and strategies.

⭐ SERVICE SPOTLIGHT

In the Accor hotel group which encompasses hotel brands such as Ibis, Novotel, Fairmont, Swissotel, Mercure and Sofitel, learning and development is provided by the organization's Académie Accor. This is a training resource supported by a global network of 18 campuses that offer over 250 training modules in every aspect of hospitality-related expertise and jobs. Courses may be attended by any employee of an Accor-brand hotel, regardless of job, family circumstance, educational background, position or seniority. The Académie Accor's primary mission is to train employees so that every hotel guest enjoys impeccable quality of service. It can train employees on-site as well as through e-learning modules, infographics, videos, virtual classrooms and other computer-mediated activities.

Source: See **www.accor.com/en/recruitment-and-careers/why-choose-accorhotels/training.html.**

Empower Employees

Many organizations have discovered that to be truly responsive to customer needs, front-line providers need to be empowered to accommodate customer requests and to recover on the spot when things go wrong. **Empowerment** means giving employees the desire, skills, tools and authority to serve the customer. Although the key to empowerment is giving employees authority to make decisions on the customer's behalf, authority alone is not enough. Employees need the knowledge and tools to be able to make these decisions, and they need incentives that encourage them to make the right decisions. Organizations do not succeed in empowering their employees if they simply tell them, 'You now have the authority to do whatever it takes to satisfy the customer'. First, employees often do not believe this statement, particularly if the organization has functioned hierarchically or bureaucratically in the past. Second, employees often do not know what it means to 'do whatever it takes' if they have not received training, guidelines and the tools needed to make such decisions.

Research suggests positive benefits to empowering front-line service workers. Some of these benefits include reduction in job-related stress, improved job satisfaction, greater adaptability and better outcomes for customers.[34] But such success does not come easily. In fact, some experts have concluded that few organizations have truly taken advantage of, or properly implemented, successful empowerment strategies.[35] Nor is empowerment the answer for all organizations. David Bowen and Edward Lawler, experts on this subject, suggest that organizations well suited to empowerment strategies are ones in which: (1) the business strategy is one of differentiation and customization, (2) customers are long-term relationship customers, (3) technology is non-routine or complex, (4) the business environment is unpredictable, and (5) managers and employees have high growth and social needs and strong interpersonal skills.[36] They also enumerate the benefits and costs of empowerment[37] as follows:

Benefits

- *Quicker online responses to customer needs during service delivery.* Employees who are allowed to make decisions on behalf of the customer can make decisions more quickly, bypassing what in the past might have meant a long chain of command, or at least a discussion with an immediate supervisor.
- *Quicker online responses to dissatisfied customers during service recovery.* When failures occur in the delivery system, customers hope for an immediate recovery effort on the part of the organization. Empowered employees can recover on the spot, and a dissatisfied customer can potentially be turned into a satisfied, even loyal, one.
- *Employees feel better about their jobs and themselves.* Giving employees control and authority to make decisions makes them feel responsible and gives them ownership for the customer's satisfaction. Decades of job design research suggest that when employees have a sense of control and of doing meaningful work, they are more satisfied. The result is lower turnover and less absenteeism.
- *Employees will interact with customers with more warmth and enthusiasm.* Employees feel better about themselves and their work, and these attitudes will spill over into their feelings about customers and will be reflected in their interactions.
- *Empowered employees are a great source of service ideas.* When employees are empowered, they feel responsible for the service outcome and they will be excellent sources of ideas about new services or how to improve current offerings.
- *Great word-of-mouth advertising from customers.* Empowered employees do special and unique things that customers will remember and tell their friends, family and associates about.

Costs

- *A potentially greater investment in selection and training.* To find employees who will work well in an empowered environment requires creative, potentially more costly selection procedures. Training will also be more expensive in general because employees need more knowledge about the company, its products and how to work in flexible ways with customers.
- *Higher labour costs.* The organization may not be able to use as many part-time or seasonal employees, and it may need to pay more for asking employees to assume responsibility.
- *Potentially slower or inconsistent service delivery.* If empowered employees spend more time with all, or even some, customers, then service overall may take longer and may annoy customers who are waiting. Empowerment also means that customers will get what they need or request. When decisions regarding customer satisfaction are left to the discretion of employees, there may be inconsistency in the level of service delivered.
- *May violate customers' perceptions of fair play.* Customers may perceive that sticking to procedures with every customer is fair. Thus, if they see that customers are receiving different levels of service or that employees are cutting special deals with some customers, they may believe that the organization is not fair.
- *Employees may 'give away the store' or make bad decisions.* Many people fear that empowered employees will make costly decisions that the organization cannot afford. Although this situation can happen, good training and appropriate guidelines will help.

To be effective at empowering staff, managers need to demonstrate that employees are valued and respected. When an employee has the authority to make a decision, they feel more empowerment.

If they make a decision that gets reversed by their manager, the empowerment dissipates. Therefore managers need to invest in their team by developing their knowledge, skills and expertise. They also need to be seen as open to new ideas through listening to their team and inviting them to contribute to decisions. If employees trust their manager and feel that the manager 'has their back' and supports them, then it is more likely that employees will feel empowered. This trust is enhanced through managers also showing appreciation to staff who undertake tasks on their own initiative.

Promote Teamwork

The nature of many service jobs suggests that customer satisfaction will be enhanced when employees work as teams. Because service jobs are frequently frustrating, demanding and challenging, a teamwork environment will help alleviate some of the stresses and strains. Employees who feel supported and feel that they have a team backing them up will be better able to maintain their enthusiasm and provide quality service.[38] 'An interactive community of co-workers who help each other, commiserate and achieve together is a powerful antidote to service burnout',[39] and, we would add, an important ingredient for service quality. By promoting teamwork, an organization can enhance the employees' *abilities* to deliver excellent service while the camaraderie and support enhance their *inclination* to be excellent service providers.

One way of promoting teamwork is to encourage the attitude that 'everyone has a customer'. That is, even when employees are not directly responsible for or in direct interaction with the final customer, they need to know whom they serve directly and how the role they play in the total service picture is essential to the final delivery of quality service. If each employee can see how he or she is somehow integral in delivering quality to the final customer and if each employee knows who to support to make service quality a reality, teamwork will be enhanced. Service blueprints (described in Chapter 8) can serve as useful tools to illustrate for employees their integral roles in delivering service quality to the ultimate customer.

Team goals and rewards also promote teamwork. When a firm rewards teams of individuals rather than basing all rewards on individual achievements and performance, team effort and team spirit are encouraged.

Provide Needed Support Systems

To be efficient and effective in their jobs, service workers require internal support systems that are aligned with their need to be customer focused. This point cannot be over-emphasized. In fact, without customer-focused internal support and customer-oriented systems, it is nearly impossible for employees to deliver quality service – no matter how much they want to. For example, a bank teller who is rewarded for customer satisfaction as well as for accuracy in bank transactions needs easy access to up-to-date customer records, a well-staffed branch (so that he or she is not constantly facing a long line of impatient customers), and supportive customer-oriented supervisors and back-office staff. In examining customer service outcomes in Australian call centres, researchers found that internal support from supervisors, teammates and other departments as well as evaluations of technology used on the job were all strongly related to employee satisfaction and ability to serve customers.[40] The following sections suggest strategies for ensuring customer-oriented internal support.

Measure Internal Service Quality

One way to encourage supportive internal service relationships is to measure and reward internal service. By first acknowledging that everyone in the organization has a customer, and then measuring customer perceptions of internal service quality, an organization can begin to develop an internal quality culture. An internal customer service audit can be used to implement a culture of internal service quality. Through the audit, internal organizations identify their customers, determine their needs, measure how well they are doing and make improvements. The process parallels market research practices used for external customers.

One risk of measuring and focusing on internal service quality and internal customers is that people can sometimes get so involved in meeting the needs of internal customers that they forget they are in business to serve the ultimate, external customers.[41] In measuring internal service quality, therefore, it is important to constantly draw the linkages between what is being delivered internally and how it supports the delivery of the final service to customers. Service blueprinting, introduced in Chapter 8, can help to illustrate these critical linkages.

Provide Supportive Technology and Equipment

When employees do not have the right equipment or their equipment fails them, they can be easily frustrated in their desire to deliver quality service. To do their jobs effectively and efficiently, service employees need the right equipment and technology.

Having the right technology and equipment can extend into strategies regarding workplace and workstation design. For example, Zappos, the online shoe retailer, provides its call centre staff with computer systems that provide comprehensive information concerning product inventory in their warehouses. This allows them to provide customers with up-to-date information and options. Corridors in the company's facilities are covered with murals and cartoons, rooms are filled with props, and workspaces are filled with personalized clutter. These are all designed to create an environment where employees feel like part of a team and are comfortable serving customers.

Develop Service-Oriented Internal Processes

To best support service personnel in their delivery of quality service on the front line, an organization's internal processes should be designed with customer value and customer satisfaction in mind. In other words, internal procedures must support quality service performance. In many companies internal processes are driven by bureaucratic rules, tradition, cost efficiencies or the needs of internal employees. Providing service- and customer-oriented internal processes can therefore imply a need for total redesign of systems. This kind of wholesale redesign of systems and processes has become known as 'process re-engineering'. Although developing service-oriented internal processes through re-engineering sounds sensible, it is probably one of the most difficult strategies to implement, especially in organizations that are steeped in tradition. Refocusing internal processes and introducing large amounts of new, supportive technology were among the changes made by British Telecom in its transition from a traditional, operations-driven company to more of a customer-focused one.

Retain the Best People

An organization that hires the right people, trains and develops them to deliver service quality, and provides the needed support must also work to retain them. Employee turnover, especially when the best service employees are leaving, can be very detrimental to customer satisfaction, employee morale and overall service quality. And, just as they do with customers, some firms spend a lot of time attracting employees but then tend to take them for granted (or even worse), causing these good employees to search for alternative jobs. Although all the strategies depicted in Figure 11.2 will support the retention of the best employees, here we focus on some strategies that are particularly aimed at this goal.

Include Employees in the Company's Vision

For employees to remain motivated and interested in sticking with the organization and supporting its goals, they need to share an understanding of the organization's vision. People who deliver service day after day need to understand how their work fits into the big picture of the organization and its goals.

SERVICE SPOTLIGHT

Insurance provider, Allianz, has a sponsorship agreement to support the Olympic Movement, including the Organizing Committees of the Olympic Games over the period 2021 through to 2028. It has used its link with the Olympics to run an internal campaign to engage and motivate its staff. It wanted a programme to attract and retain the best employees within the company. The campaign involved a roadshow of around 11 top Olympic athletes visiting each of the company's 22 UK offices. Sporting events were held for employees who were able to question athletes about competing in Olympic events. The campaign focused on the theme of 'performance' to inspire staff and encourage their collaboration to succeed.

Employees will be motivated to some extent by their pay and other benefits, but the best ones will be attracted away to other opportunities if they are not committed to the vision of the organization. Employees cannot be committed to the vision if that vision is kept secret from them. What this vision-sharing strategy means in practice is that the vision is communicated frequently to employees and that it is communicated by top managers, often by the CEO.[42]

Respected CEOs such as Richard Branson of the Virgin Group and Ingvar Kamprad of IKEA were known for communicating their vision clearly and often to employees. When the company's vision and direction are clear and motivating, employees are more likely to stay on through the inevitable rough spots on the way to accomplishing the company's goals.

Treat Employees as Customers

If employees feel valued and their needs are taken care of, they are more likely to stay with the organization. Many companies have adopted the idea that employees are also customers of the organization and that basic marketing strategies can be directed at them.[43] The products that the organization has to offer its employees are jobs (with assorted benefits) and quality of work life. To determine whether the job and work-life needs of employees are being met, organizations conduct periodic internal marketing research to assess employee satisfaction and needs.

In addition to basic internal research, organizations can apply other marketing strategies to their management of employees. For example, segmentation of the employee population is apparent in many of the flexible benefit plans and career path choices now available to employees. Organizations that are set up to meet the needs of specific segments and to adjust as people proceed through their lives will benefit from increased employee loyalty. Advertising and other forms of communication directed at employees can also increase their sense of value and enhance their commitment to the organization.[44]

Measure and Reward Strong Service Performers

If a company wants the strongest service performers to stay with the organization, it must reward and promote them. This strategy may seem obvious, but often the reward systems in organizations are not set up to reward service excellence. Reward systems may value productivity, sales or some other dimension that can potentially work *against* good service. Even those service workers who are intrinsically motivated to deliver high service quality will become discouraged at some point and start looking elsewhere if their efforts are not recognized and rewarded.

Reward systems need to be linked to the organization's vision and to outcomes that are truly important. For instance, if customer satisfaction and retention are viewed as critical outcomes, service behaviours that increase those outcomes need to be recognized and rewarded. In the Royal Bank of Scotland and National Westminster Bank, employees in branches do not receive their sales bonuses unless their branch has achieved the required customer service scores.

⭐ **SERVICE SPOTLIGHT**

Heathrow Airport Holdings Ltd operates London Heathrow Airport and is regulated by the Civil Aviation Authority(CAA). The financial income for the airport operator takes account of the quality of the service provided through the Service Quality Rebate Scheme. This scheme was introduced by the CAA to ensure the service standards that airlines and passengers could expect from Heathrow in return for the income the operator receives from the airlines using the airport. Where performance falls below a certain level, Heathrow must repay a proportion of charges that they levied back to the airlines. This provides an incentive for the airport and all of its staff to meet set standards of service quality. The rebate scheme covers the following aspects of Heathrow's performance:

- Queuing at the security search area and the availability of pier service for aircraft.
- Passenger perception of the availability of seating in the departures lounge, the quality of flight information systems, how easy it is to find their way around, the cleanliness of toilets and concourse areas within the terminal buildings, security processes and ease of use of WiFi.
- Equipment which includes lifts, escalators, and moving walkways, arrivals baggage reclaim belts, fixed electrical ground power (for aircraft on stands), stands, jetties, pre-conditioned air (for aircraft), and stand entry guidance (to assist aircraft parking).

The scheme also includes a bonus element which rewards the operator for high levels of passenger satisfaction.

Source: **https://www.heathrow.com/company/company-news-and-information/performance/airport-operations/service-quality-rebate-and-bonus-scheme.**

Companies with a goal of customer satisfaction in every service encounter often need to adjust the criteria by which employee performance is judged. Mystery shopping scores may be used in determining rewards for staff in some organizations, such as Burger King.

Aligning reward systems with customer outcomes can be challenging. Reward systems are usually well entrenched, and employees have learned over time how they need to perform within the old structures. Change is difficult both for the managers who may have created, and may still believe in, the old systems and for employees who are not sure what they need to do to succeed under the new rules. In many organizations, however, reward and incentive systems are still not matched with customer satisfaction and loyalty goals.[45]

In developing new systems and structures to recognize customer focus and customer satisfaction, organizations have turned to a variety of rewards. Traditional approaches, such as higher pay, promotions and one-off monetary awards or prizes, can be linked to service performance.

Other types of rewards include special organizational and team celebrations for achieving improved customer satisfaction or for attaining customer retention goals. In most service organizations it is not only the major accomplishments but the daily perseverance and attention to detail that move the organization forward, so recognition of the 'small wins' is also important.

In many situations, a customer's relationship is with a specific employee and may be stronger with the *employee* than with the firm. If this employee leaves the firm and is no longer available to the customer, the firm's relationship with the customer may be jeopardized.[46] Clearly, a firm should make great efforts to retain such employees; however, in spite of its best efforts, some good employees are going to leave. If the firm is not successful at retaining a key customer-contact employee, what can it do to reduce the impact on the customer? Employees could be rotated occasionally in order to ensure that the customer has exposure to, and is comfortable with, more than one employee. Firms might also form teams of employees who are responsible for interacting with each customer. In both cases, the idea is that the customer would have multiple contacts with several employees in the organization, thus reducing the firm's vulnerability to losing the customer should any one employee leave. Emphasis should also be placed on creating a positive firm image in the minds of its customers and in so doing convey that *all* its employees are capable.[47]

Customer-Oriented Service Delivery

As the examples presented in this chapter illustrate, specific approaches for hiring and energizing front-line workers take on a different look and feel across companies, based on the organization's values, culture, history and vision.[48] For example, 'developing people to deliver service quality' is accomplished quite differently at TGIF restaurants than at Disney. At Disney, the orientation and training process is highly structured, scripted and standardized. At TGIF restaurants, the emphasis is more on developing needed skills and then empowering employees to be spontaneous and non-scripted in their approach to customers. Although the style and culture of the two organizations are different, both pay special attention to all four basic themes shown in Figure 11.2. Both have made significant investments in their people, recognizing the critical roles they play.

Throughout this book we have advocated a strong customer focus. Firms that have a strong service culture clearly put an emphasis on the customer and the customer's experience. To do so, firms must also create an environment that staunchly supports the customer-contact employee because, in the organization, this person is frequently the most responsible for ensuring that the customer's experience is delivered as designed. Historically, many firms have viewed senior management as the most important people in the firm and, indeed, organizational charts reflect this view in their structure. This approach places management at the top of the structure and (implicitly) the customer at the bottom, with customer-contact employees just above them. If the organization's most important people are customers, they should be at the top of the chart, followed by those with whom they have contact. Such a view, illustrated in Figure 11.3, is more consistent with a customer-oriented focus. In effect, the role of top-level management changes from that of commanding employees to that of facilitating and supporting those employees in the organization who are closest to the customer.

Figure 11.3   Customer-focused organizational chart

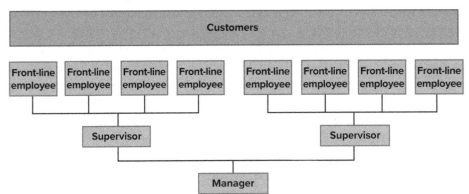

The human resource strategies that we have offered in this chapter are suggested as a means to support the customer contact employee. Indeed, a truly customer-oriented management team might actually 'flip' the services marketing triangle (discussed in Chapter 1), with customers and employees equally placed at the top – as illustrated in Figure 11.4. A statement by Michel Bon, CEO of France Telecom, succinctly summarizes the philosophy behind this approach:

> *If you sincerely believe that 'the customer is king', the second most important person in this kingdom must be the one who has a direct interaction on a daily basis with the one who is king.*[49]

Figure 11.4   Inverted services marketing triangle

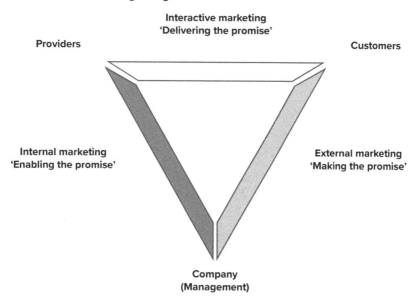

By flipping the services marketing triangle in Figure 11.4, the two groups that are the most import-ant people to the organization, customers and those who interact with customers, are placed in a position of prominence.

Summary

Because many services are delivered by people in real time, closing the service performance gap is heavily dependent on human resource strategies. The successful execution of such strategies begins with the development and nurturing of a true service culture throughout the organization.

Often service employees *are* the service, and in all cases they represent the organization in the customers' eyes. They affect service quality perceptions to a large degree through their influence on the five dimensions of service quality: reliability, responsiveness, empathy, assurance and tangibles. It is essential to match what the customer wants and needs with service employees' abilities to deliver.

In this chapter we focused on service employees to provide you with an understanding of the critical nature of their roles and an appreciation of the inherent stresses and conflicts they face. You learned that front-line service jobs demand significant investments of emotional labour and that employees confront a variety of on-the-job conflicts. Sometimes service employees are personally uncomfortable with the roles they are asked to play; at other times, the requirements of the organization may conflict with client expectations and employees must resolve the dilemma on the spot. Sometimes there are conflicting needs among customers who are being served in turn (such as in a bank teller line) or among customers being served simultaneously (as in a college classroom). At other times a front-line employee may be faced with a decision about whether to satisfy a customer or meet productivity targets (such as a dentist who is required to see a certain number of patients in a defined period of time).

Grounded in this understanding of the importance of service employees and the nature of their roles in the organization, you learned strategies for integrating appropriate human resource practices into service firms. The strategies are aimed at allowing employees to effectively satisfy customers as well as be efficient and productive in their jobs. The strategies were organized around four major human resource goals in service organizations: to hire the right people, to develop people to deliver service quality, to provide needed support systems, and to retain the best people. A company that works toward implementing these strategies is well on its way to delivering service quality through its people, thereby diminishing gap 3 – the service performance gap.

Key Concepts

Boundary spanners	234	Gig economy	234
Chatbots	238	Hiring service employees	239
Corporate culture	229	Internal customer service audit	244
Emotional labour	234	Internal marketing	239
Employee retention	233	Service culture	229
Employee satisfaction	233	Service leadership	229
Employees are the brand	232	Service profit chain	233
Employer branding	240	Subordinate service role	237
Empowerment	242		

Exercises

1   Visit the websites of companies with known world-class service cultures (such as Ritz-Carlton, FedEx or SAS airlines). How does the information conveyed on their websites reinforce these companies' service culture?

2   Review the section of the chapter on boundary-spanning roles. Interview at least two front-line service personnel regarding the stresses they experience in their jobs. How do the examples they provide relate to the sources of conflict and trade-offs described in the text?

3   Assume that you are the manager of a team of front-line customer-service employees in a credit card company. Assume that these employees work over the telephone and that they deal primarily with customer requests, questions and complaints. In this specific context:

   a   Define what is meant by *boundary-spanning roles*, and discuss the basic purposes or functions performed by participants in these roles.

   b   Discuss two of the potential conflicts that your employees may face on the basis of their roles as boundary spanners.

   c   Discuss how you, as their supervisor, might deal with these conflicts based on what you have learned.

4   Choose one or more of the human resource strategy themes (hire the right people, develop people to deliver service quality, provide needed support systems, retain the best people). Interview a manager in a service organization of your choice regarding his or her current practices within the theme you have chosen. Describe the current practices and recommend any appropriate changes for improving them.

Discussion Questions

1   Define *service culture*. Why is service culture so important? Can a manufacturing firm have a service culture? Why or why not?

2   Why are service employees critical to the success of any service organization? Why do we include an entire chapter on service employees in a marketing course?

3   What is *emotional labour*? How can it be differentiated from physical or mental labour?

4   Reflect on your own role as a front-line service provider, whether in a current job or in any full- or part-time service job you have had in the past. Did you experience the kinds of conflicts described in the boundary-spanning roles section of the chapter? Be prepared to have some concrete examples for class discussion.

5   Select a service provider (your dentist, doctor, lawyer, hair stylist) with whom you are familiar, and discuss ways this person could positively influence the five dimensions of service quality in the context of delivering his or her services. Do the same for yourself (if you are currently a service provider).

6   Describe the four basic human resource strategy themes and why each plays an important role in building a customer-oriented organization.

7   What is the difference between technical and interactive service skills? Provide examples (preferably from your own work context or from another context with which you are familiar). Why do service employees need training in both?

8   Is empowerment always the best approach for effective service delivery? Why is employee empowerment so controversial?

9   Visit the jobs page of the citizenM website at www.citizenM.com/jobs, and describe the types of people, e.g. personality, clothing tastes, etc., they are trying to recruit.

10   What reasons would you give to explain the high turnover of staff in fast-food restaurants?

Further Reading

Bernoff, J. and Schadler, T. (2010). Empowered. *Harvard Business Review*, July/August, 5–101.

Evanschitzky, H., Wangenheim, F.V. and Wünderlich, N.V. (2012). Perils of managing the service profit chain: The role of time lags and feedback loops. *Journal of Retailing*, 88(3), 356–66.

Gruman, J.A. and Saks, A.M. (2011). Performance management and employee engagement. *Human Resource Management Review*, 21(2), 123–36.

Hesket, J.L., Jones, T.O., Loveman, G.W., Earl Sasser Jr, W. and Schlesinger, L.L. (2008). Putting the service–profit chain to work. *Harvard Business Review*, July/August, 118–29.

Hogreve, J., Iseke, A., Derfuss, K. and Eller, T. (2017). The service–profit chain: A meta-analytic test of a comprehensive theoretical framework. *Journal of Marketing*, 81(3), 41–61.

Kruja, D., Ha, H., Drishti, E. and Oelfke, T. (2016). Empowerment in the hospitality industry in the United States. *Journal of Hospitality Marketing and Management*, 25(1), 25–48.

Larivière, B., Bowen, D., Andreassen, T.W., Kunz, W., Sirianni, N.J., Voss, C. and De Keyser, A. (2017). 'Service Encounter 2.0': An investigation into the roles of technology, employees and customers. *Journal of Business Research*, 79, 238–246.

Malhotra, N. and Ackfeldt, A.L. (2016). Internal communication and prosocial service behaviors of front-line employees: Investigating mediating mechanisms. *Journal of Business Research*, 69(10), 4132–39.

Schneider, B. and Bowen, D. (2010). Winning the service game: Revisiting the rules by which people co-create value. *Handbook of Service Science*, Part 1, 31–59.

Wilson, A.M. (2001). Understanding organisational culture and the implications for corporate marketing. *European Journal of Marketing*, 35(3/4), 353–67.

Chapter 12

Customers' Roles in Service Delivery

Chapter Outline

The Importance of Customers in Service Co-Creation and Delivery   254
Customers' Roles   257
Self-Service Technologies – The Ultimate in Customer Participation   262
Strategies for Enhancing Customer Participation   265
Summary and Key Concepts   271
Exercises   272
Discussion Questions   272
Further Reading   273

Learning Objectives

This chapter's objectives are to:

1 Illustrate the importance of customers in successful service delivery and co-creation of service experiences.
2 Discuss the variety of roles that service customers play: productive resources for the organization; contributors to quality and satisfaction; competitors.
3 Explain strategies for involving service customers effectively to increase both quality and productivity.

Opening Example

IKEA – Customers Create Value for Themselves

IKEA of Sweden has managed to transform itself from a small mail-order furniture company in the 1950s into the world's largest retailer of home furnishings, with over 433 stores in more than 52 markets, employing 208,000 employees. In 2018, 957 million store visits and 21.5 billion web visits generated more than 38.8 billion euros in revenues. The company sells simple Scandinavian design furnishings, charging 25 to 50 per cent less than its competitors.

Source: ©Paul2015/ Shutterstock

A key to IKEA's success is the company's relationship with its customers. IKEA has drawn the customer into its production system: 'If customers agree to take on certain key tasks traditionally done by manufacturers and retailers – the assembly of products and their delivery to customers' homes – then IKEA promises to deliver well-designed products at substantially lower prices.' In effect, IKEA's customers become essential contributors to value – they create value for themselves through participating in the manufacturing, design and delivery processes.

IKEA has made being part of the value creation process an easy, fun and pleasant experience for customers. The stores are set up with 'inspirational displays', including realistic room settings and real-life homes that allow customers to get comfortable with the furnishings, try them out and visualize the possibilities in their own homes. To make shopping easy, free pushchairs and supervised child care are provided as well as wheelchairs for those who need them.

When customers enter the store they are given catalogues, tape measures, pens and notepaper to use as they shop, allowing them to perform functions commonly done by sales and service staff. After payment, customers take their purchases to their cars on trolleys; if necessary they can rent or buy a roof rack to carry larger purchases. Thus, customers also provide furniture loading and delivery services for themselves. At home, IKEA customers then take on the role of manufacturer in assembling the new furnishings, following simple visual instructions.

IKEA prints around 200 million catalogues in 38 editions, in 17 languages for 28 countries, making its products and instructions for their use accessible worldwide. In addition to tailoring its catalogues, another key to IKEA's successful global expansion has been the company's policy of allowing each store to tailor its mix according to local market needs and budgets. For example, in its China stores, layouts reflect the design of many Chinese apartments. Because many of the apartments have balconies, the stores have a selection of balcony furnishings and displays. As Chinese kitchens are generally small, fewer kitchen items and furnishings are shown. Even IKEA's famous 'do it yourself' (DIY) assembly concept has also been adapted to some extent in China. Because fewer people have cars and therefore use public transport, IKEA has a more extensive delivery service in China than in most countries. Additionally, because labour is cheaper in China, many customers choose to have their furniture assembled for them rather than doing it themselves. In the US and UK, customers can also have their self-assembly furniture built for them using TaskRabbit, an online service that matches freelance labour to one-off jobs, which was acquired by Ikea in 2017. Although IKEA has not abandoned its DIY strategy, it has been somewhat more flexible to suit customer needs.

> IKEA's success is attributable in part to recognizing that customers can be part of the business system, performing roles they have never performed before. The company's flexible implementation of this idea through clearly defining customers' new roles and making it fun to perform these roles is the genius of its strategy. Through the process, customers co-create their own experiences and contribute to their own satisfaction.
>
> *Source: www.ikea.com.*

In this chapter we examine the unique roles played by customers in service delivery situations. Service customers are often present in the 'factory' (the place the service is produced and/or consumed), interacting with employees and with other customers. For example, in a classroom or training situation, students (the customers) are sitting in the factory interacting with the instructor and other students as they consume and co-create the educational services. Because they are present during service production, customers can contribute to, or detract from, the successful delivery of the service and to their own satisfaction. In a manufacturing context, rarely does the production facility contend with customer presence on the factory floor, nor does it rely on the customer's immediate real-time input to manufacture the product. As our opening vignette illustrates, service customers can actually produce the service themselves and to some extent are responsible for their own satisfaction. Buying IKEA furniture, customers co-create value for themselves and in the process also reduce the prices they pay.

Because customers are participants in service production and delivery, they can potentially contribute to the widening of gap 3, the service performance gap: that is, customers themselves can influence whether the delivered service meets customer-defined specifications. Sometimes customers contribute to gap 3 because they lack understanding of their roles and exactly what they should do in a given situation, particularly if the customer is confronting a service concept for the first time. Customers visiting IKEA for the first time need detailed, but simple, instructions to help them understand how to use the service effectively and get the greatest value.

At other times, customers may understand their roles but be unwilling or unable to perform for some reason. In a health club context, members may understand that to get into good physical shape they must follow the workout guidelines set up by the trainers. If work schedules or illness keep members from living up to their part of the guidelines, the service will not be successful because of customer inaction. In a different service situation, customers may choose not to perform the roles defined for them because they are not rewarded in any way for contributing their effort. When service customers are enticed through price reductions, greater convenience or some other tangible benefit, they are more likely to perform their roles willingly, as in the case of our opening vignette about IKEA.

Finally, the service performance gap may be widened not through actions or inactions on the part of the customer, but because of what *other* customers do. Other customers who are in the service outlet, either receiving the service simultaneously (passengers on an aeroplane flight) or waiting their turn to receive the service sequentially (bank customers waiting in a queue, Disneyland customers waiting to go on one of the rides), can influence whether the service is effectively and efficiently delivered.

This chapter focuses on the roles of customers in service delivery and co-creation of service experiences as well as strategies to effectively manage them.

The Importance of Customers in Service Co-creation and Delivery

Customer participation at some level is inevitable in service delivery and co-creation. Services are actions or performances, typically produced and consumed simultaneously. In many situations, employees, customers and, even, others in the service environment interact to produce the ultimate service outcome. Because they participate, customers are indispensable to the production process of service organizations, and they can actually control or contribute to their own satisfaction.[1] This view of participatory customers is consistent with the service-dominant logic of marketing which promotes the idea that customers are always co-creators of value.[2]

The importance of customers in successful service delivery is obvious if service performances are looked at as a form of drama. The drama metaphor for services (discussed in Chapter 3) suggests the reciprocal, interactive roles of employees (actors) and customers (audience) in creating the service experience. The service actors and audience are surrounded by the service setting or the servicescape (discussed in Chapter 10). The drama metaphor argues that the development and maintenance of an interaction (a service experience) relies on the audience's input as well as the actors' presentation. Through this 'services as drama' metaphor, service performances or service delivery situations are viewed as tenuous, fragile processes that can be influenced by behaviours of customers as well as by employees.[3] Service performance results from actions and interactions among individuals in both groups.

Consider the services provided by a cruise ship company. The actors (ship's personnel) provide the service through interactions with their audience (the passengers) and among each other. The audience also produces elements of the service through interactions with the actors and other audience members. Both actors and audience are surrounded by an elaborate setting (the cruise ship itself) that provides a context to facilitate the service performance. The drama metaphor provides a compelling frame of reference for recognizing the interdependent roles of actors and audience in service delivery.[4]

Recognition of the role of customers is also reflected in the definition of the *people* element of the services marketing mix given in Chapter 1: *all human actors who play a part in service delivery and thus influence the buyer's perceptions; namely, the firm's personnel, the customer, and other customers in the service environment*. Chapter 11 thoroughly examined the role of the firm's employees in delivering service quality. In this chapter we focus on the customer receiving the service and on fellow customers in the service environment.

Customer Receiving the Service

Because the customer receiving the service participates in the delivery process, he or she can contribute to narrowing or widening gap 3 through behaviours that are appropriate or inappropriate, effective or ineffective, productive or unproductive. Even in a relatively simple service such as retail, customers' actions and preparation can have an effect on service delivery. Customers who are unprepared in terms of what they want to buy can soak up the customer service representative's time as they seek advice. Similarly, shoppers who are not prepared with their credit card numbers can put the call centre representative on hold while they search for their cards or retrieve them from another room or their cars. Meanwhile, other customers and calls are left unattended, causing longer wait times and potential dissatisfaction.

The level of customer participation – low, medium or high – varies across services, as shown in Table 12.1. In some cases, all that is required is the customer's physical presence *(low level of participation)*, with the employees of the firm doing all the service production work, as in the example of an orchestral concert. Concert-goers must be present to receive the entertainment service, but little else is required once they are seated. In other situations, consumer inputs are required to aid the service organization in creating the service *(moderate level of participation)*. Inputs can include *information, effort* or *physical possessions*. All three of these are required for an accountant to effectively prepare a client's tax return: information in the form of tax history, marital status and number of dependents; effort in putting the information together in a useful fashion; and physical possessions such as receipts and past tax returns. In some situations, customers are truly co-creators of the service *(high level of participation)*. For these services, customers have important participation roles that will affect the nature of the service outcome. In a complex or long-term business-to-business consulting engagement, the client can be involved in activities such as identification of issues, shared problem-solving, ongoing communication, provision of equipment and work space, and implementation of solutions.

Table 12.1   Levels of customer participation across different services

Low: consumer presence required during service delivery	Moderate: consumer inputs required for service creation	High: customer co-creates the service
Products are standardized	Client inputs (information, materials) to customize a standard service	Active client participation guides the customized service
Service is delivered regardless of any individual purchase	Delivery of service only occurs when customer purchases	Service cannot be created apart from the customer's purchase and active participation
Payment may be the only required customer input	Customer inputs are necessary for an adequate outcome, but the service firm provides the service	Customer inputs are mandatory and co-create the outcome
Airline travel	Haircut	Marriage counselling
Hotel stay	Tax advice	Personal training
Fast-food restaurant	Full-service restaurant	Weight reduction programme

Fellow Customers

In many service contexts, customers receive the service simultaneously with other customers or must wait their turn while other customers are being served. In both cases 'fellow customers' are present in the service environment and can affect the nature of the service outcome or process. Fellow customers can either *enhance* or *detract* from customer satisfaction and perceptions of quality.[5] Some of the ways fellow customers can negatively affect the service experience are by exhibiting disruptive behaviours, causing delays, excessively crowding and manifesting incompatible needs. In restaurants, hotels, aeroplanes and other environments in which customers are in very close proximity to each other as they receive the service, crying babies, loud patrons and unruly groups can be disruptive and detract from the experiences of their fellow customers.

The customer is disappointed through no direct fault of the provider. In other cases, overly demanding customers (even customers with legitimate problems) can cause a delay for others while their needs are met. This occurrence is common in banks, post offices and customer service counters in retail stores. Excessive crowding or overuse of a service can also affect the nature of the customer's experience. For example, the quality of mobile phone networks and the ability to make a call can suffer at large social gatherings such as parades, music festivals or New Year's Eve celebrations when large numbers of customers all try to use the service in one geographical location at the same time.

Finally, customers who are being served simultaneously but who have incompatible needs can negatively affect each other. This situation can occur in restaurants, university lecture theatres, hospitals and any service establishment in which multiple segments are served simultaneously. In a study of critical service encounters occurring in tourist attractions, researchers found that customers negatively affected each other when they failed to follow either explicit or implicit 'rules of conduct'. Customers reported such negative behaviours as smoking, drinking alcohol, being verbally abusive or pushing into the line. Other times, dissatisfaction resulted when other customers were impersonal, rude, unfriendly or even spiteful.[6]

We can offer just as many examples of other customers enhancing satisfaction and quality for their fellow customers as detracting from them. Sometimes the mere presence of other customers enhances the experience – for example, at sporting events, in cinemas and in other entertainment venues. The presence of other patrons is essential for true enjoyment of these experiences. In other situations, fellow customers provide a positive social dimension to the service experience. At health clubs, churches and some resorts, such as Club Med, other customers provide opportunities to socialize and build friendships.

In some situations, customers may actually help each other achieve service goals and outcomes. The success of WW (previously known as Weight Watchers), for example, depends significantly on the camaraderie and support that group members provide each other. The study of tourist attractions mentioned earlier found that customers increased the satisfaction of others by having friendly conversations while waiting in line, by taking photographs, by assisting with children and by returning dropped or lost items.[7] An ethnographic study that observed hundreds of hours of customer interactions among travellers on the UK rail system found that customers often helped each other by: (1) providing important service-related information (e.g. schedules, interesting features en route) that can reduce trip-related anxiety; (2) engaging in enjoyable conversation, thus making the trip more pleasant; and (3) serving as someone to complain to when mishaps and service failures occurred.[8]

The influence of fellow customers in helping others is even more apparent in some online service environments such as Amazon, travel review sites and eBay. Customers will provide reviews of their experiences with the service or book or trader in order to assist others with purchasing decisions. They may also provide advice on how to use the service effectively. Computer and software suppliers often have online user groups who share ideas and solutions to issues and problems with fellow users.

⭐ SERVICE SPOTLIGHT

TomTom, the maker of satellite navigation systems for cars, has an online community of users who talk about the products and services as well as provide technical help and support to other users. It has over 50,000 registered users and operates in English, German and French. Members earn badges by sharing their 'tips & tricks', and by helping other community members. The community through their forum can provide answers to problems from a user's perspective and the company receives feedback on issues with their products and services. Since the community was established, TomTom has found that enquiries to its call centres have reduced by over 15 per cent (resulting in cost savings). Also, positive word of mouth through the community (such as the following example) may have more impact and be more trusted than corporate promotional material.

Amidst all of this negative sentiment, I'd just like to add some encouragement. HD Traffic and IQ Routes save me between twenty and forty minutes in traffic almost every single day. I have not been able to find a better, or even remotely similar, solution at any price, to my daily traffic challenges. So thank you for what has already been achieved, even if we still always crave ever more!

Source: **https://discussions.tomtom.com.**

Customers' Roles

The following subsections examine in more detail three major roles played by customers in service delivery: customers as productive resources; customers as contributors to quality and satisfaction; and customers as competitors.

Customers as Productive Resources

Service customers have been referred to as 'partial employees' of the organization – human resources who contribute to the organization's productive capacity.[9] Some management experts have suggested that the organization's boundaries be expanded to consider the customer as part of the service system. In other words, if customers contribute effort, time or other resources to the service production process, they should be considered as part of the organization. (Later in this chapter we devote a section to defining customers' jobs and strategies for managing them effectively.)

Customer inputs can affect the organization's productivity through both the quality of what they contribute and the resulting quality and quantity of output generated. In a business-to-business services context, the contributions of the client can enhance the overall productivity of the firm in both quality and quantity of service.[10] easyJet depends on customers to perform critical service roles for themselves, thus increasing the overall productivity of the airline. Passengers are asked to carry their own bags when transferring to other flights, print their own boarding passes and, in certain airports, print their own bag tags.

Customer participation in service production raises a number of issues for organizations. Because customers can influence both the quality and quantity of production, some experts believe the delivery system should be isolated as much as possible from customer inputs in order to reduce the uncertainty they can bring into the production process. This view sees customers as a major source of uncertainty – in the timing of their demands and the uncontrollability of their attitudes and actions. The logical conclusion is that any service activities that do not require customer contact or involvement should be performed away from customers: the less direct contact there is between the customer and the service production system, the greater the potential for the system to operate at peak efficiency.[11]

Other experts believe that services can be delivered most efficiently if customers are truly viewed as partial employees and their co-production roles are designed to maximize their contributions to the service creation process. The logic behind this view is that organizational productivity can be increased if customers learn to perform service-related activities they currently are not doing or are educated to perform more effectively the tasks they are already doing.[12]

For example, when self-service petrol stations first came into being, customers were asked to fill their own fuel tanks. With customers performing this task, fewer employees were needed and the overall productivity of service stations improved. Now many service stations offer customers the option of paying for their fuel at the pump by popping their credit cards into a slot on the pump and leaving the station without dealing directly with a cashier. Similarly, the introduction of many automated airline services such as self-service baggage drop-off and self-ticketing are intended to speed up the process for customers while freeing employees for other tasks.[13] Organizational productivity is increased by using customers as a resource to perform tasks previously completed by employees. In both business-to-business and business-to-consumer contexts, organizations are turning to automated and online customer service. One prominent goal with online customer service is to increase organizational productivity by using the customer as a partial employee, performing his or her own service.

★ SERVICE SPOTLIGHT

London Gatwick Airport has one of the world's largest self-service bag drop zones in its North Terminal. The technology enables passengers who have checked in online to take their bags straight to a machine upon arrival at the airport, where they can print their luggage tag, apply it to their bag and load it straight onto Gatwick's baggage sorting system. The technology automatically checks whether a bag is acceptable by determining its weight, dimensions, volume, shape, conveyability and label bar code. This state-of-the-art facility is designed to eliminate queues by allowing passengers to check-in, drop off their bag and be on their way in less than two minutes.

Although organizations derive obvious productivity benefits by involving customers as co-producers, customers do not always like or accept their new roles, especially when they perceive the purpose to be bottom-line cost savings for the company. If customers see no clear benefit to being involved in co-production (e.g. lower prices, quicker access, better quality outcome), then they are likely to resent and resist their co-production roles.

Customers as Contributors to Service Quality and Satisfaction

Another role customers can play in services co-creation and delivery is that of contributor to their own satisfaction and the ultimate quality of the services they receive. Customers may care little that they have increased the productivity of the organization through their participation, but they are likely to care a great deal about whether their needs are fulfilled. Effective customer participation can increase the likelihood that needs are met and that the benefits the customer seeks are actually attained. Think about services such as health care, education, personal fitness and weight loss, in which the service outcome is highly dependent on customer participation. In these services, unless the customers perform their roles effectively, the desired service outcomes are not possible.

Research has shown that in education, active participation by students – as opposed to passive listening – increases learning (the desired service outcome) significantly.[14] The same is true in health care; patient compliance, in terms of taking prescribed medications or changing diet or other habits, can be critical to whether patients regain their health (the desired service outcome).[15] Other research in financial and medical service settings has shown that effective co-production by customers leads to greater loyalty toward the service provider.[16] In all of these examples, the customers contribute directly to the quality of the outcome and to their own satisfaction with the service. In a business-to-business context, couriers and parcel carriers have found that in many situations customers cause their own *dissatisfaction* with the service by failing to pack shipments appropriately, resulting in breakage or delays while items are repacked. Thus, ineffective co-production can result in negative outcomes and dissatisfaction.

Research suggests that customers who believe they have done their part to be effective in service interactions are more satisfied with the service. In a study of the banking industry, bank customers were asked to rate themselves (on a scale from 'strongly agree' to 'strongly disagree') on questions related to their contributions to service delivery, as follows:

- *What they did – outcome quality of customer inputs*
  I clearly explained what I wanted the bank employee to do.
  I gave the bank employee proper information.
  I tried to cooperate with the bank employee.
  I understand the procedures associated with this service.
- *How they did it – interaction quality of customer inputs*
  I was friendly to the bank employee.
  I have a good relationship with the bank employee.
  I was courteous to the bank employee.
  Receiving this service was a pleasant experience.

Results of the study indicated that the customers' perceptions of both what they did and how they did it were significantly related to customers' satisfaction with the service they received from the bank.[17] That is to say, those customers who responded more positively to the questions listed above were also more satisfied with the bank. Research in another context showed that customers' perceptions of service quality increased with greater levels of participation. Specifically, customers (in this case members of a YMCA) who participated more in the club gave the club higher ratings on aspects of service quality than did those who participated less.[18]

Customers contribute to quality service delivery when they ask questions, take responsibility for their own satisfaction, and complain when there is a service failure. The following four scenarios illustrate the wide variations in customer participation that can result in equally wide variations in service quality and customer satisfaction.

Customers who take responsibility and providers who encourage their customers to become their partners in identifying and satisfying their own needs will together produce higher levels of service quality. In addition to contributing to their own satisfaction by improving the quality of service delivered to them,

---

SCENARIO 1

A Major International Hotel

Guest A called the desk right after check-in to report that his television was not working and that the light over the bed was burnt out; both problems were fixed immediately. The hotel staff exchanged his television for one that worked and fixed the light bulb. Later they brought him a plate of fruit to make up for the inconvenience. Guest B did not communicate to management until check-out time that his television did not work and he could not read in his bed. His complaints were overheard by guests checking in, who wondered whether they had chosen the right place to stay.

SCENARIO 2

Office of a Tax Adviser

Client A has organized into categories the information necessary to do her taxes and has provided all documents requested by the accountant. Client B has a box full of papers and receipts, many of which are not relevant to her taxes but which she brought along 'just in case'.

SCENARIO 3

An Airline Flight from London to New York

Passenger A arrives for the flight with downloaded music, reading material and wearing warm clothes; passenger A also called ahead to order a special meal. Passenger B, who arrives empty-handed, becomes annoyed when the crew runs out of blankets, complains about the magazine selection and the meal, and starts fidgeting after the movie.

SCENARIO 4

Architectural Consultation for Renovating an Office Building

Client A has invited the architects to meet with its design committee made up of managers, staff and customers in order to lay the groundwork for a major redesign job that will affect everyone who works in the building as well as customers. The committee has already formulated initial ideas and surveyed staff and customers for input. Client B has invited architects in following a decision the week previously to redesign the building; the design committee is two managers who are preoccupied with other, more immediate tasks and have little idea what they need or what customers and staff would prefer in terms of a redesign of the office space.

---

some customers simply enjoy participating in service delivery. These customers find the act of participating to be intrinsically attractive.[19] They enjoy using the Internet to obtain airline tickets, or doing all their banking via ATMs and the Internet, or refuelling their own car. Often customers who like self-service in one setting are predisposed to serving themselves in other settings as well.

⭐ **SERVICE SPOTLIGHT**

Waitrose supermarkets in the UK have installed 'Quick Check' in many of their stores. This is a self-scan system which involves customers taking a handset round the store and scanning items as they put them into their bags within their shopping trolley. Customers see a running total of their spending on the device's screen. They then pay on exiting the store without having to remove their items from the trolley. As part of the process, service personnel will occasionally rescan the items, just to make sure that everything scanned correctly and that there is no attempt at theft. The benefit to the customer is that they can bypass the usual queues at check out and there is no need for emptying a trolley and repacking.

Interestingly, because service customers must participate in service delivery, they frequently blame themselves (at least partially) when things go wrong. Why did it take so long to reach an accurate diagnosis of my health problem? Why can't I operate this self-scanning handset correctly? Why was the room we reserved for our meeting unavailable when we arrived? If customers believe they are partially (or totally) to blame for the failure, they may be less dissatisfied with the service provider than when they believe the provider is responsible.[20] A recent series of studies suggests the existence of this 'self-serving bias'. That is, when services go better than expected, customers who have participated tend to take credit for the outcome and are less satisfied with the firm than are those customers who have not participated. However, when the outcome is worse than expected, customers who have chosen to participate in service production are less dissatisfied with the service than are those who choose not to participate – presumably because the participating customers have taken on some of the blame themselves.[21]

Customers as Competitors

A final role played by service customers is that of potential competitor. If self-service customers can be viewed as resources of the firm, or as 'partial employees', they could in some cases partially perform the service or perform the entire service for themselves and not need the provider at all. Thus, in a sense customers are competitors of the companies that supply the service. Whether to produce a service for themselves (*internal exchange*) – for example, child care, home maintenance, car repair – or have someone else provide the service for them (*external exchange*) is a common dilemma for consumers.[22]

Similar internal versus external exchange decisions are made by organizations. Firms frequently choose to outsource service activities such as payroll, data processing, call centres, accounting, or maintenance and facilities management. They find that it is advantageous to focus on their core businesses and leave these essential support services to others with greater expertise. Alternatively, a firm may decide to stop purchasing services externally and bring the service production process in-house.

Whether a household or a firm chooses to produce a particular service itself or contract externally for the service depends on a variety of factors. A proposed model of internal/external exchange suggests that such decisions depend on the following:[23]

- *Expertise capacity:* the likelihood of producing the service internally is increased if the household or firm possesses the specific skills and knowledge needed to produce it. Having the expertise will not necessarily result in internal service production, however, because other factors (available resources and time) will also influence the decision. (For firms, making the decision to outsource is often based on recognizing that although they may have the expertise, someone else can do it better.)
- *Resource capacity:* to decide to produce a service internally, the household or firm must have the needed resources including people, space, money, equipment and materials. If the resources are not available internally, external exchange is more likely.

- *Time capacity:* time is a critical factor in internal/external exchange decisions. Households and firms with adequate time capacity are more likely to produce services internally than are groups with time constraints.
- *Economic rewards:* the economic advantages or disadvantages of a particular exchange decision will be influential in choosing between internal and external options. The actual monetary costs of the two options will sway the decision.
- *Psychic rewards:* these are rewards of a non-economic nature which have a potentially strong influence on exchange decisions. Psychic rewards include the degree of satisfaction, enjoyment, gratification or happiness that is associated with the external or internal exchange.
- *Trust:* in this context *trust* means the degree of confidence or certainty the household or firm has in the various exchange options. The decision will depend to some extent on the level of self-trust in producing the service versus trust of others.
- *Control:* the household or firm's desire for control over the process and outcome of the exchange will also influence the internal/external choice. Entities that desire and can implement a high degree of control over the task are more likely to engage in internal exchange.

★ SERVICE SPOTLIGHT

The travel agency outlets of Tui, a multinational travel and tourism company, have suffered from customers acting as competitors, resulting from people booking their travel and holidays directly through the Internet. Younger, independent travellers, who are used to the web and getting instant information, see little benefit in having to wait on somebody else booking their trip for them. This is particularly the case for short-haul destinations or destinations where they have been before.

The important thing to remember from this section is that in many service scenarios customers can, and often do, choose to fully or partially produce the service themselves. Thus, in addition to recognizing that customers can be productive resources and co-creators of quality and value, organizations also need to recognize the customer's role as a potential competitor.

Self-Service Technologies – The Ultimate in Customer Participation

Self-service technologies (SSTs) are services produced entirely by the customer without any direct involvement or interaction with the firm's employees. SSTs represent the ultimate form of customer participation along a continuum from services that are produced entirely by the firm to those that are produced entirely by the customer. This continuum is depicted in Figure 12.1, using the example of a service station to illustrate the various ways the same service could be delivered along all points on the continuum. At the far right end of the continuum, the service station attendant does everything from refuelling the car to taking payment. On the other end of the spectrum, the customer does everything; in between are various forms and levels of customer participation. Many service delivery options, across industries, could be laid out on this type of continuum from total customer production through total firm production.

A Proliferation of New SSTs

Advances in technology, particularly the Internet, have allowed the introduction of a wide range of self-service technologies that occupy the far left end of the customer participation continuum in Figure 12.1. These technologies have proliferated as companies see the potential cost savings and efficiencies that can be achieved,

Figure 12.1   Services production continuum

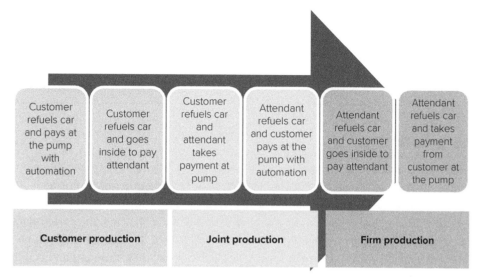

Source: Adapted from M.L. Meuter and M.J. Bitner, 'Self-service technologies: Extending service frameworks and identifying issues for research', in *Marketing Theory and Applications,* eds D. Grewal and C. Pechmann (American Marketing Association Winter Educators' Conference, 1998), pp. 12–19.

potential sales growth, increased customer satisfaction and competitive advantage. A partial list of some of the self-service technologies available to consumers includes:

- ATMs
- Self-service petrol pumps
- Airline check-in
- Self-service airline bag drop
- Hotel check-in and check-out
- Automated car rental
- Automated filing of legal claims
- Online tax returns
- Automated betting machines
- Check-in at health centres and hospitals
- Electronic blood pressure machines
- Various vending services

- Self-scanning at retail stores
- Internet banking
- Vehicle registration online
- Online auctions
- Home and car buying online
- Automated investment transactions
- Insurance online
- Public transport ticketing
- Package tracking
- Internet shopping
- Interactive voice response telephone systems
- Distance education.

The rapid proliferation of new SSTs is occurring for several reasons.[24] Many firms are tempted by the cost savings that they anticipate by shifting customers to technology-based, automated systems and away from expensive personal service. If cost saving is the only reason for introducing an SST, and if customers see no apparent benefits, the SST is likely to fail. Customers quickly see through this strategy and are not likely to adopt the SST if they have alternative options for service. Other times, firms introduce new SSTs based on customer demand. More and more, customers are expecting to find access to information, services and delivery options online or through applications on their smartphones. When they do not find what they want from a particular firm in a mobile application or online, they are likely to choose a competitor. Thus, customer demand in some industries is forcing firms to develop and offer their services via technology. In particular, there has been an explosion in mobile phone apps to assist customers in booking accommodation, track flights, undertake banking or investment transactions and provide a wide variety of information services. Using such technology can also open up new geographic, socio-economic and lifestyle markets for organizations that were not available to them through traditional channels.

★ SERVICE SPOTLIGHT

The Hilton chain of hotels has replaced room keys in many hotels with a mobile phone app. The app allows guests to check in before they arrive, even enabling them to choose which room they would like on which floor. No longer needing to queue at reception, guests can proceed straight to their room and scan their smartphone on the sensor on the door.

Customer Usage of SSTs

Some of the SSTs listed above – ATMs, self-service fuel pumps, mobile apps, Internet shopping – have been very successful, embraced by customers for the benefits they provide in terms of convenience, accessibility and ease of use.[25] Benefits to firms, including cost savings and revenue growth, can also result for those SSTs that succeed. With some services, such as grocery self-scanning systems, the early reluctance of certain customers to adopt them reflected many factors, including fear of the technology, looking incompetent in front of other customers, desire for human interaction, and a sense that 'scanning and bagging groceries is the store's job, not mine'.

Failure results when customers see no personal benefit in the new technology or when they do not have the ability to use it or know what they are supposed to do. Often, adopting a new SST requires customers to change significantly their traditional behaviours, and many are reluctant to make those changes. Research looking at customer adoption of SSTs found that 'customer readiness' was a major factor in determining whether customers would even try a new self-service option.[26] Customer readiness results from a combination of personal motivation (What is in it for me?), ability (Do I have the ability to use this SST?) and role clarity (Do I understand what I am supposed to do?). At other times, customers see no value in using the technology when compared to the alternative interpersonal mode of delivery; or the SSTs may be so poorly designed that customers may prefer not to use them.[27]

There is also a condition called self-service anxiety which can be defined as the fear and apprehension of using technology to execute a service along with the perceived social pressures of performing the service. Users of self-service technology may not only feel anxiety from the technical aspects of using the technology, but also the social aspects of performing the service in the presence of others. People may become more stressed about using self-service technology where there is a queue of people watching and waiting for them to complete their transaction.

A major problem with SSTs is that so few of them incorporate service recovery systems. In many instances, when the process fails, there is no simple way to recover on the spot. If your ATM rejects or keeps your bank card, you have to phone or visit the branch to resolve your problem. A self-service checkout in a supermarket will cease to operate if its sensor tells it that the customer hasn't put the purchased item in the bagging area. The customer then has to wait for a member of staff to reset the equipment. These failures will add to the length of the transaction and the likely dissatisfaction of the customer. It is therefore critical that organizations provide back-up systems and support for their SSTs. That may be a freephone number on the ATM machine or an employee available to support customers on self-service checkouts.

★ SERVICE SPOTLIGHT

Interactive touch-screen ordering kiosks, such as those that are being installed in McDonald's and other fast food restaurants, are being adopted because they can improve both operational efficiency and the ordering process. In operational terms, they are often easier to maintain than human service personnel as they don't need training or supervision and can operate 24/7 without a break.

> Kiosks may also be able to influence purchasing decisions during the ordering process. Customers can feel less time pressure and consider a wider range of options in comparison to verbally communicating choices to a member of staff. The kiosks can also promote combination deals to customers through clearly showing images and prices. By having the ability to customize options and confirm order accuracy, they may result in greater satisfaction with the overall customer experience.

Success with SSTs

Technologies have been successful because they offer clear benefits (such as faster service or discounts) to customers, the benefits are well understood and appreciated compared with the alternative delivery modes, and the technology is user-friendly and reliable. In addition, customers understand their roles and have the capability to use the technology.

From a strategic perspective, research suggests that as firms move into SSTs as a mode of delivery, these questions are important to ask:[28]

- What is our strategy? What do we hope to achieve through the SST (cost savings, revenue growth, competitive advantage)?
- What are the benefits to customers of producing the service on their own through the SST? Do they know and understand these benefits?
- How can customers be motivated to try the SST? Do they understand their role? Do they have the capability to perform this role?
- How 'technology ready' are our customers?[29] Are some segments of customers more ready to use the technology than others?
- How can customers be involved in the design of the service technology system and processes so that they will be more likely to adopt and use the SST?
- What forms of customer education will be needed to encourage adoption? Will other incentives be needed?
- How will inevitable SST failures be handled to regain customer confidence?

Strategies for Enhancing Customer Participation

The level and the nature of customer participation in the service process are strategic decisions that can impact an organization's productivity, its positioning relative to competitors, its service quality and its customers' satisfaction. In the following sections we will examine the strategies captured in Figure 12.2 for effectively involving customers in the service delivery process. The overall goals of a customer participation strategy will typically be to increase organizational productivity and customer satisfaction while simultaneously decreasing uncertainty due to unpredictable customer actions.

Define Customers' Roles

In developing strategies for addressing customer involvement in service delivery, the organization first determines what type of participation it wants from customers, thus beginning to define the customer's 'role'. Identifying the current level of customer participation can serve as a starting point. Customers' roles may be partially predetermined by the nature of the service, as suggested in Table 12.1. The service may require only the customer's presence (a concert, airline travel) or it may require moderate levels of input from the customer in the form of effort or information (a haircut, tax preparation) or it may require the customer to actually co-create the service outcome (fitness training, consulting, self-service offerings).

Figure 12.2   Strategies for enhancing customer participation

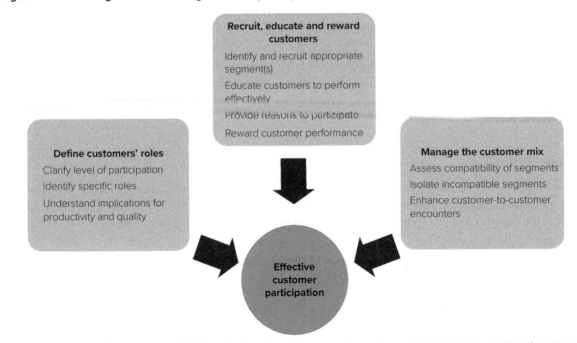

Source: Adapted from M.L. Meuter and M.J. Bitner, 'Self-service technologies: Extending service frameworks and identifying issues for research', in *Marketing Theory and Applications,* eds D. Grewal and C. Pechmann (American Marketing Association Winter Educators' Conference, 1998), pp. 12–19.

The organization may decide that it is satisfied with the existing level of participation it requires from customers but wants to make the participation more effective. For example, IKEA has positioned itself as a company whose customers are highly involved in the purchase, transportation and construction of their products. It may see no added benefit in getting customers to use self-scanning equipment at the checkout or buy their restaurant products from vending machines.

Alternatively, the organization may choose to increase the level of customer participation, which may reposition the service in the customers' eyes. Experts have suggested that higher levels of customer participation are strategically advisable when service production and delivery are inseparable, marketing benefits (cross-selling, building loyalty) can be enhanced by on-site contact with the customer, and customers can supplement for the labour and information provided by employees.[30]

Finally, the organization may decide it wants to reduce customer participation owing to all the uncertainties it causes. In such situations the strategy may be to isolate all but the essential tasks, keeping customers away from the service facility and employees as much as possible.[31] Online shopping is an extreme example of this form of service. Customers are in contact with the organization via telephone or the Internet, never see the organization's facility and have limited employee interactions. The customer's role is thus extremely limited and can interfere very little with the service delivery process.

Once the desired level of participation is clear, the organization can define more specifically what the customer's 'job' entails.[32] The customer's 'job description' will vary with the type of service and the organization's desired position within its industry. The job might entail helping oneself, helping others or promoting the company.

Helping Oneself

In many cases the organization may decide to increase the level of customer involvement in service delivery through active participation. In such situations the customer becomes a productive resource, performing aspects of the service previously performed by employees or others. IKEA is an example of customers 'helping themselves'. The result may be increased productivity for the firm and/or increased value, quality and satisfaction for the customer.

Helping Others

Sometimes the customer may be called on to help others who are experiencing the service. A child at a day-care centre might be appointed 'buddy of the day' to help a new child acclimatize into the environment. Long-time residents of retirement communities often assume comparable roles to welcome new residents. Many universities have established mentoring programmes, particularly for students from minority groups, in which experienced students with similar backgrounds help newcomers adjust and learn the system. Many membership organizations (like gyms, churches and social organizations) also rely heavily, although often informally, on current members to help orientate new members and make them feel welcome. In engaging in these types of roles, customers are again performing productive functions for the organization, increasing customer satisfaction and retention. Acting as a mentor or facilitator can have very positive effects on the person performing the role and is likely to increase his or her loyalty as well.

Promoting the Company

In some cases the customer's job may include a sales or promotional element. As you know from previous chapters, service customers rely heavily on word-of-mouth endorsements in deciding which providers to try. They are more comfortable getting a recommendation from someone who has actually experienced the service than from advertising alone. A positive recommendation from a friend, relative, colleague or an acquaintance can pave the way for a positive service experience. Many service organizations have been very imaginative in getting their current customers to work as promoters or salespeople:

- A bowling alley holds a prize draw for its regular patrons. The person whose name is drawn is given a party at the bowling alley to which he or she can invite friends for free bowling. This effectively creates a 'word-of-mouth champion' who brings new people into the establishment.
- A hotel may encourage guests to provide word of mouth recommendations by leaving reviews on TripAdvisor
- A credit card that gives customers frequent-flyer points every time they use their credit card offers 10,000 free miles to those who solicit a new credit card customer.

Individual Differences: Not Everyone Wants to Participate

In defining customers' roles it is important to remember that not everyone will want to participate.[33] Some customer segments enjoy self-service, whereas others prefer to have the service performed entirely for them. Companies that provide education and training services to organizations know that some customers want to be involved in designing the training and perhaps in delivering it to their employees. Other companies want to hand over the entire training design and delivery to the consulting organization, staying at arm's length with little of their own time and energy invested in the service. In health care, it is clear that some patients want lots of information and want to be involved in their own diagnosis and treatment decisions. Others simply want the doctor to tell them what to do. Despite all the customer service and purchase options now available via the Internet, many customers still prefer human, high-contact service delivery rather than self-service. Research has shown, for example, that customers with a high 'need for human interaction' are less likely to try new self-service options offered via the Internet and automated telephone systems.[34] Because of these differences in preferences, most companies find they need to provide service delivery choices for different market segments.

There may be dangers in imposing self-service technology as the sole delivery option for a particular service. Customers may feel frustrated about not having any choice and develop negative attitudes toward using the technology and toward the service provider. Moreover, these negative attitudes lead to adverse behaviours, such as switching to other providers or spreading negative word of mouth.[35]

Often an organization can customize its services to fit the needs of these different segments – those who want to participate and those who prefer little involvement. Banks typically customize their services by offering both automated self-service options and high-touch, human delivery options. At other times, organizations such as IKEA can effectively position themselves to specifically serve segments of customers who want a high level of participation.

SERVICE SPOTLIGHT

Retailers have invested in strategies to increase customers' liking for self-scanning tills in supermarkets. One approach has been changing the machine's voice. Tesco dispensed with the 'irritating and bossy' voice that chastised customers for an 'unexpected item in the bagging area'. Instead a less robotic friendlier voice is being used. In addition, for Christmas 2015, customers were treated to a Santa voice booming 'Ho Ho Ho Merry Christmas!' from the machine.

Source: **http://www.bbc.com/future/story/20170509-the-unpopular-rise-of-self-checkouts-and-how-to-fix-them.**

Recruit, Educate and Reward Customers

Once the customer's role is clearly defined, the organization can think in terms of facilitating that role. In a sense, the customer becomes a 'partial employee' of the organization at some level, and strategies for managing customer behaviour in service production and delivery can mimic to some degree the efforts aimed at service employees discussed in Chapter 11. As with employees, customer participation in service production and delivery will be facilitated when: (1) customers understand their roles and how they are expected to perform, (2) customers are able to perform as expected, and (3) customers receive valued rewards for performing as expected.[36] Through these means, the organization will also reduce the inherent uncertainty associated with the unpredictable quality and timing of customer participation.

Recruit the Right Customers

Before the company begins the process of educating and socializing customers for their roles, it must attract the right customers to fill those roles. The expected roles and responsibilities of customers should be clearly communicated in advertising, personal selling and other company messages. By previewing their roles and what is required of them in the service process, customers can self-select into (or out of) the relationship. Self-selection should result in enhanced perceptions of service quality from the customer's point of view and reduced uncertainty for the organization.

To illustrate, a child-care centre that requires parent participation on the site at least one-half day per week needs to communicate that expectation before it enrols any child in its programme. For some families, this level of participation will not be possible or desirable, thus precluding them from enrolling in the centre. The expected level of participation needs to be communicated clearly in order to attract customers who are ready and willing to perform their roles. In a sense, this situation is similar to a manufacturing firm exercising control over the quality of inputs into the production process.[37]

Educate and Train Customers to Perform Effectively

Customers need to be educated, or in essence 'socialized', so that they can perform their roles effectively. Through the socialization process, service customers gain an appreciation of specific organizational values, develop the abilities necessary to function within a specific context, understand what is expected of them and acquire the skills and knowledge to interact with employees and other customers.[38] Customer-education programmes can take the form of formal orientation programmes, written literature provided to customers, directional cues and signage in the service environment, and information obtained from employees and other customers.

Table 12.2   Characteristics of service that increase the importance of compatible segments

Customers are in close physical proximity to each other	Customers will more often notice each other and be influenced by each other's behaviour when they are in close physical proximity	Aeroplane flights Entertainment events Sports events
Verbal interaction takes place among customers	Conversation (or lack thereof) can be a component of both satisfying and dissatisfying encounters with fellow patrons	Full-service restaurants Cocktail lounges Educational settings
Customers are engaged in numerous and varied activities	When a service facility supports varied activities all going on at the same time, the activities themselves may not be compatible	Libraries Gyms Resort hotels
The service environment attracts a heterogeneous customer mix	Many service environments, particularly those open to the public, will attract a variety of customer segments	Public parks Public transportation Shopping centres
The core service is compatibility	The core service is to arrange and nurture compatible relationships between customers	Speed-dating events Weight-loss group programmes Mental health support groups
Customers must occasionally wait for the service	Waiting in line for service can be monotonous or anxiety producing. The boredom or stress can be magnified or lessened by other customers, depending on their compatibility	Dentists Tourist attractions Restaurants
Customers are expected to share time, space or service utensils with each other	The need to share space, time and other service factors is common in many services but may become a problem if segments are not comfortable with sharing with each other or if the need to share is intensified because of capacity constraints	Golf courses Hospitals Retirement communities Aeroplanes

Source: Adapted from C.I. Martin and C.A. Pranter, 'Compatibility management: Customer-to-customer relationships in service environments', *Journal of Services Marketing,* 3(3) (Summer 1989), pp. 5–15.

Summary

This chapter focused on the role of customers in service creation and delivery. The customer receiving the service and the fellow customers in the service environment can all potentially cause a widening of gap 3 if they fail to perform their roles effectively. A number of reasons why customers may widen the service delivery gap were suggested: customers lack understanding of their roles; customers are unwilling or unable to perform their roles; customers are not rewarded for good performance; other customers interfere; or market segments are incompatible.

Managing customers in the process of service delivery is a critical challenge for service firms. Whereas manufacturers are not concerned with customer participation in the manufacturing process, service managers constantly face this issue because their customers are often present and active partners in service production. As participants in service creation, production and delivery, customers can perform three primary roles, discussed and illustrated in the chapter: *productive resources* for the organization, *contributors* to service quality and satisfaction and *competitors* in performing the service for themselves.

Through understanding the importance of customers in service delivery and identifying the roles played by the customer in a particular context, managers can develop strategies to enhance customer participation. Strategies discussed in the text include defining the customers' roles and jobs, recruiting customers who match the customer profile in terms of desired level of participation, educating customers so they can perform their roles effectively, rewarding customers for their contributions, and managing the customer mix to enhance the experiences of all segments. By implementing these strategies, organizations should see a reduction in gap 3 due to effective, efficient customer contributions to service delivery.

Key Concepts

Customer 'codes of conduct'	270	Self-service anxiety	264
Customer participation	254	Self-service technologies	262
Customers as competitors	257	Services as drama	255
Manage the mix of customers	270		

Exercises

1   Visit a service establishment where customers can influence each other (such as a theme park, entertainment establishment, resort, shopping mall, restaurant, airline, school or hospital). Observe or interview customers and record cases of positive and negative customer influence. Discuss how you would manage the situation to increase overall customer satisfaction.

2   Interview someone regarding his or her decision to outsource a service – for example, legal services, payroll, or maintenance in a company; or cleaning, child care or pet care in a household. Use the criteria for internal versus external exchange described in the text to analyse the decision to outsource.

3   Think of a service in which a high level of customer participation is necessary for the service to be successful (gym, weight loss, educational setting, healthcare, golf lessons, or the like). Interview a service provider in such an organization to find out what strategies the provider uses to encourage effective customer participation.

4   Visit a service setting in which multiple types of customer segments use the service at the same time (such as a theatre, golf course, resort or theme park). Make your own observations or interview the manager about the organization's strategies to manage these segments effectively. Would you do anything differently if you were in charge?

Discussion Questions

1   Using your own personal examples, discuss the general importance of customers in the successful creation and delivery of service experiences.

2   Why might customer actions and attitudes cause the service performance gap to occur? Use your own examples to illustrate your understanding.

3   Using Table 12.1, think of specific services you have experienced that fall within each of the three levels of customer participation: low, medium and high. Describe specifically what you did as a customer in each case. How did your involvement vary across the three types of service situations?

4   Describe a time when your satisfaction in a particular situation was *increased* because of something another customer did. Could (or does) the organization do anything to ensure that this experience happens routinely? What does it do? Should it try to make this situation a routine occurrence?

5   Describe a time when your satisfaction in a particular situation was *decreased* because of something another customer did. Could the organization have done anything to manage this situation more effectively? If so, what?

6   Discuss the customer's role as a *productive resource* for the firm. Describe a time when you played this role. What did you do and how did you feel? Did the firm help you perform your role effectively? How?

7   Discuss the customer's role as a *contributor to service quality and satisfaction*. Describe a time when you played this role. What did you do and how did you feel? Did the firm help you perform your role effectively? How?

8   Discuss the customer's role as a potential *competitor*. Describe a time when you chose to provide a service for yourself rather than pay someone to provide the service for you. Why did you decide to perform the service yourself? What could have changed your mind, causing you to contract with someone else to provide the service?

9   Identify the main frustrations of using self-service technologies. How can these frustrations be reduced?

10   Choose a service that customers co-produce and outline the specific tasks that customers need to undertake to satisfactorily produce the service.

Further Reading

Åkesson, M., Edvardsson, B. and Tronvoll, B. (2014). Customer experience from a self-service system perspective. *Journal of Service Management*, 25(5), 677–698.

Blut, M., Wang, C. and Schoefer, K. (2016). Factors influencing the acceptance of self-service technologies: A meta-analysis. *Journal of Service Research*, 19(4), 396–416.

Fernandes, T. and Pedroso, R. (2017). The effect of self-checkout quality on customer satisfaction and repatronage in a retail context. *Service Business*, 11(1), 69–92.

Giebelhausen, M., Robinson, S.G., Sirianni, N.J. and Brady, M. K. (2014). Touch versus tech: When technology functions as a barrier or a benefit to service encounters. *Journal of Marketing*, 78(4), 113–24.

Grissemann, U.S. and Stokburger-Sauer, N.E. (2012). Customer co-creation of travel services: The role of company support and customer satisfaction with the co-creation performance. *Tourism Management*, 33(6), 1483–92.

Mende, M., Scott, M.L., van Doorn, J., Grewal, D. and Shanks, I. (2019). Service robots rising: How humanoid robots influence service experiences and elicit compensatory consumer responses. *Journal of Marketing Research*, 56(4).

Reinders, M.J., Dabholkar, P.A. and Frambach, R.T. (2008). Consequences of forcing consumers to use technology-based self-service. *Journal of Service Research*, 11(2), 107–123.

Shamdasani, P., Mukherjee, A. and Malhotra, N. (2008). Antecedents and consequences of service quality in consumer evaluation of self-service Internet technologies. *Service Industries Journal*, 28(1), 117–38.

Chapter 13

Delivering Service through Electronic Channels and Intermediaries

Chapter Outline

Multi-Channel versus Omni-Channel Delivery	275
Delivering Service through Electronic Channels	276
Delivering Service through Mobile Channels	280
Other Forms of Service Distribution	281
Direct or Company-Owned Channels	282
Franchising	283
Agents and Brokers	285
Common Issues Involving Intermediaries	288
Strategies for Effective Service Delivery through Intermediaries	289
Summary and Key Concepts	291
Exercises	291
Discussion Questions	291
Further Reading	292

Learning Objectives

This chapter's objectives are to:

1 Discuss the differences between a multi-channel and an omni-channel approach to service delivery.
2 Identify the primary channels through which services are delivered to end customers.
3 Examine the manner in which services can be delivered through technology and electronic channels.
4 Provide examples of each of the key service intermediaries.
5 View delivery of service from two perspectives – the service provider and the service deliverer.
6 Discuss the benefits and challenges of each method of service delivery.
7 Outline the strategies that are used to manage service delivery through intermediaries.

Opening Example
Shakespeare Goes Online

Shakespeare's Globe Theatre is a replica of the original Globe Theatre, an Elizabethan playhouse on the south bank of the River Thames in London, built in 1599 and destroyed by fire in 1613. It was where many of William Shakespeare's plays were originally performed. The modern reconstruction, opened in 1997 under the name 'Shakespeare's Globe Theatre', is an academic approximation based on available evidence of the 1599 and 1614 buildings.

Shakespeare's Globe Theatre has staged plays every summer since 1997 and attempts to duplicate the experience that audiences would have had in Elizabethan times. The auditorium is

Source: ©Megan Hunter

open to the sky and productions use no stage lights, microphones, speakers or amplification; all music is performed live. There is no seating at the foot of the stage and the crowding audience stands very close to the actors, adding to the feeling of a shared experience and of a community event.

To widen the audience for the performances, the theatre sought to add delivery channels. Initially, this took the form of plays being filmed and released to cinemas through Shakespeare Globe on Screen productions. This allowed theatre enthusiasts to see the plays in local cinemas in the UK, mainland Europe, USA, Canada, Australia and New Zealand. Although this was partially successful, it was clear that audiences wanted greater flexibility as to where and when they could watch a production. To address this, another delivery channel was developed: the Globe Player. This video-on-demand service allows the user to download and watch HD films of productions anywhere and anytime. Subscribers can opt between renting (around €5.50) or buying (around €14) the films. Shakespeare's Globe is also releasing an app for use on mobile phones and tablets, enabling users to browse videos as well as gain access to any films they have purchased previously.

These new electronic channels have extended the customer base for the Shakespeare's Globe Theatre from people visiting or living in London to anybody with a computer, tablet or smartphone anywhere in the world. In the first 6 months following launch, Globe Player had 100,500 users from 174 countries with 35 per cent of users accessing on mobile or tablet.

Source: www.globeplayer.tv.

Multi-Channel versus Omni-Channel Delivery

Organizations can deliver services to customers through a combination of channels that may include desktop or mobile devices, via phone, or through a physical outlet. For example, a bank may offer its services through an ATM machine, a call centre, a website, a mobile phone app and a bank branch. Customers participate in different types of purchasing situations and may choose different channels for different services or transactions. In the bank example, a customer may be happy to access their accounts through the web and ATMs, but will want to visit a bank branch when discussing a loan. Some customers may want to do all their transactions remotely, whilst others do not trust technology and want to interact with a person. To address these various needs, it may be too simplistic to rely on delivery of a service through only one channel and, increasingly, multiple channels will be required.

Strategies for multiple channels can take two forms: the first of these is a multi-channel approach and the second is an omni-channel approach. **A multi-channel strategy** simply means that the service is delivered through a range of different channels (online, telephone, agent, branch etc.). This can provide customers with a level of choice as to how they do business with the organization. However, the channels may not be directly connected to each other and customers may not be able to move seamlessly from one channel to another. In comparison, an **omni-channel strategy** is where the transition from one channel to another is seamless. An omni-channel approach joins the various customer touchpoints together so that, whatever channel or combination of channels that the customer chooses to take, the experience is consistent and unified. This means that when a customer enters a query or complaint on an organization's website or through social media, there should be no need for the customer to repeat this information when contacting a call centre or when visiting a physical outlet (the information should be visible to the employee on their tablet or computer screen). Although all organizations may want to develop an omni-channel strategy, it can be difficult as it requires significant investment in an organization's technology capabilities to enable all of the channels to capture and share information about the customer. As a result, many organizations have yet to fully embrace omni-channel; however, the expectations of consumers are likely to start driving brands to make the necessary investment.

★ SERVICE SPOTLIGHT

Disney is one of the organizations at the forefront of delivering an omni-channel experience. Its website is mobile-responsive and optimized to every device. When a visitor has booked a visit to a Disney resort, they can plan the specifics of their trip through the My Disney Experience tool. They can then use a mobile app in the park to locate attractions they earmarked in the experience tool and see estimated wait times for each attraction. The mobile app can also link to Disney's Magic Band programme which allows visitors to enter the parks, unlock their hotel rooms, check-in to FastPass lanes, connect to their Disney PhotoPass account, and charge all purchases made in the park to their Magic Band.

Source: **https://disneyworld.disney.go.com/en_GB/plan/my-disney-experience/.**

Delivering Service through Electronic Channels

The Internet has 'transformed every aspect of our lives – including how we socialize, manage our money, purchase goods and services, and gather information.'[1] Electronic channels have vastly expanded the opportunities for goods and services marketers to distribute their offerings. They differ from the other types of channel that we discuss in this chapter as they do not require direct human interaction. What they do require is some predesigned service (such as information, education or entertainment) and an electronic vehicle to deliver it. You are probably very familiar with telephone and television channels, the Internet and mobile apps. The consumer and business services that are made possible through these channels include movies on demand, interactive news and music, banking and financial services, multimedia libraries and databases, distance learning, desktop videoconferencing, remote health services and interactive network-based games.

The more a service relies on technology and/or equipment for service production and the less it relies on face-to-face contact with service providers, the less the service is characterized by inseparability and non-standardization. As you will see in the following section, using electronic channels overcomes some of the problems associated with service inseparability and allows a form of standardization not previously possible in most services. Table 13.1 summarizes the benefits and challenges of electronic distribution.

Table 13.1   Benefits and challenges in electronic distribution of services

Benefits	Challenges
Consistent delivery for standardized services	Price competition
Low cost	Inability to customize because of standardized nature of the service
Customer convenience	Lack of consistency due to customer involvement
Wide distribution	Changes in consumer behaviour
Customer choice and ability to customize	Security concerns
Quick customer feedback	Competition from widening geographies

Benefits of Electronic Channels

Consistent Delivery for Standardized Services

Electronic channels such as the Internet and mobile phone apps do not alter the service, as channels with human interaction tend to do. Unlike delivery from a personal provider, electronic delivery does not interpret the service and execute it according to that interpretation. Its delivery is likely to be the same in all transmissions. The process of booking a flight on the easyJet website or mobile phone app is the same for every customer, no matter where they are or who they are.

Low Cost

Electronic media offer more efficient means of delivery than interpersonal distribution. Critics could rightly claim that personal sales interaction is more powerful and effective but, with interactive services, companies such as Amazon are able to gain some of the credibility benefits of personal interaction (such as being able to answer individual questions or tailor the service, book recommendations and website for individuals).

Customer Convenience

With electronic channels and particularly smart phones, customers are able to access a firm's services when and where they want. 'Retailers still tell customers, "You have to come to us." But online consumers are saying, "No way – *you* have to come to *us*." My place, my time is the new mantra of consumers everywhere.'[2] Just as catalogue shopping freed working women from the perceived drudgery of having to go to the shops, e-commerce is changing the way people shop. Many companies with call centres and telephone ordering still limit their hours of availability; a real mistake if they are going to match the customer convenience of being able to order online 24 hours a day, seven days a week. For the marketer, electronic channels allow access to a large group of customers who would otherwise be unavailable to them because of busy schedules that do not allow them to shop in other ways.

⭐ **SERVICE SPOTLIGHT**

Takeaway.com is a leading online food delivery marketplace, focused on connecting consumers and restaurants through its platform in 10 European countries and Israel. The company is headquartered in the Netherlands and works with participating restaurants that deliver the food themselves. The Takeaway.com platform serves as a source of orders for these restaurants and facilitates the online payment process. Historically, restaurants were dependent on local marketing, primarily

▶ through the distribution of flyers and paper menus, which limited their reach. Takeaway.com offers restaurants access to a wider consumer-base and provides publicity at a relatively low cost, which results in an increase in orders for these restaurants. The platform is available for consumers through mobile applications and via the Takeaway website. The company derives its revenues from commission on the food ordered through the platform and, to a lesser extent, from online payment services fees. In 2018, Takeaway.com served 14.1 million active customers from 43,800 restaurants with 93.3 million meals

Source: **Figures taken from Takeaway.com Half Year 2019 Results, Amsterdam, 31 July 2019, https://corporate .takeaway.com/.**

Wide Distribution

Electronic channels do more than allow the service provider to interact with a large number of geographically dispersed consumers. They also allow the service provider to interact (often simultaneously) with a large number of intermediaries. The costs and effort to inform, promote and motivate consumers to buy through offline channels are higher than the costs to accomplish the same activities with electronic channels. A service that places an advertisement on a Google search results page only pays Google when a potential customer clicks on the advertisement and visits the organization's website. It can be far more difficult and expensive to make potential customers aware of the physical location of a service outlet and motivate them to get in their car and travel to it.

Customer Choice and Ability to Customize

Consider the options available in movies and videos to customers who use video-on-demand services. Just as Dell Computers allows customers to configure entire products to their own particular needs and desires, the Internet allows many companies to design services from the beginning. Individuals who want to renovate their kitchen may now go to many Internet sites, specify their requirements and order what they wish. Whether the supplier is a large retailer such as B&Q (www.diy.com) or a small start-up company, customers get exactly what they want.

Quick Customer Feedback

Rapid customer feedback is without doubt one of the major strengths of e-commerce. Companies can find out immediately what customers think of services and can gain far higher participation from customers in surveys. With quick customer feedback, changes can be made rapidly to service assortments, problems can be addressed immediately and the learning cycles of companies can speed up dramatically. Online customers may not be aware that they are giving feedback, but companies can monitor which web pages they access, the length of time that they spend on each page and whether they make a purchase (or at what stage they leave the website).

Challenges in Distributing Services through Electronic Channels

Price Competition

One of the traditional differences between goods and services has been the difficulty of directly comparing features and prices of services with each other. Whereas goods can typically be compared in retail settings, few retail settings exist that offer services from multiple sources. The Internet has changed all that. Services such as trivago.com and Kelkoo.com make it simple for customers to compare prices for a wide variety of services.

⭐ **SERVICE SPOTLIGHT**

ComparetheMarket.com was launched in 2006 and has grown rapidly. It is a comparison website (also known as an aggregator) and it allows customers to compare prices on a number of insurance products including car, home, van, life, pet, travel and over-50s insurance.

Insurance policies were among the first products to be successfully sold or brokered by online aggregators. Aggregators such as ComparetheMarket.com have opened up the market, making it more transparent, and forcing insurers to compete on price. They have helped insurers dramatically expand their customer reach.

In some markets, such as the United Kingdom, Italy, and Germany, aggregators hold more than one-third of the market share of the car insurance market.

Inability to Customize Due to the Standardized Nature of Electronic Services

Some of you may be on a distance learning course using video or online support materials. If you consider what you miss in learning this way compared with learning directly from a lecturer, you will understand this challenge. You may not be able to interact in real time with the lecturer, ask questions, raise points for clarification or experience the connection that you receive in person. In online classes – as in videoconferences that are springing up in many businesses – the quality of the service can also be impeded by the way the audience reacts (or does not react) in those situations. People talk among themselves, leave, laugh and criticize, among other behaviours.

Lack of Consistency Because of Customer Involvement

Although electronic channels are very effective in minimizing the inconsistency from employees or providers of service, customer variability still presents a problem. Many times, customers use the technology themselves to produce the service but often this can lead to errors or frustration unless the technology is highly user friendly. Manoeuvring online can sometimes be overwhelming, broadband speeds can vary enormously and not all websites are easy to use. Furthermore, some customers may not have computers or smartphones and, even if they do, may be reluctant to use this medium.

Changes in Consumer Behaviour

A consumer purchasing a service through electronic channels engages in very different behaviour to a consumer entering a retail store and talking to a salesperson. Considerable changes – in the willingness to search for information, in the willingness to perform some aspects of the services themselves, in the acceptance of different levels of service – are necessary when customers use electronic channels. If the website or app is slow, or if it takes too long to complete a transaction, customers will quickly move to another supplier.

Security Concerns

One issue confronting marketers using electronic channels is concern about the security of information, particularly health and financial information. Many customers are still hesitant about giving credit card numbers on the Internet. These problems can undermine consumers' trust in the Internet as a safe place to do business. Companies doing business through the Internet must continually devise ways to protect their systems from penetration, vandalism, eavesdropping and identity theft.[3] With penetration, intruders steal passwords and exploit unprotected modems and connections, actually taking over the sites. With vandalism, hackers crash corporate and other computers. To combat these problems, firewalls and other software scan for unusual activity. With eavesdropping, hackers snoop on information as it passes through multiple computers to the Internet. The typical solution is encryption software that scrambles electronic mail and other data to make it unintelligible to eavesdroppers. Finally, with identity theft, criminals steal consumers' identities in order to buy goods and services. A form of encryption technology is often used to deal with this problem, and special service companies confirm signature holders.[4]

Competition from Widening Geographies

Historically, many services were somewhat protected from competition because customers had limited choice among the providers they could physically drive or walk to. Banks, for example, supplied all local customers with current accounts, savings accounts and mortgages. In fact, it used to be said that because services could not be transported they were limited in their scope. Not any longer – and not with electronic channels. Through the Internet, many services, including financial services, can be purchased from service providers far from the local area.

Delivering Service through Mobile Channels

Smartphone Applications

The growth in smartphones and tablet computers has provided an important platform for delivering services. Software developed specifically for these platforms is called mobile application software (app). The original apps were developed to provide information retrieval, access to emails, personal calendars, personal contacts and weather information. However, they now provide information and reservation systems for hotels and airlines; communication channels; retailing channels (e.g. Amazon app); services for monitoring health and fitness (e.g. Nike+ Run Club); entertainment and games; banking and financial services; map and navigation services (e.g. Google Maps); education; transport information (e.g. Uber taxis) and many others. These all allow people to access information and services whilst they are on the move; no longer do they need to be in the service provider's premises or even in their own homes or offices. As there are no manuals or service personnel on hand when the user accesses an app, it needs to be easy to use and function in the way it is meant to. If someone is trying to check in for a flight using their mobile between meetings, or when they are in transit, simplicity and functionality are critical. The app also needs to seamlessly link with other delivery channels. A bank customer who transfers money between his bank accounts on his mobile phone wants to see that same transaction recorded on the web, at the ATM machine and on the screen of the bank employee in the local branch or in the call centre.

Smartphones also allow the service provider to provide location-based services based on the GPS information provided by the phone. The app can highlight the location of local services and car parking spaces, as well as promotional offers relevant to the individual user and details on stock levels in specific retail outlets.

The growth in location-based services and apps is likely to expand significantly as the number of smartphones continues to grow.

SERVICE SPOTLIGHT

Ted Baker, a luxury clothing brand and retailer, has introduced beacon-powered mannequins to capitalize on mobile technologies and engage with customers. Beacon mannequins throughout the store send alerts about the items that a particular mannequin is wearing and provide access to store items directly on the brand's website. The technology is enabled by a smartphone app that customers download.

▶   Martini, the drinks brand has been experimenting with beacon technology in the form of a smart ice cube. When serving the first drink, the bartender places an ice-cube shaped device into the customer's drink. This device floats around in the glass until the drink is finished and the sensor detects that it's not submerged in a liquid. When the device recognizes the empty glass, it automatically alerts the bar staff through the bartender's smartphone and places an order for a fresh glass!

Source: **https://blog.beaconstac.com/2017/09/beacon-use-cases-retail-museum-bars-restaurants-eddystone/.**

Other Forms of Service Distribution

Except for situations where electronic channels can distribute services, providers and consumers come into direct contact in service provision. Because of the inseparability of production and consumption in service, providers must either be present themselves when customers receive service or find ways to involve others in distribution. Involving others can be problematic because quality in service occurs in the service encounter between company and customer. Unless the service distributor is willing and able to perform in the service encounter as the service principal would, the value of the offering decreases and the reputation of the original service may be damaged. Chapter 11 pointed out the challenges of controlling encounters within service organizations themselves, but most service (and many manufacturing) companies face an even more formidable task: attaining service excellence and consistency when intermediaries represent them to customers. As we have indicated throughout this textbook, services are generally intangible and experiential in nature. Thus, service distribution does not typically involve moving items through a chain of firms that begins with a manufacturer and ends with a consumer, as is the case for goods distribution. In fact, many services are delivered directly from the service producer to the consumer. That is, in contrast to channels for goods, channels for services are often direct – with the creator of the service (i.e. the service principal) selling directly to and interacting directly with the customer. Examples include air travel (easyJet), opticians (Vision Express) and consulting services (Accenture). Because services cannot be owned, there are no titles or rights to most services that can be passed along a delivery channel. Because services are intangible and perishable, inventories cannot exist, making warehousing a dispensable function. In general, because services cannot be produced, warehoused and then retailed, as goods can, many channels available to goods producers are not feasible for service firms. Thus, many of the primary functions that distribution channels serve – inventorying, securing and taking title to goods – have no meaning in services, allowing the service principal to deliver the service directly to the customer.

Delivery of Service through Intermediaries

Two distinct service marketers are involved in delivering service through intermediaries: the **service principal**, or originator, and the **service deliverer**, or intermediary. The service principal is the entity that creates the service concept (whose counterpart is the manufacturer of physical goods), and the service deliverer is the entity that interacts with the customer in the actual execution of the service (whose counterpart is the distributor or wholesaler of physical goods).

Even though many of the functions that intermediaries provide for goods manufacturers are not relevant for service firms, intermediaries often deliver services and perform several important functions for service principals. First, they may co-produce the service, fulfilling service principals' promises to customers. Franchise services such as haircutting, key-making and dry-cleaning are produced by the intermediary (the franchisee) using a process developed by the service principal. Service intermediaries also make services locally available, providing time and place convenience for the customer. Because they represent multiple service principals, such intermediaries as travel and insurance agents provide a retailing function for customers, gathering together in one place a variety of choices. And, in many financial or professional services, intermediaries function as the glue between the brand or company name and the customer by building the trusting relationship required in these complex and expert offerings.

The primary types of intermediaries used in service delivery are franchisees, agents and brokers. *Franchisees* are service outlets licensed by a principal to deliver a unique service concept it has created or popularized. Examples include fast-food chains (McDonald's, Burger King), printing and design services (Minuteman Press) and hotels (Holiday Inn). **Agents and brokers** are representatives who distribute and sell the services of one or more service suppliers. Examples include insurance (AA Insurance Services), financial services (through any one of the many independent financial advisers) and travel services (American Express).

We do not include retailers in our short list of service intermediaries because most retailers – from department stores to discount stores – are channels for delivering physical goods rather than services. Retailers that sell only services (cinemas, restaurants) or retail services that support physical products (car dealers, service stations) can also be described as dealers or franchises. For our purposes in this chapter, such retailers are grouped into the franchise category because they possess the same characteristics, strengths and weaknesses as franchises.

Goods retailers, by the way, are service organizations themselves; they are intermediaries for goods and perhaps services. Manufacturing companies depend on retailers to represent, explain, promote and insure their products – all of which are pre-sale services. Manufacturers also need retailers to return, exchange, support and service products – all of which are post-sale services. These roles are increasingly critical as products become more complex, technical and expensive. For example, camera and computer firms rely on retailers carrying their products to understand and communicate highly technical information so that customers choose products that fit their needs. A retailer that leads the customer to the wrong product choice or that inadequately instructs the customer on how to use the product creates service problems that strongly influence the manufacturer's reputation.

Service principals depend on their intermediaries to deliver service to their specifications. Service intermediaries determine how the customer evaluates the quality of the company. When a McDonald's franchisee undercooks McNuggets, the customer's perception of the company – and of other McDonald's franchisees – is tarnished. When one Holiday Inn franchisee has hygiene issues, it reflects on all other Holiday Inns and on the Holiday Inn brand itself. Unless service providers ensure that the intermediary's goals, incentives and motives are consistent with their own, they lose control over the service encounters between the customer and the intermediary. When someone other than the service principal is critical to the fulfilment of quality service, a firm must develop ways to either control or motivate these intermediaries to meet company goals and standards. In the sections that follow, we discuss both direct delivery of service by the service principal and indirect delivery of the service through intermediaries.

Direct or Company-Owned Channels

Although we call this chapter 'Delivering service through electronic channels and intermediaries', it is important to acknowledge that many services are distributed directly from provider to customer. Some of these are local services – doctors, dry-cleaners and hairstylists – whose area of distribution is limited. Others are national chains with multiple outlets but are considered direct channels because the provider owns all the outlets. HSBC bank[5] is an example of a service provider with all company-owned outlets enabling service delivery to be controlled and managed in a consistent manner, thereby maintaining the bank's image.

Perhaps the major benefit of distributing through company-owned channels is that the company has complete *control* over the outlets. One of the most critical implications of this type of control is that the owner can maintain consistency in service provision. Standards can be established and will be carried out as planned because the company itself monitors and rewards proper execution of the service. Control over hiring, firing and motivating employees is also a benefit of company-owned channels. Using company-owned channels also allows the company to expand or contract sites without being bound by contractual agreements with other entities.

A final benefit of company-owned channels is that the company owns the customer relationship. In service industries in which skilled or professional workers have individual relationships with customers, a major concern is whether the loyalty the customer feels is for the company or for the individual service employee. It is well known, for example, that most people are loyal to individual hairstylists and will follow them from one place of business to another. Therefore, one of the important issues in service delivery is who owns the customer relationship – the store or the employee. With company-owned channels, the company owns both the store and the employee, and therefore has complete control over the customer relationship.

However, several disadvantages exist with company-owned channels. First, and probably the largest impediment to most service chains, the company must bear all the financial risk. When expanding, the firm must find all the capital, sometimes using it for geographical expansion rather than for other uses (such as advertising, service quality or new service development) that would be more profitable. Second, large companies are rarely experts in local markets – they know their businesses but not all markets. When adjustments are needed in business formats for different markets, they may be unaware of what these adjustments should be. This disadvantage is especially evident when companies expand into other cultures and other countries. Partnering or joint venturing is almost always preferred to company-owned channels in these situations.

When two or more service companies want to offer a service, and neither have the full financial capability or expertise, they often undertake service partnerships. These partnerships operate very much like company-owned channels except that they involve multiple owners. The benefit is that risk and effort are shared, but the disadvantage is that control and returns are also distributed among the partners. Several areas in which partnerships are common are telecommunications, high-technology services, Internet-based services and entrepreneurial services. Service partnerships also proliferate when companies expand beyond their country boundaries – typically one partner provides the business format and the other provides knowledge of the local market.

Franchising

Franchising is the most common type of distribution in services. In the UK the franchise industry is worth around 19 billion euros and employs more than 710,000 people with more than 935 franchisors licensing their brand names, business processes or formats, unique products, services or reputations in return for fees and royalties.[6] Franchising works well with services that can be standardized and duplicated through the delivery process, service policies, warranties, guarantees, promotion and branding. Body Shop[7], Domino's Pizza[8], Prontaprint[9], Toni & Guy[10] and Vision Express[11] are examples of companies that are ideal for franchise operations. At its best, franchising is a relationship or partnership in which the service provider – the franchisor – develops and optimizes a service format that it licenses for delivery by other parties – the franchisees.

★ SERVICE SPOTLIGHT

Subway, the franchised sandwich chain, was first opened in 1965 in Bridgeport, Connecticut, USA and was called Pete's Super Submarines. The first franchised Subway unit opened in 1974 and its popularity soon spread and there are now more than 42,000 Subway franchises in 100 countries worldwide. All Subway sandwiches are made on freshly baked bread and are prepared by 'sandwich artists' in front of the customer to a standardized Subway format. Franchisees receive national and local support, national and regional advertising, a two-week training programme, ongoing training for staff, store development assistance, design support; lease negotiations and construction guidance. In return, Subway charges franchisees an initial fee of around 13,500 euros and then takes 12.5 per cent of a store's gross weekly income.

Source: **Figures taken from www.businessinsider.com/what-it-costs-to-open a subway-2015-3?r=US&IR=T.**

There are benefits and disadvantages for both the franchisor and the franchisee in this relationship (see Table 13.2).

Table 13.2   Benefits and challenges in franchising

Benefits	Challenges
For franchisors	
Leveraged business format for greater expansion and revenues	Difficulty in maintaining and motivating franchisees
Consistency in outlets	Highly publicized disputes and conflict
Knowledge of local markets	Inconsistent quality
Shared financial risk and more working capital	Control of customer relationship by intermediary
For franchisees	
An established business format	Encroachment of other outlets into franchisee territory
National or regional brand marketing	Disappointing profits and revenues
Minimized risk of starting a business	Lack of perceived control over operations
	High fees

The Franchisor's Perspective

A franchisor typically begins by developing a business concept that is unique in some way. Perhaps it is a fast-food concept (such as McDonald's) with unique cooking or delivery processes. Perhaps it is a hairstylist (such as Toni & Guy) with established formats for marketing to customers, pricing and hiring employees. Or maybe it is a retail store (such as Krispy Kreme) with unique store environments, employee training, purchasing and computer systems. A franchisor typically expands business through this method because it expects the following benefits:

- *Leveraged business format for greater expansion and revenues.* Most franchisors want wider distribution – and increased revenues, market share, brand name recognition and economies of scale – for their concepts and practices than they can support in company outlets.
- *Consistency in outlets.* When franchisors have strong contracts and unique formats, they can require that service be delivered according to their specifications.
- *Knowledge of local markets.* National chains are unlikely to understand local markets as well as the business people who live in the geographic areas. With franchising, the company obtains a connection to the local market.
- *Shared financial risk and more working capital.* Franchisees must contribute their own capital for equipment and personnel, thereby bearing part of the risk of doing business.

Franchising is not without its challenges, however. Most franchisors encounter the following disadvantages:

- *Difficulty in maintaining and motivating franchisees.* Motivating independent operators to price, promote, deliver and hire according to standards the principal establishes is a difficult job, particularly when business is down.
- *Highly publicized disputes between franchisees and franchisors.* Franchisees are organizing and hiring lobbyists and lawyers to gain more economic clout. Many countries are looking at implementing legislation to boost franchisee rights.
- *Inconsistent quality.* Although some franchisees deliver the service in the manner in which the franchisor intended, other franchisees do not perform the service as well as desired. This inconsistency can undermine the company's image, reputation and brand name.
- *Customer relationships controlled by the franchisee rather than the franchisor.* The closer a company is to the customer, the better able it is to listen to that customer's concerns and ideas. When franchisees are involved, a relationship forms between the customer and the franchisee rather than between the customer and the franchisor. All customer information, including demographics, purchase history and preferences, is in the hands of the intermediary rather than the principal. This can be overcome by having a loyalty card scheme that links the customer and their transactions to the customer relationship management system of the franchisor.

The Franchisee's Perspective

From the perspective of the franchisee, one of the main benefits of franchising is obtaining an established business format on which to base a business, something one expert has defined as an 'entrepreneur in a prepackaged box, a super-efficient distributor of services and goods through a decentralized web'.[12] A second benefit is receiving national or regional brand marketing. Franchisees obtain advertising and other marketing expertise as well as an established reputation. Finally, franchising minimizes the risks of starting a business.

Disadvantages for franchisees also exist. One of the most problematic is *encroachment* – the opening of new units near existing ones without compensation to the existing franchisee. When encroachment occurs, potential revenues are diminished and competition is increased. Another frequent disadvantage involves disappointment over profits and revenues which is exacerbated by having to pay fees to the franchisor (averaging around 7–8 per cent in the UK).[13] Other disadvantages include lack of perceived control over operations and high fees. Many of these problems are due to over-promising by the franchisor, but others are caused by unrealistic expectations about what will be achieved in a franchise agreement.

Agents and Brokers

An *agent* is an intermediary who acts on behalf of a service principal (such as an estate agent) or a customer and is authorized to make agreements between the principal and the customer. Some agents, called *selling agents*, work with the principal and have contractual authority to sell a principal's output (such as travel, insurance or financial services), usually because the principal lacks the resources or desire to do so. Other agents, called *purchasing agents*, often have long-term relationships with buyers and help them in evaluating and making purchases. Such agents are frequently hired by companies and individuals to find art, antiques and rare jewellery. A *broker* is an intermediary who brings buyers and sellers together while assisting in negotiation. Brokers are paid by the party who hired them, rarely become involved in financing or assuming risk and are not long-term representatives of buyers or sellers. The most familiar examples are insurance brokers, many of whom now operate only online rather than through physical outlets.

Agents and brokers do not take title to services but instead deliver the rights to them. They have legal authority to market services as well as to perform other marketing functions on behalf of producers. The benefits and challenges in using agents and brokers are summarized in Table 13.3.

Table 13.3   Benefits and challenges in distributing services through agents and brokers

Benefits	Challenges
Reduced selling and distribution costs	Loss of control over pricing
Intermediary's possession of special skills and knowledge	Representation of multiple service principals
Wide representation	
Knowledge of local markets	
Customer choice	

Benefits of Agents and Brokers

The travel industry provides an example of both agents and brokers. Three main categories of travel intermediaries exist: tour packagers, retail travel agents and speciality channelers (including incentive travel firms, meeting and convention planners, hotel representatives and corporate travel offices). You are likely to be most familiar with traditional retail travel agents. Industry convention terms the travel companies as brokers and the individuals who work for them as travel agents or sales associates. This traditional industry is changing rapidly because of electronic channels, with online travel agents (OTAs) such as Expedia and Booking.com. These OTAs can operate using two different models:[14]

- **Agent model:** the website has direct access to the hotel's inventory of rooms and sells them, gaining a commission. The hotel collects the payment from the guest before forwarding the commission on to the OTA.
- **Merchant model:** hotels sell their rooms at discounted rates to the OTAs, which in turn mark them up, at contract-specified margins and sell to the public. The OTA collects the payment from the guest and then remits the discounted price to the hotel.

The OTAs have a significant advantage over the individual hotels as they offer a choice of hotels to travellers as well as bundled services (flight, hotel, car hire and excursions). The agreements that OTAs set up with the hotels often limit the extent to which the hotel can charge a different price from the one being offered by the OTA. Many hotels agree to this in order to have a presence in the OTA's search engine and in front of the many users of such OTA sites.

Agents and brokers, whether online or offline, offer significant benefits and challenges to the service principal. The following illustrate some of these in the travel industry.

Reduced Selling and Distribution Costs

Traditionally (before the Internet), if an airline or resort hotel needed to contact every potential traveller to promote its offerings, the costs would be exorbitant. Because most travel services are transactional, rather than long term, travellers would need to expend tremendous effort to find services that meet their needs. Online travel agents and brokers accomplish the intermediary role by assembling information from travel suppliers and offering it to travellers.

Possession of Special Skills and Knowledge

Agents and brokers have special knowledge and skills in their areas. For example, retail travel agents know the industry well and know how to access the information they do not possess, often through reference materials and online services. Tour packagers have a more specialized role – they assemble, promote and price bundles of travel services from travel suppliers, then offer these bundles either to travellers themselves or to retail travel agents. Speciality channelers have even more specialized roles. Some work in corporate travel offices to lend their skills to an entire corporation; others are business meeting and convention planners who act almost as tour packagers for whole companies or associations; and some are incentive travel firms that focus on travel recognition programmes in corporations or associations.

Wide Representation

Because agents and brokers are paid by commission rather than by salary, there is little risk or disadvantage to the service principal in extending the service offerings to a wide geography. Thus companies have representatives in many places, far more than if fixed costs such as buildings, equipment and salaries were required.

Knowledge of Local Markets

Another key benefit of agents and brokers is that they become experts in the local markets they serve. They know or learn the unique needs of different markets, including international markets. They understand what their clients' preferences are and how to adapt the principal's services to match the needs of clients. This benefit is particularly needed and appreciated when clients are dispersed internationally. Knowing the culture and taboos of a country is critical for successful selling. Most companies find that obtaining local representation by experts with this knowledge is necessary.

Customer Choice

Travel and insurance agents provide a retailing service for customers – they represent the services of multiple suppliers. If a traveller needed to visit six or eight different websites or agencies, each of which carried the services of a single supplier, imagine the effort a customer would need to make to plan a trip! Similarly, independent insurance agents have the right to sell a wide variety of insurance, which allows them to offer customers a choice. These types of agents are also able to compare prices across suppliers and get the best prices for their clients. Insurance comparison websites are good examples of this.

Challenges of Delivering Service through Agents and Brokers

Loss of Control Over Pricing

As representatives of service principals and experts on customer markets, agents and brokers are typically empowered to negotiate price, configure services and otherwise alter the marketing of a principal's service. This issue could be particularly important – and possibly detrimental – when a service provider depends on a particular (high) price to convey a level of service quality. If the price can be changed, it might drop to a level that undermines the quality image. In addition, the agent often has the flexibility to give different prices to different customers. As long as the customers are geographically dispersed, this variation will not create a problem for the service principal; however, if buyers compare prices and realize they are being given different prices, they may perceive the service principal as unfair or unethical.

Representation of Multiple Service Principals

When independent agents represent multiple suppliers, they offer customer choice. From a service principal's point of view, however, customer choice means that the agent represents – and in many cases advocates – a competitive service offering. This is the same challenge a manufacturer confronts when distributing products in a retail store. Only in rare cases are its products the only ones in a given category on the retail floor. In a service context, consider the use of independent insurance agents. These agents carry a range of insurance products from different companies, serving as a surrogate service retail store for customers. When they find a customer who needs insurance, they sell from their portfolio the offerings that best match the customer's requirements.

Common Issues Involving Intermediaries

Key problems with intermediaries include conflict over objectives and performance, difficulty controlling quality and consistency across outlets, tension between empowerment and control, and channel ambiguity.

Channel Conflict Over Objectives and Performance

The parties involved in delivering services do not always agree about how the channel should operate. Channel conflict can occur between the service provider and the service intermediary, among intermediaries in a given area, and between different types of channels used by a service provider (such as when a service principal has its own outlets as well as franchised outlets). The conflict most often centres on the parties having different goals, competing roles and rights, and conflicting views of the way the channel is performing. Sometimes the conflict occurs because the service principal and its intermediaries are too dependent on each other.

Difficulty Controlling Quality and Consistency Across Outlets

One of the biggest difficulties for both principals and their intermediaries involves the inconsistency and lack of uniform quality that result when multiple outlets deliver services. When poor performance occurs, even at a single outlet, the service principal suffers because the entire brand and reputation are jeopardized, and other intermediaries endure negative attributions to their outlets. The problem is particularly acute in highly specialized services such as management consulting or architecture, in which execution of the complex offering may be difficult to deliver to the standards of the principal.

Tension Between Empowerment and Control

McDonald's and other successful service businesses were founded on the principle of performance consistency. Both they and their intermediaries have attained profits and longevity because the company controls virtually every aspect of their intermediaries' businesses. McDonald's, for example, is famous for its demanding and rigid service standards (such as 'turn, never flip, hamburgers on the grill'), carefully specified supplies, and performance monitoring. The strategy makes sense: unless an intermediary delivers service exactly the same way the successful company outlets provide it, the service may not be as desirable to customers. From the principal's point of view, its name and reputation are on the line in each outlet, making careful control a necessity.

Control, however, can have negative ramifications within intermediaries. Many service franchisees, for example, are entrepreneurial by nature and select service franchising because they can own and operate their own businesses. If they are to deliver according to consistent standards, their independent ideas must be integrated into and often subsumed by the practices and policies of the service principal. In these situations they often feel like automatons with less freedom than they have anticipated as owners of their own businesses.

Channel Ambiguity

When control is not the chosen strategy, doubt exists about the roles of the company and the intermediary. Who will undertake market research to identify customer requirements, the company or an intermediary? Who owns the results and in what way are they to be used? Who determines the standards for service delivery, the franchisor or the franchisee? Who should train a dealer's customer service representatives, the company or the dealer? In these and other situations, the roles of the principal and its intermediaries are unclear, leading to confusion and conflict.

Strategies for Effective Service Delivery through Intermediaries

Service principals, of course, want to manage their service intermediaries to improve service performance, solidify their images and increase profits and revenues. The principal has a variety of choices, which range from strict contractual and measurement control to partnering with intermediaries in a joint effort to improve service to the customer. One of the biggest issues a principal faces is whether to view intermediaries as extensions of its company, as customers or as partners. We discuss three categories of intermediary management strategies: control, empowerment and partnering strategies.

Control Strategies

In the control strategies category, the service principal believes that intermediaries will perform best when it creates standards both for revenues and service performance, measures results and compensates or rewards on the basis of performance level. To use these strategies the principal must be the most powerful participant in the channel, possessing unique services with strong consumer demand or loyalty, or other forms of economic power.

Measurement

Some franchisors maintain control of the service quality delivered by their franchisees by ongoing measurement programmes that feed data back to the principal. Virtually all car dealers' sales and service performance is monitored regularly by the manufacturer, which creates the measurement programme, administers it and maintains control of the information. The company surveys customers at key points in the service encounter sequence: after sale, 30 days out, 90 days out and after a year. The manufacturer designs the survey instruments (some of them with the assistance of dealer councils) and obtains the customer feedback directly. On the basis of this information, the manufacturer rewards and recognizes both individuals and dealerships that perform well and can potentially punish those that perform poorly. The obvious advantage to this approach is that the manufacturer retains control; however, the trust and goodwill between manufacturers and dealers can easily be eroded if dealers feel that the measurement is used to control and punish.

Review

Some franchisors control through terminations, non-renewals, quotas and restrictive supplier sources. Expansion and encroachment are two of the tactics being used today. Another means by which franchisors exert control over franchisees is through quotas and sales goals, typically by offering price breaks after a certain volume is attained.

Empowerment Strategies

Empowerment strategies – in which the service principal allows greater flexibility to intermediaries based on the belief that their talents are best revealed in participation rather than acquiescence – are useful when the service principal is new or lacks sufficient power to govern the channel using control strategies. In empowerment strategies, the principal provides information, research or processes to help intermediaries perform well in service.

Help the Intermediary Develop Customer-Oriented Service Processes

Individual intermediaries rarely have the funds to sponsor their own customer research studies or training programmes. One way for a company to improve intermediary performance is to conduct research

In the car industry, continuous efforts are made to improve the service performance of intermediaries. For example, as a result of research undertaken with customers, Audi has recognized the need to support the digital marketing activities of their dealerships by offering dealers a standardized set of digital tools to help them generate more qualified customer leads. BMW has used research to identify the need to equip their dealers with IPads to provide their sales personnel with a tool to present the latest information on their car models to customers and increase both their efficiency and expertise.

or standard-setting studies relating to service performance, then provide the results as a service to intermediaries. Service originators can invest in training or other forms of development to improve the skills and knowledge of intermediaries and their employees.

Provide Needed Support Systems

In airlines and hotels, as well as other travel and ticketing services, the service principal's reservation system is an important support system. Holiday Inn has a franchise service delivery system that adds value to the Holiday Inn franchise and differentiates it from competitors.

Change to a Cooperative Management Structure

Companies such as TGI Fridays[15] use the technique of empowerment to manage and motivate franchisees. They develop worker teams in their outlets to hire, discipline and handle financial tasks, such as deposits and audits.

Partnering Strategies

The group of strategies with the highest potential for effectiveness involves partnering with intermediaries to learn together about end customers, set specifications, improve delivery and communicate honestly. This approach capitalizes on the skills and strengths of both principal and intermediary, and engenders a sense of trust that improves the relationship.

Alignment of Goals

One of the most successful approaches to partnering involves aligning company and intermediary goals early in the process. Both the service principal and the intermediary have individual goals that they strive to achieve. If channel members can see that they benefit the ultimate consumer of services, and in the process optimize their own revenues and profit, they begin the relationship with a target in mind.

Consultation and Cooperation

A strategy of consultation and cooperation is not as dramatic as setting joint goals, but it does result in intermediaries participating in decisions. In this approach, which could involve virtually any issue, from compensation to service quality to the service environment, the principal makes a point of consulting intermediaries and asking for their opinions and views before establishing policy. For example, when a franchisor finds that the outlets need greater support in promotion, the company can began to make customer mailings for franchisees. This approach makes the franchisees feel that they have some control over the way they do business and also generates a steady stream of improvement ideas.

Summary

Customers' expectations as to how to access a service are constantly changing and organizations need to understand the increasing importance of the Internet, smartphones and mobile apps as customer touchpoints. Organizations are also aspiring to move from a multi-channel to an omni-channel approach to service delivery.

Five forms of distribution in service were described in the chapter: electronic channels, mobile channels, direct channels, franchising and agents/brokers. Service intermediaries perform many important functions for the service principal – co-producing the service, making services locally available and functioning as the link between the principal and the customer. The focus in service distribution is on identifying ways to bring the customer and principal or its representatives together. The benefits and challenges of each type of intermediary were discussed in the chapter, and examples of firms successful in delivering services through each type were detailed. Discussion centred on strategies that could be used by service principals to improve the management of intermediaries.

Key Concepts

Agents and brokers	282	Location-based services	280
Channel ambiguity	288	Mobile apps	276
Channel conflict	288	Multi-channel	276
Control, empowerment and		Omni-channel	276
partnering strategies	289	Service deliverer	281
Electronic channels	276	Service principal	281
Franchising	283		

Exercises

1   Using the Internet, locate three services that you believe are interesting. What are the benefits of buying these services through the Internet versus elsewhere?

2   Develop a brief franchising plan for a service concept or idea that you believe could be successful.

3   Visit a franchisee and discuss the pros and cons of the arrangement from his or her perspective. How closely does this list of benefits and challenges fit the one provided in this chapter? What would you add to the list to reflect the experience of the franchisee you interviewed?

4   Select a service industry with which you are familiar. How do service principals in that industry distribute their services? Develop possible approaches to manage intermediaries using the three categories of strategies in the last section of this chapter. Which approach do you believe would be most effective? Why? Which approaches are currently used by service principals in the industry?

Discussion Questions

1   In what specific ways does the distribution of services differ from the distribution of goods?

2   Identify other service firms that are company owned and see whether the services they provide are more consistent than ones provided by franchisees.

3   Why are franchises so common in the fast-food sector?

4 List five services that could be distributed on the Internet that are not mentioned in this chapter. Why are these particular services appropriate for electronic distribution? Choose two that you particularly advocate. How would you address the challenges to electronic media discussed in this chapter?

5 List services that are sold through selling agents. Why is the use of agents the chosen method of distribution for these services? Could any be distributed in the other ways described in this chapter?

6 Look at the website www.takeaway.com. Why do you think this service has been successful?

7 What are the main differences between agents and brokers?

8 What types of services are bought through purchasing agents? What qualifies a purchasing agent to represent a buyer in these transactions? Why don't buyers themselves engage in the purchase, rather than hiring someone to do so?

9 Which of the reasons for channel conflict described in this chapter is the most problematic? Why? What can be done to address the problem you selected? Base your answer on the strategies discussed at the end of the chapter, selecting then ranking them from most to least effective.

10 Which of the three categories of strategies for effective service delivery through intermediaries do you believe is most successful? Why? Why are the other two categories less successful?

Further Reading

Ailawadi, K.L. and Farris, P.W. (2017). Managing multi-and omni-channel distribution: Metrics and research directions. *Journal of Retailing*, 93(1), 120–35.

Combs, J.G., Ketchen, D.J., Shook, C.L. and Short, J.C. (2011). Antecedents and consequences of franchising: Past accomplishments and future challenges. *Journal of Management*, 37(1), 99–126.

Evanschitzky, H., Caemmerer, B. and Backhaus, C. (2016). The franchise dilemma: Entrepreneurial characteristics, relational contracting, and opportunism in hybrid governance. *Journal of Small Business Management*, 54(1), 279–98.

Guillet, B.D. and Law, R. (2013). An examination of the relationship between online travel agents and hotels: A case study of choice hotels international and Expedia.com. *Cornell Hospitality Quarterly*, 54(1), 95–107.

Immonen, M., Sintonen, S. and Koivuniemi, J. (2018). The value of human interaction in service channels. *Computers in Human Behavior*, 78, 316–25.

Kim, E., Lin, J.S. and Sung, Y. (2013). To app or not to app: Engaging consumers via branded mobile apps. *Journal of Interactive Advertising*, 13(1), 53–65.

Rosado-Serrano, A., Paul, J. and Dikova, D. (2018). International franchising: A literature review and research agenda. *Journal of Business Research*, 85, 238–57.

Chapter 14

Managing Demand and Capacity

Chapter Outline

The Underlying Issue: Lack of Inventory Capability   295
Capacity Constraints   296
Demand Patterns   299
Strategies for Matching Capacity and Demand   300
Revenue Management   306
Queuing Strategies: When Demand and Capacity cannot be Matched   310
Summary and Key Concepts   315
Exercises   316
Discussion Questions   316
Further Reading   317

Learning Objectives

This chapter's objectives are to:

1 Explain the underlying issue for capacity-constrained services: lack of inventory capability.
2 Present the implications of time, labour, equipment and facilities constraints combined with variations in demand patterns.
3 Lay out strategies for matching supply and demand through (a) shifting demand to match capacity, or (b) adjusting capacity to meet demand.
4 Demonstrate the benefits and risks of revenue management strategies in forging a balance among capacity utilization, pricing, market segmentation and financial return.
5 Provide strategies for managing waiting lines for times when capacity and demand cannot be aligned.

Opening Example

Hilton Worldwide RMCC – Revenue Management Consolidated Centre

Revenue management is a sophisticated approach to managing supply and demand under varying degrees of constraint. The objective is to maximize the revenue (or contribution) that can be obtained from available capacity at any given point in time. It is, therefore, highly appropriate for services such as airlines, hotels and car rental.

The right revenue management decisions make an immediate and quantifiable impact on an individual hotel's profitability. Yet finding and keeping a revenue manager with the skills and experience to fit a hotel's profile is both difficult and costly.

Source: ©Willy Barton/Shutterstock

To address this challenge, Hilton Worldwide established a Revenue Management Consolidated Centre (RMCC), to 'help hotels achieve superior market share and profitability'. The RMCC operates from four locations around the world, providing Hilton Worldwide hotels with world-class revenue management talent, powerful market intelligence, cutting-edge tools and business processes. The centre manages over 45,000 rooms in 195 hotels across 35 countries, taking in city centre, convention, airport and resort hotels. Its success is dependent on finding, developing and motivating the best revenue management professionals, and then fitting their experience to the needs and profile of each individual hotel.

The RMCC provides service and cost modes tailored to each hotel, reflecting business complexity, size and market environment. The consolidated approach means Hilton Worldwide maximize cost and scale efficiencies, rapidly sharing best practice, market and trend intelligence to optimize the hotel's market share and deliver market-beating RevPAR (revenue per available room) results. The centre recruits team members from top schools' graduates and experienced professionals, who bring with them a wealth of knowledge from various markets and economies. Before starting on the job, each recruit participates in a dedicated 8-week training programme on the tools and business processes which are the foundation of RMCC's commercial focus.

Source: Darcy VanWyck, Senior Director RMCC Europe, Hilton WorldWide.

For Hilton and other hotels, managing demand and utilizing the hotel's fixed capacity of rooms, restaurants and meeting facilities can be a seasonal, weekly and, even, daily challenge. Although the hotel industry epitomizes the challenges of demand and capacity management, many service providers face similar problems. For example, tax advisers and air-conditioning maintenance services face seasonal demand fluctuations, whereas services such as commuter trains and restaurants face weekly and, even, hourly variations in customer demand. For some businesses, demand is predictable, as for a tax adviser. For others, such as management or technology consultants, demand may be less predictable, fluctuating based on customer needs and business cycles. Sometimes firms experience too much demand for the existing capacity and sometimes capacity sits idle.

Overuse or underuse of a service can directly contribute to gap 3: failure to deliver what was designed and specified. For example, when demand for services exceeds maximum capacity, the quality of service may drop because staff and facilities are over-taxed. Also, some customers may be turned away, not receiving the service at all. During periods of slow demand it may be necessary to reduce prices or cut service amenities, changing the make-up of the clientele and the nature of the service, and thus running the risk of not delivering what customers expect. For example, older travellers or business groups who are in a hotel on a weekend may resent the invasion of families and children because it changes the nature of the service they expected. At the pool, for example, collisions can occur between adults trying to swim laps and children playing water games.

In this chapter we focus on the challenges of matching supply and demand in capacity-constrained services. The service performance gap can occur when organizations fail to smooth the peaks and valleys of demand, overuse their capacities, attract an inappropriate customer mix in their efforts to build demand or rely too much on price in smoothing demand. The chapter gives you an understanding of these issues and strategies for addressing them. The effective use of capacity is frequently a key success factor for service organizations.

The Underlying Issue: Lack of Inventory Capability

The fundamental issue underlying supply and demand management in services is the lack of inventory capability. Unlike manufacturing firms, service firms cannot build up inventories during periods of slow demand to use later when demand increases. This lack of inventory capability is due to the perishability of services and their simultaneous production and consumption. An airline seat that is not sold on a given flight cannot be resold the following day. The productive capacity of that seat has perished. Similarly, an hour of a lawyer's billable time cannot be saved from one day to the next. Services also cannot be transported from one place to another or transferred from person to person. Thus Hilton's hotel services in Mallorca cannot be moved to an alternative location in off-peak months – say, to a skiing area where conditions are ideal for tourists and demand for hotel rooms is high.

The lack of inventory capability combined with fluctuating demand leads to a variety of potential outcomes, as illustrated in Figure 14.1.[1] The horizontal lines in Figure 14.1 indicate service capacity, and the curved line indicates customer demand for the service. In many services, capacity is fixed; thus capacity can be

Figure 14.1   Variations in demand relative to capacity

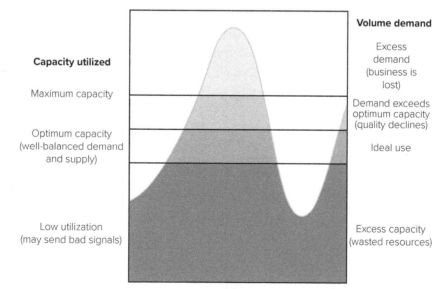

Adapted from source: Lovelock, Wintz, Jochen, *Services Marketing,* 7th edition, © 2011, ch. 9, p.230 and Palmer, *Services Marketing,* 7th edition, © 2014, ch.12, p.392. Reprinted by permission of The McGraw-Hill Companies.

designated by a flat horizontal line over a certain time period. Demand for service frequently fluctuates, however, as indicated by the curved line. The topmost horizontal line in Figure 14.1 represents maximum capacity. For example, it could represent all 160 rooms in a hotel or it could represent the approximately 70,000 seats in a large football stadium. The rooms and the seats remain constant, but demand for them fluctuates. The band between the second and third horizontal lines represents optimum capacity – the best use of the capacity from the perspective of both customers and the company (the difference between optimal and maximum capacity utilization is discussed later in the chapter). The areas in the middle of Figure 14.1 are labelled to represent four basic scenarios that can result from different combinations of capacity and demand:

1. *Excess demand.* The level of demand exceeds maximum capacity. In this situation some customers will be turned away, resulting in lost business opportunities. For the customers who do receive the service, its quality may not match what was promised because of crowding or overtaxing of staff and facilities.
2. *Demand exceeds optimum capacity.* No one is being turned away, but the quality of service may still suffer because of overuse, crowding or staff being pushed beyond their abilities to deliver consistent quality.
3. *Demand and supply are balanced at the level of optimum capacity.* Staff and facilities are occupied at an ideal level. No one is overworked, facilities can be maintained and customers are receiving quality service without undesirable delays.
4. *Excess capacity.* Demand is below optimum capacity. Productive resources in the form of labour, equipment and facilities are underutilized, resulting in lost productivity and lower profits. Customers may receive excellent quality on an individual level because they have the full use of the facilities, no waiting and complete attention from the staff. If, however, service quality depends on the presence of other customers, customers may be disappointed or may worry that they have chosen an inferior service provider.

Not all firms will be challenged equally in terms of managing supply and demand. The seriousness of the problem will depend on the extent of demand fluctuations over time and the extent to which supply is constrained. Some types of organizations will experience wide fluctuations in demand (telecommunications, hospitals, transportation, restaurants), whereas others will have narrower fluctuations (insurance, laundry, banking). For some, peak demand can usually be met even when demand fluctuates (electricity or gas supply), but for others peak demand may frequently exceed capacity (hospital emergency rooms, restaurants, hotels). Those firms that have difficulty in matching supply with fluctuations in demand, will find the issues and strategies in this chapter particularly important to their success.

To identify effective strategies for managing supply and demand fluctuations, an organization needs a clear understanding of the constraints on its capacity and the underlying demand patterns.

Capacity Constraints

For many firms, service capacity is fixed. Depending on the type of service, critical fixed capacity factors can be time, labour, equipment, facilities or (in many cases) a combination of these.

Time, Labour, Equipment, Facilities

For some service businesses, the primary constraint on service production is *time*. For example, a lawyer, a consultant, a hairdresser, a plumber and a personal counsellor all primarily sell their time. In such contexts, if the service worker is not available or if his or her time is not used productively, profits are lost. If there is excess demand, time cannot be created to satisfy it. From the point of view of the individual service provider, time is the constraint.

From the point of view of a firm that employs a large number of service providers, *labour* or staffing levels can be the primary capacity constraint. A law firm, a university department, a consulting firm, a tax accounting firm and a repair and maintenance contractor may all face the reality that, at certain times, demand for their organizations' services cannot be met because staff are already operating at peak capacity. However, it does not always make sense (nor may it be possible in a competitive labour market) to hire additional service providers if low demand is a reality a large percentage of the time.

In other cases, *equipment* may be the critical constraint. For road transport or airfreight delivery services, the lorries or aeroplanes needed to service demand may be the capacity limitation. During the Christmas holidays, DHL, TNT and other delivery service providers face this issue. Health clubs also deal with this limitation, particularly at certain times of the day (before work, during lunch hours, after work) and in certain months of the year. For network service providers, bandwidth, servers and switches represent their perishable capacity.

Finally, many firms face restrictions brought about by their limited *facilities*. Hotels have only a finite number of rooms to sell, airlines are limited by the number of seats on the aircraft, universities are constrained by the number of rooms and the number of seats in each lecture theatre, and restaurant capacity is restricted to the number of tables and seats available.

⭐ SERVICE SPOTLIGHT

Rail passenger numbers in Great Britain reached a record high in 2018/19 with total passenger demand in the morning peak having grown faster than available train seats. The statistics show that more than 230,000 passengers were standing on trains during peak hours in London. Darren Shirley, chief executive of Campaign for Better Transport, said: 'Peak-time rail is bursting at the seams. With 17 per cent of commuters not getting a seat, too many people are paying thousands of pounds to stand in aisles, vestibules and even toilet cubicles.'

Research shows that being able to get a seat on a train is a top priority for passengers. However, as there is a capacity constraint relating to the number of train services available, such congestion cannot be reduced without significant investment in new track and rolling stock.

Source: **Adapted from https://www.transport-network.co.uk/Passengers-left-standing-as-rail-bursts-at-the-seams/16037.**

Understanding the primary capacity constraint, or the combination of factors that restricts capacity, is a first step in designing strategies to deal with supply and demand issues.

Optimal versus Maximum Use of Capacity

To fully understand capacity issues, it is important to know the difference between optimum and maximum use of capacity. As suggested in Figure 14.1, optimum and maximum capacity may not be the same. Using capacity at an optimum level means that resources are fully employed but not overused and that customers are receiving quality service in a timely manner. Maximum capacity, on the other hand, represents the absolute limit of service availability. In the case of a football game, optimum and maximum capacity may be the same. The entertainment value of the game is enhanced for customers when every seat is filled, and obviously the profitability for the team is greatest under these circumstances. On the other hand, in a university classroom it is usually not desirable for students or teaching staff to have every seat filled. In this case, optimal use of capacity is less than the maximum. In some cases, maximum use of capacity may result in excessive waiting by customers, as in a popular restaurant. From the perspective of customer satisfaction, optimum use of the restaurant's capacity will again be less than maximum use.

In the case of equipment or facilities constraints, the maximum capacity at any given time is obvious. There are only a certain number of weight machines in the health club, a certain number of seats in the aeroplane and a limited amount of space in a cargo carrier. In the case of a bottling plant, when maximum capacity on the assembly line is exceeded, bottles begin to break and the system shuts down. Thus it is relatively easy to observe the effects of exceeding maximum equipment capacity.

When the limitation is people's time or labour, maximum capacity is harder to specify because people are in a sense more flexible than facilities and equipment. When an individual service provider's maximum capacity has been exceeded, the result is likely to cause decreased service quality, customer dissatisfaction, and employee burnout and turnover; but these outcomes may not be immediately observable even to the employees themselves. It is often easy for a consulting firm to take on one more assignment, taxing its employees beyond their maximum capacity, or for a dental clinic to schedule a few more appointments in a day, stretching its staff and dentists beyond their maximum capacity. Given the potential costs in terms of reduced quality and customer and employee dissatisfaction, it is critical for the firm to understand optimum and maximum human capacity limits.

Table 14.1 Constraints on capacity

Nature of the Constraint	Type of Service*
Time	Legal
	Consulting
	Accounting
	Medical
Labour	Law firm
	Accounting firm
	Consulting firm
	Health clinic
Equipment	Delivery services
	Telecommunications
	Network services
	Utilities
	Health club
Facilities	Hotels
	Restaurants
	Hospitals
	Airlines
	Schools
	Theatres
	Churches

* The examples illustrate the most common capacity constraint for each type of service. In reality, any of the service organizations listed can be operating under multiple constraints. For example, a law firm may be operating under constrained labour capacity (too few lawyers) and facilities constraints (not enough office space) at the same time.

Demand Patterns

To manage fluctuating demand in a service business, it is necessary to have a clear understanding of demand patterns, why they vary, and the market segments that comprise demand at different points in time.[2] A number of questions need to be answered regarding the predictability and underlying causes of demand.

The Recording of Demand Patterns

To begin to understand demand patterns, the organization needs to record the level of demand over relevant time periods. Organizations that have good computerized customer information systems can record this information very accurately. Others may need to record demand patterns more informally. Daily, weekly and monthly demand levels should be followed, and if seasonality is a suspected problem, graphs should be drawn for data from at least the past year. In some services, such as restaurants or health care, hourly fluctuations within a day may also be relevant. Sometimes demand patterns are intuitively obvious; in other cases, patterns may not reveal themselves until the data are collected.

Predictable Cycles

In looking at the graphic representation of demand levels, predictable cycles may be detected, including daily (variations occur by hours), weekly (variations occur by day), monthly (variations occur by day or week) and/or yearly (variations occur according to months or seasons). In some cases, predictable patterns may occur at all periods. For example, in the restaurant industry, especially in seasonal tourist locations, demand can vary predictably by month, by week, by day and by hour.

If a predictable cycle is detected, what are its underlying causes? Tax advisers can predict demand based on when taxes are due. Services catering to children and families respond to variations in school hours and term times. Retail and telecommunications services have peak periods at certain holidays and times of the week and day. When predictable patterns exist, generally one or more causes can be identified.

Random Demand Fluctuations

Sometimes the patterns of demand appear to be random – there is no apparent predictable cycle. Yet even in this case, causes can often be identified. For example, day-to-day changes in the weather may affect use of recreational, shopping or entertainment facilities. Good weather can increase the use of outdoor activities, such as amusement parks and bicycle rental, but it has the opposite effect on cinemas and art galleries. Although the weather cannot be predicted far in advance, it may be possible to anticipate demand a day or two ahead. Health-related events also cannot be predicted. Accidents, heart attacks and births all increase demand for hospital services, but the level of demand cannot generally be determined in advance. Natural disasters such as floods, fires and storms can dramatically increase the need for such services as insurance, telecommunications, builders and health care.

⭐ **SERVICE SPOTLIGHT**

Since the Syrian war began in 2011, more than two million refugees have travelled to nearby Turkey. Of these two million, approximately 350,00 settled in refugee camps, whereas the others have scattered into urban centres throughout Turkey. With this massive influx of people, Turkey has been faced with a sudden increase in demand for services such as social welfare, housing, education and, particularly, health care.

Source: www.unhcr.org/517a5d589.html.

Demand Patterns by Market Segment

An organization that has detailed records on customer transactions may be able to disaggregate demand by market segment, revealing patterns within patterns. Or the analysis may reveal that demand from one segment is predictable, whereas demand from another segment is relatively random. For example, for a bank, the visits from its business customers may occur daily at a predictable time, whereas personal account holders may visit the bank at seemingly random intervals. Health clinics often notice that walk-in or 'same-day requests to see a doctor' patients tend to concentrate their arrivals on Monday, with fewer needing immediate attention on other days of the week. Knowing that this pattern exists, some clinics schedule more future appointments (which they can control) for later days of the week, leaving more of Monday available for same-day appointments and walk-ins.

Strategies for Matching Capacity and Demand

When an organization has a clear grasp of its capacity constraints and an understanding of demand patterns, it is in a good position to develop strategies for **matching capacity and demand**. There are two general approaches for accomplishing this match. The first is to smooth the demand fluctuations themselves by shifting demand to match existing supply. This approach implies that the peaks and valleys of the demand curve (Figure 14.1) will be flattened to match as closely as possible the horizontal optimum capacity line. The second general strategy is to adjust capacity to match fluctuations in demand. This implies moving the horizontal capacity lines shown in Figure 14.1 to match the ups and downs of the demand curve. Each of these two basic strategies is described next with specific examples.

Shifting Demand to Match Capacity

With this strategy, an organization seeks to shift customers away from periods in which demand exceeds capacity – perhaps by convincing them to use the service during periods of slow demand. This change may be possible for some customers but not for others. For example, many business travellers are not able to shift their needs for airline, car rental and hotel services; leisure travellers, on the other hand, can often shift the timing of their trips. Customers who cannot shift and cannot be accommodated will represent lost business for the firm.

During periods of slow demand, the organization seeks to attract more and/or different customers to utilize its productive capacity. A variety of approaches, detailed in the following sections, can be used to shift or increase demand to match capacity. Frequently, a firm uses a combination of approaches. Ideas for how to shift demand during both slow and peak periods are shown in Figure 14.2.

Figure 14.2   Strategies for shifting demand to match capacity

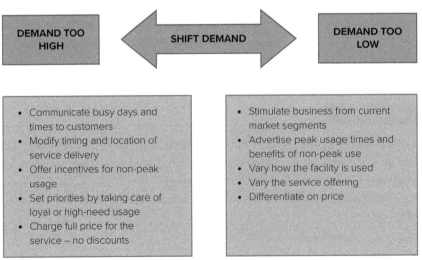

Reduce Demand During Peak Times

One strategic approach to matching capacity and demand for a service provider focuses on reducing demand during times when customer demand is at its peak for the service.

Communicate With Customers

Another approach for shifting demand is to communicate with customers, letting them know the times of peak demand so they can choose to use the service at alternative times and avoid crowding or delays. For example, signs in banks and post offices that let customers know their busiest hours and busiest days of the week can serve as a warning, allowing customers to shift their demand to another time if possible. Forewarning customers about busy times and possible waits can have added benefits. Many customer service telephone lines provide a similar warning by informing waiting customers of approximately how long it will be until they are served. Those who do not want to wait may choose to call back later when the queues are less busy or to visit the company's website for faster service.

Modify Timing and Location of Service Delivery

Some firms adjust their hours and days of service delivery to more directly reflect customer demand. Historically, UK banks were open only on weekdays. Obviously these hours did not match the times when most people preferred to do their personal banking. Now some UK banks open later in the evening and are open on Saturdays, better reflecting customer demand patterns. Online banking has also shifted demand from branches to 'anytime, anywhere' websites. Theatres accommodate customer schedules by offering matinees on weekends and holidays when people are free during the day for entertainment. Cinemas are sometimes rented during weekdays by business groups – an example of varying the service offering during a period of low demand.

Offer Incentives for Non-Peak Usage

In an attempt to shift demand away from peak times, some firms will offer incentives to encourage customers to shift their use of the service to other times. Fitness centres often offer different membership rates to customers who limit their usage to off-peak times.

Set Priorities

When demand for the service is high, and there is limited capacity, service providers can prioritize who is served by taking care of loyal or high-need customers first. Theatres often offer tickets to their regular patrons in their theatre club before tickets are offered through the box-office to other customers.

Charge Full Price

Organizations generally charge full price for service during those periods of time when they know their services are historically in high demand; no discounts are allowed during such times. One of the busiest periods of the year for airlines are those days just before and just after the Christmas period; for this reason, most airlines give priority for seating to those paying full fares and prohibit the redeeming of frequent flyer miles for bookings. Because demand is so high, customers looking for discounted or free tickets find that the days around this holiday have been 'blacked out' and they must purchase tickets at regular fares if they wish to travel.

Increase Demand to Match Capacity

Other approaches that service providers may consider in matching capacity and demand focus on increasing demand for service during times when the service is at less than full capacity.

Stimulate Business From Current Market Segments

Advertising and other forms of promotion can emphasize different service benefits to customers during peak and slow periods. Advertising and sales messages can remind customers about times when demand is low. For example, car tyre replacement centres such as Kwik Fit increase their service advertising during periods when demand is slow by sending out reminders and offering discounts for replacing more than one tyre.

Vary How the Facility is Used

One approach is to change how the service facility is used, depending on the season of the year, day of the week, or time of day. Novotel, the hotel chain, has bedrooms, restaurants and meeting facilities all available to guests 365 days and nights of the year. Yet natural demand for them varies tremendously. Because Novotel hotels cater to business travellers and business meetings, demand has a weekly cycle in addition to any seasonal fluctuations. Business travellers do not stay over weekends. Thus, demand for rooms from the hotel's primary market segment drops on Friday and Saturday nights.

To smooth the peaks and valleys of demand for its facilities, Novotel has employed a number of strategies. Group business (primarily business conferences) is pursued throughout the year to fill the lower-demand periods. A variety of special events, weddings and getaway packages are offered year round to increase weekend demand for rooms. Most city centre hotels have tried to cater to families and children at the weekends. For many working parents, weekend getaways are a primary form of relaxation and vacation. The city centre hotels cater to these couples and families by offering discounted room rates, child-oriented activities and amenities, and an environment in which families feel comfortable. At weekends, children stay free and receive a gift on arrival. The hotels also do special weekend promotions with local theme parks and visitor attractions.

Vary the Service Offering

A similar approach entails changing the nature of the service offering. For example, a ski resort that offers facilities and accommodation for skiers in the winter offer may adapt their services to attract executive development and training programmes during the summer when snow skiing is not possible. Airlines even change the configuration of their plane seating to match the demand from different market segments. Some planes may have no first-class section. On routes with a large demand for first-class seating, a significant proportion of seats may be placed in first class. The Pizza Express restaurant chain, which is primarily a sit-in restaurant, also offers take-away services in certain branches as a way to increase demand for its service.

In these examples, the service offering and associated benefits are changed to smooth customer demand for the organization's resources. Care should be exercised in implementing strategies to change the service offering, because such changes may easily imply and require alterations in other marketing mix variables – such as promotion, pricing and staffing – to match the new offering. Unless these additional mix variables are altered effectively to support the offering, the strategy may not work. Even when done well, the down-side of such changes can result in confusion in the organization's image from the customers' perspective, or a loss of strategic focus for the organization and its employees.

Differentiate on Price

A common response during slow demand is to discount the price of the service. This strategy relies on basic economics of supply and demand. To be effective, however, a price differentiation strategy depends on solid understanding of customer price sensitivity and demand curves. For example, business travellers are far less price sensitive than are families travelling for pleasure. For Novotel hotels, lowering prices during the slow summer months is not likely to increase dramatically bookings from business travellers. However, lower summer prices attract considerable numbers of families and local guests who want an opportunity to experience a good quality hotel but are not able to afford the rooms during peak season.

The maximum capacity of any hotel, airline, restaurant or other service establishment could be reached if the price were low enough. But the goal is always to ensure the highest level of capacity utilization without sacrificing profits (see Hilton example at the start of this chapter). We explore this complex relationship among price, market segments, capacity utilization and profitability later in the chapter in the section on revenue management.

Heavy use of price differentiation to smooth demand can be a risky strategy. Overreliance on price can result in price wars in an industry in which eventually all competitors suffer. Price wars are well known in the airline industry, and total industry profits often suffer as a result of airlines simultaneously trying to attract customers through price discounting. Another risk of relying on price is that customers grow accustomed to the lower price and expect to get the same deal the next time they use the service. If communications with customers are unclear, customers may not understand the reasons for the discounts and will expect to pay the same during peak demand periods. Overuse or exclusive use of price as a strategy for smoothing demand is also risky because of the potential impact on the organization's image, the potential for attracting undesired market segments, and the possibility that higher-paying customers will feel they have been treated unfairly.

Adjusting Capacity to Meet Demand

A second strategic approach to matching supply and demand focuses on adjusting capacity. The fundamental idea here is to adjust, stretch and align capacity to match customer demand (rather than working on shifting demand to match capacity, as just described). During periods of peak demand the organization seeks to stretch or expand its capacity as much as possible. During periods of slow demand it tries to shrink capacity so as not to waste resources. General strategies for adjusting the four primary service resources (time, people, equipment and facilities) are discussed throughout the rest of this section. In Figure 14.3, we summarize specific ideas for adjusting capacity during periods of peak and slow demand. Often, a number of different strategies are used simultaneously.

Figure 14.3 Strategies for adjusting capacity to match demand

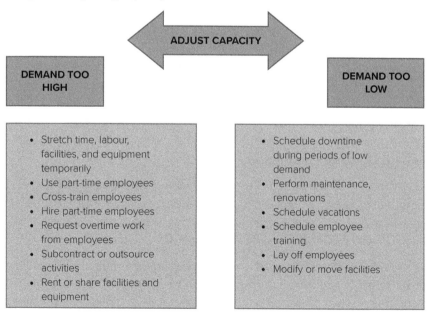

Stretch Existing Capacity

The existing capacity can often be expanded temporarily to match demand. In such cases no new resources are added; rather the people, facilities and equipment are asked to work harder and longer to meet demand:

- *Stretch time temporarily.* It may be possible to extend the hours of service temporarily to accommodate demand. A health clinic might stay open longer during flu epidemics, retailers are open longer hours during the Christmas shopping season, and accountants have extended appointment hours (evenings and Saturdays) before tax deadlines.
- *Stretch labour temporarily.* In many service organizations, employees are asked to work longer and harder during periods of peak demand. For example, consulting organizations face extensive peaks and troughs with respect to demand for their services. During peak demand, associates are asked to take on additional projects and work longer hours, and front-line service personnel in banks, tourist attractions, restaurants and telecommunications companies are asked to serve more customers per hour during busy times than during 'normal' hours or days.
- *Stretch facilities temporarily.* Theatres, restaurants, meeting facilities and classrooms can sometimes be expanded temporarily by the addition of tables, chairs or other equipment needed by customers. Or, as in the case of a commuter train, a carriage that holds a fixed number of people seated comfortably can 'expand' by accommodating standing passengers.
- *Stretch equipment temporarily.* Computers, power lines and maintenance equipment can often be stretched beyond what would be considered the maximum capacity for short periods to accommodate peak demand.

In using these types of 'stretch' strategies, the organization needs to recognize the wear and tear on resources and the potential for inferior quality of service that may go with the use. These strategies should thus be used for relatively short periods in order to allow for later maintenance of the facilities and equipment, and refreshment of the people who are asked to exceed their usual capacity. Sometimes it is difficult to know in advance, particularly in the case of human resources, when capacity has been stretched too far.

SERVICE SPOTLIGHT

Swedish Railways, along with railways in countries such as Finland, France, Germany, the Netherlands, Switzerland and Spain have expanded their capacity by using bi-level trains. Such trains, with double-decker carriages, can resolve capacity problems on a rail line via rolling stock improvements, rather than via the other options of longer trains (requiring longer platforms at stations), more trains per hour (which signalling systems may not allow) or adding extra tracks besides the existing line (which is very expensive). The double-decker design solution usually involves lowering the bottom floor to below the top level of the wheels, closer to the rails, and then adding an upper floor. Such a design fits under bridges and through tunnels whilst carrying more passengers on the same length of track.

Align Capacity With Demand Fluctuations

This basic strategy is sometimes known as a 'chase demand' strategy. By adjusting service resources creatively, organizations can in effect chase the demand curves to match capacity with customer demand patterns. Time, labour, facilities and equipment are again the focus, this time with an eye towards adjusting the basic mix and use of these resources. Specific actions might include the following:[3]

- *Use part-time employees.* In this situation, the organization's labour resource is being aligned with demand. Retailers hire part-time employees during the holiday rush, tax accountants engage temporary help during the tax return season, tourist resorts bring in extra workers during peak season. Restaurants often ask employees to work split shifts (work the lunch shift, leave for a few hours, and come back for the dinner rush) during peak mealtime hours.

- *Outsource.* Firms that find they have a temporary peak in demand for a service that they cannot perform themselves may choose to outsource the entire service. For example, in recent years, many firms have found they do not have the capacity to fulfil their own needs for technology support, web design and software-related services. Rather than try to hire and train additional employees, these companies look to firms that specialize in outsourcing these types of functions as a temporary (or sometimes long-term) solution.

- *Rent or share facilities or equipment.* For some organizations it is best to rent additional equipment or facilities during periods of peak demand. For example, express mail delivery services such as DHL will rent or lease trucks during the peak holiday delivery season. It would not make sense to buy trucks that would sit idle during the rest of the year. Sometimes organizations with complementary demand patterns can share facilities. An example is a church that shares its facilities with a pre-school during the week. The school needs the facilities Monday to Friday during the day; the church needs the facilities in the evenings and at the weekend. There are whole businesses that have been created to satisfy other businesses' fluctuating demand. For example, a firm may offer temporary office suites and clerical support to individuals who do not need such facilities and support on a continuous basis.

- *Schedule downtime during periods of low demand.* If people, equipment and facilities are being used at maximum capacity during peak periods, then it is imperative to schedule repair, maintenance and renovations during off-peak periods. This schedule ensures that the resources are in top condition when they are most needed. Vacations and training are also scheduled during slow demand periods.

- *Cross-train employees.* If employees are cross-trained, they can shift among tasks, filling in where they are most needed. Cross-training increases the efficiency of the whole system and avoids under-utilizing employees in some areas while others are being overworked. Many airlines, such as easyJet, cross-train their employees to move from ticketing to working on boarding gates to assisting with baggage if needed. In some fast-food restaurants, employees specialize in one task (like making French fries) during busy hours, and the team of specialists may number ten people. During slow hours the team may shrink to three, with each person performing a variety of functions. Grocery stores also use this strategy, with most employees able to move as needed from operating checkouts to stocking shelves to bagging groceries.

- *Modify or move facilities and equipment.* Sometimes it is possible to adjust, move or creatively modify existing capacity to meet demand fluctuations. Hotels utilize this strategy by reconfiguring rooms – two rooms with a locking door in-between can be rented to two different parties in high demand times or turned into a suite during slow demand. The airline industry offers dramatic examples of this strategy. Using an approach known as 'demand-driven dispatch', airlines have begun to experiment with methods that assign aeroplanes to flight schedules on the basis of fluctuating market needs.[4] The method depends on accurate knowledge of demand and the ability to quickly move aeroplanes with different seating capacities to flights that match their capacity. The Boeing 777 aircraft is so flexible that it can be reconfigured within hours to vary the number of seats allocated to one, two or three classes.[5] The aircraft can thus be quickly modified to match demand from different market segments, essentially moulding capacity to fit demand. Another strategy may involve moving the service to a new location to meet customer demand or even bringing the service to customers. Mobile training facilities, libraries and blood donation facilities are examples of services that physically follow customers.

★ **SERVICE SPOTLIGHT**

McDonald's has launched new mini outlets, called McDonald's to Go, in London with a reduced menu so it can meet areas where there is high demand for fast service at peak times. The first opened on Fleet Street in London, and the focus on takeaways means there is no in-store seating. It is geared to busy office workers who need to pop out for a 'grab and go' lunch that they will eat in a park or back

> at their desk. At the moment, this market segment tends to get ready-made sandwiches from small supermarkets or outlets such as Pret A Manger. A more limited menu of favourites such as Big Macs, McNuggets and Big Flavour Wraps combined with all customers ordering via a touchscreen or a smartphone app means that McDonald's staff can have more items ready at peak times.
>
> *Source:* **https://metro.co.uk/2019/08/01/mcdonalds-launches-mini-outlets-for-people-wanting-lunch-on-the-go-10499234/.**

Combining Demand and Capacity Strategies

Many firms use multiple strategies, combining marketing-driven demand management approaches with operations-driven capacity management strategies. Figuring out which is the best set of strategies for maximizing capacity utilization, customer satisfaction and profitability can be challenging, particularly when the service offering is a constellation of offerings within one service setting – for example, theme parks with rides, restaurants, shopping; hotel vacation villages with hotels, shopping, spas, pools, restaurants; or ski resorts with ski slopes, spas, restaurants and entertainment. Firms face complex problems in trying to balance demand across all the different offerings with an eye to quality and profitability.

Revenue Management

Revenue management (also referred to as *yield management*) is a term that has become attached to a variety of methods, some very sophisticated, matching demand and supply in capacity-constrained services. Using revenue management models, organizations find the best balance at a particular point in time among the prices charged, the segments sold to and the capacity used. The goal of revenue management is to produce the best possible financial return from a limited available capacity. Specifically, revenue management has been defined as 'the process of allocating the right type of capacity to the right kind of customer at the right time at the right price so as to maximize revenue or yield'.[6]

It involves a range of activities including pricing, segmentation, capacity allocation and demand modelling.

Although the implementation of revenue management can involve complex mathematical models and computer programs, the underlying effectiveness measure is the ratio of actual revenue to potential revenue for a particular measurement period:

$$\text{Yield} = \frac{\text{Actual revenue}}{\text{Potential revenue}}$$

where:

$$\text{Actual revenue} = \text{Actual capacity used} \times \text{Average actual price}$$
$$\text{Potential revenue} = \text{Total capacity} \times \text{Maximum price}$$

The equations indicate that yield is a function of price and capacity used. Recall that capacity constraints can be in the form of time, labour, equipment or facilities. Yield is essentially a measure of the extent to which an organization's resources (or capacities) are achieving their full revenue-generating potential. Assuming that total capacity and maximum price cannot be changed, yield approaches one hundred per cent as actual capacity utilization increases or when a higher actual price can be charged for a given capacity used. For example, in an airline context, a manager could focus on increasing revenue by finding ways to bring in more passengers to fill the capacity, or by finding higher-paying passengers to fill a more limited capacity. In reality, expert revenue managers work on capacity and pricing issues simultaneously to maximize revenue across different customer segments. The following shows simple yield calculations and the inherent trade-offs for two types of services: hotel and legal.

EXAMPLE

Simple Yield Calculations: Examples from Hotel and Legal Services

You can do basic yield calculations for any capacity-constrained service assuming you know the actual capacity, average price charged for different market segments, and maximum price that could be charged. Ideally, yield will approach the number 1, or 100 per cent, where:

Yield = Actual revenue/Potential revenue

We describe yield calculations for two simple examples – a 200-room hotel and a lawyer with a 40-hour work week – under different assumed pricing and usage situations. Although companies use much more complex mathematical models to determine yield, the underlying ideas are the same. The goal is to maximize the revenue-generating capability of the organization's capacity.

200-room hotel with maximum room rate of €100 per room per night

Potential revenue = 100 euros × 200 rooms = 20,000 euros per night

1   Assume: the hotel rents all its rooms at a discounted rate of 50 euros per night.

Yield = 50 euros × 200 rooms/20,000 euros = 50%

At this rate, the hotel is maximizing capacity utilization, but not getting a very good price.

2   Assume: the hotel charges its full rate, but can only rent 40 per cent of its rooms at that price, due to price sensitivity.

Yield = 100 euros × 80 rooms/20,000 euros = 40%

In this situation the hotel has maximized the per-room price, but the yield is even lower than in the first situation because so few rooms were rented at that relatively high rate.

3   Assume: the hotel charges its full rate of 100 euros for 40 per cent of its rooms and then gives a discount of 50 euros for the remaining 120 rooms.

Yield = [(100 euros × 80) + (50 euros × 120)]/
20,000 euros = 14,000 euros/20,000 euros = 70%

Clearly, the final alternative, which takes into account price sensitivity and charges different prices for different rooms or market segments, will result in the highest yield.

40 hours of a lawyer's time across a typical work week at €200 per hour maximum (private client rate)

Potential revenue = 40 hours × 200 euros per hour = 8,000 euros per week

1   Assume: the lawyer is able to bill out 30 per cent of her billable time at 200 euros per hour.

Yield = 200 euros × 12 hours/8,000 euros = 30%

In this case the lawyer has maximized her hourly rate, but has only enough work to occupy 12 billable hours.

2 Assume: the lawyer decides to charge 100 euros for non-profit or government clients and is able to bill out all 40 hours at this rate for these types of clients.

$$\text{Yield} = 100 \text{ euros} \times 40 \text{ hours}/8{,}000 \text{ euros} = 50\%$$

In this case, although she has worked a full week, yield is still not very good given the relatively low rate per hour.

3 Assume: the lawyer uses a combined strategy in which she works 12 hours for private clients and fills the rest of her time with non-profit clients at 100 euros per hour.

$$\text{Yield} = [(200 \text{ euros} \times 12) + (100 \text{ euros} \times 28)]/8{,}000 \text{ euros}$$
$$= 5{,}200 \text{ euros}/8{,}000 \text{ euros} = 65\%$$

Again, catering to two different market segments with different price sensitivities is the best overall strategy in terms of maximizing revenue-generating capacity of the lawyer's time.

Implementing a Revenue Management System

To implement a revenue management system, an organization needs detailed data on past demand patterns by market segment as well as methods of projecting current market demand. The data can be combined through mathematical programming models, threshold analysis or use of expert systems to project the best allocation of limited capacity at a particular point in time.[7] Allocations of capacity for specific market segments can then be communicated to sales representatives or reservations staff as targets for selling rooms, seats, time or other limited resources. Sometimes the allocations, once determined, remain fixed. At other times allocations change weekly, or even daily or hourly, in response to new information.

⭐ SERVICE SPOTLIGHT

Singapore International Airline has a vision for Total Offer Optimization – selling the right product to the right customer for the right (dynamic) price at the right time through the right channel. With a plethora of available data, advanced analytics segment customers into cohorts, each with their own distinctive set of preferences. With this insight, airlines now have the capability to make more targeted product offers with higher conversion rates (if the price is right). Forecasting methods consider elements such as passenger travel purpose, willingness to pay, and product preference to establish the optimal trade-off between the number of passengers buying and the price at which they are buying.

Source: **https://amadeus.com/en/insights/case-study/singapore-airlines-evolves-revenue-management-to-continue-delivering-high-quality-products-and-services.**

Research indicates that traditional revenue management approaches are most profitable when:

1. They have relatively fixed capacity
2. They have perishable inventory
3. They have different market segments or customers, who arrive or make their reservations at different times
4. They have low marginal sales costs and high marginal capacity change costs
5. The product is sold in advance
6. There is fluctuating demand.
7. Customers who arrive or reserve early are more price sensitive than those who arrive or reserve late.[8]

When these conditions are present, revenue management approaches can generally be employed to identify the best mix of service offerings to produce and sell in the period, and at what prices, to generate the highest expected revenue. These criteria exactly fit the situation for airlines, car rental agencies and many hotels – industries that have effectively and extensively used revenue management techniques to allocate capacity. In other services (entertainment, sports, fashion), those customers willing to pay the higher prices are the ones who buy early rather than late. People who really want to see a particular performance reserve their seats at the earliest possible moment. Discounting for early purchases would reduce profits. In these situations, the price generally starts out high and is reduced later to fill capacity if needed.

Interestingly, some airlines now use both these strategies effectively. They start with discounted seats for customers who are willing to buy early, usually leisure and discretionary travellers. They charge a higher fare for those who want a seat at the last minute, typically the less price-sensitive business travellers whose destinations and schedules are inflexible. However, in some cases a bargain fare can be found at the last minute as well, commonly via Internet sales, to fill seats that would otherwise go unoccupied. Online auctions and services offered by companies like Internet-based Lastminute.com serve a purpose in filling capacity at the last minute, often charging much lower fares.

Challenges and Risks in Using Revenue Management

Revenue management programmes can significantly improve revenues. However, although revenue management may appear to be an ideal solution to the problem of matching supply and demand, it is not without risks. By becoming focused on maximizing financial returns through differential capacity allocation and pricing, an organization may encounter these problems:[9]

- *Loss of competitive focus.* Revenue management may cause a firm to over-focus on profit maximization and inadvertently neglect aspects of the service that provide long-term competitive success.
- *Customer alienation.* If customers learn that they are paying a higher price for service than someone else, they may perceive the pricing as unfair, particularly if they do not understand the reasons. However, a study done in the restaurant industry found that when customers were informed of different prices being charged by time of day, week or table location, they generally felt the practice was fair, particularly if the price difference was framed as a discount for less desirable times rather than a premium for peak times or table locations.[10] Customer education is thus essential in an effective revenue management programme.
- *Overbooking.* Customers can be further alienated if they fall victim (and are not compensated adequately) to overbooking practices often necessary to make revenue management systems work effectively. Research suggests that customers who experience negative consequences of revenue management (i.e. denied service or downgrades), particularly high-value customers, subsequently reduce their number of transactions with the firm.[11]
- *Employee morale problems.* Revenue management systems take much guesswork and judgement in setting prices away from sales and reservations people. Although some employees may appreciate the guidance, others may resent the rules and restrictions on their own discretion.
- *Incompatible incentive and reward systems.* Employees may resent revenue management systems that do not match incentive structures. For example, many managers are rewarded on the basis of either capacity utilization or average rate charged, whereas revenue management balances the two factors.
- *Lack of employee training.* Extensive training is required to make a revenue management system work. Employees need to understand its purpose, how it works, how they should make decisions, and how the system will affect their jobs.
- *Inappropriate organization of the revenue management function.* To be most effective with revenue management, an organization must have centralized reservations. Although airlines and some large hotel chains and shipping companies do have such centralization, smaller organizations may have decentralized reservations systems and thus find it difficult to operate a revenue management system effectively.

Measuring the Effectiveness of Revenue Management Activities

Within each service sector, measures will be used to ascertain how well capacity has been utilized and revenue has been maximized. In the hotel industry the main measures that are used include:

Occupancy rate – the percentage share of all rooms that are occupied for a given time. To allow for rooms being renovated or used for accommodating staff, the figure is usually calculated using the total number of rooms available to guests rather than all rooms in the hotel. Some hotels also produce a percentage of beds occupied which may be different from room occupancy figures as rooms may be configured differently with one, two, three or even more beds.

Average Daily Rate (ADR) – also known as the average room rate (ARR), this represents the average rental rate per occupied room in a given period of time. It is calculated by dividing the total room revenue for a period of time by the number of rooms sold.

RevPOR (Revenue per Occupied Room) – is the total revenue (including rooms, food and beverage, etc.) divided by the number of occupied rooms. This differs from ADR since it includes ancillary spending done by guests when staying in a room.

RevPAR (Revenue per Available Room) – currently this is the most common measure used by hotels as it is simple to understand and takes account of occupancy levels and room rates. It is often used as a proxy for a hotel's profitability. It can be calculated in two ways, by either: a) dividing the rooms revenue by the number of rooms available, or b) multiplying the occupancy percentage by the average daily room rate (ADR).

Total RevPAR (Total Revenue per Available Room) – this is a measure which is growing in importance and is particularly useful in resorts or hotels where a larger component of the revenue is additional to room revenue and is calculated in a similar manner to RevPAR, by either: a) dividing the total revenue for a hotel by the number of rooms available, or b) multiplying the occupancy percentage by the revenue per available room (RevPOR).

GOPPAR (Gross Operating Profit per Available Room) – this is another measure which is growing in popularity and involves taking the total revenue of a hotel less costs and expenses and dividing it by the number of rooms available. This gives an impression of operating efficiency on a per room basis and can demonstrate whether costs are controlled properly.

All of these measures are of most use in benchmarking one hotel against others within a branded chain or against other competing hotels in a city or region. In order to enable such benchmarking to be undertaken, a number of consultancies collect data from hotels via voluntary surveys and provide blinded reports back to the participants.

Similar measures exist for other service organizations: for example, in the airline industry, revenue per available seat mile (RASM) is used (calculated by dividing operating income by available seat miles) and in freight transport there is revenue per tonne mile (RTM).

Queuing Strategies: When Demand and Capacity cannot be Matched

Sometimes it is not possible to manage capacity to match demand, or vice versa. It may be too costly – for example, most health clinics would not find it economically feasible to add additional facilities or doctors to handle peaks in demand during periods of flu epidemics; patients usually simply have to wait to be seen. Or demand may be very unpredictable and the service capacity very inflexible (it cannot be easily stretched to match unpredictable peaks in demand). Sometimes waits may occur when demand backs up because of the variability in length of time for service. For example, even though patients are scheduled by appointments in a doctor's surgery, frequently there is a wait because some patients take longer to serve than the time allotted to them.

For most service organizations, waiting customers are a fact of life at some point. Waiting can occur on the telephone (customers put on hold when they call in to ask for information, order something or make a complaint) and in person (customers queuing at the bank, post office, Disneyland or a doctor's surgery). Waiting can occur even with service transactions through the mail – delays in mail-order delivery or backlogs of correspondence on a manager's desk.

In today's fast-paced society, waiting is not something most people tolerate well. As people work longer hours, as individuals have less leisure, and as families have fewer hours together, the pressure on people's time is greater than ever. In this environment, customers are looking for efficient, quick service with no wait. Organizations that make customers wait take the chance that they will lose business or at the very least that customers will be dissatisfied.[12] Research suggests that waiting time satisfaction is nearly as important as service delivery satisfaction with respect to customer loyalty.[13] To deal effectively with the inevitability of waits, organizations can utilize a variety of queuing strategies; general strategies are described next.

Employ Operational Logic

If customer waits are common, a first step is to analyse the operational processes to remove any inefficiencies. It may be possible to redesign the system to move customers along more quickly.

★ SERVICE SPOTLIGHT

In mid-2019, Sainsbury's opened a supermarket in London with no check-out counters. All customers will scan and pay for their groceries using the SmartShop Scan, Pay & Go app which they download on their smartphone. They scan their groceries as they go round the store, pay in the app and scan a QR code before leaving which reassures them that they have paid, with no need to queue or pay at a till. The store has been tailored specifically to busy customers buying ready-to-eat products, including drinks, snacks, breakfast pots, freshly baked pastries and sandwiches that can easily and quickly be picked up, scanned and paid for. With no checkouts, staff are freed up to spend their time on the shop floor, helping customers and keeping shelves fully stocked. The experimental store aims to make grocery shopping quicker and more convenient.

When queues are inevitable, the organization faces the operational decision of what kind of queuing system to use, or how to configure the queues. Queue configuration refers to the number of queues, their locations, their spatial requirement and their effect on customer behaviour.[14] Several possibilities exist, as shown in Figure 14.4. In the multiple-queue alternative, the customer arrives at the service facility and must decide which queue to join and whether to switch later if the wait appears to be shorter in another line. In the single-queue alternative, fairness of waiting time is ensured in that the first-come, first-served rule applies to everyone; the system can also reduce the average time customers spend waiting overall. However, customers may leave if they perceive that the line is too long or if they have no opportunity to select a particular service provider. The last option shown in Figure 14.4 is the take-a-number option in which arriving customers take a number to indicate line position. Advantages are similar to the single-queue alternative with the additional benefit that customers are able to mill about, browse and talk to each other. The disadvantage is that customers must be on the alert to hear their numbers when they are called. Recent research suggests that length of the queue and perceived cost of waiting are not the only influences on customers' likelihood of staying in line. In a series of experiments and field tests, researchers showed that the larger the number of customers queuing *behind* a consumer, the more likely that consumer is to stay in the queue and wait for the service.[15]

Figure 14.4 Waiting-line configurations

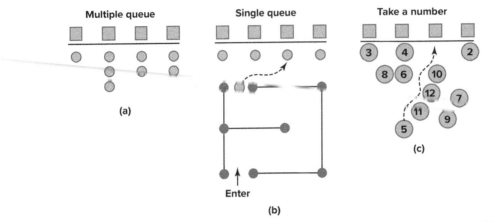

Source: J.A. Fitzsimmons and M.J. Fitzsimmons, *Service Management: Operations, Strategy, Information Technology*, 8/e, ch. 12, p. 345. © 2014 by The McGraw-Hill Companies, Inc. Reprinted by permission of The McGraw-Hill Companies.

Establish a Reservation Process

When waiting cannot be avoided, a reservation system can help to spread demand. Restaurants, transportation companies, theatres, doctors and many other service providers use reservation systems to alleviate long waits. The idea behind a reservation system is to guarantee that the service will be available when the customer arrives.

★ SERVICE SPOTLIGHT

At LEGOLAND in the UK, visitors can reduce their ride wait time with the Q-bot Ride Reservation System. The hand-held device lets visitors make ride reservations from anywhere in the Park with the flexibility to cancel or rearrange bookings. This allows visitors to enjoy the park at their leisure and when its their time to ride, the Q-Bot will let them know. There are three differently priced Q-Bot packages: Regular – the reserved ride time reflects the same time as the actual queue length; Express – reduces the waiting time by half; and Ultimate – gives near instant access to the rides and attractions.

Beyond simply reducing waiting time, a reservation system has the added benefit of potentially shifting demand to less desirable time periods. A challenge inherent in reservation systems, however, is what to do about 'no shows'. Inevitably there will be customers who reserve a time but do not show up. Some organizations deal with this problem by overbooking their service capacity on the basis of past records of no-show percentages. If the predictions are accurate, overbooking is a good solution. When predictions are inaccurate, however, customers may still have to wait and sometimes may not be served at all, as when airlines overbook the number of seats available on a flight. Victims of overbooking may be compensated for their inconvenience in such cases. To minimize the no-show problem, some organizations (such as hotels, airlines, conferences/training programmes and theatres) charge customers who fail to show up or cancel their reservations within a certain time frame.

Differentiate Waiting Customers

Not all customers necessarily need to wait the same length of time for service. On the basis of need or customer priority, some organizations differentiate among customers, allowing some to experience shorter waits for service than others. Known as 'queue discipline', such differentiation reflects management policies regarding whom to select next for service.[16] The most popular discipline is first-come, first-served. However, other rules may apply. Differentiation can be based on factors such as:[17]

- *Importance of the customer.* Frequent customers or customers who spend large amounts with the organization can be given priority in service by providing them with a special waiting area or segregated lines.
- *Urgency of the job.* Those customers with the most urgent need may be served first. This strategy is used in emergency health care. It is also used by maintenance services such as central-heating or air-conditioning repair that give priority to customers whose system is not functioning over those who call for routine maintenance.
- *Duration of the service transaction.* In many situations, shorter service jobs get priority through 'express lanes'. At other times, when a service provider sees that a transaction is going to require extra time, the customer is referred to a designated provider who deals only with these special-needs customers.
- *Payment of a premium price.* Customers who pay extra (first class on an airline, for example) are often given priority via separate check-in lines or express systems.

Make Waiting Pleasurable or at Least Tolerable

Even when they have to wait, customers can be more or less satisfied depending on how the wait is handled by the organization. Of course, the actual length of the wait will affect how customers feel about their service experience, but it is not just the actual time spent waiting that has an impact on customer satisfaction – it is how customers feel about the wait and their perceptions during it. The type of wait (for example, a standard queue versus a wait due to a delay of service) can also influence how customers will react.[18] In a classic article entitled 'The psychology of waiting lines', David Maister proposes several principles about the psychology of queuing, each of which has implications for how organizations can make waiting more pleasurable or at least tolerable.[19]

Unoccupied Time Feels Longer Than Occupied Time

When customers are unoccupied they will likely be bored and will notice the passage of time more than when they have something to do. Providing something for waiting customers to do, particularly if the activity offers a benefit in and of itself or is related in some way to the service, can improve the customer's experience and may benefit the organization as well.[20] Examples include giving customers menus to look at while waiting in a restaurant, providing interesting information to read in a dentist's office or playing entertaining music over the telephone while customers are on hold. At Disney, customers waiting to get on a ride wind their way through a themed environment, such as space tunnels or pirates' caves, that become part of the total service adventure.[21]

Pre-Process Waits Feel Longer Than In-Process Waits

If wait time is occupied with activities that relate to the upcoming service, customers may perceive that the service has started and they are no longer actually waiting. This in-process activity will make the length of the wait seem shorter and will also benefit the service provider by making the customer better prepared when the service actually does begin. Filling out medical information while waiting to see the doctor, reading a menu while waiting to be seated in a restaurant, and watching a videotape of the upcoming service event, are all activities that can both educate the customer and reduce perceptions of waiting.

Research in a restaurant context found that customers reacted less negatively to in-process waits than to either pre-process or post-process waits.[22] Other researchers have found the same for waits due to routine slowness of the process. However, if the wait is due to a service failure, then the in-process wait is viewed more negatively than the pre-process wait.[23] Thus, how customers perceive pre-process, in-process and post-process waits may depend to some extent on the cause of the wait.

Anxiety Makes Waits Seem Longer

When customers fear that they have been forgotten, or do not know how long they will have to wait, they become anxious, and this anxiety can increase the negative impact of waiting. Anxiety also results when customers are forced to choose in a multiple-line situation and they discover they have chosen the 'wrong line'. To combat waiting-line anxiety, organizations can provide information on the length of the wait. At its theme parks, Disney uses signs at intervals along the line that let customers know how long the wait will be from that point on. Using a single line also alleviates customer anxiety over having chosen the wrong line. Explanations and reassurances that no one has forgotten them help alleviate customer anxiety by taking away their cause for worry.

Uncertain Waits are Longer Than Known, Finite Waits

Anxiety is intensified when customers do not know how long they will have to wait. Healthcare providers combat this problem by letting customers know when they check in how far behind the doctor is that day. Some patients resolve this uncertainty themselves by calling ahead to ask. Maister provides an interesting example of the role of uncertainty, which he terms the 'appointment syndrome'. Customers who arrive early for an appointment will wait patiently until the scheduled time, even if they arrive very early. However, once the expected appointment time has passed, customers grow increasingly anxious. Before the appointment time the wait time is known; after that, the length of the wait is not known.

Research in an airline context has suggested that as uncertainty about the wait increases, customers become angrier, and their anger in turn results in greater dissatisfaction.[24] Research also shows that giving customers information on the length of the anticipated wait or their relative position in the queue can result in more positive feelings and acceptance of the wait and, ultimately, more positive evaluation of the service.[25]

Unexplained Waits are Longer Than Explained Waits

When people understand the causes for waiting, they frequently have greater patience and are less anxious, particularly when the wait is justifiable. An explanation can reduce customer uncertainty and may help customers estimate how long they will be delayed. Customers who do not know the reason for a wait begin to feel powerless and irritated.

Unfair Waits are Longer Than Equitable Waits

When customers perceive that they are waiting while others who arrived after them have already been served, the apparent inequity will make the wait seem even longer. This situation can easily occur when there is no apparent order in the waiting area and many customers are trying to be served. Queuing systems that work on a first-come, first-served rule are best at combating perceived unfairness. However, other approaches may be required to determine who will be served next. For example, in an emergency medical care situation, the most seriously ill or injured patients would be seen first. When customers understand the priorities and the rules are clearly communicated and enforced, fairness of waiting time should not be an issue. To understand more about perceptions of fairness, see the 'Fair treatment' section in Chapter 15.

The More Valuable the Service, the Longer the Customer Will Wait

Customers who have substantial purchases or who are waiting for a high-value service will be more tolerant of long wait times and may even expect to wait longer. For example, in a supermarket, customers who have a full cart of groceries will generally wait longer than customers who have only a few items and expect to be checked through quickly. Similarly, diners expect to wait longer for service in an expensive restaurant than they do when eating at a 'greasy spoon'.

Solo Waits Feel Longer Than Group Waits

People will wait longer when they are in a group than when they are alone because of the distractions provided by other members of the group. People also feel comfort in waiting with a group rather than alone.[26] In some group waiting situations, such as at Disneyland or when patrons are waiting in long lines to purchase concert tickets, customers who are strangers may begin to talk to each other and the waiting experience can actually become fun and a part of the total service experience.

Summary

Because service organizations lack the ability to inventory their products, the effective use of capacity can be critical to success. Idle capacity in the form of unused time, labour, facilities or equipment represents a direct drain on bottom-line profitability. When the capacity represents a major investment (for example, aircraft, expensive medical imaging equipment, lawyers and doctors), the losses associated with underuse of capacity are even more accentuated. Overused capacity is also a problem. People, facilities and equipment can become worn out over time when used beyond optimum capacity constraints. People can quit, facilities become run down and equipment can break. From the customer's perspective, service quality also deteriorates. Organizations focused on delivering quality service, therefore, have a natural drive to balance capacity utilization and demand at an optimum level in order to meet customer expectations.

This chapter has provided you with an understanding of the underlying issues of managing supply and demand in capacity-constrained services by exploring the lack of inventory capability, the nature of service constraints (time, labour, equipment, facilities), the differences in optimal versus maximum use of capacity, and the causes of fluctuating demand.

Based on a grounding in the fundamental issues, the chapter presented a variety of strategies for matching supply and demand. The basic strategies fall under two headings: *demand strategies* (shifting demand to match capacity) and *capacity strategies* (adjusting capacity to meet demand). Demand strategies seek to flatten the peaks and valleys of demand to match the flat capacity constraint, whereas supply strategies seek to align, flex or stretch capacity to match the peaks and valleys of demand. Organizations frequently employ several strategies simultaneously to solve the complex problem of balancing supply and demand.

Revenue management (also known as *yield management*) was presented as a sophisticated form of supply and demand management that balances capacity utilization, pricing, market segmentation and financial return. Long practised by the passenger airline industry, this strategy is growing in use by hotel, shipping, car rental and other capacity-constrained industries in which bookings are made in advance. Essentially, revenue management allows organizations to decide on a monthly, weekly, daily or hourly basis to whom they want to sell their service capacity and at what price.

The last section of the chapter discussed situations in which it is not possible to align supply and demand. In these unresolved capacity utilization situations, the inevitable result is customer wait. Strategies were described for effectively managing waiting lines, such as employing operational logic, establishing a reservation process, differentiating waiting customers and making waiting fun or at least tolerable.

Key Concepts

Capacity (optimum v. maximum)	297	Psychology of queuing	313
Capacity constraints	297	Queuing strategies	311
Demand patterns	296	Revenue management	303
Matching capacity and demand	300	Yield management	306

Exercises

1   Choose a local service organization that is challenged by fixed capacity and fluctuating demand. Interview the marketing manager (or another knowledgeable person) to learn: (a) in what ways capacity is constrained, (b) the basic patterns of demand, and (c) strategies the organization has used to align supply and demand. Write up the answers to these questions, and make your own recommendations regarding other strategies the organization might use.

2   Assume you manage a winter ski resort. (a) Explain the underlying pattern of demand fluctuation that is likely to occur at your resort and the management challenges it would present. Is the pattern of demand predictable or random? (b) Explain and give examples of how you might use both demand-oriented and supply-oriented strategies to smooth the peaks and troughs of demand.

3   Choose a local organization in which people have to queue for service. Design a queuing strategy for the organization.

4   Visit the website of Royal Bank of Scotland (www.rbs.co.uk), a leader in online banking. What online services does the bank currently offer? How do these online services help Royal Bank of Scotland manage the peaks and troughs of customer demand? How do its strategies to use more ATMs and other alternative delivery strategies complement the online strategies?

Discussion Questions

1   Discuss the four scenarios (excess demand, demand exceeds optimum capacity, demand and supply are balanced, excess capacity) illustrated in Figure 14.1 and presented in the text in the context of a football team selling seats for its games. What are the challenges for management under each scenario?

2   Discuss the four common types of constraints (time, labour, equipment, facilities) facing service businesses and give an example of each (real or hypothetical).

3   How does optimal capacity utilization differ from maximum capacity utilization? Give an example of a situation in which the two might be the same and one in which they are different.

4   Choose a local restaurant or some other type of service with fluctuating demand. What is the likely underlying pattern of demand? What causes the pattern? Is it predictable or random?

5   Describe the two basic strategies for matching supply and demand, and give at least two specific examples of each.

6   What is revenue management? Discuss the risks in adopting a revenue management strategy.

7   How might revenue management apply in the management of the following: a major theatre? A consulting firm? A commuter train?

8   What are the advantages and disadvantages of outsourcing?

9   Identify examples of pre-process waits and in-process waits. What can be done to reduce these waiting times?

10 Describe the four basic queuing strategies, and give an example of each one, preferably based on your own experiences as a consumer.

Further Reading

Abrate, G. and Viglia, G. (2016). Strategic and tactical price decisions in hotel revenue management. *Tourism Management*, 55, 123–32.

Borges, A., Herter, M.M. and Chebat, J.C. (2015). 'It was not that long!': The effects of the in-store TV screen content and consumers emotions on consumer waiting perception. *Journal of Retailing and Consumer Services*, 22, 96–106.

Denizci Guillet, B. and Mohammed, I. (2015). Revenue management research in hospitality and tourism: A critical review of current literature and suggestions for future research. *International Journal of Contemporary Hospitality Management*, 27(4), 526–60.

Maister, D.H. (1984). *The Psychology of Waiting Lines*. Harvard Business School.

Mauri, A.G. (2012). *Hotel Revenue Management: Principles and Practices*. Milan, Italy, Pearson.

Noone, B.M. and Mattila, A.S. (2009). Hotel revenue management and the Internet: The effect of price presentation strategy on customers' willingness to book. *International Journal of Hospitality Management*, 28(2), 272–79.

Pàmies, M.D.M., Ryan, G. and Valverde, M. (2016). Uncovering the silent language of waiting. *Journal of Services Marketing*, 30(4), 427–36.

Chapter 15

Service Recovery

Chapter Outline

The Impact of Service Failure and Recovery 320
How Customers Respond to Service Failures 323
Customers' Recovery Expectations 326
Cultural Differences in Customers' Recovery Expectations 329
Switching Versus Loyalty Following Service Recovery 330
Service Recovery Strategies 331
Service Guarantees 338
Summary and Key Concepts 342
Exercises 343
Discussion Questions 343
Further Reading 344

Learning Objectives

This chapter's objectives are to:

1. Illustrate the importance of recovery from service failures in keeping customers and building loyalty.
2. Discuss the nature of consumer complaints and why people do and do not complain.
3. Provide evidence of what customers expect and the kind of responses they want when they do complain.
4. Present strategies for effective service recovery, together with examples of what does and does not work.
5. Discuss service guarantees – what they are, the benefits of guarantees and when to use them – as a particular type of service recovery strategy.

Opening Example

Revenge on YouTube – United Airlines Breaks Guitars

Although the following service recovery failure occurred in the USA, its notoriety has spread throughout Europe and around the globe, all thanks to the power of a YouTube video.

Dave Carroll is a musician who performed in a pop-folk music band, Sons of Maxwell. The band went on tour in the USA and Canada, performing in small venues and music festivals. On 31 March 2008 the band members were flying from their hometown of Halifax, Canada to Omaha, Nebraska. During a connection in Chicago, passengers including Carroll noticed some very rough handling of luggage by United Airlines baggage handlers, including Dave's $3,500 Taylor guitar. When Carroll complained to the cabin crew, he was told that he should speak to the lead agent at the gate. Carroll did so, but was told that he should lodge his complaint with the ground staff at his destination airport in Omaha. However, on arriving at Omaha airport, he could find no ground staff as it was after midnight.

On returning to the airport in Omaha for his return flight, he spoke with a United agent who advised him that

he would need to lodge a claim at his originating airport in Halifax. Once back in Halifax, he was told he would have to phone a call centre based in India. After several calls he was told to take his guitar 1,200 miles to Chicago Airport for inspection. When he stated he couldn't travel that far, he was told to contact United Airlines central baggage centre in New York which rerouted his call back to a call centre in India. Eventually, after a number of other steps and a seven-month wait, Dave received an e-mail from United Airlines, apologizing for the damage to his guitar, but rejecting his claim for $1,200 damage because the claim had not been officially submitted within 24 hours of the flight (a requirement of the United Airlines claim policy). In response to further complaints from Carroll, he was told that his case had been closed and United Airlines would be making no further communication on the matter.

As a result, Carrol decided to write songs and produce a video about United Airline breaking guitars and posting it on YouTube. He produced the video on a budget of $150 and posted it on YouTube on Monday 6 July 2009 at 10 p.m, using Twitter and other social media channels to publicize the video. The story was picked up by consumer websites, newspapers and television channels. In less than 24 hours the video had received 24,000 views and 461 comments, most of them maligning United Airlines. By the end of July 2009, the number of views was up to 4.6 million. The song on the video became a Top 20 iTunes download in Canada and the number one country music download in the United Kingdom. At the time of writing this book, the video is still on YouTube and has received over 15 million views.

United monitored the large amount of traffic about the video and tried to enter the conversation very early on by tweeting using the airline's Twitter account that 'this has struck a chord with us' and they were trying to contact Carroll by phone to put things right. They offered Carroll compensation (which he refused – so they donated \$3,000 to a music school) and asked if they could use the video for training purposes in trying to change the United culture.

Worldwide, the video has had a major impact on the image and reputation of United Airlines. The power of online social media demonstrates the impact of negative word of mouth and the need for immediate and effective handling of customers' dissatisfaction and complaints as and when they happen.

Sources: C. Ayers (2009) 'Revenge is best served cold on YouTube', The Times, 22 July; M. Tran (2009) 'Singer gets his revenge on United Airlines and soars to fame', Guardian, 23 July; J. Deighton and L. Kornfield (2010) 'United breaks guitars', Harvard Business Review Case Study, 6 January.

In all service contexts – whether customer service, consumer services or business-to-business services – service failure is inevitable. Failure is inevitable even for the best of firms with the best of intentions, even for those with world-class service systems.

To fully understand and retain their customers, firms must know what customers expect when service failures occur, and must implement effective strategies for service recovery. Our chapter-opening vignette illustrates what can happen, particularly since the advent of social media channels and customer review sites, when companies do not address service failures effectively.

The Impact of Service Failure and Recovery

A *service failure* is generally described as service performance that falls below a customer's expectations in such a way that leads to customer dissatisfaction. Service recovery refers to the actions taken by an organization in response to a service failure. Failures occur for all kinds of reasons – the service may be unavailable when promised, it may be delivered late or too slowly, the outcome may be incorrect or poorly executed or employees may be rude or uncaring.[1] These types of failures bring about negative feelings and responses from customers. Research suggests that only a portion (45 per cent) of customers who experience a problem with service delivery actually complain to the employees serving them, and a very small number (1 to 5 per cent) complain to someone at the company headquarters.[2] This phenomenon, commonly referred to as the 'tip of the iceberg', suggests that every complaint that management receives at company headquarters represents 20 to 100 other customers who experienced the problem but did not complain. Service failures left unfixed can result in customers leaving, telling other customers about their negative experiences, leaving negative reviews online and, even, challenging the organization through consumer rights organizations or legal channels.

Service Recovery Effects

Research has shown that resolving customer problems effectively has a strong impact on customer satisfaction, loyalty, word-of-mouth communication and bottom-line performance.[3] That is to say, customers who experience service failures but who are ultimately satisfied thanks to recovery efforts by the firm will be more loyal than those whose problems are not resolved. That loyalty translates into profitability, as you learned in Chapter 7. Data from a recent Customer Rage Study verify this relationship, as shown in Figure 15.1.[4] Among customers of service businesses who complain and have their problems satisfactorily resolved, 41 per cent indicate they would definitely purchase again from the same provider – illustrating the power of good service recovery.

Figure 15.1   Unhappy customers' repurchase intentions

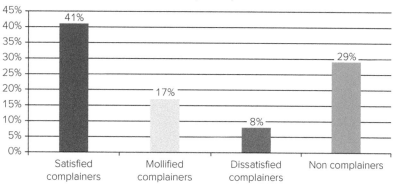

Source: 2015 Customer Rage Study, conducted by Customer Care Measurement and Consulting and the Center for Services Leadership at Arizona State University.

A well-designed, well-documented service recovery strategy also provides information that can be used to improve service as part of a continuous improvement effort. By making adjustments to service processes, systems and outcomes based on previous service recovery experiences, companies increase the likelihood of 'doing it right the first time'. In turn, this reduces costs of failures and increases initial customer satisfaction.

Unfortunately, many firms do not employ effective recovery strategies. Studies suggest as many as 63 per cent of customers who experienced a serious problem received no response from the firm.[5] There are tremendous downsides to having no service recovery or ineffective service recovery strategies. First, the Customer Rage Study mentioned earlier, and other research, has found that customers who are dissatisfied with the recovery process after making a complaint are far less likely to repurchase than those who do not complain – suggesting the power of poor service recovery![6] Second, poor recovery following a bad service experience can lead to customers who are so dissatisfied that they become 'terrorists', actively pursuing opportunities to openly criticize the company using online review sites and online social media such as Facebook. When customers experience a service failure, they talk about it to others no matter what the outcome. Research has found that customers who are satisfied with a firm's recovery efforts tell an average of nine people, whereas those customers who were dissatisfied with the response talk to an average of 22 people.[7] With the ability to share such stories on social media and the Internet, the potential reach of such dissatisfied customers is even greater. Third, repeated service failures without an effective recovery strategy in place can aggrieve even the best employees. The reduction in employee morale, and even the loss of employees, can be huge but these are often the overlooked costs of not having an effective service recovery strategy.

The Service Recovery Paradox

Occasionally some businesses have customers who are initially dissatisfied with a service experience and go on to experience a high level of excellent service recovery, seemingly leading them to be even more satisfied and more likely to repurchase than if no problem had occurred at all; that is, they appear to be more satisfied after they experience a service failure than they otherwise would have been![8] To illustrate: consider a hotel customer who arrives to check in and finds that no room is available. In an effort to recover, the hotel front-desk person immediately upgrades this guest to a better room at the original price. The customer, thrilled with this compensation, reports that he or she is extremely satisfied with this experience, is even more impressed with the hotel than before, and vows to be loyal in the future. Although such extreme instances are relatively rare, this idea – that an initially disappointed customer who has experienced good service recovery might be even more satisfied and loyal as a result – has been labelled the **service recovery paradox**. This is illustrated in Figure 15.2.

Figure 15.2 The service recovery paradox

Figure 15.2 The service recovery paradox

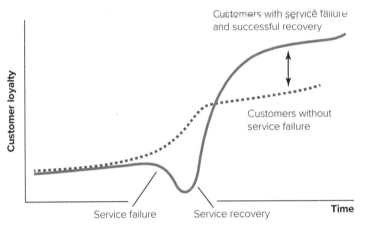

So, should a firm 'screw up' just a little so that it can 'fix the problem' superbly? If doing so would actually lead to more satisfied customers, is this strategy worth pursuing? The logical, but not very rational, conclusion is that companies should *plan to disappoint customers* so they can recover well and (hopefully!) gain even greater loyalty from them. What are the problems with such an approach?

- As we indicated earlier in this chapter, the vast majority of customers do not complain when they experience a problem. The possibility of a recovery exists only in situations in which the firm is aware of a problem and is able to recover well; if customers do not make the firm aware of the failure – and most do not – dissatisfaction is most likely to be the result.
- It is expensive to fix mistakes; re-creating or reworking a service may be quite costly to a firm.
- It would appear somewhat ludicrous to encourage service failures – after all, reliability ('doing it right the first time') is the most critical determinant of service quality across industries.
- Research suggests that even if a customer's satisfaction with the firm increases as a result of the great service recovery, repurchase intentions and image perceptions of the firm do not increase – that is, customers do not necessarily think more highly of the firm in the long run.[9]
- Although the recovery paradox suggests that a customer *may* end up more satisfied after experiencing excellent recovery, there is certainly *no* guarantee that the customer actually *will* end up more satisfied.

The recovery paradox is highly dependent on the context and situation. Although one customer may find it easy to forgive a restaurant who provides him with a gift certificate for a later date to make up for having lost his or her dinner reservation, another customer who had planned to propose marriage to his or her date over dinner may not be all that happy with the same recovery scenario.

The intrigue stimulated by the recovery paradox has led to empirical research specifically on this issue. Although anecdotal evidence provides limited support for the recovery paradox, research seems to indicate that this phenomenon is not pervasive. In one study, researchers found that only the very highest levels of customers' service recovery ratings resulted in increased satisfaction and loyalty.[10] This research suggests that customers weigh their most recent experiences heavily in their determination of whether to buy again. If the most recent experience is negative, overall feelings about the company will decrease and repurchase intentions will also diminish significantly. Unless the recovery effort is absolutely superlative, it cannot overcome the negative impression of the initial experience enough to build repurchase intentions beyond the point at which they would be if the service had been provided correctly in the first place. Other studies suggest the conditions under which a service recovery paradox is most likely to occur is when the failure is not considered by the customer to be severe, the customer has not experienced prior failures with the firm, the cause of the failure is viewed as transient by the customer, or the customer perceives that the company had little control over the cause of the failure.[11] Apparently conditions must be just right in order for the recovery paradox to be present.

Given the mixed opinions on the extent to which the recovery paradox exists, 'doing it right the first time' is still the best and safest strategy in the long run. However, when a failure does occur, then every effort at a superior recovery should be made to mitigate its negative effects. If the failure can be fully overcome, if the failure is less critical or if the recovery effort is clearly superlative, it may be possible to observe evidence of the recovery paradox.

How Customers Respond to Service Failures

Customers who experience service failures can respond in a variety of ways, as illustrated in Figure 15.3.[12] It is assumed that following a failure, dissatisfaction at some level will occur for the customer. In fact, research suggests that a variety of negative emotions can occur following a service failure, including such feelings as anger, discontent, disappointment, self-pity and anxiety.[13] These initial negative responses will affect how customers evaluate the service recovery effort and presumably their ultimate decision to return to the provider or not.[14]

Figure 15.3   Customer complaint actions following service failure

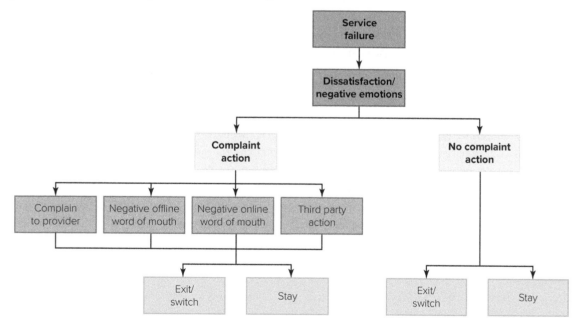

Many customers are very passive about their dissatisfaction, simply saying or doing nothing. Whether they take action or not, at some point the customers will decide whether to stay with that provider or switch to a competitor. As we have already pointed out, customers who do not complain are least likely to return. For companies, customer passivity in the face of dissatisfaction is a threat to future success.

Why People Do (and Do Not) Complain

Some customers are more likely to complain than others for a variety of reasons. These consumers believe that positive consequences may occur and that there are social benefits of complaining, and their personal norms support their complaining behaviour. They believe they should and will be provided compensation for the service failure in some form. They believe that fair treatment and good service are their due, and that in cases of service failure someone should make good. In some cases they feel a social obligation to complain – to help others avoid similar situations or to punish the service provider. A very small number of consumers have 'complaining' personalities – they just like to complain or cause trouble.

Consumers who are unlikely to take any action hold the opposite beliefs. They often see complaining as a waste of their time and effort. They do not believe anything positive will occur for them, or others, as a result of their actions. Sometimes they do not know how to complain – they do not understand the process or may not realize that avenues are open to them to voice their complaints. In some cases non-complainers may engage in 'emotion-focused coping' to deal with their negative experiences. This type of coping involves self-blame, denial and, possibly, seeking social support.[15] They may feel that the failure was somehow their fault and that they do not deserve redress.

Personal relevance of the failure can also influence whether people complain.[16] If the service failure is really important, if the failure has critical consequences for the consumer, or if the consumer has much ego involvement in the service experience, then he or she is more likely to complain. Consumers are more likely to complain about services that are expensive, high risk and ego-involving (like holidays, airline travel and medical services) than they are about less expensive, frequently purchased services (fast-food drive-through service, a taxi ride, a call to a customer service helpline). These latter services are simply not important enough to warrant the time to complain. Unfortunately, even though the experience may not be important to the consumer at that moment, a dissatisfying encounter can still drive him or her to a competitor next time the service is needed.

Finally people are more likely to complain when there are remote channels set up by service providers to make it easy for customers to provide feedback.[17] Organizations that have Twitter feeds, Facebook pages, online customer forums and online customer satisfaction surveys are more likely to find dissatisfied customers voicing their complaints.

Types of Customer Complaint Actions

When customers initiate responses following service failure, these customer complaint actions can be of various types. A dissatisfied customer can choose to complain on the spot to the service provider, giving the company the opportunity to respond immediately. This reaction is often the best-case scenario for the company, because it has a second chance at that moment to satisfy the customer, keep his or her business in the future and, potentially, avoid any negative word of mouth. Customers who do not complain immediately may choose to complain later to the provider by telephone, in writing or via the corporate website or the company's Facebook and Twitter accounts. Again, the company has a chance to recover. Researchers refer to these proactive types of complaining behaviour as *voice responses* or *seeking redress*.

Some customers choose not to complain directly to the provider but rather spread negative word of mouth about the company to friends, relatives and co-workers. This negative word-of-mouth communication can be extremely detrimental because it can reinforce the customer's feelings of negativism and spread that negative impression to others. Further, the company has no chance to recover unless the negative word of mouth is accompanied by a complaint directly to the company. In recent years, customers have taken to complaining via the Internet. A variety of websites, including web-based consumer opinion platforms such as TripAdvisor or flyertalk.com have been created to facilitate customer feedback and, in doing so, have provided customers with the opportunity of spreading negative word-of-mouth communication to a much broader audience. Some customers become so dissatisfied with a product or service failure that they construct websites or Facebook sites targeting the firm's current and prospective customers. On these sites,[18] angry customers convey their grievances against the firm in ways designed to convince other consumers of the firm's incompetence.[19]

Finally, customers may choose to complain to third parties, such as the Consumers' Association, to trading standards departments of local or national government, to a licensing authority, to a professional association or to radio or television programmes that focus on consumer issues. No matter the action (or inaction), ultimately the customers determine whether to patronize the service provider again or to switch to another provider.

Types of Complainers

Research suggests that people can be grouped into categories based on how they respond to failures. Four categories of response types were identified in a study that focused on grocery stores, car repair services, medical care, and banking and financial services:[20] *passives*, *voicers*, *irates* and *activists*. Although the proportion of the types of complainers is likely to vary across industries and contexts, it is likely that these four types of complainers will be relatively consistent and that each type can be found in all companies and industries.

Passives

This group of customers is least likely to take any action. They are unlikely to say anything to the provider, less likely than others to spread negative word of mouth and unlikely to complain to a third party. They often doubt the effectiveness of complaining, thinking that the consequences will not merit the time and effort they will expend. They feel uncomfortable complaining in public. Sometimes their personal values or norms argue against complaining. These people tend to feel less alienated from the marketplace than irates and activists.

Voicers

These customers actively complain to the service provider, but they are less likely to spread negative word of mouth, to switch patronage or to go to third parties with their complaints. *These customers should be viewed as the service provider's best friends!* They actively complain and thus give the company a second chance. As with the passives, these customers are less alienated from the marketplace than those in the other two groups. They tend to believe complaining has social benefits and therefore do not hesitate to voice their opinions. They believe that the consequences of complaining to the provider can be very positive, and they believe less in other types of complaining such as spreading word of mouth or talking to third parties. Their personal norms are consistent with complaining.

Irates

These consumers are more likely than are others to engage in negative word-of-mouth communication with friends and relatives and to switch providers. They are about average in their propensity to complain to the provider. They are unlikely to complain to third parties. These folk tend to feel somewhat alienated from the marketplace. As their label suggests, they are angrier with the provider, although they do believe that complaining to the provider can have social benefits. They are less likely to give the service provider a second chance and instead will switch to a competitor, spreading the word to friends and relatives along the way.

Activists

These consumers are characterized by above average propensity to complain on all dimensions: they will complain to the provider, they will tell others and they are more likely than any other group to complain to third parties. Complaining fits with their personal norms. As with the irates, these consumers are more alienated from the marketplace than the other groups. They have a very optimistic sense of the potential positive consequences of all types of complaining.

This is an example of a typical complaint from an irate customer appearing on the flightsfrom-hell.com website.

'I had booked my honeymoon travel tickets from Mumbai to Nice and back to Mumbai via London with *** Airlines. Let me start by saying that this has been the worst flight I have taken in my life. My honeymoon started as a flop because of *** Airlines. The staff were rude and arrogant.

I thought I had booked comfort class as my agent said that he booked me in it. While checking in I didn't realize that they had given me an economy seat. After the flight took off I realized that I am in economy. We thought there was a mistake at the check-in counter and we would get some clarity at Istanbul Airport. At the airport the guys at the counter were too busy chatting with each other to answer us properly. Their response: "What do you want us to do now? Your ticket was not premium economy." I asked him if my ticket was comfort class or not as my agent had charged me for comfort class. His response: "Why are you asking me, talk to your agent and ask him." He then turned his back and resumed his chat.

On the flight from Mumbai to Istanbul, the steward and stewardess were high-handed and were not willing to hear us out if we had any queries or wanted to make a request. We had ordered a vegetarian meal which we did not get. We had an option of chicken or fish. When we told them that we had requested vegetarian, their only response was, and I quote, "It's not mentioned in our system; there is nothing we can do about it."

Also while booking the tickets at London Gatwick, I informed the counter staff person who was punching in my details that I was unhappy with the service we got while coming from Mumbai. Her response to that was, "Why are you telling me; send a mail if you want."

Let's just say that this has been the worst experience of my life, and definitely I'm going to make it a point to try to reach each and every media source to share my experience about this ridiculous airline, and make it a point that at least my friends and family won't have to go through the experience I had to go through. Cursing myself for selecting *** Airlines for my honeymoon. Rest assured that I will not be flying with *** Airlines again.'

Source: **Adapted from complaint on www.flightsfromhell.com.**

Customers' Recovery Expectations

When they take the time and effort to complain, customers generally have high recovery expectations. They expect the firm to be accountable. They expect to be helped quickly. They expect to be compensated for their grief and for the hassle of being inconvenienced. And they expect to be treated nicely in the process.

Understanding and Accountability

In many service failure situations, customers are not looking for extreme actions from the firm; however, they are looking to understand what happened and for firms to be accountable for their actions (or inactions).[21] One study identified the eight most common 'remedies' that customers seek when they experience a serious problem;[22] three of these remedies were to have the product repaired or service fixed, be reimbursed for the hassle of having experienced a problem, and receive a product or service free of charge in the future. Interestingly, however, the other five remedies – including an apology from the firm, an explanation by the firm as to what happened, an assurance that the problem would not be repeated, a thank you for the customer's business and an opportunity for the customer to vent his or her frustrations to the firm – cost the firm very little to provide.

These five non-monetary remedies consist primarily of affording employees the opportunity to communicate with customers. Understanding and accountability are very important to many customers after a service failure; for if they perceive an injustice has occurred, someone is to blame. Customers expect an apology when things go wrong, and a company that provides an apology demonstrates courtesy and respect; customers also want to know what the company is going to do to ensure that the problem does not reoccur.[23]

Fair Treatment

Customers also want justice and fairness in handling their complaints. Service recovery experts Steve Brown and Steve Tax have documented three specific types of justice that customers are looking for following their complaints: *outcome justice, procedural justice* and *interactional justice*.[24] Outcome justice concerns the results that customers receive from their complaints; procedural justice refers to the policies, rules and timeliness of the complaint process; and interactional justice focuses on the interpersonal treatment received during the complaint process.[25] Table 15.1 shows examples of each type of justice taken from Brown and Tax's study of consumers who reported on their experiences with complaint resolution.

Table 15.1   Fairness themes in service recovery

	Fair	Unfair
Outcome justice: the results that customers receive from complaints	*'The waitress agreed that there was a problem. She took the sandwiches back to the kitchen and had them replaced. We were also given a free drink.'* *'They were very thorough with my complaint. One week later I received a coupon for a free oil change and an apology from the shop owner.'*	*'Their refusal to refund our money or make up for the inconvenience and cold food was inexcusable.'* *'If I wanted a refund, I had to go back to the store the next day. It's a 20-minute drive; the refund was barely worth the trouble.'*
Procedural justice: the policies, rules and timeliness of the complaint process	*'The hotel manager said that it didn't matter to her who was at fault, she would take responsibility for the problem immediately.'* *'The sales manager called me back one week after my complaint to check if the problem was taken care of to my satisfaction.'*	*'They should have assisted me with the problem instead of giving me a phone number to call. No one returned my calls, and I never had a chance to speak to a real person.'* *'I had to tell my problem to too many people. I had to become irate in order to talk with the manager, who was apparently the only one who could provide a solution.'*
Interactional justice: the interpersonal treatment received during the complaint process	*'The loan officer was very courteous, knowledgeable and considerate – he kept me informed about the progress of the complaint.'* *'The teller explained that they had a power outage that morning so things were delayed. He went through a lot of files [effort] so that I would not have to come back the next day.'*	*'The person who handled my complaint about the faulty air-conditioner repair wasn't going to do anything about it and didn't seem to care.'* *'The receptionist was very rude; she made it seem like the doctor's time was important but mine was not.'*

Source: Adapted from 'Recovering and learning from service failure', by S.S. Tax and S.W. Brown, MIT *Sloan Management Review* (Fall 1998), p. 79. Copyright © 1998 by Massachusetts Institute of Technology. All rights reserved.

Outcome Justice

Customers expect outcomes, or compensation, to match the level of their dissatisfaction. This compensation can take the form of actual monetary compensation, an apology, future services for free, reduced charges, repairs and/or replacements. Customers expect equity in the exchange – that is, they want to feel that the company has 'paid' for its mistakes in a manner at least equal to what the customer has suffered. The company's 'punishment should fit the crime'. Customers expect equality   that is, they want to be compensated no more or less than other customers who have experienced the same type of service failure. They also appreciate it when a company gives them choices in terms of compensation. For example, a hotel guest could be offered the choice of a refund or a free upgrade to a better room in compensation for a room not being available on arrival. Outcome justice is especially important in settings in which customers have particularly negative emotional responses to the service failure; in such situations, recovery efforts should focus on improving the outcome from the customer's point of view.[26]

However, it should also be noted that customers can feel uncomfortable if they are overly compensated.

★ SERVICE SPOTLIGHT

Early in its experience with service guarantees, Domino's Pizza offered not to charge for the pizza if the driver arrived after the 30-minute guaranteed delivery time. Many customers were not comfortable asking for this level of compensation, especially if the driver was only a few minutes late. In this case 'the punishment was greater than the crime'. For a while Domino's changed the compensation to a more reasonable reduced price for late deliveries. Later, the time guarantee was dropped altogether because of problems it caused with employees who were driving too fast in order to make their deliveries.

Procedural Justice

In addition to fair compensation, customers expect fairness in terms of policies, rules and timeliness of the complaint process. They want easy access to the complaint process, and they want things handled quickly, preferably by the first person they contact. They appreciate companies that can be adaptable in their procedures so that the recovery effort can match their individual circumstances. In some cases, particularly in business-to-business services, companies actually ask the customer, 'What can we do to compensate you for our failure?' Many times what the customer asks for is actually less than the company might have expected.

Fair procedures are characterized by clarity, speed and absence of difficulties. Unfair procedures are those that customers perceive as slow, prolonged and inconvenient. Customers also feel it is unfair if they have to prove their case – when the assumption seems to be they are wrong or lying until they can prove otherwise.

Interactional Justice

Above and beyond their expectations of fair compensation and difficulty-free, quick procedures, customers expect to be treated politely, with care and honesty. This form of fairness can dominate the other forms if customers feel the company and its employees have uncaring attitudes and have done little to try to resolve the problem. This type of behaviour on the part of employees may seem strange – why would they treat customers rudely or in an uncaring manner under these circumstances? Often it is due to lack of training and empowerment – a frustrated front-line employee who has no authority to compensate the customer may easily respond in an aloof or uncaring manner, especially if the customer is angry and/or rude.

Cultural Differences in Customers' Recovery Expectations

Service firms operating internationally, as well as those operating in multi-ethnic countries within Europe, need to be sensitive to the cultural diversity and subsequently differing expectations of service and of service recovery.

Differing Attribution Expectations

When service failures occur, customers spontaneously make assumptions about, or attribute blame for, the unexpected event. Researchers[27] have explored service recovery across cultures and found in Western countries, when the failure is caused by some external factor beyond the control of the service firm, customers will often attribute the problem to the context or situation surrounding the service failure – particularly if an explanation is offered by the firm as to what happened. Such action can diminish the blame customers attribute to the firm and its staff, thus avoiding any lowering of their perceptions of overall perceived quality.

For customers from East Asian cultures, on the other hand, a causal explanation has relatively little impact on where the blame for the failure is attributed. These customers prefer other remedies, such as a speedy resolution to the problem and a genuine apology from a manager (rather than a front-line employee) to regain 'face' in the eyes of their family and friends. East Asian customers also have a lower tolerance towards uncertain and ambiguous situations. Thus, when a failure is being remedied, these customers would prefer having a sense of control, which the firm can provide by keeping them informed of exactly what is being done to rectify the situation.

Differing Views of Outcome Justice

Western customers are more interested in, and expect to receive, tangible compensation (i.e. a discount) when a service failure occurs than are Asian customers. Offering compensation is particularly effective in restoring a sense of fairness among Western consumers as they are concerned about outcome justice. American customers, in particular, are generally more assertive and more used to 'asking for reparation' than consumers from other cultures. Previous research on service recovery in Western contexts consistently shows that compensation has a positive effect on post-recovery satisfaction and loyalty. East Asian customers, who typically tend to be high on uncertainty avoidance, prefer other types of remedies when service failure occurs. In Asian cultures there is a tendency to focus on avoidance of losses rather than on individual gains. East Asian customers emphasize the need to fit in with others and to avoid conflict and confrontation.

Differing Views of Interactional Justice

The research also suggests that, in Western cultures, offering an explanation for service failure might shift the customer's focus away from thinking that the service provider is incompetent, uncaring, or lazy. Such an explanation tends to cause Western customers to pay more attention to the situation as a cause of the failure. East Asian customers, meanwhile, are more likely to be aware of situational constraints, seek to maintain social harmony, and avoid causing a loss of face. For them, interactional fairness appears to be particularly salient. Thus, providing an explanation and treating the offended East Asian customers in a courteous, formal, and empathetic manner is more important than the compensation offered.

Procedural Justice

For service firms operating in Western countries, hassle-free and fast recovery procedures that lead to compensation for any losses or inconveniences triggered by a service failure are preferred by customers. In East Asian cultures, a genuine apology from a manager (rather than a customer-contact employee) is particularly desirable; such a procedure allows customers to regain 'face' in the eyes of their family and friends. East Asian customers would also prefer to have a sense of control, so having management constantly inform them of what is being done to rectify the situation is also appealing to them.

In service recovery, as in any service situation, companies need to be sensitive to the fact that culture and other factors play a role. Customers in all cultures expect strong service recovery but preferences for the type of recovery, or which fairness dimension to emphasize, may vary.

Switching Versus Loyalty Following Service Recovery

Ultimately, how a service failure is handled, and the customer's reaction to the recovery effort, can influence future decisions to remain loyal to the service provider or to switch to another provider. Whether customers switch to a new provider following service failure will depend in addition on a number of other factors. The magnitude and criticality of the failure will clearly be a factor in future repurchase decisions. The more serious the failure, the more likely the customer is to switch, regardless of the recovery effort.[28]

The nature of the customer's relationship with the firm may also influence whether the customer stays or switches providers. Research suggests that customers who have 'true relationships' with their service providers are more forgiving of poorly handled service failures and are less likely to switch than are those who have a 'pseudo-relationship' or a 'first-time encounter' type of relationship.[29] A true relationship is one in which the customer has had repeated contact over time with the same service provider. A first-time encounter relationship is one in which the customer has had only one contact, on a transaction basis, with the provider. A pseudo-relationship is one in which the customer has interacted many times with the same company, but with different service providers each time.

Other research reveals that the individual customer's attitude towards switching will strongly influence whether he or she ultimately stays with the provider and that this attitude toward switching will be even more influential than basic satisfaction with the service.[30] This research suggests that certain customers will have a greater propensity to switch service providers, no matter how their service failure situations are handled. Research in an online service context, for example, shows that demographic factors such as age and income, as well as individual factors such as risk aversion, will influence whether a customer continues to use an online service or switches to another provider.[31] The profile of an 'online service switcher' emerged in the research as a person who was influenced to subscribe to the service through positive word-of-mouth communication; who used the service less; who was less satisfied and less involved with the service; who had a lower income and education level; and who also had a lower propensity for taking risks.

Finally, the decision to switch to a different service provider may not occur immediately following service failure or poor service recovery, but may follow an accumulation of events. That is, service switching can be viewed as a process resulting from a series of decisions and critical service encounters over time, rather than one specific moment in time when a decision is made.[32] This process orientation suggests that companies could potentially track customer interactions and predict the likelihood of defection based on a series of events, intervening earlier in the process to head off the customer's decision to switch.

Although customers may decide to switch service providers for a variety of reasons, service failure and poor service recovery are often a cause of such behaviour. A study of approximately 500 service-switching incidents identified eight broad themes underlying the decision to defect.[33] These themes are shown in Figure 15.4.

In about 200 of the incidents, a single theme was identified as the cause for switching service providers, and the two largest categories were related to service failure. Core service failure was the cause of switching for 25 per cent of the respondents, and service encounter failure was the reason for switching services for an

Figure 15.4   Causes behind service switching

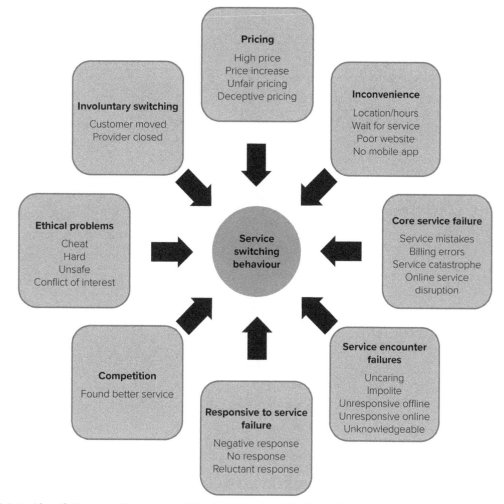

Source: Adapted from S. Keaveney, 'Customer switching behaviour in service industries: an exploratory study', *Journal of Marketing* 59 (April 1995), pp. 71–82.

additional 20 per cent of the sample. In incidents that listed two themes, 29 per cent listed core service failure and 18 per cent service encounter failure as contributing to their desire to switch providers; poor response to failure was mentioned by an additional 11 per cent of the respondents as the cause for switching. As these findings suggest, service failure can cause customers to switch companies. To minimize the impact of service failure, excellent service recovery is needed. In the next section we discuss several service recovery strategies that attempt to keep dissatisfied customers from defecting.

Service Recovery Strategies

Many companies have learned the importance of providing excellent recovery for disappointed customers. In this section we examine their strategies and share examples of benchmark companies and what they are doing. It will become clear that excellent service recovery is really a combination of a variety of strategies that need to work together, as illustrated in Figure 15.5. We discuss each of the strategies shown in the figure, starting with the basic 'do it right the first time'.

Figure 15.5 Service recovery strategies

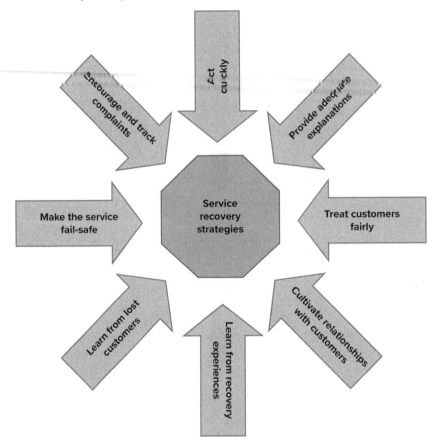

Make the Service Fail-Safe – Do it Right the First Time!

The first rule of service quality is to do it right the first time. This means recovery is unnecessary, customers get what they expect and the costs of redoing the service and compensating for errors can be avoided. As you have already learned, reliability, or doing it right the first time, is the most important dimension of service quality across industry contexts.[34]

It is frequently suggested that services adopt the quality notion of *poka yoke* to improve service reliability.[35] *Poka yoke* is a Japanese term that means 'fail safing' or 'mistake proofing'. These are automatic warnings or controls in place to ensure that mistakes are not made; essentially they are quality-control mechanisms, typically used on assembly lines. They can be devised in service settings to 'mistake-proof' the service, to ensure that essential procedures are followed and that service steps are carried out in the proper order and in a timely manner. In a hospital, setting numerous poka-yokes ensures that procedures are followed to avoid potentially life-threatening mistakes. For example, trays for surgical instruments have indentations for specific instruments, and each instrument is nested in its appropriate spot. In this way surgeons and their staff know that all instruments are in their places prior to operating.[36]

Similarly, poka-yokes can be devised to ensure that the tangibles associated with the service are clean and well maintained, and that documents are accurate and up-to-date. Poka-yokes can also be implemented for employee behaviours (checklists, role-playing and practice, reminder signs) and even for ensuring that customers perform effectively. Many of the strategies we discuss in Parts 3 and 4 of this text ('Aligning service design and standards' and 'Delivering and performing service') are aimed at ensuring service reliability and can be viewed as applications of the basic fail-safe notion of *poka yoke*.

Even more fundamentally, it is for a firm to create a culture of doing it right the first time. Within such a culture everyone understands the importance of reliability. Employees and managers aim to satisfy every customer and look for ways to improve service. Employees fully understand and appreciate the 'relationship value of a customer' concept that was presented in Chapter 7. Thus they are motivated to provide quality service *every time* and to *every customer*.

Encourage and Track Complaints

Even in an organization that aims for 100 per cent service quality, failures occur. A critical component of a service recovery strategy is thus to encourage and track complaints. Service failures can occur in a variety of ways and at numerous times throughout the service delivery process. However, in many cases it is difficult, if not impossible, for the firm to know that a service failure has occurred unless the customer informs the firm accordingly. Unfortunately, a relatively low percentage of customers (5–10 per cent) will actually complain to the firm. Thus, a major challenge facing management is how to get customers to complain when they experience a service failure and/or they are not satisfied with service delivery. So what can a firm do to elicit complaints? Here are some issues to consider:[37]

- *Develop the mind-set that complaints are good.* Too often the complaining customer is seen by employees in the organization as the *enemy* – someone to be conquered and subdued. The more prudent approach is to develop the mind-set that the complaining customer is the firm's *friend*. Complaints provide valuable feedback to the firm, giving it the opportunity not only to address the service failure for the complaining customer, but also to identify problems that other (less vocal) customers may also be experiencing. It has been suggested that complainers should be treated with the dignity and respect given to the best analysts and consultants. One company puts all customers who have complained on a VIP list. Accepting complaints is truly reflective of firms who are close to their customers.
- *Make complaining easy.* If the firm truly wants to hear from customers who experience poor service, it needs to make it easy for them to share their experiences with the firm. Sometimes customers have no idea who to speak to if they have a complaint, what the process is or what will be involved. Complaining should be easy – the last thing customers want when they are dissatisfied is to face a complex, difficult-to-access process for complaining. Customers should know where to go and/or who to talk to when they encounter problems, and they should be made to feel confident that something positive will result from their efforts. Technological advances have made it possible to provide customers with multiple avenues to complain, including freephone customer call centres, company email addresses, Twitter feeds and website feedback forms. The firm should regularly communicate to customers that complaining is easy and that it welcomes and appreciates such feedback.

⭐ SERVICE SPOTLIGHT

The following excerpt from an amusing but real interchange between a customer service representative at Sainsbury's, the supermarket chain, and a complaining customer on Twitter demonstrates a willingness to interact and empathize with customers. Not only did it make this customer happy, it also went viral and suggested that the large organization that is Sainsbury's was very approachable.

@customer
I tried to buy some battered fish from @sainsburys but it didn't have a bar cod! Marty.

@sainsburys
Were there no other packs in the plaice, or was that the sole one on the shelf? Floundering for an explanation! David.

@*customer*

I tried dropping you a line but this whole situation is giving me a haddock. What are you going to do about it? Let minnow. Marty.

@*sainsburys*

If I'm herring you right, you're looking to eel our relationship. I'll tell the store to find the shelf & fillet. David.

@*customer*

I don't think it's necessary to scale the shelves, David. There's no point doing it for the halibut. You might pull a mussel. Marty.

@*sainsburys*

I feel that some fin should be done to sort it trout. You shouldn't have that hassle when trying to spend a few squid. David.

@*customer*

Something dolphinately needs to be done about it. The quicker we sort it out the batter. Before the situation gets cray. Marty.

@*sainsburys*

Agreed, we mustn't shark the issue. Salmon should be brought to account for this mis-hake. David.

@*customer*

Sorry for carping on about this, David. With mistakes, it's just nice to be given the oppor-tuna-ty to mullet it over. Marty.

@*sainsburys*

It's ok, just needs sorted quickly. I'll get my skates on & scallop down there now. Can't be leaving you in the perch. David.

@*customer*

Don't feel gill-ty, David. It was a simple error. Good luck trawling through the products, although you're clearly a dab hand!

- *Be an active listener.* Employees should be encouraged and trained to listen actively to customers, particularly to see if they can pick up on any cues to suggest less than ideal service. A restaurant customer might respond 'fine' to the waiter's question, 'How is your meal?' However, the customer's body language and tone of voice, or the amount of food not eaten, might indicate that all is not fine. Some customers may not be assertive in voicing their displeasure, but they may drop clues to suggest that something is amiss. Employees as well as managers should be consistently listening not only to the customer's actual words but also to what he or she may really be trying or wanting to communicate.
- *Ask customers about specific service issues.* A very simple, informal way to find out about any service failure is simply to ask. Managers at one hotel with a high percentage of business travellers make it a point to be at the front desk between 7.45 a.m. and 8.45 a.m. every day, because approximately 80 per cent of their business travellers check out at that time. During the checkout process, managers avoid questions that can be answered with a simple 'yes', 'OK', or 'fine' (e.g. 'Was the room to your satisfaction?') and instead ask questions that force customers to provide specific feedback (e.g. 'How could we have

improved the technology in your room?' or 'What needs to be done to improve our gym?'). Asking customers very specific questions that cannot be answered with a simple 'yes' or 'no' may provide customers with an easy way to point out expectations that were not fulfilled.

- *Conduct short surveys.* A follow-up telephone call to a customer still in the midst of the service experience can help to identify problems in real time and thus enable real-time recovery.

⭐ SERVICE SPOTLIGHT

An example of using follow-up telephone calls is DHL Freight in Germany. It regularly calls customers the day after their consignment has been delivered to ask the customer if everything is OK with the delivery, driver and paperwork. Any problems are followed up by contact from a supervisor or senior manager.

As we have just seen, firms can utilize a number of ways to encourage and track complaints. Customer research can be designed specifically for this purpose through satisfaction surveys, critical incidents studies and lost customer research, as discussed in Chapter 6. Nowadays, freephone call centres, email, Facebook pages and the use of automated chatbots are commonplace to facilitate, encourage and track complaints. Software applications in a number of companies also allow complaints to be analysed, sorted, responded to, and tracked automatically.[38]

In some cases, technology can anticipate trouble and complaints before they happen, allowing service employees to diagnose problems before the customer recognizes they exist. At companies such as Ericsson and Siemens, information systems are being implemented to anticipate equipment failures and to send out an electronic alert to the local field technician with the nature of the problem as well as which parts and tools will be needed to make the repair – a repair the customer does not yet know is needed.

Act Quickly

Complaining customers want quick responses.[39] Thus, if the company welcomes, even encourages, complaints, it must be prepared to act on them quickly. Research conducted on service customers has found that more than one-third of all customers who have problems resolved immediately or within 24 hours are 'completely satisfied' with the action taken by the company; this compares with only 18 per cent after one week.[40] Unfortunately, many companies require customers to contact multiple employees before getting a problem resolved. Research suggests that, if a problem can be handled by the first contact, customers are satisfied with the firm's response 35 per cent of the time; however, once three or more contacts are needed, the percentage of customers who are satisfied with the response drops to 9 per cent.[41] And, of those customers who use Twitter, a staggering 81 per cent expect a same-day response to the complaints they voice via their tweets. The lesson here? A quick response to a service failure can go a long way in appeasing a dissatisfied customer.[42] The ability to provide an immediate response requires not only systems and procedures that allow quick action, but empowered employees also.

Employees must be trained and empowered to solve problems as they occur. Empowerment of employees, a practice discussed in more detail in Chapter 11, can often allow for quick responses and help placate dissatisfied customers.

Service employees have a specific and real need for recovery training. Because customers demand that service recovery take place on the spot and quickly, front-line employees need the skills, authority and incentives to engage in effective recovery. Effective recovery skills include hearing the customer's problems, taking initiative, identifying solutions, improvising and perhaps bending the rules from time to time.

Not only do employees need the authority to act (usually within defined limits), but they also should not be punished for taking action. In fact, incentives should exist that encourage employees to exercise their recovery authority. At the Ritz-Carlton, employees are authorized to spend up to 1,500 euros on behalf of the customer to solve a problem. This amount of money is rarely needed, but knowing that they have the clearance to use it encourages employees to be responsive without fear of retribution.

Sometimes employees can even anticipate problems before they arise and surprise customers with a solution. For example, the cabin crew on a flight severely delayed due to weather conditions anticipated that passengers would be hungry, particularly young children. Once in flight, they announced to the harried travellers, 'Thank you for your extreme patience in waiting with us. Now that we're on our way, we'd like to offer you complimentary beverages and dinner. Because we have a number of very hungry children on board, we'd like to serve them first, if that's OK with all of you'. The passengers nodded and applauded their efforts, knowing that hungry, crying children could make the situation even worse. The cabin crew had anticipated a problem and solved it before it escalated.

Another way that problems or complaints can be handled quickly is by building systems that allow customers to actually solve their own service needs and fix their own problems. Typically this approach is done through technology. Customers directly interface with the company's technology to perform their own customer service, which provides them with instant answers. DHL uses this strategy for its package tracking services, for example.

SERVICE SPOTLIGHT

British Telecom provides a range of self-help facilities for customers who have problems with their internet or telephone service. These include online troubleshooting diagnostic services that customers can use to check their connections and broadband speeds as well as provide them with potential steps to rectify the problems. There is also a frequently asked questions and answers section on the BT website. If the diagnostic tests or the FAQs don't recover the situation for the customer, there is an online BT community where customers can ask for help and advice from other customers. Finally, if these avenues do not help, then customers can contact customer service agents through live chat or telephone.

Provide Adequate Explanations

In many service failures, customers look to try to understand why the failure occurred. Explanations can help to defuse negative reactions and convey respect for the customer.[43] Research suggests that when the firm's ability to provide an adequate outcome is not successful, further dissatisfaction can be reduced if an adequate explanation is provided to the customer.[44] In order for an explanation to be perceived as adequate, it must possess two primary characteristics. First, the content of the explanation must be appropriate; relevant facts and pertinent information are important in helping the customer understand what occurred. Second, the style of the delivery of the explanation, or how the explanation is delivered, can also reduce customer dissatisfaction. Style includes the personal characteristics of the explanation givers, including their credibility and sincerity. Explanations perceived by customers as honest, sincere and not manipulative are generally the most effective.

Treat Customers Fairly

In responding quickly, it is also critical to treat each customer fairly. Customers expect to be treated fairly in terms of the outcome they receive, the process by which the service recovery takes place, and the interpersonal treatment received from employees attempting to address the service failure. Acknowledging a problem has occurred, apologizing for the inconvenience, and putting effort into resolving the issue are generally perceived by customers as fair treatment. In the section titled 'Customers' recovery expectations', we discussed examples, strategies and results of research that focused on fairness in service recovery. Here we remind you that fair treatment is an essential component of an effective service recovery strategy.

Cultivate Relationships with Customers

In Chapter 7, we discussed the importance of developing long-term relationships with customers. One additional benefit of relationship marketing is that, if the firm fails in service delivery, those customers who have a strong relationship with the firm are often more forgiving of service failures and more open to the firm's service recovery efforts. Research suggests that strong customer–firm relationships can help shield the firm from the negative effects of failures on customer satisfaction.[45] To illustrate: one study demonstrated that the presence of rapport between customers and employees provided several service recovery benefits, including increased post-failure satisfaction, increased loyalty intentions and decreased negative word-of-mouth communication.[46] Another study found that customers who expect the relationship to continue also tend to have lower service recovery expectations and may demand less immediate compensation for a failure, because they consider the balance of equity across a longer time horizon.[47] Thus, cultivation of strong customer relationships can provide an important buffer to service firms when failures occur.

Learn From Recovery Experiences

Problem-resolution situations are more than just opportunities to fix flawed services and strengthen ties with customers. 'They are also a valuable – but frequently ignored or underutilized – source of diagnostic, prescriptive information for improving customer service.'[48] By tracking service recovery efforts and solutions, managers can often learn about systematic problems in the delivery system that need fixing. By conducting root-cause analysis, firms can identify the sources of the problems and modify processes, sometimes eliminating almost completely the need for recovery.

⭐ SERVICE SPOTLIGHT

At Ritz-Carlton Hotels, all employees carry with them at all times service recovery forms called 'instant action forms', so that they can immediately record service failures and suggest actions to address them. Each individual employee 'owns' any complaint that he or she receives and is responsible for seeing that service recovery occurs. For example, if a maintenance employee hears a complaint from a customer while in the middle of fixing a light in the hotel corridor, he or she owns that complaint and must be sure that it is handled appropriately by the hotel before returning to the task at hand.

In turn, the employees report to management the sources of service failure and the remedies. This information is then entered into the customer database and analysed for patterns and systemic service issues that need to be fixed. If common themes are observed across a number of failure situations, changes are made to service processes or attributes. In addition, the information is entered into the customer's personal data file so when that customer stays at a Ritz-Carlton again (no matter at which hotel), employees are made aware of the prior experience, ensuring that it does not happen again for that particular customer.

Learn from Lost Customers

Another key component of an effective service recovery strategy is to learn from the customers who defect or decide to leave. Formal market research to discover the reasons customers have left can assist in preventing service failures in the future. This type of research is difficult, even painful for companies, however. No one really likes to examine their failures. Yet such examination is essential for preventing the same mistakes and losing more customers in the future.[49]

As presented in Chapter 6, lost customer research typically involves in-depth probing of customers to determine their true reasons for leaving. This information is most effectively obtained by in-depth interviews administered by skilled interviewers who truly understand the business. It may be best to have this type of research done by senior people in the company, particularly in business-to-business contexts in which customers are large and the impact of even one lost customer is great. This type of in-depth analysis often requires a series of 'why' questions or 'tell me more about that' prompts to get at the actual reason for the customer's defection.[50]

In conducting this kind of research, a firm must focus on important or profitable customers who have left – not just everyone who has dropped the company. An insurance company in Australia once began research to learn about their lost customers, only to find that the customers they were losing tended to be their least profitable customers anyway. They quickly determined that in-depth research on how to keep these unprofitable customers would not be a good investment!

Act Quickly Before Being Forced to Do so through Legislation

If an industry or large organization is not seen to be responding to the complaints of customers, national or European governmental bodies may step in and impose regulations and legislation to ensure the protection of the consumer. Many utilities, such as water, gas, electricity, telephone and broadcasting, are controlled by bodies who regulate prices and issue guidelines for service delivery. Another example is the airline industry, where the European Union introduced legislation to protect air passenger rights with regard to flight cancellations and delays. Air passengers are entitled to the following compensation in the case of arrivals delayed by over three hours:

€250 (≈ £197) for flights of up to 1,500 km
€400 (≈ £315) for flights between 1,500 km and 3,500 km
€400 (≈ £315) for all intra-community flights of more than 1,500 km
€600 (≈ £473) for flights over 3,500 km

Airlines have to pay compensation on this scale for flights that are delayed by more than three hours. Passengers are also compensated for late cancellation of their flight and should receive assistance in the event of long delays. There is therefore an incentive to address problems before the cost of addressing the issue increases as a result of having to comply with externally imposed regulations.

Service Guarantees

A guarantee is a particular type of recovery tool. In a business context, a guarantee is a pledge or assurance that a product offered by a firm will perform as promised and, if not, then some form of reparation will be undertaken by the firm. Although guarantees are relatively common for manufactured products, they have only recently been used for services. Traditionally, many people believed that services simply could not be guaranteed given their intangible and variable nature. What would be guaranteed? With a product, the customer is guaranteed that it will perform as promised and, if not, that it can be returned. With services, it is generally not possible to take returns or to 'undo' what has been performed. Scepticism about service guarantees is being dispelled, however, as more and more companies find they can guarantee their services and that there are tremendous benefits for doing so.

Companies are finding that effective service guarantees can complement the company's service recovery strategy – serving as one tool to help accomplish the service recovery strategies.

Benefits of Service Guarantees

'Service organizations, in particular, are beginning to recognize that guarantees can serve not only as a marketing tool but as a means for defining, cultivating, and maintaining quality throughout an organization.'[51] The benefits to the company of an effective service guarantee are numerous:[52]

- *A good guarantee forces the company to focus on its customers.* To develop a meaningful guarantee, the company must know what is important to its customers – what they expect and value. In many cases 'satisfaction' is guaranteed, but in order for the guarantee to work effectively, the company must clearly understand what satisfaction means for its customers (what they value and expect).
- *An effective guarantee sets clear standards for the organization.* It prompts the company to define clearly what it expects of its employees and to communicate that expectation to them. The guarantee gives employees service-oriented goals that can quickly align employee behaviours around customer strategies.

★ SERVICE SPOTLIGHT

Lands' End, the clothing retailer, publicizes its customer service guarantee on its website, stating:

> *In complete contrast to today's throwaway culture, quality counts for everything at Lands' End. We take great pride in the design and manufacture of our products to ensure their longevity and, ultimately, your satisfaction. So that you can be assured of our commitment to this, everything we sell is Quality. Guaranteed. No ifs, no buts, no problem.*

Simply put, if you're not 100 per cent happy with a purchase, you can return it at any time for an exchange or refund.

This lets employees know exactly what they should do if a customer complains. It is also clear to employees that making it right for the customer is an important company goal.

Source: see **www.landsend.co.uk** or **www.landsend.de.**

- *A good guarantee generates immediate and relevant feedback from customers.* It provides an incentive for customers to complain, thereby providing more representative feedback to the company than simply relying on the relatively few customers who typically voice their concerns. The guarantee communicates to customers that they have the right to complain.
- *When the guarantee is invoked there is an instant opportunity to recover,* thus satisfying the customer and helping customer retention.
- *Information generated through the guarantee can be tracked and integrated into continuous improvement efforts.* A feedback link between customers and service operations decisions can be strengthened through the guarantee.
- *Studies of the impact of service guarantees suggest that employee morale and loyalty can be enhanced as a result.* A guarantee generates pride among employees. Through feedback from the guarantee, improvements can be made in the service that benefit customers and, indirectly, employees.
- *For customers, the guarantee reduces their sense of risk* and builds confidence in the organization. Because services are intangible and often highly personal or ego-involving, customers seek information and cues that will help reduce their sense of uncertainty. Guarantees have been shown to reduce risk and increase positive evaluation of the service prior to purchase.[53]

The bottom line for the company is that an effective guarantee can affect profitability through building customer awareness and loyalty, through positive word of mouth, and through reduction in costs as service improvements are made and service recovery expenses are reduced. Indirectly, the guarantee can reduce costs of employee turnover through creating a more positive service culture.

Types of Service Guarantees

Satisfaction versus Service Attribute Guarantees

Service guarantees can be *unconditional satisfaction guarantees* or *service attribute guarantees*. Radisson hotels operate the 100 per cent guest satisfaction guarantee. That is, if a customer complains, they will respond speedily. If the guest remains disappointed, any staff member can evoke the 100 per cent Guest Satisfaction Guarantee, and that guest will not have to pay for their room or the service in question.

Radisson's guarantee is an unconditional satisfaction guarantee. Travelodge and Hotel ibis offer similar types of guarantee.

SERVICE SPOTLIGHT

Hotel ibis, the budget hotel chain owned by Accor, have a commitment through all of their activities to guarantee the perfect stay.

Hotel ibis demonstrate their confidence in delivering on this commitment by operating the '15-Minute Promise'. If a customer doesn't get what they expected, the hotel has 15 minutes to set it right or the specific service will be provided free of charge to the guest.

In other cases, firms offer guarantees for particular aspects of the service that are important to customers. Tesco has developed a 'One in Front' policy, which ensures that each customer should have no more than one person ahead of him or her in the checkout queue. If they do, another checkout will be opened. Pizza Hut guarantees delivery to the table in 20 minutes or the pizza is free. In both cases, the companies have guaranteed elements of the service that they know are important to customers.

External Versus Internal Guarantees

Interestingly, guarantees do not have to be just for external customers. Some companies are finding that internal service guarantees – one part of the organization guaranteeing its services to others – are effective ways of aligning internal service operations. For example, the housekeeping supplies department at Embassy Suites guarantees the housekeeping staff, its internal customer, that they can get supplies on the day they requested them. If not, the supply department pays approximately 4 euros to the housekeeper. At one direct-mail firm, the sales force guarantees to give the production department all the specifications needed to provide service to the external customer, or the offending salesperson will take the production department to lunch, will sing a song at their next department meeting, or will personally input all the specifications into the computer.[54]

Characteristics of Effective Guarantees

No matter the type of guarantee, certain characteristics make some guarantees more effective than others. These characteristics are as follows: [55]

- *Unconditional.* The guarantee should be unconditional – no strings attached. Some guarantees can appear as if they were written by the legal department (they often are), with all kinds of restrictions, proof required and limitations. Such guarantees are generally not effective.

- *Meaningful.* Guaranteeing what is obvious or expected is not meaningful to customers. For example, a water delivery company offered a guarantee to deliver water on the day promised, or a free container of water would be provided next time. In that industry, delivery on the day scheduled was an expectation nearly always met by every competitor – thus the guarantee was not meaningful to the customer. It was a bit like guaranteeing four wheels on a car! The payout should also be meaningful. Customers expect to be reimbursed in a manner that fully compensates them for their dissatisfaction, their time and for the inconvenience involved.

- *Easy to understand.* The guarantee should communicate clearly to both customers and employees. Sometimes the wording of a guarantee is confusing, the language is verbose, or the guarantee contains so many restrictions and conditions that neither customers nor employees are certain what is being guaranteed.

- *Easy to invoke.* The guarantee should be easy to invoke. Requiring customers to write a letter and/or provide documented proof of service failure are common pitfalls that make invoking the guarantee time-consuming and not worth it to the customer, particularly if the monetary value of the service is relatively low.

When to Use (or Not Use) a Guarantee

Service guarantees are not appropriate for every company and certainly not in every service situation. A guarantee is probably *not* the right strategy when:

- *Existing service quality in the company is poor.* Before instituting a guarantee, the company should fix any significant quality problems. Although a guarantee will certainly draw attention to these failures and the poor quality of the service, the costs of implementing it could easily outweigh any benefits. These costs include actual monetary payouts to customers for poor service as well as the costs associated with customer goodwill.

- *A guarantee does not fit the company's image.* If the company already has a reputation for very high quality, and in fact implicitly guarantees its service, then a formal guarantee is most likely unnecessary. For example, if Ritz-Carlton Hotels were to offer an explicit guarantee, it could potentially confuse customers who already expect the highest quality, implicitly guaranteed, from this high-end hotel chain. Research suggests that the benefits of offering a guarantee for a high-end hotel like the Ritz-Carlton may be significantly less than the benefits that a hotel of lesser standing would enjoy, and in fact the benefits might not be justified by the costs.[56]

- *Service quality is truly uncontrollable.* Uncontrollable service quality is often an excuse for not employing a guarantee, but firms encounter few situations in which service quality is truly uncontrollable. Here are a couple of examples to illustrate such situations. If success depends in large part on the participants' own effort, it would not be good practice for a training organization to guarantee that all participants will pass a particular examination on completion of the training course. The company could, however, guarantee satisfaction with the training or particular aspects of the training process. Similarly, a ferry company operating in the Western Isles of Scotland in the winter would probably not guarantee on-time departure because of the unpredictability and uncontrollability of the weather.

- *Potential exists for customer abuse of the guarantee.* Fear of opportunistic customer behaviour, including customer cheating or fraudulent invocation of service guarantees, is a common reason that firms hesitate to offer guarantees.[57] For example, at one large pizza chain, students occasionally 'cheated' the company by invoking the service guarantee without cause in order to receive free food.[58] In those situations in which abuse of the service guarantee can easily occur, firms should carefully consider the consequences of offering a guarantee. A recent study found that guarantees are more likely to be abused when offered in situations in which a large percentage of customers are not regular (repeat) customers.[59] In general, customer abuse of service guarantees is fairly minimal and not at all widespread.[60]

- *Costs of the guarantee outweigh the benefits.* As it would with any quality investment, the company will want to carefully calculate expected costs (payouts for failures and costs of making improvements) against anticipated benefits (customer loyalty, quality improvements, attraction of new customers, word-of-mouth advertising).
- *Customers perceive little risk in the service.* Guarantees are usually most effective when customers are uncertain about the company and/or the quality of its services. The guarantee can allay uncertainties and help reduce risk.[61] If customers perceive little risk, if the service is relatively inexpensive with lots of potential alternative providers, and if quality is relatively invariable, then a guarantee will likely produce little effectiveness for the company, other than perhaps delivering some promotional value.
- *Customers perceive little variability in service quality among competitors.* Some industries exhibit extreme variability in quality among competitors. In these cases a guarantee may be quite effective, particularly for the first company to offer one. Guarantees may also be effective in industries in which quality is perceived to be low overall across competitors. The first firm with a guarantee can often distinguish itself from competitors. A study of guarantees offered by several service firms in Singapore found that those companies which were unique in their industry in offering a guarantee attributed more of their success to having one than did companies in industries in which guarantees were more common.[62]

Summary

This chapter focused on the importance of an effective service recovery strategy for retaining customers and increasing positive word-of-mouth communication. Another major benefit of an effective service recovery strategy is that the information it provides can be useful for service improvement. The potential downsides of poor service recovery are tremendous – negative word of mouth, lost customers and declining business when quality issues are not addressed.

You learned how customers respond to service failures and why some complain while others do not. You learned that customers who complain expect to be treated fairly – not just in terms of the actual outcome or compensation they receive, but also in terms of the procedures that are used and how they are treated interpersonally. We pointed out that there is tremendous room for improvement in service recovery effectiveness across firms and industries.

The second half of the chapter focused on specific strategies that firms use for service recovery: (1) making the service fail-safe, or doing it right the first time, (2) encouraging and tracking complaints, (3) acting quickly, (4) providing adequate explanations, (5) treating customers fairly, (6) cultivating relationships with customers, (7) learning from recovery experiences, (8) learning from lost customers. To these, we added enacting recovery mechanisms before regulation imposes them.

The chapter ended with a discussion of service guarantees as a tool many firms use to build a foundation for service recovery. You learned the benefits of service guarantees, the elements of a good guarantee, and the pros and cons of using guarantees under various circumstances.

Key Concepts

Customer complaint actions	324	Lost customer research	335
Empowerment	335	Outcome justice	327
Fairness	327	Procedural justice	327
Interactional justice	327	Recovery expectations	326

Service failure	320	Service switching	330
Service guarantees	338	Types of complainers	325
Service recovery	320	Web-based consumer opinion platforms	324
Service recovery paradox	322		

Exercises

1   Write a letter of complaint (or voice your complaint in person) to a service organization from which you have experienced less than desirable service. What do you expect the organization to do to recover? (Later, report to the class the results of your complaint, whether you were satisfied with the recovery, what could/should have been done differently and whether you will continue using the service.)

2   Interview five people about their service recovery experiences as customers. What happened and what did they expect the firm to do? Were they treated fairly based on the definition of recovery fairness presented in this chapter? Will they give the company their custom in the future?

3   Interview a manager about the service recovery strategies used in his or her firm. Use the strategies shown in Figure 15.5 to frame your questions.

4   Reread the service spotlight relating to BT page 336. Visit BT's website for dealing with a broadband problem (https://www.bt.com/help/home/broadband). Review what the company is currently doing to help its customers solve their own problems. Compare BT's initiatives with the self-service efforts of another service provider of your choice.

5   Choose a service you are familiar with. Explain what it offers and develop a good service guarantee for it. Discuss why your guarantee is a good one, and list the benefits to the company of implementing it.

Discussion Questions

1   Why is it important for a service firm to have a strong recovery strategy? Think of a time when you received less than desirable service from a particular service organization. Was any effort made to recover? What should/could have been done differently? Do you still buy services from the organization? Why or why not? Did you tell others about your experience?

2   Discuss the benefits to a company of having an effective service recovery strategy. Describe an instance in which you experienced (or delivered as an employee) an effective service recovery. In what ways did the company benefit in this particular situation?

3   For a particular service, identify examples of unfairness in outcomes, procedures and interactions.

4   Explain the recovery paradox, and discuss its implications for a service firm manager.

5   Discuss the types of actions that customers can take in response to a service failure. Of the four types of complainer described in this chapter, which one are you? Why? As a manager, would you want to encourage your customers to be voicers? If so, how?

6   Explain the logic behind these two quotes: 'a complaint is a gift' and 'the customer who complains is your friend'.

7   Choose a firm you are familiar with. Describe how you would design an ideal service recovery strategy for that organization.

8   What are the benefits to the company of an effective service guarantee? Should every service organization have one?

9   Research and describe three service guarantees that are currently offered by companies or organizations (other than the ones already described in this chapter). Are your examples good guarantees or poor guarantees based on the criteria presented in this chapter?

10   What is the value of undertaking research with lost customers? Suggest ways in which this research could be done.

Further Reading

Cambra-Fierro, J., Melero-Polo, I. and Sese, J. (2015). Does the nature of the relationship really matter? An analysis of the roles of loyalty and involvement in service recovery processes. *Service Business*, 9(2), 297–320.

De Matos, C.A., Henrique, J.L. and Rossi, C.A.V. (2007). Service recovery paradox: A meta-analysis. *Journal of Service Research* 10 (August), 60–77.

Edvardsson, B., Tronvoll, B. and Höykinpuro, R. (2011). Complex service recovery processes: How to avoid triple deviation. *Managing Service Quality: An International Journal*, 21(4), 331–49.

Harrison-Walker, L.J. (2019). The critical role of customer forgiveness in successful service recovery. *Journal of Business Research*, 95, 376–91.

Michel, S. and Meuter, M.L. (2008). The service recovery paradox: True but overrated? *International Journal of Service Industry Management*, 19(4), 441–57.

Umashankar, N., Ward, M.K. and Dahl, D.W. (2017). The benefit of becoming friends: Complaining after service failures leads customers with strong ties to increase loyalty. *Journal of Marketing*, 81(6), 79–98.

Van Vaerenbergh, Y. and Orsingher, C. (2016). Service recovery: An integrative framework and research agenda. *Academy of Management Perspectives*, 30(3), 328–46.

Part 6
Managing Service Promises

Chapter 16 Managing External and Internal Communications

Chapter 17 Pricing of Services

The fourth provider gap illustrates the difference between service delivery and the service provider's external communications. Promises made by a service company through its media advertising, online activity and other communications may potentially raise customer expectations that serve as the standard against which customers assess service quality. Broken promises can occur for many reasons: ineffective marketing communications, over-promising in advertising or personal selling, inadequate coordination between operations and marketing, and differences in policies and procedures across service outlets.

In service companies, a fit between communications about service and actual service delivery is necessary, as shown in the figure below. Chapter 16 is devoted to the topic of managing external and internal communications – careful integration and organization of all of a service organization's external and internal communications channels. The chapter describes why this communication is necessary and how companies can do it well.

Chapter 17 deals with another issue related to managing promises, the pricing of services. In packaged goods (and even in durable goods), many customers possess enough price knowledge before purchase to be able to judge whether a price is fair or in line with competition. With services, customers often have no internal reference point for prices before purchase and consumption.

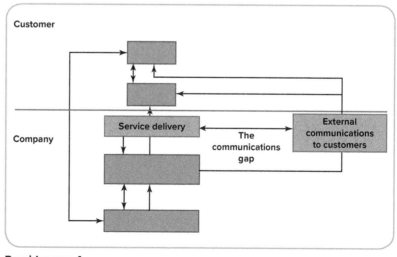

Provider gap 4

Chapter 16

Managing External and Internal Communications

Chapter Outline

The Need for Coordination in Online and Offline Marketing Communication Channels   348
Key Service Communication Challenges   350
Five Categories of Strategy to Overcome Communication Challenges   353
Summary and Key Concepts   366
Exercises   367
Discussion Questions   367
Further Reading   368

Learning Objectives

This chapter's objectives are to:

1 Discuss the key reasons for service communication challenges.
2 Introduce the concept of integrated service marketing communications.
3 Present four ways to integrate online and offline marketing communications in service organizations.
4 Present specific strategies for addressing service intangibility, managing service promises, managing customer expectations, educating customers and managing internal marketing communications.

Opening Example
Santander's Cycle Partnership

Santander UK has been awarded the title sponsorship of London's self-service bike sharing scheme for a seven-year period (2015–2022). The 11,500 bikes, 748 docking stations, and 32 service vehicles used in the scheme have been branded with the Santander Cycles name and red colour, down to the staff uniforms and membership keys. Users log more than 10 million journeys across London on the bicycles each year. The £43.75 m deal is the largest public-sector sponsorship in the world.

Source: ©LMWH/Shutterstock

The sponsorship is supported with the launch of a branded mobile phone app that enables Santander Cycles users to unlock a bike remotely and share journey information. Santander staff, known as 'cycle champions', are on call in the bank's London branches to offer advice to those using the bikes for the first time. Cyclists who have a current account with Santander also receive cashback on every journey.

The sponsorship aims to bring Santander's brand values to life. It is designed to encourage interactions between people and to embody the bank's motto 'simple, personal and fair': *simple* through events and cycle champions, *personal* through the app, and *fair* through the cashback scheme. In addition to the London scheme, Santander UK is also sponsoring a number of cycling events throughout the UK.

In 2015, television advertisements for a Santander credit card featured McLaren Honda driver Jenson Button riding a Santander Cycle to promote the new cashback offer on the card. Major public relations activity was undertaken at the launch of the new sponsorship, ensuring significant coverage over all media types.

Social media (Facebook and Twitter) are integrated in the PR for the sponsorship. On 1 April 2015, the bank even tweeted its own April Fools' joke with photographs of the first Santander Cycle-through bank. Within two months of launch, the Santander Cycles twitter feed had over 36,000 followers and around 4,000 tweets.

In 2016 and 2017, Santander expanded their sponsorship of the cycle scheme into other parts of the UK, including Milton Keynes and Swansea.

However, if Santander UK truly want to demonstrate commitment to their brand positioning (and for any integrated marketing communication campaign to work), it is important that the service activities of the organization also match the service promise that it is trying to communicate.

Source: Adapted from Parsons, R. (2015) 'Santander bike deal puts engagement first', Marketing Week, 5 March, page 6.

The message at the end of this Santander example is clear: a major cause of poorly perceived service is the difference between what a firm promises about a service and what it actually delivers. Customer expectations are shaped by both uncontrollable and company-controlled factors. Word-of-mouth communication, social media, publicity, customer generated media, customer experiences with other service providers and customer needs are key factors that influence customer expectations; they are rarely controllable by the firm. Controllable factors, such as company advertising, corporate websites, mobile apps, personal selling and promises made by service personnel also influence customer expectations. In this chapter we discuss both types of communication, but focus more heavily on the controllable factors as the ones that can be more directly influenced by the company. Accurate, coordinated and appropriate company communication – advertising, websites, social media, personal selling and other communication channels that do not over-promise or misrepresent – is essential to delivering services that customers perceive as high in quality.

Because company communications about services promise what people will do, and because people's behaviour cannot be standardized like physical goods produced by machines, the potential for a mismatch between what is communicated and perceptions of actual service delivery (provider gap 4, the communications gap) is high. By coordinating communication within and outside the organization, companies can minimize the size of this gap.

The Need for Coordination in Online and Offline Marketing Communication Channels

Marketing communication is more complex today than it used to be. In the past, customers received marketing information about goods and services from a limited number of sources, usually mass-communication ones such as television and newspapers. With a limited number of sources, marketers could easily convey a uniform brand image and coordinate promises. By contrast, today's consumers of both goods and services receive communications from a far richer variety of advertising vehicles – websites, direct mail, and interactive communication tools such as virtual communities (Facebook, LinkedIn, Twitter, YouTube, etc.), blogs, mobile phone apps, viral marketing and gaming.

In addition, consumers of services also receive additional communication from servicescapes, customer service departments and everyday service encounters with employees. These service interactions add to the variety, volume and complexity of information that a customer receives. While a company cannot control outside sources, ensuring that messages from all company sources provide a consistent message about the service brand is a major challenge for marketers of services.

Any company that disseminates information through multiple channels needs to be certain that customers receive unified messages and promises. These channels include not only marketing communication messages that flow directly from the company but also personal messages that employees send to customers. Figure 16.1 shows an enhanced version of the services marketing triangle that we presented in Chapter 1, emphasizing that the customer of services is the target of two types of communication. First, external marketing communication includes traditional channels such as advertising, corporate websites,

Figure 16.1   Communications and the services marketing triangle

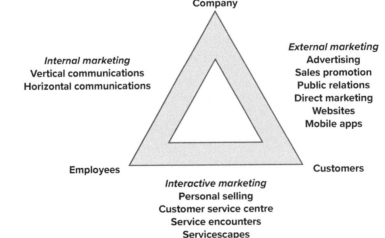

Source: Adapted from P. Kotler, *Marketing Management: Analysis, Planning, Implementation, and Control,* 9th edn, © 1997.

sales promotion and public relations. Second, interactive marketing communication involves the messages that employees give to customers through such channels as personal selling, customer service interactions, service encounter interactions and servicescapes (discussed in Chapter 10). A service company must ensure that these interactive messages remain consistent, both among themselves and with those sent through external communications. To do so, the third side of the triangle, internal marketing communications, must be managed so that information from the company to employees is accurate, complete and consistent with what customers are hearing or seeing.

The need for integrated marketing campaigns is evident in both business-to-business situations and business-to-consumer instances. In business-to-business situations, the problem often comes about because multiple parts of a service organization deal with a client and do not communicate well internally. For example, consider a large client of a major accountancy firm which provides it with audit services, taxation advice and management consultancy services. If the client organization deals with someone different for each service, the accountancy firm needs to – but may not – coordinate internally to ensure that they are sending the customer consistent messages. Not only that, but each internal division may have its own promotional campaign with different promises and messages. Think of an example from your own experience that may illustrate what happens when services marketing communications are not integrated. Have you ever seen an advertisement for a service, such as a special sandwich offer from a fast-food chain, then gone to your local outlet and found it is not available there? Did the employee behind the counter provide a reason for the sandwich offer not being available? Did he or she even realize that it was advertised for sale in all locations? This may be due to corporate advertising being changed frequently and quickly to meet competitive offerings, but the branch training in the new offerings is failing to keep pace with the changes in advertising. As a result, customers come in expecting new offerings to be available, and employees are embarrassed because they have not been informed.

This example demonstrates one of the main reasons that integrated marketing communications have not been the norm in many companies. All too often, various parts of the company are responsible for different aspects of communication. The sales department develops and executes sales communication. The marketing department prepares and disseminates advertising. A public relations firm is responsible for publicity. Functional specialists handle sales promotions, direct marketing, company websites and social media. The human resources department trains front-line employees for service interactions, and still another area is responsible for the customer service department. Rarely is one person responsible for the overall communications strategy in a company, and all too often people responsible for the different communication components do not coordinate their efforts.

Today, however, more companies are adopting the concept of integrated marketing communications (IMC), where the company carefully integrates and organizes all of its external communications channels. As a marketing executive explained it,

> *Integrated marketing communications build a strong brand identity in the marketplace by tying together and reinforcing all your images and messages. IMC means that all your corporate messages, positioning and images, and identity are coordinated across all venues. It means that your PR materials say the same things as your direct mail campaign, and your advertising has the same 'look and feel' as your website.*[1]

In this chapter we propose that a more complex type of integrated marketing communication is needed for services than for goods. External communications channels must be coordinated, as with physical goods, but both external communications and internal communication channels must be integrated to create consistent service promises. To do that, internal marketing communications channels must be managed so that employees and the company are in agreement about what is communicated to the customer. We call this more complicated version of IMC integrated services marketing communications (ISMC). ISMC requires that everyone involved with communication clearly understand both the company's marketing strategy and its promises to consumers.

Key Service Communication Challenges

Discrepancies between what is communicated about a service and what a customer receives – or perceives that they receive – can powerfully affect consumer evaluations of service quality. The main communication challenges include: (1) overcoming service intangibility, (2) management of service promises, (3) management of customer expectations, (4) educating customers and (5) achieving internal alignment. In this chapter, we first describe the challenges stemming from those factors and then detail strategies that firms have found useful in dealing with them.

Overcoming Service Intangibility

Because services are performances rather than objects, their essence and benefits are difficult to communicate to customers. Intangibility makes marketing communication for services more challenging for both marketers and consumers. The intangible nature of services creates problems for consumers both before and after purchase. Before buying services, consumers can have difficulty understanding what they will be buying. During purchase, consumers often cannot clearly see the differences among services. After purchase, consumers have trouble evaluating their service experiences.

The difficulties associated with intangibility can be divided into five properties, each of which has implications for services marketing communication. Intangibility involves incorporeal existence, abstractness, generality, non-searchability, and mental impalpability.[2]

- *Incorporeal existence.* The service product does not occupy physical space. Although the delivery mechanism may use facilities that occupy space (such as a dry-cleaning shop), the service itself (dry cleaning) does not. The implication is that showing the service is difficult, if not impossible.
- *Abstractness.* Service benefits such as financial security, fun, or health do not correspond directly with objects, making them difficult to visualize and understand. When businesses need consulting, for example, they often do not know where to begin because the concept is so vague that they do not understand the specific goals and processes, or cannot articulate what deliverables they are seeking.
- *Generality* refers to a class of things, persons, events, or properties, whereas *specificity* refers to particular objects, people, or events. Many service and service promises are described in generalities (wonderful experience, superior education, completely satisfied customers), making them difficult to differentiate from those of competitors.
- *Non-searchability.* Because service is a performance, it often cannot be previewed or inspected in advance of purchase. If we are interested in finding a doctor, a heating repair firm, a personal trainer, or virtually any service, we cannot search the options as easily as we can search the shelves in a grocery store. Considerably more effort must be expended, and what we find may not be useful. For example, if a customer needs a plumber, the information contained in a source such as the Internet does not adequately discriminate among the choices. As we discussed in Chapter 3, non-searchability is particularly true of services that are classified as either experience or credence services.
- *Mental impalpability.* Services are often complex, multidimensional, and difficult to grasp mentally. When customers have not had prior exposure, familiarity or knowledge, services are difficult to interpret. You may have experienced this when buying car insurance for the first time.

These five aspects of service intangibility make customers feel more uncertain about their purchases, and evidence indicates that the greater the risk that customers perceive in purchasing services, the more actively they will seek and rely on online or offline word-of-mouth communications to guide their choices.[3] Word of mouth can be a very convincing source of information about services for consumers, but it is not under the control of the service provider.

⭐ **SERVICE SPOTLIGHT**

Thorpe Park, a theme park in England, has seats on five big roller coasters to sell. Although the park can put out advertisements showing people enjoying its attractions, they don't really get across the emotional thrill of the rides. Thorpe Park has honed in on a social media strategy to leverage user-generated content, such as the photos that visitors take and post on Instagram to tell of their personal experience in the park. The best pictures are recognized for awards each week. Campaigns such as 'Happy Height Day', which the park runs in association with Mumsnet, a social media channel for parents, celebrate when children reach 1.4 metres, which is the minimum height for the big rides. Another social media presence creates excitement: the five vlogger videos (videos made by a video blogger) posted on YouTube relating to the Halloween 'Fright Nights'. All of these are aimed at communicating the excitement and emotions associated with the big thrill rides.

Management of Service Promises

A serious problem occurs when companies fail to manage service marketing communications – the vows made by salespeople, advertising and service personnel – and service falls short of what is promised. This sometimes occurs because the part of the company making the promise lacks the information necessary to make accurate statements. For example, salespeople often sell services, particularly new business services, before their actual availability and without having an exact date of when they will be ready for market. Demand and supply variations make service provision possible at some times, improbable at others and, generally, difficult to predict. The traditional functional structure of many companies, with their marketing and sales, operations, production, human resources, and finance departments (often called silos), also makes communication about promises and delivery difficult internally.

Management of Customer Expectations

Appropriate and accurate communication about services is the responsibility of both marketing and operations. Marketing must accurately (if compellingly) reflect what happens in actual service encounters; operations must deliver what is promised in communications. For example, when a management consulting firm introduces a new offering, the marketing and sales departments must make the offering appealing enough to be viewed as superior to competing services. In promoting and differentiating the service, however, the company cannot afford to raise expectations above the level at which its consultants can consistently perform. If advertising, websites, personal selling or any other external communication sets up unrealistic expectations, customers will be disappointed by the actual encounters.

Because of increasing deregulation and intensifying competition in the services sector, many service firms feel pressure to acquire new business and to meet or beat competition. To accomplish these ends, service firms often over-promise in selling, advertising and other company communications. In the airline industry, advertising is a constant battlefield of competing offers and price reductions to gain the patronage of customers. The greater the extent to which a service firm feels pressured to generate new customers, and perceives that the industry norm is to over-promise ('everyone else in our industry over-promises'), the greater is the firm's propensity to over-promise.

If advertising shows a smiling young worker at the counter in a Carrefour commercial, the customer expects that, at least most of the time, there will be a smiling young worker in the local Carrefour. If a brochure claims that a customer's wake-up call will always be on time at an ibis Hotel, the customer expects no mistakes. Raising expectations to unrealistic levels may lead to more initial business but invariably fosters customer disappointment and discourages repeat business.

Many product and service companies also find themselves in the position of having to actively manage customer expectations downward – to tell customers that service previously provided will be discontinued or available only at a higher price. Airlines change flight schedules and introduce charges for food. Credit card companies adjust their interest rates and change their value-added services. Hotels close their leisure facilities for refurbishment. In these situations – perhaps more than any others – the need to manage customer expectations is critical.

Educating Customers

Service companies must educate their customers. If customers are unclear about how the service will be provided, what their role in delivery involves, and how to evaluate services they have never used before, they will be disappointed. When this happens, customers will hold the service company responsible, not themselves. Errors or problems in service – even when they are 'caused' by the customer – still lead customers to defect. For this reason the firm must assume responsibility for educating customers.

For services high in credence properties – expert services that are difficult for customers to evaluate even after they have received the services – many customers do not know the criteria by which they should judge the service. For high-involvement services, such as long-term dental treatment or purchase of a first home, customers are also unlikely to comprehend and anticipate the service process. First-time home buyers rarely understand the complex set of services (surveys, conveyancing, insurance) and processes (securing a mortgage, offers and counteroffers) that will be involved in their purchases. Professionals and other providers of high-involvement services often forget that customers may be novices who must be educated about each step in the process. They assume that giving an overview at the start of the service, or providing a manual or a set of instructions, will equip the customer. Unfortunately these steps are rarely sufficient, and customers defect because they can neither understand the process nor appreciate the value received from the service.

A final condition under which **customer education** can be beneficial involves services in which demand and supply are not synchronized, as discussed in Chapter 14. If the customer is not informed about likely peaks and troughs in demand, service overloads and failures, not to mention underutilized capacity, defections are likely to result.

Achieving Internal Alignment

Multiple functions in the organization, such as marketing and operations, must be coordinated to achieve the goal of service provision. Because service advertising and personal selling promise what *people* do, frequent and effective communication across functions within the organization – horizontal communication – is critical. If internal communication is poor, perceived service quality is at risk. If company advertising and other promises are developed without input from operations, contact personnel may not be able to deliver service that matches the image portrayed in marketing efforts.

Not all service organizations advertise, but all need coordination or integration across departments or functions to deliver quality service. All need internal communication between the sales force and service providers. Horizontal communication also must occur between the human resource and marketing departments. To deliver excellent customer service, firms must be certain to inform and motivate employees to deliver what their customers expect. If marketing and sales personnel who understand customer expectations do not communicate this information to contact employees, the lack of knowledge of these employees will affect the quality of service that they deliver.

A final form of internal coordination central to providing service excellence is consistency in policies and procedures across departments and branches. If a service organization operates many outlets under the same name, whether franchised or company owned, customers expect similar performance across those outlets. If managers of individual branches or outlets have significant autonomy in procedures and policies, customers may not receive the same level of service quality across the branches.

Five Categories of Strategy to Overcome Communication Challenges

Figure 16.2 shows the major approaches to overcome the service communication challenges that we just described. The goal is to deliver service that is greater than, or equal to, promises made. Each of these approaches will be discussed in the next five sections.

Figure 16.2   Five major approaches to overcome service communication challenges

Address Service Intangibility

Approaches to address service intangibility include advertising and other communication strategies that clearly communicate service attributes and benefits to consumers, and strategies designed to encourage word-of-mouth and social media communication.

If service companies recognize the challenges they face due to intangibility, they can use selected strategies to compensate. In one way or another, each of the individual strategies we discuss here focuses on ways to make the message dramatic and memorable.

- *Use narratives to demonstrate the service experience.* Many services are experiential, and a uniquely effective approach to communicating them involves story-based appeals. Research has concluded that consumers with relatively low familiarity with a service category prefer appeals based on stories to appeals based on lists of service attributes. Furthermore, the relative advantage of the story is intensified when the novice consumer viewing it is in a happy mood rather than a sad one.[4] For example, young consumers needing their first home mortgage will react more positively to an advertisement that shows a couple in their situation finding a house they love and then a banker quickly finding them a mortgage than to an advertisement about interest rates.
- *Present vivid information.* Effective service marketing communication creates a strong or clear impression on the senses and produces a distinct mental picture. One way to use vivid information is to evoke

strong emotion, such as in British Airways' classic 'To Fly. To Serve' advertising campaign. Vividness can also be achieved by concrete language and dramatization.

- *Use interactive imagery.* One type of vividness involves what is called *interactive imagery*.[5] Imagery (defined as a mental event that involves the visualization of a concept or relationship) can enhance recall of names and facts about service. Interactive imagery integrates two or more items in some mutual action, resulting in improved recall. Some service companies effectively integrate their logos or symbols with an expression of what they do, such as the Legal & General Insurance company who use a multi-coloured umbrella in their logo to demonstrate that they provide protection. The logo of the international fast-food restaurant chain Nando's is a Portuguese cockerel, hinting at the origins of their cuisine and the fact that their meat dishes are all made with chicken.

- *Focus on the tangibles.*[6] Another way that advertisers can increase the effectiveness of services communications is to feature the tangibles associated with the service, such as showing a bank's marble columns or gold credit card. Showing the tangibles provides clues about the nature and quality of the service.

- *Use brand icons to make the service tangible.* How does an advertiser of services improve competitive differentiation and achieve strong brand awareness in a highly competitive market? Some service organizations use a character or brand icon to represent the company and generate brand visibility. One of the most enduring service brand icons is Ronald McDonald, the red-and-yellow clown that represents McDonald's and its children's charity, the Ronald McDonald House. McDonald's competitor, KFC, has its own mascot, Colonel Sanders. Advertising icons are even more critical in industries in which service is complex and difficult to understand. In the UK, talking dogs, horses and even meerkats are used by different insurance providers to generate brand visibility.

- *Use association, physical representation, documentation and visualization.* Berry and Clark propose four strategies of tangibilization: association, physical representation, documentation and visualization.[7] *Association* means linking the service to a tangible person, place or object, such as linking Virgin with Richard Branson. *Physical representation* means showing tangibles that are directly or indirectly part of the service, such as employees, buildings or equipment. *Documentation* means featuring objective data and factual information. *Visualization* is a vivid mental picture of a service's benefits or qualities, such as showing people on holiday having fun.

- *Feature service employees in communication.* Customer contact personnel are an important second audience for services advertising.[8] Featuring actual employees doing their jobs or explaining their services in communications is effective for both the primary audience (customers) and the secondary audience (employees) because it communicates to employees that they are important. Furthermore, when employees who perform a service well are featured in advertising, they become standards for other employees' behaviours. B&Q, the international DIY chain, has its own employees appearing in its advertisements.

- *Feature satisfied customers in the communication.* One way to generate positive word of mouth is to feature satisfied customers in the communications. Testimonials featuring actual service customers simulate personal communications between people and are thereby a credible way to communicate the benefits of service.

- *Encourage word-of-mouth communication.* Because services are usually high in experience and credence properties, people frequently turn to others for information rather than to traditional marketing channels. Services advertising and other external messages can generate word-of-mouth communication that extends the investment in paid communication and improves the credibility of the messages. Communications that generate talk because they are humorous, compelling or unique can be particularly effective. The Santander Cycle-through branch mentioned in the case study at the start of this chapter is a good example of this.

- *Leverage social media.* Online social media on sites such as Facebook, LinkedIn and Twitter are becoming very important avenues for consumers exchanging information about service providers and their personal experiences when interacting with them. Service organizations run the risk of their information and marketing function being performed by peer groups with user-generated content who ask/offer advice to customers, bypassing the company and the opportunity to either improve their services or recover from service failures. This may impact further on brand value as users revert to user-generated sources on social media and networks to ensure credibility, trustworthiness and expertise. It is clear that service companies that have a significant volume of customers actively engaged in user-generated content increasingly need a social media/user-generated content communication strategy. This is particularly important in the travel sector, where customers are on the move and service is a critical point of differentiation. Hotels are now responding to consumers' comments on Facebook pages and on review sites such as TripAdvisor. Many service organizations have set up their own community sites on Facebook where they can interact with customers and potential customers. Social media has also become mobile with the more recent growth of Twitter. Some travel companies are already active in this space – for example, see Chapter 4 opening example KLM will deal with customer complaints on Twitter in 'real time'. With the advent of more mobile tablet PCs like the iPad and high-quality cameras in mobile devices, it will become easier for customers to visually report/record service incidents/failures and comment on them.
- *Make use of video-sharing networks.* YouTube, Vimeo and other video-sharing networks provide opportunities to demonstrate a service or show people enjoying a service. They also allow the service provider to target niche audiences and show how the service applies to them. For example, the KLM YouTube Channel provides videos on destinations for travellers, behind-the-scenes videos for plane enthusiasts, videos aimed at children, music and games videos for the youth market as well as corporate responsibility spots, videos of events and advertisements. All of these can bring the service and the brand alive in the minds of the customer. Video networks can be accessed on mobiles, tablets, interactive TVs and computers, thereby increasing the opportunities for making a service more tangible.
- *Aim messages at influencers.* Improved technologies are now allowing companies to identify online influencers. These are people with more connections than others and therefore more ability to influence others about services. When identified, these individuals can be 'seeded' by giving them information about the service, inviting them to participate in special events, and otherwise encouraging them to know and communicate about a service. Many hotels offer free hotel stays to travel bloggers in return for blogs about the hotel and its facilities.

⭐ SERVICE SPOTLIGHT

Starwood Resorts has been using Instagram influencers since it first advertised on the Instagram platform in 2014. One of its campaigns involved five travel-related Instagram influencers. These influencers were used to help promote two new properties in Paris, Le Metropolitan and Le Dokhan. Each influencer would post photos and content about their experiences at the hotels, and to increase bookings, a link to LiketoKnow.it (a European e-shopping/blogging site) was included in the description. When a post was 'liked', that user would get an email from that website with booking information, or the user could book directly through the influencer's post. Starwood Resorts now has more than 500,000 followers and earned thousands more with the help of the influencers.

Source: **https://www.socialtables.com/blog/hotel-sales/influencer-marketing/.**

Manage Service Promises

In manufacturing physical goods, the departments that make promises and those that deliver them can operate independently. Goods can be fully designed and produced, and then turned over to marketing for promotion and sale. In services, however, the sales and marketing departments make promises about what other employees in the organization will fulfil. Because what employees do cannot be standardized to the same extent as physical goods, greater coordination and management of promises are required. This coordination can be accomplished by creating a strong service brand and by coordinating all of the company's marketing communications.

Creating a Strong Service Brand

Branding plays a special role in service companies:

> Strong brands enable customers to better visualize and understand intangible products. They reduce customers' perceived monetary, social, or safety risk in buying services, which are difficult to evaluate prior to purchase. Strong brands are the surrogates when the company offers no fabric to touch, no trousers to try on, no watermelons or apples to scrutinize, no automobile to test.[9]

In contrast to branding in product situations, where each individual product has its own brand, the primary brand in service is frequently the company itself. The focus of brand creation is on raising the awareness, meaning and equity of the company among key target audiences. For example, companies like KLM, Radisson, DHL and Vodafone all focus communication and information on their companies rather than individual services that the company offers. Therefore, the brand becomes the company's method of integrating marketing communication.

1. The *company's presented brand* is that part of the brand image that the company controls and disseminates through all of its activities. Advertising, the brand name itself, websites, employees, facilities and all other types of information dissemination must be coordinated and controlled.

2. The brand is also influenced by *non-controllable external brand communications* about the company over which the company has no power. This may include online review sites as well as press reports, comments from pressure groups, etc. These sources of communication are potent because they are perceived by customers to be credible and unbiased, but they can have either positive or negative effects on the service brand. McDonald's is frequently criticized in the press or by pressure groups for its environmental record or in relation to its impact on obesity.

3. *Customer experience with the company* – the actual interactions with company employees and other firm manifestations – is another element that shapes the brand and is likely to be more powerful than any marketing messages. No matter how effective and unified advertising is for a service, actual experiences disproportionately provide meaning to customers.

These three inputs lead to *brand awareness*, the customer's recall and recognition of the brand, and *brand associations*, the elements and activities that customers associate with the brand. These inputs also lead to *brand preference*, the customer's positive or negative attitudes towards the brand, and *brand loyalty*, the extent to which customers wish to maintain a relationship with the brand. These all largely emanate from customer experience, but are also shaped by the company's presented brand and word of mouth/ press comment etc. The higher and more positive each of these elements are, the stronger the brand image and the higher the *brand equity* a company has. Brand equity is the value of customer goodwill and positive attitudes that a company builds up over time. Higher brand equity is usually associated with higher sales and greater customer brand loyalty. Figure 16.3 is a service-branding model that shows the relationships among the main elements in creating a strong service brand.

Figure 16.3   A service branding model

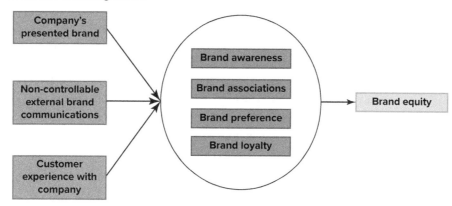

Coordinate External Communication

For any organization, one of the most important yet challenging aspects of managing brand image involves coordinating all the external communication vehicles that send information to customers. This task has become far more challenging in recent years, because a notable trend is the proliferation of new media. Not only are traditional communication vehicles such as advertising, websites, sales promotion, public relations, direct marketing and personal selling proliferating, but many forms of new media are now available to marketers. As demonstrated in the Santander campaign set out at the start of this chapter, advertising, sponsorship, use of social media, YouTube and events all add to the tools available and may increase the complexity of coordinating a common brand message across all communication channels. However, the main communication channels are as follows:

Websites are the company's own online communication to customers. A disconnect often exists between the look, feel and content of a company's website and its advertising, usually because different parts of the company (or different advertising vendors) are responsible for creating these vehicles. When websites are coordinated in theme, content and promises – as they are in DHL advertising – a company is better able to match service delivery with promises because the promises themselves are consistent. It is important that usability testing is undertaken on a website. This involves observing representative users performing tasks, such as product or information searches on a site. For a site to be successful, it must enable the user to complete a task, such as identify the opening hours of a gym, and do so in a timely and user-friendly manner. If a website is difficult to use or is unclear, people will leave and search a competitor's site.

Search engine optimization involves achieving the highest position in search engines' listing of results for a specific combination of keywords entered by search engine users. The higher a company ranks in the search engine results pages, the more visitors its website is likely to attract. To improve a website's ranking, it is important to understand how Google and other search engines compile their listing using software processes called spiders or robots to crawl around sites that are registered with that search engine. The main influencing factors are the keywords on the page and the website's metadata, including title page tags as well as links to the site from other web pages. The benefits of focusing on search engine optimization is that it has a highly targeted impact, as it puts an organization's service in front of people who are searching for that service.

Traditional advertising is any paid form of non-personal presentation and promotion of a company's offerings by an identified sponsor. Traditional advertising vehicles include television, radio, newspapers, magazines and outdoor signage. Because advertising is paid, marketers control the creative appeals, placement and timing. Internet advertising is now grabbing a bigger share of companies' advertising budgets and should be synchronized with traditional advertising vehicles. MasterCard's highly successful worldwide

'Priceless' advertising campaign lists three or four tangible items and their prices, followed by a key customer benefit that is 'priceless'. The campaign is an example of solid synchronization because it is 'extraordinarily flexible, and carries a brand message that is not only relevant globally but also adapts well to different media, different payment channels, different markets'.[10] The campaign, now seen in 96 countries and 47 languages, has generated strong brand recall and has received a number of the advertising industry's prestigious awards.

Online advertising. A major factor contributing to the success of Internet advertising is the availability of approaches that are more popular than the banner advertisement which dominated the medium for years. Banner advertisements[11] still account for the largest category of Internet advertisements, but their effectiveness as a marketing tool is being seriously questioned. Click-through rates, the most common measure of effectiveness, have dropped from 10 per cent to 0.025 per cent over the years. Analysts suggest the following reasons for the drop:

- *Banner clutter.* As spending increased, so did the number of advertisements, which reduced the novelty and created sites filled with banners that often led to no value. Just as with other advertising clutter, users learned to stop paying attention.
- *Boring banners.* Although the potential to create fun and interactive banner advertisements existed, many advertisers simply created me-too banners that were low on content and creativity.
- *Built-in banners.* Once advertisers started using animation and other colourful attention-getting devices, the advertisements became intrusive, interfering with the users' surfing stream and with the time they spent on sites. Some advertisements took so long to download that they delayed and derailed users' interactions on the web.

Advertisers had to face the fact that their hopes for banner advertisements were not being fulfilled, at least as measured simply by click-through rates. Improved advertising approaches have been developed, with the most significant being search-based advertising, or paid search advertising. In this form of advertising, which currently represents the largest share of online spending among all online advertisement formats, advertisers pay only when qualified leads are delivered to their websites. With AdWords, a pay-per-click advertising service offered by Google, advertisers buy the rights to words and terms related to their business. When a consumer searches Google using one of those keywords, the advertiser's Uniform Resource Locator (URL), along with its name and description, appears at the top of the search results. The advertiser pays only when a user clicks on the advertisement. Marketers recognize that managing their media planning and buying strategy as a whole, rather than as segregated channels, maximizes campaign effectiveness. For this reason, more and more advertisers are adding online advertising to their traditional advertising buys. Today, online advertising accounts for a small percentage of total advertising expenditures, largely because the medium is not as costly as television or print. In the future, as consumers spend more time on the web, Internet advertising will become even more important than before.

Social media advertising: Because social networks gather such a large amount of user information, social media advertising is able to target an audience more precisely than many other media channels. Facebook can not only target audiences based on location, language, age and other common demographics, it can also target people based on their interests and behaviours. The advertisements will appear on the right-hand side of a user's Facebook page. Twitter distinguishes between three kinds of Twitter ads: *Promoted Tweets* are messages that appear directly in the timelines of targeted Twitter users; *Promoted Accounts* invite targeted Twitter users to follow a brand; *Promoted Trends* give users' stories the top position on the trending topic list for 24 hours. Twitter targeting is especially valuable in reaching people based on the size and relevance of their networks.

Mobile apps: The average person has 26 mobile apps stored on his or her smartphone. These generally combine fun and social elements with rewards, discounts and ways of buying or reserving a service. They can create high visibility and build brand recognition as smartphone users check their devices many times a day. They create a direct marketing channel that potentially can build engagement and customer loyalty.

They can be as a relevant for a small coffee shop or a hair salon as they can be for a major multinational corporation. However, to be successful mobile apps need to have features that the user values, while at the same time being well branded and easy to use. It can be a way of staying closer to customers, simply by being at their fingertips at all times.

Sales promotion includes short-term incentives such as coupons, premiums, discounts and other activities that stimulate customer purchases and stretch media spending. The fast-food industry, including McDonald's, Burger King and Wendy's, offers premiums like action figures that link the chains' offerings to current movies and television shows.

Public relations covers the activities that build a favourable company image through publicity, relations with the news media and community events. Sir Richard Branson, founder of Virgin Atlantic Airways, is a master at obtaining publicity for his airline. When launching the airline, he claimed, 'I knew that the only way of competing with British Airways and the others was to get out there and use myself to promote it'.[12] In the years since the airline was launched, his publicity-winning stunts have included recording the fastest time across the Atlantic Ocean in a speedboat, flying a hot-air balloon across the Atlantic Ocean and from Japan to Canada, dressing up in everything from a stewardess's uniform to a bikini on Virgin flights, and being photographed in his bath. Sir Branson has his own online blog, Twitter feed, Facebook and Google Plus accounts to communicate his thoughts and maintain his high profile. All of these have links to the Virgin group website.

⭐ SERVICE SPOTLIGHT

IKEA, the home furniture store, sought media coverage in the UK by launching a pop-up Breakfast in Bed Café, where tables were replaced with beds and sleeping was encouraged. In this experiential activation, customers could book a slot at the IKEA Breakfast in Bed Café, either in the morning for breakfast, or in the afternoon for tea and a 'siesta'. The café was set up with IKEA furnishings and the dining room was specifically designed to resemble a homely eatery. As well as providing a breakfast menu, which comprised toast, tea, fresh juice and an array of traditional Swedish treats, the Breakfast in Bed Café also offered a 'pillow menu' to ensure optimum comfort. Once fed, guests were served sleep-inducing teas as chilled-out music filled the room and IKEA's sleep specialists gave out tips to get a great night's sleep. With these tips in mind, guests could then enjoy a power nap in one of nine beds. Despite its short run-time and so little marketing prior to the event, this activation generated a large amount of buzz, with hundreds of comments and shares, and thousands of likes on social media.

Direct marketing involves the use of mail, telephone, email and text messaging to communicate directly with specific consumers to obtain a direct response. It can be delivered in the form of a campaign for a particular service or in the form of a newsletter. Direct marketing by email has registered significant growth as the physical costs are substantially less than direct mail or telephone. However, response rates to any of these forms of direct marketing can be low unless customers have opted in to receive the service provider's newsletters and regular updates. In May 2018, the European Union launched an updated legal framework for data protection entitled the General Data Protection Regulation (GDPR) which applies across Europe (including the UK). Similar legislation exists in other parts of the world, for example Australia has the Federal Privacy Act and South Africa has the Protection of Personal Information Act. Such legislation requires every organization to ask potential recipients if they wish to opt in to receiving direct marketing material. This means that individuals are only likely to opt in if they are positively inclined towards the service brand or have an existing business relationship.

Viral marketing is the seeding of interesting content on websites, blogs or by email that people will want to see and pass on through their online networks and friends. It requires a video clip, a TV advertisement, a song or a picture that is seen as being sufficiently funny, clever or shocking to make it compulsive viewing. A good example is the video that launched the Domino's Pizza app. It translates a users' stomach rumbles into a personalized recommendation of a specific pizza to satisfy their hunger. The Tummy Translator app uses what Domino's calls 'Gastro-Acoustic-Enterology' and is designed to help drive sales as well as showing the range of options on its menu.

Personal selling is face-to-face presentation by a representative from the firm to make sales and build customer relationships. One way that personal selling and advertising are integrated in business-to-business companies is through the development of advertising materials that salespeople distribute to customers. This approach not only creates an integrated message to customers, but also keeps salespeople fully informed of the promises the company is making.

Manage Customer Expectations

Accurately promising when and how service will be delivered is one of the most important ways to close the communication gap. Among the most effective strategies to manage customer expectations are: to make realistic promises; to offer service guarantees, options and tiered-value offerings; and to communicate criteria customers can use to assess service.

Make Realistic Promises

The expectations that customers bring to the service affect their evaluations of its quality: the higher the expectation, the better the delivered service must be to be perceived as high quality. Therefore, promising reliability in advertising is appropriate only when reliability is actually delivered. It is essential for a firm's marketing or sales department to understand the actual levels of service delivery (percentage of times the service is provided correctly, or percentage and number of problems that arise) before making promises about reliability. To be appropriate and effective, communications about service quality must accurately reflect what customers will actually receive in service encounters.

Probably the simplest and most important point to remember is to promise what is possible. Many companies hope to create the perception that they provide high-quality service by claiming it in marketing communications, but this strategy can backfire when the actual service does not live up to the promises raised in advertising. In line with the strategies we discuss in the next section, all service communications should promise only what is possible and not attempt to make services more attractive than they actually are.

Offer Service Guarantees

As discussed in Chapter 15, service guarantees are formal promises to customers about aspects of the service that they will receive. Although many services carry implicit service satisfaction guarantees, their true benefits – an increase in the likelihood of a customer choosing or remaining with the company – come only when the customer knows that guarantees exist and trusts that the company will stand behind them.

Offer Choices

One way to set proper expectations is to give customers options for aspects of service that are meaningful, such as time and cost. A lawyer charging 100 euros per hour, for example, might offer clients the choice between a price increase of 10 euros per hour or a reduction in the number of minutes comprising the session (such as 50 minutes). With the choice, clients can select the aspect of the trade-off (time or money) that is most meaningful to them. Making the choice solidifies the client's expectations of service.

This strategy is effective in business-to-business situations, particularly in terms of speed versus quality. Customers who are time-conscious often want reports, proposals or other written documents quickly. When asked to provide a 10-page proposal for a project within three days, an architectural firm responded that it could provide either a two-page proposal in three days or a 10-page proposal in a week. Its customer selected the latter option, recognizing that the deadline could be extended. In most business-to-business services, speed is often essential but threatens performance. If customers understand the trade-off and are asked to make a choice, they are likely to be more satisfied because their service expectations for each option become more realistic.

Create Tiered-Value Service Offerings

Product companies are accustomed to offering different versions of their products with prices commensurate with the value customers perceive. Cars with different configurations of features carry price tags that match not their cost but their perceived value to the customer. This same type of formal bundling and pricing can be accomplished in services, with the extra benefit of managing expectations.

Credit card companies offer tiered-value service offerings. American Express has multiple levels of credit card services based on the type of service provided: the traditional green card offers basic service features, the gold card additional benefits and the platinum card still more. Two advantages of tiered offerings are: (1) the practice puts the burden of choosing the service level on the customer, thereby familiarizing the customer with specific service expectations, and (2) the company can identify which customers are willing to pay more for higher service levels.

The opportunity to set expectations accurately is present at the time of purchase: when customers make the decision is the moment they can be reminded of the terms of the agreement if they request support that is above the level in the contract.

Communicate the Criteria and Levels of Service Effectiveness

At times companies can establish the criteria by which customers assess service. Consider a business customer who is purchasing market research services for the first time. Because market research is an expert service, it is high in credence properties that are hard for customers to judge. Moreover, the effectiveness of this type of service differs, depending on the objectives the client brings to the service. In this situation a service provider can teach the customer the criteria by which to evaluate the service. The provider that teaches the customer in a credible manner will have an advantage in shaping the evaluation process.

As an example, consider research company A, which communicates the following criteria to the customer: (1) a low price signals low quality, (2) reputation of the firm is critical, and (3) person-to-person interviews are the only type of customer feedback that will provide accurate information. A customer who accepts these criteria will evaluate all other suppliers using them. If research company B had talked to the customer first, consider these (very different!) criteria and their impact on the buyer: (1) market research companies with good reputations are charging for their reputation, not their skill, (2) telephone interviews have been found to work as well as person-to-person interviews, and (3) price does not indicate quality level.

The same approach can be used with service *levels* rather than evaluative criteria. For example, if research company B provides four-day turnaround on the results of its data analysis, the company has just set the customer's expectation level for all other suppliers.

Manage Customer Education

As discussed in Chapter 12, customers must perform their roles properly for many services to be effective. If customers forget to perform their roles, or perform them improperly, disappointment may result. For this reason, communication to customers can take the form of customer education.

Prepare Customers for the Service Process

On a return trip from Singapore on Singapore Airlines, a customer neglected to heed the airline's warning that return flights must be confirmed 24 hours in advance. On arriving at the airport to return home, they found that their seat had been given to another customer who had conformed to the airline's request for confirmation. Depending on the perspective taken, you could argue that either the company or the customer was right in this situation. Whose responsibility is it to make sure that customers perform their roles properly?

Companies can avoid such situations by preparing customers for the service process, and companies may need to prepare the customer often, even every step of the way, for the subsequent actions the customer needs to take. A business-to-business example will help illustrate this strategy.

Customers of management consulting services purchase intangible benefits: marketing effectiveness, motivated workforces, culture change. The very fact that companies purchase these services usually indicates that they do not know how to perform them on their own. Many clients will also not know what to look for along the way to judge progress. In management consulting and other complex service situations, the effective provider prepares the customer for the service process and creates structure for the customer. At the beginning of the engagement, the management consulting firm establishes checkpoints throughout the process, at which times progress will be evaluated, and leads the customer to establish objectives for project completion. Because customers do not know what that progress will look like, the consulting firm takes the lead in setting goals or criteria to be examined at those times.

A similar approach is effective with individual service customers. Do you remember registration at the beginning of your first university semester or term? How aware were you of the steps in the process and what to do after each one? It is unlikely that directions, even in great detail, made you feel confident and competent in the new service experience. You may have required step-by-step – 'next call this telephone number or go to page B' – guidance.

As these examples show, whenever a customer is inexperienced or a service process is new or unique, education about what to expect is essential.

Confirm Performance to Standards and Expectations

Service providers sometimes provide service, even explicitly requested service, yet fail to communicate to the customer that it has been accomplished. These providers stop short of getting credit for their actions when they do not reinforce actions with communication about their having fulfilled the request. This situation may happen under one or more of the following conditions:

- The customer cannot evaluate the effectiveness of a service.
- The decision-maker in the service purchase is a person different from the users of the service.
- The service is invisible.
- The provider depends on others to perform some of the actions to fulfil customer expectations.

When customers cannot evaluate service effectiveness, usually because they are inexperienced or the service is technical, the provider may fail to communicate specific actions that address client concerns because the actions seem too complex for the customer to comprehend. In this situation, the service provider can improve perceptions by translating the actions into customer-friendly terms. A personal injury lawyer who aids a client with the medical and financial implications of an accident needs to be able to tell the client in plain language that he or she has performed the necessary actions.

When the decision-maker in service purchases is different from the users of the service, a wide discrepancy in satisfaction may exist between decision-makers and users. An example is in the purchase of information technology products and services in a company. The decision-maker – the manager of information technology or someone in a similar position – makes the purchase decisions and understands the service promises. If users are not involved in the purchase process, they may not know what has been promised and may be dissatisfied.

Customers are not always aware of everything that is done behind the scenes to serve them well. Most services have invisible support processes. For instance, doctors frequently request diagnostic tests to rule out possible causes for illness. When these tests come back negative, doctors may neglect to inform patients. Many hairstyling firms have guarantees that ensure customer satisfaction with haircuts, permanents and colour treatments. However, only a few of them actively communicate these guarantees in advertising because they assume customers know about them. The firm that explicitly communicates the guarantee may be selected over others by a customer who is uncertain about the quality of the service. Making customers aware of standards or efforts to improve service that are not readily apparent can improve service quality perceptions.

Clarify Expectations After the Sale

When service involves a handover between sales and operations, as it does in most companies, clarifying expectations with customers helps the service delivery arm of the company to align with customer expectations. Salespeople are motivated and compensated to raise customer expectations – at least to the point of making the sale – rather than to communicate realistically what the company can provide. In these situations, service providers can avoid future disappointment by clarifying what was promised as soon as the handover is made.

Teach Customers to Avoid Peak Demand Periods and Seek Slow Demand Periods

Few customers want to face queues or delays in receiving services. In the words of two researchers: 'At best, waiting takes their time, and at worst, they may experience a range of unpleasant reactions – feeling trapped, tired, bored, angry, or demeaned'.[13] In a bank setting, researchers tested three strategies for dealing with customer waits: (1) giving customers prior notice of busy times, (2) having employees apologise for the delays, and (3) assigning all visible employees to serving customers. Only the first strategy focuses on educating customers; the other two involve managing employees. Researchers expected – and confirmed – that customers warned of a wait in line tended to minimize the negative effects of waiting to justify their decision to seek service at peak times. In general, customers given a card listing the branch's busiest and slowest times were more satisfied with the banking service. The other two strategies, apology and all tellers serving, showed no effects on satisfaction.[14] Educating customers to avoid peak times benefits both customers (through faster service) and companies (by easing the problem of over-demand).

Manage Internal Marketing Communication

The fifth major category of strategies necessary to match service delivery with promises involves managing internal marketing communications. Internal marketing communications can be both vertical and horizontal. *Vertical communications* are either downward, from management to employees, or upward, from employees to management. *Horizontal communications* are those across functional boundaries in an organization.

Create Effective Vertical Communications

Companies that give customer-contact employees adequate information, tools and skills allow them to perform successful interactive marketing. Some of these skills come through training and other human resource efforts discussed in Chapter 11, but some are provided through *downward communication*. Among the most important forms of downward communication are company newsletters and magazines, corporate television networks, email, briefings, videos, internal promotional campaigns, and recognition programmes. One of the keys to successful downward communication is keeping employees informed of everything that is being conveyed to customers through external marketing. Employees should see company advertising before it is aired or published and should be familiar with the website, mailings and direct selling approaches being used. If these vertical communications are not present, both customers and employees suffer – customers will not receive the same messages from employees that they hear in company external marketing, and employees will feel uninformed and 'in the dark' about what their company is doing. In such circumstances, customers come asking for services that have been marketed externally but not internally, making the employees feel uninformed, left out and helpless.[15]

Sell the Brand Inside the Company

Having knowledge about what the company is doing in marketing communications is one aspect of internal marketing, but it is not enough. It is important to market the company's brand and brand message to employees so that they can deliver the brand values to customers. There are three principles for selling the brand internally:[16] choose the right moment to educate and inspire employees, link internal and external marketing, and bring the brand alive for employees.

Choosing the right moment is essential, because employees don't have the capacity, or the willingness, to absorb too many change initiatives, and the company therefore has to be selective in identifying opportunities when it can create enthusiasm for the brand. This may be at a time when new services are launched, when a company acquires another company, after refurbishment or when new geographical markets are being entered. When the Savoy hotel reopened after a major refurbishment, Fairmont Hotels (the parent company) spent a large amount of time and effort on communicating the Savoy brand values to the staff.

Linking internal and external marketing means that employees need to hear the same message from management that customers hear. If customers hear that serving them is most important but employees are told that cost savings matter more, employees will be confused and unable to deliver the brand values. One of the best ways to link the two types of communication is to create advertising that targets both customers and employees. Bringing the brand alive to employees involves creating a strong emotional connection between employees and the company. Singapore Airlines connects with its employees through the company's grace, formal dress, quiet tone and Asian food. On the other hand, Aloft hotels builds its connection with the millennial staff by adopting a more casual, younger image with staff wearing gingham button-down tops, paired with Noble Jeans and a funky, cool, striped knit tie.

Create Effective Upward Communication

Upward communication is also necessary in closing the gap between service promises and service delivery. Employees are at the front line of service, and they – more than anyone else in the organization – know what can and cannot be delivered. They know when service breakdowns are occurring and, very often, why they are happening. Having open communication channels from employees to management can prevent service problems from happening and minimize them when they do take place. Managers can encourage upward communication by setting up staff suggestion schemes where employees can put forward ideas and complaints. These used to take the form of physical suggestion boxes where staff dropped their written ideas, but now they tend to be online virtual suggestion boxes. Managers can also survey their employees to gauge their attitudes and obtain suggestions for improvement. Some companies, as can be seen in the following Body Shop example, appoint employee representatives to feed back on staff views and who may, within some organizations, be a member of the management board.

⭐ SERVICE SPOTLIGHT

The Body Shop, the cosmetic retail chain, has an internal communicator network. In every department, there is a 'Communicator' who is responsible for ensuring that upward, downward and horizontal communications happen in that area. These communicators work closely with their managers to ensure that communication meetings are held regularly in each department. This is supplemented in the individual retail stores with 'Public Relations Officers' who perform a similar role, ensuring that communication happens both internally with staff as well as within the local community through the media and local organizations.

An employees' suggestion scheme called Idea Boards encourages employees to produce ideas on how the company can improve what it does. These ideas are forwarded to the people who can implement them and feedback is provided to the employees through the Ideas Board and the internal newsletter.

Create Effective Horizontal Communications

Horizontal communication – communication across functional boundaries in an organization – facilitates coordinated efforts for service delivery. This task is difficult because functions typically differ in goals, philosophies, outlooks and views of the customer, but the payoff is high. Coordination between marketing and operations can result in communication that accurately reflects service delivery, thus reducing the gap between customer expectations and actual service delivery. Integration of effort between marketing and human resources can improve the ability of each employee to become a better marketer. Coordination between finance and marketing can create prices that accurately reflect the customer's evaluation of a service. In service firms, all these functions need to be integrated to produce consistent messages and to narrow the service gaps.

One important strategy for effective horizontal communications is to open channels of communication between the marketing department and operations personnel. For example, when a company creates advertising that depicts the service encounter, it is essential that the advertising accurately reflects what customers will experience in actual service encounters. Exaggeration puts service quality perceptions at risk, especially when the firm is consistently unable to deliver to the level of service portrayed in the advertising. Coordination and communication between advertising and service providers are pivotal in delivering service that meets expectations.

Featuring actual employees doing their jobs or explaining the services they provide, a strategy we mentioned earlier in this chapter, is one way to coordinate advertising portrayals and the reality of the service encounter. To create this type of advertising, the advertising department or agency interacts directly with service employees, facilitating horizontal communications. Similar benefits can be achieved if employees are included in the advertising process in other ways, such as by being shown advertising in its pre-test forms.

Another important strategy for horizontal communications involves opening channels of communication between sales and operations. Mechanisms for achieving this goal can be formal or informal and can include annual planning meetings, retreats, team meetings or workshops in which departments clarify service issues. In these sessions the departments can interact to understand the goals, capabilities and constraints of the other. Some companies hold 'gap workshops' at which employees from both functions meet for a day or two to try to understand the difficulties in matching promises made through selling with delivery accomplished by operations personnel.[17]

Likewise, involving the operations staff in face-to-face meetings with external customers allows operations personnel to understand the salesperson's role and the needs and desires of customers more readily. Rather than filtering customers' needs through the sales force, operations employees can witness at first hand the pressures and demands of customers. A frequent and desirable outcome of this strategy is the operations staff giving better service to the internal customer – the salesperson – as they become aware of their own roles in satisfying both external and internal customers.

Align Back-Office and Support Personnel with External Customers through Interaction or Measurement

As companies become increasingly customer focused, front-line personnel develop improved skills in discerning what customers require. As they become more knowledgeable about, and empathetic toward, external customers, they also experience intrinsic rewards for satisfying customers. Back-office or support personnel, who typically do not interact directly with external customers, miss out on this bonding and, as a consequence, fail to gain the skills and rewards associated with it.

Interaction: Companies are creating ways to facilitate the interaction between back-office and support personnel and external customers. Scottish and Southern Energy, a utilities provider, facilitates such interaction by regularly getting support staff (such as finance and human resource personnel) to handle customers' calls in the company's call centres.

When actual interaction is difficult or impossible, some companies video customers during the purchase and consumption process in their service facilities to vividly portray customers' needs and requirements and to show all personnel the support that front-line people need in order to deliver to meet customer expectations.

Measurement: When company measurement systems are established, employees are sometimes judged on the basis of how they perform for the next internal customer in the chain. Although this approach provides feedback in terms of how well the employees are serving the internal customer, it lacks the motivation and rewards that come from seeing their efforts affect the end-customer.

★ SERVICE SPOTLIGHT

FedEx has aligned internal personnel with the external customer using measurement. FedEx's service quality indicator (SQI) computes the number of daily company-wide service failures. To clearly communicate customer fail points to internal employees, the company has created linking measures to trace the causes to each internal department. For example, the company's IT department affects overall service quality delivered by the company and therefore has sub-measures that provide feedback on how the department's work is impacting on the SQI.

Create Cross-Functional Teams

Another approach to improving horizontal communications to better serve customers is to involve employees in cross-functional teams to align their jobs with end-customer requirements. For example, if a team of telecommunications service representatives is working to improve interaction with customers, back-office people such as computer technicians, engineers or training personnel can become part of the team. The team then learns the requirements and, together, sets goals for achieving them, an approach that directly creates communications across the functions.

The cross-functional team approach can best be explained by the example of an advertising agency. The individual in an advertising agency who typically interacts directly with the client is the account executive (often called a 'suit' by the creative staff). In the traditional agency, the account executive visits the client, uncovers client expectations, elicits a brief, and then interacts with the various departments in the agency (art, copywriting, production, traffic and media buying) that will perform the work. All functions are specialized and, in the extreme case, get direction for their portion of the work right from the account executive. In a cross-functional team, representatives from all functional areas meet with the account executive, and even with the client, to collectively discuss the account and approaches to address this particular client's needs. Each team member brings his or her function's perspective and opens communication. All members can then understand the constraints and schedules of the other groups.

Summary

Discrepancies between service delivery and external communications have a strong effect on customer perceptions of service quality. In this chapter we discussed the role of, and need for, integrated services marketing communications in minimizing these discrepancies. We described external, interactive and internal marketing communications based on the service triangle and emphasized the need to coordinate all three of its dimensions to deliver service that meets customer expectations. We also discussed the factors that lead to challenges in services marketing communications, including: overcoming service intangibility; management of service promises; and management of customer expectations, educating customers, and achieving internal alignment.

We then offered strategies to address each of these service communications challenges. To address service intangibility, we described specific strategies such as the use of vivid imagery and tangible icons in communications, as well as ways to maximize the use of word-of-mouth communication. To manage service promises, we delineated the need for a strong service brand and coordinated external communications. To manage customer expectations, we suggested the need for making realistic promises, extending service guarantees, offering choices, creating tiered-value service offerings and communicating the criteria and levels of service effectiveness. To manage customer education, we emphasized the need to prepare customers for the service process, to make performance conform to standards and expectations, to clarify expectations after the sale and to teach customers how to avoid peak demand periods. Finally to manage internal alignment, we discussed internal branding in addition to effective vertical communication, horizontal communication, aligning teams and support staff.

Key Concepts

Advertising	348	Paid search advertising	358
Banner advertisement	358	Personal selling	360
Corporate websites	348	Public relations	349
Customer education	352	Sales promotion	349
Customer expectations	347	Search engine optimization	357
Direct marketing	349	Service promises	349
Horizontal communications	363	Services marketing triangle	348
Integrated marketing communications		Social media advertising	358
(IMC)	349	Tangibilization strategies	354
Integrated services marketing		Tiered-value service offerings	361
communications (ISMC)	349	Usability testing	357
Internal marketing	349	Vertical communications	363
Mobile apps	358	Viral marketing	359

Exercises

1 Explore each area of the DHL website (ww.dhl.com) and make a list of the types of information you find based on the three categories of marketing communication (external, interactive, internal) discussed in this chapter. What additional information do you find useful on the site?

2 Find five effective service advertisements in newspapers and magazines. Using the criteria given in this chapter, identify why they are effective. Then critique them and discuss ways in which they could be improved.

3 Examine the contents of Sir Richard Branson's blog site (www.virgin.com/richard-branson). How does this strengthen or weaken the Virgin brand?

Discussion Questions

1 Which of the key reasons for provider gap 4 discussed at the beginning of this chapter is the easiest to address in a company? Which is the hardest to address? Why?

2 Review the five general strategies for achieving integrated services marketing communications. Would all these strategies be relevant in goods firms? Which would be most critical in goods firms? Which would be

most critical in services firms? Are there any differences between those most critical in goods firms and those most critical in services firms?

3   What are the most effective Internet advertisements that you have seen? Why are they effective?

4   Using the section on managing customer expectations, put yourself in the position of your lecturer, who must reduce the amount of 'service' provided to the students in your class. Give an example of each strategy in this context. Which of the strategies would work best with you (the student) in managing your expectations? Why?

5   Why are social media channels like Facebook and YouTube so important in service firms? Are they important in product firms?

6   What other strategies can you suggest for taking advantage of online social media channels?

7   In which form of internal marketing communication – vertical or horizontal – would you invest if you had to choose between them as CEO of an organization? Why?

8   What other strategies can you add to the four offered in the section on customer education? What types of education do you expect from service firms? Give an example of a firm from which you have received adequate customer education. What firm has not provided you with adequate customer education?

9   Discuss the proposition that the interaction between companies and customers in online social media results in customer expectations being raised about service employees being more open and flexible during a service encounter in the physical environment.

Further Reading

Ashley, C. and Tuten, T. (2015). Creative strategies in social media marketing: An exploratory study of branded social content and consumer engagement. *Psychology & Marketing*, 32(1), 15–27.

Chaffey, D. and Ellis-Chadwick, F. (2019). *Digital Marketing*. Pearson UK.

De Veirman, M., Cauberghe, V. and Hudders, L. (2017). Marketing through Instagram influencers: The impact of number of followers and product divergence on brand attitude. *International Journal of Advertising*, 36(5), 798–828.

Miles, S.J. and Mangold, W.G. (2014). Employee voice: Untapped resource or social media time bomb? *Business Horizons*, 57(3), 401–11.

Ots, M. and Nyilasy, G. (2015). Integrated marketing communications (IMC): Why does it fail? An analysis of practitioner mental models exposes barriers of IMC implementation. *Journal of Advertising Research*, 55(2), 132–45.

Pescher, C., Reichhart, P. and Spann, M. (2014). Consumer decision-making processes in mobile viral marketing campaigns. *Journal of Interactive Marketing*, 28(1), 43–54.

Punjaisri, K. and Wilson, A.M. (2011). Internal branding process: Key mechanisms, outcomes and moderating factors. *European Journal of Marketing*, 45(9/10), 1521–37.

Punjaisri, K., Wilson, A. and Evanschitsky, H. (2009). Internal branding: An enabler of employees' brand-supporting behaviours. *Journal of Service Management*, 20(2), 209–26.

Chapter 17

Pricing of Services

Chapter Outline

Three Key Ways that Service Prices are Different for Consumers	371
Approaches to Pricing Services	375
Dynamic Pricing	379
Adapting the Price	380
Summary and Key Concepts	384
Exercises	384
Discussion Questions	384
Further Reading	385

Learning Objectives

This chapter's objectives are to:

1 Discuss three major ways that service prices are perceived differently from goods prices by customers.
2 Articulate the key ways that pricing of services differs from pricing of goods from a company's perspective.
3 Demonstrate what value means to customers and the role that price plays in value.
4 Describe strategies that companies use to price services.
5 Give examples of pricing strategy in action.

Opening Example

British Airways Restructures its Economy Airfares

In May 2016, British Airways launched a new structure for economy airfares on its short-haul flights, aimed at improving transparency and addressing the needs of different market segments. The new fare structure gives a choice of three fares allowing customers to only pay for the benefits and services that they need. The three categories are: Basic – for those want the lowest possible fare; Plus – for those who want benefits to make their journey simpler and easier; and Plus Flex – for those whose personal schedule is likely to change.

The details are set out in the table below:

Source: ©Jarretera/Shutterstock

	Basic	Plus	Plus Flex
2 pieces of hand baggage	✓	✓	✓
1 checked bag	For a **fee**	✓	✓
Choose seats	For a **fee**	Yes – free from **48 hours** before departure	Yes – free at **any** time
Change flights on day of travel	For a **fee** + fare difference	Yes – free until **1 hour** before departure	Yes – free until **1 hour** before departure
Change flights at any time	For a **fee** + fare difference	For a **fee** + fare difference	Fare difference may apply
Full refund if you cancel	**No**	**No**	✓

For British Airways, this price bundling approach is aimed at aligning the company's offering more closely to the needs of its customers.

Source: www.britishairways.com.

According to one of the leading experts on pricing, most service organizations use a 'naive and unsophisticated approach to pricing without regard to underlying shifts in demand, the rate that supply can be expanded, prices of available substitutes, consideration of the price–volume relationship, or the availability of future substitutes'.[1] What makes the pricing of services more difficult than pricing of goods? What approaches work well in the context of services?

This chapter builds on three key differences between customer evaluation of pricing for services and goods: (1) customers often have inaccurate or limited reference prices for services, (2) price is a key signal of quality in services, and (3) monetary price is not the only price relevant to service customers. As we demonstrate, these three differences can have a profound impact on the strategies companies use to set and administer prices for services.

This chapter also discusses common pricing structures, including cost-based, competition-based, and demand-based pricing. One of the most important aspects of demand-based pricing is perceived value, which must be understood by service providers so that they price in line with offerings and customer expectations. For that reason we also describe how customers define value, and discuss pricing strategies in the context of value.

Three Key Ways that Service Prices are Different for Consumers

What role does price play in consumer decisions about services? How important is price to potential buyers, compared with other factors and service features? Service companies must understand how pricing works, but first they must understand how customers perceive prices and price changes. In the next three subsections, we describe what we know about the ways that customers perceive the cost of services, and each is central to effective pricing.

Customer Knowledge of Service Prices

To what extent do customers use price as a criterion in selecting services? How much do consumers know about the costs of services? Before you answer these questions, take the services pricing quiz in Figure 17.1. Were you able to fill in a price for each of the services listed? If you were able to answer the questions on the basis of memory, you have internal *reference prices* for the services. A reference price is a price point in memory for a good or a service; it can consist of the price last paid, the price most frequently paid or the average of all prices customers have paid for similar offerings.[2]

To see how accurate your reference prices for services are, you can compare them with the actual price of these services from the providers in your town or city. If you are like many consumers, you feel quite uncertain about your knowledge of the prices of services, and the reference prices you hold in memory for services are not generally as accurate as those you hold for goods. There are many reasons for this difference.

Service Variability Limits Knowledge

Because services are not created on a factory assembly line, service firms have great flexibility in the configurations of services they offer. Firms can conceivably offer an infinite variety of combinations and permutations, leading to complex and complicated pricing structures. How did you answer the questions about prices for an annual car service? If you are like most consumers, you probably wanted more information

Figure 17.1   What do you know about the prices of services?

What do the following services cost in your town or city?

Service	Price?
An annual service for a car	
A grocery home delivery	
Legal help with a divorce	
Laundering a dress or suit	
Rental of a car for one day	
One hour of house-cleaning	
Room at an ibis hotel	
Haircut	
Repairing a leaking tap	

before you offered a reference price. You probably wanted to know what type of service the service centre is providing. Does it include an oil change and new brakes? What types of diagnostic tests will be undertaken? How long does it take? What is its purpose? If the service is undertaken simply as a regular annual service, you may expect to pay less than if it is occasioned by some problem that you are having with your car. The point we want to illustrate here is that a high degree of variability often exists across providers of services. Not every service centre defines a service for a car in the same way.

Providers are Unwilling to Estimate Prices

Another reason customers lack accurate reference prices for services is that many providers are unable or unwilling to estimate price in advance. For example, legal services providers are rarely willing – or even able – to estimate a price in advance. The fundamental reason is that they do not know themselves what the services will involve until they have fully examined the client's situation, or until the process of service delivery (such as a court trial) unfolds. In a business-to-business context, companies will obtain bids or estimates for complex services, such as consulting or construction, but this type of price estimation is typically not undertaken with end-consumers; therefore, they often buy services such as car servicing without advance knowledge about the final price of the service.

Individual Customer Needs Vary

Another factor that results in the inaccuracy of reference prices is that individual customer needs vary. Some hairstylists' service prices vary across customers on the basis of hair length, type of haircut and whether a conditioning treatment and styling are included. Therefore, if you were to ask a friend how much he or she spent on a haircut from a particular stylist, the chances are that your cut from the same stylist may cost a different price. In a similar vein, a service as simple as a hotel room will have prices that vary greatly: by size of room, time of year, type of room availability and individual versus group rate. These two examples are for very simple services. Now consider a service purchase as idiosyncratic as cosmetic surgery from a dentist or help from a lawyer. In these and many other services, customer differences in need will play a strong role in the price of the service.

Collection of Price Information is Overwhelming in Services

Still another reason customers lack accurate reference prices for services is that customers feel overwhelmed with the information they need to gather. With most goods, retail stores display the products by category to allow customers to compare and contrast the prices of different brands and sizes. Rarely is there a similar display of services in a single outlet. If customers want to compare prices (of dry-cleaning, for example), they must call or drive to individual outlets, or search various websites.

The fact that consumers often possess inaccurate reference prices for services has several important managerial implications. Promotional pricing (as in couponing or special pricing) may be less meaningful for services, for which price anchors typically do not exist. Perhaps that is why price is not featured in service advertising as much as it is featured in advertising for goods. Promotional pricing may also create problems if the promotional price (such as a 30 euro cut and blow dry special from a salon) is the only one customers see in advertising, for it could become the customer's anchor price, making the regular price of 50 euros for a future purchase seem high by comparison.

The absence of accurate reference prices also suggests that advertising actual prices for services the customer is not used to purchasing may reduce uncertainty and overcome a customer's inflated price expectations for some services. For example, a marketing research firm's advertisements citing the price for a simple study (such as 7,500 euros) would be informative to business customers who are not familiar with the costs of research studies and therefore would be guessing at the cost. By featuring price in advertising, the company overcomes the fear of high cost by giving readers a price anchor.

Prices are not Visible

One requirement for the existence of customer reference prices is *price visibility* – the price cannot be hidden or implicit. In many services, particularly financial services, most customers know about only the rate of return and not the costs they pay in the form of fund management and insurance fees.

For all the reasons discussed here, many customers do not see the price at all until *after* they receive certain services. Of course, in situations of urgency, such as in the case of accident or illness, customers must make the decision to purchase without respect to cost. And if cost is not known to the customer before purchase, it cannot be used as a key criterion for purchase, as it often is for goods. Price is likely to be an important criterion in *repurchase,* however. Furthermore, monetary price in repurchase may be an even more important criterion than in initial purchase.

The Role of Non-Monetary Costs

Economists have long recognized that monetary price is not the only sacrifice consumers make to obtain products and services. Demand, therefore, is not just a function of monetary price but is influenced by other costs as well. Non-monetary costs represent other sources of sacrifice perceived by consumers when buying and using a service (see Figure 17.2). Time costs, search costs, convenience costs and psychological costs often enter into the evaluation of whether to buy or rebuy a service, and may at times be more important concerns than monetary price. Customers will trade money for these other costs.

- *Time costs.* Most services require direct participation of the consumer and thus consume real time: time waiting as well as time when the customer interacts with the service provider. Consider the investment you make to exercise, see a doctor or get through the crowds to watch a concert or a football game. Not only are you paying money to receive these services, but you are also expending time. Time becomes a sacrifice made to receive service in multiple ways. First, because service providers cannot completely control the number of customers or the length of time it will take for each customer to be served, customers are likely to expend time waiting to receive the service. Waiting time for a service is frequently longer and less predictable than waiting time to buy goods. Second, customers often have to wait for an available appointment from a service provider. Virtually everyone has expended waiting time to receive services.
- *Search costs.* The effort invested to identify and select among services you desire – your search costs – are often higher for services than for physical goods. Prices for services are rarely displayed on shelves of service establishments for customers to examine as they shop, so these prices are often known only when a customer has decided to experience the service. As an example, how well did you estimate the costs of an hour of house-cleaning in the price quiz? As a student, it is unlikely that you regularly purchase

Figure 17.2   Monetary and non-monetary costs

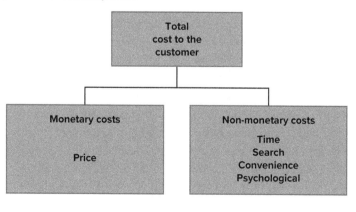

house-cleaning, and you probably have not seen the price of an hour of cleaning displayed in any retail store. Another factor that increases search costs is that each service establishment typically offers only one 'brand' of a service (with the exception of brokers in insurance or financial services), so a customer must initiate contact with several different companies to get information across sellers. Price comparisons for some services (travel, insurance and hotels, for example) have been facilitated through price comparison sites on the Internet, reducing search costs.

- *Convenience costs.* There are also convenience (or, perhaps more accurately, inconvenience) costs of services. If customers have to travel to a service, they incur a cost, and the cost becomes greater when travel is difficult, as it is for elderly persons. Further, if service hours do not coincide with customers' available time, they must arrange their schedules to correspond to the company's schedule. And if consumers have to expend effort and time to prepare to receive a service (such as removing furniture before getting a carpet laid), they make additional sacrifices.

- *Psychological costs.* Often the most painful non-monetary costs are the psychological costs incurred in receiving some services. Fear of not understanding (insurance), fear of rejection (bank loans), fear of outcomes (medical treatment or surgery) – all these fears constitute psychological costs that customers experience as sacrifices when purchasing and using services. New services, even those that create positive change, bring about psychological costs that consumers factor into the purchase of services. While many petrol stations now offer self-checkout at the pump, the number of customers who use them has not lived up to expectations. Many customers are worried about getting confused and facing embarrassment in front of other customers when they cannot use them quickly enough.

⭐ SERVICE SPOTLIGHT

At Disneyland Paris, the waiting time for popular rides (such as *Big Thunder Mountain*, *Crush's Coaster* and *Ratatouille: The Adventure*) is often in excess of 60 minutes. Combined with shorter waits on other attractions on an average day, a family visiting the park may spend 4 to 5 hours waiting and only 30 to 40 minutes on the actual rides.

Non-Monetary Cost Priorities

Everybody will have different cost priorities. Some people will wait longer or travel further to get their car serviced, to save money. Others will be more concerned about convenience and will seek the nearest car service centre, no matter what the price. Quality may be more important to others and they will travel further for a car service centre that they perceive as employing better mechanics.

Reducing Non-Monetary Costs

The managerial implications of these other sources of sacrifice are compelling. First, a firm may be able to increase monetary price by reducing time and other costs. For example, a services marketer can reduce the perceptions of time and convenience costs when use of the service is embedded in other activities (such as when a convenience store provides utility bill payment services, sells stamps and serves coffee along with selling products). Second, customers may be willing to pay to avoid the other costs. Many customers willingly pay extra to have items delivered to their home – including restaurant meals – rather than transporting the services and products themselves. Some customers also pay a premium for fast check-in and checkout when hiring cars, for reduced waiting time in a professional's office (as in so-called 'executive appointments' where, for a premium price, a busy executive comes early in the morning and does not have to wait) and to avoid doing the work themselves (such as paying one and one-half times the price per litre to avoid having to refuel a rental car before returning it). If time or other costs are pivotal for a given service, the company's advertising can emphasize these savings rather than monetary savings.

Many other services save time, thus actually allowing the customer to 'buy' time. Household cleaning services, lawn care, babysitting, online shopping, home banking, home delivery of groceries, decorating and carpet cleaning – all these services represent net gains in the discretionary time of consumers and can be marketed that way. Services that allow the customer to buy time are likely to have monetary value for busy consumers.

Price as an Indicator of Service Quality

One of the intriguing aspects of pricing is that buyers are likely to use price as an indicator of both service costs and service quality – price is at once an attraction variable and a repellent.[3] Customers' use of price as an indicator of quality depends on several factors, one of which is the other information available to them. When service cues to quality are readily accessible, when brand names provide evidence of a company's reputation or when the level of advertising communicates the company's belief in the brand, customers may prefer to use those cues instead of price. In other situations, however, such as when quality is hard to detect or when quality or price varies a great deal within a class of services, consumers may believe that price is the best indicator of quality. Many of these conditions typify situations that consumers face when purchasing services.[4] Another factor that increases the dependence on price as a quality indicator is the risk associated with the service purchase. In high-risk situations, many of which involve credence services such as restaurants or management consulting, the customer will look to price as a surrogate for quality.

Because customers depend on price as a cue to quality and because price sets expectations of quality, service prices must be determined carefully. In addition to setting prices to cover costs or match competitors, companies must select the price points that convey the appropriate quality signal. Pricing too low can lead to inaccurate inferences about the quality of the service. Pricing too high can set expectations that may be difficult to match in service delivery.

Approaches to Pricing Services

Rather than repeat the basics of pricing that are common across products and services and are set out in many standard marketing textbooks, we want to emphasize in this chapter the way that services prices and pricing differ from the customer's and the company's perspective. We discuss these differences in the context of the three pricing structures typically used to set prices: (1) cost-based, (2) competition-based, and (3) demand-based pricing. These categories are the same bases on which goods prices are set, but adaptations must be made in services. Figure 17.3 shows the three structures interrelating because companies need to consider each of the three to some extent in setting prices. In the following sections we describe in general each basis for pricing and discuss challenges that occur when the approach is used in services pricing. Figure 17.3 summarizes those challenges.

Cost-Based Pricing

In cost-based pricing, a company determines expenses from raw materials and labour, adds amounts or percentages for overhead and profit, and thereby arrives at the price. This method is widely used by industries such as utilities, contracting, wholesaling and advertising. The basic formula for cost-based pricing is

$$\text{Price} = \text{Direct costs} + \text{Overhead costs} + \text{Profit margin}$$

Direct costs involve materials and labour that are associated with delivering the service, overhead costs are a share of fixed costs, and the profit margin is a percentage of full costs (direct + overhead).

Figure 17.3 Three basic marketing price structures and challenges associated with their use for services

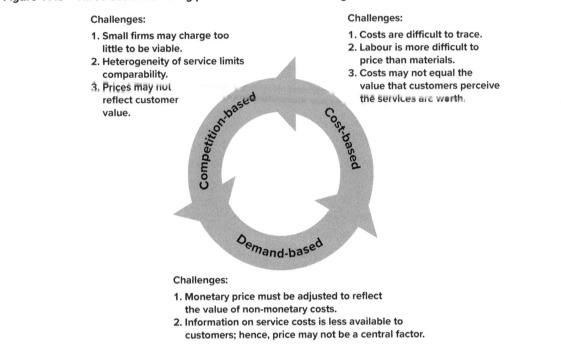

Challenges:
1. Small firms may charge too little to be viable.
2. Heterogeneity of service limits comparability.
3. Prices may not reflect customer value.

Challenges:
1. Costs are difficult to trace.
2. Labour is more difficult to price than materials.
3. Costs may not equal the value that customers perceive the services are worth.

Challenges:
1. Monetary price must be adjusted to reflect the value of non-monetary costs.
2. Information on service costs is less available to customers; hence, price may not be a central factor.

Special Challenges in Cost-Based Pricing for Services

One of the major difficulties in cost-based pricing for services involves defining the units in which a service is purchased. Thus the price per unit – a well-understood concept in pricing of manufactured goods – is a vague entity. For this reason many services are sold in terms of input units rather than units of measured output. For example, most professional services (such as consulting, engineering, architecture, psychotherapy and tutoring) are sold by the hour.

What is unique about services when using cost-based approaches to pricing? First, costs are difficult to trace or calculate in services businesses, particularly where multiple services are provided by the firm.[5] Consider how difficult it must be for a bank to allocate teller time accurately across its current, savings and money market accounts in order to decide what to charge for the services. Second, a major component of cost is employee time rather than materials, and the value of people's time, particularly non-professional time, is not easy to calculate or estimate.

An added difficulty is that actual service costs may under-represent the value of the service to the customer. A local tailor charges 10 euros for taking in a seam on a 350-euro ladies' suit jacket and an equal 10 euros for taking in a seam on a pair of 30-euro trousers. The tailor's rationale is that both jobs require the same amount of time. What she neglects to see is that the customer would pay a higher price – and might even be happier about the alterations – for the expensive suit jacket, and that 10 euros is too high a price for the trousers.

Examples of Cost-Based Pricing Strategies Used in Services

Cost-plus pricing is a commonly used approach in which component costs are calculated and a mark-up added. In product pricing, this approach is quite simple; in service industries, however, it is complicated because the tracking and identification of costs are difficult. The approach is typically used in industries in which cost must be estimated in advance, such as construction, engineering and advertising. In construction or engineering, bids are solicited by clients on the basis of the description of the service desired. Using their knowledge of the costs of the components of the service (including the raw materials such as stone and timber), labour (including both professional and unskilled) and margin, the company estimates and presents to the client a price for the finished service. A contingency amount – to cover the possibility that costs may be higher than estimated – is also stated because in large projects specifications can change as the service is provided.

Fee for service is the pricing strategy used by professionals; it represents the cost of the time involved in providing the service. Consultants, psychologists, accountants and lawyers, among other professionals, charge for their services on an hourly basis. Virtually all psychologists and lawyers have a set hourly rate they charge to their clients, and most structure their time in increments of an hour.

One of the most difficult aspects of this approach is that record-keeping is tedious for professionals. Lawyers and accountants must keep track of the time they spend for a given client, often down to 10-minute increments. For this reason the method has been criticized because it does not promote efficiency and sometimes ignores the expertise of the lawyers (those who are very experienced can accomplish much more than novices in a given time period, yet billings do not always reflect this). Clients often fear padding of their legal bills, and they frequently audit them. Despite these concerns, the hourly bill dominates the industry, with the majority of revenues billed this way.[6]

Competition-Based Pricing

The competition-based pricing approach focuses on the prices charged by other firms in the same industry or market. Competition-based pricing does not always imply charging the identical rate others charge but rather using others' prices as an anchor for the firm's price. This approach is used predominantly in two situations: (1) when services are standard across providers, such as in the dry-cleaning industry, and (2) in oligopolies characterized by few large service providers, such as in the airline or rental car industry. Difficulties involved in provision of services sometimes make competition-based pricing less simple than it is in goods industries.

Special Challenges in Competition-Based Pricing for Services

Small firms may charge too little and not make margins high enough to remain in business. Many family-owned service establishments – dry-cleaning, retail and fast food outlets, among others – cannot deliver services at the low prices charged by chain operations.

Further, the heterogeneity of services across and within providers makes this approach complicated. Bank services illustrate the wide disparity in service prices. Customers buying current accounts, money orders or foreign currency, to name a few services, find that prices are rarely similar across providers. For example, there are likely to be major differences in overdraft charges between banks, and the commission and exchange rates quoted for foreign currency transactions can also differ significantly. Banks claim that they set fees high enough to cover the costs of these services. The wide disparity in prices probably reflects banks' difficulty in determining prices as well as their belief that financial customers do not shop around nor discern the differences (if any) among offerings from different providers. A banking expert makes the point that 'It's not like buying a litre of milk . . . . Prices aren't standardized'.[7] Only in very standardized services (such as dry-cleaning) are prices likely to be remembered and compared.

Examples of Competition-Based Pricing in Services Industries

Price signalling occurs in markets with a high concentration of sellers. In this type of market, any price offered by one company will be matched by competitors to avoid giving a low-cost seller a distinct advantage. The airline industry exemplifies price signalling in services. When any competitor drops the price of routes, others match the lowered price almost immediately.

Going-rate pricing involves charging the most prevalent price in the market.

⭐ **SERVICE SPOTLIGHT**

Rental car pricing is an illustration of this technique (and an illustration of price signalling, because the rental car market is dominated by a small number of large companies). For years, the prices set by one company (Hertz) have been followed by the other companies. When Hertz instituted a new pricing plan that involved 'no mileage charges, ever', other rental car companies imitated the policy. They then had to raise other factors such as base rates, size and type of car, daily or weekly rates and drop off charges to continue to make profits. Prices in different geographic markets, even cities, depend on the going rate in that location, and customers often pay different rates in contiguous cities in the same country.

Demand-Based Pricing

The two approaches to pricing just described are based on the company and its competitors rather than on customers. Neither approach takes into consideration that customers may lack reference prices, may be sensitive to non-monetary prices and may judge quality on the basis of price. All these factors can be accounted for in a company's pricing decisions. The third major approach to pricing, *demand-based pricing*, involves setting prices consistent with customer perceptions of value: prices are based on what customers will pay for the services provided.

The buyer's perception of total value prompts their willingness to pay a particular price for a service. To translate the customer's value perceptions into an appropriate price for a specific service offering, the marketer must answer a number of questions. What benefits does the service provide? How important is each of these benefits? How much is it worth to the customer to receive a particular benefit from a service? At what price will the service be economically acceptable to potential buyers? In what context is the customer purchasing the service?

Special Challenges in Demand-Based Pricing for Services

The most important thing a company must do – and often a difficult thing – is to estimate the value to customers of the company's services. Value may be perceived differently by consumers because of idiosyncratic tastes, knowledge about the service, buying power and ability to pay. In this type of pricing, what the consumers value – not what they pay – forms the basis for pricing. Therefore its effectiveness rests solely on accurately determining what the market perceives the service to be worth.

When the services are for the end-consumer, most often service providers will decide that they cannot afford to give each individual exactly the bundle of attributes he or she values. They will, however, develop different bundles of attributes to address specific segments; for example, an airline will provide economy, premium economy, business class and first class offerings for different customer segments, but it will not provide a bespoke service for each passenger. On the other hand, when tailored services are sold to businesses (or, in the case of high-end services, to end-customers), the company can deliver different bundles to each customer. For example, an airline providing flights on a private jet may be able to provide senior executives and celebrities with the exact bundle of attributes they desire.

One of the most complex and difficult tasks of services marketers is setting prices internationally. If services marketers price on the basis of perceived value and if perceived value and willingness to pay differ across countries (which they often do), then service firms may provide essentially the same service but charge different prices in different countries. Here, as in pricing domestically, the challenge is to determine the perceived value, not just to different customers but to customers in different parts of the world.

Examples of Demand-Based Pricing in Service Industries

With demand-based pricing, a service marketer may charge different prices to different groups of customers for what are perceived to be different benefits or quality levels of the service, even though there may not be corresponding differences in the costs of providing the service to each of these groups. This form of market segmentation pricing is based on the premise that segments show different price elasticities of demand and desire different values from a service. Non-monetary costs and benefits must be factored into the calculation of perceived value to the customer. When services require time, inconvenience, psychological and search costs, the monetary price may need to be lower to compensate. And when services save time, inconvenience, psychological and search costs, the customer may be willing to pay a higher monetary price. The challenge is to determine the value to customers of each of the non-monetary aspects involved.

Services marketers often price by *client category*, based on the recognition that some groups find it difficult to pay a recommended price. Health clubs will typically offer student memberships, recognizing that this segment of customers has limited ability to pay full price. In addition to the lower price, student memberships may also carry with them reduced hours of use, particularly in peak times. The same line of reasoning leads to memberships for retired people who are less able to pay full price but are willing to patronize the clubs during daytime hours when most full-price members are working. In the British Airways example, at the start of this chapter, some business customers will pay more to have the flexibility of the 'Plus Flex' ticket whereas other customers may seek a cheaper fare as they do not want or value the flexibility option so highly.

Companies can configure service bundles that reflect price and service points appealing to different groups in the market. Hotels, for example, offer standard rooms at a basic rate but then combine amenities and tangibles related to the room to attract customers who are willing to pay more for the executive floor, spa baths, additional beds and sitting areas.

Dynamic Pricing

Dynamic pricing is the use of price to manage demand for a service by capitalizing on customer sensitivity to prices. It builds on the three basic marketing price structures of cost, competition and demand. Certain services such as passenger transportation, hotels, concerts and sporting events have a finite amount of supply alongside significant fluctuations in demand. It is a form of technology-led pricing frequently used as part of a revenue management/yield management model (discussed in Chapter 1). It involves the buying and selling of goods and services in markets in which prices move quickly in response to supply and demand fluctuations. Dynamic pricing is estimated to account for more than 40 per cent of total online transactions. For example, airlines adjust their fares for a particular flight frequently, sometimes several times a day, as the flight's departure date nears, to reflect customer demand and the time remaining until the departure date.

Special Challenges in Dynamic Pricing for Services

As stated in Chapter 14, dynamic pricing requires very detailed data on past demand patterns at different price points by market segment as well as methods of projecting likely market demand. The mathematical programming models behind dynamic pricing require a combination of the cost-based information, competition-based information and market information in order to best calculate the likely demand at different price points. The collection of real-time information in each of these areas can require significant effort and financial investment.

Examples of Dynamic Pricing in Service Industries

In addition to dynamic pricing being undertaken by the service provider directly, dynamic prices can also be offered through third-party sites such as comparison websites (aggregators), group buying sites or on auction sites.

Comparison websites or *aggregators* are website portals or search utilities that enable clients to gain several quotes or prices via an electronic e-quote form. In the insurance sector, they include websites such as comparethemarket.com, gocompare.com and confused.com; in flights and travel, they include sites such as skyscanner.net, trivago.com, trainline.com and expedia.com; in restaurants they include 5pm.co.uk; and in utilities, uswitch.com and moneysupermarket.com. These aggregators conclude agreements with a number of suppliers to provide a comparative quote to potential customers based on pre-determined list of specified needs as disclosed by them. These prices also change.

⭐ SERVICE SPOTLIGHT

Online flight aggregator skyscanner.net was born out of the difficulties of one of its founders in finding cheap flights to ski resorts. In 2002, convinced they could do better, he and a group of other IT professionals developed the concept at weekends while continuing to work as contractors. In November 2016, Ctrip, the largest travel firm in China, bought Skyscanner for $1.75 billion. The company now receives more than 35 million monthly visitors from some 230 countries with particularly strong growth in Russia, Italy, Spain and China. In addition, their mobile search apps have been installed on 35 million devices. The company's technology searches millions of Internet sites for flights and then compares and contrasts each offering for their relative advantages, such as cost, time and date of departure and destination. It also books the flight. The site is now available in 30 languages and the company has offices in the UK, Singapore, Beijing, Shenzhen, Miami, Barcelona, Sofia and Budapest. The service has recently expanded to include hotels and car rental.

Group buying sites work on the concept that the greater the number of people who want to buy a service, the lower the price will be for everyone. Groupon is an example of a site that operates in 18 countries within Europe. Each day, Groupon features a variety of service offers from spa treatments to restaurants in major cities. By promising service businesses a minimum number of customers (a form of collective buying power), they can offer discounts. If the minimum number of customers for a particular deal is reached, then the customer gets the service at the discounted rate. If not enough people sign up, then the specific deal is cancelled for all customers. On some sites, the greater the number of people who want to buy the service, the lower the price will be for everyone. Sellers generally group the prices of the product being sold based on the number of buyers. For example, for 5 to 10 buyers, the price for each buyer is 100 euros; for 10 to 20 buyers, the price for each buyer is 95 euros, and so on. Word of mouth is critical, because interested buyers are encouraged to enlist their friends and relatives to get a cheaper price for the whole group. Sellers motivate this action by placing an 'Invite Your Friend' icon right next to the service or price information. Advantages of this form of dynamic pricing are that the price decreases as a greater number of people bid, and the exact service and its specifications are known to buyers when bidding.

Online auction sites such as eBay are generally used for auctioning products rather than services. However, eBay has seen some growth in auctions of vacations, hotel stays and holiday property rentals. Luxurytraveldiary.com is a UK website that offers auctions that allow customers to bid for travel related products and hotel packages – the highest bid at the end of the auction period gets the hotel package at that price. Online auctions of this type represent dynamic pricing because customers pay what they are willing and compete with each other on the service they desire.

Adapting the Price

In this section we describe the various approaches available for adapting the price of a service to attract different customer groups and address different service situations.

Attracting the Bargain Hunters

When price is the most important determinant of value to a customer, the company focuses mainly on price. This focus does not mean that the quality level and intrinsic attributes are always irrelevant, just that price dominates in importance. The following pricing strategies can be targeted at this situation.

Discounting

Service providers offer discounts or price cuts to communicate to price sensitive buyers that they are receiving value. Airlines such as British Airways, easyJet and Ryanair advertise short periods of two to three months when ticket prices within Europe will be discounted. Ryanair occasionally advertises free seats where the passenger only pays taxes and administration charges for a flight. These attract customers to try their flights and help fill planes during off-peak periods. Discounting also brings traffic to the company's website which may result in flights other than the free ones being booked.

Odd Pricing

Odd pricing is the practice of pricing services just below the exact amount to make buyers perceive that they are getting a lower price. For example, dry-cleaners charge 2.98 euros for a shirt rather than 3.00 euros, health clubs have membership fees priced at 33.90 euros per month rather than 34 euros, and haircuts are 19.50 euros rather than 20.00 euros. Odd prices suggest discounting and bargains and are therefore appealing to customers for whom value means low price.

Penetration Pricing

Penetration pricing is a strategy in which new services are introduced into a market at low prices to stimulate trial and widespread use. The strategy is appropriate when: (1) sales volume of the service is very sensitive to price, even in the early stages of introduction; (2) it is possible to achieve economies in unit costs by operating at large volumes; (3) a service faces threats of strong potential competition very soon after introduction; and (4) there is no class of buyers willing to pay a higher price to obtain the service.[8] Penetration pricing can lead to problems when companies then select a 'regular' increased price. Care must be taken not to penetrate with so low a price that customers feel the regular price is outside the range of acceptable prices. Some freight transport companies use a penetration approach when entering a new geographical market in order to attract potential customers away from existing carriers.

Attracting Status Seekers

When the customer is concerned principally with the value components of the service, price is not the primary concern. The more desirable intrinsic attributes a given service possesses, the more highly valued the service is likely to be and the higher the price the marketer can set. The following pricing strategies can be targeted at this situation.

Prestige Pricing

Prestige pricing is a special form of demand-based pricing by service marketers who offer high-quality or status services. For certain services – restaurants, health clubs, airlines and hotels – a higher price is charged for the luxury end of the business. Some customers of service companies who use this approach may actually value the high price because it represents prestige or a quality image and may give them a higher level of status among their friends and associates (particularly if they can promote it on their social media pages). Others prefer purchasing at the high end because they are given preference in seating or accommodation and are entitled to other special benefits. In prestige pricing, demand may actually increase as price increases because the costlier service has more value in reflecting quality, status or prestige.

Skimming Pricing

Skimming pricing, a strategy in which new services are introduced at high prices with large promotional expenditures, is an effective approach when services are major improvements over past services. In this situation customers are more concerned about obtaining the service before anyone else than about the cost of the service, allowing service providers to skim the customers most willing to pay the highest prices. New restaurants with celebrity chefs may implement this when opening in a new city.

Attracting Convenience Seekers

Some customers define value as including not just the benefits they receive but also the time, money and effort they put into the service. The following pricing strategies can be targeted at this situation.

Price Framing

Because many customers do not possess accurate reference prices for services, services marketers are more likely than product marketers to organize price information (**price framing**) for customers so they know how to view it. Sites such as Groupon let customers know the actual values of the offers being made as well as the discounted prices in the offer. Customers naturally look for price anchors as well as familiar services against which to judge focal services.

Price Bundling

Some services are consumed more effectively in conjunction with other services; other services accompany the products they support (such as extended service warranties, training and expedited delivery). When customers find value in a package of services that are interrelated, **price bundling** is an appropriate strategy. Bundling, which means pricing and selling grouped together rather than individual services, has benefits to both customers and service companies. As an example, a health club customer may be able to contract for aerobics classes at 10 euros per month, weight machines at 15 euros and the swimming pool at 15 euros – or the group of three services for 27 euros (a price incentive of 13 euros per month). Customers find that bundling simplifies their purchase and payment, and companies find that the approach stimulates demand for the firm's service line, thereby achieving cost economies for the operations as a whole while increasing net contributions.[9] Bundling also allows the customer to pay less than when purchasing each of the services individually, which contributes to perceptions of value.

The effectiveness of price bundling depends on how well the service firm understands the bundles of value that customers or segments perceive, and on the complementarity of demand for these services. Effectiveness also depends on the right choice of services from the firm's point of view. Because the firm's objective is to increase overall sales, the services selected for bundling should be those with a relatively small sales volume without the bundling to minimize revenue loss from discounting a service that already has a high sales volume.

> **★ SERVICE SPOTLIGHT**
>
> Subway offers **value pricing** with their 3-euro lunch saver menu. This includes a 15 cm sub sandwich and a drink. Rivals Burger King, McDonald's and other fast-food restaurants have similar product ranges. The terminology used may vary from 'meal deals' to 'king savers' but they all represent a bundled offering at a low price.

Complementary Pricing

Services that are highly interrelated can be leveraged by using **complementary pricing**. This pricing includes three related strategies – captive pricing, two-part pricing and loss leadership.[10] In captive pricing, the firm offers a base service or product and then provides the supplies or peripheral services needed to continue using the service. In this situation the company could offload some part of the price for the basic service to the peripherals. For example, photocopier rental services often drop the price for installation to a very low level, then compensate by charging enough for the ink, paper and maintenance contracts to make up for the loss in revenue. With service firms, this strategy is often called *two-part pricing* because the service price is broken into a fixed fee plus variable usage fees (also found in telephone services and health clubs). *Loss leadership* is the term typically used in retail stores when providers place a familiar service on special offer, largely to draw the customer to the store and then reveal other levels of service available at higher prices.

Attracting Performance Seekers

In service industries in which outcome is very important but uncertainty is high, the most relevant aspect of value is the *result* of the service. In personal injury lawsuits, for example, clients value the settlement they receive at the conclusion of the service. From tax accountants, clients most value cost savings. From universities and colleges, students most value getting a job upon graduation. In these and other situations, an appropriate value-based pricing strategy is to price on the basis of results or outcome of the service.

The most prevalent form of results-based pricing is a practice called *contingency pricing* used by lawyers. Contingency pricing is the major way that personal injury and certain consumer cases are billed. In this approach, lawyers do not receive fees or payment until the case is settled, when they are paid a percentage of the money that the client receives. Therefore, only an outcome in the client's favour is compensated. From the client's point of view, the pricing makes sense, in part because most clients in these cases are unfamiliar with and possibly intimidated by law firms. Their biggest fears are high fees for a case that may take years to settle. By using contingency pricing, clients are ensured that they pay no fees until they receive a settlement.

In these and other instances of contingency pricing, the economic value of the service is hard to determine before the service, and providers develop a price that allows them to share the risks and rewards of delivering value to the buyer. Partial contingency pricing, now being used in commercial law cases, is a version in which the client pays a lower fee than usual but offers a bonus if the settlement exceeds a certain level. Results-based pricing is demonstrated clearly in the online 'pay-per-click' advertising industry today. Rather than buying media with estimated audiences, companies that buy advertisements on Google pay only for users who actually respond to their ads by clicking on them.

Attracting Multiple Segments

Time, place, quantity and incentive differentials have all been used effectively by service firms to attract different segments of a market.

Time differentials involve price variations that depend on when the service is consumed. Off-peak rail fares, airline tickets that include a Saturday night stay, and health spas in the off-season are time differentials that reflect slow periods of service. By offering lower prices for underused time periods, a service company can smooth demand and also gain incremental revenue.

Place differentials are used for services in which customers have a sensitivity to location. The front row at concerts, centre court in tennis or basketball, beach-side rooms in hotels – all these represent place differentials that are meaningful to customers and that therefore command higher prices.

Quantity differentials are usually price decreases given for volume purchasing. This pricing structure allows a service company to predict future demand for its services. Customers who buy a booklet of coupons for a tanning salon or facial, a quantity of tokens for toll roads or ferries, or packages of advertising spots on radio or television, are all responding to price incentives achieved by committing to future services. Corporate discounts for airlines, hotels and rental cars exemplify quantity discounts in the business context; by offering lower prices, the service provider locks in future business.

Summary

This chapter began with three key differences between customer evaluation of pricing for services and goods: (1) customers often have inaccurate or limited reference prices for services, (2) price is a key signal to quality in services, and (3) monetary price is not the only relevant price to service customers. These three differences can have a profound impact on the strategies that companies use to set and administer prices for services. The chapter next discussed common pricing structures, including cost-based, competition-based, demand-based and dynamic pricing. Central to the discussion were the specific challenges in each of these structures and the services pricing techniques that have emerged in practice.

Finally, we considered how prices can be adapted for different customer segments and situations. These included attracting: (1) bargain hunters, (2) status seekers, (3) convenience seekers, (4) performance seekers, and (5) multiple segments.

Key Concepts

Aggregators	379	Odd pricing	381
Comparison websites	379	Online auction sites	380
Competition-based pricing	377	Penetration pricing	381
Complementary pricing	382	Perceived value	378
Cost-based pricing	375	Prestige pricing	381
Demand-based pricing	378	Price bundling	382
Discounting	381	Price framing	382
Dynamic pricing	379	Reference prices	371
Group buying sites	379	Results-based pricing	383
Market segmentation pricing	379	Skimming pricing	382
Non-monetary costs	373	Value pricing	382

Exercises

1   List five services for which you have no reference price. Now put yourself in the role of the service provider for two of those services and develop pricing strategies. Be sure to include in your description which of the value definitions you believe customers will possess and what types of strategies would be appropriate given those definitions.

2   In the next week, find three price lists for services (such as from a restaurant, drycleaner or hairstylist). In each case, identify what the pricing base is and what strategy is being used. How effective is each one?

3   Consider that you are the owner of a new health club and can prepare a value/price package that is appealing to students. Describe your approach. How does it differ from existing offerings?

Discussion Questions

1   Which approach to pricing (cost-based, competition-based, demand-based or dynamic pricing) is the most fair to customers? Why?

2   Is it possible to use a combination of these approaches simultaneously when pricing services? If you answer yes, describe a service that is priced this way.

3   For what consumer services do you have reference prices? What makes these services different from others for which you lack reference prices?

4   Name three services you purchase in which price is a signal of quality. Do you believe that there are true differences across services that are priced high and those that are priced low? Why or why not?

5   Describe the non-monetary costs involved in the following services: getting a car loan, belonging to a health club, attending an executive education class, and getting dental braces.

6   What are the implications of comparison websites or aggregators for a service organization trying to differentiate its offering?

7   Why are auction sites such as eBay more suited to products rather than services?

Further Reading

Bilotkach, V., Gaggero, A.A. and Piga, C.A. (2015). Airline pricing under different market conditions: Evidence from European low-cost carriers. *Tourism Management*, 47, 152–63.

Greenleaf, E.A., Johnson, E.J., Morwitz, V.G. and Shalev, E. (2016). The price does not include additional taxes, fees, and surcharges: A review of research on partitioned pricing. *Journal of Consumer Psychology*, 26(1), 105–24.

Indounas, K.A. and Avlonitis, G.J. (2009). Pricing objectives and their antecedents in the services sector. *Journal of Service Management*, 20(3), 342–74.

Kienzler, M. and Kowalkowski, C. (2017). Pricing strategy: A review of 22 years of marketing research. *Journal of Business Research*, 78, 101–10.

Schlereth, C. and Skiera, B. (2012). Measurement of consumer preferences for bucket pricing plans with different service attributes. *International Journal of Research in Marketing*, 29(2), 167–80.

Viglia, G., Mauri, A. and Carricano, M. (2016). The exploration of hotel reference prices under dynamic pricing scenarios and different forms of competition. *International Journal of Hospitality Management*, 52, 46–55.

Part 7
Service and the Bottom Line

Chapter 18 The Financial Impact of Service Quality

In this final section of the text, we discuss one of the most important questions about service that managers have been debating for many years: is excellent service profitable to an organization? We pull together research and company experience to answer this question. We present our own model of how the relationship works and consider some alternative models that have been used. Our model shows how service quality has offensive effects (gaining new customers) and defensive effects (retaining customers).

We also discuss several important performance models in this chapter including customer equity which compares investments in service with expenditures on other marketing activities. The balanced scorecard is an approach that includes multiple company factors including financial, customer, operational and innovative measures. The balanced scorecard allows a company to measure performance from the customer's perspective (Chapter 9), from the employee's perspective (Chapter 11) and from an innovation and new service perspective (Chapter 8). Thus, in Chapter 18 we synthesize the measurement issues that underlie the provision of service and offer a way for companies to demonstrate that service is accountable financially. We also present an approach called strategic performance mapping that helps companies integrate all elements of their balanced scorecards. These models help companies understand more accurately their benefits from investments in service excellence.

Chapter 18

The Financial Impact of Service Quality

Chapter Outline

Service and Profitability: The Direct Relationship 389
Offensive Marketing Effects of Service: Attracting More and Better Customers 391
Defensive Marketing Effects of Service: Customer Retention 392
The Key Drivers of Service Quality, Customer Retention and Profits 394
Customer Equity and Return on Marketing 394
Company Performance Measurement: The Balanced Performance Scorecard 397
Summary and Key Concepts 401
Exercises 402
Discussion Questions 402
Further Reading 403

Learning Objectives

This chapter's objectives are to:

1 Examine the direct effects of service on profits.
2 Consider the effect of service on getting new customers.
3 Evaluate the role of service in keeping customers.
4 Discuss what is known about the key service drivers of overall service quality, customer retention and profitability.
5 Discuss the balanced performance scorecard that allows for strategic focus on measurements other than financials.

Opening Example

Zappos – The Value of Investing in Service Quality

Zappos, the world's biggest online shoe retailer, sells shoes, clothing and accessories internationally from its base in Las Vegas, Nevada, in the USA. The success of the company is partly attributed to its loyal customers: 75 per cent of Zappos orders come as repeat business. This loyalty is engendered by the organization's obsessive focus on service quality. Customer focus is reflected in its consumer-friendly, highly intuitive website and fast, free shipping (in both directions). Service is evidenced by the company's vast model selection, including special sizes, and its more than 2.9 million items in stock.

Source: ©Poring Studio/Shutterstock

Whilst the majority of orders are placed directly on the Internet, calls are also made to the Zappos call centre which is staffed 24 hours per day. The call centre operators are there to solve customer problems, even if that means helping a customer to find a non-stocked item by searching competitors' websites. Call-takers are encouraged to take as much time as necessary to assist customers with their orders, answer their questions, troubleshoot their problems and build a relationship with the customer. Zappos' current record for the longest customer service call is 10 hours, 51 minutes. Zappos employees are held accountable for 'wowing' customers with outstanding service. They routinely send handwritten thank-you notes to customers and have been known to also send bouquets of flowers or boxes of chocolates in sympathy or in celebration.

The key characteristics of the Zappos service are:

- Easy-to-find contact information
- 24/7 call centre
- 365-day return policy
- Free shipping and returns
- No automated telephone answer routing system
- Friendly, solution-oriented representatives
- Representatives don't use scripts
- Unlimited length of call
- Representatives are empowered to help
- No up-selling by representatives.

This focus on the customer and service quality resulted in significant financial returns. Zappos, now owned by Amazon, has increased its revenue to over one billion dollars.

Source: See www.zappos.com and www.digitalistmag.com/future-of-work/2018/06/13/zappos-ceo-shows-exactly-why-doing-good-is-good-business-06175847.

Virtually all companies hunger for evidence and tools to ascertain and monitor the payoff and payback of new investments in service. Many managers still see service and service quality as costs rather than as contributors to profits, partly because of the difficulty involved in tracing the link between service and financial returns. Determining the financial impact of service parallels the age-old search for the connection between advertising and sales. Service quality's results – like advertising's results – are cumulative and, therefore, evidence of the link may not come immediately or even quickly after investments and, like advertising, service quality is one of many variables – among them pricing, advertising, efficiency and image – that simultaneously influence profits. Furthermore, spending on service per se does not guarantee results, because strategy and execution must both also be considered.

In recent years, however, researchers and company executives have sought to understand the relationship between service and profits, and have found strong evidence to support the relationship. For example, a study examined the comparative benefits of revenue expansion and cost reduction on return on quality. The research addressed a common strategic dilemma faced by executives: whether to reduce costs through the use of quality programmes, such as Six Sigma, that focus on efficiencies and cost-cutting, or to build revenues through improvements to customer service, customer satisfaction and customer retention.[1] Using managers' reports as well as secondary data on firm profitability and stock returns, the study investigated whether the highest return on quality was generated from cost-cutting, revenue expansion or a combination of the two approaches. The results suggest that firms that adopt primarily a revenue expansion emphasis perform better and have higher return on quality than firms that emphasize either cost reduction or both revenue expansion and cost reduction together.[2]

Executives are also realizing that the link between service and profits is neither straightforward nor simple. Service quality affects many economic factors in a company, some of them leading to profits through variables not traditionally in the domain of marketing. For example, the traditional total quality management approach expresses the financial impact of service quality in lowered costs or increased productivity. These relationships involve operational issues that concern marketing only in the sense that marketing research is used to identify service improvements that customers notice and value.

More recently, other types of evidence have become available on which to examine the relationship between service and profitability. The overall goal of this chapter is to synthesize that recent evidence and to identify relationships between service and profits. This chapter is divided into six sections, paralleling the chapter's objectives. In each section we assess the evidence and identify what is currently known about the topics. The chapter is organized using a conceptual framework linking all the variables in the topics.

Service and Profitability: The Direct Relationship

Figure 18.1 shows the underlying question at the heart of this chapter. The executives of leading service companies such as British Airways and Disney were willing to trust their intuitive sense that better service would lead to improved financial success. Without formal documentation of the financial payoff, they have committed significant resources over the years to improving service and were richly rewarded for their leaps of faith. However, executives in other companies are sometimes reluctant to invest in service, waiting for solid evidence of its financial soundness.

Figure 18.1   The direct relationship between service and profits?

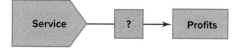

Profits and Service

A study examining 15 years of audited returns (between 2000 and 2014) found that the stock returns on companies with higher levels of customer satisfaction do better than the market average. The recorded cumulative returns were 518 per cent over the years studied, compared with a 31 per cent increase for the S&P 500 top companies in the USA and similar results were found with UK companies.[3] As discussed in Chapter 5, customer satisfaction is a broader concept than service quality, but service quality is almost always an important driver of customer satisfaction across all types of industries. A review by Gupta and Zeithaml[4] of two decades of studies examining the links between customer satisfaction, service quality and firm performance, resulted in several important recurring findings across studies. Because so many studies were examined in the review, only a subset are mentioned here, but the complete list of sources can be found in the published review itself.

Studies that were reviewed used a variety of metrics for financial performance: profit, stock price, Tobin's q (ratio of the market value of a firm divided by the replacement cost of its tangible assets), return on assets (ROA), return on investment (ROI), abnormal earnings, and cash flows. Here is what the authors concluded:

Generalization 1: Improvement in Customer Satisfaction has a Significant and Positive Impact on Firms' Financial Performance

Many studies have shown a strong link between customer satisfaction and firm profitability. For example, one comprehensive study by Anderson, Fornell and Mazvancheryl[5] using 200 of the *Fortune* 500 firms across 40 industries showed that a 1 per cent change in ACSI (as measured by the American Customer Satisfaction Index on a 0–100 scale) is associated with 1.016 per cent change in shareholder value as measured by Tobin's q. This implies that a 1 per cent improvement in satisfaction for these firms will lead to an increase in firm's value of approximately 190 million euros. Supporting this finding, a similar study by Gruca and Rego[6] found that a 1-point increase in ACSI results in an increase of around 38 million euros in a firm's net operational cash flow next year and a decrease of 4 per cent in cash flow variability.

In a service-industry study using data from almost 8,000 customers of a national hotel chain, researchers found that return on investment in service quality (e.g. cleanliness) was almost 45 per cent. Another study showed that a 1-point improvement in satisfaction (on a 7-point scale) increased ROA by 0.59 per cent.

Collectively, these studies show a strong and positive impact of customer satisfaction on firm performance. They further provide a rough benchmark about the size of the impact: a 1 per cent change in ACSI can lead to a 160 to 190 million euros' improvement in firm value. In sum, these results provide a strong guideline to firms about how much they should spend on improving customer satisfaction.

Generalization 2: The Link Between Satisfaction and Firm Performance is Asymmetric

An *asymmetric relationship* means that increases in customer satisfaction do not always have the same impact on firm performance as decreases in customer satisfaction. For example, a study by Anderson and Mittal[7] found that a 1 per cent increase in satisfaction led to 2.37 per cent increase in ROI, whereas a 1 per cent drop in satisfaction reduced ROI by 5.08 per cent. Another study by Nayyar[8] found that positive news about customer service led to an increase in compounded annualized rate (CAR) of about 0.46 per cent, whereas reports of reductions in customer service were met with declines in CAR of about half or 0.22 per cent. Also, Anderson and Mittal[9] found that the impact on ROI of a drop in satisfaction was twice that of an increase in satisfaction. In contrast, another study found that negative news of customer service had only half the impact on CAR that positive news produces.

Generalization 3: The Strength of the Satisfaction-Profitability Link Varies Across Industries as Well as Across Firms Within an Industry

The strength of the relationships among customer satisfaction, service quality and profitability is not consistent across industries. In a study by Ittner and Larcker,[10] the impact was found to be stronger in service industries than in durable and non-durable manufacturing firms. In that study, the ACSI had a positive but insignificant impact on market value of durable and non-durable manufacturing firms, and a positive and significant impact on the market value of transportation, utility and communication firms. The effect was strongly negative for retailers. Anderson and Mittal[11] also found that trade-offs between customer satisfaction and productivity (e.g., labour productivity) were more likely for services than for goods. Specifically, a simultaneous 1 per cent increase in both customer satisfaction and productivity is likely to increase ROI by 0.365 per cent for goods, but only 0.22 per cent for services.

In addition to the differences found in the studies cited, Anderson and Mittal's study[12] found that, while a 1 per cent change in satisfaction had an *average* impact of 1.016 per cent on shareholder value (Tobin's q), the impact ranged from 2.8 per cent for department stores to –0.3 per cent for discount stores. Anderson and Mittal's[13] study again found that industry characteristics explain 35 per cent of the variance in cash flow growth and 54 per cent of the variance in cash flow variability. They also found that the influence of customer satisfaction on cash flow growth is greatest for low-involvement, routinized and frequently purchased products (e.g., beer and fast food).

While this summary represents a considerable improvement over what we knew in the past, companies are very eager to learn more. This general information about the relationships among customer satisfaction, service quality, and financial performance will help them understand that investing in customer satisfaction and service quality is beneficial. Thus, indications are that the investments are worthwhile and that not investing can be harmful to firms.

Although some companies continued to approach the relationship at a broad level, others have focused more specifically on particular elements of the relationship: for example, the relationship between service quality and either customer acquisition or retention.

SERVICE SPOTLIGHT

Colt, a provider of networked communication services, has embarked on a transformation initiative aimed at improving service quality and the customer experience. Its aim is to make Colt 'the most customer oriented business in its industry', with an NPS target of 60 by 2020.

That's quite a challenge as some of Colt's competitors still record very low, or even negative NPS scores. So Colt looked at what drives different aspects of NPS and then broke NPS down into its constituent parts and built a programme of work to determine which levers it needed to pull to make a difference to each of those components. Aspects that are being addressed include reducing quote, order and delivery time; improving data accuracy; reducing reworks; reducing customer queries; reducing service delivery workload; reducing inbound calls; and providing transparency to customers on what's going on with their service at all times. Progress has been good with Colt's NPS increasing and the company has established a link between improved customer service and income. It has found that an increase in one NPS point is equivalent to a share of wallet increase and churn reduction amounting to €8.6m in revenue over three years. Listening to customers, understanding what's important to them and making improvements based on that is directly resulting in revenue growth.

Source: **www.colt.net.**

Offensive Marketing Effects of Service: Attracting More and Better Customers

Service quality can help companies attract more and better customers to the business through offensive marketing.[14] Offensive effects (shown in Figure 18.2) involve market share, reputation and price premiums. When service is good, a company gains a positive reputation and through that reputation a higher market share and the ability to charge more than its competitors for services. These benefits were documented in a multi-year, multi-company study called PIMS (profit impact of marketing strategy). The PIMS research shows that companies offering superior service achieve higher than normal market share growth and that service quality influences profits through increased market share and premium prices as well as lowered costs and less rework.[15] The study found that businesses rated in the top fifth of competitors on relative service quality average an 8 per cent price premium over their competitors.[16]

Figure 18.2 Offensive marketing effects of service on profits

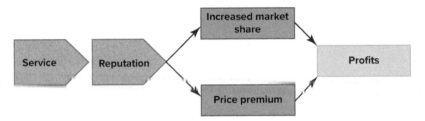

To document the impact of service on market share, a group of researchers described their version of the path between quality and market share, claiming that satisfied customers spread positive word of mouth, which leads to the attraction of new customers and then to higher market share. They claim that advertising service excellence without sufficient quality to back up the communications will not increase market share.[17]

★ SERVICE SPOTLIGHT

With revenues in excess of €988 million and customers in more than 80 countries, the Finnish company Stora Enso is one of the world's leading paper, packaging and wood products producers. The company is keen to build their competitive differentiation by focusing on criteria like service quality, product quality, delivery reliability and new product development. Its operations and processes have become fundamental to establishing new best practices focused on improving customer satisfaction. The implementation of these practices has resulted in significant improvements in the company's net promoter score (NPS – see Chapter 5). In one year, an additional 7 million euros of sales revenue was obtained from customers who had previously been detractors about the company (awarding a NPS of 6 or below) but had moved to become passives (NPS – 7–8) or promoters (NPS score 9–0).[18]

Defensive Marketing Effects of Service: Customer Retention

When it comes to keeping the customers a firm already has – an approach called *defensive marketing*[19] – researchers and consulting firms have often documented and quantified the financial impact of existing customers. In Chapter 7 we explained that customer defection, or 'customer churn', is widespread in service businesses. Customer defection is costly to companies because new customers must replace lost customers, and replacement comes at a high cost. Getting new customers is expensive; it involves advertising, promotion and sales costs as well as start-up operating expenses. New customers are often unprofitable for a period of time after acquisition. In the insurance industry, for example, the insurer does not typically recover selling costs until the third or fourth year of the relationship. Capturing customers from other companies is also an expensive proposition: a greater degree of service improvement is necessary to make a customer switch from a competitor than to retain a current customer.

Service plays a critical role – if not the critical role – in retaining customers. Providing consistently good service is not as easy to duplicate and therefore is likely to be the cementing force in customer relationships. In general, the longer a customer remains with a company, the more profitable the relationship is for the organization: 'Served correctly, customers generate increasingly more profits each year they stay with a company. Across a wide range of businesses, the pattern is the same: the longer a company keeps a customer, the more money it stands to make.'[20] The money a company makes from retention comes from four sources (shown in Figure 18.3): costs, volume of purchases, price premium and word-of-mouth communication. This section provides research evidence for many of the sources.

Figure 18.3   Defensive marketing effects of service on profits

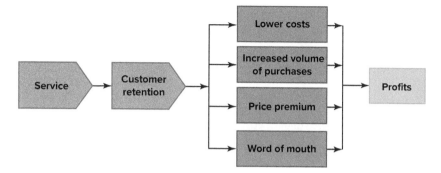

Lower Costs

Attracting a new customer is five times as costly as retaining an existing one. Consultants who have focused on these relationships assert that customer defections have a stronger effect on a company's profits than market share, scale, unit costs and many other factors usually associated with competitive advantage.[21] They also claim that, depending on the industry, companies can increase profits from 25 to 85 per cent by retaining just 5 per cent more of their customers.

Consider the following facts about the role of service quality in lowering costs:

- 'Our costs of not doing things right the first time were from 25 to 30 per cent of our revenue' (David F. Colicchio, regional quality manager, Hewlett-Packard Company).[22]
- Bain and Company, a consulting organization specializing in retention research, estimates that in the life insurance business, a 5 per cent annual increase in customer retention lowers a company's costs per policy by 18 per cent.

Volume of Purchases

Customers who are satisfied with a company's services are likely to increase the amount of money they spend with that company or the types of services offered. A customer satisfied with a broker's services, for example, will likely invest more money when it becomes available. Similarly, a customer satisfied with a bank's current account services is likely to open a savings account with the same bank and to use the bank's loan services as well. Companies are aiming to increase their 'share of wallet' through satisfying the customer. 'Share of wallet' means the **percentage** of a customer's spending for a type of service that goes to one particular company.

Price Premium

Evidence suggests that a customer who notices and values the services provided by a company will pay a price premium for those services. Most of the service quality leaders in industry command higher prices than their competitors: DHL collects more for overnight delivery than the national postal services, Hertz rental cars cost more than Budget cars, and staying at the Ritz-Carlton is a more expensive undertaking than staying at the Sofitel.

Word-of-Mouth Communication

In Chapter 3 we described the valuable role of word-of-mouth communications in purchasing service. Because word-of-mouth communication is considered more credible than other sources of information, the best type of promotion for a service may well come from other customers who advocate the services provided by the company. Word-of-mouth communication brings new customers to the firm, and the financial value of this form of advocacy can be calibrated by the company in terms of the promotional costs it saves as well as the streams of revenues from new customers.

The Key Drivers of Service Quality, Customer Retention and Profits

Understanding the relationship between overall service quality and profitability is important, but it is perhaps more useful to managers to identify specific drivers of service quality that most relate to profitability (shown in Figure 18.4). Doing so will help firms understand what aspects of service quality to change to influence the relationship, and therefore where to invest resources.

Figure 18.4   The key drivers of service quality, customer retention and profits

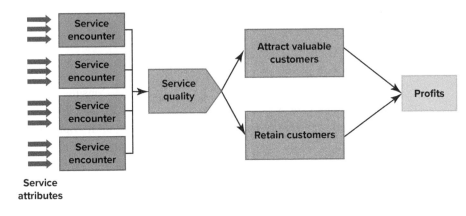

Most evidence for this issue has come from examining the aspects of service (such as empathy, responsiveness and tangibles) on overall service quality, customer satisfaction and purchase intentions rather than on financial outcomes such as retention or profitability. As you have discovered in this text, service is multifaceted, consisting of a wide variety of customer-perceived dimensions including reliability, responsiveness and empathy, and resulting from innumerable company strategies such as technology and process improvement. In research exploring the relative importance of service dimensions on overall service quality or customer satisfaction, the bulk of the support confirms that reliability is most critical; but other research has demonstrated the importance of customization and other factors. Because the dimensions and attributes are delivered in many cases with totally different internal strategies, resources must be allocated where they are most needed, and study in this topic could provide direction.

Table 18.1 shows a list of the questions that businesses still need to know more about this topic and the others in this chapter.

Some companies and researchers have viewed the effect of specific service encounters on overall service quality or customer satisfaction and the effect of specific behaviours within service encounters. For example, Marriott Hotels conducted extensive customer research to determine what service elements contribute most to customer loyalty. They found that four of the top five factors came into play in the first ten minutes of the guest's stay – those that involved the early encounters of arriving, checking in and entering the hotel rooms. Other companies have found that mistakes or problems that occur in early service encounters are particularly critical, because a failure at early points results in greater risk for dissatisfaction in each ensuing encounter.

Customer Equity and Return on Marketing

Although the marketing concept has articulated a customer-centred view since the 1960s, marketing theory and practice have only become incrementally customer centred. For example, marketing has only recently decreased its emphasis on short-term transactions and increased its focus on long-term customer

Table 18.1   Service quality and the economic worth of customers: businesses still need to know more

Topic	Key Research Questions
Service quality and profitability: the direct relationship	1. What methodologies need to be developed to allow companies to capture the effect of service quality on profit? 2. What measures are necessary to examine the relationship in a consistent, valid and reliable manner? 3. Does the relationship between service quality and profitability vary by industry, country, category of business (e.g. in services companies versus goods companies, in industrial versus packaged goods companies) or other variables? 4. What are the moderating factors of the relationship between service quality and profitability? 5. What is the optimal spending level on service in order to affect profitability?
Offensive effects of service quality	1. What is the optimal amount of spending on service quality to obtain offensive effects on reputation? 2. To obtain offensive effects, are expenditures on advertising or service quality itself more effective? 3. In what ways can companies signal high service quality to customers to obtain offensive effects?
Defensive effects of service quality	1. What is a loyal customer? 2. What is the role of service in defensive marketing? 3. How does service compare in effectiveness to other retention strategies such as price? 4. What levels of service provision are needed to retain customers? 5. How can the effects of word-of-mouth communication from retained customers be quantified? 6. What aspects of service are most important for customer retention? 7. How can defection-prone customers be identified?
Perceptions of service quality, behavioural intentions and profits	1. What is the relationship between customer purchase intentions and initial purchase behaviour in services? 2. What is the relationship between behavioural intentions and repurchase in services? 3. Does the degree of association between service quality and behaviour change at different quality levels?
Identifying the key drivers of service quality, customer retention and profits	1. What service encounters are most responsible for perceptions of service quality? 2. What are the key drivers in each service encounter? 3. Where should investments be made to affect service quality, purchase, retention and profits? 4. Are key drivers of service quality the same as key drivers of behavioural intentions, customer retention and profits?

relationships. Much of this refocus stems from the changing nature of the world's leading economies, which have undergone a century-long shift from the goods sector to the service sector.

Because service often tends to be more relationship based, this structural shift in the economy has resulted in more attention to relationships and therefore more attention to customers.

This customer-centred view is starting to be reflected in the concepts and metrics that drive marketing management, including such metrics as customer value and voice of the customer. For example, the concept of brand equity, a fundamentally product-centred concept, is now being challenged by the customer-centred concept of *customer equity*, defined as the total of the discounted lifetime values summed over all the firm's customers.

In other words, customer equity is obtained by summing up the customer lifetime values of the firm's customers. In fast-moving and dynamic industries that involve customer relationships, products come and go but customers remain. Customers and customer equity may be more central to many firms than brands and brand equity, although current management practices and metrics do not yet fully reflect this shift. The shift from product-centred thinking to customer-centred thinking implies the need for an accompanying shift from product-based metrics to customer-based metrics.

Using Customer Equity in a Strategic Framework

Consider the issues facing a typical marketing manager or marketing-oriented CEO: how do I manage my brand? How will my customers react to changes in service and service quality? Should I raise price? What is the best way to enhance the relationships with my current customers? Where should I focus my efforts? Determining customer lifetime value, or customer equity, is the first step, but the more important step is to evaluate and test ideas and strategies using lifetime value as the measuring stick. At a very basic level, strategies for building customer relationships can affect five basic factors: retention rate, referrals, increased sales, reduced direct costs and reduced marketing costs.

Rust, Zeithaml and Lemon[23] have developed an approach based on customer equity that can help business executives answer their questions. The model that represents this approach is shown in Figure 18.5. In this context, customer equity is an approach to marketing and corporate strategy that finally puts the customer – and, more important, strategies that grow the value of the customer – at the heart of the organization. The researchers identify the drivers of customer equity – value equity, brand equity and relationship equity – and explain how these drivers work, independently and together, to grow customer equity. Service strategies are prominent in both value equity and relationship equity. Within each of these drivers are specific, incisive actions ('levers') that the firm can take to enhance its overall customer equity.

Figure 18.5   The customer equity model

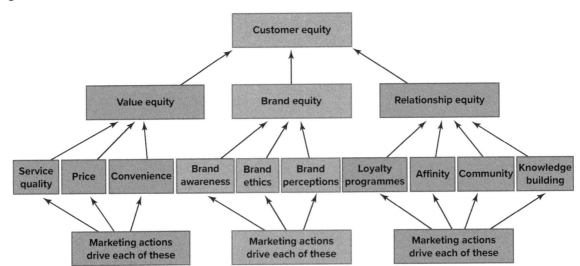

Sources: Adapted from R.T. Rust, K.N. Lemon and V.A. Zeithaml (2004) 'Return on marketing: using customer equity to focus marketing strategy', *Journal of Marketing*, 68, no. 1 (January 2004), pp. 109–27; R. Rust, V. Zeithaml and K. Lemon (2000) *Driving Customer Equity*, New York: Free Press, 2000.

Why is Customer Equity Important?

For most firms, customer equity – the total of the discounted lifetime values of all the firm's customers – is certain to be the most important determinant of the long-term value of the firm. Although customer equity will not be responsible for the entire value of the firm (consider, for example, physical assets, intellectual property, research and development competencies, etc.), the firm's current customers provide the most reliable source of future revenues and profits – and provide a focal point for marketing strategy.

Although it may seem obvious that customer equity is key to long-term success, understanding how to grow and manage customer equity is much more complex. Growing customer equity is of utmost importance, and doing it well can lead to significant competitive advantage.

Calculating Return on Marketing Using Customer Equity

Return on marketing enables companies to look at all competing marketing strategy options and trade them off on the basis of projected financial return. This approach allows companies not just to examine the impact of service on financial return but also to compare the impact of service with the impact of branding, price changes and all other marketing strategies. Using the customer equity model, firms can analyse the drivers that have the greatest impact, compare the drivers' performance with that of competitors' drivers, and project return on investment from improvements in the drivers. The framework enables 'what-if' evaluation of marketing return on investment, which can include such criteria as return on quality, return on advertising, return on loyalty programmes and, even, return on corporate citizenship, given a particular shift in customer perceptions. This approach enables firms to focus marketing efforts on strategic initiatives that generate the greatest return.

Company Performance Measurement: The Balanced Performance Scorecard

Traditionally, organizations have measured their performance almost completely on the basis of financial indicators such as profit, sales and return on investment. This short-term approach leads companies to emphasize financials to the exclusion of other performance indicators. Today's corporate strategists recognize the limitations of evaluating corporate performance on financials alone, contending that these income-based financial figures measure yesterday's decisions rather than indicate future performance. This recognition came when many companies' strong financial records deteriorated because of unnoticed declines in operational processes, quality or customer satisfaction.[24] In the words of one observer of corporate strategy:

> *Financial measures emphasize profitability of inert assets over any other mission of the company. They do not recognize the emerging leverage of the soft stuff – skilled people and employment of information – as the new keys to high performance and near-perfect customer satisfaction . . . . If the only mission a measurement system conveys is financial discipline, an organization is directionless.*[25]

For this reason, companies began to recognize that balanced scorecards – strategic measurement systems that captured other areas of performance – were needed. The developers of balanced scorecards defined them as follows:

> *a set of measures that gives top managers a fast but comprehensive view of the business . . . [that] complements the financial measures with operational measures of customer satisfaction, internal processes, and the organization's innovation and improvement activities – operational measures that are the drivers of future financial performance.*[26]

Having a firm handle on what had been viewed as 'soft' measures became the way to help organizations identify customer problems, improve processes and achieve company objectives. Balanced scorecards have become extremely popular. One recent report indicates that more than one-half of the largest companies worldwide use them.

As shown in Figure 18.6, the balanced scorecard captures three perspectives in addition to the financial perspective: customer, operational and learning. The balanced scorecard brings together, in a single management report, many of the previously separated elements of a company's competitive agenda and forces senior managers to consider all the important measures together. The scorecard has been facilitated by recent developments in software that allow companies to create balanced scorecards, automating and integrating measurements from all parts of the company.

Figure 18.6   Sample measurements for the balanced scorecard of a service

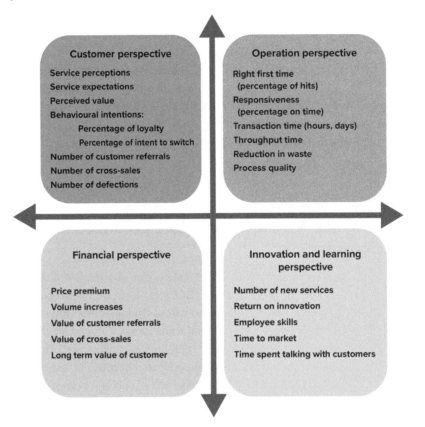

Source: Adapted from *Harvard Business Review,* an excerpt from J.R.S. Kaplan and D.P. Norton (1992) 'The balanced scorecard measures that drive performance', *Harvard Business Review* (January–February 1992).

Methods for measuring financial performance are the most developed and established in corporations, having been created more than 400 years ago. In contrast, efforts to measure market share, quality, innovation, human resources and customer satisfaction have only recently been created. Companies can improve their performance by developing this discipline in their measurement of all four categories.

Customer Perceptual Measures

Customer perceptual measures are leading indicators of financial performance. As we discussed in this chapter, customers who are not happy with the company will defect and will tell others about their dissatisfaction.

⭐ **SERVICE SPOTLIGHT**

The French-owned EDF Group uses an adapted balanced scorecard approach to link overall objectives to continuous improvement to create a strategy-linked culture throughout the whole of its organization. The scorecard they use reflects the Group's strategic vision in the form of five ambitions, with associated performance measures. The five ambitions are to meet shareholder expectations, care for customers, be a positive point of reference (corporate reputation), be safe and responsible and maximize staff satisfaction. These ambitions do not in themselves follow the traditional balanced scorecard template but they are seen as the issues that are critical to an energy provider. The balanced scorecard is EDF Group's corporate-wide strategic reference framework for decisions at local and operational levels including decisions relating to service delivery.

As we also discussed, perceptual measures reflect customer beliefs and feelings about the company and its products and services, and can predict how the customer will behave in the future. Overall forms of the measurements we discussed in Chapter 6 (shown in the customer perspective box of Figure 18.6) are measures that can be included in this category. Among the measures that are valuable to track are overall service perceptions and expectations, customer satisfaction, perceptual measures of value and behavioural intention measures, such as loyalty and intent to switch. A company that notices a decline in these numbers should be concerned that the decline will translate into less profit for the company.

Operational Measures

Operational measures involve the translation of customer perceptual measures into the standards or actions that must be set internally to meet customers' expectations. Although virtually all companies count or calculate operational measures in some form, the balanced scorecard requires that these measures stem from the business processes that have the greatest effect on customer satisfaction. In other words, these measures are not independent of customer perceptual measures but instead are intricately linked with them. In Chapter 9 we called these customer-linked operational measures *customer-defined standards* – operational standards determined through customer expectations and calibrated the way the customer views and expresses them.

Financial Measures

One way that service leaders are changing financial measurement is to calibrate the defensive effect of retaining and losing customers. The monetary value of retaining customers can be projected through the use of average revenues over the lifetimes of customers. The number of customer defections can then be translated into lost revenue to the firm and become a critical company performance standard:

> *Ultimately, defections should be a key performance measure for senior management and a fundamental component of incentive systems. Managers should know the company's defection rate, what happens to profits when the rate moves up or down and why defections occur.*

> Reichheld, F.F. and Sasser, W.E. (1990). Zero defections: Quality comes to services.
> *Harvard Business Review*, 68(5), 105–111.

Companies can also measure actual increases or decreases in revenue from retention or defection of customers by capturing the value of a loyal customer, including expected cash flows over a customer's lifetime or lifetime customer value (as described in Chapter 7). Other possible financial measures (as shown in Figure 18.6) include the value of price premiums, volume increases, customer referrals and cross-sales.

Innovation and Learning

The final area of measurement involves a company's ability to innovate, improve and learn – by launching new products, creating more value for customers and improving operating efficiencies. This measurement area is most difficult to capture quantitatively but can be accomplished using performance-to-goal percentages. For example, a company can set a goal of launching ten new services a year, then measure what percentage of that goal it does achieve. If four new services are launched, its percentage for the year is 40 per cent, which can then be compared with subsequent years.

Effective Non-Financial Performance Measurements

According to field research conducted in 60 companies and survey responses from 297 senior executives, many companies do not identify and act on the correct non-financial measures.[27] One example involves a bank that surveyed satisfaction only from customers who physically entered the branches, a policy that caused some branch managers to offer free food and drinks in order to increase their scores. According to the authors of the study, companies make four major mistakes:

1 *Not linking measures to strategy.* Companies can easily identify hundreds of non-financial measures to track, but they also need to use analysis that identifies the most important drivers of their strategy. Successful organizations use value-driver maps, tools that lay out the cause-and-effect relationships between drivers and strategic success. Figure 18.7 shows the causal model developed by a successful fast-food chain to understand the key drivers of shareholder value. The factors on the right were identified as most important in leading to the concepts on the left, and the sequence of concepts from top to bottom show the relationships among company strategies (such as selection and staffing) and intermediate results (such as employee and customer satisfaction) that result in financial results (such as sustained profitability and shareholder value). The study found that fewer than 30 per cent of the firms surveyed used this causal modelling approach.

2 *Not validating the links.* Only 21 per cent of companies in the study verify that the non-financial measures lead to financial performance. Instead, many firms decide what they are going to measure in each category and never link the categories. Many managers believed that the relationships were self-evident instead of conducting analysis to validate the linkages. It is critical that companies pull together all their data and examine the relationships among the categories.

3 *Not setting the right performance targets.* Companies sometimes aim too high in setting improvement targets. Targeting 100 per cent customer satisfaction might seem to be a desirable goal, but many companies expend far too many resources to gain too little improvement in satisfaction. The study's authors found that a telecommunications company aiming for 100 per cent customer satisfaction was wasting resources because customers who were 100 per cent satisfied spent no more money than those who were 80 per cent satisfied.[28]

4 *Measuring incorrectly.* Companies need to use metrics with statistical validity and reliability. Organizations cannot measure such a complex phenomenon as customer satisfaction with one or two simple measures, nor can they use inconsistent methodologies to measure the same concept. Another problem that companies may encounter is trying to use quantitative metrics to capture qualitative results for important factors such as leadership and innovation.

Creating a balanced scorecard in and of itself does not improve performance. Companies will not reap the benefits of techniques such as the balanced scorecard unless they effectively address how to measure non-financial performance.

Figure 18.7   The measures that matter most: a causal model for a fast-food company shows the critical drivers of performance and the concepts that lead to shareholder value

Source: Adapted from C.D. Ittner and D.F. Larcker (2003) 'Coming up short on nonfinancial performance measurement', *Harvard Business Review* (November 2003), pp. 88–95.

Summary

Each of the sections in this chapter assessed the evidence and identified what is known about the relationship between service and profitability. The chapter used a conceptual framework to link all the variables in these topics: (1) the direct relationship between service and profits; (2) offensive effects of service quality, the ability to obtain new customers; (3) defensive effects of service quality, the ability to retain existing customers; and (4) key drivers of service quality, customer retention and profits. Considerable progress has been made in the investigation of service quality, profitability and the economic worth of customers, but managers are still lacking many of the answers that would help them make informed decisions about service quality investments. The customer equity model was also discussed as a way of measuring the return on marketing. The chapter concluded with a discussion of the balanced scorecard, which offers a strategic approach for measuring all aspects of a company's performance.

Key Concepts

Balanced scorecard	397	Offensive marketing	391
Customer equity	396	Share of wallet	393
Defensive marketing	392		

Exercises

1 Use a web search engine to locate three software companies that make balanced scorecard software. What are their current offerings? How can these software firms help individual companies understand the concepts and relationships discussed in this chapter? Which of the three companies would you select based on the information you have found?

2 Interview a local firm to find out what it knows about its key drivers of financial performance. What are the key service drivers of the firm? Does the company know whether these service drivers relate to profit?

3 Select a service industry (such as fast food) or a company (such as McDonald's) that you are familiar with, either as a customer or as an employee, and create a balanced scorecard. Describe the operational, customer, financial and learning measures that could be used to capture performance.

Discussion Questions

1 Why has it been difficult for executives to understand the relationship between service improvements and profitability in their companies?

2 To this day, many companies believe that service is a cost rather than a revenue producer. Why might they hold this view? How would you argue the opposite view?

3 What is the difference between offensive and defensive marketing? How does service affect each of these?

4 If the costs of retaining an existing customer are lower than the costs of attracting a new customer, why do many insurance companies offer lower prices to new customers?

5 Discuss the proposition that 100 per cent customer satisfaction is a goal that is not ever achievable nor profitable.

6 What are the main sources of profit in defensive marketing?

7 What are the main sources of profit in offensive marketing?

8 How will the balanced scorecard help you understand and document the information presented in this chapter? Which of the sections that discuss different aspects of the relationship between service quality and profits can it illuminate?

Further Reading

Elbanna, S., Eid, R. and Kamel, H. (2015). Measuring hotel performance using the balanced scorecard: A theoretical construct development and its empirical validation. *International Journal of Hospitality Management*, 51, 105–14.

Fornell, C., Mithas, S., Morgeson, F. and Krishnan, M.S. (2006). Customer satisfaction and stock prices: High returns, low risk. *Journal of Marketing*, 70(1), 3–14.

Jääskeläinen, A., Laihonen, H. and Lönnqvist, A. (2014). Distinctive features of service performance measurement. *International Journal of Operations & Production Management*, 34(12), 1466–86.

Kaplan, R.S. (2012). The balanced scorecard: Comments on balanced scorecard commentaries. *Journal of Accounting and Organizational Change*, 8(4), 539–45.

Kaplan, R.S. and Norton, D.P. (1996). *Balanced Scorecard: Translating Strategy into Action*. Cambridge: Harvard Business School Press.

Neely, A. (Ed.). (2007). *Business Performance Measurement: Unifying Theory and Integrating Practice*. Cambridge: Cambridge University Press.

Raithel, S., Sarstedt, M., Scharf, S. and Schwaiger, M. (2012). On the value relevance of customer satisfaction. Multiple drivers and multiple markets. *Journal of the Academy of Marketing Science*, 40(4), 509–25.

Wilson, A.M. (2000). The use of performance information in the management of service delivery. *Marketing Intelligence and Planning*, 18(3), 127–34.

Case Section

Chapter Outline

Case 1 CitizenM: Redesigning Consumers' Hotel Experiences

Case 2 Amazon: Delivering Service through Electronic Channels and Intermediaries

Case 3 The John Lewis and Partners Customer Experience

Case 4 McDonald's: Designing Services Processes and Innovations

Case 5 Music Festivals and the Price of Live Performances

Case 6 Marriott International: Opportunity Window for Customer Experience

Case 7 Turkish Airlines: Enhancing the Customer Experience

Case 8 Starbucks: Key Elements of the 'Starbucks Experience'

CASE 1   CITIZENM: REDESIGNING CONSUMERS' HOTEL EXPERIENCES

This case was written by Professor Kate L. Daunt, Cardiff Business School, Cardiff University, UK.

Introduction

Frustrated at the stagnation and monotony of the hotel industry, in 2008 co-founders of the hotel brand citizenM, Michael Levie and Rattan Chadha, blasted onto the hotel scene with disruptive force by offering affordable luxury for the modern traveller. In order to identify a profitable gap in the marketplace, Levie and Chadha undertook market research to understand the factors on which the hotel industry competes and the factors most important to customers. The new-entrant hoteliers concluded that while the hotel industry aims to compete on a plethora of factors, only three of these factors determine why frequent travellers book five-star hotels over three-star hotels: the luxurious servicescape, the luxurious sleeping environment and prime location. Alternatively, travellers were found to choose three-star hotels over five-star establishments because of the price and the feeling that five-star hotels are too pretentious, formal and unwelcoming. Armed with this information, Levie and Chadha created a master list to pinpoint which features, typical to hotel offerings, citizenM could eliminate, reduce, raise and create (Kim and Mauborgne, 2017).

First on the hit-list to eliminate were typical hotel design facets and offerings that were shown to offer little value to consumers. These included the front desk, concierge service and full-service restaurant. Levie and Chadha's market research showed that the front-desk does not bring value to the customer, it exists for the benefit of the hotel to aid in the processing of people (i.e. assign guests rooms) and payments. Underpinned by a customer-orientation, the traditional front desk was removed from the citizenM blueprint. Porters were also added to the eliminate list. Levie and Chadha found that modern travellers travel light, often with only carry-on luggage, therefore removing the need for porters and eliminating a guest's negative experiences of having to wait for their luggage to arrive to their room and the awkward moment of tipping the porter for their service. Driven by an understanding that modern travellers seek to explore the local culture and cuisine, the traditional full-service restaurant (and accompanying professional kitchen) was also added to the eliminate list, freeing up physical space in the hotel within which Levie and Chadha could innovate (Vermeulen, 2015; Kim and Mauborgne, 2017).

The reduced list focused on customers' wants with laser precision to craft the service offering and associated servicescape. At odds with the typical hotel market offering, Levie and Chadha understood that because customers typically spend little time in their hotel rooms beyond when they are sleeping, guest room types, room size and price were reduced comparative to the industry standard, while the quality of the sleeping environment was recognized as an important raise factor with a focus on bed size, shower power and the quality of linens used. Situating the hotels in a prime location, offering free high-speed Internet access and free on-demand movies were also recognized as factors that should be raised relative to the competition because of their perceived importance to consumers. Finally, driven by an innate understanding of the factors that modern travellers value, Levie and Chadha's create list comprised non-industry standard features including: 3-minute self-check-in (customers hate to wait), a communal living environment (travellers want access to social environments) and multi-tasking employees (customers want access to friendly employees who can own and solve their problems). Armed with this deep understanding of modern hotel customers' needs and wants, the game-changing brand of citizenM was born. It is a brand that year-on-year attracts the highest guest rankings, the highest rate of guest occupancies (for which citizenM achieves a staggering 80 per cent higher than industry average), the lowest employee costs and the highest profit per square foot in the global hotel industry (Kim and Mauborgne, 2017). Additionally, citizenM continues to win multiple industry awards for its achievements in design, guest reviews and is poll position among 'the best' hotels in the world.

citizenM's first hotel opened its doors at Amsterdam's Schiphol airport in 2008, quickly followed by further hotel openings in Amsterdam city centre, Glasgow, London, Rotterdam, New York, Paris and beyond (Vermeulen, 2015). citizenM employs an inventive strategy to create an instantly recognizable design which entails typically purchasing (rather than leasing) buildings and utilizing, where possible, prefabricated modular design. That is, citizenM bedrooms are all identical in size and design and are built offsite using modular construction techniques to exact design specifications before being transported to the hotel's location and stacked into place, Lego® style, using a crane. Interestingly, this build technique hasn't limited citizenM's (upwards) growth ambitions, with the brand owning the tallest modular hotel in the United States, citizenM New York Bowery located in lower Manhattan, which towers at 22 storeys and comprises 210 modular units which were constructed in and shipped from Poland (Marani, 2018). This innovative approach to construction keeps costs low, build quality and consistency high, considerably speeds up the time it takes to bring a new citizenM hotel to market and allows for the micromanaging of every facet of the citizenM's servicescape design (Mest, 2017).

Mission, Positioning and Target Market

Underpinned by Levie and Chadha's eliminate, reduce, raise and create master list, citizenM demonstrates an unrivalled understanding of its target market which has enabled the firm to produce a meaningful and value-led mission and positioning within the marketplace. According to citizenM's website, the company mission is to *become the leading transformational hotel; inspiring a new generation of modern travellers in the big cities of the world by offering an affordable luxury lifestyle, while providing sustained premium returns to stakeholders* (citizenM.com, n.d.). Thus, their mission is to disrupt. At the core of this mission is the firm's transformational and innovative positioning and genuine focus on the customer experience from the customer's perspective. In an interview, Levie states *our aim is not to reply on marketing to sell hotel rooms. It is*

to create a hotel experience that in itself becomes our marketing, because people can't stop recommending it and sharing pictures of it on Facebook and Instagram' (Kim and Mauborgne, 2017). In this sense, citizenM aims to create a hotel experience that is so positive, it not only secures customer loyalty, it also fosters positive word-of-mouth between consumer groups. Therefore, removing the need for and the associated costs of traditional advertising methods. citizenM has successfully generated change and innovation in an industry which has been incredibly slow to evolve and innovate. If asked to imagine a typical hotel room, we might picture the following: a mid-sized carpeted room containing a double-sized bed with a chocolate on the pillow, windows draped with fabric curtains in traditional, muted earth-toned colours. A television mounted on a shelf above a dark wood desk which contains a pen, notepad, room service menu and leaflet stating the charges for Wi-FI. citizenM's rooms do not reflect this image. If personified, the traditional hotel room is a somewhat old-fashioned yet dependable individual, while citizenM is the cool kid who loves to break the rules. citizenM achieves its positioning of 'affordable luxury' via curating a fresh, fun and surprising servicescape to evoke feelings of luxury, escapism and foster positive emotions, while also using technology to promote convenience and a seamless service experience (see Table 1).

An important ingredient of citizenM's success is the firm's ability to identify and satisfy a previously untapped segment of the hotel market. citizenM make their target market known to all by embedding it into the brand's DNA. The term citizenM derives from 'mobile citizens of the world' and aims to tap into the growing generation of well-informed frequent travellers. A consumer's age and gender are not important to citizenM, but rather the brand employs four avatars to pinpoint its target consumers, labelled: business traveller, cultural traveller, fashionista (who travels to shop) and explorer (Allchin, 2012). These individuals are described as being open-minded and *cross continents as easily as they cross streets* (citizenM.com, n.d.). Such customers are turned-off by the traditional, old-fashioned hotel experience, are value-conscious, enjoy spending time in environments that are inspirational and contemporary and seek genuine, rather

Table 1   Comparison of traditional hotel marketing offering versus citizenM

	Traditional hotel	citizenM
Marketing positioning	• Business OR leisure • Serious	• Business and leisure • Fun
Employees	• Doorman • Porter • Receptionist • Concierge • Restaurant server • Housekeeping • Maintenance • Telephone reservation team	• Multi-tasking ambassador • Website
Servicescape	• Lobby • Full-service restaurant • Traditional design • Minimal use of customer-facing technology • Single or double beds • A chocolate on your pillow • A light switch • Pay-for-view movies • TV with 5 channels • Rooms of different sizes and grades (i.e. standard and superior) • Sink in the bathroom • Premium branded toiletries	• Living room • Canteen • Contemporary design • Maximum use of customer-facing technology • King-sized beds • An iPad by your bed • Controllable mood lighting • Free-to-view movies • TV with multiple channels and the ability to stream content straight from your device • Modular rooms of one size (small) and one grade (great)
Service experience	• Formal and scripted • 15-minute check-in time • Check-in/out with employee • Free slow Wi-Fi, pay for premium Wi-Fi, Wi-Fi hotspots • Loyal customers collect points for each visit	• Informal and unscripted • 3-minute check-in time • Check-in/out with self-service kiosk • Free fast Wi-Fi in all areas of the hotel • Loyal customers get 10 per cent off every booking

Source: Kate Daunt

than scripted, customer service experiences (Anon, 2017a). Levie explains: '*citizenM provides affordable luxury for the people. Since day one it has aimed to create a new, hybrid hotel that answers to the frustrations of many travellers. Its secret is giving everything that they want, and nothing that they don't. This means citizenM can keep its prices low, even in the middle of hyper busy urban centres. Our properties give every guest a perfect night's sleep, an inspiring place to meet and a continuous reason to smile with genuine, friendly touches . . . while it takes its aim of providing a stylish and affordable hotel very seriously, citizenM also has a sense of humour*' (Brown, 2018).

Servicescape Design: The citizenM Lobby and Communal Areas

citizenM embraces a holistic understanding of the power of servicescapes and this focus includes the location of their hotels. citizenM intentionally locate in sites that are attractive to their target market. The firm isn't interested in residing in the depths of the countryside with limited transport links. Rather, the hotels are positioned at the very heart of the metropolis. Look to TripAdvisor to discover the busiest, trendiest and most vibrant area of any given city and this is where you are also likely to find citizenM who aim to be part of the neighbourhood's fabric and draw inspiration from the local community (Brown, 2018). However, while the firm recognizes the strategic importance of location to the success of the brand, by their own admission they have made errors. In an interview Chadha explains: '*Downtown Glasgow* (citizenM's second hotel to open) *was a mistake . . . it doesn't attract our target customers . . . when the bars close, they bring the party back to the hotel. That's not what we intended*' (Welsh, 2014).

However, when knocked back, citizenM continues to bounce back. An example of this resilient attitude can be seen in the development of one of citizenM's hotels in London, England. This was an ambitious project. citizenM planned to locate what remains one of its biggest properties to date, directly opposite one of the most recognizable landmarks in London – the historic Tower of London, famous for its gruesome past, current housing of the Queen's collections of jewels and the fancily dressed Beefeater guards. However, with history comes heritage and associated heritage protection rules and regulations. To add further woe, the residents in the local area strongly objected to the planned building. Yet, citizenM fought on, working with the planners and regulators and three years later they were given permission to build. The result is a stark juxtaposition of a branded, modern, glass-flanked building against the foreboding ancient brick castle and fortress (Anon, 2017a).

Because citizenM has eliminated reception desks, the concierge and porters, the entrance and first physical encounter with a citizenM hotel is not typical of what you might expect from a hotel. Yet, while tweaked to the local location, all citizenM entrance and communal areas have a look and feel that is distinctively recognizable as the brand. Typically, this

Source: ©Roberto La Rosa/Shutterstock

open-plan ground floor space comprising integrated living areas uses design strategies to divide the space into three separate zones. These are labelled the living room, the canteen and the self-check-in area. The living room space could be described as curated chaos (citizenM.com, n.d.). Underpinned by a diverse mix of furniture from Swiss firm Vitra, which is aesthetically similar to IKEA but with a premium tone, the servicescape works hard to portray the brand image, make functional use of the physical space and evoke positive emotions. For example, in keeping with the local area, the citizenM Tower of London proudly exhibits a distinct kitsch Britannia vibe. Here, the walls from floor to ceiling feature a built-in shelving matrix which is adorned with eye-catching and curious artefacts, paintings, photographs and memorabilia. These include a vintage police helmet, union flag, framed sketch of a royal castle and pair of antique leather riding boots. A supportive structural pillar is given a citizenM makeover and is adorned with a wrap of wallpaper which repeats a black and white portrait of a young Queen Elizabeth II (Fountain, 2016). The effect is paradoxically busy yet soothing; it is clear that detail matters to the citizenM design team.

Considering customers' needs to work and play, the brand uses servicescape design to facilitate different customer activities. For example, well-spaced wooden tables and chairs positioned next to power points are available for guests who wish to work formally on a laptop, spread out their paperwork and hold a meeting without fear that the table next to them is eavesdropping on their conversation. By contrast, in the same open-space area an alternative zone is created with the use of large comfortable fabric chairs and small coffee tables cocooned by a large fluffy floor rug, all which centre around a wall-mounted flat screen television and are flanked by walls on either side containing a library full of contemporary and classical literature. Here, the servicescape signals that customers are welcome to chat, relax and while the day away. Clever use of lighting also aids the zoning effect of the living room space and enhances customer's visual perceptions. For example, ceiling lighting devices labelled reflecting holons are used to help layer light, create atmosphere and distinguish one relaxation area from another (Yu, Bae and Wu, 2018). These cream-coloured lights look something akin to a hot-air balloon festival, the multiple different illuminated shapes and sizes hang from the ceiling, floating elegantly and casting a cosy glow on those sat below. Large glass windows and dashes of plants and greenery introduce biophilic elements into the servicescape and successfully bring the outside in, flooding the area with natural daylight (Browning, 2016).

Moving on to the eating space labelled canteenM, this zoned area offers canteen-style seating which centres around a bar area in which ambassadors can create cocktails or artisan coffees for guests. Facilitating self-service, the servicescape design features tray stations, cutlery cubbies and open refrigerators from which customers can grab a locally produced sandwich or cold alcoholic or non-alcoholic beverage. A chalk board features the small selection of hot foods available to order and the materials employed in this area signal cleanliness and hygiene, distinct from the cosy fabrics of the living room space. CanteenM is available for guests to use day or night, replaces the need for room service and provides customers with a further area in which to work, relax and consume refreshments (Vermeulen, 2015).

Clearly designed with the customer journey in mind, close to the canteen and logically situated near the entrance and elevators, is the third zone of citizenM's integrative living area: the self-check-in space, populated with several desks containing screens akin to airport self-check-in terminals (Anon, 2017b). Using touch-screen technology, check-in takes less than three minutes, in which time guests can recall their booking and issue themselves with a RFID room key which can also double up as a payment method in the canteen (citizenM.com, n.d.). Somewhat ingeniously, the room keys are manufactured to contain a hole through which a plastic tie can be fed, converting the key into a luggage tag for the trip home, while loyal canteenM customers can engage in sustainable behaviour and reuse their room key on subsequent visits to any citizenM hotel (citizenM.com, n.d.). Given that many citizenM customers check-in independently, without the aid of an employee, the firm uses signage featuring white and red text against a black background, to welcome its target customers and set the tone for a guest's stay. The sign reads: *'To all travellers long and short haul. To the weary, the wise and the bleary-eyed. To the suits, weekenders, fashion baggers and affair-havers. To the explorers, adventurers and dreamers. To all locals of the world from Amsterdam, Boston, Cairo to Zagreb. To all who travel the world with wide eyes and big hearts. To all who are independent yet united in a desire for positive travelling. To those who are smarter than a dolphin with a university degree and realize that you can have luxury for not much cash. To those who need a good bed, a cold drink and big fluffy towels. To all who are mobile citizens of the world. citizenM welcomes you all'* (Fountain, 2016). The brand's use of inspirational quotes and quirky imagery continues into the elevators and corridors leading to guests' rooms. For example, one elevator contains the image of an elephant head on businessman's smartly dressed torso complete with suit and briefcase with the caption 'wise citizen', while a long corridor contains stencilled quotations of 'wisdom and advice from around the world' including *'to get an energy boost in the afternoon, eat lively witchetty grubs (Australia)'* (Fountain, 2016).

Servicescape Design: The citizenM Bedroom

In line with the evolution of technology, consumers' needs and customer experience demands, the modular built citizenM bedrooms have undergone multiple iterations since the hotel's initial launch. The first room housed the shower and lavatory in separate cylinders, whereas the second room iteration combined these to increase design efficiencies. Reportedly, room version 3.0 is currently being tested in citizenM's experience centre. Chadha notes, *'the design is constantly changing – we're not standing still'* (Anon, 2017a). By industry standards, citizenM rooms are small and are designed to house a maximum of two guests. The king-sized bed, which takes up a third of the room's floor space, is slotted between the room's walls (left to right) and is positioned against a window (Murphy, 2017). The beds are square in shape so that duo customers can decide to sleep either facing the television, which is mounted on a wall at the end of the bed, or they can choose to relocate, placing their pillows under the window allowing guests to exit the bed without the need to climb over their companion – genius! (citizenM.com, n.d.). The bed is furnished with a Sealy mattress, plump pillows and Frette bed linen, thus providing customers with comfort akin to a 5-star hotel (Robbins, 2012). The white structure of the bed is constructed with a red tab which guests can pull to reveal a large drawer in which they can stow their luggage, creating space-saving efficiencies (Fountain, 2016). A further distinctive feature of a citizenM bedroom is the placement of bathroom-related facilities. The sink is mounted on a white fixture in the main bedroom area which is cleverly designed to also contain a lamp, mini-bar, towel holder and further storage. The shower and lavatory are concealed within a frosted glass pod. Toiletries by perfumer Alessandro Gualtieri (Robbins, 2012) are ergonomically placed and guests can choose between citizenAM or citizenPM bodywash depending on their mood. The slick black packaging for the toiletries is adorned with white text containing narratives designed to make guests smile. For example, citizenPM reads: '*Shower/Shampoo designed for citizens who live by the night, dance with the dark and don't wake up until the sun goes down. citizenPM shower gel and shampoo will make you feel like you're about to walk out into wonderland and that somehow everything tonight will just fall into place. You never know, it just might*'. Alternatively, citizenAM soap states: '*Designed to turn even the longest-haul traveller into a sparkling clean and nice-smelling human being again*' (Fountain, 2016).

A distinguishing feature of a citizenM hotel room is its use of technology which is embedded into the servicescape. Docked next to every citizenM bed is an iPad which the firm label a moodpad (Murphy, 2017) and describe as a personal butler (citizenM.com, n.d.). Via this tablet, customers can operate the blackout blinds, use the free fast Wi-Fi to stream content from their personal smartphone to the television (i.e. YouTube), control the room temperature and personalize the lighting colour for the room. A guest wanting to watch one of the many free-to-stream movies simply need select 'movie mode' for the blinds to close, the lighting to dim and the movie selector to pop up on the television (Tallon, 2016). All that's missing is a popcorn machine. As with other areas of the servicescape design, citizenM has gone through a period of trial and error to achieve the correct balance of technology in guests' rooms. International hotel designer, James Sloan notes '*citizenM had too much tech. It's scaled back now and the experience is much better. . .technology for technology's sake actually frustrates guests*' (Anon, 2017c). A further quirk of the citizenM room can be found with the presence of a pillow doll which can be either human or animal shaped. These rag dolls are often posted on social media by guests and are discussed at length on travel review websites, representing the tactile and interactive nature of the citizenM servicescape. Finally, bedrooms contain a small, yet functional desk with lamp and chair.

The citizenM Ambassador

Underpinning the physical servicescape design of the hotel is the essential human element of the citizenM employee, the ambassador. As with other facets of the citizenM servicescape design, the firm breaks from standard industry protocol in how they recruit, task and utilize frontline employees. Chadha explains: '*There's no reception, no concierge, our ambassadors are there to help find whatever you want. . .They don't grab your bag or bug you every five minutes. If you need something, ask. Otherwise we leave you alone. Our ambassador training takes 10 weeks and begins with a casting on the hotel site. Many of our ambassadors are from drama school. We don't often take people from the hospitality industry because they pick up bad habits. We look for people who are genuine, who might even become friends with the client*' (Welsh, 2014). Personality is key to the recruitment process and in order to allow ambassadors the freedom to fully serve individual customer needs, citizenM ditches scripted interactions in favour of fostering natural and authentic interactions between ambassadors and guests (citizenM.com, n.d.). In an era where consumers are increasingly sensitive to and frustrated by perceived employee insincerity and cynicism, this strategy seems a smart move.

The citizenM Virtual Servicescape

Crucial to citizenM's business model is a slick website with intuitive user-friendly functionality. Because citizenM hires fewer employees than is the industry standard, the website must act as a workhorse for the brand and fulfil many of roles traditionally performed by employees. These include acting as a travel agent, offering information traditionally provided by a concierge, taking payments and being a receptionist (Robbins, 2012). In keeping with the physical servicescape design of the citizenM hotels, the webpage exhibits the distinctive black, red and white colour scheme. Headlining the homepage is a slick contemporary, professionally filmed video, showing attractive people enjoying citizenM cities and hotel features. Bright colours and motion are used to grab the viewer's attention. As browsers scroll down the page they are greeted with large, beautifully styled and lit images of citizenM's facilities and the contents of citizenM's social media feed. Chadha is clear that social media constitutes an important form of data to the hotel: '*it has given us the chance to receive direct feedback, but also connect with our guests on a more individual level. . .We have also taken a lot of the guest feedback from social media into consideration when building future hotels. The hotel is built for them, so if they have an opinion, we want to hear it*' (O'Neill, 2013).

Underpinning citizenM's use of data is an industry-defining data management programme and associated software which enables the firm to pump real-time data from both sides of the line of invisibility to the heart of the business, enabling the firm to monitor and identify fail points prior to the customer even realizing that there is an issue (Wolfe, 2015). This software and data management system also enables the firm to monitor immediate costs and simultaneously implement effective changes. For example, changing suppliers can represent a long, unattractive and laborious process for many hoteliers. However, citizenM's data system enables the firm to monitor costs, quality and speed of supplier activities and easily switch to an alternative supplier when needed (PhocusWire, 2018).

The citizenM Voyage to Date and Future Travel Plans

citizenM's growth trajectory is impressive: after a little over 20 years in the business, the hotel now boasts 30 hotels in 11 countries, totalling 7000 rooms. The firm's expansion can be roughly mapped from Europe, to the USA, to Asia and this expansion looks set to continue with further hotels currently under development in Los Angeles, Miami, San Francisco, Seattle, Washington, Geneva and Paris (which will grow the Paris portfolio size to five hotels, signalling that Paris really is the 'city of love' for the brand). Rumoured expansion plans also point to further hotel openings in Asia and entrance into the Australasian market (citizenM.com, n.d.). The citizenM website affirms '*we are not stopping our exploration any time soon. . .We want to offer our signature affordable luxury wherever our travel-thirsty citizens dream of going next. Which is everywhere*' (citizenM.com, n.d.).

References

Allchin, Josie (2012). 'Bedding in Culture' *Marketing Week*, 4 July.

Anon (2017a). Focus Q&A – Robin Chadha, *Design Curial*, 16 November. Available at www.designcurial.com/news/focus-qa---robin-chadha-5971003/ accessed 26 July 2019].

Anon (2017b). citizenM Now Open for Business at Paris La Défence, Design Exchange, 13 June. Available at www.demagazine.co.uk/design/citizenm-now-open-for-business-at-paris-la-defense [accessed 26 July 2019].

Anon (2017c). When 'Design' Becomes 'User Experience'. Available at www.independenthotelshow.co.uk/news/42-when-design-becomes-user-experience [accessed 26 July 2019].

Brown, Piers (2018). BHN's Piers Brown Talks to citizenM COO Michael Levie About the Brand's Evolution and Expansion Plans. Available at www.boutiquehotelnews.com/home/features/2018/10/22/quick-qa-michael-levie,-citizenm/ [accessed 26 July 2019].

Browning, Bill (2016). Human Spaces 2.0: Biophilic Design in Hospitality. Available at http://interfaceinc.scene7.com/is/content/InterfaceInc/

Interface/Americas/WebsiteContentAssets/Documents/Reports/Hosp-Human%20Spaces/wc_am-interfacehospitalityhumanspaces8252017.pdf [accessed 23 August 2019].

Fountain, Daniel (2016). citizenM Tower of London, *Hotel Designs*, 7 December. Available at https://hoteldesigns.net/latest-hotel-review/review-citizenm-tower-of-london/ [accessed 26 July 2019].

Kim, W. Chan and Renée Mauborgne (2017). *Blue Ocean Shift Beyond Competing: Proven Steps to Inspire Confidence and Seize New Growth*. Macmillan, London.

Marani, Matthew (2018). Stacks on Stacks: Take a Look Behind the Construction of the Tallest Modular Hotel in the US, *The Architect's Newspaper*, 21 December. Available at https://archpaper.com/2018/12/citizenm-new-york-bowery-hotel-modular-construction/#gallery-0-slide-0 [accessed 25 July 2019].

Mest, Elliott (2017). Two NYC Hotels Come Together Piece by Piece, *Hotel Management*, 232, 2, 16-17.

Murphy, Matt (2017). citizenM Shoreditch: The Dutch Chain Bringing Style to London's 'Budget' Boutique Hotel Scene, *The Independent*, 23 March. Available at https://www.independent.co.uk/travel/hotels/citizenm-shoreditch-hotel-review-east-london-budget-dutch-chain-budget-a7645861.html [accessed 23 August 2019].
O'Neill, Thomas (2013). Creative Partners: How citizenM is Reinventing the Affordable Hotel Experience, 2 September. Available at https://www.thedrum.com/news/2013/09/02/creative-partners-how-citizenm-reinventing-affordable-hotel-experience [accessed 21 June 2019].

PhocusWire (2018). citizenM on the Unhappy Marriage of Tech and Hotel Companies. 1 August. Available at https://www.youtube.com/watch?v=JdCSFhj0hqM [accessed 23 August 2019].

Robbins, Tom (2012). Prefab Rooms and Linen by Frette: Hotel Insider Stylish, High-tech and Cheap: Is citizenM the Future of Hospitality?, *Financial Times*, 14 July, London.

Tallon, Lucy (2016). citizenM Hotel, You Beautifully Designed Thing, Medium.com. Available at https://medium.com/common-good/citizenm-hotel-you-beautifully-designed-thing-810d4a8e6c73 [accessed 26 July 2019].

Vermeulen, Freek (2015). 3 Steps to Break Out in a Tired Industry, *Harvard Business Review*, 1 May. Available at https://hbr.org/2015/05/3-steps-to-break-out-in-a-tired-industry [accessed 23 June 2019].

Welsh, Liz (2014). Reinventing the Posh Hotel, *Inc. Magazine*, 36, 5, 120–122.

Wolfe, Frank (2015). How the citizenM Brand is Getting Technology Right, *Hotel Management*, 230, 10, 15.

www.citizenM.com (n.d.) [accessed 26 July 2019].

Yu, Hui., Ge Bae and Liang Wu (2018). Application of Perception Theory in Hotel Interior Design, *Open Journal of Applied Sciences*, 8, 285–295.

This case was written by Dr Fiona Whelan-Ryan, WIT School of Business, Waterford Institute of Technology, Ireland.

Source: ©rvlsoft/Shutterstock

Introduction

Amazon is a leading global online retailer and, in the US, it has surpassed Walmart as the country's biggest retailer (Johnson, 2014). The Amazon website was originally developed in 1994 as an online retailer of books, with the site evolving and expanding to sell electronics, music, DVDS, furniture, clothing, personal care products, jewellery and other miscellaneous items for personal use and for the home. Similar to eBay, users can purchase and sell items using Amazon's online marketplace system. In 2007 Amazon launched Kindle, its iconic e-reader; in 2008, Amazon acquired the audiobook company Audible. The current design of the Amazon logo features an arrow underneath the word 'Amazon', beginning at the 'A' and ending at the 'Z'. This design is meant to portray the message that Amazon sells everything from 'A' to 'Z'.

Amazon continuously innovates in both online and offline retailing experiences for customers. In September 1999, Amazon launched a third-party seller marketplace, Amazon Auctions (originally called zShops), where consumers could search for rare and collectable books sold by third-party retailers. Today, half of all merchandise sold on the Amazon site comes from third-party sellers, small businesses and entrepreneurs (Howard, 2016). In November 2000, Amazon Auctions and zShops evolved into Amazon Marketplace, a service that allows customers to sell used books, CDs, DVDs, and other products alongside new items online. This arrangement enhances customer experience in gaining access to a wider choice of products from a range of suppliers with the convenience of purchasing them through a single check-out process (Chaffey, 2018). Today, Amazon offers more than 330 million products sold by other companies (Duhigg, 2019). Amazon warehouses, referred to as fulfilment centres, employ a workforce of the more than 250,000 full-time associates to support this global network. Amazon Fulfilment comprises employees, technology and innovation to deliver products to customers. Furthermore, in 2015 Amazon opened the first of its 15 physical bookstores in the United States.

Amazon generates revenue based on fixed fees or sales commissions per-unit and it also receives profits from advertising (Amazon.com, 2018). Physical gross merchandise, specifically third-party sales, has grown from 3 per cent of the total in 1999 to 58 per cent (Amazon.com, 2018) of sales on Amazon by independent third-party sellers (mostly small- and medium-sized businesses). However, despite Amazon's dominance in e-commerce, online sales are not the most important profit engine for the company. In 2003, Amazon made a significant move to offering web services (AWS) by licensing its platform to other e-commerce sites and currently this continues to be one of the company's major sources of revenue and this has generated the majority of Amazon's operating income since 2016. Amazon Web Services is the world's most comprehensive and broadly adopted cloud platform, offering over 165 fully featured services from data centres globally (Brigham, 2019). Amazon Web Services comprise services to help build business applications, customer engagement, database storage facilities, game technology, media services and robotics and other B2B solutions.

Amazon is guided by four principles: *'customer obsession rather than competitor focus, passion for invention, commitment to operational excellence, and long-term thinking'* (Amazon.com, 2019) and, irrespective of its innovative developments,

Source: ©SWNS/Alamy Stock Photo

Amazon maintains this original ethos and mission of putting the customer at the heart of everything it does. However, according to critics, this is sometimes to their detriment as many suppliers feel they are being put under pressure regarding their margins. Amazon has also been roundly criticized in the press for placing undue pressure on their employees who experience less than favourable working conditions (DePillis and Sherman, 2018).

Amazon Customers

Amazon identifies three sets of consumers it seeks to serve: customers, seller customers and developer customers. Its customer base is global, B2C, C2C, C2B and B2B orientated. Amazon offers a customer-centric, quality-driven, metrics-focused platform that serves all its customers in an optimal way. Amazon is one of the biggest e-commerce companies in Europe and is a major player, especially in the UK and Germany (E-commerce News Europe, 2019). The European market is a major part of Amazon's international business. As European customers increasingly favour e-commerce, automation and digitalization, Amazon is playing a key role in reshaping and challenging the B2C retail sector in fashion, media, entertainment, pharmacy and the B2B sector in cloud computing, logistics, financial services and healthcare (Tzortzakis, 2019). The number of international and US Prime Amazon Prime subscribers are 59.5 million and 58.5 respectively. Prime memberships are available in 17 countries: Austria, Australia, Belgium, Canada, China, France, Germany, India, Italy, Japan, Luxembourg, Mexico,

the Netherlands, Singapore, Spain, the UK and the US. Germany is Amazon's largest foreign market, accounting for nearly one-third of its international net sales in 2017. Much of its success is attributable to its wide-ranging product offering and low prices (Enberg, 2018).

Amazon has approximately 285 million active customer accounts (defined as accounts that have purchased in the past 12 months) worldwide and the company's success can be attributed to its obsessive focus on its customers. Amazon's websites offer an easy and convenient way to shop, with low prices, great choice and comprehensive product information. A series of personalization features ensure that the site content and communication with customers is current, insightful and relevant, and provides a unique buying experience for Amazon's millions of customers. Two key strategies for the business are the dramatic expansion in the range of products Amazon sells and a persistent focus on lowering prices. As Jeff Bezos, founder and CEO of Amazon.com commented in 2002, *'There are two types of retailers: those that work hard to raise prices and those that work hard to lower prices. Though both models can be successful, we've decided to relentlessly follow the second model'* (Amazon.com, 2002).

Amazon Business

Some of the forces that have transformed the business-to-consumer landscape (B2C) are also being transferred to the B2B landscape (Rossolillo, 2019). In 2015 Amazon expanded into B2B e-commerce and introduced Amazon Business which offers millions of products to business customers. Everything is available: from IT and lab equipment, office equipment and supplies, education and food service supplies (Post, 2019). Amazon Business serves millions of customers around the world and provides purchasing solutions to registered businesses of any size with products and services that are tailored for business, government organizations and the education sector (Sheetz, 2019). Amazon.com (2019) argues that companies can reduce costs, save time and effort, ensure greater visibility and control over organizational expenditure and promote easy reconciliation of accounts. Amazon offers an Amazon Business Prime membership programme for business customers who want free shipping on more than 100 million items, plus other benefits. By 2018 it was reported that Amazon was already generating $10 billion (USD) in annual sales (Betters-Picaro, 2019).

Amazon Partnerships

From 1998 onwards, as Amazon grew, its share price growth facilitated partnerships and/or acquisitions with a wide range of companies in different sectors such as Drugstore.com (pharmacy), Living.com (furniture), Pets.com (pet supplies), Wineshopper.com (wines), HomeGrocer.com (groceries), Sothebys.com (auctions) and Kozmo.com (urban home delivery). These partners pay Amazon for valuable placement and exposure on the Amazon site, which promotes and drives traffic to their own sites. The Amazon retail platform enables other retailers to sell products online using the Amazon user interface and infrastructure through their 'Syndicated Stores' programme. In recent years, Amazon has tended to invest in or acquire companies in sectors such as Table 1 below.

New Partnerships–Amazon's Move to Healthcare

In January 2018, Amazon developed a not-for-profit joint venture with JPMorgan Chase and multinational corporation Berkshire Hathaway. Subsequently renamed Haven, the company has stated that it aims to use data and technology more effectively to provide improved, cheaper healthcare for the collective three companies' 1.2 million employees and their family members (Fleming, 2019). Observers claim that Haven is using digital technologies to innovate

and develop employee healthcare benefits, experimenting in facilitation of GP access, remote patient monitoring, digital health-care delivery and reducing prescription drug costs.

It is notable that Amazon are moving into the healthcare provision market and joining forces with medical organizations (public and private) and bodies such as the UK's National Health Service (NHS). The NHS has joined forces with Amazon to allow elderly people, blind people and other patients who cannot easily search for health advice on the Internet to access the information through Alexa, Amazon's AI-powered voice assistant device. The UK's National Health Service (the NHS) envisages that patients asking Alexa for health advice will ease pressure on the NHS, with Amazon's algorithm using information from the NHS website to provide answers to questions. The NHS Long-term Plan aims to iteratively improve the quality of patient care and health outcomes and relieve pressure on the health service by making more services available digitally. Matthew Gould, chief executive of NHSX, which is overseeing the digital drive has stated that: 'Part of our mission at NHSX is to give citizens the tools to access services and information directly, and partnerships such as this are an important part of achieving this' (Siddique, 2019).

Electronic Channels of Distribution

Since 1995, Amazon has established itself as the world's leader in e-commerce. Amazon.com and its European websites such as Amazon.co.uk, Amazon.it, Amazon.de and Amazon.fr are online stores that ship 45 million products around the world, offering 24/7 customer service, daily deals and promotions, and the ability to track purchases and delivery times. Amazon's success is the direct result of a strong user shopping experience. The

Table 1   Amazon's investment in a variety of sectors

Business	Business and consumer	Consumer
Artificial intelligence	Publishing	Clothing & accessories
Business and cloud services	Media production & entertainment	Home services
Financial services	Hardware options	Food & beverage products
Social commerce & network initiatives	Transportation & logistics	Miscellaneous consumer products

Amazon shopping experience clearly emphasizes product search and online purchasing from the very beginning of the user's experience whether for first-time users or returning customers and content tailored to the current user. Once they have established the website's product search and online shopping capabilities, users will most likely want to take advantage of those features right away – starting with search. Amazon uses cookies to keep a user logged in, and that user's shopping habits are tracked and stored server-side. Amazon dynamically customizes the user's experience based on prior searches, page views, wish-list additions, written reviews and, ultimately, purchases. Customized content for the browser includes related items displayed and recommended items, based on prior activity, are increasingly tailored to their tastes and habits.

After an order has shipped, customers can track their orders on Amazon.fr, Amazon.co.uk, Amazon.de, Amazon.it, Amazon.es etc. in the 'From Your Orders' section where customers can find tracking information in their order details. If an order includes multiple items, each may have separate delivery dates and tracking information.

The Amazon App

In 2011 Amazon rolled out the Amazon app, making it even easier to shop online and offering customers faster and better search capabilities including voice and image search. Shopping lists can be managed easily by simply tapping, holding and dragging to add items to lists. Tracking each package by receiving shipping notifications also enables consumers to be aware of when important gifts will arrive (Day one staff, 2018). In 2017 Amazon rolled out augmented reality (AR) views on the app as well which enables customers to select and position virtual furniture and other items in their homes and in 2019 Amazon subsequently rolled out Amazon Showroom a tool that lets you place virtual furniture in a virtual room (Perez, 2017; Gottsegen, 2019).

Amazon Prime

Amazon Prime was built on the foundation of unlimited fast delivery. Prime members receive unlimited One-Day Delivery on millions of eligible items across all categories; unlimited same-day delivery to a number of large cities and metropolitan areas. Two-hour scheduled same-day delivery slots with Prime Now are offered at no extra charge between 8 am and 10 pm across more than 30 per cent of the population in selected postcodes in the UK. Over 100 million paid members worldwide also enjoy the many benefits of Prime over and above unlimited fast delivery. Throughout Europe, Amazon Prime offers unlimited access to award-winning movies and TV shows with Prime Video; unlimited access to over 2 million songs with Prime Music; access to Prime Day deals; access to Audible Channels for Prime; unlimited access to thousands of books and magazines with Prime Reading; Access to Prime Wardrobe; unlimited photo storage with Prime Photos; access to Twitch Prime; early access to select Lightning Deals; one free pre-released book a month with Amazon First Reads and more.

Amazon Prime Air is a future delivery system that will get deliveries to customers in 30 minutes or less using small drones. Amazon is committed to making Prime Air available to customers worldwide as soon as they are permitted to do so. This technology is currently being developed, tested, refined and rolled out, subject to aviation and drone safety regulations. Once operational, Prime Air will enhance the overall safety and efficiency of ground transportation services by affording people to skip an extra car journey, reducing pressure on road networks. Small, electrically powered drones will perform deliveries efficiently, cleanly and reduce the overall environmental footprint (Misener, 2015).

Source: ©happyphotons/Shutterstock

Amazon and E-Commerce – Evolving Strategies

The advantages of service principals co-operating and partnering with Amazon include the low cost of getting a product to market and the flexibility the platform offers. Amazon is a long-established and well-recognized online retailer and that experience is unrivalled. Furthermore, Amazon has a proven business model and technological infrastructure that is highly effective. Amazon has a global following of customers who use many of its services on a continuous basis (Breslin, 2019). However, there are inherent risks in having over-dependence on one e-commerce site and thereby maintaining a narrow approach to channel strategy. Manufacturers may also experience a lack of control of over their brand reputation, ownership of the overall pricing strategy, improved margins and greater control over their ability to fulfil orders. To mitigate these risks, manufacturers are developing new e-commerce strategies to diversify their online strategy over the next five years in a number of ways. Firstly, by focusing on direct-to-consumer online stores, developing the use of other channels and, to a lesser extent, selling using social media and B2B portals. However, according to findings from a study conducted on behalf of B2B online in 2017 by Luzern and WBR Insights, the future belongs to companies who diversify their e-commerce strategy. The study findings also noted that European brands operate in a market that is not as competitive as the United States which has implications for e-commerce Omni-channel and multi-channel development into the future. It has been suggested that the future of retail lies in the development of a multi-channel strategy and Amazon's position as the world's largest online retailer and Omni-channel is being diluted in the process as Amazon has sought to develop multi-channels into offline retail (primarily in the US) (Serrano, 2019).

Challenges

Anti-Competitive Practices

Amazon and its main competitors, agents and service principals have experienced a variety of challenges since the company's inception and continued development, primarily in the area of anti-competitive practices. The company has been challenged on its alleged use of patents as an anti-competitive practice, namely the '1-click patent', which was initially challenged by Barnes and Noble and other industry leaders. In 2008, sales representatives of Amazon's Booksurge division started contacting publishers of print on demand titles to inform them that for Amazon to continue to sell and distribute their POD-produced titles, they would be required to sign exclusive agreements with Amazon's own Booksurge POD company. A number of publishers considered this to amount to monopolistic behaviour and challenged this move under anti-trust law. Furthermore in 2008, Amazon UK was heavily criticized for attempting to prevent publishers from direct selling at discount from their own website. Amazon UK withdrew from sale key titles from the publisher Hachette Livre UK and the withdrawal was seen as an intention to put pressure on the publishers to provide what book traders deemed to be unreasonable levels of discount. In 2013, Amazon agreed to end its price parity for marketplace sellers in the European Union in response to investigations from the UK Office of Fair Trade.

Additionally, in 2015 Amazon announced that Apple TV and Google Chromecast products would not be sold on Amazon.com within a month of the press release, citing reasons around preventing 'customer confusion'. The decision was roundly criticized as a strategy to remove competition from Amazon Fire TV Products. In 2017, Apple and Amazon reached a new agreement and Amazon began to sell Apple TV products again. Furthermore in 2019, Amazon and Google reached a new arrangement and announced it would add Chromecast support to the Prime Video mobile app and Google in turn announced it would restore access to YouTube on Fire TV. Amazon has been criticized for engaging in unfair competitive practices and predatory pricing. In 2019 Senator Elizabeth Warren called for additional scrutinizing and dismembering of platforms that engage in unfair competition. For example, she noted that Amazon collects information from its third-party sellers to identify successful products and launches 'Amazon Basics' versions that compete with them (Sussman, 2019).

Direct Selling

In 2014, Amazon and Hachette became involved in another dispute over agency pricing (Johnson, 2014). Agency pricing is usually dictated by the agent (such as Hachette) who determines the price of a book; typically, however, Amazon dictates the discount level of a book. High-profile authors became involved; hundreds of writers, including Stephen King, James Patterson, Lee Childs and John Grisham, signed a petition stating: 'We encourage Amazon in the strongest possible terms to stop harming the livelihood of the authors on whom it has built its business. None of us, neither readers nor authors, benefit when books are taken hostage'. Hachette maintained it wanted to broker a fairer deal with Amazon that valued the role of authors and their publishers (Chapman, 2014). One could argue that Amazon's tough stance on negotiations and hard-bargaining benefits the consumer in terms of competitive pricing.

Conversely, massive challenges have been experienced by high street book store companies like Barnes and Noble, Waterstones and Borders because of online book retailing and also the introduction of digital/e-books. Amazon is renowned to be a tough negotiator in terms of margins and yet enables publishers to reach wider markets. For example, in the UK, Waterstones, one of the largest traditional bookstores, found competition with online competitors so expensive and challenging that, eventually, in 2012 it entered a partnership arrangement where Amazon markets and distributes its books online in return for a commission online. Amazon has created a tiered performance-based incentive system to encourage affiliates to sell more Amazon products (Chaffey, 2018).

Customer Reviews and Controversies

By June 2011, Amazon had moved into the publishing business and had begun to seek positive reviews from established authors in exchange for increased promotion of their own books. Amazon actively encouraged customer reviews, as having a high volume of reviews was and is important to both customers and sellers alike; it improves conversion rates and raises products higher in the Amazon search results.

Data mining tools are effectively used by Amazon to enhance the overall customer experience with recommendations being given to sellers and to customers in terms of products, pricing and promotional considerations. For organizations (producers) and consumers alike, it is easy to filter and compare customer reviews with ease of access to both positive and negative reviews. This allows consumers the opportunity to gain a thorough knowledge of a product through customer reviews, giving the shopper peace of mind and helping them to make a more informed purchase decision. The user is not pressured into purchasing an item but feels that the decision of whether to buy a product is completely under their control.

However, a number of cases emerged that challenged the reliability of Amazon reviews. A study at Cornell University in 2011 asserted that 85 per cent of Amazon's high-status consumer reviewers 'had received free products from publishers, agents, authors and manufacturers' (Lowery, 2011). Since 2016 Amazon has not permitted users to be compensated or incentivized in the form of free or discounted products for writing reviews (Hanbury, 2018).

Improving Employee Working Conditions

Amazon employs in excess of 750,000 employees world wide (Amazon, 2019). It raised its minimum wage for employees in 2018. However, it was reported that the elimination of bonuses and stock options as well as increased demands on productivity negated the effect of the wage increase (Sainato, 2019). Furthermore there have been suggestions that challenging physical working conditions such as workplace injuries, a lack of air conditioning in some fulfilment centres, excessive work hours, physical labour, a paucity of rest periods and the pressure to maintain a delivery schedule, even during difficult weather conditions and especially during peak demand periods, are the reality for many Amazon employees (Hamilton and Cain, 2019). Some workers have resorted to going on strike over the poor working conditions and are seeking to increase the minimum wage for night-time shift workers (Kaori Gurley, 2019). Bezos has continually refuted the criticisms relating to unfavourable working conditions and Amazon has responded by uploading blogs and press release statements on its minimum wage rate and the benefits it offers full-time employees, including quality health insurance, a retirement savings programme, generous parental leave and paid time off (Schwär, 2018; Carney, 2019).

Conclusion

Amazon has truly evolved from an online bookstore to offering consumers, online and offline, physical shopping experiences that embrace all technology has to offer for the convenience of the consumer. Amazon has expanded to be one of the biggest and most well-respected companies in the world. With a growing presence in other countries, Amazon has positioned itself as a formidable global company. Amazon successfully evolved from solely serving B2C customers to serving B2B markets offering innovative Amazon Web Services as well as Amazon Business Services and Amazon health-care initiatives. Amazon continues to evolve offering both omni- and multi-channel experiences to their customers. Businesses are seeking ways to lessen their dependence on Amazon as a primary channel of distribution and in turn, Amazon is seeing ways to expand its markets through the development of its own retail stores such as Amazon Books, Amazon Go and Amazon Pop Ups indicating that the future of retail lies in offline as well as online developments and innovations. With its expansions in product offerings, innovative products, programming and delivery services, Amazon has demonstrated its potential to continue to grow on an unprecedented scale. Its success is mainly attributable to its approach to its customer. As described in its mission statement, everything Amazon does is about 'enhancing the customer experience'.

References

Amazon.com (2002) Amazon.com, Company Reports, https://ir.aboutamazon.com/annual-reports [accessed 10 October 2019].

Amazon.com (2018) AboutAmazon.com, https://ir.aboutamazon.com/annual-reports [accessed 10 October 2019].

Amazon.com (2019) Amazon Parcels, http://parcelsapp.com/en/shops/amazon [accessed 12 October 2019].

Amazon.co.uk (2019) Track Your Package, https://www.amazon.co.uk/gp/help/customer/display.html?nodeId=201910530 [accessed 20 December 2019].

Barilliance, https://www.barilliance.com/amazon-omnichannel-strategy/ [accessed 12 December 2019].

Betters-Picaro, E. (2019) 'What is Amazon Business and how does it work?' 6 August 2019, ZDNet.com. https://www.zdnet.com/article/what-is-amazon-business-and-how-does-it-work/ [accessed 21 May 2020].

Breslin, S. (2019) '4 Benefits of Selling on Amazon Instead of Your Own Store', *Repricerexpress*, https://www.repricerexpress.com/benefits-selling-on-amazon-instead-store/ [accessed 12 December 2019].

Brigham, K. (2019) 'How Amazon makes money', *CNBC*, https://www.cnbc.com/2019/02/12/how-amazon-makes-money.html [accessed 12 December 2019]

Carney, J. (2019) 'Raising the minimum wage is something all companies and Congress should get behind', *The Amazon Blog Day one* [accessed 7 January 2020].

Chaffey, D. (2018) Amazon.com case study – 2018 update, *Smart Insights*, https://www.smartinsights.com/digital-marketing-strategy/online-business-revenue-models/amazon-case-study/ [accessed 11 December 2019].

Chapman, G. (2014) 'Authors call on readers in Amazon book battle', Phys Org, 3 July 2014, https://phys.org/news/2014-07-authors-readers-amazon.html [accessed 20 December 2019].

Day one staff (2018) 'Shop anytime, anywhere, in more ways than ever', *The Amazon Blog Day one*, https://blog.aboutamazon.com/shopping/shop-anytime-anywhere-in-more-ways-than-ever [accessed 12 October 2019].

DePillis, L. and Sherman, I. (2018) 'Amazon's Extraordinary 25-Year Revolution', *CNN Business*, https://edition.cnn.com/interactive/2018/10/business/amazon-history-timeline/index.html [accessed 11 December 2019].

Duhigg, C. (2019) 'Is Amazon Unstoppable?', *New Yorker*, https://longform.org/posts/is-amazon-unstoppable. [accessed 12 December 2019] Farfan, B. (2019) 'Amazon's Mission Statement', the balance small business, https://www.thebalancesmb.com/amazon-mission-statement-4068548 [accessed 12 December 2019].

E-commerce News Europe (2019) Amazon in Europe, https://ecommercenews.eu/amazon-in-europe/ [accessed 20 December 2019].

Enberg, J. (2018) Amazon Around the World, *eMarketer*, https://www.emarketer.com/content/amazon-around-the-world [accessed 20 December 2019].

Feiner, L. (2019) 'Amazon is spending billions on Internet satellites, self-driving cars and more as revenue growth slows', *CNBC*, https://www.cnbc.com/2019/05/17/amazon-makes-several-start-up-investments-revenue-growth-slows.html [accessed 12 December 2019].

Fleming, N. (2019) 'Does Amazon have answers for the future of the NHS?', *The Guardian Online*, https://www.theguardian.com/technology/2019/aug/24/alexa-nhs-future-amazon-artificial-intelligence-healthcare [accessed 23 December 2019].

Gottsegen, G. (2019) 'Amazon Showroom lets you customise furniture in a virtual living room', *C|net*, https://www.cnet.com/news/amazon-showroom-lets-you-customize-furniture-in-a-virtual-living-room/ [accessed 12 December 2019].

Hamilton, I. and Cain, A. (2019) 'Amazon warehouse employees speak out about the "brutal" reality of working during the holidays, when 60-hour weeks are mandatory and ambulance calls are common', *Business Insider*, 19 February 2019, https://www.businessinsider.com/amazon-employees-describe-peak-2019-2?r=US&IR=T [accessed 21 May 2019].

Hanbury, M. (2018) 'Amazon has an underground subculture that trades reviews for deals – and the company is finally cracking down', *Business Insider*, https://www.businessinsider.com/amazon-bad-review-practices-crackdown-2018-4?r=US&IR=T [accessed 12 December 2019].

Henry, Z. (2017) 'Amazon Has Acquired or Invested in More Companies than you Think', *Inc.com*, https://www.inc.com/magazine/201705/zoe-henry/will-amazon-buy-you.html [accessed 12 December 2019].

Howard, D. (2016) 'Amazon: Half of all merchandise sold now comes from third-party sellers', *Retail Dive*, 17 November 2016, https://www.retaildive.com/news/amazon-half-of-all-merchandise-sold-now-comes-from-third-party-sellers/430677/ [accessed 15 April 2020].

Johnson, D. (2014) 'Did Judge Denise Cote accidentally screw Amazon?', Melville House Books, LINK and https://www.retaildive.com/news/amazon-half-of-all-merchandise-sold-now-comes-from-third-party-sellers/430677/ [accessed 11 December 2019].

Kaori Gurley, L. (2019) '60 Amazon Workers Walked Out Over Warehouse Working Conditions', https://www.vice.com/en_us/article/pa7qny/60-amazon-workers-walked-out-over-warehouse-working-conditions [accessed 7 January 2020].

Lowery, G. (2011) 'Study unmasks the secret world of Amazon's reviewers', *Chronicle Online*, Cornell University, http://www.news.cornell.edu/stories/June11/PinchAmazon.html [accessed 11 December 2019].

Luzern and WBR Digital (2017) 'Are brands too dependent on Amazon for their e-commerce Strategy?', *B2B Online*, https://b2bonlineeu.wbresearch.com/are-brands-too-dependent-on-amazon-for-their-ecommerce-strategy-ty-u

Misener, P. (2015) 'Why we're excited by Europe's pragmatic drone regulation policy', *The Amazon Blog* https://cdn2.hubspot.net/hubfs/2419671/LuzernWBRReport24ppWEB.pdf [accessed 11 December 2019].

Perez, S. (2017) 'Amazon adds an AR shopping feature to its iOS app', *TechCrunch*, https://techcrunch.com/2017/11/01/amazon-adds-an-ar-shopping-feature-to-its-ios-app/ [accessed 12 December 2019].

Post, J. (2019) 'Amazon Business: What it is and how it could benefit you', *Business News Daily*, https://www.businessnewsdaily.com/9637-what-is-amazon-business.html [accessed 12 December 2019].

Rossolillo, N. (2019) 'Business-to-Business Services Are Finally Entering the 21st Century', *The Motley Fool*, https://www.fool.com/investing/2019/04/17/business-to-business-services-are-finally-entering.aspx [accessed 12 December 2019].

Sainato, M. (2019) 'Revealed: Amazon touts high wages while ignoring issues in its warehouses' in *The Guardian*, 7 August 2019, https://www.theguardian.com/technology/2019/aug/06/

amazon-workers-minimum-wage-injuries-working-conditions [accessed 21 May 2020].

Schwär, (2018) 'Jeff Bezos responded to reports of poor working conditions at Amazon – here's what he said', *Business Insider Deutschland*, 26th April 2018, https://www.businessinsider.com/jeff-bezos-responded-to-reports-on-amazon-warehouse-working-conditions-2018-4?r=US&IR=T [accessed 7 January 2020].

Serrano, S. (2019) 'What Amazon Teaches Us about OmniChannel Strategy in 2019', *Barilliance*, https://www.barilliance.com/amazon-omnichannel-strategy/ [accessed 21 December 2019].

Sheetz, M. (2019) 'There's a business growing within Amazon that could one day be worth more than retail or cloud', *CNBC*, https://www.cnbc.

com/2019/03/19/amazon-business-could-be-worth-more-than-core-retail-e-commerce.html [accessed 12 December 2019].

Siddique, H. (2019) 'NHS teams up With Amazon to bring Alexa to patients', *The Guardian Online*, https://www.theguardian.com/society/2019/jul/10/nhs-teams-up-with-amazon-to-bring-alexa-to-patients [accessed 23 December 2019].

Sussman, S. (2019) 'How Amazon Controls its Marketplace', *The American Prospect*, https://prospect.org/economy/amazon-controls-marketplace/, [accessed 12 December 2019].

Tzortzakis I. (2019) 'Amazon's Expansion in Europe', *Eurofound*, https://www.eurofound.europa.eu/publications/article/2019/amazons-expansion-in-europe, [accessed 21 December 2019].

CASE 3   THE JOHN LEWIS AND PARTNERS CUSTOMER EXPERIENCE

This case was written by Dr Christopher Pich, Dr Mojtaba Poorrezaei and Dr Sheilagh Resnick, Nottingham Business School, Nottingham Trent University, UK.

Source: ©Red Confidential/Shutterstock

'When you're part of it, you put your heart into it. At John Lewis and Partners, we're more than employees – we're owners. That's why we're all called Partners. And that's why we all go above and beyond to offer quality products and outstanding service to the people who matter most – you, our customers. Because for us, it's personal. (John Lewis Group Strategic Report, 2019)

Established in 1864, John Lewis and Partners (JLP) is one of the UK's leading department store chains, operating across the country from 51 stores and with an established online, omni-channel platform (John Lewis, 2019). Indeed, JLP is positioned as a premium, high-end retailer selling quality products, services and brands ranging from electronics, homeware, fashion, cosmetics, haberdashery and gifts to name but a few (Gwynn, 2018). However, JLP did not begin life with this all-encompassing department store format and in fact the organization, founded by none other than John Lewis, started life as a humble, single, family-run drapery business. Twenty-five years after its establishment, the organization expanded beyond drapery to include must-have products, and the latest fashions, furnishings and latest technologies. Furthermore, the organization evolved in terms of its management and developed into a cooperative or 'Partnership' –

owned and governed by its employees, who came to be known as *partners* (Paranque and Willmott, 2014). Partners work at all levels of the organization and serve on various boards and committees to lead the business but also hold the boards-committees to account. In addition, partners are rewarded with an annual bonus calculated from the annual profits. For example, in the financial year 2018–2019, partners were awarded a bonus of 3 per cent, which cost the organization £44.7m, although this was a reduction from 5 per cent (£74 million) awarded in 2017–2018 (John Lewis Group Strategic Report, 2018).

JLP has seen considerable growth in recent years with sales in 2018-19 up 1.3 per cent and with increased customer satisfaction, as measured by the Net Promoter Score, increased for the fourth year in a row. Figure 1 shows a consistent growth in JLP annual sales revenue from 2009 to 2018.

JLP has become one of the UK's best-loved department store chains among partners and customers, even boasting a Royal Warrant from HM The Queen as a prestigious supplier of haberdashery and household goods to the Royal Household. Since its birth in 1864, JLP has continued to abide by its pricing policy of 'Never Knowingly Undersold', championed as its promise to customers on quality, service and price. Under this policy, customers have been challenged with the proposition that if they can buy products, services and brands more cheaply elsewhere, the organization will match the competitors' price or if customers have recently bought products, services and brands from JLP, the difference will be paid (John Lewis, 1925). This pricing policy which represents a 'promise of value' continues to this day (John Lewis, 1925).

JLP continue to assess and improve its omni-channel offering, monitoring changing trends and habits and ensuring the organization remains relevant to consumers and differentiated from competitors. Furthermore, new strategies and tactics are routinely deployed by JLP to remain innovative, inspiring and distinctive in terms of products,

Figure 1   Annual sales revenue of John Lewis in the United Kingdom (UK) from 2009 to 2018 (in million GBP)

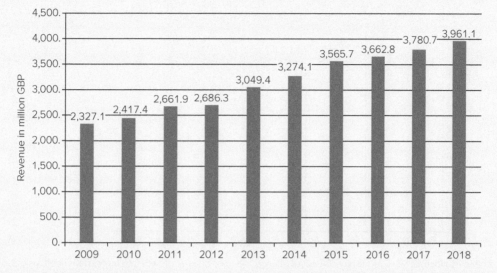

Source: Sabanoglu, T., 2019. Annual sales revenue of John Lewis in the United Kingdom (UK) from 2009 to 2019. Statista (18/10/2019). Available from: https://www.statista.com/statistics/420216/john-lewis-revenue-uk-united-kingdom/

services and communications. Indeed, JLP was a pioneer of the 'click and collect' initiative (Baldwin, 2019), which enabled customers to shop online through the JLP website and pick-up their products in store often as early as 24 hours after purchasing. This service offering, involving the integration of online and offline customer service, was highly innovative compared with direct competitors when it was launched in 2008 (Smithers, 2015). The 'click and collect' service remains a staple feature of the JLP experience and continues to evolve. For example, in May 2019, JLP launched a pilot scheme to allow customers to 'click and collect' from Co-op stores across the country including cities such as Manchester, Nottingham and London (Jahshan, 2019). The uptake for this new delivery feature is yet to be seen and it is unknown whether this pilot will be rolled out to all Co-op stores.

Today, JLP is one of the UK's largest employee-owned organizations with over 83,000 partners. In fact, JLP is a retail giant and serves as the parent company of two related yet distinct brands: *John Lewis & Partners* and *Waitrose & Partners*. Waitrose & Partners is a chain of British supermarkets, which forms the food retail division and was founded as a separate entity to JLP in 1904. Founded by Wallace Wyndham 'Waite', Arthur 'Rose' and David Taylor (Taylor left the business in 1908), the small store began life selling a wide range of

high-quality grocery products. From 1904 to 1937, Waitrose expanded, opening new grocery stores in towns and cities across the South of England and in October 1937 the supermarket chain decided to join the JLP (Waitrose, 2019).

Partners continue to make decisions on how the business is run and to adhere to the principles developed in John Lewis 1929, which form part of the organization's constitution. This in turn allows partners to understand their responsibilities and rights as employee-owners (John Lewis Group Strategic Report, 2019).

UK Retailing – Turbulent Times

The UK is the sixth largest retail sector in the world with sales of £358 billion and employing £2.8 million people (John Lewis Group Strategic Report, 2019). Historically, retail involved shops and people and was goods based. Today, retail is undergoing 'seismic' shifts driven by changes in consumer behaviour and technology and, as a result, the market is under attack from many different sides. The performance of the UK high street is one of decline; customer footfall in town centres has decreased every year since 2013 and, in the last 10 years, has fallen by 17 per cent (Grimsey, 2018). The number of shops lying empty in town centres has soared with consumer

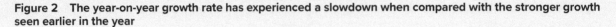

Figure 2   The year-on-year growth rate has experienced a slowdown when compared with the stronger growth seen earlier in the year

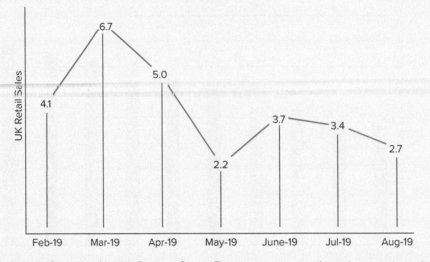

Source: Office for National Statistics – Monthly Business Survey. The year-on-year growth rate has experienced a slowdown when compared with the stronger growth seen earlier in the year. ONS (18/10/2019). Available from: https://www.ons.gov.uk/businessindustryandtrade/retailindustry/bulletins/retailsales/august2019

confidence impacted by political and economic uncertainty, Brexit, and an underlying shift in the nature of consumer behaviour (Retail Trends, 2019). As a result, margins are being eroded by reducing sales, increasing costs and a lack of consumer confidence. Annual sales continue to fall, reflecting the changing nature of the retail landscape (Retail Sales, 2019) and we are entering the era of cautious consumption. As illustrated in Figure 2, there is a significant drop in UK retail sales from March to May 2019 and continuing decline post June 2019.

UK shoppers in the future will shop 'smarter' (Retail Outlook, 2019) and, according to Retail Outlook 2019, shoppers also say they will shop around more, buy more items on promotion, and buy more Own Label products. Similarly, customers who spend on clothing intend to buy fewer items and/or buy them at discounted prices and at sales times.

In addition to economic uncertainty, technology and evolving consumer behaviour are challenging the capabilities of retailers to their limits. The way in which consumers shop has changed through e-commerce, which now accounts for 20 per cent of UK retail sales. Multi-channel retailing is a model whereby retailers use a combination of two or more integrated channels, most commonly the Internet and a store, to sell products and services to customers (Lewis, Whysall, Foster, 2014) and is focused on offering a seamless integrated shopping experience

to the customer. Multi-channel has developed further towards an omni-channel model, which involves a more synergetic integration of channels, the aim of which is to create an overall brand experience for customers, regardless of the channel or the stage they are in during the purchasing process (Cummins, Peltier, Dixon, 2016).

For many retailers, online is fast becoming the main channel and a shift from a store-based past to a digital future is likely to continue into the future. Nowadays, customers no longer purchase solely in-store or online instead, they shop across channels and do so by searching for information in one channel, and completing the purchase in another (Lee, Chan, Chong, Thadou, 2019). As customers demand an integrated purchasing experience across channels, many retailers have moved to omni-channel retailing to remain competitive.

The ability to access multiple channels and access to the Internet has also changed the nature of the consumer by the provision of up-to-date information through web-based sites, blogs and social media. Customers are now able to research goods and services before purchase, with many shoppers often better informed than store staff. Many are more tech 'savvy' and are becoming experts at taking advantage of online offers. Mobile applications allow comparative price checks, reviews, rankings/ratings while in store or shopping online. As a result, sales and promotional activity have remained a feature of the market with discounting ever more ongoing as retailers fight to grow the top-line in an intensely competitive market place. Shoppers now regularly consult a consumer review site prior to purchase and are critiquing goods and services through review sites as customer views and comments can have more authenticity and value than traditional advertising and other communication strategies. Customers also have the ability to skewer brands on blogs and social media. If the brand promise is broken, the shopping experience disappoints or if a purchase costs more than expected, expect them to spread the word!

Shoppers expect a consistent experience across every touch point of their shopping journey. They also want control over which payment methods they use, and control over their time; they don't want to visit a store only to find the product is out of stock. For retailers, a critical part of their competitive differentiation must be to cater to shoppers' preferred ways of researching, browsing and buying to deliver a seamless on and off-line relationship. They must go beyond selling a product or service to delivering customer experiences.

The retail industry is experiencing challenging times; retailers large and small, national and international continue to face pressures and JLP is not an exception. For example, operating profit for 2018-2019 was £117.4m (Figure 1). However, the organization has experienced weaker sales across some departments and borne higher operating costs (Experience: The new battle in retail, 2019). As a result, it recently unveiled the first loss in the firm's 155-year history of £25.9m for the first six months of 2019 (Prynn, and English, 2019). In response, JLP has launched a major restructuring programme to reduce management and head office roles (John Lewis, 2019), to merge the management departments of its high street department stores and Waitrose grocery chain (John Lewis, 2019) and seeks to reduce costs with its landlords (John Lewis, 2019). Although JLP is under pressure to address this profit decline, it is taking action to safeguard the retailer as one of the UK's most trustworthy, quintessentially British, high-street brands, and has embarked on delivering a new customer experience strategy.

Customer Experience Strategy

Over the last decade, there has been a shift from consumption of the product to the consumption of the service. Customer research, which has traditionally focused on measurements of satisfaction and service quality, has broadened to acknowledge that consumption has experiential qualities (Hirschman and Holbrook, 1982). Within this change is the growing importance of a service experience (Pine and Gilmore, 1998). Customer experience is a recent concept, defined as a process for enabling hedonic consumption, which can result in holistic customer value or experiences (Jain & Aagja, and Bagdare, 2017). It encompasses cognitive, affective and emotional responses and involves the whole customer purchasing journey across different touchpoints and multiple channels (Verhoef, Lemon, Parasuraman, Roggeveen, Tsiros & Schlesinger, 2009). The use of multiple channels for customer shopping, aided by the availability of Internet-enabled smartphones and other devices, is fast becoming the mainstream shopping model (Beck & Rygl, 2015). This has changed the way customers can access goods and services and thus created new channels, which can enable different shopping experiences.

The digitalization era has also altered consumer behaviour. Expectations of service have changed as customers now have the choice of multiple points of interaction with a retailer. While the introduction of technology-enabled touchpoints might improve the customer experience, it could equally diminish it. Retailers and other service providers need to contend with new e-service features, such as mobile apps, chat-bots and interactive websites, all of which might have both positive and negative impact on the customer experience. The challenge of implementing customer interactions with technology is the reason why customer experience has become a top management priority over the last decade. What really matters for customers in their interaction with a retailer is their overall experience across different touchpoints, known as cumulative experience, and defined as: *'The cumulative customer experience comprises a retrospective assessment of all encounter experiences that contribute to the relationship with the service'* (Ciuchita, Mahr, & Odekerken-Schröder, 2019).

Indeed, the cumulative customer experience is what counts in order to achieve customer satisfaction. From a service perspective, it is not only important that satisfaction with each single encounter matters, but that overall satisfaction with the whole customer journey contributes significantly to the perception of customer experience. In other words, new features of e-service offered to a customer should be aligned with other interaction points both online and offline to deliver an overall excellent experience. The ability to deliver this is how retailers can both differentiate themselves from and outperform competitors. Due to technological advancements and availability of online shopping data, retailers now have a better understanding of customer data collected via their interaction with various touchpoints. This data has enabled companies to deliver more personalized customer experiences by enabling bespoke relevant product and service suggestions and incentives within both the online and offline environments. JLP is an example of a successful retailer, which has differentiated itself from other competitors by effective management of the customer experience.

Winning Approach

In 2017, JLP piloted a new 'concierge-style' shopping experience initiative designed to increase footfall and improve its customer experience offerings (Jajshan, 2017). These initiatives included the introduction of an in-store 'Experience Desk' and of 'Service Partners', who symbolize the 'face' of JLP and can be called upon to give 'tours' of the store, make bookings for in-store events and address any questions or concerns about the customer experience (Jajshan, 2017). This strategy of enhancing the JLP customer experience is also part of the organization's internal environment and culture with its emphasis on employee engagement and empowerment of partners. For example, JLP aims to empower partners through learning, engaging all partners with a sense of purpose, rewards, inspiring and community-led leadership and a belief in the importance of well-being. In addition, JLP was ranked 18 out of 49 of large businesses in terms of 'Britain's Healthiest Workplace' and scored 71 per cent job satisfaction from partners (John Lewis Group Strategic

Report, 2019). Therefore, JLP maintains that it values the impact of its business and recognizes that the decisions made about all its stakeholders are important to the well-being of the organization and society at large. Furthermore, JLP states: *'We work to build brand trust and loyalty and provide customers with increasingly personalised, unique and exclusive products and services that are authentic and inspiring. And because we're partners, we're invested to build that trust and loyalty'* (John Lewis Group Strategic Report, 2019).

JLP's differentiation strategy has focused on the customer experience to stand out from all other retailers and has been introduced to respond to changes in customers' needs for more one-to-one interactions and personalized experiences. In-store spa facilities, demo kitchens, food innovation studios, personalized shoppers and other concierge-style service are examples of its in-store experiential events, which aim to deliver personalized service experiences. The ultimate goal of these various touchpoints is to maximize customers' interaction with the store, which can create a memorable experience. Although technological developments have revolutionized the service industry and condensed the traditional service life cycle, JLP has taken a holistic view of customer experience in which technology-enabled interactions are imbedded throughout the customer journey. Both online and offline touchpoints are designed to respond to customer's expectations and thus to improve the customer experience. In addition, the retailer has offered individualized experience through the Partnership model as highlighted by this statement: *'Our Partnership strategy means we are focused on differentiation not scale and offering our customers increasingly personalised, unique and exclusive products that are authentic and inspiring. Customers also trust us to curate ethically sourced products and services'* (John Lewis Group Strategic Report, 2019).

Although many traditional retailers have been negatively affected by online competition, JLP has embraced online touchpoints to shape a memorable customer journey. In some experiential events, both online and offline touchpoints are combined to respond to customer enquiries. A bespoke customer collection point is available to facilitate the online order and in-store collection. JLP has introduced a

Photograph of unidentified people visiting John Lewis and Partners shopping mall, Oxford Circus, London UK, 2019.
Source: ©TK Kurikawa/Shutterstock

new app whereby customers are informed by a stylist about the new arrivals of their favourite brand. Personal stylists interact with customers via this app, and in-store appointments to deliver a complete style and beauty make over experience are available. These appointments can also be made via the Experience Desk in the store.

The Experience Desk

The 'Experience Desk' acts as a vehicle to communicate personalized styling services, gift experiences, advice on technology, introductions to personal shoppers and up-to-date knowledge on products, technology and services. The desk continues to be rolled out to all stores, playing a part in differentiating JLP as it acts as a physical manifestation of the brand and demonstrates its identity and values in action. The Experience Desk is a: '. . .*place to discover our exclusive events and workshops, book selected services or purchase one of our special experience gifts*' (John Lewis, 2019).

It is the place in the store where online and offline experience are joined together to deliver an excellent experience and where customers can experience personalized interaction with JLP. But, despite the significant investment made by JLP into their customer experience strategy, there appears to be limited awareness and recognition of these in-store initiatives. In addition, many customers are often confused what the experience 'desk' signifies. For

example, one customer questioned the relevance of the desk, did not understand what it represented and questioned whether it was a place to give 'feedback to staff about your experience?' another customer revealed: '*I don't know what the desk is all about. Is it somewhere to pay for goods when it is busy? Or is it to return unwanted products and gifts? I'm confused*' (John Lewis Customer 1, 2019). Likewise, another JLP customer highlighted: '*Is it a place to collect online orders, I think they call it 'click and collect' or is it where you report problems? Actually, I don't know what it's all about*' (John Lewis Customer 2, 2019).

This has raised an important question about the success of the newly implemented desk, which aims to build a bridge between online and offline encounters and to support the customer experience strategy, which JLP hopes will continue to grow sales and profits in difficult trading times.

References

2019 Retail Outlook (online). Available at https://www.pwc.co.uk/industries/retail-consumer/insights/retail-outlook.html

Baldwin, C. (2016), 'John Lewis pioneers Clipper's latest click and collect facility', *Essential Retail*, https://www.essentialretail.com/news/57480654d17d2-john-lewis-pioneers-clippers-latest-click-collect-facility/ [accessed 17 October 2019].

Beck, N. and Rygl, D. (2015), 'Categorization of multiple channel retailing in Multi-, Cross-, and Omni-Channel Retailing for retailers and retailing'. *Journal of Retailing and Consumer Services*, 27, 170–178. http://doi.org/10.1016/j.jretconser.2015.08.001

Ciuchita, R., Mahr, D., and Odekerken-Schröder, G. (2019), 'Deal with it: How coping with e-service innovation affects the customer experience'. *Journal of Business Research*, 103, 130-141. https://doi.org/10.1016/j.jbusres.2019.05.036

Cummins, S., Peltier, J.W., Dixon, A. (2016), 'Omni-channel research framework in the context of personal selling and sales management'. *Journal of Research in Interactive Marketing*. 10 (1), 2–16.

Experience: The new battle in retail (2019). (online). Available at http://www.adyen.com.

Grimsey, W. (2018), *The Grimsey Review 2* (online). Available at http://www.vanishinghighstreet.com/wp-content/uploads/2018/07/GrimseyReview2.pdf.

Gwynn, Simon. (2010), 'John Lewis and Waitrose unveil 'modern, progressive' new brand identity', *Campaignlive.co.uk*, https://www.campaignlive.co.uk/article/john-lewis-waitrose-unveil-modern-progressive-new-brand-identity/1491742, [accessed 5 October 2019].

Hirschman, E. and Holbrook, M. (1982), 'Hedonic Consumption: Emerging Concepts, Methods and Propositions'. *Journal of Marketing, 46*(3), 92-101. doi:10.2307/1251707

Jahshan, E. (2019), 'John Lewis to trial click-and-collect at Co-op stores', *Retail Gazette*, https://www.retailgazette.co.uk/blog/2019/05/john-lewis-to-trial-click-and-collect-at-co-op-stores/ [accessed 17 October 2019].

Jain, R. & Aagja, J. and Bagdare, S. (2017), 'Customer experience – a review and research agenda'. *Journal of Service Theory and Practice.* 27. 10.1108/JSTP-03-2015-0064.

Jajshan, Elias. (2017), 'John Lewis unveils details of new concierge shopping experience', *Retail Gazette*, https://www.retailgazette.co.uk/blog/2017/10/john-lewis-unveils-new-concierge-shopping-experience-service/ [accessed 6 October 2019].

John Lewis axes third of top jobs in restructuring, *BBC News*, https://www.bbc.co.uk/news/business-49890058 [accessed 7 October 2019].

John Lewis Group Strategic Report, *Annual report 2019*, John Lewis Partnership plc, London..

John Lewis seeks discounts from some landlords, *BBC News*, https://www.bbc.co.uk/news/business-49918002 [accessed 9 October 2019].

John Lewis Customer 1 (2019) – Authors' Interview, Research Project, Nottingham Business School, Nottingham Trent University.

John Lewis. (2019). Homepage. [online] John Lewis & Partners. Available at: https://www.johnlewis.com/ [accessed 5 October 2019].

John Lewis (1925) – Never Knowingly Undersold – https://www.creativereview.co.uk/never-knowingly-undersold/

John Lewis (1925) – Never Knowingly Undersold. Available from: https://www.creativereview.co.uk/never-knowingly-undersold/

Lee, Z.W.Y., Chan, T.K.H. and Chong, A.Y.-L., Thadou, D.R. (2019), 'Customer engagement through omnichannel retailing: The effects of channel integration quality'. *Industrial Marketing Management*, 77 (February), 90-101.

Lewis, J., Whysall, P. and Foster, C. (2014), 'Drivers and technology-related obstacles in moving to multichannel retailing'. *International Journal of Electronic Commerce*, 18 (4), 43–68.

Office for National Statistics – Monthly Business Survey. The year-on-year growth rate has experienced a slowdown when compared with the stronger growth seen earlier in the year. ONS [18/10/2019]. Available from: https://www.ons.gov.uk/businessindustryandtrade/retailindustry/bulletins/retailsales/august2019

Paranque, Bernard. and Willmott, Hugh. (2014), 'Cooperatives-saviours or gravediggers of capitalism? Critical performative and the John Lewis Partnership', *Organization*, 21(5), 604-625.

Photograph of unidentified people visit John Lewis and partners shopping mall Oxford Circus London UK. 2019. [photograph]. At: London, England.

Pine, B.J. and Gilmore, J.H. (1998), 'Welcome to the Experience Economy'. *Harvard Business Review*, 76, 97-105.

Prynn, Jonathan. and English, Simon. (2019), 'No-deal Brexit alert as John Lewis unveils first loss in 155 years', *Evening Standard Online*, https://www.standard.co.uk/news/politics/nodeal-brexit-alert-as-john-lewis-unveils-first-loss-in-155-years-a4234826.html [accessed 7 October 2019].

Retail Trends2019: *Retail Re-invented* (online). Available at https://www2.deloitte.com/uk/en/pages/consumer-business/articles/retail-trends.html.

Retail Sales, Great Britain: August 2019 (online). Available at https://www.ons.gov.uk/businessindustryandtrade/retailindustry/bulletins/retailsales/aaugust2019

Sabanoglu, T., 2019. Annual sales revenue of John Lewis in the United Kingdom (UK) from 2009 to 2019. *Statista* [18/10/2019]. Available from: https://www.statista.com/statistics/420216/john-lewis-revenue-uk-united-kingdom/

Smithers, R. (2015), 'John Lewis to charge for 'click and collect', *The Guardian Online,* https://www.theguardian.com/business/2015/jul/01/john-lewis-to-charge-for-click-and-collect [accessed 17 October 2019].

Verhoef, P., Lemon, K., Parasuraman, A. P., Roggeveen, A., Tsiros, M. and Schlesinger, L. (2009), 'Customer Experience Creation: Determinants, Dynamics and Management Strategies'. *Journal of Retailing.* 85. 31-41. 10.1016/j.jretai.2008.11.001

Waitrose, https://www.waitrose.com/home/about_waitrose/corporate_information/company_history.html [Accessed 17 October 2019].

CASE 4   McDONALD'S: DESIGNING SERVICES PROCESSES AND INNOVATIONS

This case was written by Dr Fiona Whelan-Ryan, WIT School of Business, Waterford Institute of Technology, Ireland.

Overview of McDonald's

McDonald's is a well-established fast food restaurant franchise throughout Europe. It is one of the leading restaurant franchises in 2018 in terms of units with only Subway operating a greater number of units (Lock, 2019a). McDonald's is a widely recognized global franchise brand through which the vast majority of McDonald's restaurants – more than 80 per cent worldwide and nearly 90 per cent in the US – are owned and operated by approximately 5,000 independent, small and mid-sized business people. Ray Kroc joined the company in 1954, after the McDonald brothers had franchised six locations. In 1955 he founded the McDonald's Corporation and five years later bought the exclusive rights to the McDonald's name (McDonald's Corp, 2019a). Kroc's vision for the company was that there would be 1,000 McDonald's restaurants solely in the United States. Yet, McDonald's continued to grow and expand into international markets beginning in 1967 opening in Canada and Puerto Rico. Today, the company has over 36,000 restaurants in over 100 nations. McDonald's is the most valuable fast food brand in the world with an estimated brand value of about 130.4 billion US dollars (Lock, 2019b). McDonald's has enjoyed considerable growth with around 3.7 million visits every day to its restaurants (Ingenico, 2018).

According to Statista.com, in 2018, the European country in which McDonald's operated and franchised the majority of its establishments was Germany. France (including Monaco) accounted for the second largest number of McDonald's restaurants in 2018 with 1,463 units (Lock, 2019a). While Europe is a significant market for McDonald's, the company is more strongly represented in its native country of the United States. In 2018, the US accounted for nearly 14,000 McDonald's restaurants out of the 38,000 McDonald's establishments worldwide. In terms of revenue, the US market accounted for the largest share of the company's total revenue in 2018 (Lock, 2019b). Through the end of 2018, the business was structured into the following segments that combined markets with similar characteristics and ownership structure, and reflected how management reviewed and evaluated operating performance:

- US – the company's largest segment.
- International lead markets – established markets including Australia, Canada, France, Germany, the U.K. and related markets.
- High growth markets – markets that the company believes have relatively higher restaurant expansion and franchising potential including China, Italy, Korea, the Netherlands, Poland, Russia, Spain, Switzerland and related markets (McDonald's Corp, 2018).

Physical Service Delivery Channels

Due to the inseparable nature of services, direct face-to-face contact is often required between the service provider and their customers. Although some of the pre-requisite elements can be carried out online, inevitably with food and beverage delivery processes there will be a direct encounter between the provider and the customer. Therefore, service intermediaries such as agents, brokers, call centres and, in this case, franchises play an important role in accessibility and delivery of products and services. Service principals are dependent on their intermediaries (franchisees) to deliver their products and services with attention to specifications in their operations relating to consistency in the overall customer service experience.

Virtual and Electronic Service Delivery Channels

Electronic channels have transformed how service orientated companies manage and deliver their service offerings. Electronic channels include the Internet, mobile technology, especially apps, and using voice-based and AI technology to deliver services and enhance the customer experience. McDonald's has invested heavily in equipment and technological innovations to remain competitive in the market, delivering products and services effectively and efficiently to their customers.

Electronic Channels (Distribution and Technology)

McDonald's is constantly evolving, devising and implementing effective and efficient service distribution strategies to improve the customer experience with new technologies. But there is a parallel effort to improve the customers' and employees' day-to-day experience and enhance food production and food service ability (Morgan, 2019). McDonald's has outlined a long-term global growth strategy focused on enhancing digital capabilities such as kiosk ordering, delivery systems and accelerating deployments of its Experience of the Future restaurants (EOTFs) (Dignan, 2018) with a pilot to-go location opened in London in 2019 (McDonald's Corp, 2019b).

Delivering Service through Electronic and Mobile Channels

McDonald's continues to focus on a customer-centric approach at the core of its business, focusing on three key areas: food, value and the customer experience. Additionally, McDonald's is focused on enhancing the overall customer experience through three identified growth accelerators: Experience of the Future ('EOTF'), digital and delivery; i.e. McDonald's with hospitable, friendly service and ever-improving convenience for customers on their terms (Lauchlan, 2018). McDonald's electronic channels have vastly expanded opportunities to distribute their offerings. They differ from other delivery channels as they do not require direct human interaction. While human interaction may form some part of the process, there is significantly less direct interaction experienced by the provider and the customer. The Internet, smartphone apps, automation and AI are electronic channels and mobile channels that offer advantages for McDonald's and their customers alike (Ingenico, 2018). These advances in technology afford marketers the opportunity to promote

and engage interactively with consumers and allow consumers the opportunity to access information as well as products and services in a more dynamic and engaging format.

The McDonald's App

Source: ©Jimmy Tudeschi/Shutterstock

The McDonald's app allows customers to order in their own time. Using the app, customers can select from their favourite McDonald's items, customize their own meal, or choose from 'available deals' using the 'add deal to mobile order' button. Customers can pay using their credit card and the card will not be charged until they have received their order through UberEats. Customers can add or remove a payment card using the checkout and 'my account' screens. Subsequently, customers can check in at any participating McDonald's restaurant to pick up their meal however they want – getting food brought to their car, avoiding the queues inside the restaurant or grabbing their order in the drive thru.

In the UK and Ireland, McDonald's, along with its franchisees, is leading the way in tuning in to how consumers pay and their preferences, rolling out a click and collect app, in-store kiosks and drive thru contactless payments, all aimed at handling contactless cards and Apple and Google Pay mobile payments. The franchise chain has signed up with Ingenico Group to create a modern, seamless payment structure to be able to offer customers this wide variety of payment options that allow consumers to quickly and easily pay how they want via the McDonald's Click and Collect app, through in-restaurant self-service order screens or when using a drive thru (Hospitality Technology, 2018). This technology has been successfully deployed to all McDonald's restaurants across the UK and Ireland. Jon Braithwaite, Director of IT, McDonald's

Restaurants Limited, elaborated on the strategy: 'We believe that this payment solution is one of the most advanced in the retail sector and is a critical component to delivering excellent experience for our customers. Leveraging Ingenico's experience of implementing complex payment programmes, our teams have been able to deliver the new service ahead of schedule, on budget and with the outstanding performance level we expected. Ingenico's payment security expertise, scale and commitment to innovation give us the confidence that we have the right partner to support our needs now and into the future' (Skeldon, 2018). These sentiments were reinforced by Ian Benn, Senior Vice President, Commercial, Enterprise Retail, Ingenico Group, who added: '*Throughout its history, McDonald's has been a leader in customer service innovation. Ingenico is very proud to be able to play a part in that story, speeding up service, adding new payment options and staying ahead of the pace*' (Jones, 2019).

McDonald's business is built on consistency, speed and convenience. It has ascertained that facilitating quick and easy ordering and payment options is essential as it builds and ensures customer loyalty and retention. Consumers do not want to queue; they want to order quickly and easily, regularly doing so on their own device electronically. In the UK, electronic payments have overtaken cash in many outlets. With the sharp uptake of contactless technology – now more than one in three transactions according to UK finance – which shows no signs of slowing down (McDonald's Corp, 2019c).

Benefits of Electronic Channels (Internet and Mobile Apps)

McDonald's digital app, which notifies consumers of deals and promotions, has paid off. Store sales benefit from the app and the app also complements the fast food company's efforts to promote its restaurants and their daily deals. The mobile app is driving customers to promotions. 'We also see deeper penetration as customers take advantage of value offers,' analyst Andy Barish has observed, estimating gains in same-store sales of 3 per cent (Kim, 2018). In terms of customer (sales) promotions, if a deal is available for redemption through Mobile Order & Pay, customers will see an 'Add Deal to Mobile Order' button below the code when viewing the deal in the McDonald's app. To redeem the deal, customers can choose the 'Add Deal to Mobile Order' button then customize the items in this order (Dawson 2018).

Showcasing In-Store

Source: ©Sorbis/Shutterstock

In recent years, McDonald's has rolled out Evoke's touchscreen ordering system. It has effectively decreased demand for point-of-sale staff and could consequently decrease the wage bill significantly. However, McDonald's has demonstrated how technology does not replace interaction with staff – instead, it can complement and enhance the consumer experience, responding to a greater demand for personalized and customized service using technology. The introduction of touchscreen ordering is fast becoming the norm in fast food outlets, but retailers in other markets need to consider the opportunities this specific development could have for their own high-street presence – as long as they use it correctly.

By implementing a touchscreen channel, retailers such as McDonald's provide customers with greater opportunities for both online browsing and in-store exploration. While the technology itself is a means of enabling and enhancing sales, its clever use within the store in terms of combining it with a stock check facility, an item finder or an ordering form can provide a customized service at a key location in-store, encouraging more footfall and product exploration to an increasingly empowered and technologically-advanced consumer. McDonald's robustly defended its introduction of touchscreens by claiming they allowed staff to better serve customers – not replace them. Examples of enhancing the customer experience include its table service option whereby after ordering food, customers can pick up a plastic table number and have someone deliver the food to their table (Cannon, 2019). Touchscreens, when not enabling customers to order their food, display video advertisements for other McDonald's products and special promotions such as particular deals. It means that no opportunity for promotion is wasted. McDonald's has committed to technology for the future and there is already strong evidence from customers and employees alike that it has been a success (Dawson, 2018). The blueprint is one that can be easily followed by even the newest retailers taking their place on the high street (McDonald's Corp, 2018).

The popularity and utilization of self-order kiosks continues to grow over time, and in France, Italy and Spain, well over half of all in-restaurant visits involve orders being placed through the kiosk. Germany has made a strong push to grow digital engagement in 2018 through digital calendar promotions, and enjoys success, driving sales and guest count growth, as well as increased app downloads. In 2019, the Company report suggests that McDonald's continues to utilize digital initiatives to engage customers, grow awareness and adoption of digital offerings, and support menu offerings (Morgan, 2019).

The 'To-Go' Option

The McDonald's to-go location in London has harnessed technology in terms of customer requirements of accessibility, ease of ordering, speed and convenience. Customers order via touchscreen kiosks and quickly pick up their food to go as there is no seating in the restaurant. McDonald's is providing an option for busy customers on the go to get their food even faster than before. Instead of being full of tables and chairs, the restaurant features touch screens for customers to order. The pilot location in London is much smaller than a typical McDonald's. Even the menu is streamlined, making only popular items like fries, chicken nuggets and the classic Big Mac available. After ordering, customers move to the collection area, where they queue for their order. Since customers can only order through the kiosks, all employees work on fulfilling the orders, which gets the food to customers much faster (Morgan, 2019).

The to-go option is one of the biggest changes to McDonald's since it introduced the drive-thru in the 1970s, and it has the potential to set the pace for a new wave of restaurants. The to-go location works from both an effective and efficiency-based perspective in a busy urban location with high footfall. McDonald's has yet to announce plans to expand the to-go location to other parts of the world, reinforcing their underlying commitment to the original restaurant brand while also wanting to serve customers in the best way possible. However, if the to-go location proves successful, it is likely this option will be expanded to further locations (Morgan, 2019).

Distribution Partnering Strategies – Intermediaries

In January 2016, McDonald's launched a home delivery service, initially in three Florida cities, through a partnership with Uber Eats. Subsequently, in 2017, McDonald's launched its long-awaited home delivery trial in Europe after teaming up with Uber's takeaway service across parts of the UK. The fast food giant is offering its 'McDelivery' service through Uber Eats, with orders available from 22 locations across London and another 10 restaurants in Leeds and Nottingham (Williams, 2017).

Customers order their McDonald's food through the Uber Eats app, which then uses Uber couriers to deliver the food. McDelivery is available on breakfast, lunch and dinner menus from 7 am to 2 am, although customers must live within a radius of 1.5 miles of restaurants in the trial. Claude Abi-Gerges, a McDonald's franchisee who owns and operates five of the London restaurants participated in the trial, noted that the service provides a new level of convenience for customers (Rodger, 2017). '*It's the next chapter in how we get freshly made, great-tasting food to our customers in a way that suits them and fits around their busy lives,*' he added (Rodger, 2017; Williams, 2017).

Uber Eats: Test Drone Delivery with McDonald's

Uber, the ride-sharing and food delivery company, is developing and testing more innovative forms of delivery in terms of its food delivery service using drones to speed up the delivery of McDonald's meals (Dickey, 2019). The company's Uber Eats platform is collaborating with San Diego State University and with the fast food restaurants such as McDonald's in San Diego to examine how drones could be used to improve deliveries in high-density urban areas, after it was granted permission by the Federal Aviation Administration (FAA) to commence tests. Uber suggests that the project will not only decrease delivery times, but also expand the number of culinary choices available to customers. The drones will not ensure full delivery as the plan is to still include hand deliveries by an Uber Eats driver, who will meet the drone at a drop-off location and bring it to the customer's requested location. In the future, drones could be instructed to land at a specified through QR code correspondence (Harris, 2019).

Future Innovation for Effective Service Delivery

Automation and technology play an important role in interactions that can afford to be transactional rather than relational, especially for customer service interactions optimized around speed and efficiency (Gavett, 2015). Technological innovations offer the customer greater autonomy and choice in placing an order through a self-serve kiosk, reviewing payment options, ordering and collecting from a counter or table service. While McDonald's claims that customers are favourably disposed towards using the self-serve kiosks because it gives them more time to customize their orders, the reality is that automation will be replacing much of the human workforce in coming years in many sectors. It is widely predicted that fast-food employees will be affected by developments in technological innovations in more efficient and effective operations in areas such as food preparation, ordering suggestions for customers (thanks to AI) and food service and delivery to the customer (Dodds, 2019). McDonald's has started to replace human servers with voice-based technology in some of its drive-thru restaurants. This technology is being implemented with the help of a voice technology company called Apprente, which McDonald's acquired in October 2019 (BBC, 2019). Apprente specializes in building voice-based agents that can take orders in multiple languages

and accents. McDonald's has been testing this technology in several locations and expects it will allow for *'faster, simpler and more accurate order taking'* (Khalid, 2019).

Source: ©RMC42/Shutterstock

As well as voice-based technological acquisitions, in 2019 McDonald's acquired an Israeli-based AI machine-learning start-up called Dynamic Yield for a reported $300 million (USD). Dynamic Yield's *'decision technology'* will be built into new electronic menu boards located at McDonald's drive-thrus to provide a more personalized customer experience. McDonald's high-tech menu boards have been compared with Amazon's online shopping site which constantly offers similar or complementary items or suggestions for future purchases as it tracks your previous and current search activity. This is one of the first instances of using decision technology aimed at the point of sale in terms of endeavouring to augment the customer experience (McDonald's Corp, 2019d). This implies that the items on the menu could change even as a customer is ordering, as the technology driving the menu boards will consider internal, extraneous and contemporaneous factors, such as current weather conditions; so it might suggest cold drinks on a hot day and, dependent on how busy the restaurant is, it might push items in terms of suggestions to customers that are quicker to prepare. McDonald's has rolled out this technology in 8,000 outlets in the US, subsequently rolling out the menu boards in 14,000 of its US restaurants and expanding into other markets and has begun work to integrate the technology into all of its digital customer experience touchpoints, such as self-order kiosks and McDonald's global mobile app (McDonald's Corp, 2019e).

McDonald's CEO, Steve Easterbrook, has indicated that the company has further plans for investment in technology and innovations through systems such as wireless beacons to detect customer's smartphones and licence recognition technology so that the menu board could adjust its items based on a customer's recent purchases (Locker, 2019). Consequently, big data and, in this case, customer data could be shared across the entire chain of restaurants rather than being confined to a single outlet, further enhancing the power of the technology and its ability to boost sales. McDonald's can glean invaluable insights into the trends and behaviours in the market, particularly customer behaviour, by gathering data on its 68 million daily customers (Gibson, 2019). This technology innovation strategy embraces artificial intelligence in order to maximize revenue and profits, a trend that is common across service-orientated businesses in recent years. Combining the AI technology with big data, such as customer data gathered via loyalty programs and apps, enables these companies to offer a more personalized customer experience (Mogg, 2019).

Conclusion

Technology is constantly evolving and at a rapid pace. Likewise, customers' expectations and their need for autonomy and instant access to products and services have similarly advanced. McDonald's is committed to delivering the best possible experience for its customers and staff. In light of this commitment, McDonald's has stated that it is its '*mission to embody a culture of innovation*' (McDonald's, 2019). McDonald's is continuously embracing a culture of innovation in devising and implementing effective and efficient service distribution strategies to improve the customer experience with new technologies. High-tech innovation enables faster, simpler and more accurate ordering.

Adaptations in processes and delivery systems have been achieved by investment in advanced technology capabilities and human resources built on several key initiatives that the company has introduced over the last number of years: from the acquisition of Dynamic Yield, an AI system that improves the order-making and order-taking experience, to the expansion of McDelivery, as well as the development of McDonald's global mobile app, mobile order and pay, acquisition and development of McD tech labs, namely Apprente (a conversational voice-based technology start-up), which will facilitate faster, more accurate drive-thru ordering systems, to indoor and outdoor digital menu boards and self-order kiosks. These technological advances offer opportunities to develop and enhance productivity, high quality, positive and personalized experiences to meet rising expectations – benefiting both customers and restaurant employees and ultimately the company's bottom line.

References

BBC (2019) 'McDonald's uses AI for ordering at drive-throughs', *BBC News Online*, 11 September 2019, https://www.bbc.com/news/technology-49664633 [accessed 17 October 2019].

Cannon, J. (2019) 'McDonald's latest tech move aims to bring voice-based, conversational ordering to the dining experience', *MarTech Today*, https://marketingland.com/mcdonalds-latest-tech-move-aims-to-bring-voice-based-conversational-ordering-to-the-dining-experience-267223 [accessed 17 October 2019].

Dawson, J. (2018) Why retailers cannot ignore McDonald's' touchscreen innovation, https://www.shiftmagazine.com/authors/james-dawson.html [accessed 17 October 2019].

Dickey, M.R. (2019) 'Uber will start testing Eats drone delivery', 12 June 2019, https://techcrunch.com/2019/06/12/uber-will-start-testing-eats-drone-delivery/ [accessed 17 October 2019].

Dignan, L. (2018) 'Food factory AI: How McDonald's automation lets the crew focus more on customers', ZDnet.com, https://www.zdnet.com/article/food-factory-ai-how-mcdonalds-automation-lets-the-crew-focus-more-on-customers/ [accessed 17 October 2019].

Dodds, L. (2019) 'The future of fast food: From robot chefs to lab-grown meat, what will eating out be like in a decade?', *The Telegraph Online*, https://www.telegraph.co.uk/technology/2019/07/30/future-fast-food-robot-chefs-lab-grown-meat-will-eating-like/ [accessed 17 October 2019].

Gavett, G. (2015) 'How Self-Service Kiosks Are Changing Customer Behavior', 11 March 2015, https://hbr.org/2015/03/how-self-service-kiosks-are-changing-customer-behavior [accessed 17 October 2019].

Gibson, K. (2019) 'McDonald's wants to become the Amazon of fast-food', CBS News Online, 26 March 2019, https://www.cbsnews.com/news/mcdonalds-dynamic-yield-personalize-digital-menus-based-on-traffic-weather/ [accessed 17 October 2019].

Harris, J. (2019) 'McDonald's drive-thru will use AI to have your food ready before you even order', North Wales Live, https://www.dailypost.co.uk/news/uk-world-news/mcdonalds-drive-thru-use-ai-16037654 [accessed 28 November 2019].

Hospitality Technology (2018) 'McDonald's UK, Ireland Locations Select Ingenico as Payment Solution Provider', 15 May 2018, https://hospitalitytech.com/mcdonalds-uk-ireland-locations-select-ingenico-payment-solution-provider [accessed 17 October 2019].

Ingenico Group (2018) 'McDonald's selects Ingenico as its long-term Payment Solution Provider', 15 May 2018, https://www.ingenico.com/press-and-publications/press-releases/all/2018/05/mcdonalds-selects-ingenico-as-its-long-term-payment-solution-provider.html [accessed 17 October 2019].

Jones, R. (2019) 'One in 10 adults in UK have gone "cashless", data shows', *The Guardian Online,* https://www.theguardian.com/money/2019/jun/06/adults-uk-cashless-contactless-payments [accessed 17 October 2019].

Khalid, A. (2019) 'McDonald's plans to bring AI voice technology to its drive-thrus', 9 October 2019, *Endgadget,* https://www.engadget.com/2019-09-10-mcdonald-plans-to-bring-ai-voice-technology-to-its-drive-thrus.html?guccounter=1&guce_referrer=aHR0cHM-6Ly93d3cuZ29vZ2xlLmNvbS91cmw_c2E9dCZyY-3Q9aiZxPSZlc3JjPXMmc291cmNlPXdlYiZjZD0x-JnZlZD0yYWhVS0V3amxfdVhmcXV2b0FoVUt-TaFVJSGNCZURTOFFGakFBZWdRSUFSQUIm-dXJsPWh0dHBzJTNBJTJGJTJGd3d3LmVuZ2FkZ-2V0LmNvbSUyRjIwMTktMDktMTAtbWNkb25h-bGQtcGxhbnMtdG8tYnJpbmctYWktdm9pY2Ut-dGVjaG5vbG9neS10by1pdHMtZHJpdmUtdGhy-dXMuaHRtbCZ1c2c9QU92VmF3MDJaeDRk-d0lGR0RVdkk0UnduNTBSdA&guce_referrer_sig=AQAAAJjqZ-gOAUVnEu_FNhU9dC4QTF-V6o2RKFU76SC6BE9HVMoLJNO1mJeEgASN-xGMNeDdbY2_-jpPP05Jya-pnjnIIh0wCQ6c2gF-MR8tiqUHn14tnHPuD7_pu7s8crDvi1LYsqRB16-fzCMWB5QiAynJwogT1ZKeKSjgVz8ZGMqAICIj [accessed 15 April 2020].

Kim, T. (2018) 'Buy McDonald's shares because its mobile deal app usage is surging, Jeffries says', CNBC Markets Online, https://www.cnbc.com/2018/08/28/buy-mcdonalds-shares-because-its-mobile-deal-app-usage-is-surging.html [accessed 19 December 2019].

Lauchlan, S. (2018) 'Digital and delivery – McDonald's growth accelerators that are paying off', diginomica.com https://diginomica.com/digital-and-delivery-mcdonalds-growth-accelerators-that-are-paying-off [accessed 17 October 2019].

Lock, S. (2019a) 'Number of McDonald's restaurants in Europe from 2016 to 2018, by country', Statista.com/statistics/256044/mcdonalds-restaurants-in-europe/ 11 September 2019 [accessed 17 October 2019].

Lock, S. (2019b) 'Brand value of the 10 most valuable fast food brands worldwide in 2019 (in million U.S. dollars)', https://www.statista.com/statistics/273057/value-of-the-most-valuable-fast-food-brands-worldwide/ 11 September 2019 [accessed 17 October 2019].

Locker, M. (2019) 'McDonald's is spending $300 million to be more like Amazon', Fast Company, 26 March 2019, https://www.fastcompany.com/90325388/mcdonalds-tries-to-be-more-like-amazon-with-300-million-ai-bet [accessed 17 October 2019].

McDonald's (2018) Annual Report, http://www.annualreports.com/HostedData/AnnualReports/PDF/NYSE_MCD_2018.pdf [accessed 17 October 2019].

McDonald's (2019) 'We are investing in the future of McDonald's through the agreement to acquire Apprente, a voice-based tech start-up', https://news.mcdonalds.com/stories/company-news-details/acquistion-of-Apprente-a-voice-based-tech-start-up [accessed 19 December 2019].

McDonald's Corp (2019a) 'The Ray Kroc Story', http://www.mcdonalds.ie/iehome/our_story/

our_history/the_ray_kroc_story.html [accessed 17 October 2019].

McDonald's Corp (2019b) Our Business Model, https://corporate.mcdonalds.com/corpmcd/about-us/our-business-model.html [accessed 17 October 2019].

McDonald's Corp (2019c) 'McDonald's Global Headquarters Restaurant Updates International Menu Items with Favorites from India, Sweden, Switzerland, Malaysia and Belgium', 6 June 2019, https://news.mcdonalds.com/stories/about-our-food/global-menu-mhq-june-2019 [accessed 17 October 2019].

McDonald's Corp (2019d) 'Mobile Order and Pay', https://www.mcdonalds.com/us/en-us/mobile-order-and-pay.html [accessed 17 October 2019].

McDonald's Corp (2019e) 'McDonald's to Acquire Dynamic Yield, Will Use Decision Technology to Increase Personalization and Improve Customer Experience', *Cision PR Newswire*, 26 March 2019, https://www.prnewswire.com/il/news-releases/mcdonald-s-to-acquire-dynamic-yield-will-use-decision-technology-to-increase-personalization-and-improve-customer-experience-839722580.html [accessed 17 October 2019].

Mogg, T. (2019) 'McDonald's to use A.I. to tempt you into extra purchases at the drive-thru', 26 March 2019, *Digital Trends*, https://www.digitaltrends.com/cool-tech/mcdonalds-uses-ai-to-tempt-you-into-extra-purchases-at-the-drive-thru/ [accessed 17 October 2019].

Morgan, B. (2019) 'The Sign of a Future Restaurant: The McDonald's To-Go Location', *Forbes.com*, https://www.forbes.com/sites/blakemorgan/2019/08/22/a-sign-of-the-future-restaurant-the-new-mcdonalds-to-go-location/#3f67d7a3d7fd [accessed 17 October 2019].

Rodger, J. (2017) 'McDonald's have finally launched their UK home delivery service', CoventryLive, 23 June 2017, https://www.coventrytelegraph.net/whats-on/food-drink-news/mcdonalds-home-delivery-uk-mcdelivery-13227826 [accessed 17 October 2019].

Skeldon, P. (2018) 'McDonald's serves up quick and easy mobile ways to buy and pay', *InternetRetailing* 4 June 2018, https://internetretailing.net/mobile-theme/mobile-theme/mcdonalds-serves-up-quick-and-easy-mobile-ways-to-buy-and-pay-17845 [accessed 17 October 2019].

Williams, H. (2017) 'McDonald's teams up with Uber to bring long awaited home delivery trial to Europe', *Independent.ie/Business World*, https://www.independent.ie/business/world/mcdonalds-teams-up-with-uber-to-bring-long-awaited-home-delivery-trial-to-europe-35855306.html [accessed 17 October 2019].

CASE 5   **MUSIC FESTIVALS AND THE PRICE OF LIVE PERFORMANCES**

This case was written by Dr Fiona Whelan-Ryan, WIT School of Business, Waterford Institute of Technology, Ireland.

Introduction

As consumers search for opportunities to engage in unique events, as well as digitally record and share them, music festivals have become an increasingly popular part of an individual's summer and often punctuate their social planning. Most music festivals offer festival attendees a rich experience in terms of access to various genres of music, leading artists, spoken word (including comedy), well-being and mindfulness initiatives, wide-ranging and high quality food and beverage offerings, camping, glamping and luxury camper vans on-site, all of which collectively appeal to families and generation Y and Z consumers alike. In this highly competitive market, and in light of the fact that festival-goers' expectations have become increasingly sophisticated, festival organizers/promoters are increasingly challenged to continue to further develop their festivals, attracting the most popular music artists while charging festival attendees premium prices. Festivals are often sold out even before headlining acts are disclosed and publicized. Ticket re-selling agents snap up as many tickets as they can and then re-sell them at extortionate prices to potential attendees.

Most artists depend on music festivals as well, as a way of promoting their own tours in order to maintain their relationships with their fans, and they are also dependent on festivals as a primary revenue stream. Festival promoters in turn often pay extraordinary fees to book headline acts that will attract high levels of demand for their festival. Music festival promoters continuously manage many different variables when planning and running a festival. These range from paying artists' agents, controlling overheads such as staging, lighting, sound systems and marquees, as well as exorbitant insurance fees and other health and safety related costs in addition to hoping that the weather is not too inclement. Consequently, promoters rely heavily on sponsorship to offset some of the costs and build a certain level of revenue for a festival. Furthermore, promoters must continue to develop their event offerings and continuously evolve festivals, particularly in terms of developing new initiatives. This can include proactively trying to address contemporary issues and embracing important social values, such as the introduction of sustainability and diversity initiatives, for example Glastonbury becoming a plastic-free festival, through to sourcing sustainable partners, fossil-free venues, offering more meat-free and vegan foods, with fewer air miles and more diverse acts in terms of gender balance (Dawson, 2019).

Source: ©dwphotos/Shutterstock

The Growth of Music Festivals

Music festivals offer a blend of dynamic and rich experiences, including live performances from a variety of artists and various cultural genres, coupled with a variety of complementary offerings, with a collective atmosphere of a cross-section of different fans. Music festivals are niche and offer a unique theme and a genre which allows for people of all music tastes to seek out a festival that matches their interests and enables them to see their favourite acts live. The number of festivals continues to grow at a rapid pace, a development that fits well with the increasing demand for experiences (Consultancy. uk, 2017). Recovering economies, socio-cultural, technological and consumer trends and accelerating interests in experiences throughout Europe and the UK have collectively contributed to a growth in attendance and demand for music festivals. For countries, regions and more specifically communities, music festivals provide opportunities to boost the local economy. Advancements in audio-visual technology and sophisticated social media campaign engagement by organizers and festival-goers alike have also accelerated growth in the popularity of music festivals. Environmental impact is a key concern for many festival organizers as well as festival-goers in terms of recycling and transport initiatives. Safety is similarly a joint concern for both parties. The use of digital technologies for scanning and avoiding queues for entering and exiting particular areas of a festival, and in terms of queuing for food and beverages and other facilities, is also a priority (Mintel, 2019).

Increased corporate sponsorship, growing sophistication in marketing and social media engagement, and millennial trends have been significant players in driving the massive growth of music festivals over the last decade. As it now so easy and cost-effective to hear a vast selection of high-quality music on demand, it's the overall *'experience'* more than anything that drives attendance. This includes the experience of the live performances, pyrotechnics, miscellaneous entertainment stands and all those added extras that many festivals have learned to cultivate so much faster than their concert-organizing counterparts (Giovarruscio, 2016). Furthermore, for artists, music streaming and digitization of music offerings has changed the way musicians and bands operate throughout the world. Most income is generated by artists' touring. In 2002 David Bowie predicted: *'Music itself is going to become like running water or electricity. . . . You'd better be prepared for doing a lot of touring because that's the only unique situation that's going to be left'* (Pareles, 2002).

Festivals also popularize specific regions which can lead to increased tourism (Miller, 2020). Music festivals around the world continue to grow with each passing year. Festivals have adapted much more successfully to shifts in consumer demand for live music. Tickets for the biggest, most expensive music festivals cost roughly as much as one might spend for a typical one-band concert and, although festival prices are on the increase, a live

music festival in the UK currently sets an attendee back about €178 (Statista, 2019), whereas a ticket to just one concert by Drake in 2019 racked up a fee of over €250. Festival attendance is at its highest level in four years in spite of the UK's biggest festival, Glastonbury, taking its traditional 'fallow year' off in 2018. Half (49 per cent) of Generation Z (consumers aged 16 to 19 years) attended a music festival in the last year. They are joined by 43 per cent of millennials (aged 20 to 39 years), and 19 per cent of Generation X (40 to 54-year-olds). Such is Britain's love of live music that, according to Mintel (2019), a staggering 61 per cent of festival-goers would prioritize going to a music festival over a holiday within the UK; and 57 per cent would prioritize this over a European holiday.

The music scene has evolved over time. In the past, music artists used to tour to promote a newly released album, whereas these days artists release music to promote a tour. The reason is primarily down to the fact that it is difficult for artists to earn a living from music sales in the age of the Internet as the money an artist makes from someone listening to a track on Spotify is a minimal amount. So, an increase in ticket prices for live music concerts and festivals was always inevitable. Artists who are keen to avoid the drudgery of touring can play at a significant festival and make as much money over a one-off show. Music promoters have multiple challenges, between having to book in advance and pay artists enough to secure their performances, needing to sell a certain number of tickets in order to be successful, the additional costs of insurance, the risks of bad weather and also contending with anti-social behaviour of a smaller amount of festival-goers who can also affect the reputation of the festival and the safety of other festival-goers (Gajanan, 2019).

Carlos Chirinos, a professor of clinical music and global health at New York University suggests that millennials and Gen Z consumers are more likely to spend money on experiences over material goods, contending that sharing a clip from a Billie Eilish or Cardi B performance with one's Instagram followers is more gratifying than buying something expensive. This 'experiential economy' has expanded and Chirinos contends that music festivals have become more popular as audiences are keen to connect with their favourite artists and with other festival-goers and fans as well (Gajanan, 2019). A 2019 Deloitte survey of millennials, a group that makes up at least 45 per cent of the 32 million people who attend music festivals, highlights their most highly ranked reason for attending a music festival or concert is to see a particular artist (45 per cent); however, more and more festival-goers are motivated by the social aspect of a live event. This includes enjoying time with friends/family (41 per cent), meeting new people (19 per cent) and to take pictures/selfies (15 per cent). Meanwhile, as many as seven in ten (69 per cent) event-goers say that the range of alternative activities (e.g. non-music) available at a music event is important, up from 64 per cent in 2018. Health, adventure and immersive themes are continuing to be combined with music and this has become increasingly popular, as 48 per cent of those aged 19 and under attend music events for the entire experience (Mintel, 2019).

Organizing Music Festivals

Most music festivals do not make money for at least two to three years but costs and lower margins must be managed and leveraged against future potential profits. Music festivals have become highly competitive and are always subject to potential mergers or take-overs by rival organizers. To survive, every festival must find its own niche. Music festivals are costly to host and while at face value they seem to have access to a captive audience and significant revenue streams, their bottom line and profit margins are seriously eroded. The main expenses include performers, site hire, staging, utilities, waste disposal, printing and signage, marketing, technology, equipment hire, insurance, infrastructure, security, staffing, photography and videography, VAT and payments to the Performing Rights Society (PRS). Revenue streams include tickets, sponsorships, on-site accommodation including camping and glamping, traders, merchandising, food and beverage facilities and other entertainment elements such as amusement rides, marquees hosting well-being events, comedy, spoken word, silent discos, eco-sites, facilities and entertainment for children and so on (Nielsen, 2019).

Experienced festival and event organizers and promoters usually operate in a specific sector, e.g. the music sector, and have access to financial backing, including sponsorship deals to plan and organize

the festival. Potential sponsors, their products/services, brands and corporate values and their actual and potential target markets must correlate with or complement the type of event that is being staged. It is most challenging for inexperienced event organizers and for organizers of a new festival to identify and access appropriate sponsors with sufficient financial support. It is vital for event organizers to have identified potential sponsors and developed sponsorship deals with them in advance of a festival, as it is not enough to rely on revenue from ticket sales to ensure that event is feasible (Bradshaw, 2017). To access sponsorship, event organizers need to find potential sponsors, sell appropriate sponsorship offers and develop appropriate sponsorship deals. Merchandising also forms an integral part of most music festivals for the organizers and artists alike. For the artists there are numerous revenue streams including streaming, downloading, vinyl, CD, merchandising, publishing, live, sponsorship, performing rights, airplay, synchronization and innumerable B2B services. Artists today can effectively use digital media such as Twitter, Facebook, Instagram, podcasts and blogs to build their own communities (Murphy, 2019).

Music Festival Promoters

There are very few music festival promoters that have established themselves globally (Lewis, 2020). The leading music promoter in the world in 2018 was Live Nation, with 49.52 million tickets sold (see Figure 1). Live Nation (the world's leading live entertainment company) topped the ranking of leading promoters by ticket sales substantially, selling over four times more than AEG Presents, who ranked second with just under 11.6 million sales. Live Nation Entertainment serves markets globally and dominates the music promotion and ticketing industry, and has operated under that name since the Live Nation–Ticketmaster merger in 2010 (Statista, 2020).

Attending Music Festivals – The Costs

Attending music festivals is expensive. A three-day pass for the 2019 Coachella music festival in California cost $429 (USD) or €391 (euro). Tickets

Figure 1 Leading global music promoters in 2018

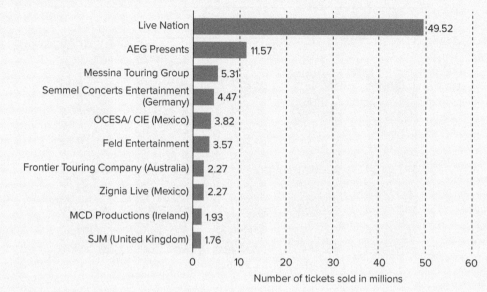

Source: Data from Statista 2020

for the Glastonbury Festival in the UK went for £253 ($321 USD) or €293 (euro). According to economist Alan Krueger, music festivals are a bargain. In his recently released book *Rockonomics*, Krueger (2019) highlights the phenomenal increase in concert ticket prices over the past 40 years. The rising cost of concerts, Krueger explains, is mostly due to what economists refer to as 'Baumol's cost disease' (Baumol and Bowen, 1966). This is the idea that certain industries experience rapid productivity growth because of the effect of achieving greater economies of scale in maximizing output as a result of investment in machinery, equipment and technology. It suggests that industries that are more 'people intensive' such as the performing arts, realistically cannot incur as much productivity growth in relative terms as human input is relatively more expensive (Kopf, 2019).

Average Price of Music Festival Tickets in Europe 2014–2018

In 2016, European recorded music industry revenues amounted to roughly 4.3 billion euros, an increase for the second year in a row after an otherwise steady decrease since 2001. The UK is the leading music market in Europe in terms of both total recorded music revenues and digital music revenues, followed by Germany and France. However, when looking at a ranking of European countries by recorded music revenues per capita, the UK ranks second after Norway and is closely followed by two other Scandinavian markets, Sweden and Denmark. The average price of music festival tickets in Europe has increased over the last few years (see Figure 2). In 2018, the average cost of a ticket was just over 178 euros, which is up from an average of 163 euros in 2017 and 146 euros the year before that. This is part of the ever-changing characteristics of the music industry. The UK hosted the highest number of festivals, with 27 major music events taking place that year (Statista.com, 2019). Weekend festival tickets cost approximately 236 euros or more, which excludes transport, tents and the food and beverage expenses that are also incurred when attending a festival. Festival-goers spent an average of €316 to attend a festival and this includes pre-festival purchases such as tents and clothing as well as food and alcohol during the festival and excludes the price of a ticket (Livewire, 2017).

The following sections describe two significantly different festivals: one of the leading festivals in the world and one of the worst festivals ever run.

Glastonbury

The Glastonbury festival is a five-day festival of contemporary performing arts. Set in 900 acres of

Figure 2   Average price of music festivals 2014–2018

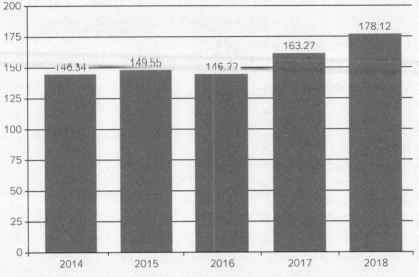

Source: Data from Statista 2020

countryside in England's south-west, Glastonbury has its own claim to fame: the title of 'the largest green-field music and performing arts festival in the world'. The first incarnation of the festival was in 1970 and was disappointing in terms of numbers, with attendance at about 1,500. A ticket then cost £1 (€18 in today's money) whereas entry to the full weekend event in 2017 was about €271. Approximately 200,000 people attend each day (BBC News, 2018). Glastonbury festival was due to celebrate its fiftieth anniversary in 2020 and it had been suggested that attendance might have been expanded to a capacity of 210,000, if the local council and organizers could agree on it (Trendell, 2020). However, an online statement released on 18 March 2020 by the organizers of the festival, Michael and Emily Eavis, announced that Glastonbury 2020 was cancelled as a result of the global pandemic Covid-19, based on government sanctions (Glastonbury Festival, 2020).

The difference in pricing of festivals is notable in ticket costs, in which Glastonbury topped. Festival-goers may have achieved almost the impossible in terms of getting their hands on tickets for the festival, but additional economic costs incurred in terms of transport, accommodation, food and beverages are also significant. For example, a pint of beer costs €5.30 to €5.70 at Glastonbury (Consultancy.uk 2017).

Source: ©marietta peros/Shutterstock

Fyre Festival

In April 2017, approximately 5,000 festival-goers spent hundreds to thousands of dollars for tickets to a luxury music festival on a private island in the Bahamas. Promotions for the much-hyped event, called Fyre Festival, promised 'a place where the tropical sun shines all day, and our celebrations ignite the night. This is an invitation to unplug, connect with something deeper, and hunt for something bigger'. Tickets cost $500 to 1,500 (USD), the staggering equivalent of €457 to €1,370 (euro). Festival-goers were promised luxury accommodation, gourmet food and the chance to socialize with celebrities. But the reality was closer to a catastrophe that played out in real-time on social media, whereby tents were provided and not luxury villas as promised and cold cheese sandwiches comprised the gourmet food on offer. A-list acts promoted as headliners dropped out in the days leading up to the festival and attendees immediately started to leave en masse. Multiple lawsuits were launched against the event's organizers, who included Ja Rule and Fyre Media CEO, Billy McFarland, with the latter now serving a six-year prison sentence for fraud. Essentially, McFarland greatly underestimated the cost and time it would take to organize a music festival (Huddleston, 2019).

Pricing Approaches and Strategies for Festival Tickets

Music festivals have become a significant business proposition over the last 50 years since the incarnation of Woodstock and Glastonbury. These festivals have expanded with multiple stages, multiple experiences in live music acts, leading DJs, well-being initiatives, camping and glamping options, increasingly sophisticated food and beverage offerings over a series of minimum three to five days at top ticket prices. Niche or smaller music festivals have gained in popularity (Gajanan, 2019). According to Krueger (2019) price discrimination with in music sector is critical. For example, charging different prices for standing versus seating, or for VIP access as opposed to general access, is standard. Furthermore, price bundling and early-bird pricing all form part of an integral part of festival pricing and, more specifically, music festival pricing.

Pricing tickets for festivals is an art and a science. Festival and other event organizers want to sell as many tickets as possible, but if pricing is too low, profit margins are compromised. Conversely, pricing too high can have a negative impact on demand for tickets (Sawyer, 2019). 'One of the biggest mistakes event creators make is not spending enough time on pricing', suggests Nels Gilbreth, VP, Pricing and Monetization at Eventbrite. 'People are afraid to charge differently for things like VIP tickets or early bird tickets, but these are so common to the consumer.' Implementing a tiered pricing approach can attract more market segments and stimulate demand at a series of price points. The main advantage of implementing a tiered pricing approach is that organizers are offering a variety of ticket types and price points that inevitably attract more customers, appealing to those who perceive a greater value in higher prices while serving others who may only be able to afford the lower tiered price. The utilization of event management systems and revenue management technology support event management, allowing for increased pricing flexibility for an event and in terms of accepting payments. It also allows the organizer to monitor demand and more actively manage ticket prices (Eventsforce, 2019).

Pricing Approaches

A tiered pricing approach that appeals to a variety of festival-goers/target markets may be used and is categorized in Table 1.

Pricing Strategies

Eventbrite, a global digital platform for creating, sharing and communicating about events from music festivals to marathons, offers advice on planning, organizing, pricing and communicating about events (Eventbrite, 2019). Pricing strategies incorporate the pricing and promotion of specific types of tickets for

Table 1   Pricing approaches for music festivals

Standard ticket	Standard general admission ticket per day or a standard festival package (e.g. over the specific number of days).
Special access	Provides attendees something extra for a higher price. For example, VIP, early access, or a backstage pass.
Targeted discount	Allocates discounts to all groups that can 'prove' membership of specific groups. For example, students, children/family tickets.
Group discounts	Offer discounts for higher volume/group purchases, for example, a group of six tickets for one overall price.

Source: Sawyer, 2019

a particular event that appeal to specific target markets and stimulate demand at various price points. The following are pricing strategies that Eventbrite (2019) recommend.

- Generate advance interest with early bird (discounted) tickets: Stimulate demand from innovator-consumers and price-sensitive festival-goers by incentivizing interested attendees to buy their ticket early, by offering an exclusive discount to early bird purchasers. It is important to set a specific time-frame and parameters for potential attendees to avail of the early-bird discount (Eventsforce, 2019).
- Utilize dynamic pricing: A time-based pricing strategy implies that organizers will set a series of prices to sell 'waves' of tickets. Organizers will set one price for the first wave of tickets and, once those are sold out, they move to the next (slightly more expensive) tier. The utilization of this type of dynamic pricing strategy is a useful way to gauge how much attendees are willing to pay.
- Incentivize for valued customers and repeat (loyal) festival-goers and fans who are prepared to pay more with VIP offerings: VIP packages drive interest in a festival and also drive ticket sales. Some festival-goers are prepared to pay more for additional experiences such as: avoiding queues, 'meet and greets', VIP seating, access to specific areas and a higher quality of food and beverage offerings. Organizers need to ensure that the experience VIPs pay for is worth the extra cost they incur.
- Consider charging higher prices for tickets sold on-site on the day(s) of the festival: Selling tickets on the day, on-site at a higher price, is also feasible for attendees who have decided to attend last minute and show up at concert stalls/gates if capacity allows, with unsold tickets. It implies that optimum capacity is realized for the event at an optimum price point, thereby increasing revenue.
- Reconfigure pricing for membership/affiliation and sponsors: Membership of a particular organization or professional body and the utilization of corporate tickets form part of a pricing strategy that is often useful when it applies to the sponsors of a particular event.

- Offer and price for bundling (experiences): Offering festival-goers a ticket price that is inclusive of a series of days of the festival and that may also include other sub-events that form part of the festival, or additional offerings such as on-site accommodation and food and beverage options, may be considered.
- Offer group discounts: Offering a group discount (but limited to a specific number of tickets e.g. six persons) and for families often is deemed to be a value-based proposition for some festival-goers.

Re-Sale of Tickets

European consumers have consistently reported problems when buying tickets for cultural and sports events based on negative experiences with some unauthorized re-selling websites (BEUC, 2019). There are specific regulations in a number of countries which prohibit or restrict the re-sale of tickets in one way or another. For example, the re-selling of tickets at more than face value (e.g. in Denmark or Belgium) is prohibited. But, in most countries, there are no specific rules or regulations in place. Consumers who cannot attend an event should be able to re-sell their ticket(s) to another person. However, the current situation where big companies are making huge profits on re-selling tickets to consumers at excessively inflated prices is perceived to be unfair and unacceptable. Consumers should also have an opportunity to buy a ticket from the primary seller for the face value. Unfortunately, this is often impossible due to tickets disappearing almost instantly from the main ticketing agent and primary market in order to be re-sold minutes later for much higher prices on unauthorized ticket re-selling websites. A solution, already in effect in some countries, is to restrict the field of action of re-sellers, e.g. by allowing ticket re-sale at no more than the original seller's price of the ticket. In some countries there are websites which allow a fair re-sale of event tickets for not more than the price initially paid for them.

Ticket re-sellers are often referred to as ticket brokers or secondary ticket sellers. The main four ticket re-sellers include Viagogo, StubHub, Seatwave and GetMeIn. These ticket re-sellers have been accused of misleading pricing and have been subject to the action against 'drip pricing', where VAT, booking and delivery fees were added at the end of the booking process (Johnson, 2018). In 2018, Kilimanjaro Live, which was promoting Ed Sheeran's UK stadium tour, cancelled more than 10,000 tickets in an attempt to encourage fairer prices. Stuart Galbraith, of Kilimanjaro Live, disclosed that he had successfully negotiated with GetMeIn, Seatwave and StubHub to ensure they would not re-sell tickets for the tour. 'The only agency which listed against our wishes and ignored all our correspondence was Viagogo', he reported. 'We're achieving exactly what Ed wanted, which is "we want you to come in and pay this [fixed] price"' (Johnson, 2018).

An ongoing [legal] challenge in relation to re-sale of tickets has observed that these re-seller companies can move their offices from one country to another in order to avoid legal action. This has been the case for the most infamous of these re-selling websites, Viagogo. In 2018, Digital Minister Margot James advised UK consumers not to use Viagogo, one of the main four secondary ticket re-sellers, after the Advertising Standards Authority (ASA) had referred Viagogo to the National Trading Standards. Viagogo has not respected a UK court order secured by the Competition and Markets Authority (Johnson, 2018). The UK authority announced it would take new legal action. In the interim, Viagogo relocated to Switzerland and then on to the US. In the UK, the consumer advocacy group *Which?* has also conducted extensive research on this topic and shared the evidence with its national authority. From January 2019, national authorities working together at European level possess stronger powers and are able to fine or close down websites following an investigation. BEUC and its members, national consumer organizations, have called for the network of national consumer authorities (the CPC network) to launch a formal coordinated enforcement action and effectively stop ongoing breaches of EU consumer protection law by Viagogo (BEUC, 2019).

The Future of Music Festivals

Technology is influencing and shaping all socio-cultural interactions as we know them. Technologically-enhanced music festival experiences will continue to evolve and develop: from overall staging, incredible lighting displays, state-of-the-art sound quality, to VR-elements such as holograms of stars (often departed), to interactive apps that allow fans to send requests for specific hits or shout-outs, to the exciting anticipatory build-up on social media. Festival-goers' overall comfort, safety and security may be enhanced with personalized wristbands embedded with radio frequency identification (RFID) that tags link attendees' credit card details to all festival areas and on-site vendors, thereby reducing queues and reducing the need for cash and deterring petty crime. Wearable technology may also assist promoters in building up a more complete data profile of festival-goers and their activities and experiences on-site. iBeacon technology first appeared at an event at South By Southwest (SXSW) in 2015 and has since been used at various digital events in Australia to connect audiences with brands, locations and each other (hello, lost friend) as festival-goers can opt-in for location-based notifications. iBeacon provides geo-tagged information such as advising on the length of queues at popular performances, or which marquee or specific area that your are friends currently in, and is potentially just as appealing and lucrative for on-site merchandisers who can trigger promotions when an attendee passes the vendors' location. Other technological advances will, over time, include virtual reality and augmented reality, which will allow attendees to get up close and personal with on-stage experiences, in chill-out areas or even 'hanging out with the band' (Dragani, 2019).

Conclusion

Music festivals are here to stay and are only set to become increasingly sophisticated as time progresses. Music artists depend on these festivals and likewise promoters and festivals are dependent on the artists to generate interest and demand for tickets. The limited number of promoters in this sector has raised questions in terms of the potential for monopolistic behaviours and anti-competitive practices. Furthermore, this sector requires additional regulation in the area of ticket re-sales agents. Currently, promoters, festival-goers and regulatory bodies are still playing catch-up with these predatory organizations. Most music festivals have developed their own

USPs, ESPs and niche market(s) and their ticket pricing reflects this phenomenon. Festival-goers have higher expectations around their festival experience and this is inevitably reflected in ticket pricing structures. Fees commanded by popular artists such as Lizzo, Billie Eilish, Drake, Ed Sheeran and many more performers have soared as have insurance costs. Promoters are heavily dependent on sponsorship deals to boost their revenue streams. Event and revenue management systems greatly assist with the management of pricing structures and distribution of tickets and other services such as the ability to reserve on-site accommodation for events. Online systems and digital communications platforms continue to play an invaluable role in promoting events and communicating with festival-goers, artists communicating with their fans, as well as festival-goers communicating with everyone else. The costs incurred by promoters, and the stakes promoters have to contend with are high, but critically the ticket prices and non-monetary costs incurred by festival-goers continue to soar and promoters only have one chance to pull off the event and get it right!

References

Baumol, William J. and William G. Bowen (1966) *Performing Arts: The Economic Dilemma*, New York: The Twentieth Century Fund.

BBC News (2018) 'Music Festivals: What's the world's biggest?' *BBC News Online*, https://www.bbc.com/news/world-44697302 [accessed 24 January 2020].

BEUC (2019) The European Commission Organisation, https://www.beuc.eu/publications/beuc-x-2019-034_resale_of_tickets_-_questions_and_answers.pdf [accessed 27 January 2020].

Bradshaw, G. (2017) 'How to Find Music Festival Sponsors', *Attendstar*, https://www.attendstar.com/find-music-festival-sponsors/ [accessed 29 January 2020].

Consultancy.uk (2017) 'Top 10 largest music festivals in the UK', 16 June 2017, https://www.consultancy.uk/news/13576/top-10-largest-music-festivals-in-the-uk [accessed 29 January 2020].

Dawson, B. (2019) 'Predicting how sustainable music festivals will be in 20 years', *Dazed*, https://www.dazeddigital.com/music/article/45702/1/sustainable-music-festivals-in-20-years-oya-oslo-norway-climate-change [accessed 30 January 2020].

Deloitte (2019) 'The Deloitte Global Millennial Survey 2019: Societal discord and technological transformation create a "generation disrupted"', https://www2.deloitte.com/global/en/pages/about-deloitte/articles/millennialsurvey.html [accessed 28 January 2020].

Dragani, R. (2019) Augmented reality will change concerts forever', *Verizon.com*, Fourth Industrial Revolution, 31 July 2019, https://www.verizon.com/about/our-company/fourth-industrial-revolution/augmented-reality-will-change-concerts-forever [accessed 15 April 2020].

Eventbrite (2019) About Eventbrite, https://www.eventbrite.com/about/ [accessed 29 January 2020].

Eventsforce (2019) '7 Pricing Strategies to Drive Event Ticket Sales', Eventsforce Blog, 5 August 2019, https://www.eventsforce.com/blog/7-pricing-strategies-to-drive-event-ticket-sales/ [accessed 29 January 2020].

Gajanan, M. (2019) 'How Music Festivals Became a Massive Business in the 50 Years since Woodstock', *Time Magazine Online*, 14 August 2019, https://time.com/5651255/business-of-music-festivals/ [accessed 28 January 2020].

Giovarruscio, A. (2016) 'Why Festivals Are More Important than Ever', *Digital Music News*, 28 July 2016, https://www.digitalmusicnews.com/2016/07/28/festivals-more-popular/ [accessed 24 January 2020].

Glastonbury Festival (2020) 'A Statement from the Glastonbury Festival', 18 March 2020, https://www.glastonburyfestivals.co.uk/a-statement-from-glastonbury-festival/ [accessed 15 April 2020].

Huddleston, T. (2019) 'Fyre Festival: How a 25-year-old scammed investors out of $26 million', *CNBC*, 22 August 2019, https://www.cnbc.com/2019/08/18/how-fyre-festivals-organizer-scammed-investors-out-of-26-million.html [accessed 22 May 2020].

Johnson, C. (2018) 'Don't buy tickets from Viagogo, minister warns', *BBC News Online*, 30 May 2018, https://www.bbc.com/news/business-44299981 [accessed 27 January 2020].

Kopf, D. (2019) 'Economics explains why there are so many music festivals now', *Quartz*, https://qz.com/quartzy/1655137/economics-explains-why-there-are-so-many-music-festivals/ [accessed 24 January 2020].

Krueger, A.B. (2019) *Rockonomics*, NY: Currency, Penguin Random House.

Lewis, J. (2020) 'Top concert promoters every independent artist should know', *Omari MC*, https://www.omarimc.com/top-concert-promoters-every-independent-artist-should-know/ [accessed 30 January 2020].

Livewire (2017) 'Festival-goers to spend €253m attending Irish music festivals this year', *Livewire Festival Insider*, http://archive.livewire.ie/livewire-festival-insider-music/ [accessed 13 February 2020].

Miller, K.D. (2020) 'The Benefits of Full Engagement at Music Festivals', *Positive Psychology*, https://positivepsychology.com/power-of-engagement-at-music-festivals/ [accessed 20 January 2020].

Mintel Press Office (2019) 'Raving Mad: UK Music Festival Attendance at Highest Level in Four Years', 23 August 2019, Mintel Press Office, https://www.mintel.com/press-centre/leisure/raving-mad-uk-music-festival-attendance-at-highest-level-in-four-years [accessed 20 January 2020].

Murphy, G. (2019) '2020 – 'Where is the Money in Today's Music World?', *Journal of Music Online*, 24 October 2019, https://journalofmusic.com/focus/2020-where-money-todays-music-world [accessed 20 January 2020].

Nielsen, F. (2019) 'How Much Does a Music Festival Cost to Put On? 18 Expenses to Plan For', *Billetto*, 2 July 2019, https://billetto.co.uk/blog/how-much-does-music-festival-cost/ [accessed 29 January 2020].

Pareles, J. (2002) David Bowie, 21st Century Entrepreneur, *The New York Times*, 9 June 2002, https://www.nytimes.com/2002/06/09/arts/david-bowie-21st-century-entrepreneur.html [accessed 24 January 2020].

Sawyer, K. (2019) 'Four Ways to Make More Money with Tiered Pricing', *Eventbrite Blog*, 27 March 2019, https://www.eventbrite.com/blog/make-money-tiered-pricing-ds00/ [accessed 29 January 2019].

Statista.com (2019) 'Average price of music festival tickets in Europe from 2014 to 2018', Statista Research Department, November 14, 2019. Statista.com, https://static1.statista.com/statistics/687719/music-festivals-ticket-prices-in-europe/ [accessed 24 January 2020].

Statista (2020) 'Leading music promoters worldwide in 2018, by number of tickets sold', https://www.statista.com/statistics/304982/leading-music-promoters-worldwide/#statisticContainer [accessed 30 January 2020].

Trendell, A. (2020) 'Glastonbury Festival 2020 could be set to get even bigger', *NME*, https://www.nme.com/news/music/glastonbury-festival-2020-could-be-set-to-get-even-bigger-capacity-camping-2592991 [accessed 24 January 2020].

CASE 6   MARRIOTT INTERNATIONAL: OPPORTUNITY WINDOW FOR CUSTOMER EXPERIENCE

This case was written by Mariusz Soltanifar, Hanze University of Applied Sciences, Groningen, the Netherlands.

Introduction

From an adventurous vacation, to trying delicious food in Rome or discovering beautiful views and outdoor activities in Vancouver, Marriott International wants to be there for you, not only with accommodation but with assisting you in planning each step of your journey. During a time in which the consumption of luxurious commodities is taking a more prominent stance within the world's stage, these increases in demand compel daring entrepreneurs to fill in the gaps in the supply chain.

John Williard Marriott founded one of the (soon-to-become) leading hotel companies in the world, Marriott International. Marriott began as the A&W Root Beer stand in 1927, operated by John Williard Marriott and his wife Alice, whose objective was to satisfy the thirst of the citizens of Washington, USA. During succeeding years they developed into catering and then into accommodation: in the years from 1957, the company's founders and its successors opened their first motor hotel in Arlington, Virginia, and undertook other endeavours to grow and become the diverse, global enterprise it is known as today (Marriott International, 2020b). Their vision was to become the leading provider and facilitator of luxury, leisure and business experiences. Today, Marriott operates and franchises hotels and licenses vacation ownership resorts across the globe.

Source: ©JHVEPhoto/Shutterstock

Marriott International's Expansion and Consolidation

In November 2016, Marriott acquired Starwood Hotels & Resorts Worldwide, becoming the world's largest hotel chain. According to CNBC (2016) this acquisition provided Marriott with two major benefits. First, it gave Marriott more leverage with corporate travel departments who often look for one giant chain to house all of their employees. Second, it provided Marriott more power over Expedia and Priceline, the two giant online travel agencies that sell rooms on behalf of hotel companies in exchange for a commission. This acquisition also emphasized their commitment of 'doing whatever it takes to take care of the customer'. Marriott aims to enhance the lives of customers by creating and enabling unsurpassed vacation and leisure experiences. The company vows to be an unfailing provider of satisfactory services, which is reflected in a set of distinctive features that form their competitive advantages. These are presented to the public in quarterly earnings conference calls. During the second-quarter earnings conference call in 2018, the company highlighted the massive scale of operations, access to luxury properties which benefit the entire organization and proprietary booking channels as advantages that differentiate Marriott from any other hotel chain. The CEO, Arne Sorenson, also emphasized the vibrant, expanded loyalty programme and innovative strategies that support Marriott's ability to keep a leading position in the market and to outperform other industry benchmarks.

The year 2018 marked significant steps in the company's development. Marriott undertook a multitude of activities. These included the acquisition of management and franchise agreements of 816 properties, comprising 125,000 rooms. Marriott also built 500 new properties, comprising more than 80,000 rooms across its 30 respective sub-brands (Marriott International News Center, 2019). In contrast to having 3,500 lodging properties located in 70 countries in 2011, the company stated that it was in possession of more than 6,900 properties and 1.3 million rooms in 130 countries and territories, as of 31 December 2018 (Marriott International News Center, 2019). In the same year, the company recorded a revenue of $20,758m and a net income of $1,907m (Marriott Annual Report, 2018) and Marriott International keeps expanding. As highlighted in Marriott's news centre, the hotel chain plans to open new hotels all over the world, including Tokyo, Melbourne, Mexico City and Reykjavik. All in all, more than 30 luxury properties are planned to open in 2020, speaking to the momentum that sub-brands such as St. Regis, the Ritz-Carlton and EDITION have with affluent travellers.

Integrating more brands and existing loyalty programmes, for instance by acquiring Starwood (including its Starwood Preferred Guest programme (SPG)), into one loyalty programme means the company has more to offer its customers and aims to appeal to customers considering them as their hotel of choice more often. This development has led to Marriott possessing the world's largest loyalty programme, namely Marriott Bonvoy, that has proven to be the best way to deepen loyalty through unique customer experiences (Carmody, 2020). The Bonvoy loyalty programme replaced the previous three loyalty brands that the company had: Marriott Rewards, the Ritz-Carlton Rewards, and Starwood Preferred Guest.

Source: ©Stakon/Shutterstock

Marriott International continues to expand into further strategic destinations around the world while ensuring continuous improvement in quality (Marriott International News Center, 2019). All of

which aligns with the company's core values: putting people first, embracing change, acting with integrity and the pursuit of excellence (Marriott International, 2020). However, a huge loyalty programme would not suffice to maintain customer relationships. The companies who use loyalty programmes as a standard procedure need to innovate them constantly to keep appealing to their customers. Marriott is no different. Loyalty programmes offered as a standard procedure might lose their ability to do what they were designed to do (i.e. maintain customer loyalty). Standard loyalty programmes might result in the frustration of customers after joining them, and lead to a bad user experience, through offering unappealing rewards compared to competitors. However, it appears that Marriott knows how to handle that. The hotel chain doesn't simply focus on offering discounted rooms, or offers such as getting the tenth night free, but more on experiences of travellers. For example, the company offers a separate front desk line to help speed the check-in and check-out process. David Flueck, Senior Vice President of Global Loyalty at Marriott, emphasizes that the new generation of millennials value experiences over material things. Thus, in order to drive true emotional loyalty, loyalty programmes are moving now from being points collection programmes to being full experiences (Carmody, 2020). This shift away from product and towards experiences is one that can be seen across the travel landscape. People no longer just want a comfy bed to rest their head, they also want to explore new places and try new things. Special treatment offers for the returning customers are no longer enough. As a result, the type and form of loyalty programme at Marriott has been reshaped by the needs of the new generation of millennials. A good example of Marriott differentiating its loyalty programme from a standard collection of points was allowing its guests a unique opportunity to meet with Chef Daniel Boulud, a world-famous chef who has restaurants in New York City, and to prepare one of his famous meals. This was a unique experience not only for foodies seeking unique culinary experiences but also for each hotel guest. These sorts of experiential benefits are certainly memorable customer experiences and encourage word-of-mouth (WOM) support from their best customers. WOM benefits associated with loyal customers go way beyond the direct financial impact on the firm. Notably, the hotel chain benefits from free advertising provided through WOM communication, including WOM endorsements or from 'customer voluntary performance'. This is aided by Marriott's Facebook page, where it posts highly shareable social media content, which has close to 3 million followers (Marriott Hotels, 2020). For instance, one can expect that hosting a members-only event featuring Imagine Dragons in Bangkok will empower the company to attract new customers who will share such experiences with their network. The more Marriott's customers share their unique experiences with the brand, the more of their peers covet similar experiences for themselves. As such, relationship marketing is not only beneficial to its customers but to the company itself. The hotel has even created a *Moments* experience platform to utilize the potential of loyal customer reviews, where experiences can be shared.

Appealing Email Strategy

Besides a well-designed Marriott Bonvoy loyalty programme, the company uses a well-thought-out email strategy. Like other hotel chains squeezed by Google and Airbnb, Marriott has been working to distinguish itself through specialized offerings for members like Bonvoy. The features of the new loyalty programme have been promoted in the first multi-million-dollar global media campaign that runs across TV and cinema, as well as in Marriott's various original content channels, including its dedicated travel magazine *Marriott Bonvoy Traveler* and on hotel websites, all in an effort to showcase various travellers' experiences, from swimming to commenting on a good meal to playing chess. Email marketing is also widely used by Marriott. Split over a period of two months, Marriott's email communication stream provides nine different touchpoints, each one delivering a unique message and call-to-action, thus providing just enough information without burdening the customer. Trigger-based, depending on the customer's behaviour, the emails further underscore the 'right time, right message' approach. This Early Month On Book (EMOB) marketing is focused mainly on educating and reminding the customer of the existing additional service provider's features, such as a mobile app, for

example, and thereby driving voluntary activation and long-term use. It is also a great example of how companies can utilize the effectiveness of the low-cost marketing channels, such as email, and build better customer relationships (Johnson, 2019).

Not Only Customers Benefit from Loyalty Programmes

Multiple benefits offered through Marriott's loyalty programme manifest themselves in social and economic dimensions. Through recurrent bookings, customers build trust and confidence in Marriott, along with a sense of reduced anxiety and comfort in knowing that their expectations will be met in reality. Being acquainted with the booking process, payment procedure, and staying over at a location the customer chooses leads to trust and confidence in the service offered. Additionally, the customers may develop a sense of familiarity and a social relationship with Marriott, creating a desire to come back or explore a Marriott hotel at different locations. As such, Marriott becomes a part of the social support system of its guests. The social support benefits resulting from a long-term relationship with a hotel chain contribute to a better quality of life (personal and/or work life) above and beyond the technical benefits of the service provided. These close personal and professional relationships that are developed between service providers and clients builds a great basis for the customer's loyalty and willingness to book a hotel room again.

Loyal hotel customers may serve as mentors and, because of their experience with the provider, help other customers understand the explicit or implicit rules of conduct when staying at a Marriott hotel. Other than this, loyal customers may, because of their experience with and knowledge of the provider, be able to contribute to the co-production of the service by assisting in service delivery. Often more experienced customers can make the service employees' job easier by giving hints on how to improve the service and participating in customer surveys. For example, offering questionnaires to complete regarding the satisfaction level before and after staying brings the benefits for the hotel as well. While customers receive a discounted price for booking a room for filling the questionnaire, Marriott gathers insights on the functionality of the services offered, such as how the restaurant menu could be improved. Another benefit of customer retention that Marriott receives is employee retention. It is easier for a firm to retain employees when it has a stable base of satisfied customers (Ferguson, 2017; Frey, Bayon and Totzek, 2013). Lastly, economic benefits such as increased purchases or a reduced need for marketing efforts, are to be gained as well.

Building Long-Lasting Relationships

The demands of the digital age and its influences on business operations mean Marriott International faces the growing challenge of how to retain a customer's loyalty when the fiercest competition is only a click away. To counter this, the company undertakes a set of distinct business initiatives which allows it to obtain competitive advantage over other market players; this includes the formation of their loyalty programme. One of the unprecedented steps the company took to manage customer relationships was bringing all brands together under one loyalty programme, Marriott Bonvoy, in February 2019. The Bonvoy loyalty programme emphasizes individuality and personalization, which in turn lays the foundation for facilitating trust and increasing customer engagement (Mobile Marketing, 2019). The many opportunities induced by these efforts signifies the need for robust customer relationship management, which is marked by customer segmentation to allow for more personal conversation. The aim of the programme is to provide a cohesive story for travellers, optimize rewards and streamline consumer choice (Fleming, 2019). The programme includes an app and offers a reward plan for the hotel company's most loyal customers. For example, it allows users to search by location rather than brand so it can showcase all the options across its portfolio. Marriott Bonvoy provides a wide array of different services customized to the customers personal needs, such as helpful staff willing to guide guests each step of the journey and provide clear instructions. Cleanliness, organization, and elegance are other features that stand out and grasp attention of the hotel guests. Through this, Marriott shows a set of distinct hotel features, that allow for the company to

form a competitive advantage over its competitors, as it increases customer satisfaction. The majority of interaction instituted by the loyalty programme can be found in the 'Marriott app'. The functionality of the app allows users to autonomously check-in with a pre-programmed key card available on the individual's smartphone (Borison, n.d.) and enter the hotel bedroom without the need of an actual room key; as such, check-in queues can be avoided. Perhaps even better, one can also make a request for room service, housekeeping and other amenities via their phone (Mobile Marketing, 2019). However, these implications do provide challenges as well, for instance raising the question: how does one market the app without being intrusive? And even more complicated: how does one retain its app users? On a similar note, Fleming (2019) highlights that managing the expectations of a huge range of travellers, and having to combine Marriott's various schemes into one programme, has been a challenge. Although Marriott claims that on average guests will receive 20 per cent more points under the new scheme than the old one, there are some, particularly on the SPG Starwood Preferred Guest (SPG) programme, who lost out. For example, if a hotel guest had an SPG status based on their number of hotel stays, according to Ewen (2018) the new programme may result in a lower elite level. Another loss for SPG loyalty programme holders was the late checkout until 4pm benefit for Gold members; that is now not guaranteed but is based on availability. Airline partnerships, such as with Delta, Emirates and China, have also been removed, taking away related bonuses with SkyMiles and Starpoints. Furthermore, cash and points redemptions have been devalued and SPG Flights redemption options are no longer available (Ewen, 2018).

Customer Profitability Segmentation Strategy

Marriott uses customer profitability segments as a strategy for focusing relationship marketing efforts. The company utilizes the following customer pyramid in order to differentiate between customers relative to their amount of stays, as well as money spent (see Figure 1). The goal is to reward them according to the aforementioned criteria with different benefit packages.

Figure 1   Customer pyramid

- The *Member* tier represents the least profitable members who stay up to 9 nights annually at any Marriott Hotel. Their benefits are complimentary in-room Internet access, member rates and mobile check-in/services.
- The *Silver Elite* tier is the second lowest tier and represents customers who stay for 10 to 24 days per year. In addition to the benefits granted to previous tiers, customers from this tier receive 10 per cent bonus points, are allowed to check out late and are allowed to use the dedicated elite reservation line.
- The *Gold Elite* tier represents customers who stay between 25 and 49 nights annually. It carries the same benefits as the previous tiers but also grants customers points such as an in-hotel welcome gift and an enhanced room upgrade.
- The *Platinum Elite* tier represents customers who stay for 50 to 74 nights per year and provides the same benefits as the previous tiers, along with a lounge access, a guaranteed room type and an annual choice benefit (e.g. 5 suite night awards or gift points).
- The *Titanium Elite* represents customers who stay for 75 to 99 nights annually and provides all the previous' tiers benefits, along with a superior variant of the annual choice benefit, along with a 48 hour guaranteed room availability.
- The *Ambassador Elite* tier represents customers who stay 100+ nights per year and have a $20,000 annual qualifying spend. Its customers enjoy all the aforementioned benefits along with a personal point of contact that is available and

at their service during their stay, and the opportunity to check in and out at any time (Marriott International, 2020).

Other hotel chains, such as Hilton and Hyatt also provide loyalty programmes, though they have some distinctive benefits. Compared to Marriott Bonvoy, Hilton Honors only provides four different customer segmentation categories but with a similar perk distribution (Miller, 2018):

- The *Member* category: Complimentary Internet, late check-out – depending on availability, without any requirements.
- The *Silver* category: All member benefits, 20 per cent point bonus, 5th night free on award bookings, requires 4 stays or 10 nights.
- The *Gold* category: All Silver benefits, 80 per cent points bonus, room upgrades (subject to availability), Continental breakfast, requires 20 stays, 40 nights, or 75,000 base points.
- The *Diamond* category: All Gold benefits, 100 per cent points bonus, Executive Lounge access, one-year Diamond status extension, requires 30 stays, 60 nights or 120,000 base points.

Hilton's programme distributes earned points per $1 dollar spent by its customers and the higher the customer's membership category, the higher its points earnings. As can be clearly distinguished, Marriott ensures a more elaborate customer retention plan for its most loyal customers (e.g. from Ambassador Elite).

Hyatt, one of Marriott's main competitors, also segments its customer benefit system similarly to Marriott, though this hotel chain also provides slightly fewer status tiers:

- *World of Hyatt Member* Complimentary standard Internet, waived resort fees on award stays, complimentary continental breakfast for two, early check-in at 12 p.m. (depending on availability), late check-out at 2 p.m. (depending on availability), one category room upgrade (subject to availability), with no further requirements.
- *World of Hyatt Discoverist* All member benefits, 10 per cent point bonus, premium Internet, free breakfast, 2 p.m. late checkout, earn one point per dollar spent at American Airlines with the AAdvantage, complimentary upgrades to preferred rooms (higher floors, corner rooms, or better views that fall into the same category of the room type booked), requires: stay 10 nights or obtain 25,000 Base Points or hold 3 qualifying meetings/events in a calendar year.
- *World of Hyatt Explorist* All Discoverist benefits, 20 per cent point bonus, upgrade to the best room, excluding suites and rooms with club lounge access, 72 hours guaranteed availability, requires: stay 30 nights or obtain 50,000 Base Points or hold 10 qualifying meetings/events in a calendar year.
- *World of Hyatt Globalist* All Explorist benefits, 30 per cent points bonus, upgrade to the best room, 4 p.m. late check-out, club lounge access, complimentary full breakfast daily for each registered guest (up to 2 adults and 2 children), 4 suite upgrades after 60 qualifying nights or 100,000 Base Points each calendar year, 1 upgrade is used per stay up to 7 nights, complimentary parking on free night awards at participating hotels and resorts, Guest of Honor program for family and friends to enjoy Globalist benefits when booking an award stay for them, access complimentary fitness classes, requires: stay 60 nights or obtain 100,000 Points or hold 20 qualifying meetings/events in a calendar year.

Unique to Hyatt, the hotel chain also provides a system called 'milestone rewards' which, depending on the customer's earned base points (points that count toward tier status) or spent nights, confers certain benefits (e.g. club lounge access awards, suite upgrades, $100 gift card, bonus points).

Extending the Loyalty Offering

As part of its strategy to build customer relationships, Bonvoy launched a new 'Eat Around Town' programme, allowing members to earn points at their favourite restaurants across the United States. Members can earn Marriott Bonvoy points at over 11,000 restaurants that participate in the 'Eat Around Town' programme. The collected points can be redeemed for free nights at more than 7,000 participating hotels in 132 countries and territories through Marriott Bonvoy Moments (Marriott, 2019). One of Marriott's goal is to improve the customer's experiences through the integration of the Rewards Network (a leading fintech company for the restaurant industry that was brought to life in collaboration with Marriott Bonvoy) along with Marriott's relationships with prominent individuals in the sports, music, and cooking industries. This allows members to have incredible and exclusive experiences with Marriott Bonvoy Moments, the company's travel experiences marketplace. *Marketing Week* claims that the 'Moments' programme offers loyal customers the opportunity to be rewarded with a total of 120,000 experiences across 1,000 destinations globally, such as local city tours or even attending the Oscars (Fleming, 2019). These experiences are possible through Marriott's collaboration with multiple partners, such as NFL and Universal Music Group. For example, a recent partnership with Manchester United offers Bonvoy's members the opportunity to experience unique football moments, such as being a kit manager for a day or stadium announcer. Additionally, Marriott collaborates with JP Morgan Chase, which enables members to obtain points through making purchases with their cards VISA and/ or American Express cards.

Data Breach

The criticisms that Marriott received by moving to a single loyalty programme were accompanied by a high-profile data breach that impacted as many as 383 million customer records in late 2018 (Gressin, 2018; Grigonis, 2019). Marriott International, which bought Starwood Hotels & Resorts in 2016 for $13.3 billion, revealed it had discovered a massive security breach involving guests who had stayed at

Starwood-branded properties from 2014 through to 10 September 2018. The data that had been compromised included payment card numbers with expiry dates and passport numbers (Marriott, 2018). During the incident, Marriott claimed that an internal security tool alerted the company to the breach but an investigation showed the unauthorized access began in 2014 (Grigonis, 2019). Additionally, around 327 million guests had non-payment-related data compromised, which included the name of the hotel guest, mailing address, phone number, email address, passport number, SPG account data, birth date, and gender, along with details like arrivals and departures, reservation dates and communication preferences (Whitakker, 2018). Other guests had more limited data compromised, such as name, email, and mailing address. Fortunately, the breach only included the Starwood Preferred Guest loyalty programme and guests who booked at a Marriott-owned property from another booking platform were not affected. The Starwood data breach put customers from around the world at risk of identity theft and fraud. In response to the data breach, Marriott offered its customers the opportunity to sign up for the Webwatcher service free of charge for one year. Webwatcher monitors Internet sites where personal information is shared and generates an alert to the consumer if evidence of the consumer's personal information is found. Besides changing passwords, enabling two-factor authentication or freezing credit cards, such services can prevent criminals from using the compromised information to open new lines of credit in name of Marriott customers. In the age of digitalization, while booking a room is just a click away, issues of data security are crucial for Marriott, in addition to government fines for Marriott for violating the European Union's General Data Protection Regulations (GDPR) and a massive loss of customer trust, as a result of the data breach.

Marriott Continues to Grow

Not withstanding the data breach, Marriott International continues to be the largest hotel chain in the world in terms of revenue (Statista, 2020) and continues to strengthen its relationship marketing strategy to keep recurring customers and to fulfil their expectations. Relationship marketing at the company delivers numerous benefits, for the customers and also for the company itself. Well-designed, executed and constantly improving loyalty is a crucial factor that helps the company to maintain its distance between its competitors. For that, Marriott International continues to increase its room inventory while exhibiting steady progress on several key hospitality-industry metrics and delivers meaningful experiences through the Marriott Bonvoy loyalty programme. The hotel chain has put the loyalty member at the centre of what they are doing. Having a focus on hotel guests and the service culture, and providing a friendly, and attentive service are no longer enough, because a feeling of authenticity remains an integral component of the overall customer experience (Shankman, 2014). This authenticity is especially crucial to the new generation of customers, millennials, who demand ethical practices and value experiences over services (Deloitte, 2019). That's why today's Marriott Bonvoy's loyalty programme is focused on delivering authentic travel experiences to customers rather than simply delivering hotel services; as such, this has led to navigating across Marriott's portfolio, driving channels on Marriott.com and app which have been expanded more than ever before.

References

Borison, R. (n.d.). 'Marriott Hotels debuts innovative mobile check-in feature via app.' Available at: https://www.retaildive.com/ex/mobilecommercedaily/marriott-hotels-debuts-innovative-mobile-check-in-feature-via-app

Carmody (2020) https://www.inc.com/bill-carmody/marriott-reveals-best-way-to-retain-your-best-customers-and-its-not-what-you-think.html

CNBC (2016). 'Marriott buys Starwood, becoming world's largest hotel chain.' Retrieved from https://www.cnbc.com/2016/09/23/marriott-buys-starwood-becoming-worlds-largest-hotel-chain.html

Deloitte (2019). 'The Deloitte Global Millennial Survey 2019.' Available at: https://www2.deloitte.com/global/en/pages/about-deloitte/articles/millennialsurvey.html

Ewen, N. (2018). 'What SPG Members Have Lost in the Marriott Integration.' Available at: https://thepointsguy.com/guide/what-spg-members-have-lost-marriott-integration/

Ferguson, G. (2017, November 21). 'Why Are Long-Term Employees Important?' Available at: https://smallbusiness.chron.com/longterm-employees-important-40711.html

Fleming (2019) 'Inside the launch of Marriott's new loyalty programme'. MarketingWeek. Accessed 15 March, 2020 from: https://www.marketingweek.com/marriott-loyalty-programme/

Frey, R.-V., Bayón, T. and Totzek, D. (2013) 'How Customer Satisfaction Affects Employee Satisfaction and Retention in a Professional Services Context', *Journal of Service Research*, 16(4), pp. 503–517. doi: 10.1177/1094670513490236

Gressin, S. (2018) 'The Marriott data breach', *Consumer Information*, Federal Trade Commission. https://www.consumer.ftc.gov/blog/2018/12/marriott-data-breach

Grigonis, H.K. (2019) 'Marriott suffers a massive breach of its data base. Here's how to to protect yourself.' *Digital Trends*, January 2019. https://www.digitaltrends.com/business/marriott-starwood-preferred-guest-breach/

Johnson, N. (2019) 'Marriott Bonvoy's EMOB Email Marketing Stream Makes Our Hearts Skip a Beat', *Media Logic* https://www.medialogic.com/blog/financial-services-marketing/emob-marketing-email/

Lock, S. (2020). Marriott International – Statistics & Facts. *Statista* Retrieved January 15, 2020, from https://www.statista.com/topics/1872/marriott-international/

Marriott International. (2018). Marriott International, Inc. 2018 Annual report. Available at: https://www.marriott.com/culture-and-values/core-values.mi

Marriott International. (2020a). Core Values & Heritage. Available at: https://www.marriott.com/culture-and-values/core-values.mi

Marriott International. (2020b). Hotels & Resorts. Available at: https://www.marriott.com/loyalty/member-benefits.mi Marriott Hotels (2020). Facebook Page. Available at: https://www.facebook.com/Marriott/

Marriott International News Center (2019). 'Marriott International Sets New Record for Growth in 2018 Fueling Global Expansion and Adding Choice for Travelers.' Available at: https://news.marriott.com/news/2019/01/22/marriott-international-sets-new-record-for-growth-in-2018-fueling-global-expansion-and-adding-choice-for-travelers

Miller, A. (2017, August 1). The World of Hyatt Loyalty Program — Full Review [Updated 2020]. Available at: https://upgradedpoints.com/hotel-loyalty-programs/the-world-of-hyatt/

Mobile Marketing. (November 2019). 'What are the key factors for hospitality loyalty apps?' *Mobile Marketing*. Available at https://mobilemarketingmagazine.com/hospitality-loyalty-apps-top-features-which-drive-engagement-kumulos

Shankman (2014) https://skift.com/2014/10/29/interview-marriott-international-ceo-on-authenticity-and-the-guest-experience/

Whittakker (2018) https://techcrunch.com/2018/11/30/starwood-hotels-says-500-million-guest-records-stolen-in-massive-data-breach/?guccounter=1

CASE 7   **TURKISH AIRLINES: ENHANCING THE CUSTOMER EXPERIENCE**

This case was written by Mariusz Soltanifar, Hanze University of Applied Sciences, Groningen, the Netherlands.

Source: ©Dux Croatorum/Shutterstock

Introduction

Today, air travel has revolutionized how people explore the world. If you're feeling inspired to marvel at the sunrise at Copacabana Beach in Rio de Janeiro, or walk around the floating flower markets and bohemian neighbourhoods in Amsterdam, you're simply a plane ticket away. Not only is the world easier to travel around but it is also now far more accessible. People have the opportunity to fly and visit their families and friends wherever they live at any time, or do business across the world, all through a quick flight purchase online. Whatever the reason might be, Turkish Airlines' mission is to appeal to these wishes.

Founded in 1933 (İstanbul-Anadolu Agency, 2019), with a staff of just 24 people and an initial budget of TRY 180,000 (approx. 30K USD) (Turkish Airlines, 2019a), Turkish Airlines has grown to become one of the leading aviation organizations in the world. With a recorded revenue of $2,855m, and an accompanying $753min net profit in 2018 (Turkish Airlines, 2018a), the company intends to become the preferred European air carrier while maintaining its prominence in Turkey. Part of the company's market position today stems from a wide range of travelling possibilities. In 2013, the company already had a large flight network, covering 197 international destinations in 104 countries (Turkish Airlines, 2013). Since then, the organization

has expanded its flight coverage to an extra 21 countries (Curran, 2019). With an order for 212 aircraft in the first half of 2013 (Alcácer and Çekin, 2016), Turkish Airlines had moved to double its size and became one of the industry's top-ten players. Today, according to Forbes, Turkish Airlines serves more destinations in the world than any other airline carrier (Olmsted, 2018). An important reason for this success is the strategic locations for the company's operations. Situated in the geographical heart of the planet, Turkish Airlines has access to four prime regions – Asia, Europe, Africa and the Middle East – and continues to earn notable distinction for serving more destinations than any major carrier (Curran, 2019). The demand for purchasing tickets is increasing, therefore the company keeps expanding. According to The World Tourism Organization, Turkish Airlines currently has 339 planes and maintains approximately 10,000 flights per week (Curran, 2019). Its large fleet of aircraft enables the company to operate in two major segments: Air Transport (Aviation) and Technical Maintenance Operations (Technical). The Aviation segment is involved in the domestic and international passenger and cargo air transportation. The Technical segment offers repair and maintenance service in the civil aviation sector and gives technical and infrastructural support related to the airline industry (Business Insider, 2020). In 2018, Turkish Airlines transported 75.2 million passengers which translated into an 82 per cent occupancy rate, an annual rise of 10 per cent, served by more than 35,000 employees (Ahval, 2020).

An Elevated Experience in the Sky

Each travel experience at Turkish Airlines starts by booking a flight. To ensure convenient and quick access to information, the company website aims to provide clear data, supplemented by the aesthetic appeal of website design. For instance, the company recently redesigned its logo of a bird to include a wave graphic that aims to reflect the seven continents of the world (Design Week, 2019). A new visual identity and corporate design, along with various social media channels, support the company's branding and consistent messaging to its customers. Online review sites such as Airline Quality (2020) and Trust Pilot (2020) also provide anecdotal insights from which potential customers can derive a clear picture of how the company operates. All of these factors are important when seeking to gain competitive advantage over neighbouring air travel providers such as Lufthansa, Air France, British Airways, the fast-growing Gulf Airlines Emirates, Etihad, and Qatar Airways. Price, service, localization and other unique amenities are key considerations while competing with these airlines.

In consideration of the needs of different consumers, Turkish Airlines distinguishes between different modes of travelling. Within the economy class, customers have the opportunity to choose between a variety of tailored alternatives such as 'EcoFly', 'ExtraFly' and 'Primefly'. These allow customers to choose from a variety of rates of refund and rates of checked baggage (Turkish Airlines, 2020a). Even passengers flying economy class get extended benefits in comparison to other airlines and are able to arrange hotel reservations and car rental (Turkish Airlines, 2020). These services are designed to take care of every moment of the passenger's travelling experience. When selecting business class, customers can be assured of travelling while having a pleasant experience, enjoying award-winning dishes, with use of the latest in-flight entertainment system and enjoying more comfortable seating (Turkish Airlines, 2020).

From special passenger lounges to streamlined self-check-in areas, for the last few years Turkish Airlines has been redesigning every point of contact between the brand and its passengers. The airline has placed modern screens on all the aircraft, with a wide range of entertainment. The company has also looked to improve the variety of food provided during the flight to enrich the dining experience. With a menu that corresponds to the seasons, the talented chefs rank fifth in the 'Best Business Class Onboard Catering' 2019 awards (World Airline Awards, 2020). The attentive and helpful flight attendants, comfortable seating, and punctual flight arrival (Airline Quality, 2020) are just a few of the compliments in

which passengers express their experience. In-flight Internet services offered also influence the customers' perception and enable them to stay connected during the flight.

The continuous improvement is visible across the entire organization at Turkish Airlines, with a business model managed through all processes. Meanwhile, implementation efficiency is enhanced by updating information and communication technology systems infrastructures, improving operational and commercial efficiency and increasing employee productivity and commitment. This includes, for instance, targeted efforts in the area of fuel efficiency to reduce costs while mitigating greenhouse gas emissions (Turkish Airlines, 2018b). Turkish Airlines managed to save 29,608 tons of fuel which resulted in a 93,267 tons of greenhouse gas emissions reduction. In 2019, Turkish Airlines aimed to decrease its electrical energy consumption, natural gas consumption, water consumption per person by 5 per cent compared to 2018 (Turkish Airlines, 2018b).

From One of the Worst to One of the Most Highly Reputed Airlines

Today, Turkish Airlines is among one of the preferred airlines thanks to its large flight network and high-quality service delivered to customers. The company enhances its brand recognition with memorable commercials featuring world-renowned celebrities and attractive flight promotions. Using this approach, Turkish Airlines bolsters the loyalty of existing customers while also reaching out to its target passenger segment. The quality of service provided by Turkish Airlines has significantly improved over the years (Olmsted, 2018). Several strategic decisions have contributed to this such as, for instance, customer satisfaction surveys that are conducted at all stages of travelling – including pre-, during and post-flight – in order to proactively deliver process improvements and new concepts of travel experience. A Customer Experience Panel has been created with the aim of providing customer satisfaction-oriented studies. It is a digital platform that provides operations data and real-time monitoring of market research on performance measures and the satisfaction of passengers. The platform tracks indicators at all customer service touchpoints via a single panel and provides reports for management to review and act upon.

Rising Competition Threatens Profits

Unique customer experience and brand identity for Turkish Airlines involves every part of the customer journey before, during and after flight, whether it's serving traditional Turkish coffee and tea at 35,000 feet with Flying Chefs or making the arrival lounge at Istanbul Airport as special and relaxing as the flying experience. Like other air carriers in the Gulf region, such as Emirates Airline, Etihad Airways, and Qatar Airways, Turkish Airlines is hiring sports stars and other celebrities for their marketing and sponsorship campaigns, featuring, for instance, Lionel Messi (viewed over 140 million times on YouTube) and launching their new in-flight catering concepts. The airline also seeks, like the big three, to boost the size of its fleet and its passenger capacity. As communicated recently by Ali Serdar Yakut, Chief Information Office at Turkish Airlines, the company aims to have more than 500 planes by the end of 2023 (Cisco, n.d.). The frequency of flights offered and huge investment in new fleet are key to cope with the challenges posed by these competitors, but foremost is the quality of services offered. The quality of service determines customer experience and there is much to compete for against Emirates, Etihad and Qatar Airways.

Personalized Travel with Emirates

Emirates focuses on its top-paying customers, who are not as inclined to make purchases based on price as Turkish Airlines passengers, and it also has a higher proportion of business and first-class seats than its peers. Emirates puts less emphasis on filling every seat in the plane. Emirates' load factor, a measure of seats sold per plane, is roughly 78 per cent, compared with the industry average of more than 80 per cent as reported by the *Wall Street Journal* (Wall and Parasie, 2018). By pouring billions of dollars into its fleet of planes, in-flight entertainment and wine lists, Emirates has a relatively small but fiercely loyal group of the world's biggest-spending travellers. In 2017, the airline spent $56 million on its collection of fine French wines alone (Wall and Parasie, 2018). Similarly to Turkish Airlines, Emirates is looking into the future and has fears of being overthrown by tech giants, such as Google, who hold massive amounts of customer data. Privatized services like ground transportation, entertainment, restaurant bookings and hotel stays could all be developed and delivered with a high margin to customers, with the use of technology. Instead of waiting to be overtaken, Emirates wants to provide these services itself. To do that, it is building a proprietary information-technology system that will rely on huge amounts of data and artificial intelligence (AI). AI will be used to anticipate customers' travel needs before, during and even after the flight. The ultimate goal is for Emirates' passengers to be able to make arrangements for their entire trips on the airline's website. AI will assist Emirates by offering various activities and entertainment based on the established personal preferences of passengers (Parasie, 2018). In addition, AI will use factors such as age and gender to help expand on the airlines' services by predicting what passengers might be interested in. From pickup at home to drop-off at the hotel, Emirates is trying to accomplish personalized travel with the aim to make high-end passengers' journeys as seamless and pleasurable as possible. AI will be used to better meet customers' expectations, for example, passengers drinking a certain red wine in an Emirates lounge should be welcomed with a glass of the same wine once on board. Similarly, passengers watching a favourite movie on their tablet on the way to the airport should be able to arrive on board and continue watching it on the plane. The airline is also shifting more into concierge services, including booking hard-to-get restaurant reservations and offering all-in-one holiday packages at Dubai's resorts (Wall and Parasie, 2018). Regarding privacy and data security issues, Emirates asks for the permission of passengers to collect the needed information through every data point.

Both Turkish Airlines and Emirates are highly committed to engaging existing and potential customers through various types of advertising and sponsorships, with a great emphasis on culture and sports. Yet the marketing and sales spent by both parties differs significantly. In 2019, Turkish Airlines spent 1.1 billion dollars and Emirates spent 1.7 billion dollars. The airlines communicate with their diverse audiences by targeting relevant demographic factors with the use of technology to generate the data required for ensuring that customers receive practical and timely information based on their preferences. Turkish Airlines utilized digital advertising by launching a project on Spotify named 'Spotify – Free Your Senses'. The concept of 'Five Senses' was transformed into an interactive experience with destination suggestions tailored according to user preferences. As part of the project, which went online in eight countries, travellers on the Spotify platform were directed to microsites in their language via premium advertising. Users were offered destination suggestions on the page customized according to their preferences. They went on to listen to playlists on this page via Spotify and shared posts on their social media accounts. The advertising was listened to 5,270,864 times and viewed 3,667,871 times (Turkish Airlines, 2020c). Emirates are also actively engaging in digital advertising. Emirates is now the world's most followed airline on Instagram, LinkedIn and YouTube; it produced a large volume of content in 2019, covering everything from the launch of new routes, its vegan meal offering and changing the landing gear on an A380, to in-flight marriage proposals. Other marketing efforts include organizing different events such as the Turkish Airlines World Golf Club organized in 63 countries in 2018, or the Emirates Airline Dubai Jazz Festival, which hosted hundreds of acts from all over the world to perform to more than 500,000 fans (Emirates, 2019).

Digital Elements of Air Travel at Etihad

For Etihad Airways, enhancing customer experience is a priority. A key building block of their digital strategy is to really understand their passengers' preferences and the experiences they want. The airline is constantly seeking to bring innovation by implementing the most relevant revolutionizing technologies.

Luxury with Qatar Airways

The Qsuite was introduced by Qatar Airways in 2017 and features the industry's first-ever double bed in business class, as well as privacy panels that stow away, allowing passengers in adjoining seats to create their own private room, another first of its kind in the industry (Anderson, 2019). In 2019 the airline introduced new improvements to its economy class: new seats, a new entertainment system and a new cuisine aimed at boosting the comfort and satisfaction levels of its customers (Rosen, 2019).

Relocating to a New Hub in Istanbul

Additional challenges to maintain Turkish Airlines' leading position with regard to customer experience are arising from Istanbul Airport competing with other hubs such as Dubai and Singapore. In order to provide a unique customer experience, similarly to Etihad and Qatar Airways, Turkish Airlines continues to develop its airport hub. In April 2019, the company relocated to the new Istanbul Airport (Deutsche Welle, 2019). The new hub covers 76.5 square kilometres, making it three times bigger than the former Atatürk airport and six times the area of London Heathrow. The transportation of its hub operations was unprecedented in the aviation industry. The company flew 337 of its planes to the new location (Deutsche Welle, 2019). With its relocation to its new hub in Istanbul, the company aims to utilize its features of strategic location at the crossroads of Europe, Africa and the Middle East, aiming for 200 million passengers a year. Turkish Airlines has the geographical advantage of being closer to Europe, allowing it to easily serve any destination with narrow body aircraft, which is one reason why Turkish Airlines serves so many more destinations in Europe than the Gulf carriers. On the Europe and Asia border, the Istanbul hub means Turkish Airlines can offer short-haul flights and more fuel-efficient planes than other carriers. The company is also part of the Star Alliance, which comprises a large number of air travel organizations that make use of each other's hubs to allow for easier connections, and a wider reach of possible destinations. Additionally, the new hub provides Turkish Airlines with the opportunity to highlight the urban credentials of Istanbul, a city with a rich heritage and a modern, vibrant and entrepreneurial community. While comparing Istanbul to the cities of competitor airlines from Dubai, Abu Dhabi and Doha, this was a huge differentiator. By 2028, the Turkish hub is set to operate six runways and service 200 million passengers per year (Deutsche Welle, 2019). In comparison, the world's busiest airport Hartsfield-Jackson Atlanta International, saw 104 million guests in 2018. While using its location benefits, Turkish Airlines could make its hub one of the world's largest airports by international passenger numbers (*The Economist*, 2019).

Source: ©fivetonine/Shutterstock

Although the relocation to the new hub delivers economic benefits for Turkish Airlines and the country itself, environmental activists argued that the massive development would destroy forests and wildlife (Deutsche Welle, 2016). Ever since the project's inception in 2009, aviation experts have also expressed their concerns. The unstable ground, the local bird population and the Black Sea's changeable weather (strong winds and fog that pose a safety threat to air traffic) are three commonly shared concerns (as reported by *The Guardian*, 2019). Workers involved in building the new hub in Istanbul also protested against harsh working and poor living conditions, bad food, delays in wages and fatal accidents during the construction.

Regardless of these concerns, today Istanbul Airport (see image above) is equipped with cutting-edge technology that accelerates all processes at the airport. In order to achieve this, various teams visited and researched the most advanced airports from around the world to improve upon and implement various technological solutions into the new airport in Istanbul. While it is ahead for the moment, the challenging issue is that technology is always changing and almost as fast as it is implemented it becomes outdated. With such a large financial investment, the decision-makers around such a massive project have to remain one step ahead of the game to ensure they remain competitive and at the forefront of the technological changes (Coleman, 2019). An example of this is that Turkish Airlines keeps expanding their Self-Service Technology (SST) devices, in order to constantly improve consumer experience. Take for instance, the self-service check-in kiosks that are used to facilitate and accelerate the flight-booking procedure and avoid long queues and other waiting times (Turkish Airlines, 2020b). There are several uses of SST in Istanbul's new airport which greatly contribute to the consumer experience. These include an app (İGA) which grants better and faster consumer service relative to the passenger's location, self-service bag-drop and extended RFID (radio frequency identification) baggage tracking, automated border control, smart retail, and smart parking (Passenger Self Service, 2017). RFID is used to transfer data and automatically identify and track baggage tags at the airport. As such, bags can be identified and tracked without the need for human intervention.

Securing Customer Data

In a digitized world, where the demands of data protection and the frequency of cyber attacks is increasing, security has become paramount for business success. In order to meet these demands, in 2018 Turkish Airlines introduced a series of data system innovations to their CRM platform developed in line with its customer-focused vision. The corporation's CRM systems are compliant with the Turkish Personal Data Protection Law, and the General Data Protection Regulation (GDPR) which came into force in Europe. Thanks to efficient data management, the corporation's CRM system allows customers a variety of personalized offers based on their needs and preferences. The integrated automatic survey application also laid the groundwork for continuous measurement and improvement of customer satisfaction. Customers might be concerned regarding the imminent dangers associated with the increasingly digitized buyer experience, including data collection techniques and the accompanying threats of cyber-attacks. As such, Turkish Airlines needs proactive instigation of in-depth visibility services, as well as incident response and detection applications. Considering the approximate 80 million customers who are served yearly, Turkish Airlines needs to make sure it has effective security of sensitive data. Turkish Airlines' Vice President of Information Technology Governance, Kadir Yildiz, stated that the primary goal is to ensure customer satisfaction at all cost. In order to fulfil this promise, the airline recently upgraded to Cisco AMP for Endpoints and Cisco Umbrella (Cisco, n.d.). Furthermore, Turkish Airlines has implemented ransomware and file-less malware protection. By pioneering new technology, Turkish Airlines can understand their customers better and also increase the efficiency of their operations (Cisco, n.d.).

Initiatives for Enhancing the Customer Experience

Turkish Airlines keeps expanding its services, for both economy and business class passengers. In 2018, for example, Turkish Airlines drew much attention with its 'Fly Good Feel Good' initiative. To deliver an exemplary flying experience, the company combined under a single umbrella all that needs to be done before, during and after a flight for an all-round comfortable trip. To more effectively address passenger needs, Turkish Airlines implemented this initiative that guides passengers on all issues that may have a positive effect on the travelling experience, from pre-flight preparation to cabin exercises, sleep to yoga and meditation. Fly Good Feel Good covers a wide range of issues, including informative videos accessible via the in-flight entertainment system covering topics such as flying with infants and children, on-board nutrition, air travel during pregnancy, prevention of nose and ear congestion during a flight and reducing the effects of a possible 'jet-lag' after the flight. In addition, the airline bar offers passengers healthy snack options such as dried strawberries and dried apples. Fly Good Feel Good aims at enhancing the flying experience with a laser focus on customer satisfaction.

Another service offered to all passengers is the Press Reader application that gives passengers digital access to over 7,000 newspapers and magazines, in over 60 languages. There is also a clever strategy behind using this service. Turkish Airlines passengers are directed to the application one day before their flight via email and the website. As a result, passengers benefit from the application free-of-charge for 48 hours in addition to using it in the passenger lounges and on their flight. Turkish Airlines personnel may also access the application without any limitations.

In the situation where a passenger experiences a long layover, the traveller is encouraged to make use of the airline's unique 'Tour Istanbul', a guided tour of the city's top interesting and estimated historical sites. This kind of service is offered to any connecting international passenger in any class who faces a long layover of 6 hours or more, free of charge (Turkish Airlines, 2020d). As such, each passenger not only has a chance to admire the beauty of the city, from elaborate underground cisterns through the famed 'Blue Mosque' to the World Heritage Site Topkapi Palace, but Turkish Airlines offers customers the round-trip door to door service from the airport for free.

Business class services also keep expanding. Turkish Airlines offers an exclusive transfer service for destinations in the USA and Canada featuring premium segment vehicles and chauffeurs to help them travel to and from the airport. Istanbul Bosphorus Experience is another service that welcomes those passengers who have connection times of seven hours or more between their flights. Designed for business class customers, Istanbul Bosphorus Experience service takes passengers to a private yacht via VIP-designated vehicles and offers them a one-hour guided Bosphorus tour and a meal, before transporting them back to the airport for their next flight. Forbes (Olmsted, 2018) argues that Turkish Airlines has one of the best business classes in the world from well-designed, ergonomic lay flat seats, standout cuisine and battery-powered candles on tray tables to simulate a candlelit restaurant dinner, just to name a few exceptional services that business customers get. The Exclusive Drive programme for business class passengers is another distinctive feature through which the company meets sophisticated needs, differentiating itself from its competitors.

While trying to secure the best customer experience, in 2018 Turkish Airlines pulled out of Skytrax World Airline Audit, after Lufthansa became the first European airline to get a Skytrax 5-star rating. The company said that its aim is to provide the best possible experience to its customers and would therefore only take into account the reviews reported directly by its passengers (GTP, 2018). In fact, Turkish Airlines won quite a few awards through Skytrax, including awards for being the best airline in Southern Europe, for having the best business class on-board catering, for having the world's best business class lounge, and for having the best business class dining lounge. The company has been ranked 24 in the Skytrax *the world's top 100 airlines 2019* (Skytrax, 2019). Other than this, the organization was crowned 'Europe's Best Airline' between 2010 and 2015 (Turkish Airlines n.d.). After withdrawing from Skytrax in 2018, Turkish Airlines has been downgraded to a 3-star airline rating by Skytrax (Skytrax, 2018) for the quality of its on-board product and staff service, and the Turkish Airlines home base airport service. Other 3-star airlines include for instance American, United, Air India, easyJet and Ryanair. As such, Skytrax has been criticized for providing a lack of disclosure regarding the connection between the airlines they consult for, and the ratings they give to airlines. It seems like there's a conflict of interest if Skytrax is getting money from airlines to help them improve their onboard product, when they're also rating those airlines. For example, in the case of Etihad, they pulled out of Skytrax when they were a 4-star airline, but wanted to participate when they were rated a 5-star airline.

Criticisms of Turkish Airlines' Customer Service

Although, Turkish Airlines is performing well, recent developments in the African market might possibly weaken its leading position in certain markets. On 16 December 2019, the Federal Government of Nigeria issued a ban to Turkish Airline flights entering the country. The ban is in connection with the ongoing baggage handling issues. Turkish Airlines makes a lot of money by charging excess and oversize baggage fees. Recently, it has not been restricting the number of bags that passengers are allowed to check-in. This means that its aircraft's hold cargo cannot hold all the bags. Even if the airline is aware that the hold is full, it does not restrict anyone from booking extra bags. Even if the plane is at maximum capacity, and bags have to be left behind, the airline will continue to take money for luggage it knows it cannot transport. Apparently Turkish Airlines is leaving behind way too many bags belonging to passengers on their flights to and from Nigeria. This practice has caused problems and frustration for passengers and has led to repeated cases of poor passenger treatment, as claimed by the Nigerian Civil Aviation Authority (NCAA). With regard to this situation, Live And Lets Fly reported that, on one flight to Nigeria, the airline left a staggering 85 per cent of passenger bags in Istanbul. The issue of handling excessive baggage by Turkish Airlines has also affected the Abuja and Lagos airports in Nigeria, facing serious crises controlling the passengers at the airport whenever they arrive without their baggage. The Nigerian government has suspended all Turkish Airlines operations to Nigeria until a time when the airline is ready to operate with the right size of aircraft that can transport all passengers with their baggage at the same time.

Besides recent baggage handling issues, Turkish Airlines has been exposed to criticism of the services offered. A recent study on e-complaints revealed various weaknesses in services with regard to luggage, operational services, employees, sales, customer services and flight services. The online complaints of Turkish Airlines were submitted between February 2018 and February 2019 on one of the most-visited customer complaint website in Turkey, 'www.sikayetvar.com'. Customers shared their dissatisfaction with the restrictions on the maximum weight of passenger luggage, and the requirement to pay an extra fee in case of exceeding these limits. Such complaints constituted 5 per cent of all complaints, followed by lost baggage (10 per cent) and damaged baggage (13 per cent). The compensation regarding cancelled or delayed flights was also an issue, although other observed issues such as disrespectful and impolite employees (3 per cent), negligent and irresponsible employees (5 per cent), and uninformed employees

(3 per cent) seem to take a recurring stance in the feedback (Dergipark, 2019).

Conclusion

Turkish Airlines continues to soar. Relocating to the new Istanbul hub gives this fast-growing flagship airline a platform to challenge Gulf rivals for regional dominance. Even though political unrest and security concerns have made troubles for Turkish Airlines, the carrier's high-quality service and product offerings remain unchanged, ensuring that each guest leaves the aircraft with memorable experiences. However, the company needs to address the issues of baggage handling and other recent complaints, in order to maintain its meteoric rise and challenge the Gulf-based airlines. As such, Turkish Airlines can take further steps to consolidate its position as one of the world's leading airlines with added momentum from its new home in Istanbul Airport.

References

All Accessed 15 February 2020.

Ahval. (2020, January 10) Turkish Airlines passenger numbers fall by 1.1 percent in 2019. Available at: https://ahvalnews.com/turkish-airlines/turkish-airlines-passenger-numbers-fall-11-percent-2019

Airline Quality (2020) https://www.airlinequality.com/airline-reviews/turkish-airlines/page/1/

Alcácer, J., and Çekin, Esel. (2016) "Turkish Airlines: Widen Your World." *Harvard Business School Case*, 716-408, September 2015. (Revised July 2016.)

Anderson, M. A. (2019) 'Take Off Around The World With Qatar Airways And Its Never-Before-Offered Roundtrip Fares.' *Forbes.* https://www.forbes.com/sites/maryannanderson/2020/01/10/take-off-with-qatar-airways-around-the-world-with-never-before-offered-roundtrip-fares/#539955b136e6

Business Insider (2020) https://markets.businessinsider.com/stocks/turk_hava_yollari/company-profile

Cisco (n.d.) Cisco Case Study: Turkish Airlines. Available at: https://www.cisco.com/c/en/us/about/case-studies-customer-success-stories/turkish-airlines.html

Coleman, L. (2019) 'How this airport is planning to dominate the $35B airline industry.' *Forbes.* 12 May 2019. Available at: https://www.forbes.com/sites/laurencoleman/2019/05/12/how-this-airport-is-planning-to-dominate-the35b-airline-industry/#160bc7a2113d

Curran, A. (2019). 'Turkish Airlines Now Fly To An Incredible 125 Countries – Simple Flying.' 1 August 2019. Available at: https://simpleflying.com/turkish-airlines-125-countries/

Dergipark (2019). 'A survey on e-complaints: the case of Turkish Airlines.' *Journal of Tourism, Leisure and Hospitality.* Available at: http://dergipark.org.tr/tr/download/article-file/777389

Design Week (2019) https://www.designweek.co.uk/issues/11-17-march-2019/turkish-airlines-goes-global- with-new-brand-identity/

Deutsche Welle (2019) 'Turkish Airlines leaves Ataturk International Airport with massive move to new Istanbul hub.' *Deutsche Welle.* April 2019. Available at: https://www.dw.com/en/turkish-airlines-leaves-ataturk-international-airport-with-massive-move-to-new-istanbul-hub/a-48238827

Deutsche Welle (2016) 'New airport: Turbulence for the environment.' *Deutsche Welle.* October 2016. Available at: https://www.dw.com/en/new-airport-turbulence-for-the-environment/a-36038659

Emirates (2019) Annual Report 2018-19 Emirates Group. Available at: https://cdn.ek.aero/downloads/ek/pdfs/report/annual_report_2019.pdf

GTP (2018) 'Turkish Airlines Withdraws from Skytrax Audit.' *Greek Travel Pages.* 15 June 2018. Available at: https://news.gtp.gr/2018/06/15/turkish-airlines-withdraws-from-skytrax-audit/

İstanbul-Anadolu Agency (2019, September 12). 'Turkish Airlines carries some 50M passengers in 8 months – Latest News.' Available at: http://www.hurriyetdailynews.com/turkish-airlines-carries-some-50m-passengers-in-8-months-146505

Olmsted, L. (2018, February 5). 'Why Turkish Airlines Is Great Choice For Your Travels – Business Or Leisure.' Available at: https://www.forbes.com/sites/larryolmsted/2018/02/05/why-turkish-airlines-is-great-choice-for-your-travels-business-or-leisure/#3a6402342363

Parasie, N. (2018) 'Emirates aims to sell more than flights.' *Wall Street Journal* 18 May. https://www.

wsj.com/articles/emirates-air-aims-to-sell-more-than-flights-1526868540

PassengerSelfService. (2017, October 15). 'Istanbul new airport use of smart technology.' Available at: https://www.passengerselfservice.com/2017/10/istanbul-new-airport-use-smart-technology/

Rosen, E. (2019). 'Qatar Airways Shows Off New Economy Seats And Meals.' Available at: https://www.forbes.com/sites/ericrosen/2019/03/06/qatar-airways-new-economy-seats-meals/#322481f04f7f

SKYTRAX. (2018). 'Turkish Airlines Customer Reviews' *SKYTRAX*. Available at: https://www.airlinequality.com/airline-reviews/turkish-airlines/page/1/

SKYTRAX. (2019). 'The World's Top 100 Airlines 2019' *SKYTRAX*. Available at: https://www.worldairlineawards.com/worlds-top-100-airlines-2019/

SKYTRAX. (n.d.). 'The World's Best Business Class Airlines 2019' *SKYTRAX*. Available at: https://www.worldairlineawards.com/worlds-best-business-class-airlines-2019/

The Economist (2019) 'Turkish Airlines takes on Emirates, Etihad and Qatar Airways.' 11 April. Available at: https://www.economist.com/business/2019/04/11/turkish-airlines-takes-on-emirates-etihad-and-qatar-airways

The Guardian (2019) 'Turkish Airlines is switching to a new Istanbul airport – all in 45 hours.' April 2019. Available at: https://www.theguardian.com/cities/2019/apr/06/turkish-airlines-switching-to-new-airport-all-in-45-hours

Turkish Airlines. (2013). 'The best airline in Europe which flies the most countries in the world.' Available at: https://investor.turkishairlines.com/documents/ThyInvestorRelations/download/icerikler/turkish_airlines_fact_sheet_eng_ver1.pdf

Turkish Airlines. (2018a). Annual Report. Available at: https://investor.turkishairlines.com/documents/ThyInvestorRelations/THY__FRAE__2018_ENG_v2.pdf

Turkish Airlines. (2018b). Sustainability Report 2018. Available at: https://investor.turkishairlines.com/documents/ThyInvestorRelations/download/yillik_raporlar/surdurulebilirlik-rapor-haziran-2019-v6-en.pdf

Turkish Airlines (2019a). History. Available at: https://investor.turkishairlines.com/en/turkishairlines/history

Turkish Airlines. (2019b). Turkish Airlines, Europe's Best Airline for past 5 years. Available at: https://www.turkishairlines.com/en-us/press-room/awards/turkish-airlines-the-best-in-europe-for-the-last-five-years/index.html

Turkish Airlines. (2020a). Booking. Available at: https://www.turkishairlines.com/en-jp/flights/booking/

Turkish Airlines. (2020b). Check-in. Available at: https://www.turkishairlines.com/en-int/any-questions/check-in/

Turkish Airlines. (2020c). Follow Turkish Airlines on Social Media. Available at: https://www.turkishairlines.com/en-int/any-questions/get-in-touch/social-media/

Wall, R. and Parasie, N. (2018) 'Chateau-Margaux for Seat 2A: Emirates Rewrites Rules for Airlines.' *Wall Street Journal* 12 July. Available at: https://www.wsj.com/articles/chateau-margaux-for-seat-2a-emirates-rewrites-rules-for-airlines-1531406181

World Airline Awards (2020). Available at: https://www.worldairlineawards.com/worlds-best-business-class-airlines-2019/

Turkish Airlines. (2020d). 'Unique Istanbul experiences free with Turkish Airlines.' Available at: https://www.turkishairlines.com/en-jp/flights/fly-different/touristanbul/?gclid=-CjwKCAiAjrXxBRAPEiwAiM3DQt-xzp_rjDcUcgBwSQ6ZHKV56GrV43b2f2vFqBqB1L_TxKVeVQ5ltxoCMrkQAvD_BwE

CASE 8   STARBUCKS: KEY ELEMENTS OF THE 'STARBUCKS EXPERIENCE'

This case is adapted from a case written by Arthur A. Thompson, University of Alabama, USA.

Introduction

Since its founding in 1987 as a modest nine-store operation in Seattle, Washington, Starbucks has become the premier roaster, marketer, and retailer of speciality coffees in the world, with over 30,100 store locations in 78 countries as of April 2019 and expected annual sales of more than $26 billion in fiscal year 2019, ending 30 September, 2019. In addition to its flagship Starbucks brand coffees and coffee beverages, Starbucks' other brands included Teavana teas, Seattle's Best Coffee, Evolution Fresh juices and smoothies, Ethos bottled waters, and Princi and LaBoulange pastries, breads and snack foods. In addition to the products, the Starbucks Experience is built around store design, employee engagement and social responsibility.

Store Design and Ambience

Store Design

Starting in 1991, Starbucks created its own in-house team of architects and designers to ensure that each store would convey the right image and character. Stores had to be custom-designed because the company didn't buy real estate and build its own freestanding structures. Instead, each space was leased in an existing structure, making each store different in size and shape. Most stores ranged in size from 1,000 to 1,500 square feet and were located in office buildings, downtown and suburban retail centres, airport terminals, university campus areas, and busy neighbourhood shopping areas convenient for pedestrian foot traffic and/or drivers. A few were in suburban malls. Four store templates, each with its own colour combinations, lighting scheme, and component materials, were introduced in 1996; all four were adaptable to different store sizes and settings.

But as the number of stores increased rapidly over the next 20-plus years, greater store diversity and layouts quickly became necessary. Some stores were equipped with special seating areas to help make Starbucks a desirable gathering place where customers could meet and chat or simply enjoy a peaceful interlude in their day. Flagship stores in high-traffic, high-visibility locations had fireplaces, leather chairs, newspapers, couches and lots of ambience. Increasingly, the company began installing drive-through windows at locations where speed and convenience were important to customers and locating kiosks in high-traffic supermarkets, building lobbies, the halls of shopping malls, and other public places where passers-by could quickly and conveniently pick up a Starbucks beverage and/or something to eat.

A new global store design strategy was introduced in 2009. Core design characteristics included the celebration of local materials and craftsmanship, a focus on reused and recycled elements, the exposure of structural integrity and authentic roots, the absence of features that distracted from an emphasis on coffee, seating layouts that facilitated customer gatherings, an atmosphere that sought to engage all five customer senses (sight, smell, sound, hearing, and feel), and flexibility to meet the needs of many customer types (*Restaurants and Institutions*, 2009). Each new store was to be a reflection of the environment in which it operated and be environmentally friendly. In 2010, Starbucks began an effort to achieve LEED (Leadership in Energy and Environmental Design) Certification for all new company-owned stores (a LEED-certified building had to incorporate green building design, construction, operations, and maintenance solutions (Starbucks 2009a)).

To better control average store opening costs, the company centralized buying, developed standard contracts and fixed fees for certain items, and consolidated work under those contractors who displayed good cost control practices. The retail operations group outlined exactly the minimum amount of equipment each core store needed, so that standard items could be ordered in volume from vendors at 20 to 30 per cent discounts, then delivered just in time to the store site either from company warehouses or the vendor. Modular designs for display cases were developed. The layouts for new and remodelled stores were developed on a computer, with software that allowed the costs to be estimated as the design evolved. All this cut store opening and remodelling costs significantly and shortened the process to about 18 weeks.

Store Ambience

Starbucks management viewed each store as a billboard for the company and as a contributor to building the company's brand and image. The company goes to great lengths to make sure the store fixtures, the merchandise displays, the colours, the artwork, the banners, the music and the aromas all blend to create a consistent, inviting, stimulating environment that evokes the romance of coffee and signals the company's passion for coffee. To try to keep the coffee aromas in the stores pure, smoking is banned and employees are asked to refrain from wearing perfumes or colognes. Prepared foods are kept covered so customers smell coffee only. Colourful banners and posters are used to keep the look of the Starbucks stores fresh and in keeping with seasons and holidays. All these practices reflect a conviction that every detail matters in making Starbucks stores a welcoming and pleasant 'third place' (apart from home and work) where people can meet friends and family, enjoy a quiet moment alone with a newspaper or book, or simply spend quality time relaxing – and most importantly, have a satisfying experience.

Employee Engagement

Howard Schultz, a former chairman and chief executive officer of Starbucks, deeply believed that Starbucks' success was heavily dependent on customers having a very positive experience in its stores. This meant having store employees who are knowledgeable about the company's products, who pay attention to detail in preparing the company's espresso drinks, who eagerly communicate the company's passion for coffee and who possess the skills and personality to deliver consistent, pleasing customer service. Many of the baristas are aged in their twenties and working part-time, going to college on the side or pursuing other career activities. Schultz viewed the company's challenge as one of attracting, motivating and rewarding store employees in a manner that would make Starbucks a company that people would want to work for and that would generate enthusiastic commitment and higher levels of customer service. Moreover, Schultz wanted to send all Starbucks employees a message that cements the trust that had been built between management and the company's workforce.

Instituting Health Care Coverage for All Employees

One of the requests that employees had made to the prior owners of Starbucks back in the 1980s was to extend health care benefits to part-time workers. Their request had been turned down, but Schultz believed that expanding health care coverage to include part-timers was something the company needed to do. He knew from having grown up in a family that struggled to make ends meet how difficult it was to cope with rising medical costs. In 1988, Schultz went to the board of directors with his plan to expand the company's health care coverage to include part-timers who worked at least 20 hours per week. He saw the proposal not as a generous gesture but as a core strategy to win employee loyalty and commitment to the company's mission. Board members resisted because the company was then unprofitable and the added costs of the extended coverage would only worsen the company's bottom line. But Schultz argued passionately that it was the right thing to do and wouldn't be as expensive as it seemed. He observed that if the new benefit reduced staff turnover, which he believed was likely, then it would reduce the costs of hiring and training– which equalled about $3,000 per new hire. He further pointed out that it cost $1,500 a year to provide an employee with full benefits. Part-timers, he argued, were vital to Starbucks, constituting two-thirds of the company's workforce. Many were baristas who knew the favourite drinks of regular customers; if the barista left, that connection with the customer was broken. Moreover, many part-time employees were called upon to open the stores early, sometimes at 5:30 or 6 a.m.; others had to work until closing, usually 9 p.m. or later. Providing these employees with health care benefits, he argued, would signal that the company honoured their value and contribution.

The board approved Schultz's plan and part-timers working 20 or more hours were offered the same health coverage as full-time employees starting in late 1988. Starbucks paid 75 per cent of an employee's health care premium; the employee paid 25 per cent. Over the years, Starbucks extended its health coverage to include preventive care, prescription drugs, dental care, eye care, mental health and chemical dependency. Coverage was also offered for unmarried partners in a committed relationship. Since most Starbucks employees were young and comparatively healthy, the company had been able to provide broader coverage while keeping monthly payments relatively low.

A Stock Option Plan for Employees

By 1991, the company's profitability had improved to the point where Schultz could pursue a stock option plan for all employees, a programme he believed would have a positive, long-term effect on the success of Starbucks (Schultz, 2012). Schultz wanted to turn every Starbucks employee into a partner, give them a chance to share in the success of the company and make clear the connection between their contributions and the company's market value. Even though Starbucks was still a private company, the plan that emerged called for granting stock options to every full-time and part-time employee in proportion to their base pay. In May 1991, the plan, dubbed Bean Stock, was presented to the board. Although board members were concerned that increasing the number of shares might unduly dilute the value of the shares of investors who had put up hard cash, the plan received unanimous approval. The first grant was made in October 1991, just after the end of the company's fiscal year in September; each partner was granted stock options worth 12 per cent of base pay. When the Bean Stock programme was initiated, Starbucks dropped the term 'employee' and began referring to all of its people as 'partners' because every member of the Starbucks workforce became eligible for stock option awards after six months of employment and 500 paid work hours.

Starbucks went public in June 1992, selling its initial offering at a price of $17 per share. Starting in October 1992 and continuing through October 2004, Starbucks granted each eligible employee a stock option award with a value equal to 14 per cent of base pay. Beginning in 2005, the plan was modified to tie the size of each employee's stock option awards to three factors: (1) Starbucks' success and profitability for the fiscal year, (2) the size of an employee's base wages, and (3) the price at which the stock option could be exercised. Since becoming a public company, Starbucks stock had split 2-for-1 on six occasions. Performance-based stock awards to employees totalled about 5 million shares in fiscal 2017; these shares had an average value of $54.30 on the date of the grant and vested in two equal annual instalments beginning two years from the grant date.

Starbucks' Stock Purchase Plan for Employees

In 1995, Starbucks implemented an employee stock purchase plan that gave partners who had been employed for at least 90 days an opportunity to purchase company stock through regular payroll deductions. Partners who enrolled could devote anywhere from 1 to 10 per cent of their base earnings (up to an annual maximum of $25,000) to purchasing shares of Starbucks stock. After the end of each calendar quarter, each participant's contributions were used to buy Starbucks stock at a discount of 5 per cent of the closing price on the last business day of each calendar quarter (until March 2009, the discount was 15 per cent). Roughly 30 per cent of Starbucks partners participated in the stock purchase plan during the period 2000 to 2011. Participation has eroded in the past three fiscal years due to Starbucks' flat stock price performance since October 2015. In fiscal 2018, about 600,000 shares were purchased under this plan.

The Workplace Environment

Starbucks management believed its competitive pay scales and comprehensive benefits for both full-time and part-time partners (employees) allowed it to attract motivated people with above-average skills and good work habits. An employee's base pay was determined by the pay scales prevailing in the geographic region where an employee worked and by the person's job, skills, experience, and job performance.

About 90 per cent of Starbucks' partners were full-time or part-time baristas, paid on an hourly basis. In 2019, after six months of employment, baristas at company-owned stores in the United States could expect to earn about $11–$12 per hour; the national average pay for Starbucks baristas in 2019 was around $400 per week. Hourly-paid shift supervisors earned about $13–$14 an hour; store managers earned about $50,000, and salaries for district managers were in the $75,000 to $85,000 range.

Starbucks was named to *Fortune*'s list of the '100 Best Companies to Work For' 14 times during the 1988–2019 period. Surveys of Starbucks partners conducted by *Fortune* magazine in the course of selecting companies for inclusion on its annual list indicated that full-time baristas liked working at Starbucks because of the camaraderie, while part-timers were particularly pleased with the health insurance benefits (Starbucks, 2009b).

Schultz's approach to offering employees good compensation and a comprehensive benefits package was driven by his belief that sharing the company's success with the people who made it happen helped everyone think and act like an owner, build positive long-term relationships with customers, and do things in an efficient way. Schultz's rationale, based on his father's experience of going from one low-wage, no-benefits job to another, was that if you treat your employees well, that is how they will treat customers.

Starbucks' fringe benefit program me, 2019

- Medical, dental, and vision coverage.
- Sick pay, up to 40 hours per year.
- Paid vacations (up to 120 hours annually for hourly workers with 5 or more years of service at retail stores and up to 200 hours annually for salaried and non-retail hourly employees with 10 or more years of service).
- Seven paid holidays.
- One paid personal day every six months for salaried and non-retail hourly partners only.
- Mental health and chemical dependency coverage.
- 401(k) retirement savings plan – partners age 18 or older with 90 days of service were eligible to contribute from 1 per cent to 75 per cent of their pay each pay period (up to the annual IRS dollar limit – $18,500 for calendar year 2018). Partners age 50 and older had a higher IRS annual limit ($24,500 for calendar year 2018). Starbucks matched 100 per cent of the first 5 per cent of eligible pay contributed each pay period. Starbucks' matching contributions to the 401(k) plans worldwide totalled $111.7 million in fiscal 2018 and $101.4 million in fiscal 2017.
- Short- and long-term disability.
- Stock purchase plan – eligible employees could buy shares at a 5 per cent discount through regular payroll deductions of between 1 and 10 per cent of base pay.
- Life insurance coverage equal to annual base pay for salaried and non-retail employees; coverage equal to $5,000 for store employees. Supplemental coverage could be purchased in flat dollar amounts of $10,000, $25,000, and $45,000.
- Short-term disability coverage (partial replacement of lost wages/income for 26 weeks, after a short waiting period); hourly employees can purchase long-term disability coverage.
- Company-paid long-term disability coverage for salaried and non-retail employees.
- Accidental death and dismemberment insurance.
- Adoption assistance. Reimbursement of up to $10,000 to help pay for qualified expenses related to the adoption of an eligible child.
- Financial assistance programme for employees that experience a financial crisis.
- Stock option plan (Bean stock). Shares were granted to eligible partners, subject to the company's achievement of specified performance targets and the employee's continued employment through the vesting period. Vesting occurred in two equal annual instalments beginning two years from the grant date. The company's board of directors determined how many shares were to be granted each year and also established the specified performance targets. About 9.5 million shares were granted in fiscal year 2018.
- Pre-tax payroll deductions for work-related commuter expenses.

- A free coffee or tea product each week.
- An in-store discount of 30 per cent on purchases of beverages, food, and merchandise.
- A college achievement plan featuring full tuition reimbursement every semester for employees enrolled in Arizona State University's top ranked online degree programmes. As of March 2018, some 1,282 Starbucks employees had graduated and over 10,000 were currently working toward their degrees.
- Gift-matching benefits – Starbucks matched up to $1,500 per fiscal year for individual contributions of money or volunteer time to eligible nonprofit organizations.

Source: Information in the Careers section at www.starbucks.com, accessed 28 May 2019; and company 2018 10-K Report, pp. 80–82.

Employee Training and Recognition

To accommodate its strategy of rapid store expansion, Starbucks put in systems to recruit, hire and train baristas and store managers. Every partner/barista hired for a retail job in a Starbucks store received at least 24 hours' training in their first two to four weeks. Training topics included coffee history, drink preparation, coffee knowledge, customer service and retail skills, plus a four-hour workshop on 'Brewing the Perfect Cup'. Baristas spent considerable time learning about beverage preparation: grinding the beans, steaming milk, learning to pull perfect (18- to 23-second) shots of espresso, memorizing the recipes of all the different drinks, practising making the different drinks and learning how to customize drinks to customer specifications. There were sessions on cash register operations, how to clean the milk wand on the espresso machine, explaining the Italian drink names to unknowing customers, making eye contact with customers and interacting with them, and taking personal responsibility for the cleanliness of the store. And there were rules to be memorized: milk must be steamed to at least 150 degrees Fahrenheit but never more than 170 degrees; every espresso shot not pulled within 23 seconds must be tossed; never let coffee sit in the pot more than 20 minutes; always compensate dissatisfied customers with a Starbucks coupon that entitles them to a free drink.

There were also training programmes for shift supervisors, assistant store managers, store managers and district managers that went much deeper, covering not only coffee knowledge and information imparted to baristas but also the details of store operations, practices and procedures as set forth in the company's operating manual, information systems and the basics of managing people. In addition, there were special career development programmes, such as a coffee masters programme for store employees and more advanced leadership skills training for shift supervisors and store management personnel. When Starbucks opened stores in a new market, it sent a Star team of experienced managers and baristas to the area to lead the store opening effort and to conduct one-on-one training following the basic orientation and training sessions.

To recognize and reward partner contributions, Starbucks had created a partner recognition programme consisting of different awards and programmes (sbuxrecognition.com, 2018). Examples included: Partner of the Quarter Awards (for one partner per store per quarter) for significant contributions to their store and demonstrating behaviours consistent with the company's mission and values; Spirit of Starbucks awards for making exceptional contributions to partners, customers and community while embracing the company's mission and values; a Manager of the Quarter for store manager leadership; Green Apron Awards where partners could recognize fellow partners for how they bring to life the company's mission, values, and customer commitment; and Bravo and Team Bravo! awards for above and beyond the call of duty performance and achieving exceptional results.

In 2019, Starbucks' stated values were:

- Creating a culture of warmth and belonging, where everyone is welcome.
- Delivering our best in all we do, holding ourselves accountable for results.
- Acting with courage, challenging the status quo and finding new ways to grow our company and each other.
- Being present, connecting with transparency, dignity, and respect.

The website also states: '*We are performance-driven, through the lens of humanity*'. In addition to being expected to live by the company's values, all Starbucks personnel are expected to conform to the highest standards of ethical conduct and to take all legal and ethical responsibilities seriously (Starbucks, 2019).

Starbucks' Corporate Social Responsibility Strategy

Howard Schultz's effort to 'build a company with soul' included a long history of doing business in ways that were socially and environmentally responsible. A commitment to do the right thing has been central to how Starbucks operated since Howard Schultz first became CEO in 1987, and one of the core beliefs at Starbucks was that 'the way to build a great, enduring company is to strike a balance between profitability and a social conscience' (Starbucks, 2019). The specific actions comprising Starbucks' social responsibility strategy have varied over the years but the intent of the strategy was consistently one of contributing positively to the communities in which Starbucks had stores, being a good environmental steward, and conducting the company's business in ways that earned the trust and respect of customers, partners/employees, suppliers, and the general public.

In 2019, Starbucks' corporate social responsibility (CSR) strategy had five main elements:

1. *Ethically sourcing all of its products.* This CSR element had two main aspects: (a) all of the company's actions and collaborative efforts in purchasing the company's supplies of coffee, tea and cocoa that were aimed at providing loans and technical assistance to the small family farms that grew these products, paying prices for these products that improved the living standards and economic well-being of the farmers and their communities, and trying to institute better soil-management and sustainable farming practices; and (b) striving to buy the manufactured products and services it needed from suppliers who not only adhered to strict food safety and product quality standards, and

certain Starbucks-specified operating practices, but also signed an agreement pledging compliance with the company's global Supplier Code of Conduct. This code of conduct included (Starbucks, 2020):

- Demonstrating commitment to the welfare, economic improvement, and sustainability of the people and places that produce products and services for Starbucks.
- Adherence to local laws and international standards regarding human rights, workplace safety and worker compensation and treatment.
- Meeting or exceeding national laws and international standards for environmental protection and minimizing negative environmental impacts of the supplier's operations.
- Commitment to measuring, monitoring, reporting and verification of compliance to this code.
- Pursuing continuous improvement of these social and environmental principles.

Verification of compliance was subjects to audits by Starbucks personnel or acceptable third parties. From time to time, Starbucks had temporarily or permanently discontinued its business relationship with suppliers who failed to comply or failed to work with Starbucks to correct a non-complying situation.

2. *Community involvement and corporate citizenship.* Active engagement in community activities and display of good corporate citizenship had always been core elements in the way Starbucks conducted its business. Starbucks stores and employees regularly volunteered for community improvement projects and initiatives that would have a meaningful impact on the localities in which Starbucks had a presence. In fiscal 2011 Starbucks sponsored a special global month of service in which more than 60,000 employees in 30 countries volunteered for over 150,000 service hours and completed 1,400 community-service projects; every year since, Starbucks has held a Global Month of Service.

The company had a goal of having 100 per cent of its stores worldwide participating in community service projects. Recently, through a strategic alliance with Feeding America, Starbucks had instituted a 'food share' programme to rescue food that would otherwise spoil in its stores to donate to organizations providing meals to needy families and homeless people. Management estimated that, when the programme was fully operational in all Starbucks stores, the food donations would help provide 50 million meals per year. As of 2017, some 5 million meals from 2,700 stores had been donated.

3. *Environmental stewardship.* Initiatives here included a wide variety of actions to increase recycling, reduce waste, be more energy efficient, use renewable energy sources, conserve water resources, make all company facilities as green as possible by using environmentally friendly building materials and energy-efficient designs, and engage in more efforts to address climate change. Beginning in January 2011, all new company-owned retail stores globally were built to achieve Leadership in Energy and Environmental Design (LEED) certification; as of 2017 Starbucks had built more than 1,500 LEED-certified stores in 20 countries. The company's goal was to have 10,000 greener retail stores by 2025. In 2008, Starbucks set a goal of reducing water consumption by 25 per cent in company-owned stores by 2015, and after two years had implemented proactive measures that had decreased water use by almost 22 per cent. Starbucks had invested in renewable energy since 2005, and it achieved a milestone in 2015 by purchasing the equivalent of 100 per cent of the electricity consumption of all company-operated stores worldwide from renewable energy sources, primarily utilizing Renewable Energy Credits from the United States and Canada and through green electricity-supply contracts across Europe. Starbucks was the number one purchaser of renewable electricity in its sector on the EPA's Green Power Partnership National Top 100 list. In North Carolina and Washington State, Starbucks has invested in a solar farm and a wind farm that delivers enough energy to power more than 700 Starbucks stores.

By 2011, nearly 80 per cent of company-owned Starbucks stores in North America were recycling cardboard boxes and other back-of-store items; there were front-of-store recycling bins in place in all company-owned locations where there were municipal recycling capabilities (50 per cent of company-owned stores in the United States as of year-end 2015). Since 1985, Starbucks had given a $0.10 discount to customers who brought reusable cups and tumblers to stores for use in serving the beverages they ordered. In 2018, a programme was in place to double the recycled content, recyclability, and reusability of the cups in which beverages were served by 2022, and an initiative had been launched to empower 10,000 Starbucks employees to be 'sustainability champions' by 2020. Stores participated in Earth Day activities each year with in-store promotions and volunteer efforts to educate employees and customers about the impacts their actions had on the environment.

4. *Creating opportunities to help people achieve their dreams.* The chief initiatives here included hiring 100,000 young people aged 16 to 24 years who were disconnected from work and school by 2020, hiring at least 25,000 veterans and military spouses by 2025, welcoming and employing 10,000 refugees across the 75 countries in which Starbucks stores were located by 2022, and expanding partner participation in the company's college achievement plan that covered full-tuition reimbursement for admission to one of Arizona State University's online degree programmes. Starbucks had initiated a programme to make 'Youth Opportunity' grants to support mentoring, work placement and apprenticeship programmes for young people, and in 2017, in partnership with 50 other employers, had committed to hiring, training, and advancing the careers of 100,000 young people aged 16 to 24 years by 2020.

5. *Charitable contributions.* The Starbucks Foundation, set up in 1997, oversaw a major portion of the company's philanthropic activities; it received the majority of its funding from Starbucks Coffee Company and private donations. Over the years, the Starbucks Foundation had made close to 200 grants to nonprofit organizations such as the American Red Cross for relief efforts to communities experiencing severe damage from earthquakes, hurricanes, tornadoes, floods, and other natural disasters, Save the Children for efforts to improve education, health, and nutrition, the Global Fund and Product (RED)™ to provide medicine to people in Africa with AIDS, and a wide assortment of community-building efforts. Donations were made in cash and in-kind contributions.

The Starbucks Foundation helps support organizations, creating pathways to lifelong opportunity and programmes which create job and training opportunities for people who may face barriers, through Opportunity for All grants. In 2019, the Foundation awarded $1.4 million in grants to 63 programmes and organizations ranging from $10,000 to $50,000 per grant (Starbucks Foundation, 2019a).

Water, sanitation, and hygiene education programmes in water-stressed countries were supported through the Starbucks Foundation's Ethos Water Fund. For each bottle of Ethos water purchased at Starbucks stores, Starbucks donated $0.05 ($0.10 in Canada) to the Ethos© Water Fund. Since 2005, the Fund has made over $15 million in grants, benefiting more than 500,000 people around the world (Starbucks Foundation, 2019b).

Starbucks has been named on the *Corporate Responsibility Magazine*'s list of the 100 Best Corporate Citizens on numerous occasions; this list is based on more than 360 data points of publicly available information in seven categories: Environment, Climate Change, Human Rights, Philanthropy, Employee Relations, Financial Performance, and Governance. Over the years, Starbucks has received over 25 awards from a diverse group of organizations for its philanthropic, community service and environmental activities.

Conclusion

To be successful at selling coffee, Starbucks has built the customer experience around store design and employee engagement. It has supported this with a strategy of corporate social responsibility by contributing positively to the communities in which Starbucks has stores in a manner that attempts to earn the trust and respect of customers, employees, suppliers, and the general public.

References

Restaurants and Institutions (2009). 'Starbucks Plans New Global Store Design', *Restaurants and Institutions*, June 25, 2009, accessed at www.rimag.com on December 29, 2009.

Sbuxrecognition.com (2018). Information posted at www.sbuxrecognition.com, accessed June 1, 2018.

Schultz, H. (2012) pp. 131–136, *Pour Your Heart Into It: How Starbucks built a company one cup at a time.* Hachette UK.

Starbucks (2009a). Starbucks Global Responsibility Report for 2009, p. 13. Green Building. Available at: https://globalassets.starbucks.com/assets/359fba8443174461b674acdec0885479.pdf

Starbucks (2009b). Company news release, May 21, 2009, accessed at www.starbucks.com on June 14, 2010.

Starbucks (2019). Posted at https://www.starbucks.com/careers/working-at-starbucks/culture-and-values, accessed June 19, 2019.

Starbucks (2019). Starbucks Company Profile, accessed June 09, 2019, https://www.starbucks.com/about-us/company-information/starbucks-company-profile

Starbucks (2020). Starbucks Supplier Code of Conduct. Available at: https://globalassets.starbucks.com/assets/21687912103D4C1BB7E52CFFF9203E92.pdf, accessed May 4, 2020.

Starbucks Foundation (2019a). Starbucks Stories and News. Available at: https://stories.starbucks.com/press/2019/the-starbucks-foundation-2019-opportunity-for-all-grants/

Starbucks Foundation (2019b). The Starbucks Foundation was created as part of our commitment to strengthen communities. Available at: https://www.starbucks.com/responsibility/community/starbucks-foundation

Endnotes

Chapter 1

1   Source: www.forbes.com – *The Forbes Global 2000* (published April 2014).

2   J.B. Quinn, J.J. Baruch and P.C. Paquette, 'Technology in services', *Scientific American*, 257, no. 6 (December 1987), pp. 50–8.

3   C.H. Lovelock, 'Classifying services to gain strategic marketing insights', *Journal of Marketing*, 47 (Summer 1983), pp. 9–20.

4   Ibid.

5   R.H.K. Vietor, *Contrived Competition* (Cambridge, MA: Harvard University Press, 1994).

6   M. Sawhney, S. Balasubramanian and V.V. Krishnan, 'Creating growth with services', *Sloan Management Review* (Winter 2004), pp. 34–43.

7   J.A. Alexander and M.W. Hordes, *S-Business: Reinventing the Services Organization* (New York: SelectBooks, 2003); R. Oliva and R. Kallenberg, 'Managing the transition from products to services', *International Journal of Service Industry Management* 14, no. 2 (2003), pp. 160–72.

8   J. Pine and J. Gilmore, *The Experience Economy* (Boston: Harvard Business School Press, 1999).

9   Source: Anderson, L., Ostrom, A., Corus, C., Fisk, R., Gallan, A., Giraldo, M., Mende, M., Mulder, M., Rayburn, S., Rosenbaum, M., Shirahada, K., & Williams, J. (2013). Transformative service research: An agenda for the future. Journal of Business Research, 66, 1203–1210.

10 S.L. Vargo and R.F. Lusch, 'Evolving to a new dominant logic for marketing', *Journal of Marketing*, 68 (January 2004), pp. 1–17.

11 S.L. Vargo and R.F. Lusch, 'Service dominant logic: continuing the evolution', *Journal of the Academy of Marketing Science*, 36,1 (2008), pp. 1–10.

12 C. Grönroos, 'Value co-creation in service logic: A critical analysis', *Marketing Theory*, 11/3 (2011), pp. 279–301.

13 C. Grönroos and P. Voima (2013) Critical service logic: making sense of value creation and co-creation. *Journal of the Academy of Marketing Science*, 41(2), 133–150

14 E. Gummesson and F. Polese, 'B2B is not an island', *Journal of Business and Industrial Marketing*, 24, nos 5/6 (2009), pp. 337–50.

15 L.p. Willcocks and R. Plant, 'Getting from bricks to clicks', *Sloan Management Review* (Spring 2001), pp. 50–9.

16 G. Eysenbach, E.R. Sa and T.L. Diepgen, 'Shopping around the Internet today and tomorrow: towards the millennium of cybermedicine', *British Medical Journal* 319 (1999), p. 1294.

17 M.J. Bitner, S.W. Brown and M.L. Meuter, 'Technology infusion in service encounters', *Journal of the Academy of Marketing Science* 28 (Winter 2000), pp. 138–49.

18 M.J. Bitner, 'Self-service technologies: what do customers expect?', *Marketing Management* (Spring 2001), pp. 10–11.

19 R. Hallowell, 'Service in e-commerce: findings from exploratory research', Harvard Business School, Module Note, N9-800-418, 31 May 2000.

20 A. Parasuraman and C.L. Colby, *Techno-Ready Marketing: How and Why Your Customers Adopt Technology* (New York: Free Press, 2001).

21 L. Berry, *Discovering the Soul of Service* (New York: Free Press, 1999).

22 R.T. Rust, C. Moorman and p.R. Dickson, 'Getting return on quality: revenue expansion, cost reduction, or both?' *Journal of Marketing* 66 (October 2002), pp. 7–24.

23 J.L. Heskett, T.O. Jones, G.W. Loveman, W.E. Sasser Jr and L.A. Schlesinger, 'Putting the service–profit chain to work', *Harvard Business Review* (March–April 1994), pp. 164–74.

24 E.W. Anderson and V. Mittal, 'Strengthening the satisfaction –profit chain', *Journal of Service Research* 3, no. 2 (November 2000), pp. 107–20.

25 Discussion of these issues is found in many services marketing publications. The discussion here is based on V.A. Zeithaml, A. Parasuraman and L.L. Berry, 'Problems and strategies in services marketing', *Journal of Marketing* 49 (Spring 1985), pp. 33–46.

26 For research supporting the idea of goods–services continua, see D. Iacobucci, 'An empirical examination of some basic tenets in services: goods–services continua', in *Advances in Services Marketing and Management*, eds T.A. Swartz, D.E. Bowen and S.W. Brown (Greenwich, CT: JAI Press, 1992), vol. 1, pp. 23–52.

27 S.L. Vargo and R.F. Lusch, 'The four service marketing myths', *Journal of Service Research* 6 (May 2004), pp. 324–35.

28 C. Lovelock and E. Gummesson, 'Whither services marketing? In search of a new paradigm and fresh perspectives', *Journal of Services Research* 7 (August 2004), pp. 20–41.

29 E.J. McCarthy and W.D. Perrault Jr, *Basic Marketing: A Global Managerial Approach* (Burr Ridge, IL: Richard D. Irwin, 1993).

30 B.H. Booms and M.J. Bitner, 'Marketing strategies and organizational structures for service firms', in *Marketing of Services*, eds J.H. Donnelly and W.R. George (Chicago: American Marketing Association, 1981), pp. 47–51.

31 Ibid.
32 E. Langeard, J. Bateson, C. Lovelock and p. Eiglier,
    *Marketing of Services: New Insights from Consumers
    and Managers* (Cambridge, MA: Marketing Sciences
    Institute, 1981).

Chapter 2

1 The gaps model of service quality that provides the
   structure for this text was developed by and is fully
   presented in V.A. Zeithaml, A. Parasuraman and
   L.L. Berry, *Delivering Quality Service: Balancing Customer
   Perceptions and Expectations* (New York: Free Press, 1990).

Chapter 3

1 P. Nelson, 'Information and consumer behaviour',
   Journal of Political Economy 78, no. 20 (1970),
   pp. 311–29.
2 M.R. Darby and E. Karni, 'Free competition and
   the optimal amount of fraud', *Journal of Law and
   Economics* 16 (April 1973), pp. 67–86.
3 T.S. Robertson, *Innovative Behavior and
   Communication* (New York: Holt, Rinehart & Winston,
   1971).
4 M. Laroche, G.H.G. McDougall, J. Bergeron and Z. Yang,
   'Exploring how intangibility affects perceived risk',
   Journal of Service Research 6, no. 4 (May 2004), pp.
   373–89; K.B. Murray and J.L. Schlacter, 'The impact
   of services versus goods on consumers' assessment of
   perceived risk and variability', *Journal of the Academy
   of Marketing Science* 18 (Winter 1990),
   pp. 51–65; M. Laroche, J. Bergeron and C. Goutaland,
   'How intangibility affects perceived risk: the moderating
   role of knowledge and involvement', *Journal of Services
   Marketing* 17, no. 2 (2003), pp. 122–40.
5 M. Laroche et al., 'Exploring how intangibility affects
   perceived risk'.
6 R.F. Lusch, S.W. Brown and G.J. Brunswick, 'A general
   framework for explaining internal vs. external
   exchange', *Journal of the Academy of Marketing Science*
   10 (Spring 1992), pp. 119–34.
7 M.L. Meuter, A.L. Ostom, R.I. Roundtree and M.J. Bitner,
   'Self-service technologies: understanding customer
   satisfaction with technology-based service encounters',
   Journal of Marketing 64 (July 2000), pp. 50–64; M.J. Bitner,
   'Self-service technologies: what do customers expect?',
   Marketing Management (Spring 2001), pp. 10–11.
8 J.H. Gilmore and B.J. Pine II, 'The experience is the
   marketing', report from Strategic Horizons LLP (2002).
9 See, for example, B.J. Pine II and J.H. Gilmore, *The
   Experience Economy* (Boston, MA: Harvard Business
   School Press, 1999); B.H. Schmitt, *Experiential
   Marketing* (New York: Free Press, 1999); B.H. Schmitt,
   Customer Experience Management (Hoboken, NJ: John
   Wiley & Sons, 2003).
10 S.J. Grove and R.P. Fisk, 'Service theater: an analytical
    framework for services marketing', in *Services
    Marketing,* 4th edn, ed. C. Lovelock (Englewood Cliffs,
    NJ: Prentice Hall, 2001), pp. 83–92.
11 S.J. Grove, R.P. Fisk and M.J. Bitner, 'Dramatizing the
    service experience: a managerial approach', in *Advances
    in Services Marketing and Management,* vol. 1, eds T.A.
    Swartz, D.E. Bowen and S.W. Brown (Greenwich, CT: JAI
    Press, 1992), pp. 91–121.
12 Grove, Fisk and Bitner, 'Dramatizing the service
    experience'.
13 Grove and Fisk, 'Service theater'.
14 Ibid.
15 Grove, Fisk and Bitner, 'Dramatizing the service
    experience'.
16 Ibid.
17 Ibid.
18 M.R. Solomon, C. Surprenant, J.A. Czepiel and
    E.G. Gutman, 'A role theory perspective on dyadic
    interactions: the service encounter', *Journal of
    Marketing* 49 (Winter 1985), pp. 99–111.
19 Ibid.
20 R.F. Abelson, 'Script processing in attitude formation and
    decision making', in *Cognition and Social Behavior,* eds
    J.S. Carroll and J.S. Payne (Hillsdale, NJ: Erlbaum, 1976).
21 R.A. Smith and M.J. Houston, 'Script-based evaluations
    of satisfaction with services', in *Emerging Perspectives
    on Services Marketing,* eds L. Berry, G.L. Shostack and
    G. Upah (Chicago, IL: American Marketing Association,
    1982), pp. 59–62.
22 J.E.G. Bateson and M.K.M. Hui, 'Crowding in the service
    environment', in *Creativity in Services Marketing:
    What's New, What Works, What's Developing,* eds
    M. Venkatesan, D.M. Schmalensee and C. Marshall (Chicago,
    IL: American Marketing Association, 1986), pp. 85–8.
23 J. Baker, 'The role of the environment in marketing
    services: the consumer perspective', in *The Services
    Challenge: Integrating for Competitive Advantage,* eds
    J.A. Czepiel, C.A. Congram and J. Shanahan (Chicago, IL:
    American Marketing Association, 1987), pp. 79–84.
24 C.L. Martin and C.A. Pranter, 'Compatibility
    management: customer-to-customer relationships in
    service environments', *Journal of Services Marketing* 3
    (Summer 1989), pp. 43–53.
25 Ibid.
26 N. Bendapudi and R.p. Leone, 'Psychological implications
    of customer participation in coproduction', *Journal of
    Marketing* 67 (January 2003), pp. 14–28.
27 L.A. Bettencourt, A.L. Ostrom, S.W. Brown and R.I.
    Roundtree, 'Client co-production in knowledge-intensive
    business services', *California Management Review* 44,
    no. 4 (Summer 2002), pp. 100–28.
28 S. Dellande, M.C. Gilly and J.L. Graham, 'Gaining
    compliance and losing weight: the role of the service

provider in health care services', *Journal of Marketing* 68 (July 2004), pp. 78–91; M.L. Meuter, M.J. Bitner, A.L. Ostrom and S.W. Brown, 'Choosing among alternative service delivery modes: an investigation of customer trials of self-service technologies', *Journal of Marketing* (2005), pp. 61–83.

29 C.K. Prahalad and V. Ramaswamy, 'The new frontier of experience innovation', *Sloan Management Review* (Summer 2003), pp. 12–18.

30 A.F. Firat and A. Venkatesh, 'Liberatory postmodernism and the reenchantment of consumption', *Journal of Consumer Research* 22, no. 3 (December 1995), pp. 239–67.

31 M.P. Gardner, 'Mood states and consumer behavior: a critical review', *Journal of Consumer Research* 12 (December 1985), pp. 281–300.

32 Ibid., p. 288.

33 S.S. Tomkins, 'Affect as amplification: some modifications in theory', in *Emotion: Theory, Research, and Experience,* eds R. Plutchik and H. Kellerman (New York: Academic Press, 1980), pp. 141–64.

34 L.L. Berry, L.P. Carbone and S.H. Haeckel, 'Managing the total customer experience', *Sloan Management Review* (Spring 2002), pp. 85–9.

35 V.S. Folkes and V.M. Patrick, 'The positivity effect in perceptions of services: seen one, seen them all?', *Journal of Consumer Research* 30 (June 2003), pp. 125–37.

36 B.D. Keillor, G.T.M. Hult and D. Kandemir, 'A study of the service encounter in eight countries', *Journal of International Marketing* 12, no. 1 (2004), pp. 9–35.

37 D.E. Murphy, 'New East Europe retailers told to put on a happy face', *Los Angeles Times,* 26 November 1994, pp. A1, A18.

38 E. Arnould, L. Price and G. Zinkhan, *Consumers*, 2nd edn (New York: McGraw-Hill, 2004).

39 For excellent coverage of buyer behaviour in organizations, see M.D. Hutt and T.W. Speh, *Business Marketing Management,* 8th edn (Mason, OH: South-Western, 2004), ch. 3.

40 Ibid., pp. 68–9.

41 Ibid., pp. 62–7.

Chapter 4

1 The model on which this chapter is based is taken from V.A. Zeithaml, L.L. Berry and A. Parasuraman, 'The nature and determinants of customer expectations of service', *Journal of the Academy of Marketing Science* 21, no. 1 (1993), pp. 1–12.

2 R.B. Woodruff, E.R. Cadotte and R.L. Jenkins, 'Expectations and norms in models of consumer satisfaction', *Journal of Marketing Research* 24 (August 1987), pp. 305–14.

3 J.A. Miller, 'Studying satisfaction, modifying models, eliciting expectations, posing problems, and making meaningful measurements', in *Conceptualization and Measurement of Consumer Satisfaction and Dissatisfaction,* ed. H.K. Hunt (Bloomington, IN: Indiana University School of Business, 1977), pp. 72–91.

4 W.H. Davidow and B. Uttal, 'Service companies: focus or falter', *Harvard Business Review* (July–August 1989), pp. 77–85.

5 A. Parasuraman, L.L. Berry and V.A. Zeithaml, 'Understanding customer expectations of service', *Sloan Management Review* 32 (Spring 1991), p. 42.

6 L.L. Berry, A. Parasuraman and V.A. Zeithaml, 'Ten lessons for improving service quality', Marketing Science Institute, Report No. 93–104 (May 1993).

7 D. Bowen, 'Leadership aspects and reward systems of customer satisfaction', speech given at CTM Customer Satisfaction Conference, Los Angeles, 17 March 1989.

8 D.L. Davis, J.G. Guiltinan and W.H. Jones, 'Service characteristics, consumer research, and the classification of retail services', *Journal of Retailing* 55 (Fall 1979), pp. 3–21; and W.R. George and L.L. Berry, 'Guidelines for the advertising of services', *Business Horizons* 24 (May–June 1981), pp. 52–6.

9 E.R. Cadotte, R.B. Woodruff and R.L. Jenkins, 'Expectations and norms in models of consumer satisfaction', *Journal of Marketing Research* 14 (August 1987), pp. 353–64.

10 Parasuraman, Berry and Zeithaml, 'Understanding customer expectations', p. 40.

11 Davidow and Uttal, 'Service companies'.

12 W. Boulding, A. Kalra, R. Staelin and V.A. Zeithaml, 'A dynamic process model of service quality: from expectations to behavioral intentions', *Journal of Marketing Research* 30 (February 1993), pp. 7–27.

13 R.T. Rust and R.L. Oliver, 'Should we delight the customer?', *Journal of the Academy of Marketing Science* 28 (Winter 2000), pp. 86–94.

14 T.S. Gross, *Positively Outrageous Service* (New York: Warner Books, 1994).

15 J. Clemmer, 'The three rings of perceived value', *Canadian Manager* (Summer 1990), pp. 30–2.

16 Rust and Oliver, 'Should we delight the customer?'.

17 Parasuraman, Berry and Zeithaml, 'Understanding customer expectations', p. 41.

18 See http://corporate.ritzcarlton.com.

Chapter 5

1 For more discussion of the debate on the distinctions between quality and satisfaction, see A. Parasuraman, V.A. Zeithaml and L.L. Berry, 'Reassessment of expectations as a comparison standard in measuring service quality: implications for future research', *Journal of Marketing* 58 (January 1994), pp. 111–24;

R.L. Oliver, 'A conceptual model of service quality and service satisfaction: compatible goals, different concepts', in *Advances in Services Marketing and Management*, vol. 2, eds T.A. Swartz, D.E. Bowen and S.W. Brown (Greenwich, CT: JAI Press, 1994), pp. 65–85; M.J. Bitner and A.R. Hubbert, 'Encounter satisfaction vs. overall satisfaction vs. quality: the customer's voice', in *Service Quality: New Directions in Theory and Practice*, eds R.T. Rust and R.L. Oliver (Newbury Park, CA: Sage, 1993), pp. 71–93; D.K. Iacobucci, A. Grayson and A.L. Ostrom, 'The calculus of service quality and customer satisfaction: theory and empirical differentiation and integration', in *Advances in Services Marketing and Management*, vol. 3, eds T.A. Swartz, D.E. Bowen and S.W. Brown (Greenwich, CT: JAI Press, 1994), pp. 1–67; P.A. Dabholkar, C.D. Shepherd and D.I. Thorpe, 'A comprehensive framework for service quality: an investigation of critical conceptual and measurement issues through a longitudinal study', *Journal of Retailing* 7, no. 2 (Summer 2000), pp. 139–73; and J.J. Cronin Jr, M.K. Brady and G.T.M. Hult, 'Assessing the effects of quality, value, and customer satisfaction on consumer behavioral intentions in service environments', *Journal of Retailing* 7 (Summer 2000), pp. 193–218.

2 See in particular, Parasuraman, Zeithaml and Berry, 'Reassessment of expectations'; Oliver, 'A conceptual model of service quality'; and M.K. Brady and J.J. Cronin Jr, 'Some new thoughts on conceptualizing perceived service quality: a hierarchical approach', *Journal of Marketing* 65 (July 2001), pp. 34–49.

3 A. Parasuraman, V.A. Zeithaml and L.L. Berry, 'SERVQUAL: a multiple-item scale for measuring consumer perceptions of service quality', *Journal of Retailing* 64 (Spring 1988), pp. 12–40.

4 Parasuraman, Zeithaml and Berry, 'Reassessment of expectations'.

5 Oliver, 'A conceptual model of service quality'.

6 See V. Mittal, P. Kumar and M. Tsiros, 'Attribute-level performance, satisfaction, and behavioral intentions over time', *Journal of Marketing* 63 (April 1999), pp. 88–101; L.L. Olsen and M.D. Johnson, 'Service equity, satisfaction, and loyalty: from transaction-specific to cumulative evaluations', *Journal of Service Research* 5 (February 2003), pp. 184–95.

7 Olsen and Johnson, 'Service equity, satisfaction, and loyalty'.

8 R.L. Oliver, *Satisfaction: A Behavioral Perspective on the Consumer* (New York: McGraw-Hill, 1997).

9 For a more detailed discussion of the different types of satisfaction, see E. Arnould, L. Price and G. Zinkhan, *Consumers*, 2nd edn (New York: McGraw-Hill, 2004), pp. 754–96.

10 S. Fournier and D.G. Mick, 'Rediscovering satisfaction', *Journal of Marketing* 63 (October 1999), pp. 5–23.

11 Oliver, *Satisfaction*, ch. 2.

12 A. Ostrom and D. Iacobucci, 'Consumer trade-offs and the evaluation of services', *Journal of Marketing* 59 (January 1995), pp. 17–28.

13 For more on emotions and satisfaction, see Oliver, *Satisfaction*, ch. 11; and L.L. Price, E.J. Arnould and S.L. Deibler, 'Consumers' emotional responses to service encounters', *International Journal of Service Industry Management* 6, no. 3 (1995), pp. 34–63.

14 L.L. Price, E.J. Arnould and P. Tierney, 'Going to extremes: managing service encounters and assessing provider performance', *Journal of Marketing* 59 (April 1995), pp. 83–97.

15 Source: Pedragosa, V., Biscaia, R., & Correia, A. (2015). The role of emotions on consumers' satisfaction within the fitness context. *Motriz: Revista de Educação Física*, 21(2), 116–124.

16 For more on attributions and satisfaction, see V.S. Folkes, 'Recent attribution research in consumer behavior: a review and new directions', *Journal of Consumer Research*, 14 (March 1988), pp. 548–65; and Oliver, *Satisfaction*, ch. 10.

17 A.R. Hubbert, 'Customer co-creation of service outcomes: effects of locus of causality attributions', doctoral dissertation, Arizona State University, Tempe, Arizona (1995).

18 Ibid.

19 For more on fairness and satisfaction, see E.C. Clemmer and B. Schneider, 'Fair service', in *Advances in Services Marketing and Management*, vol. 5, eds T.A. Swartz, D.E. Bowen and S.W. Brown (Greenwich, CT: JAI Press, 1996), pp. 109–26; Oliver, *Satisfaction*, ch. 7; and Olsen and Johnson, 'Service equity, satisfaction, and loyalty'.

20 Fournier and Mick, 'Rediscovering satisfaction'.

21 See, for example: C. Fornell, M.D. Johnson, E.W. Anderson, J. Cha and B.E. Bryant, 'The American Customer Satisfaction Index: nature, purpose, and findings', *Journal of Marketing*, 60 (October 1996), pp. 7–18; C. Fornell, 'A national customer satisfaction barometer: the Swedish experience', *Journal of Marketing*, 56 no. 1 (1992), pp. 6–21.

22 E.W. Anderson, C. Fornell and D.R. Lehmann, 'Customer satisfaction, market share, and profitability: findings from Sweden', *Journal of Marketing*, 58 (July 1994), pp. 53–66.

23 M. Bruhn and M.A. Grund, 'Theory, development and implementation of national customer satisfaction indices: the Swiss index of customer satisfaction (SWICS)', *Total Quality Management* 11, no. 7 (2000), pp. S1017–S1028; A. Meyer and F. Dornach, 'The German customer barometer', (http://www.servicebarometer.com/de/); Norwegian customer satisfaction barometer (www.kundebarometer.com).

24 F.F. Reichheld, 'The one number you need to grow', *Harvard Business Review*, December 2003, pp. 46–53.

25 T.L. Keiningham, B. Cooil, L. Akjoy, T.W. Andreassen and J. Weiner, 'The value of different customer satisfaction and loyalty metrics in predicting customer retention, recommendation and share of wallet', *Managing Service Quality*, 17 no. 4 (2007), pp. 361–84.

26 Adapted from: N. Clark (2010) 'The satisfaction manifesto: secret of good service', *Marketing*, 3 November, p. 29.

27 C. Grönroos, 'A service quality model and its marketing implications', *European Journal of Marketing* 18 (1984), pp. 36–44.

28 R. Rust and R. Oliver, 'Service quality: insights and managerial implications from the frontier', in *Service Quality: New Directions in Theory and Practice*, eds R.T. Rust and R.L. Oliver (Thousand Oaks, CA: Sage, 1994).

29 Ibid.

30 See C. Grönroos, 'A service quality model and its marketing implications', *European Journal of Marketing* 18, no. 4 (1984), pp. 36–44; R.T. Rust and R.L. Oliver, 'Service quality insights and managerial implications from the frontier', in *Service Quality: New Directions in Theory and Practice*, eds R.T. Rust and R.L. Oliver (Thousand Oaks, CA: Sage, 1994), pp. 1–19; M.J. Bitner, 'Managing the evidence of service', in *The Service Quality Handbook*, eds E.E. Scheuing and W.F. Christopher (New York: AMACOM, 1993), pp. 358–70.

31 Parasuraman, Zeithaml and Berry, 'SERVQUAL: a multiple-item scale'. Details on the SERVQUAL scale and the actual items used to assess the dimensions are provided in Chapter 6.

32 Ibid.

33 For a review of what is known about service quality delivery via the Web see, V.A. Zeithaml, A. Parasuraman and A. Malhotra, 'Service quality delivery through websites: a critical review of extant knowledge', *Journal of the Academy of Marketing Science*, 30, no. 4 (2002), pp. 362–75.

34 V. Zeithaml, A. Parasuraman and A. Malhotra, 'A conceptual framework for understanding e-service quality: implications for future research and managerial practice', Marketing Science Institute Working Paper, Report No. 00-115 (2001).

35 Holloway, B.B. and Beatty, S.E.(2008), Satisfiers and Dissatisfiers in the Online Environment: A Critical Incident Assessment, *Journal of Service Research*, 10(4), 347–364.

36 R. Normann, *Service Management: Strategy and Leadership in the Service Business*, 3rd edn (Chichester: John Wiley & Sons, 2000).

37 'How Marriott makes a great first impression', *The Service Edge* 6, no. 5 (May 1993), p. 5.

38 A.G. Woodside, L.L. Frey and R.T. Daly, 'Linking service quality, customer satisfaction, and behavioral intention', *Journal of Health Care Marketing* 9 (December 1989), pp. 5–17.

39 G.L. Shostack, 'Planning the service encounter', in *The Service Encounter*, eds J.A. Czepiel, M.R. Solomon and C.F. Surprenant (Lexington, MA: Lexington Books, 1985), pp. 243–54.

40 Ibid.

41 For detailed discussions of the critical incident technique, see J.C. Flanagan, 'The critical incident technique', *Psychological Bulletin* 51 (July 1954), pp. 327–58; M.J. Bitner, J.D. Nyquist and B.H. Booms, 'The critical incident as a technique for analyzing the service encounter', in *Services Marketing in a Changing Environment*, eds T.M. Bloch, G.D. Upah and V.A. Zeithaml (Chicago, IL: American Marketing Association, 1985), pp. 48–51; S. Wilson-Pessano, 'Defining professional competence: the critical incident technique 40 years later', paper presentation to the Annual Meeting of the American Educational Research Association, New Orleans (1988); I. Roos, 'Methods of investigating critical incidents', *Journal of Service Research* 4 (February 2002), pp. 193–204; D.D. Gremler, 'The critical incident technique in service research', *Journal of Service Research* 7 (August 2004), pp. 65–89.

42 For a complete discussion of the research on which this section is based, see M.J. Bitner, B.H. Booms and M.S. Tetreault, 'The service encounter: diagnosing favorable and unfavorable incidents', *Journal of Marketing* 54 (January 1990), pp. 71–84; M.J. Bitner, B.H. Booms and L.A. Mohr, 'Critical service encounters: the employee's view', *Journal of Marketing* 58, no. 4 (1994), pp. 95–106; D. Gremler and M.J. Bitner, 'Classifying service encounter satisfaction across industries', in *Marketing Theory and Applications*, eds C.T. Allen et al. (Chicago, IL: American Marketing Association, 1992), pp. 111–18; and D. Gremler, M.J. Bitner and K.R. Evans, 'The internal service encounter', *International Journal of Service Industry Management* 5, no. 2 (1994), pp. 34–56.

43 Bitner, Booms and Mohr, 'Critical service encounters'.

44 Bitner, 'Managing the evidence of service'.

Chapter 6

1 A. Wilson, *Marketing Research: An Integrated Approach*, 3rd edn (London: FT Prentice-Hall, 2011).

2 Wilson, *Marketing Research: An Integrated Approach*.

3 This section is based on a comprehensive assessment of the critical incident technique in D.D. Gremler, 'The critical incident technique in service research', *Journal of Service Research* 7 (August 2004), pp. 65–89.

4 Ibid.

5 F. Buttle, 'SERVQUAL: review, critique, research agenda', *European Journal of Marketing* 30, no.1 (1996), pp. 8–32.

6 C. Grönroos, *Service Management and Marketing*, 3rd edn (Chichester: John Wiley & Son, 2007).

7   J. Cronin and S. Taylor, 'Measuring service quality: a reexamination and extension', *Journal of Marketing* 56 (1992), pp. 55–68.

8   See http://www.slm-leisure.co.uk.

9   E. Day, 'Researchers must enter consumer's world', *Marketing News*, 17 August 1998, p. 17.

10   Adapted from A.M. Wilson, 'The use of mystery shopping in the measurement of service delivery', *The Service Industries Journal* 10, no. 9 (1998), pp. 148–63.

11   P.R. Magnusson, J. Mathing and P. Kristensson, 'Managing user involvement in service innovation: experiments with innovating end users', *Journal of Service Research* 6 (November 2003), pp. 111–24.

12   V.A. Zeithaml, A. Parasuraman and L.L. Berry, *Delivering Quality Service: Balancing Customer Perceptions and Expectations* (New York: Free Press, 1990), p. 28.

13   A. Parasuraman, V.A. Zeithaml and L.L. Berry, 'Moving forward in service quality research', Marketing Science Institute Report No. 94–114, (September 1994).

14   A. Wilson, *Marketing Research: An Integrated Approach*, 3rd edn (London: FT Prentice-Hall, 2011).

15   Ibid.

16   'Baldridge winner co-convenes quality summit', *Executive Report on Customer Satisfaction*, 30 October 1992.

17   M.J. Bitner, B. Booms and L. Mohr, 'Critical service encounters: the employee's viewpoint', *Journal of Marketing* 58 (October 1994), pp. 95–106.

18   Zeithaml, Parasuraman and Berry, *Delivering Quality Service*, p. 64.

19   'Empowerment is the strength of effective suggestion systems', *Total Quality Newsletter*, August 1991.

Chapter 7

1   L.L. Berry and A. Parasuraman, *Marketing Services* (New York: Free Press, 1991), ch. 8.

2   G. Knisely, 'Comparing marketing management in package goods and service organizations', a series of interviews appearing in *Advertising Age*, 15 January, 19 February, 19 March and 14 May 1979.

3   This discussion is based on M.D. Johnson and F. Selnes, 'Customer portfolio management: toward a dynamic theory of exchange relationships', *Journal of Marketing* 68 (April 2004), pp. 1–17.

4   R.M. Morgan and S.D. Hunt, 'The commitment-trust theory of relationship marketing', *Journal of Marketing* 58 (July 1994), pp. 20–38; N. Bendapudi and L.L. Berry, 'Customers' motivations for maintaining relationships with service providers', *Journal of Retailing* 73 (Spring 1997), pp. 15–37.

5   Johnson and Selnes, 'Customer portfolio management'.

6   Ibid.

7   See also D. Siredeshmukh, J. Singh and B. Sabol, 'Customer trust, value, and loyalty in relational exchanges', *Journal of Marketing* 66 (January 2002), pp. 15–37.

8   See C. Huffman and B. Kahn, 'Variety for sale: mass customization or mass confusion?' *Journal of Retailing* 74 (Winter 1998), pp. 491–513; B.J. Pine and J.H. Gilmore, 'Welcome to the experience economy', *Harvard Business Review* 76 (July–August 1998), pp. 97–105; B.J. Pine, D. Peppers and M. Rodgers, 'Do you want to keep your customers forever?', *Harvard Business Review* 73 (March–April 1995), pp. 103–14.

9   C. Gronroos, *Service Management and Marketing*, 3rd edn (Chichester: John Wiley & Sons, 2007).

10   The three types of relational benefits discussed in this section are drawn from K.P. Gwinner, D.D. Gremler and M.J. Bitner, 'Relational benefits in service industries: the customer's perspective', *Journal of the Academy of Marketing Science* 26 (Spring 1998), pp. 101–14.

11   See M.B. Adelman, A. Ahuvia and C. Goodwin, 'Beyond smiling: social support and service quality', in *Service Quality: New Directions in Theory and Practice*, eds R.T. Rust and R.L. Oliver (Thousand Oaks, CA: Sage Publications, 1994), pp. 139–72; and C. Goodwin, 'Private roles in public encounters: communal relationships in service exchanges', unpublished manuscript, University of Manitoba (1993).

12   E.J. Arnould and L.L. Price, 'River magic: extraordinary experience and the extended service encounter', *Journal of Consumer Research* 20 (June 1993), pp. 24–45.

13   N. Bendapudi and R.P. Leone, 'How to lose your star performer without losing customers, too', *Harvard Business Review* (November 2001), pp. 104–15.

14   Gwinner, Gremler and Bitner, 1998.

15   R. Dhar and R. Glazer, 'Hedging customers', *Harvard Business Review* 81 (May 2003), pp. 86–92.

16   D.D. Gremler and S.W. Brown, 'The loyalty ripple effect: appreciating the full value of customers', *International Journal of Service Industry Management* 10, no. 3 (1999), pp. 271–91.

17   L.A. Bettencourt, 'Customer voluntary performance: customers as partners in service delivery', *Journal of Retailing* 73 (Fall 1997), pp. 383–406.

18   S.J. Grove and R.P. Fisk, 'The impact of other customers on service experiences: a critical incident examination of "getting along"', *Journal of Retailing* 73 (Spring 1997), pp. 63–85.

19   L.L. Price, E.J. Arnould and A. Hausman, 'Commercial friendships: service provider–client relationship dynamics', in *Frontiers in Services*, eds R.T. Rust and R.L. Oliver (Nashville, TN: Vanderbilt University, 1996).

20   Source: F.F. Reichheld, 'Loyalty and the renaissance of marketing', Marketing Management, vol. 2, no. 4 (1994), 105–113.

21   Additional frameworks for calculating lifetime customer value that include a variety of other variables can be found in W.J. Reinartz and V. Kumar, 'The impact of customer relationship characteristics on profitable lifetime duration', *Journal of Marketing* 67 (January 2003), pp. 77–99; Dhar and Glazer, 'Hedging customers';

H.K. Stahl, K. Matzler and H.H. Hinterhuber, 'Linking customer lifetime value with shareholder value', *Industrial Marketing Management* 32, no. 4 (2003), pp. 267–79.

22 S. Gupta, D.R. Helmann and J.A. Stuart, 'Valuing customers', *Journal of Marketing Research* 41 (February 2004), pp. 7–18.

23 S. Vargo, 'Toward a transcending conceptualization of relationship', *Journal of Business & Industrial Marketing*, 24(5/6) (2009), pp. 373–379.

24 For more on customer profitability segments and related strategies, see V.A. Zeithaml, R.T. Rust and K.N. Lemon, 'The customer pyramid: creating and serving profitable customers', *California Management Review* 43 (Summer 2001), pp. 118–42.

25 D. Brady, 'Why service stinks', *BusinessWeek,* 23 October 2000, pp. 118–28.

26 Dhar and Glazer, 'Hedging customers'.

27 D. Rosenblum, D. Tomlinson and L. Scott, 'Bottomfeeding for blockbuster businesses', *Harvard Business Review* 81 (March 2003), pp. 52–9.

28 See P.C. Verhoef, K.N. Lemon, A. Parasuraman, A. Roggeveen, M. Tsiros and L.A. Schlesinger, 'Customer experience creation: Determinants, dynamics and management strategies', *Journal of Retailing* 85(1) (2009), pp. 31–41.

29 See T.A. Burnham, J.K. Frels and V. Mahajan, 'Consumer switching costs: a typology, antecedents, and consequences', *Journal of the Academy of Marketing Science* 32 (Spring 2003), pp. 109–26; F. Selnes, 'An examination of the effect of product performance on brand reputation, satisfaction, and loyalty', *European Journal of Marketing* 27, no. 9 (2003), pp. 19–35; P.Klemperer, 'The competitiveness of markets with switching costs', *Rand Journal of Economics* 18 (Spring1987), pp. 138–50.

30 T.L. Huston and R.L. Burgess, 'Social exchange in developing relationships: an overview', in *Social Exchange in Developing Relationships,* eds R.L.Burgess and T.L. Huston (New York: Academic Press, 1979), pp. 3–28; L. White and V. Yanamandram, 'Why customers stay: reasons and consequences of inertia in financial services', *Managing Service Quality* 14, nos 2/3 (2004), pp. 183–94.

31 See J.P. Guiltinan, 'A classification of switching costs with implications for relationship marketing', in *Marketing Theory and Practice,* eds Terry L. Childers et al. (Chicago, IL: American Marketing Association, 1989), pp. 216–20; Klemperer, P., 'The competitiveness of markets with switching costs', *The RAND Journal of Economics* 18, no. 1 (Spring 1987), pp. 138–50; C. Fornell, 'A national customer satisfaction barometer: the Swedish experience', *Journal of Marketing* 56 (January 1992), pp. 6–21; P.G. Patterson and T. Smith, 'A cross-cultural study of switching barriers and propensity to stay with service providers', *Journal of Retailing* 79 (Summer 2003), pp. 107–20.

32 See Bendapudi and Berry, 'Customers' motivations for maintaining relationships with service providers'; H.S. Bansal, P.G. Irving and S.F. Taylor, 'A three-component model of customer commitment to service providers', *Journal of the Academy of Marketing Science* 32 (Summer 2004), pp. 234–50.

33 Berry and Parasuraman, *Marketing Services,* pp. 136–42.

34 For more information on cautions to be considered in implementing rewards strategies, see L. O'Brien and C. Jones, 'Do rewards really create loyalty?', *Harvard Business Review* (May–June 1995), pp. 75–82; and G.R. Dowling and M. Uncles, 'Do customer loyalty programs really work?', *Sloan Management Review* (Summer 1997), pp. 71–82.

35 Kim, J.W., Choi, J.H., Qualls, W. and Han, K.S. (2008), 'It takes a marketplace community to raise brand commitment: The role of online communities', *Journal of Marketing Management,* Vol. 24 Nos. 3–4, pp. 409–31.

36 D.D. Gremler and S.W. Brown, 'Service loyalty: its nature, importance, and implications', in *Advancing Service Quality: A Global Perspective,* eds B. Edvardsson, S.W. Brown, R. Johnston and E.E. Scheuing (Jamaica, NY: International Service Quality Association, 1996), pp. 171–80; H. Hansen, K. Sandvik and F. Selnes, 'Direct and indirect effects of commitment to a service employee on the intention to stay', *Journal of Service Research* 5 (May 2003), pp. 356–68.

37 C.W. Hart, 'Made to order', *Marketing Management* 5 (Summer 1996), pp. 11–23.

38 R. Brooks, 'Alienating customers isn't always a bad idea', P. Carroll and S. Rose, 'Revisiting customer retention', *Journal of Retail Banking* 15, no. 1 (1993), pp. 5–13.

39 J. Dahl, 'Rental counters reject drivers without good records', *The Wall Street Journal,* 23 October 1992, P.B1.

40 See L.C. Harris and K.L. Reynolds, 'The consequences of dysfunctional customer behavior', *Journal of Service Research* 6 (November 2003), p. 145 for cites; also, see A.A. Grandey, D.N. Dickter and H.P. Sin, 'The customer is *not* always right: customer aggression and emotion regulation of service employees', *Journal of Organizational Behavior* 25 (2004), pp. 397–418.

41 K. Ohnezeit, recruiting supervisor for Enterprise Rent-A-Car, personal communication, 12 February 2004.

42 See Harris and Reynolds, 'The consequences of dysfunctional customer behavior'.

43 S.M. Noble and J. Phillips, 'Relationship hindrance: why would consumers not want a relationship with are tailer?', *Journal of Retailing,* 80, no. 4 (2004), pp. 289–303.

44 For a detailed discussion on relationship ending, see A. Halinen and J. Tähtinen, 'A process theory of relationship ending', *International Journal of Service Industry Management* 13, no. 2 (2002), pp. 163–80.

45 M. Schrage, 'Fire your customers', *The Wall Street Journal,* 16 March 1992, p. A8.

Chapter 8

1   D.H. Henard and D.M. Szymanski, 'Why some new products are more successful than others', *Journal of Marketing Research* (August 2001), pp. 362–75.

2   M.J. Bitner and S.W. Brown, 'The Service Imperative', *Business Horizons 50th Anniversary Issue,* 51 (January–February 2008), pp. 39–46.

3   Sources: M.J. Bitner and S.W. Brown, 'The Service Imperative', *Business Horizons* 50th *Anniversary Issue,* 51 (January–February 2008), pp. 39–46; 'Succeeding through Service Innovation', a white paper published by the University of Cambridge Institute for Manufacturing and IBM, October 2007; and Organisation for Economic Co-operation and Development, 'Promoting Innovation in Services', 2005.

4   Ostrom, A. L., Parasuraman, A., Bowen, D. E., Patrício, L., & Voss, C. A. (2015). Service research priorities in a rapidly changing context. *Journal of Service Research,* 18(2), 127–159.

5   European Commission, ESIC European Service Innovation Centre Discussion Paper, "Service Innovation Policy - A Benchmarking Review". January 2015.

6   G.L. Shostack, 'Understanding services through blueprinting', in *Advances in Services Marketing and Management,* vol. 1, eds T.A. Swartz, D.E. Bowen and S.W. Brown (Greenwich, CT: JAI Press, 1992), pp. 75–90, quote from p. 76.

7   For excellent reviews of research and issues in new services development see *Journal of Operations Management* 20 (2002), special issue on New Issues and Opportunities in Service Design Research; A. Johne and C. Story, 'New service development: a review of the literature and annotated bibliography', *European Journal of Marketing* 32, no. 3/4 (1998), pp. 184–251; B. Edvardsson, A. Gustafsson, M.D. Johnson and B. Sanden, *New Service Development and Innovation in the New Economy* (Lund: Studentlitteratur AB, 2000).

8   B. Schneider and D.E. Bowen, 'New services design, development and implementation and the employee', in *Developing New Services,* eds W.R. George and C. Marshall (Chicago, IL: American Marketing Association, 1984), pp. 82–101.

9   S. Michel, S.W. Brown and A.S. Gallan, 'An expanded and strategic view of discontinuous innovations: deploying a service dominant logic', *Journal of the Academy of Marketing Science* 36 (Winter 2008).

10   For a discussion of these adaptations and related research issues, see M.V. Tatikonda and V.A. Zeithaml, 'Managing the new service development process: synthesis of multidisciplinary literature and directions for future research', in *New Directions in Supply Chain Management: Technology, Strategy, and Implementation,* eds T. Boone and R. Ganeshan (New York: AMACOM, 2002), pp. 200–36; B. Edvardsson et al., *New Service Development and Innovation in the New Economy.*

11   A. Griffin, 'PDMA research on new product development practices: updating trends and benchmarking best practices', *Journal of Product Innovation Management* 14 (1997), pp. 429–58; S. Thomke, 'R&D comes to services: Bank of America's pathbreaking experiments', *Harvard Business Review,* 81 (April 2003), pp. 70–9.

12   R.G. Cooper, 'Stage gate systems for new product success', *Marketing Management* 1, no. 4 (1992), pp. 20–9.

13   M. Iansiti and A. MacCormack, 'Developing products on Internet time', *Harvard Business Review* (September–October 1997), pp. 108–17.

14   A. Khurana and S.R. Rosenthal, 'Integrating the fuzzy front end of new product development', *Sloan Management Review* (Winter 1997), pp. 103–20.

15   Iansiti and MacCormack, 'Developing products on Internet time'.

16   M.E. Porter, *Competitive Strategy* (New York: Free Press, 1980).

17   Khurana and Rosenthal, 'Integrating the fuzzy front end'; see also R.G. Cooper, S.J. Edgett and E.J. Kleinschmidt, *Portfolio Management for New Products* (Reading, MA: Addison-Wesley, 1998).

18   D. Rigby and C. Zook, 'Open-market innovation', *Harvard Business Review* (October 2002), pp. 80–9.

19   D. Leonard and J.F. Rayport, 'Spark innovation through empathic design', *Harvard Business Review* (November–December 1997), pp. 103–13.

20   J. Surowiecki, *The Wisdom of Crowds* (Doubleday Publishing, 2005).

21   R. Cross, A. Hargadon, S. Parise and R.J. Thomas, 'Together we innovate', *The Wall Street Journal,* September 15–16 (2007), p. R6.

22   Shostack, 'Service design'.

23   E.E. Scheuing and E.M. Johnson, 'A proposed model for new service development', *Journal of Services Marketing* 3, no. 2 (1989), pp. 25–34.

24   Shostack, 'Service design', p. 35.

25   Maxey, 'Testing, testing, testing'.

26   The service blueprinting section of the chapter draws from the pioneering works in this area: G.L. Shostack, 'Designing services that deliver', *Harvard Business Review* (January–February 1984), pp. 133–9; G.L. Shostack, 'Service positioning through structural change', *Journal of Marketing* 51 (January 1987), pp. 34–43; J. Kingman-Brundage, 'The ABCs of service system blueprinting', in *Designing a Winning Service Strategy,* eds M.J. Bitner and L.A. Crosby (Chicago, IL: American Marketing Association, 1989), pp. 30–3.

27   Shostack, 'Understanding services through blueprinting', pp. 75–90.

28   These key components are drawn from Kingman-Brundage, 'The ABCs'.

29   S. Flieb and M. Kleinaltenkamp, 'Blueprinting the service company: managing service processes efficiently', *Journal of Business Research* 57 (2004), pp. 392–404.

30 For coverage of the practical benefits of blueprinting, see, E. Gummesson and J. Kingman-Brundage, 'Service design and quality: applying service blueprinting and service mapping to railroad services', in *Quality Management in Services,* eds P. Kunst and J. Lemmink (Assen/Maastricht: Van Gorcum, 1991).

31 Shostack, 'Understanding services through blueprinting'.

32 D. Getz, M. O'Neill and J. Carlsen, 'Service quality evaluation at events through service mapping', *Journal of Travel Research* 39 (May 2001), pp. 380–90.

33 Cooper et al., *Portfolio Management for New Products.*

34 Froehle et al., 'Antecedents of new service development effectiveness'; Henard and Szymanski, 'Why some new products are more successful than others'; Edvardsson et al., *New Service Development and Innovation in the New Economy.*

35 Cooper et al., *Portfolio Management for New Products.*

36 See ibid. for an excellent discussion and coverage of multiple methods for managing product and service portfolios.

37 S.S. Tax and I. Stuart, 'Designing and implementing new services: the challenges of integrating service systems', *Journal of Retailing* 73 (Spring 1977), pp. 105–34.

38 R.G. Cooper, C.J. Easingwood, S. Edgett, E.J. Kleinschmidt and C. Storey, 'What distinguishes the top performing new products in financial services?', *Journal of Product Innovation Management* 11 (1994), pp. 281–99.

39 B. Edvardsson, L. Haqlund and J. Mattson, 'Analysis, planning, improvisation and control in the development of new services', *International Journal of Service Industry Management* 6, no. 2 (1995) pp. 24–35.

Chapter 9

1 T. Levitt, 'Industrialization of service', *Harvard Business Review* (September–October 1976), pp. 63–74.

2 B.S. Lunde and S.L. Marr, 'Customer satisfaction measurement: does it pay off?' (Indianapolis, IN: Walker Customer Satisfaction Measurements, 1990).

3 '2015 Customer Rage Study' conducted by Customer by Customer Care Measurement and Consulting in collaboration with the Center for Services Leadership at Arizona State University's W.P. Carey School of Business.

4 S. Banker, "A Leading Computer Manufacturer's Perfect Order Journey," *Forbes,* 3 February 2016 www.forbes.com/sites/stevebanker/2016/02/03/a-leading-computer-manufacturers-perfect-order-journey/print/.

5 D.E. Hansen and P.J. Danaher, 'Inconsistent performance during the service encounter: what's a good start worth?', *Journal of Service Research* 1 (February 1999), pp. 227–35.

6 'Taking the measure of quality', *Service Savvy* (March 1992), p. 3.

Chapter 10

1 The term *servicescape* used throughout this chapter, and much of the content of this chapter, are based, with permission, on M.J. Bitner, 'Servicescapes: the impact of physical surroundings on customers and employees', *Journal of Marketing* 56 (April 1992), pp. 57–71. For recent contributions to this topic, see *Servicescapes: The Concept of Place in Contemporary Markets,* ed. J.F. Sherry Jr (Chicago, IL: NTC/Contemporary Publishing, 1998); and M.J. Bitner, 'The servicescape', in *Handbook of Services Marketing and Management,* eds T.A. Swartz and D. Iacobucci (Thousand Oaks, CA: Sage Publications, 2000), pp. 37–50.

2 L.P. Carbone, *Clued In: How to Keep Customers Coming Back Again and Again* (Upper Saddle River, NJ: Prentice Hall, 2004). See also L.L. Berry and N. Bendapudi, 'Clueing in customers', *Harvard Business Review* (February 2003), pp. 100–6.

3 J.H. Gilmore and B.J. Pine II, 'The experience is the marketing', *Strategic Horizons* (2002), an e-Doc; B.J. Pine II and J.H. Gilmore, *The Experience Economy: Work Is Theater and Every Business Is a Stage* (Boston, MA: Harvard Business School Press, 1999); B.H. Schmitt, *Experiential Marketing* (New York: Free Press, 1999).

4 For reviews of environmental psychology, see D. Stokols and I. Altman, *Handbook of Environmental Psychology* (New York: John Wiley, 1987); S. Saegert and G.H. Winkel, 'Environmental psychology', *Annual Review of Psychology* 41 (1990), pp. 441–77; and E. Sundstrom, P.A. Bell, P.L. Busby and C. Asmus, 'Environmental psychology 1989–1994', *Annual Review of Psychology* 47 (1996), pp. 485–512.

5 See M.R. Solomon, 'Dressing for the part: the role of costume in the staging of the servicescape', in *Servicescapes: The Concept of Space in Contemporary Markets,* ed. J.F. Sherry Jr (Chicago, IL: NTC/Contemporary Publishing, 1998), pp. 81–108; and A. Rafaeli, 'Dress and behavior of customer contact employees: a framework for analysis', in *Advances in Services Marketing and Management,* vol. 2, eds T.A. Swartz, D.E. Bowen and S.W. Brown (Greenwich, CT: JAI Press, 1993), pp. 175–212.

6 See http://www.dezeen.com/20i4/07/18/christopher-jenner-eurostar-london-ticket-hall-redesign/.

7 D. Michaels, 'Business-class warfare: rival airlines scramble to beat BA's reclining bed seats', *The Wall Street Journal,* 16 March 2001, p. B1.

8 See www.citizenm.com.

9 For recent research documenting the effects of music on consumers, see J. Baker, D. Grewal and A. Parasuraman, 'The influence of store environment on quality inferences and store image', *Journal of the Academy of Marketing Science* 22 (Fall 1994), pp. 328–39; J.C. Chebat, C. Gelinas-Chebat and P. Filliatrault, 'Interactive effects of musical and visual cues on time perception:

an application to waiting lines in banks', *Perceptual and Motor Skills* 77 (1993), pp. 995–1020; L. Dube, J.C. Chebat and S. Morin, 'The effects of background music on consumers' desire to affiliate in buyer–seller interactions', *Psychology and Marketing* 12, no. 4 (1995), pp. 305–19; J.D. Herrington and L.M. Capella, 'Effects of music in service environments: a field study', *Journal of Services Marketing* 10, no. 2 (1996), pp. 26–41; J.D. Herrington and L.M. Capella, 'Practical applications of music in service settings', *Journal of Services Marketing* 8, no. 3 (1994), pp. 50–65; M.K. Hui, L. Dube and J.C. Chebat, 'The impact of music on consumers' reactions to waiting for services', *Journal of Retailing* 73 (Spring 1997), pp. 87–104; A.S. Mattila and J. Wirtz, 'Congruency of scent and music as a driver of in-store evaluations and behavior', *Journal of Retailing* 77 (Summer 2001), pp. 273–89; L. Dube and S. Morin, 'Background music pleasure and store evaluation: intensity effects and psychological mechanisms', *Journal of Business Research* 54 (November 2001), pp. 107–13; J. Bakec, A. Parasuraman, D. Grewal and G.B. Voss, 'The influence of multiple store environment cues as perceived merchandise value and patronage intentions', *Journal of Marketing* 66 (April 2002), pp. 120–41.

10 For recent research documenting the effects of scent on consumer responses, see D.J. Mitchell, B.E. Kahn and S.C. Knasko, 'There's something in the air: effects of congruent and incongruent ambient odor on consumer decision making', *Journal of Consumer Research* 22 (September 1995), pp. 229–38; and E.R. Spangenberg, A.E. Crowley and P.W. Henderson, 'Improving the store environment: do olfactory cues affect evaluations and behaviors?' *Journal of Marketing* 60 (April 1996), pp. 67–80.

11 See www.singaporeair.com.

12 See J.M. Sulek, M.R. Lind and A.S. Marucheck, 'The impact of a customer service intervention and facility design on firm performance', *Management Science* 41, no. 11 (1995), pp. 1763–73; P.A. Titus and P.B. Everett, 'Consumer wayfinding tasks, strategies, and errors: an exploratory field study', *Psychology and Marketing* 13, no. 3 (1996), pp. 265–90; C. Yoo, J. Park and D.J. MacInnis, 'Effects of store characteristics and instore emotional experiences on store attitude', *Journal of Business Research* 42 (1998), pp. 253–63; K.L. Wakefield and J.G. Blodgett, 'The effect of the servicescape on customers' behavioral intentions in leisure service settings', *Journal of Services Marketing* 10, no. 6 (1996), pp. 45–61.

13 T.R.V. Davis, 'The influence of the physical environment in offices', *Academy of Management Review* 9, no. 2 (1984), pp. 271–83.

14 J.C. Ward and J.P. Eaton, 'Service environments: the effect of quality and decorative style on emotions, expectations, and attributions', in *Proceedings of the American Marketing Association Summer Educators'*
Conference, eds. R. Achrol and A. Mitchell (Chicago, IL: American Marketing Association 1994), pp. 333–4.

15 A. Rapoport, *The Meaning of the Built Environment* (Beverly Hills, CA: Sage Publications, 1982); R.G. Golledge, 'Environmental cognition', in *Handbook of Environmental Psychology,* vol. 1, eds D. Stokols and I. Altman (New York: John Wiley, 1987), pp. 131–74.

16 M.P. Gardner and G. Siomkos, 'Toward a methodology for assessing effects of in-store atmospherics', in *Advances in Consumer Research,* vol. 13, ed. R.J. Lutz (Ann Arbor, MI: Association for Consumer Research, 1986), pp. 27–31.

17 M.J. Bitner, 'Evaluating service encounters: the effects of physical surroundings and employee responses', *Journal of Marketing* 54 (April 1990), pp. 69–82.

18 J.C. Ward, M.J. Bitner and J. Barnes, 'Measuring the prototypicality and meaning of retail environments', *Journal of Retailing* 68 (Summer 1992) pp. 194–220.

19 Adapted from J.F. Sherry Jr, 'The soul of the company store: Nike Town Chicago and the emplaced brandscape', in *Servicescapes: The Concept of Place in Contemporary Markets,* ed. J.F. Sherry Jr (Chicago: NTC/Contemporary Publishing Company, 1998), pp. 109–46. Copyright © 1998 by NTC Business Books. Reprinted by permission of NTC Contemporary Books. The initial quotation is from 'Nike Town Comes to Chicago,' Nike press release, 2 July 1992, as quoted in ibid., p. 109.

20 See, for example, Mehrabian and Russell, *An Approach to Environmental Psychology;* J.A. Russell and U.F. Lanius, 'Adaptation level and the affective appraisal of environments', *Journal of Environmental Psychology* 4, no. 2 (1984), pp. 199–235; J.A. Russell and G. Pratt, 'A description of the affective quality attributed to environments', *Journal of Personality and Social Psychology* 38, no. 2 (1980), pp. 311–22; J.A. Russell and J. Snodgrass, 'Emotion and the environment', in *Handbook of Environmental Psychology,* vol. 1, eds D. Stokols and I. Altman (New York: John Wiley, 1987), pp. 245–81; J.A. Russell, L.M. Ward and G. Pratt, 'Affective quality attributed to environments', *Environment and Behavior* 13 (May 1981), pp. 259–88.

21 See, for example, M.S. Sanders and E.J. McCormick, *Human Factors in Engineering and Design,* 7th edn (New York: McGraw-Hill, 1993); and D.J. Osborne, *Ergonomics at Work,* 2nd edn (New York: John Wiley, 1987).

22 Mehrabian and Russell, *An Approach to Environmental Psychology;* Russell and Snodgrass, 'Emotion and the environment'.

23 A. Mehrabian, 'Individual differences in stimulus screening and arousability', *Journal of Personality* 45, no. 2 (1977), pp. 237–50.

24 Carbone, *Clued In;* Berry and Bendapudi, 'Clueing in customers'; Gilmore and Pine, 'Experience is the marketing'; Pine and Gilmore, *The Experience Economy;* Schmitt, *Experiential Marketing.*

25 A. Mehrabian and J.A. Russell, *An Approach to Environmental Psychology* (Cambridge, MA: Massachusetts Institute of Technology, 1974).

26 R. Donovan and J. Rossiter, 'Store atmosphere: an environmental psychology approach', *Journal of Retailing* 58 (Spring 1982), pp. 34–57.

27 D.J. Bennett and J.D. Bennett, 'Making the scene', in *Social Psychology through Symbolic Interactionism*, eds G. Stone and H. Farberman (Waltham, MA: Ginn-Blaisdell, 1970), pp. 190–6.

28 J.P. Forgas, *Social Episodes* (London: Academic Press, 1979).

29 R.G. Barker, *Ecological Psychology* (Stanford, CA: Stanford University Press, 1968).

30 For a number of excellent papers on this topic spanning a range from toy stores to bridal salons to cybermarketspaces to Japanese retail environments and others, see J.F. Sherry Jr, ed., *Servicescapes: The Concept of Place in Contemporary Markets*.

31 Sherry, 'The soul of the company store: Nike Town Chicago and the emplaced brandscape', in *Servicescapes: The Concept of Place in Contemporary Markets*, ed. J.F. Sherry Jr (Chicago, IL: NTC/Contemporary Publishing, 1998), pp. 109–46.

32 E.J. Arnould, L.L. Price and P. Tierney, 'The wilderness servicescape: an ironic commercial landscape', in *Servicescapes: The Concept of Place in Contemporary Markets*, ed. J.F. Sherry Jr (Chicago, IL: NTC/Contemporary Publishing, 1998), pp. 403–38.

33 This section is adapted from M.J. Bitner, 'Managing the evidence of service', in *The Service Quality Handbook*, eds E.E. Scheuing and W.F. Christopher (New York: AMACOM, 1993), pp. 358–70.

34 F.D. Becker, *Workspace* (New York: Praeger, 1981).

Chapter 11

1 S.M. Davis, *Managing Corporate Culture* (Cambridge, MA: Ballinger, 1985).

2 C. Grönroos, *Service Management and Marketing* (Lexington, MA: Lexington Books, 1990), p. 244.

3 See K.N. Kennedy, F.G. Lassk and J.R. Goolsby, 'Customer mind-set of employees throughout the organization', *Journal of the Academy of Marketing Science*, 30 (Spring 2002), pp. 159–71.

4 R. Hallowell, D. Bowen and C. Knoop, 'Four Seasons goes to Paris', *Academy of Management Executive* 16, no. 4 (2002), pp. 7–24; J.L. Heskett, L.A. Schlesinger and E.W. Sasser Jr, *The Service Profit Chain* (New York: Free Press, 1997); B. Schneider and D.E. Bowen, *Winning the Service Game* (Boston, MA: Harvard Business School Press, 1995).

5 Berry, *Discovering the Soul of Service*, p. 40.

6 Hallowell, Bowen and Knoop, 'Four Seasons goes to Paris'.

7 For an excellent discussion of the complexities involved in creating and sustaining a service culture, see Schneider and Bowen, *Winning the Service Game*, ch. 9. See also M.D. Hartline, J.G. Maxham III and D.O. McKee, 'Corridors of influence in the dissemination of customer-oriented strategy to customer-contact service employees', *Journal of Marketing* 64 (April 2000), pp. 35–50.

8 Adapted from: R. Preston, 'Smiley Culture: Pret A Manger's Secret Ingredients', *The Telegraph* 9 March, 2012

9 This quote is most frequently attributed to J. Carlzon of Scandinavian Airline Systems.

10 See, for example, H. Rosenbluth, 'Tales from a nonconformist company', *Harvard Business Review* (July–August 1991), pp. 26–36; and L.A. Schlesinger and J.L. Heskett, 'The service-driven service company', *Harvard Business Review* (September–October 1991), pp. 71–81.

11 B. Schneider and D.E. Bowen, 'The service organization: human resources management is crucial', *Organizational Dynamics* 21, (Spring 1993), pp. 39–52.

12 D.E. Bowen, S.W. Gilliland and R. Folger, 'How being fair with employees spills over to customers', *Organizational Dynamics* 27 (Winter 1999), pp. 7–23.

13 See J.L. Heskett, T.O. Jones, G.W. Loveman, W.E. Sasser Jr and L.A. Schlesinger, 'Putting the service–profit chain to work', *Harvard Business Review* (March–April 1994), pp. 164–74; G.W. Loveman, 'Employee satisfaction, customer loyalty, and financial performance', *Journal of Service Research* 1 (August 1998), pp. 18–31; A. Rucci, S.P. Kirn and R.T. Quinn, 'The employee–customer profit chain at Sears', *Harvard Business Review* (January–February 1998), pp. 82–97; and R. Hallowell and L.L. Schlesinger, 'The service–profit chain', in *The Handbook of Services Marketing and Management*, eds T.A. Swartz and D. Iacobucci (Thousand Oaks, CA: Sage Publications, 2000), pp. 203–22.

14 J. Pfeffer, *The Human Equation* (Boston, MA: Harvard Business School Press, 1998); and A.M. Webber, 'Danger: toxic company', *Fast Company* (November 1998), pp.152–62.

15 M.K. Brady and J.J. Cronin Jr, 'Customer orientation: effects on customer service perceptions and outcome behaviors', *Journal of Service Research* 3 (February 2001), pp. 241–51.

16 L.A. Bettencourt and K. Gwinner, 'Customization of the service experience: the role of the frontline employee', *International Journal of Service Industry Management* 7, no. 2 (1996), pp. 3–20.

17 For research on the influence of front-line employee behaviours on customers, see D.D. Gremler and K.P. Gwinner, 'Customer–employee rapport in service relationships', *Journal of Service Research* 3 (August 2000), pp. 82–104; K. de Ruyter and M.G.M. Wetzels, 'The impact of perceived listening behavior in

voice-to-voice service encounters', *Journal of Service Research* 2 (February 2000), pp. 276–84; T.J. Brown, J.C. Mowen, D.T. Donavan and J.W. Licata, 'The customer orientation of service workers: personality trait effects of self- and supervisor performance ratings', *Journal of Marketing Research* 39 (February 2002), pp. 110–19.

18   A. Hochschild, *The Managed Heart: Commercialization of Human Feeling* (Berkeley, CA: University of California Press, 1983).

19   T. Hennig-Thurau, M. Goth, M. Paul and D.D. Gremler, 'Are all smiles created equal? How employee–customer emotional contagion and emotional labor impact service relationships', *Journal of Marketing* 70 (July 2006), pp. 58–73.

20   A. Hochschild, 'Emotional labor in the friendly skies', *Psychology Today* (June 1982), pp. 13–15.

21   For additional discussion on emotional labour strategies, see R. Leidner, 'Emotional labor in service work', *Annals of the American Academy of Political and Social Science* 561, no. 1 (1999), pp. 81–95.

22   Quoted from C.L. Macdonald and C. Sirianni, *Working in the Service Society* (Philadelphia: Temple University Press, 1996), p. 4.

23   Quoted from B.F. Ashforth and R.H. Humphrey, 'Emotional labor in service roles: the influence of identity', *Academy of Management Review* 18 (1993), p. 93.

24   B. Shamir, 'Between service and servility: role conflict in subordinate service roles', *Human Relations* 33(10) (1980), pp. 741–56.

25   M.D. Hartline and O.C. Ferrell, 'The management of customer-contact service employees: an empirical investigation', *Journal of Marketing* 60 (October 1996), pp. 52–70; J. Singh, J.R. Goolsby and G.K. Rhoads, 'Burnout and customer service representatives', *Journal of Marketing Research* 31 (November 1994), pp. 558–69; L.A. Bettencourt and S.W. Brown, 'Role stressors and customer-oriented boundary-spanning behaviors in service organizations', *Journal of the Academy of Marketing Science* 31 (Fall 2003), pp. 394–408.

26   B. Shamir, 'Between service and servility: role conflict in subordinate service roles', *Human Relations* 33, no. 10 (1980), pp. 741–56.

27   E.W. Anderson, C. Fornell and R.T. Rust, 'Customer satisfaction, productivity, and profitability: differences between goods and services', *Marketing Science* 16, no. 2 (1997), pp. 129–45.

28   For discussions of internal marketing, see L.L. Berry and A. Parasuraman, 'Marketing to employees', in *Marketing Services*, L.L. Berry and A. Parasuraman (New York: Free Press, 1991), ch. 9; C. Grönroos, 'Managing internal marketing: a prerequisite for successful external marketing', in *Service Management and Marketing*, C. Grönroos (Lexington, MA: Lexington Books, 1990), ch. 10.

29   Berry and Parasuraman, 'Marketing to employees', p. 153.

30   This section on hiring for service competencies and service inclination draws from work by B. Schneider and colleagues, specifically, B. Schneider and D. Schechter, 'Development of a personnel selection system for service jobs', in *Service Quality: Multidisciplinary and Multinational Perspectives*, eds S.W. Brown, E. Gummesson, B. Edvardsson and B. Gustavsson (Lexington, MA: Lexington Books, 1991), pp. 217–36.

31   J. Hogan, R. Hogan and C.M. Busch, 'How to measure service orientation', *Journal of Applied Psychology* 69, no. 1 (1984), pp. 167–73. See also Brown et al., 'The customer orientation of service workers'; and D.T. Donovan, T.J. Brown and J.C. Mowen, 'Internal benefits of serviceworker customer orientation: job satisfaction, commitment, and organizational citizenship behaviors', *Journal of Marketing* 68 (January 2004), pp. 128–46.

32   For a detailed description of a model selection system for telephone sales and service people, see Schneider and Schechter, 'Development of a personnel selection system'.

33   R. Normann, 'Getting people to grow', *Service Management* (New York: John Wiley, 1984), pp. 44–50.

34   J.C. Chebat and P. Kollias, 'The impact of empowerment on customer contact employees' roles in service organizations', *Journal of Service Research* 3 (August 2000), pp. 66–81.

35   C. Argyris, 'Empowerment: the emperor's new clothes', *Harvard Business Review* 76 (May–June 1998), pp. 98–105.

36   D.E. Bowen and E.E. Lawler III, 'The empowerment of service workers: what, why, how, and when', *Sloan Management Review* (Spring 1992), pp. 31–9.

37   Reprinted from 'The empowerment of service workers: what, why, how, and when', by D.E. Bowen and E.E. Lawler, *Sloan Management Review* (Spring 1992), pp. 31–9, by permission of the publisher. Copyright © 1992 by Massachusetts Institute of Technology. All rights reserved.

38   J.H. Gittell, 'Relationships between service providers and their impact on customers', *Journal of Service Research* 4 (May 2002), pp. 299–311.

39   Berry and Parasuraman, 'Marketing to employees', p. 162.

40   A. Sergeant and S. Frenkel, 'When do customer-contact employees satisfy customers?', *Journal of Service Research* 3 (August 2000), pp. 18–34.

41   Reprinted from K. Albrecht, *At America's Service* (Homewood, IL: Dow-Jones-Irwin, 1988), pp. 139–42, as discussed in B. Schneider and D.E. Bowen, *Winning at the Service Game* (Boston, MA: Harvard Business School Press, 1995), pp. 231–2. Copyright © 1988 by Dow-Jones-Irwin. Reprinted by permission of The McGraw-Hill Companies.

42   O. Gadiesh and J.L. Gilbert, 'Transforming corneroffice strategy into frontline action', *Harvard Business Review* (May 2001), pp. 73–9.

43 L.L. Berry, 'The employee as customer', *Journal of Retail Banking* 3 (March 1981), pp. 33–40.

44 M.C. Gilly and M. Wolfinbarger, 'Advertising's internal audience', *Journal of Marketing* 62 (January 1998), pp. 69–88.

45 See Schneider and Bowen, *Winning the Service Game*, ch. 6, for an excellent discussion of the complexities and issues involved in creating effective reward systems for service employees.

46 N. Bendapudi and R.P. Leone, 'Managing business-to-business customer relationships following key contact employee turnover in a vendor firm', *Journal of Marketing* 66 (April 2002), pp. 83–101.

47 Ibid.

48 J.R. Katzenbach and J.A. Santamaria, 'Firing up the front line', *Harvard Business Review* (May–June 1999), pp.107–17.

49 Quoted in D. Stauffer, 'The art of delivering great customer service', *Harvard Management Update* 4, no. 9 (September 1999), pp. 1–3.

Chapter 12

1 See B. Schneider and D.E. Bowen, *Winning the Service Game* (Boston, MA: Harvard Business School Press, 1995), ch. 4; L.A. Bettencourt, 'Customer voluntary performance: customers as partners in service delivery', *Journal of Retailing* 73, no. 3 (1997), pp. 383–406; P.K. Mills and J.H. Morris, 'Clients as "partial" employees: role development in client participation', *Academy of Management Review* 11, no. 4 (1986), pp. 726–35; C.H. Lovelock and R.F. Young, 'Look to customers to increase productivity', *Harvard Business Review* (Summer 1979), pp. 9–20; A.R. Rodie and S.S. Kleine, 'Customer participation in services production and delivery', in *Handbook of Services Marketing and Management*, eds T.A. Swartz and D. Iacobucci (Thousand Oaks, CA: Sage Publications, 2000), pp. 111–26; C.K. Prahalad and V. Ramaswamy, 'Co-opting customer competence', *Harvard Business Review* (January–February 2000), p. 7; N. Bendapudi and R.P. Leone, 'Psychological implications of customer participation in co-production', *Journal of Marketing* 67 (January 2003), pp. 14–28.

2 S.L. Vargo and R.F. Lusch, 'Evolving to a new dominant logic for marketing' *Journal of Marketing* 68 (January 2004), pp.1–17; and R.F. Lusch, S.L. Vargo and M.O. O'Brien, 'Competing through service: insights from service-dominant logic', *Journal of Retailing* 83, no. 1 (2007), pp. 5–18.

3 S.J. Grove, R.P. Fisk and M.J. Bitner, 'Dramatizing the service experience: a managerial approach', in *Advances in Services Marketing and Management*, vol. 1, eds T.A. Swartz, D.E. Bowen and S.W. Brown (Greenwich, CT: JAI Press, 1992), pp. 91–122.

4 For an interesting view of work and business as theatre, see B.J. Pine II and J.H. Gilmore, *The Experience Economy: Work Is Theatre and Every Business a Stage* (Boston, MA: Harvard Business School Press, 1999).

5 See S.J. Grove and R.P. Fisk, 'The impact of other customers on service experiences: a critical incident examination of "Getting Along"', *Journal of Retailing* 73, no. 1 (1997), pp. 63–85; C.I. Martin and C.A. Pranter, 'Compatibility management: customer-to-customer relationships in service environments', *Journal of Services Marketing* 3 (Summer 1989), pp. 5–15.

6 Grove and Fisk, 'The impact of other customers on service experiences'.

7 Ibid.

8 K. Harris and S. Baron, 'Consumer-to-consumer conversations in service settings', *Journal of Service Research* 6 (February 2004), pp. 287–303.

9 See P.K. Mills, R.B. Chase and N. Margulies, 'Motivating the client/employee system as a service production strategy', *Academy of Management Review* 8, no. 2 (1983), pp. 301–10; D.E. Bowen, 'Managing customers as human resources in service organizations', *Human Resource Management* 25, no. 3 (1986), pp. 371–83; and Mills and Morris, 'Clients as "partial" employees'.

10 L.A. Bettencourt, A.L. Ostrom, S.W. Brown and R.I. Rowntree, 'Client co-production in knowledge-intensive business services', *California Management Review*, 44, no. 4 (2002), pp. 100–28.

11 R.B. Chase, 'Where does the customer fit in a service operation?', *Harvard Business Review* (November–December 1978), pp. 137–42.

12 Mills et al., 'Motivating the client/employee system'.

13 M. Adams, 'Tech takes bigger role in air services', *USA Today*, 18 July 2001, p. 1.

14 See D.W. Johnson, R.T. Johnson and K.A. Smith, *Active Learning: Cooperation in the College Classroom* (Edina, MN: Interaction Book Company, 1991).

15 S. Dellande, M.C. Gilly and J.L. Graham, 'Gaining compliance and losing weight: the role of the service provider in health care services', *Journal of Marketing* 68 (July 2004), pp. 78–91.

16 S. Auh, S.J. Bell, C.S. Mcleod and E. Shih, 'Co-production and customer loyalty in financial services', *Journal of Retailing* 83, no. 3 (2007), pp. 359–70.

17 S.W. Kelley, S.J. Skinner and J.H. Donnelly Jr, 'Organizational socialization of service customers', *Journal of Business Research* 25 (1992), pp. 197–214.

18 C. Claycomb, C.A. Lengnick-Hall and L.W. Inks, 'The customer as a productive resource: a pilot study and strategic implications', *Journal of Business Strategies* 18 (Spring 2001), pp. 47–69.

19 J.E.G. Bateson, 'The self-service customer – empirical findings', in *Emerging Perspectives in Services Marketing*, eds L.L. Berry, G.L. Shostack and G.D. Upah (Chicago, IL: American Marketing Association, 1983), pp. 50–3.

20 V.S. Folkes, 'Recent attribution research in consumer behavior: a review and new directions', *Journal of Consumer Research* 14 (March 1988), pp. 548–65; and M.J. Bitner, 'Evaluating service encounters: the effects of physical surroundings and employee responses', *Journal of Marketing* 54 (April 1990), pp. 69–82.

21 Bendapudi and Leone, 'Psychological implications of customer participation in co-production'.

22 R.F. Lusch, S.W. Brown and G.J. Brunswick, 'A general framework for explaining internal vs. external exchange', *Journal of the Academy of Marketing Science* 10 (Spring 1992), pp. 119–34.

23 Ibid.

24 See M.J. Bitner, A.L. Ostrom and M.L. Meuter, 'Implementing successful self-service technologies', *Academy of Management Executive* 16 (November 2002), pp. 96–109.

25 See P. Dabholkar, 'Consumer evaluations of new technology-based self-service options: an investigation of alternative models of service quality', *International Journal of Research in Marketing* 13 (1), pp. 29–51; F. Davis, 'User acceptance of information technology: system characteristics, user perceptions and behavioral impact', *International Journal of Man–Machine Studies* 38 (1993), pp. 475–87; L.M. Bobbitt and P.A. Dabholkar, 'Integrating attitudinal theories to understand and predict use of technology-based self-service', *International Journal of Service Industry Management* 12, no. 5 (2001), pp. 423–50; J.M. Curran, M.L. Meuter and C.F. Surprenant, 'Intentions to use self-service technologies: a confluence of multiple attitudes', *Journal of Service Research* 5, no. 3 (2003), pp. 209–24.

26 M.L. Meuter, M.J. Bitner, A.L. Ostrom and S.W. Brown, 'Choosing among alternative service delivery modes: an investigation of customer trial of self-service technologies', *Journal of Marketing*, 69 (2005), pp. 61–83.

27 M.L. Meuter, A.L. Ostrom, R.I. Roundtree and M.J. Bitner, 'Self-service technologies: understanding customer satisfaction with technology-based service encounters', *Journal of Marketing* 64 (July 2000), pp. 50–64.

28 Meuter et al., 'Choosing among alternative service delivery modes'; see also Y. Moon and F.X. Frei, 'Exploding the self-service myth', *Harvard Business Review*, 78 (May–June 2000), pp. 26–7; Bitner et al., 'Implementing successful self-service technologies'.

29 A. Parasuraman and C.L. Colby, *Techno-Ready Marketing: How and Why Your Customers Adopt Technology* (New York: Free Press, 2001).

30 Bowen, 'Managing customers as human resources'.

31 Chase, 'Where does the customer fit in a service operation?'

32 See Schneider and Bowen, *Winning the Service Game*, ch. 4. The four job descriptions in this section are adapted from M.R. Bowers, C.L. Martin and A. Luker, 'Trading places, employees as customers, customers as employees', *Journal of Services Marketing* 4 (Spring 1990), pp. 56–69.

33 Bateson, 'The self-service customer'.

34 Meuter et al., 'Choosing among alternative service delivery modes'.

35 Reinders, M. J., Dabholkar, P. A., & Frambach, R. T. (2008). Consequences of forcing consumers to use technology-based self-service. *Journal of Service Research* 11(2), 107–123.

36 Bowen, 'Managing customers as human resources'; and Schneider and Bowen, *Winning the Service Game*, ch. 4; Meuter et al., 'Choosing among alternative service delivery modes'; Dellande et al., 'Gaining compliance and losing weight'.

37 C. Goodwin and R. Radford, 'Models of service delivery: an integrative perspective', in *Advances in Services Marketing and Management*, vol. 1, eds T.A. Swartz, D.E. Bowen and S.W. Brown (Greenwich, CT: JAI Press, 1992), pp. 231–52.

38 S.W. Kelley, J.H. Donnelly Jr and S.J. Skinner, 'Customer participation in service production and delivery', *Journal of Retailing* 66 (Fall 1990), pp. 315–35; and Schneider and Bowen, *Winning the Service Game*, ch. 4.

39 Bowen, 'Managing customers as human resources'.

40 Ibid.; see also L.C. Harris and K.L. Reynolds, 'The consequences of dysfunctional customer behavior', *Journal of Service Research* 6 (November 2003), pp. 144–61.

41 Martin and Pranter, 'Compatibility management'.

Chapter 13

1 R. Woodall, C. Colby and A. Parasuraman, 'E-volution to revolution', *Marketing Management*, March/April 2007, pp. 27–38.

2 G. Hamel and J. Sampler, 'The e-corporation', *Fortune*, 7 December 1998, pp. 80–92.

3 D. Clark, 'Safety first', *Wall Street Journal*, 7 December 1998, P. R14.

4 Ibid.

5 See www.hsbc.com.

6 Nat West/British Franchise Association Survey (2018) 2018 Franchise landscape https://www.business.natwest.com/content/dam/natwest_com/Business_and_Content/PDFs/NatWest-Franchise-Report-2018.pdf

7 See www.thebodyshop.com.

8 See www.dominos.co.uk.

9 See www.prontaprint.com.

10 See www.toniandguy.co.uk.

11 See www.visionexpress.com.

12 A.E. Serwer, 'Trouble in franchise nation', *Fortune*, 6 March 1995, pp. 115–29.

13 2013 Nat West/British Franchise Association Survey.

14 R.S. Toh, P. Raven and F. DeKay, 'Selling rooms: Hotels vs. third-party websites', *Cornell Hospitality Quarterly* 52.2 (2011): 181–189.

15 See www.fridays.com.

Chapter 14

1 C. Lovelock, 'Getting the most out of your productive capacity', in *Product Plus* (Boston, MA: McGraw-Hill, 1994), ch. 16.

2 Portions of this section are based on C.H. Lovelock, 'Strategies for managing capacity-constrained service organizations', in *Managing Services: Marketing, Operations, and Human Resources*, 2nd edn (Englewood Cliffs, NJ: Prentice Hall, 1992), pp. 154–68.

3 Lovelock, 'Getting the most out of your productive capacity'.

4 M.E. Berge and C.A. Hopperstad, 'Demand driven dispatch: a method for dynamic aircraft capacity assignment, models, and algorithms', *Operations Research* 41 (January–February 1993), pp. 153–68.

5 Lovelock, 'Getting the most out of your productive capacity'.

6 I.C.L. Ng, 'The future of pricing and revenue models' *Journal of Revenue and Pricing Management*, 9(3) (2010): 525–548.

7 S.E. Kimes, 'Yield management: a tool for capacity-constrained service firms', *Journal of Operations Management* 8 (October 1989), pp. 348–63.

8 R. Desiraji and S.M. Shugan, 'Strategic service pricing and yield management', *Journal of Marketing* 63 (January 1999), pp. 44–56; and Fitzsimmons and Fitzsimmons, *Service Management*, ch.13, p. 403.

9 Kimes, 'Yield management'.

10 S.E. Kimes and J. Wirtz, 'Has revenue management become acceptable? Findings from an international study on the perceived fairness of rate fences', *Journal of Service Research* 6 (November 2003), pp. 125–35.

11 F.V. Wangenheim and T. Bayon, 'Behavioral consequences of overbooking service capacity', *Journal of Marketing* 71 (October 2007), pp. 36–47.

12 For research supporting the relationship between longer waits and decreased satisfaction, quality evaluations and patronage intentions see Clemmer and Schneider, 'Toward understanding and controlling customer dissatisfaction'; A.T.H. Pruyn and A. Smidts, 'Customer evaluation of queues: three exploratory studies', *European Advances in Consumer Research* 1 (1993), pp. 371–82; S. Taylor, 'Waiting for service: the relationship between delays and evaluations of service', *Journal of Marketing* 58 (April 1994), pp. 56–69; K.L. Katz, B.M. Larson and R.C. Larson, 'Prescription for the waiting-in-line blues: entertain, enlighten, and engage', *Sloan Management Review* (Winter 1991), pp. 44–53; S. Taylor

and J.D. Claxton, 'Delays and the dynamics of service evaluations', *Journal of the Academy of Marketing Science* 22 (Summer 1994), pp. 254–64; D. Grewal, J. Baker, M. Levy and G.B. Voss, 'The effects of wait expectations and store atmosphere on patronage intentions in service-intensive retail stores', *Journal of Retailing* 79 (Winter 2003), pp. 259–68.

13 F. Bielen and N. Demoulin, 'Waiting time influence on the satisfaction-loyalty relationship in services', *Managing Service Quality* 17, no. 2 (2007), pp. 174–93.

14 J.A. Fitzsimmons and M.J. Fitzsimmons, *Service Management*, 3rd edn (New York: Irwin/McGraw-Hill, 2000), ch. 11.

15 R. Zhou and D. Soman, 'Looking back: exploring the psychology of queuing and the effect of the number of people behind', *Journal of Consumer Research* 29 (March 2003), pp. 517–30.

16 Fitzsimmons and Fitzsimmons, *Service Management*, ch. 11.

17 Lovelock, 'Getting the most out of your productive capacity'.

18 For an excellent review of the literature on customer perceptions of and reactions to various aspects of waiting time, see S. Taylor and G. Fullerton, 'Waiting for services: perceptions management of the wait experience', in *Handbook of Services Marketing and Management*, eds T.A. Swartz and D. Iacobucci (Thousand Oaks, CA: Sage Publications, 2000), pp. 171–89.

19 D.A. Maister, 'The psychology of waiting lines', in *The Service Encounter*, eds J.A. Czepiel, M.R. Solomon and C.F. Surprenant (Lexington, MA: Lexington Books, 1985), pp. 113–23.

20 S. Taylor, 'The effects of filled waiting time and service provider control over the delay on evaluations of service', *Journal of the Academy of Marketing Science* 23 (Summer 1995), pp. 38–48.

21 A. Bennett, 'Their business is on the line', *The Wall Street Journal*, 7 December 1990, p. B1.

22 L. Dube-Rioux, B.H. Schmitt and F. Leclerc, 'Consumer's reactions to waiting: when delays affect the perception of service quality', in *Advances in Consumer Research*, vol. 16, ed. T. Srull (Provo, UT: Association for Consumer Research, 1988), pp. 59–63.

23 M.K. Hui, M.V. Thakor and R. Gill, 'The effect of delay type and service stage on consumers' reactions to waiting', *Journal of Consumer Research* 24 (March 1998), pp. 469–79.

24 Taylor and Fullerton, 'Waiting for services'.

25 M.K. Hui and D.K. Tse, 'What to tell consumers in waits of different lengths: an integrative model of service evaluation', *Journal of Marketing* 60 (April 1996), pp. 81–90.

26 J. Baker and M. Cameron, 'The effects of the service environment on affect and consumer perception of waiting time: an integrative review and research propositions', *Journal of the Academy of Marketing Science* 24 (Fall 1996), pp. 338–49.

Chapter 15

1   For research that shows different types of service failures, see M.J. Bitner, B.H. Booms and M.S. Tetreault, 'The service encounter: diagnosing favorable and unfavorable incidents', *Journal of Marketing* 54 (January 1990), pp. 71–84; and S.M. Keaveney, 'Customer switching behavior in service industries: an exploratory study', *Journal of Marketing* 59 (April 1995), pp. 71–82.

2   Information provided by TARP Worldwide Inc, based on data from 10 studies (representing responses from more than 8,000 customers) conducted in 2006 and 2007. Companies from the following industries were included: retail (stores, catalogue and online) auto financing and insurance (property/casualty).

3   For research on important outcomes associated with service recovery, see S.S. Tax, S.W. Brown and M. Chandrashekaran, 'Customer evaluations of service complaint experiences: implications for relationship marketing', *Journal of Marketing* 62 (April 1998), pp. 60–76; S.S. Tax and S.W. Brown, 'Recovering and learning from service failure', *Sloan Management Review* (Fall 1998), pp. 75–88; A.K. Smith and R.N. Bolton, 'An experimental investigation of customer reactions to service failure and recovery encounters', *Journal of Service Research* 1 (August 1998), pp. 65–81; S.W. Kelley, K.D. Hoffman and M.A. Davis, 'A typology of retail failures and recoveries', *Journal of Retailing* 69 (Winter 1993), pp. 429–52; R.N. Bolton, 'A dynamic model of the customer's relationship with a continuous service provider: the role of satisfaction', *Marketing Science* 17, no. 1 (1998), pp. 45–65; A.K. Smith and R.N. Bolton, 'The effect of customers' emotional responses to service failures on their recovery effort evaluations and satisfaction judgments', *Journal of the Academy of Marketing Science* 30 (Winter 2002), pp. 5–23.

4   Information is based on data from 10 studies conducted in 2006 and 2007, TARP Worldwide Inc.

5   2015v and 2013 National Customer Rage Studies conducted by Customer Care Alliance in collaboration with the Center for Service Leadership at Arizona State University's W.P. Carey School of Business.

6   S.S. Tax and S.W. Brown, 'Recovering and learning from service failure', *Sloan Management Review* (Fall 1998), pp. 75–88;

7   2015 Customer Rage Study, conducted by Customer Care Measurement and Consulting and the Center for Services Leadership at Arizona State University.

8   See C.W. Hart, J.L. Heskett and W.E. Sasser Jr, 'The profitable art of service recovery', *Harvard Business Review* 68 (July–August 1990), pp. 148–56; M.A. McCollough and S.G. Bharadwaj, 'The recovery paradox: an examination of consumer satisfaction in relation to disconfirmation, service quality, and attribution based theories', in *Marketing Theory and Applications*, eds C.T. Allen et al. (Chicago, IL: American Marketing Association, 1992), p. 119.

9   C.A. de Matos, J.L. Henrique and C.A.V. Rossi, 'Service recovery paradox: a meta-analysis', *Journal of Service Research* 10 (August 2007), pp. 60–77.

10 Smith and Bolton, 'An experimental investigation of customer reactions to service failure and recovery encounters'.

11 V.P. Magnini, J.D. Ford, E.P. Markowski and E.D. Honeycutt Jr., 'The service recovery paradox: justifiable theory or smoldering myth?', *Journal of Services Marketing* 21, no. 3 (2007), pp. 213–25; J.G. Maxham III and R.G. Netemeyer, 'A longitudinal study of complaining customers' evaluations of multiple service failures and recovery efforts', *Journal of Marketing* 66 (October 2002), pp. 57–71; M.A. McCullough, L.L. Berry and M.S. Yadav, 'An empirical investigation of customer satisfaction after service failure and recovery', *Journal of Service Research* 3 (November 2000), pp. 121–37.

12 For research foundations on typologies of customer responses to failures, see R.L. Day and E.L. Landon Jr, 'Towards a theory of consumer complaining behavior', in *Consumer and Industrial Buying Behavior*, eds A. Woodside, J. Sheth and P. Bennett (Amsterdam: North-Holland, 1977); J. Singh, 'Consumer complaint intentions and behavior: definitional and taxonomical issues', *Journal of Marketing* 52 (January 1988), pp. 93–107; and J. Singh, 'Voice, exit, and negative word-of-mouth behaviors: an investigation across three service categories', *Journal of the Academy of Marketing Science* 18 (Winter 1990), pp. 1–15.

13 Smith and Bolton, 'The effect of customers' emotional responses to service failures'.

14 Ibid.

15 N. Stephens and K.P. Gwinner, 'Why don't some people complain? A cognitive–emotive process model of consumer complaining behavior', *Journal of the Academy of Marketing Science* 26 (Spring 1998), pp. 172–89.

16 Ibid.

17 A.S. Mattila and J. Wirtz, 'Consumer complaining to firms: the determinants of channel choice', *Journal of Services Marketing*, 18, no. 2 (2004), pp. 147–55.

18 Many such websites exist; examples include www.untied.com (for United Airlines experiences), www.starbucked.com (for Starbucks), and www.walmartsucks.com (for Wal-Mart).

19 J.C. Ward and A.L. Ostrom, 'Online complaining via customer-created websites: a protest framing perspective', working paper, W.P. Carey School of Business, Arizona State University (2004).

20 J. Singh, 'A typology of consumer dissatisfaction response styles', *Journal of Retailing* 66 (Spring 1990), pp. 57–99.

21 J.R. McColl-Kennedy and B.A. Sparks, 'Application of fairness theory to service failures and service recovery',

Journal of Service Research 5 (February 2003), pp. 251–66; M. Davidow, 'Organizational responses to customer complaints: what works and what doesn't', *Journal of Service Research* 5 (February 2003), pp. 225–50.

22 2007 National Customer Rage Study conducted by Customer Care Alliance.

23 Davidow, 'Organizational responses to customer complaints'.

24 See Tax, Brown and Chandrashekaran, 'Customer evaluations of service complaint experiences'; Tax and Brown, 'Recovering and learning from service failure'.

25 Tax and Brown, 'Recovering and learning from service failure'.

26 Smith and Bolton, 'The effect of customers' emotional responses to service failures'.

27 A.S. Mattila and P.G. Patterson, 'Service recovery and fairness perceptions in collectivist and individualist Contexts', *Journal of Services Research* 6 (May 2004), pp. 336–46; A.S. Mattila and P.G. Patterson, 'The impact of culture on consumers' perceptions of service recovery efforts', *Journal of Retailing* 80 (Fall 2004), pp. 196–206.

28 McCullough, Berry and Yadav, 'An empirical investigation of customer satisfaction after service failure and recovery'.

29 A.S. Mattila, 'The impact of relationship type on customer loyalty in a context of service failures', *Journal of Service Research*, 4 (November 2001), pp. 91–101; see also R.L. Hess Jr, S. Ganesan and N.M. Klein, 'Service failure and recovery: the impact of relationship factors on customer satisfaction', *Journal of the Academy of Marketing Science* 31 (Spring 2003), pp. 127–45; R. Priluck, 'Relationship marketing can mitigate product and service failures', *Journal of Services Marketing* 17, no. 1 (2003), pp. 37–52.

30 H.S. Bansal and S.F. Taylor, 'The service provider switching model (SPSM)', *Journal of Service Research* 2 (November 1999), pp. 200–18.

31 S.M. Keaveney and M. Parthasarathy, 'Customer switching behavior in online services: an exploratory study of the role of selected attitudinal, behavioral, and demographic factors', *Journal of the Academy of Marketing Science* 29, no. 4 (2001), pp. 374–90.

32 I. Roos, 'Switching processes in customer relationships', *Journal of Service Research* 2 (August 1999), pp. 68–85.

33 Keaveney, 'Customer switching behavior in service industries'.

34 A. Parasuraman, V.A. Zeithaml and L.L. Berry, 'SERVQUAL: a multiple-item scale for measuring consumer perceptions of service quality', *Journal of Retailing* 64 (Spring 1988), pp. 64–79.

35 R.B. Chase and D.M. Stewart, 'Make your service failsafe', *Sloan Management Review* (Spring 1994), pp. 35–44.

36 Ibid.

37 Sources: Tax and Brown, 'Recovering and learning from service failure'; O. Harari, 'Thank heaven for complainers', *Management Review* 81 (January 1992), p. 59.

38 L.M. Fisher, 'Here comes front-office automation', *Strategy and Business* 13 (Fourth Quarter, 1999), pp. 53–65; and R.A. Shaffer, 'Handling customer service on the web', *Fortune*, 1 March 1999, pp. 204, 208.

39 Davidow, 'Organizational responses to customer complaints'.

40 2015 Customer Rage Study, conducted by Customer Care Measurement and Consulting and the Center for Services Leadership at Arizona State University.

41 Ibid.

42 R. Holmes, "How to Keep Client Rants from Going VIral" Wall street Journal (December 9, 2013) http://blogs.wsj .com/accelerators/2013/12/09/ryan-homes-how-to-keep-client-rants-from-going-viral/

43 L.L. Berry and K. Seiders, 'Serving unfair customers', *Business Horizons* 51 (January/February 2008), pp. 29–37.

44 J. Dunning, A. Pecotich and A. O'Cass, 'What happens when things go wrong? Retail sales explanations and their effects', *Psychology and Marketing* 21, no. 7 (2004), pp. 553–72; McColl-Kennedy and Sparks, 'Application of fairness theory to service failures and service recovery'; Davidow, 'Organizational responses to customer complaints'.

45 Hess, Ganesan and Klein, 'Service failure and recovery: the impact of relationship factors on customer satisfaction'; Priluck, 'Relationship marketing can mitigate product and service failures'.

46 T. DeWitt and M.K. Brady, 'Rethinking service recovery strategies: the effect of rapport on consumer responses to service failure', *Journal of Service Research* 6 (November 2003), pp. 193–207.

47 Hess, Ganesan and Klein, 'Service failure and recovery: the impact of relationship factors on customer satisfaction'.

48 L.L. Berry and A. Parasuraman, *Marketing Services* (New York: Free Press, 1991), p. 52.

49 F.F. Reichheld, 'Learning from customer defections', *Harvard Business Review* (March–April 1996), pp. 56–69.

50 Ibid.

51 A.L. Ostrom and C.W.L. Hart, 'Service guarantees: research and practice', in *Handbook of Services Marketing and Management*, eds T. Swartz and D. Iacobucci (Thousand Oaks, CA: Sage Publications, 2000), pp. 299–316.

52 See ibid.; C.W.L. Hart, 'The power of unconditional guarantees', *Harvard Business Review* (July–August 1988), pp. 54–62; and C.W.L. Hart, *Extraordinary Guarantees* (New York: AMACOM, 1993).

53 A.L. Ostrom and D. Iacobucci, 'The effect of guarantees on consumers' evaluation of services', *Journal of Services Marketing* 12, no. 5 (1998), pp. 362–78; S.B. Lidén and P. Skålén, 'The effect of service guarantees on service recovery', *International Journal of Service Industry Management* 14(1) (2003), pp. 36–58.

54 Example cited in Ostrom and Hart, 'Service guarantees'.

55 These characteristics are proposed and discussed in C.W.L. Hart, 'The power of unconditional guarantees', *Harvard Business Review* 66 (July–August 1988), pp. 54–62; C.W.L. Hart, *Extraordinary Guarantees* (New York: AMACOM, 1993).

56 J. Wirtz, D. Kum and K.S. Lee, 'Should a firm with a reputation for outstanding service quality offer a service guarantee?', *Journal of Services Marketing* 14, no. 6 (2000), pp. 502–12.

57 J. Wirtz, 'Development of a service guarantee model', *Asia Pacific Journal of Management* 15 (April 1998), pp. 51–75.

58 Ibid.

59 J. Wirtz and D. Kum, 'Consumer cheating on service guarantees', *Journal of the Academy of Marketing Science* 32 (Spring 2004), pp. 159–75.

60 Wirtz, 'Development of a service guarantee model'.

61 Ostrom and Iacobucci, 'The effect of guarantees'.

62 Wirtz, 'Development of a service guarantee model'.

Chapter 16

1   P.G. Lindell, 'You need integrated attitude to develop IMC', *Marketing News*, 26 May 1997, p. 5.

2   B. Mittal, 'The advertising of services: meeting the challenge of Intangibility', *Journal of Service Research* 2 (August 1999), pp. 98–116.

3   H.S. Bansal and P.A. Voyer, 'Word-of-mouth processes within a services purchase decision context', *Journal of Service Research* 3 (November 2000), pp. 166–77.

4   A.S. Mattila, 'The role of narratives in the advertising of experiential services', *Journal of Service Research* 3 (August 2000), pp. 35–45.

5   K.L. Alesandri, 'Strategies that influence memory for advertising communications', in *Information Processing Research in Advertising*, ed. R.J. Harris (Hillsdale, NJ: Erlbaum, 1983).

6   L.L. Berry and T. Clark, 'Four ways to make services more tangible', *Business* (October–December 1986), pp. 53–4.

7   Ibid.

8   W.R. George and L.L. Berry, 'Guidelines for the advertising of services', *Business Horizons* (May–June 1981), pp. 52–6.

9   L.L. Berry, 'Cultivating service brand equity', *Journal of the Academy of Marketing Science 28* (Winter 2000), pp. 128–37.

10 See www.mastercardinternational.com.

11 Sources: K.J. Bannan, 'Seven ways to make online advertising work for you', *Advertising Age*, 11 October 2004, p. 11; R. Bayani, 'Banner ads – still working after all these years?', *Link-up* (November/December 2001), pp. 2, 6.

12 P. Denoyelle and J.-C. Larreche, 'Virgin Atlantic Airways – ten years later', INSEAD Case (1995).

13 E.C. Clemmer and B. Schneider, 'Managing customer dissatisfaction with waiting: applying social-psychological theory in a service setting', in *Advances in Services Marketing and Management*, vol. 2, eds T. Schwartz, D.E. Bowen and S.W. Brown (Greenwich, CT: JAI Press, 1993), pp. 213–29.

14 Ibid.

15 L.L. Berry, V.A. Zeithaml and A. Parasuraman, 'Quality counts in services, too', *Business Horizons* (May–June 1985), pp. 44–52.

16 C. Mitchell, 'Selling the brand inside', *Harvard Business Review* 80 (January 2002), pp. 5–11.

17 V.A. Zeithaml, A. Parasuraman and L.L. Berry, *Delivering Quality Service: Balancing Customer Perceptions and Expectations* (New York: Free Press, 1990), p. 120.

Chapter 17

1   K. Monroe, 'The pricing of services', *Handbook of Services Marketing*, eds C.A. Congram and M.L. Friedman (New York: AMACOM, 1989), pp. 20–31.

2   Ibid.

3   Ibid.

4   V.A. Zeithaml, 'The acquisition, meaning, and use of price information by consumers of professional services', in *Marketing Theory: Philosophy of Science Perspectives*, eds R. Bush and S. Hunt (Chicago, IL: American Marketing Association, 1982), pp. 237–41.

5   C.H. Lovelock, 'Understanding costs and developing pricing strategies', *Services Marketing* (New York: Prentice Hall, 1991), pp. 236–46.

6   A. Stevens, 'Firms try more lucrative ways of charging for legal services', *The Wall Street Journal*, 25 November 1994, pp. B1ff.

7   J.L. Fix, 'Consumers are snarling over charges', *USA Today*, 2 August 1994, pp. B1–B2.

8   Monroe, 'The pricing of services'.

9   Monroe, 'The pricing of services'.

10 G.J. Tellis, 'Beyond the many faces of price: an integration of pricing strategies', *Journal of Marketing* 50 (October 1986), pp. 146–60.

Chapter 18

1   R.T. Rust, C. Moorman and P.R. Dickson, 'Getting return on quality: revenue expansion, cost reduction, or both?', *Journal of Marketing* 66 (October 2002), pp. 7–24.

2   Ibid.

3   C. Fornell, F.V. Morgeson III and G.T.M. Hult (2016). Stock returns on customer satisfaction do beat the

market: gauging the effect of a marketing intangible. Journal of Marketing, 80(5), 92–107.

4   S. Gupta and V. Zeithaml, 'Customer metrics and their impact on financial performance', *Marketing Science* 25 (November–December 2006), pp. 718–39.

5   E. Anderson, C. Fornell and S. Mazvancheryl, 'Customer satisfaction and shareholder value', *Journal of Marketing* 68 (2004), pp. 172–85.

6   T.S. Gruca and L. L. Rego, 'Customer satisfaction, cash flow and shareholder value', *Journal of Marketing* 69 (2005), pp. 115–30.

7   E. Anderson and V. Mittal, 'Strengthening the satisfaction-profit chain', *Journal of Service Research 3* (2000), pp. 107–20.

8   P. Nayyar, 'Stock market reactions to customer service changes', *Strategic Management Journal* 16(1) (1995), pp. 39–53.

9   E. Anderson and V. Mittal, 'Strengthening the satisfaction-profit chain'.

10   C. Ittner and D. Larcker, 'Are non-financial measures leading indicators of financial performance? An analysis of customer satisfaction', *Journal of Accounting Research,* 36 (3) (1998), pp. 1–35.

11   E. Anderson and V. Mittal, Strengthening the satisfaction-profit chain'.

12   Ibid.

13   Ibid.

14   C. Fornell and B. Wernerfelt, 'Defensive marketing strategy by customer complaint management: a theoretical analysis', *Journal of Marketing Research* 24 (November 1987), pp. 337–46; see also C. Fornell and B. Wernerfelt, 'A model for customer complaint management', *Marketing Science* 7 (Summer 1988), pp. 271–86.

15   B. Gale, 'Monitoring customer satisfaction and market-perceived quality', *American Marketing Association Worth Repeating Series,* no. 922CS01 (Chicago, IL: American Marketing Association, 1992).

16   Ibid.

17   R.E. Kordupleski, R.T. Rust and A.J. Zahorik, 'Why improving quality doesn't improve quality (or whatever happened to marketing?)', *California Management Review* 35 (1993), pp. 82–95.

18   See www.storaenso.com.

19   Fornell and Wernerfelt, 'Defensive marketing strategy by customer complaint management' also Fornell and Wernerfelt, 'A model for customer complaint management'.

20   F. Reichheld and E. Sasser, 'Zero defections: quality comes to services', *Harvard Business Review* (September–October 1990), p. 106.

21   Ibid., p. 105.

22   D.F. Colicchio, regional quality manager, Hewlett-Packard Company, personal communication.

23   R.T. Rust, K.N. Lemon and V.A. Zeithaml (2004). Return on marketing: Using customer equity to focus marketing strategy. Journal of marketing, 68(1), 109–127.

24   R.S. Kaplan and D.P. Norton, 'The balanced scorecard – measures that drive performance', *Harvard Business Review* (January–February 1992), pp. 71–9.

25   Kaplan and Norton, 'The balanced scorecard'.

26   S. Silk, 'Automating the balanced scorecard', *Management Accounting* (May 1998), pp. 38–42.

27   The material in this section comes from C.D. Ittner and D.F. Larcker, 'Coming up short on nonfinancial performance measurement', *Harvard Business Review* (November 2003), pp. 88–95.

28   Ibid., p. 92.

Index

A

Abercrombie & Fitch scent in
    stores 215
Abi-Gerges, Claude 433
Abstractedness, tangibility and 350
Accenture 7, 58, 125
Accident insurance customers, principal
    expectations of 76
Accor Hotels 6
    Accor brands training
      resources 242
Acquaintances, customers as 132–3
Active relational customer
    expectations 134
Adaptation of prices 380–83
Adequate service expectations
    influencing factors 70
    sources of 69–72
Adjustment of capacity to meet
    demand 303–4
Advertising channels 348–9
Aesthetics, differences across
    cultures 55–6
Agent model intermediaries 286
Agents and brokers 282
    benefits and challenges in use of 286
    benefits of 286–7
    challenges of service delivery
      through 287
    customer choice 287
    local market knowledge 287
    loss of control over pricing, challenge
      of 287
    multiple service principals, challenge
      of representation of 287
    reduction of selling and distribution
      costs 286
    representation width 287
    skills and knowledge of 286–7
Air France 72
    service standards 198
Airbnb, peer-to-peer room rental 105
Airline cabin crews, provision of Apple
    iPads for 234
Airline flights, passengers on 260
Alabama University 465–72
Alibaba new service developments 165
Alignment of capacity with demand
    fluctuations 304–6
Allchin, Josie 406
Allianz 3
    sponsorship of Olympic
      Movement 246
Alternatives, evaluation of service
    alternatives 43, 46
Amazon 11, 44–5, 133, 148, 161, 210
    Alexa 11
Amazon, delivering service through
    electronic channels and
    intermediaries (case study) 413–21

Amazon App 116
Amazon Auctions 413
Amazon Books 419
Amazon Business Prime 415
Amazon Business Services 419
Amazon Fulfilment 413
Amazon Go 419
Amazon Kindle 413
Amazon Marketplace 413
Amazon Pop Ups 419
Amazon Prime 416
Amazon Web Services 413, 419
anti-competitive practices 417
augmented reality (AR) 416
business 414–15
Business-to-business (B2B)
    solutions 413, 417
Business-to-customer (B2C)
    solutions 413
challenges 417–19
continuous innovation 413
customer reviews, controversies
    and 418
customers 414
direct selling 418
e-commerce and, evolving
    strategies 417
electronic channels of
    distribution 415–16
employee working conditions,
    challenge of improvement of
    418–19
evolution of 419
Fire TV 417
growth potential 419
healthcare, move to 415, 419
investment in variety of sectors 415
leading global online retailer 413
partnerships 415
principles, guidance by 413–14
revenue generation 413
Ambient conditions 213, 214–15
American Customer Satisfaction Index
    (ACSI) 86, 390
American Express 191, 361
    Centurion Card 134
American Express Australia, use of big
    data by 108
American Marketing Association 143
Anderson, E.W. and Mittal, V. 390–91
Anderson, E.W., Fornell, C. and
    Mazvancheryl, S. 390
Ansoff, H.I. 166
Apple 8, 130, 147
    airline cabin crews, provision of
      Apple iPads for 234
    customer connections 232
Apple TV 417
Approaches to pricing of services 375–9
Appropriate service standards, factors
    necessary for 185–8

APS Bank branch interior redesign 212
Artificial intelligence (AI) 434, 458
    listening to customers 109
    technology 165, 431, 435
    voice assistant device 415
Asda
    customer listening programme 125
    customer-perception tracker
      survey 113
Assets, return on (ROA) 390
Assurance dimension of service
    delivery 233
Attribution of dissatisfaction 53
Audit of internal customer service 244–5
Augmented reality (AR) 206
AXA Group 3, 4, 90

B

Back-office and support personnel,
    alignment with customers by
    interaction or
measurement 365–6
Bain & Company 393
Balanced performance
    scorecard 397–401
Balanced scorecard of service,
    measurements for 398
Banco Santander 3, 161, 354, 357
    Cycle Partnership 347
Banner advertisement 358
Bargain-hunters, attraction of 381
Barnes & Noble 418
Behaviours and actions, measurements
    for 197
Behaviours in servicescape 218–19
Benefits of electronic channels 277–8
Benetton 125
Berkshire Hathaway 415
Berry, Leonard 14, 89, 145
Berry, L.L. and Clark, T. 354
Berry, L.L., Parasuraman, A. and
    Zeithaml, V.A. 68
Best people
    competing for 240
    retention of 245–8
Betters-Picaro, E. 415
Bezos, Jeff 44–5, 418–19
Bi-level trains of on European
    railways 304
Biases
    biased interpretation 160
    negative or positive 53–4
Big data analytics 107–8
Bitner, M.J. 18, 208, 213
Blecharczyk, Nathan 105
Blueprinting 170–79
    backstage contact employee
      actions 171

bank cash machine 175
benefits and uses of applications 176
blueprint components 171–2
building a blueprint 176–9
contact employee actions, mapping
   of 178
customer actions 171
customer identification 178
definition of 170–71
evidence of service at each customer
   action step, adding of 179
examples of 172–4
frequently asked questions
   about 176–7
interaction, line of 172
internal interaction, line of 172
linking contact activities to needed
   support functions 178–9
mapping process from customer
   perspective 178
onstage contact employee
   actions 171
overnight hotel stay 172–4
physical evidence 172
reading and using service
   blueprints 174–6
service process identification 178
support processes 171–2
technology actions, mapping of 178
technology-delivered self-service 174
visibility, line of 172
BMW 3
BNP Paribas 3, 120
Bodies of people, services directed at 5
Body Shop internal communicator
   network 364
Boots the Chemists Advantage
   Card 144
Booz-Allen & Hamilton 164
Borders Books 418
Boulud, Daniel 449
Boundary-spanning roles 234–9
Bowers, M.J. 164
B&Q 354
Brady, Michael 89
Brand loyalty 54
Brand personification, employees
   and 231–2
Branson, Richard 354
Breslin, S. 417
Brigham, K. 413
British Airways (BA) 13, 72, 109, 187,
   359, 381, 389
British Telecom (BT) 125
   self-help facilities 336
Brodie, Brian 82
Brokers *see* Agents and brokers
Brown, Piers 407, 408
Browning, Bill 409
Budget Rentals 393
Building customer relationships 103,
   129–55
   acquaintances, customers as 132–3
   active relational customer
      expectations 134
   business-to-business
      relationship 150
   core service provision 143–4
   customer expectations, types of 134
   customer experience
      management 143–4
   customer is not *always* right 149–52

customer profitability segments
   140–42
customer pyramid 141
customers
   not wanting relationships 151–2
   relationship value of 137–9
   relationships with, evolution
      of 132–4
customization bonds 148
difficult customers 150–51
discussion questions 154
dysfunctional customers 150–51
ending business relationships 152
example, Starbucks App 130–31
exercises 153–4
financial relationship bonds 146–7
firing customers, difficulties of 152–3
frequent-flyer programmes 146
friends, customers as 133
further reading 154–5
interpersonal bonds 147
intrusive organizations 151
irritating customers 151
key concepts 153
learning objectives 129
lifetime value 138
   calculation of, example of 138
   estimation of 138
linking customer relationship value
   to firm value 139
market segment incompatibility,
   customer and 149–50
online brand communities 147
partners, customers as 133–4
passive relational customer
   expectations 134
profitability tiers
   business decision-making
      using 142
   customer pyramid 140–41
   view of customers on 141–2
relationship bonds 145–9
relationship challenges 149–53
relationship development 132
relationship development model 143
relationship development
   strategies 143–9
relationship endings 152
relationship marketing 131–7
   benefits for customers and
      firms 135–7
   benefits for firms 136
   confidence benefits 135
   customer behaviour benefits 136–7
   customer irritation with 151
   economic benefits 136
   goal of 134–5
   human resource management
      (HRM) benefits 137
   negativity towards 151–2
   social benefits 135–6
   special treatment benefits 136
relationship strategies, levels of 146
relationship value
   of customers 137–9
   factors influencing 137–8
   service dominant logic perspective
      on 139
retention strategies 144
service spotlights
   American Express Centurion
      Card 134

Boots the Chemists Advantage
   Card 144
difficult clients 152
Mastercard customer
   relationship 147
Royal Caribbean Cruises
   customization 148
social bonds 148
structural bonds 149
Triodos Bank mission 142
Virgin Airlines Flying Club 140
social relationship bonds 147–8
strangers, customers as 132
structural bonds 149
summary 153
switching
   barriers to 144–5
   costs of 145
   customer inertia on 144–5
time-consuming customers 151
touchpoints 144
transactional customer
   expectations 134
unattractive customers 151
unprofitability in long-term of
   customers 150
word-of-mouth communication 136–7
Bundling prices 382
Burger King 65, 359
Business analysis 168
Business strategy development (or
   review) 165–6
Business-to-business (B2B)
   relationship 28, 46, 51, 69, 91, 96,
      117, 125, 180, 186, 320, 328, 372
   building customer relationships 136,
      147, 149, 150, 151
   communications management 349,
      360–61, 362
   customers' roles in service
      delivery 255, 258, 259
Button, Jensen 347
Buying centres 58

C

Cafe Nero 204
Cameron, G. 82
Capacity
   capacity constraints 296–8
   demand and, queuing strategies for
      balancing 310–15
   demand and, strategies for
      matching 300–306
   optimal vs maximum use of 297–8
   shifting demand to match 300–301
Capita 7
Car industry intermediary
   performance 290
Car insurance consumers, principal
   expectations of 76
Car repair consumers, principal
   expectations of 76
Cardiff Business School 405–12
Carney, J. 419
Carrefour 7, 351
Case studies 405–72
   Amazon, delivering service
      through electronic channels and
      intermediaries 413–21

Case studies (*Continued*)
  CitizenM, redesign of consumers'
    hotel experiences 405–12
  John Lewis & Partners, customer
    experience 422–9
  Marriott International, opportunity
    window for customer
    experience 448–55
  McDonalds, designing services
    processes and innovations 430–37
  Music Festivals, pride of live
    performances at 138–17
  Starbucks, key elements of the
    'Starbucks Experience' 465–72
  Turkish Airlines, enhancement of
    customer experience 456–64
Chadha, Rattan 405
Chaffey, D. 413, 418
Champions League football 158
Chapman, G. 418
Chatbots 238
Chesky, Brian 105
ChiantiBanca Restaurant Experience
  Banking 208
Childs, Lee 418
Chirinos, Carlos 439–40
Chision 109
CitizenM
  boutique hotels 210
  employer branding 241–2
CitizenM, redesign of consumers' hotel
  experiences (case study) 405–12
  bedrooms 409–10
  Chadha, Rattan 405
  CitizenM Ambassadors 410
  construction, innovation in 406
  design 406
  employee costs 405
  employee dispositions 407
  first (and further) openings 406
  future travel plans 411
  growth trajectory 411
  guest occupancies 405
  Levie, Michael 405
  lobby, communal areas and 408–9
  marketing position 407
  marketplace, identification of
    profitable gap in 405
  mission positioning 406–7
  modern travellers, requirements of 405
  service experience 407
  servicescape 407
  servicescape design 408–9, 409–10, 411
  target market 406–7
  traditional hotel offering, comparison
    with 407
  typical hotel design facets,
    elimination of 405
  vitrual sercoscape 411
Claridges in London 148
Clarification of expectations after
  sale 363
Closing gaps in service quality 34
Club Med 44, 210
'Clue management' 206–7
Co-creation and delivery of services,
  importance of customers in 254–7
Coca Cola 204
Cognition, environment and 216
Colicchio, David F. 393
Collection of price information
  overwhelming services 372

Colt, customer orientation at 391
Combining demand and capacity
  strategies 306
Commercialization 169
Communication challenges, categories
  of strategy for overcoming 353–66
Communication upwards
  through employees 124–6
  through employees, objectives
    of 124–5
  through employees, research
    for 125–6
Communications (external and internal)
  management of 345, 346–68
  advertising channels 348–9
  back-office and support personnel,
    alignment with customers by
    interaction or measurement 365–6
  banner advertisement 358
  clarification of expectations after
    sale 363
  communication challenges,
    categories of strategy for
    overcoming 353–66
  coordination of external
    communication 357–60
  corporate websites 348–9
  cross-functional teams, creation
    of 366
  customer education 352
  management of 353, 361–3
  customer expectations 347–8
  management of 351–2, 353, 360–61
  direct marketing 349, 359
  discussion questions 367–8
  education of customer 352
  effective horizontal communication,
    creation of 365
  effective upward communication,
    creation of 364
  effective vertical communications,
    creation of 363
  example, Santander's Cycle
    Partnership 347
  exercises 367
  external communication
    coordination 357–60
  further reading 368
  horizontal communications 363
    creation of effectiveness in 365
  intangibility of service, dealing
    with 350–51, 353–5
  integrated marketing
    communications (IMC) 349
  integrated service marketing
    communications (ISMC) 349
  interaction, alignment of back-
    office and support personnel with
    customers by 365–6
  internal alignment, achievement
    of 352
  internal brand selling 364
  internal marketing 349
  internal marketing communication,
    management of 353, 363–6
  key concepts 367
  learning objectives 346
  measurement, alignment of back-
    office and support personnel with
    customers by 366
  mobile apps 358–9
  online advertising 358

online and offline marketing
  communication channels, need for
  coordination on 348–9
paid research advertising 358
peak demand periods, teaching
  avoidance of 363
performance confirmation to
  standards and expectations 362–3
personal selling 360
preparation of customers for service
  process 361–2
public relations 359
public relations channels 349
realsim in promises 360
sales promotion 359
sales promotion channels 349
search engine optimization 357
selling brand inside company 364
service brands, creation of strength
  in 356–7
service communication
  strategies 350–52
service effectiveness, communication
  of criteria and levels of 361
service guarantees 360
service intangibility, addressing
  350–51, 353–5
service options, offering of 360–61
service performance, confirmation to
  standards and expectations 362–3
service process, preparation of
  customers for 361–2
service promises, management
  of 351, 353, 356–60
service spotlights
  Body Shop internal communicator
    network 364
  FedEx alignment of internal
    personnel with customers using
    measurement 366
  IKEA Breakfast in Bed Café 359
  Starwood Resorts Instagram
    influencers 355
  Thorpe Park social media
    strategy 351
services marketing triangle 348
slow demand periods, teaching
  seeking out of 363
social media advertising 358
summary 366–7
tangibilization 354
tiered-value service offerings 361
traditional advertising 357–8
usability testing 357
vertical communications 363
  creation of effectiveness in 363
viral marketing 359–60
websites 357
Company-owned electronic
  channels 282–3
Company performance
  measurement 397–401
Company vision, inclusion of
  employees in 245–6
ComparetheMarket.com 279
Comparison websites
  (aggregators) 379–80
Compatibility management 270
  service characteristics for
    improvements in 271
Compatibility of service
  customers 51

Competition
  competition-based pricing 371, 377–8
  competition-based pricing for
    services, examples of 377–8
  competition-based pricing for
    services, special challenges for 377
  competition tracking 121
  competitors, customers as 257, 261–2
  meeting customer expectations
    and 78–9
Complaint actions following service
    failure 323
  activist complainers 325
  complainer types 325–6
  irate complainers 325
  passive complainers 325
  quick action before legislative force
    is applied 338
  reasons for taking (and not
    taking) 324
  speed of 335–6, 338
  types of 324–5
  voicers of complaint 325
Complaint handling, custoumer-defined
    standards by segment 195
Complaint on flightsfromhell.com 326
Complaint service, provision of
    adequate explanation 336
Complaint solicitation 111, 112
Complaint tracking 333–5
Complementary pricing 382–3
Compounded annualized rate
    (CAR) 390
Concepts
  development and evaluation of 167–8
  see also Key concepts
Confidentiality 123
Conflict, sources of 237–8
Consumer behaviour 39, 40–60
  aesthetics, differences across
    cultures 55–6
  alternatives, evaluation of 43, 46
  attribution of dissatisfaction 53
  biases, negative or positive 53–4
  brand loyalty 54
  buying centres 58
  compatibility of service
    customers 51
  consumer choice of service 43–8
  consumer decision-making and
    evaluation of services, stages in 43
  consumer experience during service
    delivery 48–52
  credence qualities 41–3
  culture, role of 54–7
  customer co-production 51
  differences among consumers 54–8
  discussion questions 59
  dissatisfaction, attribution of 53
  drama, service provision as 49–50
  emotion and mood 51–2
  Europe, housing ownership in 56
  evaluation continuum for product
    types 42
  examples
    evaluation on self-service 47–8
    travelling millennials and buying
      behaviour 41
  exercises 59
  experience qualities 41–3
  further reading 60
  global differences 54–7

group decision-making 57
  hierarchy of needs (Maslow) 43–4
  households, decision-making in 57
  housing ownership in Europe 56
  information search 43, 44–6
  key concepts 58–9
  learning objectives 40
  manners and customs, differences
    across cultures 55
  material culture, differences in 55
  mood and emotion 51–2
  need recognition 43–4
  organizations, decision-making
    in 57–8
  perceived risk 45–6, 47
  positive moods 52
  post-experience evaluation 52–4
  postmodern human behaviour 51
  processes, services as 49
  purchase of service 43, 46
  search qualities 41–3
  self-service technologies (SSTs) 47–8
    categories and examples of 47
    problems with 48
    strong feelings and beneficial uses
      for 47–8
  service delivery, consumer
    experience during 48–52
  service provision as drama 49–50
  service roles and scripts 50
  service spotlights
    Crowne Plaza Hotel, London
      Docklands 45
    IKEA co-production 51
    Spotify 47
    Starbucks in Australia 55
  summary 58
  theatre, service as 49–50
  values and attitudes, differences
    across cultures 55
  word-of-mouth communication 45, 53
Contingency pricing 383
Convenience costs 374
Convenience seekers, attraction
    of 382–3
Cooper, R.G. 164
Coordination of external
    communication 357–60
Core service provision 143–4
Cornell University 418
Corporate culture 229
Corporate websites 348–9
Cost-based pricing 371, 375–7
  for services, special challenges
    for 376
  strategies for services 376–7
Costa Coffee experience, redesign
    for 204
Credence qualities 41–3
Critical incident studies 111, 113
Critical incident technique (CIT) 113
Critical role of employees, example
    of 228
Cronin, Joseph 89
Cross-functional working 222
  cross-functional teams, creation of 366
Crowdsourcing 167
  innovation by Giffgaff 158
Crowne Plaza Hotel, London
    Docklands 45
Culture, role in consumer
    behaviour 54–7

Cumulative perceptions, transaction
    versus 83–4
Current market segments, stimulation
    of business from 302
Currently served markets, new services
    for 161
Customer attraction, offensive
    marketing and 391–2
Customer centricity 88
  customer satisfaction and 88
Customer co-production 51
Customer communication and balance
    of capacity with demand 301
Customer databases 106–8
Customer-defined service
    standards 156, 183–202
  appropriate service standards,
    factors necessary for 185–8
  behaviours and actions,
    measurements for 197
  complaint handling, consumer-
    defined standards by segment 195
  customer, not company-defined
    standards 187–8
  customer expectations, translation
    into behaviours and actions 193–4
  customization 186
    strategy for, standardization
      compared with 186
  determination of appropriate
    standards 194–5
  development of 191–200
  discussion questions 202
  example, DHL Freight, understanding
    service standards from customer
    perspective 184
  exercises 201
  feedback about employee
    performance, provision of 200
  formal service targets and goals 186–7
  further reading 202
  goal-setting 187
  hard customer-defined
    standards 189–90
  key concepts 201
  learning objectives 183
  measurements for standards,
    development of 196–8
  measures against standards, tracking
    of 199–200
  Net Promoter Score (NPS) 197
  one-time fixes 190–91
  process for setting customer-defined
    standards 192
  service encounter, identification of
    existing or desired sequence 192
  service performance indices,
    development of 200
  service spotlights
    Air France/KLM service
      standards 198
    FedEx hard measurements for
      international operations 197
    hotels and one-time fixes 191
    Integrated Service Solutions (ISS)
      standards of service 187
    Northern Ireland Education
      Department customer service
      standards 195–6
    Scottish and Southern Energy
      (SSE) Energy Supplier
      Guaranteed Standards 188

Customer-defined service standards
(*Continued*)
Zappos and service
standardization 186
service standards, calibration of 185
SERVQUAL surveys 197
soft and hard measures, linkage for
speed of complaint handling 194
soft customer-defined
standards 190, 191
soft measurements 197–8
standardization of service 186
behaviours and actions 185
summary 201
target levels
measures and, updating of 200
standards, establishment of 198–9
types of 189–91
Customer delight, customer
satisfaction and 88
Customer education 352
management of 353, 361–3
Customer equity
concept of 396
importance of 397
model for 396
return on marketing and 394–7
return on marketing using,
calculation of 397
in strategic framework 396
Customer expectations 39, 61–80
accident insurance customers,
principal expectations of 76
adequate service expectations
influencing factors 70
sources of 69–72
car insurance consumers, principal
expectations of 76
car repair consumers, principal
expectations of 76
communications (external and
internal) management of 347–8
competition, meeting customer
expectations and 78–9
customer expectations,
management of 74
customer service expectations,
escalation of 78
delighting the customer, questions
about 77
desired expectations, sources of 68–9
desired service
influencing factors 71
sources of 72–3
discussion questions 80
dual customer expectation levels 65
encounter expectations *versus*
overall expectations 72
equipment repair customers,
principal expectations of 76
example. KLM, social media and
customer expectations 62
exceeding customer expectations 74–6
exceeding customer service
expectations 77–8
exercises 79–80
explicit service promises 72–3
possible influence strategies for 75
further reading 80
hotel consumers, principal
expectations of 76
implicit service promises 72, 73

implicit service promises, possible
influence strategies for 75
importance of 63
influencing factors 68–74
key concepts 79
lack of knowledge of (provider gap
1) 28–9, 35–6
lasting service intensifiers 69
possible influence strategies for 75
learning objectives 61
levels of expectation 63–5
management of 74, 351–2, 353,
360–61
issues involving 74–9
online and offline word-of-mouth
communications 72, 73
past experience 72, 73
possible influence strategies for 75
perceived service alternatives 69, 70
possible influence strategies for 75
personal needs 68–9
possible influence strategies for 75
personal service philosophy 69
predicted service 69, 71–2
influencing factors 71
possible influence strategies for 75
sources of 72–3
property insurance customers,
principal expectations of 76
self-perceived service role 69, 70–71
possible influence strategies for 75
service delivery 'reality check' 76
service expectations, meaning and
types of 63–8
service spotlight
easyJet flight duration strategy 78
future hotels, technology and 65
Ibis Hotels Satisfaction
Guarantee 73
Premier Inn hub concept 66–7
situational factors 69, 71
possible influence strategies for 75
summary 79
temporary service intensifiers 69–70
possible influence strategies for 75
translation into behaviours and
actions 193–4
types of 134
'unrealistic' customer expectations,
dealing with 74–6
use of marketing research to
understand 109–10
vehicle rental/leasing customers,
principal expectations of 76
word-of-mouth communications,
possible influence strategies for 75
zone of tolerance 66–8
service dimensions and 67–8
Customer experience
management 143–4
Customer focus, maintenance of 22
Customer-focused organization
chart 248
Customer gap 27, 35, 39
Customer is not *always* right 149–52
Customer knowledge of service
prices 371–3
Customer mix, management of 270–71
Customer needs research 111, 113–14
Customer-oriented service
delivery 248–9
Customer panels 111, 119–20

Customer participation 254–5
levels across services 256
self-service technologies and 262–5
strategies for enhancement of 265–71
Customer perceptions of service 39,
81–102
American Customer Satisfaction
Index (ACSI) 86
cumulative perceptions, transaction
versus 83–4
customer centricity 88
customer satisfaction and 88
customer delight, customer
satisfaction and 88
customer perceptions 82–4
customer satisfaction 84–8
attributions for service success or
failure 85
consumer emotions 85
definition of 84
determination of 84–6
ensuring high level of 88
family members, co-workers and
other consumers 86
perceptions of equity and
fairness 86
product and service features 84–5
delighting customers 88
Deutsche Kundenbarometer 86
discussion questions 101–2
empathy 91
e-service quality (e-SQ) 91–4
evidence of service 99–100
example, Virgin Money, changing
perceptions at 82
further reading 102
hotel visit, service encounter cascade
for 94
Institute of Customer Service 86
key concepts 100–101
learning objectives 81
national customer satisfaction
indices 86–8
Nordic model of service
experience 89
Norsk Kundebarometer 86
one-stop-shop concept 88
outcome, interaction and physical
environment quality 88
promise keeping, customer
satisfaction and 88
promises kept 88
quality-satisfaction link 83
RATER (reliability, assurance,
tangibles, empathy,
responsiveness) 83, 89
Reichheld's Net Promoter metric 87
relationship building 88
customer satisfaction and 88
reliability 90
responsiveness 91
satisfaction *versus* service
quality 82–3
service encounters
adaptability theme 96, 97, 98, 99
building blocks of customer
perceptions 94–9
coping theme 96, 97, 98, 99
critical incident technique 96
encounter cascade 94
face-to-face encounters 96
importance of 95

'moment of truth' and 94
remote encounters 95–6
service recovery theme 96, 97, 98, 99
sources of pleasure and displeasure in 96–9
spontaneity theme 96, 97, 98, 99
telephone encounters 96
themes 97–9
types of 95–6
service quality 89–94
assurance inspiring trust and confidence 89, 90
customer judgements on dimensions of 92–3
dimensions of 89–91, 92–3
empathy and treating customers as individuals 89, 91
reliability and delivering on promises 89, 90
responsiveness and being willing to help 89, 91
satisfaction *versus* 82–3
tangibles representing service physically and virtually 89, 90–91
service recovery 88
customer satisfaction and 88
service spotlights
Emirates service 91
fitness centres, consumer satisfaction with 85
Skyscanner service quality 93–4
Temkin Group Net Promoter Industry Benchmarks 88
Whistl reliability 90
SERVQUAL 89
staff superiority 88
customer satisfaction and 88
summary 100
Swedish Customer Satisfaction Barometer 86
Swiss Index of Customer Satisfaction (SWICS) 86
tangibles 90
transaction *versus* cumulative perceptions 83–4
United Kingdom Customer Satisfaction Indicator (UKCSI) 86
Customer profitability segments 140–42
Customer pyramid 141
Customer receiving service 255
Customer recovery expectations 326–30
Customer relationships
cultivation of 337
evolution of 132–4
see also Building customer relationships
Customer satisfaction 84–8
attributions for service success or failure 85
consumer emotions 85
definition of 84
determination of 84–6
ensuring high level of 88
family members, co-workers and other consumers 86
perceptions of equity and fairness 86
product and service features 84–5
surveys of 111, 114–16

surveys of, disconfirmation paradigm 116
Customer service 8
expectations of, escalation of 78
Customers
as competitors 257, 261–2
as contributors to service quality and satisfaction 259–61
customer-defined, *not* company-defined standards 187–8
difficult customers 150–51
economic worth of, service quality and 395
education of 352
fellow customers, dealing with 256–7
individual differences between, attitudes to participation and 267–8
irritating customers 151
needs of, variation in 372
not wanting relationships 151–2
relationship value of 137–9
responses to service failures 323–6
retention of, defensive marketing and 392–3
service receipt by customers 255
time-consuming customers 151
treating employees as 246
treatment of customers following complaints, fairness of 336–7
unattractive customers 151
unprofitability in long-term of customers 150
see also Lost customers
Customers' roles in service delivery 226, 252–73
airline flight, passengers on 260
co-creation and delivery of services, importance of customers in 254–7
compatibility management 270
service characteristics for improvements in 271
competitors, customers as 257, 261–2
customer mix, management of 270–71
customer participation 254–5
levels across services 256
self-service technologies and 262–5
strategies for enhancement of 265–71
customer receiving service 255
customers as competitors 257, 261–2
customers as contributors to service quality and satisfaction 259–61
customers' individual differences, attitudes to participation and 267–8
discussion questions 272–3
exercises 272
fellow customers, dealing with 256–7
further reading 273
helping oneself 266–7
helping others 267
hotel guests, complaints by 260
IKEA, value creation by customers at 253–4
importance of customers in service co-creation and delivery 254–7
inappropriate customer participation, avoidance of 269–70
key concepts 272

learning objectives 252
negative customer outcomes, avoidance of 269–70
office building renovation, architectural consultation for 260
performance of customers, education and training for effectiveness in 268–9
productive resources, customers as 257–8
promoting the company 267
recruitment of
education and rewards for customers 268–70
right customers 268
rewards for customer contributions 269
roles of customers 257–62
defining customers' roles 265–8
self-service anxiety 264
self-service technologies (SSTs) 262–5
customer usage of 264–5
proliferation of new services 262–4
success with 265
service delivery, unique role of customers in 254
service quality and satisfaction, customers as contributors to 259–61
service receipt by customers 255
service spotlights
Emirates customer classification scheme 270
Gatwick self-service bag drop zones 258
Hilton hotels mobile phone app services 264
interactive touch-screen ordering kiosks 264–5
self-scanning tills, strategies for popularisation of 268
TomTom online community of users 257
Tui and customers acting as competitors 262
Waitrose "Quick Check" self-scan system 261
'services as drama' 255
services production continuum 263
strategies for enhancement of customer participation 265–71
summary 271–2
tax advice, customers seeking 260
Customization 186
customization bonds 148
strategy of, standardization compared with 186
Cycles of demand patterns, predictability of 299

D

Data analytics 108
Data mining 108
Database marketing research 111
Daunt, Kate L. 405–12
Defensive marketing effects of service 392–3, 395
Delighting customers 88

Delighting customers (*Continued*)
  questions about 77
Delivering service through
  electronic channels 276–80
  intermediaries, strategies for
    effectiveness 289–90
  mobile channels 280–81
Delivery of quality in service, strategies
  for use of people in 239–48
Delivery timing and location
  modification to balance of capacity
    with demand 301
Dell Computer 8, 12, 174, 189, 190
Demand and capacity
  management 226, 293–317
  adjustment of capacity to meet
    demand 303–4
  alignment of capacity with demand
    fluctuations 304–6
  capacity
    demand and, queuing strategies for
      balancing 310–15
    demand and, strategies for
      matching 300–306
    optimal vs maximum use of 297–8
    shifting demand to match 300–301
  capacity constraints 296–8
  combining demand and capacity
    strategies 306
  current market segments, stimulation
    of business from 302
  customer communication and balance
    of capacity with demand 301
  cycles of demand patterns,
    predictability of 299
  delivery timing and location
    modification to balance of capacity
      with demand 301
  demand, adjustment of capacity to
    meet 303–4
  demand and capacity strategies,
    combinations of 306
  demand fluctuations, alignment of
    capacity with 304–6
  demand patterns 299–300
    market segments and 300
    predictable cycles of 299
    recording of 299
  demand reduction during peak
    times 301
  demand relative to capacity,
    variations in 295
  differentiation of waiting
    customer 312–13
  discussion questions 316
  equipment constraint on
    capacity 296–7, 298
  examples
    Hilton Worldwide Revenue
      Management Consolidated
      Centre (RMCC) 294
    yield calculations 307–8
  exercises 316
  explained waits feel shorter than
    unexplained waits 314
  facilities constraint on capacity
    296–7, 298
  facilities usage, variations
    of 302
  further reading 317
  increasing demand to match
    capacity 301–3

inventory capability, underlying issue
  of lack of 295–6
key concepts 315
known, finite waits feel shorter than
  uncertain waits 314
labour constraint on capacity 296–7,
  298
learning objectives 293
market segments, demand patterns
  and 300
non peak use, offer of incentives
  for 301
operational logic, employment
  of 311–12
optimal vs maximum use of
  capacity 297–8
peak time reduction in demand 301
pleasurable waiting (or tolerable
  waiting), development of 313–15
pre-process waits feel longer than
  in-process waits 313
price differentiation to match
  demand with capacity 302–3
pricing to balance of capacity with
  demand 301
priority setting to balance of capacity
  with demand 301
psychology of queuing 313–15
queuing strategies 310–15
random demand fluctuations 299
reservation process, establishment
  of 312
revenue management 303, 306–10
  average daily rate (ADR)
    measurement 310
  challenges and risks in use of 309
  gross operating profit per
    available room (GOPPAR)
    measurement 310
  measurement of effectiveness of
    activities 310
  occupancy rate measurement 310
  revenue per available room
    (RevPAR) measurement 310
  revenue per occupied room
    (RevPOR) measurement 310
  system for, implementation
    of 308–9
  total revenue per available
    room (Total RevPAR)
    measurement 310
service offerings, variations of 302
service spotlights
  bi-level trains of on European
    railways 304
  McDonalds to Go 305–6
  rail capacity in UK 297
  Sainsbury's Smartshop Scan, Pay
    and Go app 311
  Singapore Airlines Total Offer
    Optimization 308
  Turkey, capacity for Syrian
    refugees in 299
service value, customer waiting time
  and 314
shifting demand to match
  capacity 300–301
strategies for adjusting capacity to
  match demand 303
stretching existing capacity to meet
  demand 304
summary 315

time constraint on capacity
  296–7, 298
unfair waits feel longer than
  equitable waits 314
unoccupied tome feels longer than
  occupied time 313
waiting, anxiety makes it seem
  longer 314
waiting customer
  differentiation 312–13
waiting in groups feels less long than
  sole waiting 315
waiting-line configurations 312
yield calculations, example of 307–8
yield management 306–10
Demand-based pricing 371, 378–9
Demand-based pricing for services,
  examples of 378–9
Demand-based pricing for services,
  special challenges for 378
Demand fluctuations, alignment of
  capacity with 304–6
Demand patterns 299–300
  market segments and 300
  predictable cycles of 299
  recording of 299
Demand reduction during peak times 301
Demand relative to capacity, variations
  in 295
DePillis, L. and Sherman, L. 414
Desired expectations, sources of 68–9
Desired service
  influencing factors 71
  sources of 72–3
Determination of appropriate
  standards 194–5
Deutsche Kundenbarometer 86
Deutsche Telekom 3, 4
Development of
  business strategies 165–6
  customer-defined service
    standards 191–200
  new service strategies 166
  pleasurable waiting (or tolerable
    waiting) 313–15
  relationships 143–9
  service culture with employees 230
  service-oriented internal
    processes 245
  service performance indices 200
DHL 46, 187, 190, 357, 393
DHL Freight
  follow-up calls 335
  understanding service standards
    from customer perspective 184
Differences among consumers 54–8
Differentiation of waiting
  customer 312–13
Differentiator, servicescape as 211–12
Difficult clients 152
Difficult customers 150–51
Direct channels 282–3
Direct marketing 349, 359
Disconfirmation paradigm 116
Discounting 381
Discovering the Soul of Service
  (Berry, L.) 14
Discussion questions
  building customer relationships 154
  communications (external and
    internal) management of 367–8
  consumer behaviour 59

customer-defined service
    standards 202
customer expectations 80
customer perceptions of
    service 101–2
customers' roles in service
    delivery 272–3
demand and capacity
    management 316
electronic channels and
    intermediaries, service delivery
    through 290–91
employees' roles in service
    delivery 250–51
listening to customers 128
physical and virtual
    servicescape 224
pricing of services 384–5
service innovation and design 181
service quality, financial impact
    of 402
service quality, gaps model of 38
service recovery 343–4
services 23–4
Disney 204–5
Disney omni-channel experience 276
Disney (Walt Disney Company) 49, 94,
    96, 185, 389
Disneyland Paris 8, 49, 57, 187
Disneyland Paris, waiting times at 374
Dissatisfaction, attribution of 53
Domino's Pizza
    'Gastro-Acoustic-Enterology' 360
Domino's Pizza outcome justice on
    delivery delays for 328
Drama, service provision as 49–50
Drivers of service quality, customer
    retention and profits 295, 394
Dual customer expectation levels 65
Duhigg, C. 413
Dynamic pricing 379–80
    examples in service industries
        of 379–80
    for services, examples of 379–80
    for services, special challenges
        for 379
    special challenges for
        services in 379
Dysfunctional customers 150–51

E

Easterbrook, Steve 435
EasyJet 21, 381
    flight duration strategy 78
    online customer community 112
    online flight tracker 13
Eavis, Michael and Emily 442
eBay 11, 161, 413
E-commerce 4
E-Commerce News Europe 414
Economic worth of customers, service
    quality and 395
EDF Energy 7
    balanced scorecard approach 399
Edge 204
Effective horizontal communication,
    creation of 365
Effective services marketing research
    programme, elements in 110–20

Effective upward communication,
    creation of 364
Effective vertical communications,
    creation of 363
Eilish, Billie 446
Einstein, Albert 190
Electronic channels
    benefits of 277–8
    challenges of service delivery
        through 278–80
    delivering service through 276–80
Electronic channels and intermediaries,
    service delivery through 226,
    274–92
    agent model 286
    agents and brokers 282, 285–7
        benefits and challenges in use
            of 286
        benefits of 286–7
        challenges of service delivery
            through 287
        customer choice 287
        local market knowledge 287
        loss of control over pricing,
            challenge of 287
        multiple service principals,
            challenge of representation
            of 287
        reduction of selling and
            distribution costs 286
        representation width 287
        skills and knowledge of 286–7
    benefits of electronic channels 277–8
    common issues involving
        intermediaries 288
    company-owned channels 282–3
    delivering service through
        electronic channels 276–80
        intermediaries, strategies for
            effectiveness 289–90
        mobile channels 280–81
    direct channels 282–3
    discussion questions 290–91
    electronic channels
        benefits of 277–8
        challenges of service delivery
            through 278–80
        delivering service through 276–80
    electronic distribution
        benefits and challenges of 277
        customer behaviour change,
            challenge of 279
        customer choice, benefits of 278
        customer convenience, benefits
            of 277
        customer involvement, challenge
            of lack of consistency and 279
        customization, benefits of ability
            in 278
        low cost, benefits of 277
        price competition, challenge of 278
        quick customer feedback, benefits
            of 278
        security concerns, challenge
            of 279–80
        standardization and inability to
            customize 279
        standardized services, consistent
            delivery of 277
        wide distribution, benefits of 278
        widening geographies, challenge of
            competition from 280

example, Shakespeare goes
    online 275
exercises 290
franchisees 282
franchising 283–5
    benefits and challenges of 284
    franchisee's perspective 285
    franchisor's perspective 284–5
further reading 291
intermediaries
    alignment of costs with 290
    channel ambiguity 288
    channel conflict over objectives
        and performance 288
    common issues involving 288
    consultation and cooperation
        with 290
    control strategies 289
    cooperative management structure,
        change to 290
    customer-oriented processes,
        development for 289–90
    delivery of service through 281–2
    empowerment and control,
        tensions between 288
    empowerment strategies 289–90
    measurement strategy for control
        of 289
    partnering strategies 290
    quality and consistency across
        outlets 288
    review strategy for control of 289
    strategies for effective delivery
        through 289–90
    support systems, provision of 290
key concepts 290
learning objectives 274
merchant model 286
mobile channels, delivering service
    through 280–81
multi-channel vs omni-channel
    delivery 275–6
omni-channel delivery 276
service deliverer 281
service distribution, other forms
    of 281–2
service principal 281
service spotlights
    car industry intermediary
        performance 290
    ComparetheMarket.com 279
    Disney omni-channel
        experience 276
    Martini beacon technology 281
    Subway sandwich chain
        franchise 283–4
    Takeaway.com 277–8
    Ted Baker's beacon
        mannequins 280
smartphone applications 280
summary 290
Emirates
    customer classification scheme 270
    personalized travel with 458–9
    service 91
Emotion
    environment and 216–17
    mood and 51–2
Emotional labour 234
    appropriate bahaviours, teaching
        of 236
    deep acting 236

Emotional labour (*Continued*)
  demanding customers, passing to
    management of 237
  emotional management skills,
    teaching of appropriate bahaviours
    and 236
  employee breaks and dealing
    with 236–7
  employee views, airing of 236
  management on front line for dealing
    with 236
  occurrence of 235
  physical work environment and 236
  screening for emotional labour
    abilities 235–6
  strategies for management of 235–7
  surface acting 236
Empathy
  customer perceptions of service
    and 91
  empathic design 166
  service delivery and 234
Employee empowerment 242–4
  benefits of 243
  costs of 243
Employees
  behaviours of, effect on service
    quality dimensions 233–4
  satisfaction of, customer satisfaction
    and profits 232–3
  upward communication through
    124–6
Employees' roles in service
    delivery 226, 227–51
  assurance dimension of service
    delivery 233
  audit of internal customer
    service 244–5
  best people
    competing for 240
    retention of 245–8
  boundary-spanning roles 234–9
  brand personification, employees
    and 231–2
  chatbots 238
  company vision, inclusion of
    employees in 245–6
  conflict, sources of 237–8
  corporate culture 229
  customer-focused organization
    chart 248
  customer-oriented service
    delivery 248–9
  delivery of quality in service, strategies
    for use of people in 239–48
  development of a service culture 230
  discussion questions 250–51
  emotional labour 234
    appropriate bahaviours, teaching
      of 236
    deep acting 236
    demanding customers, passing to
      management of 237
    emotional management skills,
      teaching of appropriate
      bahaviours and 236
    employee breaks and dealing
      with 236–7
    employee views, airing of 236
    management on front line for
      dealing with 236
    occurrence of 235

physical work environment
    and 236
  screening for emotional labour
    abilities 235–6
  strategies for management
    of 235–7
  surface acting 236
empathy in service delivery 234
employee behaviours, effect on
  service quality dimensions 233–4
employee empowerment 242–4
  benefits of 243
  costs of 243
employee satisfaction, customer
  satisfaction and profits 232–3
employer branding 240–41
equipment support, provision of 245
example, critical role of
  employees 228
exercises 250
further reading 251
gig economy 234
hiring the right people 239–41
human resource strategies for
  delivering service quality through
  people 239
inter-client conflicts 238
interactive skills, training for 241
internal service quality, measurement
  of 244–5
inverted services marketing
  triangle 249
key concepts 250
learning objectives 227
organization chart, customer-
  focused 248
organization/client conflicts 237
people, strategies for delivering
  service quality through 239–48
person/role conflicts 237
preferred employer, aim of
  being 240–41
profits, employee satisfaction,
  customer satisfaction and 232–3
quality/productivity trade-offs 238–9
reliability of service delivery 233
service competences, hiring for 240
service culture 229–31
  development of 230
  transportation of 230–31
service employees, critical
  importance of 231–4
service inclination, hiring for 240
service leadership 229–30
service-oriented internal processes,
  development of 245
service performers, rewards for
  246–8
service profit chain 233
service quality
  dimensions of, effect of employee
    behaviours on 233–4
  strategies for delivering with
    people 239–48
service spotlights
  Accor brands training
    resources 242
  airline cabin crews, provision of
    Apple iPads for 234
  Allianz sponsorship of Olympic
    Movement 246
  Apple customer connections 232

CitizenM employer branding 241–2
Heathrow Service Quality Rebate
  Scheme 247
McDonald's way, service culture
  and 231
Pret a Manger service culture
  230–31
Starbucks community
  cultivation 241
Virgin Group brand values 229–30
summary 249–50
support systems, provision of 244–5
teamwork, promotion of 244
technical skills, training for 241
technological support, provision
  of 245
transporting a service culture 230–31
treating employees as customers 246
vision of company, inclusion of
  employees in 245–6
Employer branding 240–41
Enabling both customers and
  employees 12
Enberg, J. 414
Encounter expectations *versus* overall
  expectations 72
Ending business relationships 152
ENEL 3
Enterprise Rent-a-Car 151
Eon 120
Equipment constraint on capacity
  296–7, 298
Equipment repair customers, principal
  expectations of 76
Equipment support, provision of 245
Ergonomics 217–18
Ericsson 8, 96
E-service quality (e-SQ) 91–4
ESOMAR 124
Estimation of prices, providers
  unwillingness to 372
Ethics in marketing research 123–4
Ethnography (market-oriented) 118
Etihad, digital elements of air travel
  at 459
Europcar 190–91
Europe
  Bi-level trains of on European
    railways 304
  geographical service clusters in 159
  housing ownership in 56
European Union (EU) 124
  General Data Protection Regulation
    (GDPR) 124
Eurostar customer areas
  makeover 210
Eurostat 4
Evaluation continuum for product
  types 42
Evaluation on self-service 47–8
Evidence
  of service 99–100
  updating and modernization of 222
Evolution of services 11–13
Examples
  Airbnb, peer-to-peer room
    rental 105
  Costa Coffee experience,
    redesign for 204
  critical role of employees 228
  crowdsourcing innovation -
    Giffgaff 158

DHL Freight, understanding service standards from customer perspective 184
evaluation on self-service 47–8
Giffgaff crowdsourcing innovation 158
Hilton Worldwide Revenue Management Consolidated Centre (RMCC) 294
KLM, social media and customer expectations 62
Ritz-Carlton Hotels, service quality gaps and 26–7
Santander's Cycle Partnership 347
Service Industries in Europe 3
Shakespeare goes online 275
Starbucks App 130–31
travelling millennials and buying behaviour 41
Virgin Money, changing perceptions at 82
yield calculations 307–8
YouTube revenge for broken guitars on United Airlines 319–20
Exceeding customer expectations 74–6
Exceeding customer service expectations 77–8
Exercises
  building customer relationships 153–4
  communications (external and internal) management of 367
  consumer behaviour 59
  customer-defined service standards 201
  customer expectations 79–80
  customers' roles in service delivery 272
  demand and capacity management 316
  electronic channels and intermediaries, service delivery through 290
  employees' roles in service delivery 250
  listening to customers 127
  physical and virtual servicescape 224
  pricing of services 384
  service innovation and design 181
  service quality, financial impact of 402
  service quality, gaps model of 38
  service recovery 343
  services 23
Exit surveys 111, 116–17
Expanded marketing mix for services 20
Expedia 63–4, 174
  post-introduction evaluation 170
Experian 106
Experiences
  experience qualities 41–3
  services as 8
Explanation for complaints, adequacy of 336
Explicit service promises 72–3

possible influence strategies for 75
External communication coordination 357–60

F

Facebook 11, 62, 109, 130, 148, 167, 347, 348, 355, 358
Facilitator, servicescape as 211
Facilities
  constraints on capacity 296–7, 298
  usage of, variations of 302
Fail-safe service 332–3
Failure of service 320
  impact of service failure and recovery 320–23
  see also Service failures
Fair Trade, UK Office for 417
Fairmont Hotels 364
Fairness themes in service recovery 327
Farshid Moussavi's retail space for Victoria Beckham's fashion label 214
FedEx
  alignment of internal personnel with customers using measurement 366
  hard measurements for international operations 197
Feedback about employee performance, provision of 200
Fellow customers, dealing with 256–7
Finance Innovation Competitiveness Cluster in France 159
Financial relationship bonds 146–7
Financial Times 11
Firing customers, difficulties of 152–3
First Group 218
Fitness centres, consumer satisfaction with 85
Fleming, N. 415
Flexibility, maintenance of degree of 180
Flueck, David 449
Forbes 3
Ford Sync Emergency Assistance technology 10
Formal service targets and goals 186–7
Fortune 500 Companies 390
Fountain, Daniel 408, 409, 410
Franchisees 282
Franchising 283–5
  benefits and challenges of 284
  franchisee's perspective 285
  franchisor's perspective 284–5
Frequent-flyer programmes 28, 136, 146, 267
Frey, Thomas 65
Friends, customers as 133
Front-end planning for innovation 164, 165–8
Further reading
  building customer relationships 154–5
  communications (external and internal) management of 368

consumer behaviour 60
customer-defined service standards 202
customer expectations 80
customer perceptions of service 102
customers' roles in service delivery 273
demand and capacity management 317
electronic channels and intermediaries, service delivery through 291
employees' roles in service delivery 251
listening to customers 128
physical and virtual servicescape 225
pricing of services 385
service innovation and design 182
service quality, financial impact of 403
service quality, gaps model of 38
service recovery 344
services 24
Future expectations research 111, 120
Future hotels, technology and 65

G

Gap scores, tracking of 121
Gaps model of service quality, illustration of 34
Gatwick self-service bag drop zones 258
Gebbia. Joe 105
General Data Protection Regulation (EU, GDPR) 124
General Foods 14
Generality, tangibility and 350
Geographical service clusters in Europe 159
Giffgaff crowdsourcing innovation 158
Gig economy 234
Global differences in consumer behaviour 54–7
Global reach of services, extension of 12–13
Go Pro 147
Goal-setting 187
Going-rate pricing 377–8
Goods versus services 15
Goodwill 123
Google 357, 358
Google Chromecast 417
Google Home 11
Gottsegen, G. 416
Gould, Matthew 415
Grewal, D. and Pechmann, C. 143
Grisham, John 418
Grönroos, C. 18, 89, 134
Group buying sites 379, 380
Group decision-making 57
Groupon 382

Grove, S.J. and Fisk, R.p. 49–50
Gruca, T.S. and Rego, L.L. 390
Guarantees of service 338–42
Gupta, S. and Zeithaml, V. 390

H

Hachette Livre UK 417, 418
Hamilton, I. and Cain, A. 418
Hanbury, M. 418
Hanze University of Applied Sciences, Groningen 448–55, 456–64
Hard customer-defined standards 189–90
Harley Dadidson Owners Groups 147
Harvard Business Review 398, 399
Harvard Business School 14
Heathrow Service Quality Rebate Scheme 247
Helping oneself 266–7
Helping others 267
Heraldscotland.com 82
Hertz Rentals 393
Heterogeneity of services 16
Hewlett-Packard 7, 8, 393
Hierarchy of needs (Maslow) 43–4
High-performance service innovations 179–80
Hilton Hotels
    Innovation Gallery 168–9
    loyalty programme 452
    mobile phone app services 264
    Worldwide Revenue Management Consolidated Centre (RMCC) 294
Hiring the right people 239–41
H&M 210
Holiday Inns 131
Holloway, R.B. and Beatty, S.E. 93
Horizontal communications 363
    creation of effectiveness in 365
Hotel consumers, principal expectations of 76
Hotel guests, complaints by 260
Hotel visits, service encounter cascade for 94
Hotels and one-time fixes 191
Households, decision-making in 57
Housing ownership in Europe 56
Howard, D. 413
HSBC Holdings 3, 4, 6
Human factors design 217–18
Human resource strategies for delivering service quality through people 239
Hyatt Hotels, loyalty programme 452–3

I

Ibis Hotels 351
    guarantee of perfect stay 340
    Satisfaction Guarantee 73
IBM 4, 7, 28
Ideas generation 166–7
IKEA 161
    Breakfast in Bed Café 359
    co-production 51
    IKEA Place 206
    value creation by customers at 253–4

Impact magazine 105, 106–7
Implementation of service innovation 164, 168–70
Implicit service promises 72, 73
    possible influence strategies for 75
Importance of
    customer expectations 63
    customers in service co-creation and delivery 254–7
Importance/performance matrices 122
Inappropriate customer participation, avoidance of 269–70
Incompleteness risk 160
Incorporeal existence, tangibility and 350
Increasing demand to match capacity 301–3
Individual behaviours in serviscape 218–19
Individual customer needs, variation in 372
Individual responses, variations in 218
Influencing factors on customer expectations 68–74
Information from marketing research, use of 123
Information search 43, 44–6
Information technology (IT) 4, 8, 89, 222, 366, 380, 434
ING Direct 90, 147
ING Group 3
Innovation
    innovative service offerings 11
    successes in, predictors of 158
    see also Service innovation and design
Inseparability 16–17
    resulting marketing implications 17
Institute of Customer Service 86
Intangibility 6, 16
    of service, dealing with 350–51, 353–5
Intangible actions 4
Intangible possessions of people, services directed at 5
Integrated marketing communications (IMC) 349
Integrated service marketing communications (ISMC) 349
Integrated Service Solutions (ISS) 185
Integrated Service Solutions (ISS) standards of service 187
Integration of new services 179
Inter-client conflicts 238
Interaction, alignment of back-office and support personnel with customers by 365–6
Interactive marketing 33–4
Interactive skills, training for 241
Interactive touch-screen ordering kiosks 264–5
InterContinental Hotels Group (IHG) KnowledgeNet 123
Intermediaries 288
    alignment of costs with 290
    channel ambiguity 288
    channel conflict over objectives and performance 288
    common issues involving 288
    consultation and cooperation with 290
    control strategies 289

cooperative management structure, change to 290
customer-oriented processes, development for 289–90
delivery of service through 281–2
empowerment and control, tensions between 288
empowerment strategies 289–90
measurement strategy for control of 289
partnering strategies 290
quality and consistency across outlets 288
review strategy for control of 289
strategies for effective delivery through 289–90
support systems, provision of 290
Internal alignment, achievement of 352
Internal brand selling 364
Internal marketing 349
Internal marketing communication, management of 353, 363–6
Internal responses to servicescape 216–18
Internal service quality, measurement of 244–5
Internet as service 13
Internet of Things (IoT) 11, 12
    service innovation through 163–4
Interpersonal bonds 147
Intesa Sanpaolo 3
Intrusive organizations 151
Inventory capability, underlying issue of lack of 295–6
Inverted services marketing triangle 249
Investment, return on (ROI) 390
Invisibility of prices 373
iPad 62, 82
    airline cabin crews, provision of Apple iPads for 234
Irritating customers 151

J

James, Margot 445
John Lewis & Partners, customer experience (case study) 422–9
    'click and collect' initiative 423
    consumer behaviour 424
    cooperative management 422
    cumulative customer experience 425–6
    customer experience strategy 425
    differentiation strategy 426–7
    digitalization era 425
    economic uncertainty 424
    employee-ownership 423
    e-service features 425
    experience desk 427
    growth trajectory 422
    John Lewis and Partners (JLP), establishment of (1864) 422
    multi-channel retailing 424
    'Never Knowingly Undersold' 422
    omni-channel offering, continuous improvement aim 422–3
    omni-channel platform 422
    online retailing 424–5
    popularity 422

restructuring programme 425
Royal Warrant 422
sales revenue 423
'smarter shopping,' effects of 424
touch-point shopping 425
turbulent times for UK retail 423–5
Waitrose & Partners 423
winning approach 426–7
year-on-year growth rate 424
Johnson, D. 413, 418
Journal of Marketing 208, 213
Journal of Marketing 6, 9, 15,
89, 396
*Journal of the Academy of Marketing
Science* 18
JP Morgan Chase 415

K

Kaori Gurley, J. 418
Kaplan, J.R.S. and Norton, D.P. 398
Keiningham, Timothy 87
Key concepts
building customer
relationships 153
communications (external
and internal) management
of 367
consumer behaviour 58–9
customer-defined service
standards 201
customer expectations 79
customer perceptions of
service 100–101
customers' roles in service
delivery 272
demand and capacity
management 315
electronic channels and
intermediaries, service delivery
through 290
employees' roles in service
delivery 250
listening to customers 127
physical and virtual
servicescape 223
pricing of services 384
service innovation and
design 181
service quality, financial impact
of 402
service quality, gaps
model of 38
service recovery 342–3
services 23
Key ways service prices differ for
consumers 371–5
KFC 354
Khurana, A. and
Rosenthal, S.R. 164
Kim, W.C. and
Mauborgne, R. 405, 406
King, Stephen 418
KLM 13, 72, 190–91, 210, 355
service standards 198
social media and customer
expectations 62
Known, finite waits feel shorter than
uncertain waits 314
Kotler, P. 18, 348

Krueger, Alan 441
Kwik Fit 117

L

Labour constraint on capacity 296–7,
298
Lands' End customer service
guarantee 339
Lasting service intensifiers 69
possible influence strategies for 75
Learning objectives
Building customer relationships 129
Communications (external and
internal) management of 346
Consumer behaviour 40
Customer-defined service
standards 183
Customer expectations 61
Customer perceptions of service 81
Customers' roles in service
delivery 252
Demand and capacity
management 293
Electronic channels and
intermediaries, service delivery
through 274
Employees' roles in service
delivery 227
Listening to customers 104
Physical and virtual
servicescape 203
Pricing of services 369
Service innovation and design 157
Service quality, financial impact
of 387
Service quality, gaps model of 25
Service recovery 318
Services 2
Legal & General Insurance 354
Lego 167
Levels of expectation 63–5
Levie, Michael 405
Lifetime value 138
calculation of, example of 138
estimation of 138
LinkedIn 348, 355
Linking customer relationship value to
firm value 139
Listening gap 103
Listening to customers 103, 104–28
artificial intelligence (AI) 109
big data analytics 107–8
communication upward through
employees 124–6
objectives of 124–5
research for 125–6
competition tracking 121
complaint solicitation 111, 112
confidentiality 123
critical incident studies 111, 113
critical incident technique (CIT) 113
customer databases 106–8
customer expectations, use
of marketing research to
understand 109–10
customer needs research 111, 113–14
customer panels 111, 119–20
customer satisfaction surveys 111,
114–16

disconfirmation paradigm 116
data analytics 108
data mining 108
database marketing research 111
disconfirmation paradigm 116
discussion questions 128
effective services marketing research
programme, elements in 110–20
employees, upward communication
through 124–6
ethics in marketing research 123–4
ethnography (market-oriented) 118
example, Airbnb, peer-to-peer room
rental 105
exercises 127
exit surveys 111, 116–17
further reading 128
future expectations research 111, 120
gap scores, tracking of 121
goodwill 123
importance/performance
matrices 122
information from marketing
research, use of 123
key concepts 127
learning objectives 104
lost customer follow-up 111, 120
market-oriented ethnography 111,
118
marketing research 106, 109–10
elements for effectiveness in
services research 110–20
ethics in 123–4
findings of, analysis and
interpretation of 121–3
research objectives for
services 110
use of information from 123
use to understand customer
expectations 109–10
monitoring user-generated content
and netnography 108–9
mystery shopping 111, 118–19
netnography 109
online ethnography 109
performance tracking 121
post-transaction surveys 111, 116–17
process checkpoint
evaluations 117–18
professionalism 123
relationship surveys 114–16
disconfirmation paradigm 116
research approaches, primary
objectives and 111
research objectives for services 110
research programmes 109–10
service expectation meetings and
reviews 111, 117
service spotlights
American Express Australia, use of
big data by 108
Asda customer listening
programme 125
Asda customer-perception tracker
survey 113
EasyJet online customer
community 112
InterContinental Hotels Group
(IHG) KnowledgeNet 123
Telefónica O$_2$ loyalty
programme 113–14
Ticketmaster data analysis 106–7

Listening to customers (*Continued*)
Transport for London, mystery shopping at 119
Volvo ethnographic approach in research 118
services marketing research programmes 109–10
SERVPERF instrument 116
SERVQUAL surveys 111, 114–16
perception statements in 115
Sport and Leisure Management 116
summary 126–7
trust 129
upward communication 124–6
elements of effective programme for 124
employee suggestions 126
executive visits to customers 125
managers' listening to customers 125
managers' listening to employees 126
objectives of 124–5
research for 125–6
research on intermediate customers 125
research on internal customers 126
user-generated content and netnography, monitoring of 108–9
zones of tolerance charts 121–2
Live Nation Entertainment 106
LLoyds Banking Group 3
London Underground 199, 200
Loss leadership 383
Lost customers
follow-up on 111, 120
learning from 337–8
research on 335
Lovelock, C.H. 4
Lower costs, defence with 393
Lowery, G. 418
Loyalty vs switching following service recovery 330–31
Lufthansa 6
Lusch, Bob 9
Luxurytraveldiary.com 380
Luzern & WBR Digital 417

M

McDonald's 64–5, 204, 206, 356, 359
to Go 305–6
McDonald's way, service culture and 231
Ronald MacDonald House 354
UK restaurant redesign 222
McDonald's, designing services processes and innovations (case study) 430–37
Abi-Gerges, Claude 433
Amazon online shopping and 434
benefits of electronic channels (Internet and Mobile Apps) 432
big data, customer data and 435
drone delivery 433–4
Dynamic Yield AI machine-learning start-up 434, 435
Easterbrook, Steve 435
electronic channels (distribution and technology) 431

electronic service delivery channels 430–33
Experience of the Future restaurants (EOTFs) 431
'McDelivery' service 433
McDonald's App 431–2
McDonald's restaurants
disposition of 430
operational arrangements 430
'mission to embody a culture of innovation' 435
mobile and electronic channels, delivering service through 431
overview of McDonalds 430
physical service delivery channels 430
processes and delivery systems, adaptations in 435
self-order kiosks 433
showcasing in-store 432–3
structure of McDonalds business 430
touchscreen channels 432–3
Uber Eats and 433–4
virtual delivery channels 430–33
voice-based technological acquisitions 434
MacGillavry, K and Wilson, A. 184
Major innovations 161
Making service fail-safe 332–3
Management of service expectations, issues involving 74–9
Manners and customs, differences across cultures 55
Marani, Matthew 406
Market-oriented ethnography 111, 118
Market Research Society 105, 106–7, 124
Market segments
demand patterns and 300
incompatibility of, customer and 149–50
segmentation pricing 379
Market testing 169
Marketing
customer equity and return on 394–7
price structures, service provision and 376
return on, calculation using customer equity 397
Marketing Magazine 88
Marketing Management: Analysis, Planning, Implementation, and Control (Kotler, P.) 18, 348
Marketing mix
people 19–20
physical evidence 20–21
place 20
price 20
process 20, 21–2
product 20
promotion 20
Marketing News 121
Marketing research 106, 109–10
elements for effectiveness in services research 110–20
ethics in 123–4
findings of, analysis and interpretation of 121–3
research objectives for services 110
use of information from 123
use to understand customer expectations 109–10

Marketing Science Institute 14, 68
Marketing Week 347
Marriott Hotels 94, 95, 167, 192, 205, 394
Marriott International, new concept testing 161
Marriott International, opportunity window for customer experience (case study) 448–55
Boulud, Daniel 110
customer profitability segmentation strategy 451–3
customer pyramid 452
data breach 453–4
development, 2018 significant year for 448–9
Early Month On Book (EMOB) marketing 450
email strategy 450
expansion and consolidation 448–50
Expedia, power over 448
Facebook page 450
Flueck, David 449
foundations 448
growth trajectory 454
Hilton Hotels, loyalty programme 452
Hyatt Hotels, loyalty programme 452–3
loyalty offering, extension of 453
loyalty programmes 449, 450–51
Marriott Bonvoy 449, 450, 451
Marriott Bonvoy Traveler 450
Marriott International News Center 449
Moments experience platform 450
Priceline, power over 448
relationship building 451
Sorenson, Arne 448
Starwood Preferred Guest programme (SPG) 449, 451
sub-brands 449
vacation and leisure experiences 448
word-of-mouth (WOM) communications 449–50
Martini beacon technology 281
Maslow, Abraham 43–4
MasterCard 357–8
customer relationship 147
Material cultures, differences in 55
McFarland, Billy 443
McLaren Honda 347
Measurements
alignment of back-office and support personnel with customers by 366
against standards, tracking of 199–200
for standards, development of 196–8
Mental impalpability, tangibility and 350
Merchant model 286
Mest, Elliott 406
Microsoft 125
Minds of people, services directed at 5
Misener, P. 416
Mobile apps 358–9
Mobile channels, delivering service through 280–81
Monetary and non-monetary costs 373
Monitoring user-generated content, netnography and 108–9
Mood and emotion 51–2
M&S (Marks and Spencer) 149

Multi-channel vs omni-channel delivery 275–6
Multiple segments, attraction of 383
Murphy, Matt 410
Music Festivals, pride of live performances at (case study) 438–47
advance interest, generation of 444
Advertising Standards Authority (ASA) 445
anti-competitive practices 445–6
artists and music festivals 438
attending music festivals 440–43
average price of festival tickets in Europe (2014-2018) 441
average price of music festivals (2014-2018) 442
Chirinos, Carlos 439–40
corporate sponsorship 439, 440
costs of attending music festivals 440–43
Deloitte survey (2019) 440
Drake 446
dynamic pricing 444
Eavis, Michael and Emily 442
Eilish, Billie 446
Eventbrite pricing suggestions 444
festival-goers' expectations 438
future of music festivals 445
Fyre Festival 442–3
Generation Z 439–40
GetMeIn 444–5
Glastonbury 438, 439, 441
attendance at 442
ticket costs for 441–2
global music promoters (2018) 441
group discounts 444
growth of music festivals 438–40
iBeacon 445
James, Margot 445
Kilimanjaro Live 445
Krueger, Alan 441
Live Nation 440
Livewire 441
Lizzo 446
McFarland, Billy 443
membership and sponsors, reconfiguration of prices for 444
merchandising 440
monopolistic behaviours 445–6
music festival promotors 440
on-site ticket prices 444
organizing music festivals 440
Performing Rights Society (PRS) 440
price bundling 444
pricing approaches 443–4
pricing strategies 443–4
re-sale of tickets 438, 444–5
resale of tickets, ongoing legal challenge on 445
revenue streams 440
richness of experience 438
Rockonomics (Krueger, A.) 441
Seatwave 444–5
Sheeran, Ed 445, 446
South By Southwest (SXSW) 445
sponsorship deals 439, 440
strategies for festival ticketing 443–4
StubHub 444–5
ticket re-selling agents 438
tourism and popularity of 439
unauthorized re-selling websites 444
valued customers, incentivization of 444
Viagogo 444–5
wearable technology 445
MyCustomer.com 62
Mystery shopping 111, 118–19

N

Nando's 354
National customer satisfaction indices 86–8
National Health Service (UK, NHS) 415
Nayyar, P. 390
Need recognition 43–4
Negative customer outcomes, avoidance of 269–70
Net Promoter Score (NPS) 114, 391, 392
customer-defined service standards and 197
Netflix 3, 148, 162
Netnography 109
New Product Management for the 1980s (Booz-Allen & Hamilton) 164
New service development processes 160–61
New service strategy development 166
New service strategy matrix 166
NHS (National Health Service) Choices Health Apps Library 12
Nike 8
Nike Town 216, 219
servicescape design 217
Noble Jeans 364
Non-financial performance measurements, mistakes in 400
Non-monetary cost priorities 374
Non-monetary costs, reduction of 374–5
Non-monetary costs, role of 373–5
Non-peak use, offer of incentives for 301
Non-searchability, tangibility and 350
Nordic model of service experience 89
Norsk Kundebarometer 86
Northern Ireland Education Department customer service standards 195–6
Nottingham Business School 422–9
Novotel 210

O

Odd pricing 381
Offensive marketing effects of service 391–2, 395
Office building revovation, architectural consultation for 260
Oliver, Richard L. 84
Omni-channel delivery 276
One-stop-shop concept 88
One-time fixes 190–91
O'Neill, Thomas 411
Online advertising 358
Online and offline marketing communication channels, need for coordination on 348–9
Online and offline word-of-mouthcommunications 72, 73
Online auction sites 380
Online brand communities 147
Online ethnography 109
Operational logic, employment of 311–12
Optimal vs maximum use of capacity 297–8
Ordering kiosks, interactive and touch-screen 264–5
Organisation for Economic Co-operation and Development (OECD) 159
Organization chart, customer-focused 248
Organization/client conflicts 237
Organizations, decision-making in 57–8
Outcome, interaction and physical environment quality 88
Oversimplification 159–60

P

Package, servicescape as 210
Paid research advertising 358
Parasuraman, A., Zeithaml, V.A. and Berry, L.L. 15
Parasuraman, Parsu 89, 145
Parsons, R. 347
Partners, customers as 133–4
Passive relational customer expectations 134
Past experience 72, 73
possible influence strategies for 75
Patterson, James 418
Payback in technology investments 13
Peak demand periods, teaching avoidance of 363
Peak time reduction in demand 301
Penetration pricing 381
People
bodies of people, services directed at 5
person/role conflicts 237
services marketing and 19
strategies for delivering service quality through 239–48
Perceived risk 45–6, 47
Perceived service alternatives 69, 70
possible influence strategies for 75
Perceived value 378
Perez, S. 416
Performance confirmation to standards and expectations 362–3
Performance measurement 397–401
performance measures that matter 401
Performance of customers, education and training for effectiveness in 268–9
Performance seekers, attraction of 383
Performance to promises, failure to match (provider gap 4) 33–4, 37
Performance tracking 121
Perishability (and resulting marketing implications) 17

Person/role conflicts 237
Personal needs 68–9
   possible influence strategies
      for 75
Personal selling 360
Personal service philosophy 69
Philips Electronics services
   innovations 162–3
Philips Lifeline service 163
Phillips moodpad 210
PhocusWire 411
Physical and virtual servicescape 156,
   202–25
   ambient conditions 213, 214–15
   augmented reality (AR) 206
   behaviours in servicescape 218–19
   'clue management' 206–7
   cognition, environment and 216
   cross-functional working 222
   differentiator, servicescape as
      211–12
   discussion questions 224
   emotion, environment and 216–17
   ergonomics 217–18
   evidence, updating and
      modernization of 222
   example, Costa Coffee experience,
      redesign for 204
   exercises 224
   facilitator, servicescape as 211
   further reading 225
   human factors design 217–18
   individual behaviours in
      servicescape 218–19
   individual responses, variations
      in 218
   internal responses to
      serviscape 216–18
   key concepts 223
   learning objectives 203
   package, servicescape as 210
   physical and virtual evidence 205–8
      recognition of strategic impact
         of 220
      of service, blueprinting of 221
   physical environment, framework for
      understanding 213
   physical evidence
      affect on customer
         experience 206–8
      elements of 205
      examples from customer
         perspective 207
      opportunities, assessment and
         identification of 221
      strategy, guidelines for 220–22
   physical servicescape
      environmental dimensions
         of 213–16
      underlying framework 212–13
   physiology, environment
      and 217–18
   screeners of environmental
      stimuli 218
   service spotlights
      Abercrombie & Fitch scent in
         stores 215
      APS Bank branch interior
         redesign 212
      ChiantiBanca Restaurant
         Experience Banking 208

Eurostar customer areas
   makeover 210
Farshid Moussavi's retail space
   for Victoria Beckham's fashion
   label 214
McDonalds UK restaurant
   redesign 222
Nike Towns and servicescape
   design 217
Quantas and Hamilton Island
   virtual reality experience 206
Tyne and Wear Metro, impact
   of environment on behaviour
   at 219
servicescape 204
servicescape complexity 209
servicescape effects on behaviour,
   framework for understanding
   212–20
servicescape usage 208, 209
signs, symbols and artefacts 213,
   215–16
social interactions in servicescape 219
socializer, servicescape as 211
spatial layout and functionality 213,
   215
stimulus-organism-response
   theory 212
strategic roles of servicecape,
   clarification of 221
strategic roles of servicescape
   210–12
summary 222–3
typology of servicescapes 208–9
virtual environment-user
   relationships in service
   organisations, framework for
   understanding 220
virtual reality (VR) 205
virtual servicescapes 205
   underlying framework 219–20
Physical environment, framework for
   understanding 213
Physiology, environment and 217–18
Pich, Christopher 422–9
Pine and Gilmore 8
Pizza Hut 185
Place differentials, prices and 383
Pleasurable waiting (or tolerable
   waiting), development of 313–15
Poka-yoke fail-safe service 332
Pokémon GO 206
Poltrona Frau 210
Poorrezaei, Mojtaba 422–9
Portfolio management for new
   products 179
Positive moods 52
Post, J. 414
Post-experience evaluation 52–4
Post-introduction evaluation 169–70
Post-transaction surveys 111,
   116–17
Postmodern human behaviour 51
Pre-process waits feel longer than in-
   process waits 313
Predicted service 69, 71–2
   influencing factors 71
   possible influence strategies for 75
   sources of 72–3
Preferred employer, aim of being
   240–41

Premier Inn hub concept 66–7
Premium prices, defence with 393
Preparation of customers for service
   process 361–2
Prestige pricing 381
Pret a Manger service culture 230–31
Price adaptation 380–83
Price as indicator of service quality 375
Price bundling 382
Price differentiation to match demand
   with capacity 302–3
Price framing 382
Price information, services
   overwhelmed by collection of 372
Price premiums, defence with 393
Price signalling 377
Prices not visible 373
Prices of services, knowledge of 371
PriceWaterhouseCoopers 58
Pricing of services 345, 369–85
   adaptation of prices 380–83
   approaches to 375–9
   bargain-hunters, attraction of 381
   bundling prices 382
   collection of price information
      overwhelming services 372
   comparison websites
      (aggregators) 379–80
   competition-based pricing 371,
      377–8
      for services, examples of 377–8
      for services, special challenges
         for 377
   complementary pricing 382–3
   contingency pricing 383
   convenience costs 374
   convenience seekers, attraction
      of 382–3
   cost-based pricing 371, 375–7
      for services, special challenges
         for 376
      strategies for services 376–7
   customer knowledge of service
      prices 371–3
   customer needs, variation in 372
   demand-based pricing 371, 378–9
      for services, examples of 378–9
      for services, special challenges
         for 378
   discounting 381
   discussion questions 384–5
   dynamic pricing 379–80
      examples in service industries
         of 379–80
      for services, examples of 379–80
      for services, special challenges
         for 379
      special challenges for services
         in 379
   estimation of prices, providers
      unwillingness to 372
   exercises 384
   further reading 385
   going-rate pricing 377–8
   group buying sites 379, 380
   individual customer needs,
      variation in 372
   invisibility of prices 373
   key concepts 384
   key ways service prices differ for
      consumers 371–5

learning objectives 369
loss leadership 383
market segmentation pricing 379
marketing price structures, service
 provision and 376
monetary and non-monetary
 costs 373
multiple segments, attraction of 383
non-monetary costs
 priorities for 374
 reduction of 374–5
 role of 373–5
odd pricing 381
online auction sites 380
penetration pricing 381
perceived value 378
performance seekers, attraction of 383
place differentials, prices and 383
prestige pricing 381
price adaptation 380–83
price as indicator of service
 quality 375
price bundling 382
price framing 382
price information, services
 overwhelmed by collection of 372
price signalling 377
prices not visible 373
prices of services, knowledge of 371
providers unwillingness to estimate
 prices 372
psychological costs 374
quantity differentials, prices and 383
reference prices 371
results-based pricing 383
search costs 373–4
segmentation pricing by market,
 elasticities of demand and 379
service prices, customer knowledge
 of 371–3
service prices, key differences for
 consumers 371–5
service quality, price as indicator
 of 375
service spotlights
 Disneyland Paris, waiting times
  at 374
 rental car going-rate
  pricing 378
 scyscanner.net online flight
  aggregator 380
 Subway value pricing 382
service variability limits
 knowledge of 371–2
skimming pricing 382
status seekers, attraction of 381–2
summary 384
time costs 373
time differentials, prices and 383
two-part pricing 383
variability in service limits,
 knowledge of 371–2
Pricing to balance of capacity with
 demand 301
Priority setting to balance of capacity
 with demand 301
Process, services marketing and 21
Process checkpoint evaluations 117–18
Process for setting customer-defined
 standards 192
Processes, services as 49
Procter & Gamble 14

Productive resources, customers
 as 257–8
Products, services as 7–8
Professionalism 123
Profitability and service, direct
 relationship between 389–91, 395
Profitability tiers
 business decision-making using 142
 customer pyramid 140–41
 view of customers on 141–2
Profits, employee satisfaction,
 customer satisfaction and 232–3
Profits, service and 389–91
 asymmetric relationship between
  satisfaction and financial
  performance 390
 customer satisfaction, financial
  performance and 390
 performance setting targets 400
 profitability-satisfaction link,
  variability of 390–91
 validation of profitability-satisfaction
  links 400
Project choice 179
Promise keeping, customer satisfaction
 and 88
Promises kept 88
Promoting the company 267
Property insurance customers,
 principal expectations of 76
Provider gaps 28–37
Providers' unwillingness to estimate
 prices 372
Prudential 3
Psychological costs 374
Psychology of queuing 313–15
Public relations 359
Public relations channels 349
Purchase of service 43, 46
Purchase volumes, defence with 393

Q

Qatar Airways, luxury with 459
Quality/productivity trade-offs 238–9
Quality-satisfaction link 83
Quantas Airways 205
 Hamilton Island virtual reality
  experience 206
Quantity differentials, prices and 383
Queuing strategies 310–15

R

Radian6 109
Radical innovations 161, 162
Radisson Blu 56
Rail capacity in UK 297
Random demand fluctuations 299
RATER (reliability, assurance,
 tangibles, empathy,
 responsiveness) 83, 89
Reading suggestions see Further reading
Realsim in promises 360
Recovery expectations of
 customers 326–30
Recovery experiences, learning
 from 337

Recovery from service failures, impact
 of failure and 320–23
Recruitment
 education and rewards for
  customers 268–70
 of the right customers 268
Red Bull 147
Reference prices 371
Reichheld, F.F. and Sasser, W.E. 399
Reichheld, Frederick 87
 Net Promoter metric of 87
Relationship bonds 145–9
Relationship building 88
 customer satisfaction and 88
Relationship challenges 149–53
Relationship development 132
 model for 143
 strategies for 143–9
Relationship endings 152
Relationship enhancement 179–80
Relationship marketing 131–7
 benefits for customers and
  firms 135–7
 benefits for firms 136
 confidence benefits 135
 customer behaviour benefits 136–7
 customer irritation with 151
 economic benefits 136
 goal of 134–5
 human resource management (HRM)
  benefits 137
 negativity towards 151–2
 social benefits 135–6
 special treatment benefits 136
Relationship strategies, levels of 146
Relationship surveys 114–16
 disconfirmation paradigm 116
Relationship value
 of customers 137–9
 factors influencing 137–8
 service dominant logic perspective
  on 139
Relationships with customers
 cultivation of 337
 see also Building customer
  relationships
Reliability 90
 of service delivery 233
Rental car going-rate pricing 378
Repurchase intentions of unhappy
 customers 321
Research approaches, primary
 objectives and 111
Research objectives for services 110
Research programmes 109–10
Reservation process, establishment
 of 312
Resnick, Sheilagh 422–9
Responsiveness 91
Results-based pricing 383
Retention strategies 144
Return on investment (ROI) 179
Revenue management 303
 average daily rate (ADR)
  measurement 310
 challenges and risks in use of 309
 gross operating profit per available
  room (GOPPAR)
  measurement 310
 measurement of effectiveness of
  activities 310
 occupancy rate measurement 310

Revenue management (*Continued*)
  revenue per available room
    (RevPAR) measurement 310
  revenue per occupied room
    (RevPOR) measurement 310
  system, implementation of 308–9
  total revenue per available room
    (Total RevPAR) measurement 310
Rewards for customer
    contributions 269
Right-first-time service 332–3
Ritz-Carlton Hotels 77–8, 191, 393
  service quality gaps and 26–7
  service recovery forms 337
Robbins, Tom 410, 411
Roche, Dee 62
Rockonomics (Krueger, A.) 441
Roles of customers 257–62
  defining customers' roles 265–8
Rolls-Royce 11
  TotalCare® programme 163–4
Rossolillo, N. 414
Royal Bank of Scotland (RBS) 199
Royal Caribbean Cruises
    customization 148
Rust, R. and Oliver, R. 89
Rust, R.T., Zeithaml, V.A. and Lemon,
    K.N. 396
Ryanair 381

S

Sage Accounting Software 185
Sainato, M. 418
Sainsbury's
  customer interaction and
    empathy 333–4
  Smartshop Scan, Pay and Go app 311
Sales promotion 359
Sales promotion channels 349
SAP 147
Satisfaction *versus* service quality 82–3
Schorr, James L. 131
Schultz, Howard 466–7, 468, 470
Schwär, Ariel 419
Scottish and Southern Energy (SSE)
    Energy Supplier Guaranteed
    Standards 188
Screeners of environmental stimuli 218
Search costs 373–4
Search engine optimization 357
Search qualities 41–3
Segmentation pricing by market,
    elasticities of demand and 379
Self-perceived service role 69, 70–71
  possible influence strategies for 75
Self-scanning tills, strategies for
    popularisation of 268
Self-service anxiety 264
Self-service technologies (SSTs) 12,
    47–8
  categories and examples of 47
  customer usage of 264–5
  Customers' roles in service
    delivery 262–5
  problems with 48
  proliferation of new services 262–4
  strong feelings and beneficial uses
    for 47–8
  success with 265

Selling brand inside company 364
Serrano, S. 417
Service brands, creation of strength
    in 356–7
Service communication strategies
    350–52
Service competences, hiring for 240
Service contexts 6–9
Service culture 229–31
  development of 230
  transportation of 230–31
Service delivery
  consumer experience during 48–52
  new ways for 11–12
  'reality check' on 76
  service deliverer 281
  unique role of customers in 254
Service design and standards, lack of
    delivery of (provider gap 3) 31–2,
    36–7
Service development and testing 168
Service distribution, other forms
    of 281–2
Service dominant logic 9–10
Service effectiveness, communication
    of criteria and levels of 361
Service employees, critical importance
    of 231–4
Service encounters
  adaptability theme 96, 97, 98, 99
  building blocks of customer
    perceptions 94–9
  coping theme 96, 97, 98, 99
  critical incident technique 96
  encounter cascade 94
  face-to-face encounters 96
  identification of existing or desired
    sequence 192
  importance of 95
  'moment of truth' and 94
  remote encounters 95–6
  service recovery theme 96, 97,
    98, 99
  sources of pleasure and displeasure
    in 96–9
  spontaneity theme 96, 97, 98, 99
  telephone encounters 96
  themes 97–9
  types of 95–6
Service expectations
  expectation meetings and
    reviews 111, 117
  meaning and types of 63–8
Service failures
  accountability for 326–7
  attribution expectations 329–30
  complaint actions following 323
  customer responses to 323–6
  customer understanding of 326–7
  fair treatment of customers
    following 327–8, 336–7
  interactional justice following 327,
    328, 329
  outcome justice following 327, 328,
    329
  procedural justice following 327, 328,
    329–30
  recovery and, impact of 320–23
Service guarantees
  benefits of 339–40
  communications management
    and 360

effective guarantees, characteristics
    of 340–41
  external vs internal guarantees 340
  satisfaction vs service attribute
    guarantees 340
  service recovery and 338–42
  types of 340–41
  use of (when and when not to
    use) 341–2
Service improvements 161–2
Service inclination, hiring for 240
Service Industries in Europe 3
Service innovation and design 156,
    157–82
  biased interpretation 160
  business analysis 168
  business strategy development (or
    review) 165–6
  commercialization 169
  concept development and
    evaluation 167–8
  crowdsourcing 167
  currently served markets, new
    services for 161
  discussion questions 181
  empathic design 166
  example, crowdsourcing innovation
    (Giffgaff) 158
  exercises 181
  Finance Innovation Competitiveness
    Cluster in France 159
  flexibility, maintenance of degree
    of 180
  front-end planning for 164, 165–8
  further reading 182
  geographical service clusters in
    Europe 159
  high-performance service
    innovations 179–80
  ideas generation 166–7
  implementation of 164, 168–70
  incompleteness risk 160
  innovation successes, predictors
    of 158
  integration of new services 179
  Internet of Things (IoT), service
    innovation through 163–4
  key concepts 181
  learning objectives 157
  major innovations 161
  market testing 169
  new service development
    processes 160–61
  new service strategy
    development 166
  new service strategy matrix 166
  oversimplification 159–60
  portfolio management for new
    products 179
  post-introduction evaluation 169–70
  project choice 179
  radical innovations 161, 162
  relationship enhancement 179–80
  return on investment (ROI) 179
  service blueprinting 170–79
    backstage contact employee
      actions 171
    bank cash machine 175
    benefits and uses of
      applications 176
    blueprint components 171–2
    building a blueprint 176–9

contact employee actions, mapping of 178
customer actions 171
customer identification 178
definition of 170–71
evidence of service at each customer action step, adding of 179
examples of 172–4
frequently asked questions about 176–7
interaction, line of 172
internal interaction, line of 172
linking contact activities to needed support functions 178–9
mapping process from customer perspective 178
onstage contact employee actions 171
overnight hotel stay 172–4
physical evidence 172
reading and using service blueprints 174–6
service process identification 178
support processes 171–2
technology actions, mapping of 178
technology-delivered self-service 174
visibility, line of 172
service development and testing 168
service improvements 161–2
service innovations
descriptions of 159–60
development of, stages in 164–70
policy on, challenges of 158–60
service line extensions 161
service-related cluster initiatives 159
'Service Research Priorities in a Rapidly Changing Context' (2015) 159
service spotlights
Alibaba new service developments 165
Expedia post-introduction evaluation 170
Hilton Innovation Gallery 168–9
Marriott International new concept testing 161
Philips Electronics services innovations 162–3
Rolls-Royce TotalCare® programme 163–4
start-up businesses 161
style changes 162
subjectivity risk 160
success, consideration of multiple measures of 179–80
summary 180
Service innovations
descriptions of 159–60
development of, stages in 164–70
policy on, challenges of 158–60
Service intangibility, addressing 350–51, 353–5
Service leadership 229–30
Service line extensions 161
Service Management and Marketing (Grönroos, C.) 18
Service marketers, challenges and questions for 17–18
Service offerings, variations of 302

Service options, offering of 360–61
Service organizations 6–7
Service-oriented internal processes, development of 245
Service performance, confirmation to standards and expectations 362–3
Service performance indices, development of 200
Service performers, rewards for 246–8
Service prices
customer knowledge of 371–3
key differences for consumers 371–5
Service principal 281
Service process, preparation of customers for 361–2
Service profit chain 14, 233
Service promises, management of 351, 353, 356–60
Service provision as drama 49–50
Service quality 89–94
assurance inspiring trust and confidence 89, 90
customer judgements on dimensions of 92–3
design and standards, errors in selection of (provider gap 2) 29–30, 36
dimensions of 89–91, 92–3
dimensions of, effect of employee behaviours on 233–4
empathy and treating customers as individuals 89, 91
perceptions of 395
price as indicator of 375
quality gaps model audit 35–7
reliability and delivering on promises 89, 90
responsiveness and being willing to help 89, 91
satisfaction and, customers as contributors to 259–61
satisfaction versus 82–3
strategies for delivering with people 239–48
tangibles representing service physically and virtually 89, 90–91
Service quality, financial impact of 386, 387–403
balanced performance scorecard 397–401
balanced scorecard of service, measurements for 398
company performance measurement 397–401
customer attraction, offensive marketing and 391–2
customer equity
concept of 396
importance of 397
model for 396
return on marketing and 394–7
return on marketing using, calculation of 397
in strategic framework 396
customer retention, defensive marketing and 392–3
defensive marketing effects of service 392–3, 395
discussion questions 402
drivers of service quality, customer retention and profits 295, 394

economic worth of customers, service quality and 395
exercises 402
further reading 403
key concepts 402
learning objectives 387
lower costs, defence with 393
marketing
customer equity and return on 394–7
return on, calculation using customer equity 397
non-financial performance measurements, mistakes in 400
offensive marketing effects of service 391–2, 395
performance measurement 397–401
performance measures that matter 401
premium prices, defence with 393
price premiums, defence with 393
profitability and service, direct relationship between 389–91, 395
profits, service and 389–91
asymmentric relationship between satisfaction and financial performance 390
customer satisfaction, financial performance and 390
performance setting targets 400
profitability-satisfaction link, variability of 390–91
validation of profitability-satisfaction links 400
purchase volumes, defence with 393
service quality, perceptions of 395
service spotlights
Colt, customer orientation at 391
EDF Group balanced scorecard approach 399
Stora Enso net promotor score (NPS) 392
'share of wallet' aim 393
shareholder value, performance measures and 401
summary 401–2
volume purchases, defence with 393
word-of-mouth communication, defence with 393
Zappos, value of investing in service quality 388
Service quality, gaps model of 25–38
closing gaps 34
customer expectations, lack of knowledge of (provider gap 1) 28–9, 35–6
customer gap 27, 35, 39
discussion questions 38
example, Ritz-Carlton Hotels 26–7
exercises 38
further reading 38
gaps model of service quality, illustration of 34
interactive marketing 33–4
key concepts 38
learning objectives 25
performance to promises, failure to match (provider gap 4) 33–4, 37
provider gaps 28–37
service design and standards, lack of delivery of (provider gap 3) 31–2, 36–7

Service quality, gaps model of
  (Continued)
  service quality design and standards,
    errors in selection of (provider gap
    2) 29–30, 36
  service quality gaps model audit 35–7
  service spotlight, standards set by
    external bodies 30–31
  service strategy, use of gaps model
    for assessment of 35
  summary 35
Service receipt by customers 255
Service recovery 226, 318–44
  complaint actions following service
    failure 323
    activist complainers 325
    complainer types 325–6
    irate complainers 325
    passive complainers 325
    quick action before legislative
      force is applied 338
    reasons for taking (and not
      taking) 324
    speed of 335–6, 338
    types of 324–5
    voicers of complaint 325
  complaint service, provision of
    adequate explanation 336
  complaint tracking 333–5
  customer perceptions of service and 88
  customer recovery expectations
    326–30
  customer relationships, cultivation
    of 337
  customer responses to service
    failures 323–6
  customer satisfaction and 88
  discussion questions 343–4
  example, YouTube revenge for
    broken guitars on United
    Airlines 319–20
  exercises 343
  explanation for complaints, adequacy
    of 336
  fail-safe service 332–3
  failure of service 320
  fairness themes in service
    recovery 327
  further reading 344
  guarantees of service 338–42
  Ibis Hotels guarantee of perfect
    stay 340
  impact of service failure and
    recovery 320–23
  key concepts 342–3
  learning objectives 318
  lost customer research 335
  lost customers, learning
    from 337–8
  loyalty vs switching following
    service recovery 330–31
  making service fail-safe 332–3
  paradox of 321–3
  poka-yoke fail-safe service 332
  recovery effects 320–21
  recovery expectations of
    customers 326–30
  recovery experiences, learning
    from 337
  recovery from service failures,
    impact of failure and 320–23

relationships with customers,
  cultivation of 337
repurchase intentions of unhappy
  customers 321
right-first-time service 332–3
service failures
  accountability for 326–7
  attribution expectations 329–30
  complaint actions following 323
  customer responses to 323–6
  customer understanding of 326–7
  fair treatment of customers
    following 327–8, 336–7
  interactional justice following 327,
    328, 329
  outcome justice following 327,
    328, 329
  procedural justice following 327,
    328, 329–30
  recovery and, impact of 320–23
service guarantees 338–42
  benefits of 339–40
  effective guarantees,
    characteristics of 340–41
  external vs internal
    guarantees 340
  satisfaction vs service attribute
    guarantees 340
  types of 340–41
  use of (when and when not to
    use) 341–2
service spotlights
  British Telecom self-help
    facilities 336
  complaint on flightsfromhell.
    com 326
  DHL Freight follow-up
    calls 335
  Domino's Pizza outcome justice on
    delivery delays for 328
  Lands' End customer service
    guarantee 339
  Ritz-Carlton service recovery
    forms 337
  Sainsbury's customer interaction
    and empathy 333–4
service switching, causes bearing
  on 331
strategies for 331–8
summary 342
switching vs loyalty following
  330–31
treatment of customers following
  complaints, fairness of 336–7
web-based consumer opinion
  platforms 324–5
Service-related cluster initiatives 159
'Service Research Priorities in a
  Rapidly Changing Context'
  (2015) 159
Service roles and scripts 50
Service spotlights
  Abercrombie & Fitch scent in
    stores 215
  Accor brands training resources 242
  Air France/KLM service
    standards 198
  airline cabin crews, provision of
    Apple iPads for 234
  Alibaba new service
    developments 165

Allianz sponsorship of Olympic
  Movement 246
American Express Australia, use of
  big data by 108
American Express Centurion
  Card 134
Apple customer connections 232
APS Bank branch interior
  redesign 212
Asda customer listening
  programme 125
Asda customer perception tracker
  survey 113
bi-level trains of on European
  railways 304
Body Shop internal communicator
  network 364
Boots the Chemists Advantage
  Card 144
British Telecom self-help
  facilities 336
car industry intermediary
  performance 290
ChiantiBanca Restaurant Experience
  Banking 208
CitizenM employer branding 241–2
Colt, customer orientation at 391
ComparetheMarket.com 279
complaint on flightsfromhell.
  com 326
Crowne Plaza Hotel, London
  Docklands 45
DHL Freight follow-up calls 335
difficult clients 152
Disney omni-channel
  experience 276
Disneyland Paris, waiting times
  at 374
Domino's Pizza outcome justice on
  delivery delays for 328
easyJet flight duration
  strategy 78
easyJet online customer
  community 112
easyJet online flight tracker 13
EDF Energy 7
EDF Group balanced scorecard
  approach 399
Emirates customer classification
  scheme 270
Emirates service 91
Eurostar customer areas
  makeover 210
Expedia post-introduction
  evaluation 170
Farshid Moussavi's retail space
  for Victoria Beckham's fashion
  label 214
FedEx alignment of internal
  personnel with customers using
  measurement 366
FedEx hard mearurements for
  international operations 197
fitness centres, consumer satisfaction
  with 85
Ford Sync Emergency Assistance
  technology 10
future hotels, technology
  and 65
Gatwick self-service bag drop
  zones 258

Heathrow Service Quality Rebate Scheme 247
Hilton hotels mobile phone app services 264
Hilton Innovation Gallery 168–9
hotels and one-time fixes 191
Ibis Hotels Satisfaction Guarantee 73
IKEA Breakfast in Bed Café 359
IKEA co-production 51
Integrated Service Solutions (ISS) standards of service 187
interactive touch-screen ordering kiosks 264–5
InterContinental Hotels Group (IHG) KnowledgeNet 123
Lands' End customer service guarantee 339
Marriott International new concept testing 161
Martini beacon technology 281
Mastercard customer relationship 147
McDonalds to Go 305–6
McDonalds UK restaurant redesign 222
McDonald's way, service culture and 231
NHS (National Health Service) Choices Health Apps Library 12
Nike Towns and servicescape design 217
Northern Ireland Education Department customer service standards 195–6
Philips Electronics services innovations 162–3
Premier Inn hub concept 66–7
Pret a Manger service culture 230–31
Quantas and Hamilton Island virtual reality experience 206
rail capacity in UK 297
rental car going-rate pricing 378
Ritz-Carlton service recovery forms 337
Rolls-Royce TotalCare® programme 163–4
Royal Caribbean Cruises customization 148
Sainsbury's customer interaction and empathy 333–4
Sainsbury's Smartshop Scan, Pay and Go app 311
Scottish and Southern Energy (SSE) Energy Supplier Guaranteed Standards 188
self-scanning tills, strategies for popularisation of 268
Siemens 8
Singapore Airlines Total Offer Optimization 308
Skyscanner service quality 93–4
skyscanner.net online flight aggregator 380
social bonds 148
Spotify 47
standards set by external bodies 30–31
Starbucks community cultivation 241
Starbucks in Australia 55
Starwood Resorts Instagram influencers 355

Stora Enso net promotor score (NPS) 392
structural bonds 149
Subway sandwich chain franchise 283–4
Subway value pricing 382
Takeaway.com 277–8
Ted Baker's beacon mannequins 280
Telefónica O₂ loyalty programme 113–14
Temkin Group Net Promoter Industry Benchmarks 88
Thorpe Park social media strategy 351
Ticketmaster data analysis 106–7
TomTom online community of users 257
Transport for London, mystery shopping at 119
Triodos Bank mission 142
Tui and customers acting as competitors 262
Turkey, capacity for Syrian refugees in 299
Tyne and Wear Metro, impact of environment on behaviour at 219
Virgin Airlines Flying Club 140
Virgin Group brand values 229–30
Volvo ethnographic approach in research 118
Waitrose "Quick Check" self-scan system 261
Whistl reliability 90
Zappos and service standardization 186
Service standards, calibration of 185
Service strategy, use of gaps model for assessment of 35
Service switching, causes bearing on 331
Service value, customer waiting time and 314
Service variability, knowledge limitations and 371–2
Services 2–24
  bodies of people, services directed at 5
  customer focus, maintenance of 22
  customer service 8
  discussion questions 23–4
  enabling both customers and employees 12
  evolution of 11–13
  example, Service Industries in Europe 3
  exercises 23
  expanded marketing mix for services 20
  experiences, services as 8
  further reading 24
  global reach of services, extension of 12–13
  goods versus services 15
  heterogeneity 16
  innovative service offerings 11
  inseperability 16–17
    resulting marketing implications 17
  intangibility 6, 16
  intangible actions 4

intangible possessions of people, services directed at 5
Internet as service 13
key concepts 23
learning objectives 2
Lovelock's classification of 4
marketing mix
  people 19–20
  physical evidence 20–21
  place 20
  price 20
  process 20, 21–2
  product 20
  promotion 20
minds of people, services directed at 5
payback in technology investments 13
people, services marketing and 19
perishability (and resulting marketing implications) 17
physical evidence, services marketing and 20–21
process, services marketing and 21
products, services as 7–8
self-service technologies 12
service contexts 6–9
service delivery, new ways for 11–12
service dominant logic 9–10
Service Industries in Europe 3
service marketers, challenges and questions for 17–18
service organizations 6–7
'service-profit chain' 14
service spotlight
  easyJet online flight tracker 13
  EDF Energy 7
  Ford Symc Emergency Assistance technology 10
  NHS (National Health Service) Choices Health Apps Library 12
  Siemens 8
services, meaning of 3–6
services impacting on marketing activities, characteristics of 15–19
services marketing
  differences in 14
  rationale for 14
  services marketing triangle 18–19
servuction system model 21
summary 22–3
tangibility spectrum 6
tangible actions 4
tangible possessions of people, services directed at 5
technology and service 11–13
  paradoxes and dark side of 13
traditional marketing mix (product, price, place [distribution] and promotion) 19
transformative service 8–9
value creation 9
value-in-use creation model 10
'Services as drama' 255
Services marketing research programmes 109–10
Services marketing triangle 18–19, 348
Services production continuum 263
Servicescapes
  complexity of 209

Servicescapes (*Continued*)
effects on behaviour, framework for
understanding 212–20
physical and virtual 204
typology of 208–9
usage 208, 209
see also Physical and virtual
servicescape
'Servicescapes: the impact of physical
surroundings on customers and
employees' (Bitner, M.J.) 208, 213
SERVPERF instrument 116
SERVQUAL surveys
customer-defined service
standards 197
customer perceptions and 89
listening to customers and 111,
114–16
perception statements in 115
Servuction system model 21
Shakespeare goes online 275
'Share of wallet' aim 393
Shareholder value, performance
measures and 401
Sheeran, Ed 445, 446
Sheetz, M. 414
Shell 3
Shifting demand to match
capacity 300–301
Shostack, G. Lynn 6, 167
Siddique, H. 415
Siemens 3, 8, 28
service spotlight on 8
Signs, symbols and artefacts 213,
215–16
Singapore Airlines 21, 210, 214, 361, 364
Total Offer Optimization 308
Situational factors 69, 71
possible influence strategies for 75
Sivadas, E. 121
Six Sigma 389
Skimming pricing 382
Skyscanner
service quality 93–4
skyscanner.net online flight
aggregator 380
Sloan Management Review 164
Slow demand periods, teaching seeking
out of 363
Smartphone applications 280
Social bonds , service spotlight on 148
Social interactions in servicescape 219
Social media advertising 358
Social relationship bonds 147–8
Socializer, servicescape as 211
Soft and hard measures, linkage for
speed of complaint
handling 194
Soft customer-defined standards 190,
191
Soft measurements 197–8
Soltanifar, Mariusz 448–55, 456–64
Sorenson, Arne 448
S&P 500 Companies 389
Spatial layout and functionality 213, 215
Sport and Leisure Management 116
Spotify 130, 148
service spotlight on 47
Staff superiority, customer satisfaction
and 88
Standardization

customer-defined service
standards 186
of service behaviours and
actions 185
Standards set by external bodies 30–31
Starbucks 3, 56, 109, 140, 147, 149, 167,
204, 210
in Australia 55
community cultivation 241
Starbucks App 130–31
Starbucks, key elements of the
'Starbucks Experience' (case
study) 465–72
ambience in-store 466
American Red Cross 472
Bean Stock programme 467
Best Company to Work For 468
'Brewing the Perfect Cup'
workshop 469
charitable contributions 472
community involvement, corporate
citizenship and 470–71
Corporate Citizenship award 472
corporate social responsibility
strategy 470–72
dreams, creation of opportunities for
achievement of 471
Earth Day activities 471
employee engagement 466–70
environmental stewardship 471
EPA Green Power Partnership 471
ethical sourcing 470
founding in Seattle 465
fringe benefit program (2019) 468–9
Global Fund 472
Green Apron Awards 469
health care for all employees 466–7
hygiene education programmes 472
Leadership in Energy and
Environmental Design (LEED) 471
partner contributions, rewards
for 469
Partner of the Quarter Awards 469
performance-driven 470
Product (RED)™ 472
recognition of employees 469–70
recycling 471
Renewable Energy Credits 471
sanitation education
programmes 472
Schultz, Howard 466–7, 468, 470
soil management 470
Starbucks Foundation 472
stock option plan for employees 467
stock purchase for employees 467
store design, customer experience
and 465–6, 472
Supplier Code of Conduct 470
sustainable farming 470
training of employees 469–70
values, statement of 469
workplace environment 467–8
'Youth Opportunity' grants 471
Start-up businesses 161
Starwood Resorts Instagram
influencers 355
Status seekers, attraction of 381–2
Stefan Floridian Waters 214
Stimulus-organism-response theory 212
Stora Enso Net Promotor Score
(NPS) 392

Strangers, customers as 132
Strategic roles of servicescape 210–12
clarification of 221
Strategies for
adjusting capacity to match
demand 303
control of intermediaries 289
delivery of quality in service, use of
people in 239–48
effectiveness of
intermediaries 289–90
enhancement of customer
participation 205–11
management of emotional
labour 235–7
matching capacity and
demand 300–306
possible influence 75
queuing strategies for balancing
demand and capacity 310–15
service communication 350–52
service recovery 331–8
Stretching existing capacity to meet
demand 304
Structural bonds 149
Structural bonds, service spotlight
on 149
Style changes 162
Subjectivity risk 160
Subway
sandwich chain franchise 283–4
value pricing 382
Success, consideration of multiple
measures of 179–80
Summaries
building customer relationships 153
communications (external and
internal) management of 366–7
consumer behaviour 58
customer-defined service
standards 201
customer expectations 79
customer perceptions of
service 100
customers' roles in service
delivery 271–2
demand and capacity
management 315
electronic channels and
intermediaries, service delivery
through 290
employees' roles in service
delivery 249–50
listening to customers 126–7
physical and virtual
servicescape 222–3
pricing of services 384
service innovation and design 180
service quality, financial impact
of 401–2
service quality, gaps model of 35
service recovery 342
services 22–3
Support systems, provision
of 244–5
Surowiecki, James 167
Sussman, S. 417
Swedish Customer Satisfaction
Barometer 86
Swiss Index of Customer Satisfaction
(SWICS) 86